HUMAN DEVELOPMENT

GRACE J. CRAIG
THE UNIVERSITY OF MASSACHUSETTS AT AMHERST

PRENTICE-HALL, INC., ENGLEWOOD CLIFFS, NEW JERSEY

To Talli

*whose encounter with each
developmental task proclaims the
tough and tender dialogue of life*

Library of Congress Cataloging in Publication Data

Craig, Grace J.
  Human development.

  Bibliography: p. 475
  Includes indexes.
  1. Developmental psychology. I. Title.
BF713.C7   155   75-33185
ISBN 0-13-444760-3

Printed in the United States of America

10 9 8 7 6 5 4 3 2 1

PRENTICE-HALL INTERNATIONAL, INC., London
PRENTICE-HALL OF AUSTRALIA, PTY./LTD., Sydney
PRENTICE-HALL OF CANADA, LTD., Toronto
PRENTICE-HALL OF INDIA PRIVATE LIMITED, New Delhi
PRENTICE-HALL OF JAPAN, INC., Tokyo

Part and chapter opening illustrations by Jean Callan King/Visuality

CONTENTS

This text is designed to introduce the field of developmental psychology to a wide range of college level students. It is an integrated study of the full life span with comprehensive coverage of basic developmental concepts and principles, discussion of developmental issues, as well as trends in research and their applications. Throughout the book, there is an attempt to include issues, concepts, and research drawn from the related disciplines of biology, sociology, and anthropology. Although this text has full life span coverage and perspective, it is also appropriate for courses in Childhood and Adolescence. It can be used in a single semester or quarter term course or, with the use of supplements, for full year courses.

There is no single, right way to teach a developmental psychology course. Any good instructor will adapt the materials to suit his or her own style, interest, and expertise. This text combines aspects of a topical and chronological organization. There are separate chapters discussing such current issues as intelligence, self-concept development over the life span, research methods, comparative developmental theories, genetics and genetic counseling, and language development. Following the initial topical chapters, the text is primarily organized in chronological fashion. Many of these sections were written as independent units so that the instructor could select his or her own organization.

This text attempts to preserve the controversial, the challenging, and the complex by presenting such issues in a clear, informal, and readable manner. Thus the student is exposed to the personal and professional dialogue of human development. Examples are illustrated using the results of research literature and also the student's own personal experiences. To assist both student and instructor, chapters contain an outline, summary, suggested readings, and review questions. In addition, a glossary, extensive bibliography, and subject and name indexes are provided at the end of the book.

Such a book as this owes much to countless individuals—to mentors and colleagues, to students, to assistants, and to friends. Many of these sources of ideas, insights, and observations must remain unnamed. Nevertheless, this book could not have been completed without the constant involvement of some key people—the patience of my family, in particular my husband Ralph, the continued guidance and support of the Prentice-Hall staff, most notably, Patricia Balassi, Neale Sweet, and Patricia McDermott, the tireless, dedicated attention to detail and pursuit of accuracy by my research assistant, Jeff Moss, the general assistance of Jean Stein, Jane Barrett, and Jan Buessem, and the comments, criticisms, and suggestions of my colleagues in Human Development and in Psychology, particularly, Ellis G. Olim and Alfred L. Karlson. Professor Karlson has also written the supplementary material accompanying this text which includes the *Study Guide and Workbook, Test Items,* and *Instructor's Manual.*

G. J. C.

The University of Massachusetts
at Amherst

PART I
HUMAN DEVELOPMENT:
AN INTEGRATED STUDY OF THE LIFE SPAN

DEVELOPMENT: PERSPECTIVES, PROCESSES, AND RESEARCH METHODS

The sperm—fragile and microscopic—strives against great odds to reach the ovum and unite with it to begin a new organism.

The helpless human newborn struggles to breathe on its own. Soon its vocal, motor, and systemic functions are exercised regularly.

The infant stretches, reaches, pulls, and finally walks and manipulates objects.

The baby is delighted when her smile calls forth an affectionate response. She greets new textures and sights with surprise and wonder.

The child forms an attachment to someone close to him, and as his physical and emotional needs are met, he learns to trust the world.

The delinquent youth struggles to maintain his loyalty and self-respect. The invalid seeks whatever measure of independence and autonomy is possible.

The adult discovers beauty in art and nature and feels a childlike wonder at the new experience.

Adolescents, young adults, parents, and aged couples discover and rediscover the meaning of relationships with others. Whether sensitive and fragile, sturdy and releasing of self-expression, stormy and anxious, or quietly comfortable and comforting, these relationships are a necessary and continuing part of a person's development.

Complex and rich, full of quest and challenge, the process of human development is the product of many strands: biological, cultural, intellectual, and psychodynamic. It is a process that begins with conception and continues to old age and death. In this book, therefore, our aim will be to examine developmental principles and processes throughout the human life span and across several disciplines. We shall investigate the human organism at all ages and stages, from the point of view of biology, anthropology, and sociology, as well as psychology.

LIFE SPAN STAGES.

Newborn. (*Jan Lukas, Rapho Guillumette.*)

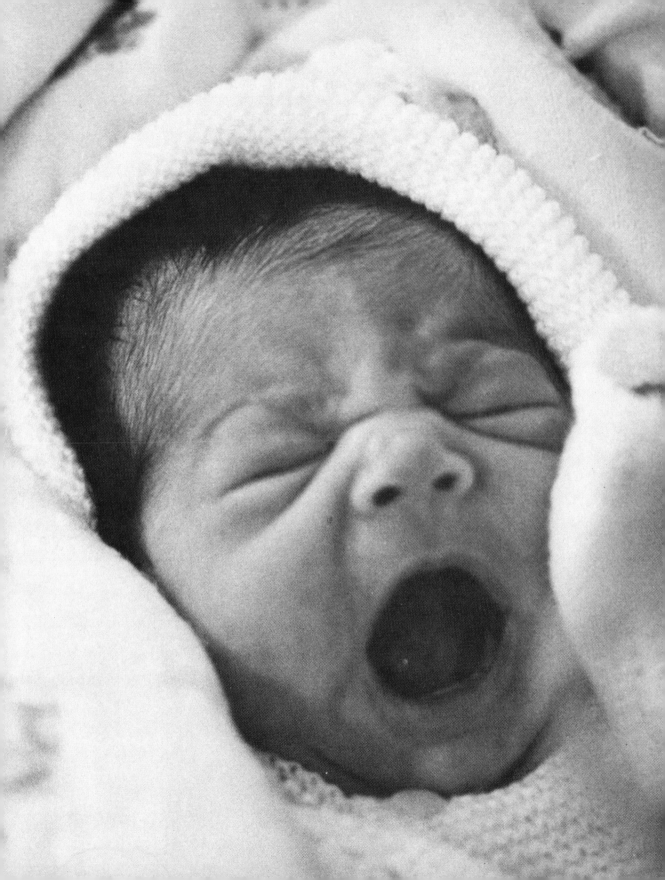

Infancy. (*Hella Hammid, Rapho Guillumette.*)

Middle childhood. (*Al Lowry, Photo Researchers.*)

Early childhood. (*Bruce Roberts, Rapho Guillumette.*)

Adolescence. (*Ken Heyman.*)

Early adulthood. (*Photo Researchers.*)　　　　Middle adulthood. (*Chester Higgins, Jr., Rapho/Photo Researchers.*)

Aging. (*Al Kaplan, DPI.*)

Despite the variety of influences that may affect it, the process of human development is fairly consistent and potentially explicable. Difficulties in understanding human growth and behavior often lie within those who try to explain and predict them. Whenever we evaluate what a person can or cannot do, whenever we try to predict what he should do —in short, any time we pass judgment on the behavior of another human being—we tend to bring to our conclusions an accumulation of values and standards based on our own experiences and environment.

For example, those who have been reared in a middle-class American suburban environment might expect a normal 3-year-old to be able to ride a tricycle. Any child of this age who cannot do so might be thought to have some sort of motor problem. However, the child who is brought up in an apartment in a large city, or a child born and reared in a country that does not view the tricycle as an essential part of a child's experience, cannot and should not be expected to climb on a tricycle and pedal away. Similarly, the suburban child should not be expected either to be knowledgeable in the way of city streets or to be at ease with barnyard animals.

The same considerations must be given to children's development of sexual behavior and value systems. One culture may forbid, or at least strongly disapprove of, the very behavior that another culture encourages, and the values of a culture form the basis for the behavior and judgment of its members. A child gradually learns what is "right" and "normal," and tries to behave accordingly, as he develops.

Middle-class America, for example, generally discourages sex play and nudity among children, frowns on homosexuality at any stage of development, and disapproves strongly of incest and extramarital sex. In contrast, the Marind Anim tribe of New Guinea encourages sex play and nudity among young children and expects homosexual relations to occur between adolescent boys and older relatives. The tribe's ceremonies include one in which a bride must have public intercourse with male members of the husband's family before the husband is permitted to touch her. The tribal women are also encouraged to engage in extramarital sex, so long as they do it with their husband's knowledge and approval (Van Baal, 1966). To attempt to understand human behavior and development without knowledge of and reference to such cultural variations would be a rather futile exercise.

In the study of human development, we must also be aware of the full human life span. Just as the explanation of adult behavior depends upon an understanding of child development, so too should the study of child development include an awareness of the potential of adulthood (Neugarten, 1969). It is important to examine the processes and experiences of childhood that have contributed to adult behavior. It is also instructive to look at the physical and psychological characteristics of maturity toward which the child is moving. We recognize self-reflection, decision making, and goal orientation in adults, but we often overlook the behavioral cues in children that would indicate the emergence of such characteristics. We become more sensitive to the significance of developmental change in children once we view such change in terms of the full context of human life.

Historically, attitudes toward childhood and childrearing have varied widely. In the Middle Ages, for example, children were not thought of as separate entities at all. While they were infants, they were largely ignored as human beings; and when they were no longer infants they were considered small adults, to be treated to the same conversation, jokes, music, food, and other entertainment as were enjoyed by full-size adults (Aries, 1960; Plumb, 1971). Brueghel, the famous medieval artist, depicted children taking part in the dances and feasts of the grownups. Other painters, too, failed to distinguish between children and their elders, except in relative stature. Clothing, hair styles, and activities were the same for persons of all ages.

HISTORICAL AND CROSS-CULTURAL PERSPECTIVES

In Peter Brueghel the Elder's "Children's Games," painted in 1560, little distinction is made between the children and the adults. (*Kunsthistorisches Museum, Vienna; Peter Adelberg, European Art Color.*)

By 1600, the concept of childhood innocence was beginning to be accepted, and an effort was made to protect the child from the excesses and sins of the adult world. By the eighteenth century, this attitude was fully supported, at least by the upper and middle classes, and children were treated as persons with an identity of their own (Plumb, 1971). What we know today as the "generation gap" may be simply the result of the twentieth-century exaggeration of this separation of youths and their elders. Because children and adolescents have been placed in a world apart, they have filled that world with symbols, vocabulary, attitudes, and actions that are often incomprehensible to adults.

Discipline of children has also varied through the years. Harsh physical punishment was the rule in parts of Ancient Greece just as it was in nineteenth-century America. Terrorizing children with stories of ghosts and monsters was long a popular form of control (DeMause, 1974). The encouraging change that has taken place in this century is not only that methods of childrearing have become more humane, but also that all of our preconceptions about children and their development are being questioned (Mead, 1972). Impulses that once seemed dangerous, such as thumb-sucking and masturbation, are now being accepted as part of a child's normal activity (Wolfenstein, 1951). Rigid schedules for feeding, toilet training, and play have given way to reliance on self-demand, readiness, and self-expression. Parents are no longer afraid to relax and enjoy their children but are free to let their own feelings of what is "right" for their children and their situation guide their decision making.

Attitudes toward children vary across cultures as well as across centuries. For example, Russians swaddle newborns tightly because they view the infants as strong creatures who need to be restrained from injuring themselves. The French, on the other hand, regard babies as fragile, vulnerable creatures and swaddle them to protect them (Mead, 1972).

Among the Ik people of Uganda, children are turned out of the house when they are about 3 years of age (Turnbull, 1972). They are made to sleep in the open and provide their own shelter. The children of the tribe band together for protection against the elements and against older children. Even when the children fight viciously among themselves the adults do not interfere. As a result, only the strongest children survive to take their places in adult society. Children, like the aged, are looked upon by the Ik as useless, expendable burdens. Although this harsh treatment is an extreme example, it serves to illustrate that what middle-class Americans may regard as normal childrearing practices are by no means generally accepted in other cultures.

The historical and cultural differences in attitudes toward children and childrearing are sometimes the result of varying social and economic problems. The Ik, for example, are a dying tribe for whom mere survival is a difficult, daily problem. That children would seem a terrible burden to these people is, therefore, not surprising. More affluent societies may look on children and childrearing as more joyful experiences because they can literally afford to do so. But even within social groups where finding enough to eat and a place to live are not problems, habits, customs, myths, and misconceptions continue to have an impact on childrearing practices.

Central to the concerns of developmental psychologists are the processes by which change takes place. There is no clear agreement on how a child acquires a nearly full grammar of his native language by the time he is 5 years old; or why reminiscing seems to be such an essential part of aging; or even how a child learns to read, or to assume a sex role, or express love, grief, or hostility. Nevertheless, there are some common terms and concepts used by developmental psychologists—and by sociologists, anthropologists, and educators as well—to investigate and debate the issues.

DEVELOPMENTAL PROCESSES

Development can be defined as the changes in the structure, thought, or behavior of a person which occur as a function of both biological and environmental influences. Usually these changes are progressive and cumulative. They result in increased size of the person, increased complexity of activity, and integration of organization and function. For example, the motor development of the infant progresses from random waving of arms and legs to purposeful reaching, grasping, creeping, and walking. The development of cognitive processes moves toward the ability to conceptualize and to think in abstract terms. The acquisition of a vocabulary is a first step in the use of symbols, a skill which paves the way for learning to read and deal with number concepts.

Development

Some development, such as prenatal growth, is primarily biological while other development may be highly dependent on the environment. Learning a foreign language while residing in a foreign country, or acquiring the speech patterns and accent of one's family, are examples of development which is strongly related to the environment. Most development, however, cannot be so neatly categorized as either biological or environmental, since it involves an interaction of both elements.

Biological changes in the structure and function of an organism consist of growth, aging, and maturation. *Growth* is an increase in size, function, or complexity up to some point of optimal maturity. *Aging*, on the other hand, refers to the same kind of biological evolution beyond the point of optimal maturity. Aging does not necessarily imply decline or deterioration. Just as aging often improves the qualities of some cheeses and wines, it may also contribute to the improvement of human judgment and insight.

Biological Processes of Development

Maturation refers to the emergence of an organism's genetic potential. It consists of a series of preprogrammed changes which comprise alterations not only in the organism's structure and form but also in its complexity, integration, organization, and function. Faulty nutrition or illness may delay the process of maturation, but proper nutrition, good health, or even encouragement and teaching will not necessarily speed it up dramatically (Shirley, 1933). This holds true across the life span and for such seemingly unrelated processes as an infant's motor development and an adolescent's development of secondary sex characteristics with the accompanying emotional complications.

Processes of Environmental Influence

The environment exerts an influence on an individual every minute of every day. Lights, sounds, heat, food, drugs, feelings of safety—all can create biological or psychological stress or comfort. These elements can fulfill basic needs; their absence can cause anxiety or physical distress. Some of these environmental influences are temporary and situational. Others, if repeated or constant, will have a more lasting, even permanent, effect on the organism. The effect may be physical (stunted growth, for example) or behavioral.

Learning is the basic developmental process by which an individual's behavior is changed by the environment. Learning is a relatively permanent change in behavior or in the capacity for behavior resulting from either experience or practice. Clearly, learning algebra and learning ballet are somewhat different types of learning, just as are learning to avoid a hot stove and learning to avoid strangers.

Psychologists do not agree on the generalities of even those basic processes of learning which they can identify and describe. In the next chapter we shall look at different theories advanced by some of the best-known of these scientists. Most psychologists do agree, however, that at least one of the basic processes in learning is the process called conditioning.

Throughout this book, we shall discuss more complex aspects of learning such as concept learning, verbal mediation, hypothesis testing, modeling and imitation, and learning sets. We shall also examine cognitive models of insight, discovery, and understanding as bases for explaining human development and behavior.

Socialization is the lifelong process by which an individual acquires the attitudes, beliefs, customs, values, roles, and expectations of a culture or a social group. One of the functions of socialization is to help the individual participate effectively in a group and in society in general (Goslin, 1969).

Children are socialized into various *roles* at both simultaneous and successive ages. In adulthood, for example, a man may be expected to perform in the roles of employee, husband, neighbor, community member, and father. A woman may be faced with an even greater variety of roles. In addition to being an employee, neighbor, community member, wife, and mother, she may have "roles within roles." As wife, she may be responsible for a large portion of the family's budgeting and may also serve as a sort of social director; as mother, she will be disciplinarian, teacher, nurse, chauffeur, nutritionist, and psychologist. Each new role brings with it new socialization, and the socialization is always based on the attitudes, expectations, and values of the surrounding social group.

Just as the learner changes as the roles he must perform change, so too are other people in the environment affected by what takes place within the learner. Socialization is always a two-way process because it occurs in a social environment (Goslin, 1969). An infant is socialized by his experience within the family, but the other family members must learn new roles because of the presence of the infant. A child who is accustomed to throwing tantrums must learn new behaviors when he enters school; at the same time, the teacher must learn to deal with tantrum behavior. The same interplay exists between a humane, dedicated nurse and a rude, uncooperative patient. The person who is learning a new role often creates new roles for others.

Socialization does not stop when an individual leaves childhood but continues on in adulthood and old age. Then, however, much of the socialization is consciously sought, sometimes in anticipation of the expected life change. A person about to change jobs may take a course to strengthen certain vocational skills. A man facing retirement may develop a hobby or join a social group in preparation for the time when he will have a great many leisure hours to fill.

Throughout the life span, human behavior is modified by changes in the social environment, and the human being will find himself required to play a variety of roles. The effectiveness of the socialization process can be measured by the success of an individual's interaction with those persons around him.

We come now to a question that is a continuing source of debate among psychologists: How much of our behavior is attributable to maturation and how much depends upon learning? We know that there are certain behaviors such as sitting, standing, or walking, which develop primarily because of the body's maturational unfolding. Yet even this body potential can sometimes be affected by drugs, inadequate nutrition, fatigue, disease, restriction, or emotional stress. Other behaviors are even more difficult to categorize on an either-or basis. A child may be born with the capacity for speech, but he must *learn* a language. An infant may spontaneously demonstrate certain emotional behaviors, such as distress or even anger. Yet he must *learn* to want something that is unattainable before he can develop the level of frustration that will produce a tantrum, and he then must learn when tantrum behavior can and should occur (Hebb, 1966).

Interaction of Developmental Processes

The important point to remember is that most behavior is a product of the interaction of maturation and learning. Certain limits or characteristics of behavior may be built into an individual's genetic blueprint through heredity, but even these factors can be affected by the environment. Anne Anastasi (1958) points out, for example, that an inherited susceptibility to a disease, such as asthma or diabetes, can result in the onset of the disease because of environmental factors. The disease, in turn, may affect the individual's socialization or intellectual development if it prevents his participation in social or athletic events and interferes with his school attendance. The same type of interaction can be seen in the relationship between inherited physical characteristics such as body type, skin color, or height, which affect a person's self-concept and social acceptance. His behavior may be based on stereotyped expectancies (fat people are jolly, short men are insecure) held by himself as well as by others.

TIMING. The interaction of learning and maturation may depend upon the particular point in time of development when an environmental effect occurs. An example of the crucial nature of such timing is a *critical period*, a point in time during which—and only during which—a particular environmental factor can have an effect. Several such periods occur during prenatal development of the infant, when certain chemicals, drugs, or diseases can adversely affect the development of specific body organs only within a very precise time.

Another example of crucial timing is found among baby ducks and geese in the wild. The formation of an early relationship with the mother is crucial to the survival of the young birds. They must follow their mother and learn from her if they are to survive. This relationship is formed quite suddenly, dramatically, and permanently within the first few hours after the birds are hatched in a process called *imprinting*. The birds display a pattern of peeping and following behaviors released by the mother bird or by almost any large moving object of an appropriate size and shape. However, there is a critical period during which the process must occur. If the mother bird first appears on the scene 2 or 3 days after the baby is hatched, the duckling's fear response will have matured sufficiently so that imprinting cannot take place. This process will be discussed in detail in Chapter 10.

There are other types of periods in which the individual is more or less sensitive to environmental influences. An *optimal period* is similar to a critical period in that it is the particular time when a specific behavior develops most successfully as a result of the interaction of maturation and learning. But an optimal period does not have the all-or-nothing quality of a critical period. Although there is an optimal time for a behavior to develop, the behavior can be learned at an earlier or later date. *Readiness* refers to a point in time when an individual has matured sufficiently for a particular learning to take place. This individual may not be able to learn the activity or behavior prior to this maturational point, but it is not crucial that he learn it the moment he becomes ready. For example, a child's cognitive development may be such that he is not able to learn subtraction until he is 6 years old. If, for some reason, he is not taught to subtract until age 6½ or 7, however, the opportunity will not have been lost forever, as would be true of a process for which there is a critical period.

The precise nature of timing as it applies to human development is not yet known. Are there critical periods for the·learning of certain behaviors? Or are there only sensitive periods? Are there optimal periods when a person can learn to read, acquire athletic skills, or learn to speak a foreign language? Can an understanding of imprinting shed any light on the nature of human attachment relationships? These are some of the questions we shall examine in our study of development.

To study any subject, we need a method or approach, a set of goals and guidelines toward which to work, and a way to evaluate the results we achieve. In this section and the next we shall examine several methods that are commonly used to investigate the study of human development.

Most breakthroughs and new theories in the sciences have been stimulated by an astute observation of some event. Someone saw something different, asked questions about it, continued to observe it, tested its limits, and arrived at some basis for generalization and prediction. This simple example illustrates the observational method at work.

On Saturday afternoon John Parker watches television for three hours. That evening he complains of a headache and an upset stomach. On Sunday afternoon he also watches television for three hours, and he again mentions a headache and only picks at his food at suppertime. On Monday he watches no television and his wife observes that he seems to feel fine and eats well at suppertime. Over the next several weeks, Mrs. Parker notices that her husband experiences headaches and an upset stomach only on the days when he watches television for more than an hour. She has made a generalization about his behavior based upon her repeated observations.

Parents, professionals, and students, as well as researchers, rely on observation in their work. They look for patterns of behavior, whether in a patient, a criminal, a student, customers and employees, or a piece of machinery, in order to diagnose problems and come up with solutions. In the study of human development, we can learn from what may at first appear to be rather insignificant acts of behavior.

Suppose, for example, that we look at the picture of a house and a tree drawn by a 6-year-old. Immediately, we may notice that the picture is "childlike," not "adultlike." On closer observation, we might notice that the house sits directly on the ground, or the chimney is at a strange angle, or the tree is almost perpendicular to the hill and is somewhat out of proportion. Are these just "errors" resulting from the child's poor motor coordination? Are they the idiosyncrasies of one particular child?

Jean Piaget, an astute observer of children, assumes that children's drawings are not just reproductions of what the children see; rather, he considers that the drawings represent the way children think, the way children construct *reality*. The pictures reveal the understanding, and lack of understanding, children have about relationships between objects in the world. Each child has certain cognitive limitations. He may see things only from his point of view, or he may focus on only one relationship at a time. In a child's experiences, things that are "on" something else are usually related in a perpendicular way. There-

A 6-year-old's drawing. (*Shawn Riley, Lafayette, Indiana.*)

fore, the chimney on the roof of a house relates at a perpendicular angle to the roof—not to the house or the ground. If the child wants to draw a tree on a hillside, he may place the tree perpendicular to the side of the hill. When he draws the tree, he focuses on that tree and gives it a size related to its importance, rather than the physical size in proportion to the hill. Our point here is not to interpret the drawing but rather to highlight keen observation as the basis for hypothesis.

The Validity of Observation

Before we can use our observations as the basis for generalizations about human behavior, we must first make sure that the observations are valid. Are they true? Do they really mean what they have been proposed to mean? In addition, we must be sure that our observations are reliable, that we have defined what we are looking at, that our conclusions are logical, and that our generalizations are restricted to the facts at hand.

RELIABILITY. For an observation to be valid, it must be reliable. *Reliability* refers to the extent to which an experiment or observation will produce the same results each time it is repeated. A reliable measurement, therefore, is dependable, repeatable, and consistent. For example, let us consider again the drawing we used to illustrate Piaget's conclusions.

1. Is our observation of the drawing consistent over time? (That is,

are the chimney and tree often slanted, or always slanted, when the child draws such a picture?)

2. Is our observation consistent across children? (Do many 6-year-olds set chimneys and trees at an angle?)
3. Is our observation consistent across observers? (Will anyone looking at the picture see that the tree and chimney are at an angle?)

Thus, before we can begin to build a theory based on crooked chimneys and trees, we must be sure we have identified a dependable, repeatable, consistent observation—in other words, a reliable phenomenon.

DEFINITION OF TERMS. Basically, there are two kinds of definitions: theoretical and operational. A theoretical definition of intelligence, for example, might be: the ability to adapt to one's environment. An operational definition could be: intelligence consists of those behaviors that are measured on the Stanford-Binet test. Someone who defines intelligence in a different way might get different results when interpreting the same material. The researcher must use a definition of his study topic that describes the techniques of observation and measurement employed in his research—an *operational definition*. His work is more meaningful if he also has a theoretical definition of his subject.

To carry the point one step further, consider the problem of studying aggressive behavior. We might be able to agree on a theoretical definition of aggression as the intent to injure, hurt, or destroy. But how do we measure intent? What aggressive behavior do we observe? To answer these questions, we need an operational definition of our research topic. We might operationally define aggression as the hitting, kicking, punching, and verbal insults one child directs at others. On the other hand, we might decide on an operational definition that categorizes aggression as the hitting, kicking, punching, and verbal insults children use in doll play. One definition measures direct aggression, the other indirect or fantasy aggression. Correct definitions of terms are very important, for the results of research may differ because different things are being observed and measured.

CONSISTENT LOGIC. A number of problems in research studies may be caused by faulty logic. A major one results from an arbitrary decision about what constitutes causality. For example, if we find that female college students who smoke have lower grades than female college students who do not smoke, can we conclude that smoking *causes* low grades among women? Or could we perhaps conclude that low grades cause smoking? Or does some additional variable cause both grades and smoking to vary together? In other words, are women who are highly anxious, or fat, or socially maladjusted, more likely to smoke *and* get poor grades?

LIMITED GENERALIZATION. Each observation occurs in a particular setting, under specific conditions, with certain individuals of a specified age, past history, culture, and so forth. Any generalization must be limited to those same situations, settings, and people. For example, Mrs. Parker cannot conclude that all people, or even all adult males, who watch several hours of television will show ill effects. Nor can Piaget generalize his findings to children of a different age or from a different culture.

Blocks to Good Observations

Since observation is a relatively simple technique that is available to everyone, it would seem that the field of developmental psychology, as well as many other areas, would be flooded with new knowledge, exciting breakthroughs, and sound theories arising from its use. Unfortunately, there are several factors that serve as obstacles to good observation.

OBSERVER BIAS. Many of us see what we expect to see or what we want to see. We either do not notice or refuse to believe that which conflicts with our preconceptions. Whether a bias results from prejudice, stereotyping, or lack of experience, it will serve to invalidate the conclusions of an observation. An observer who is studying athletic skills in females may do a less than honest job if he is convinced that women either cannot or should not be skilled in this area. An observer who is studying social development among children in a minority group may do an inadequate job if he is unaware of the socialization patterns of the group he is studying.

INSENSITIVITY. When we observe things every day, we become accustomed to them and fail to recognize their significance. For example, the seat locations which students choose in a classroom may tell us something about the social groups to which they belong and about their popularity, leadership, and feelings of isolation. But if we see these students in the classroom several times a week, we may overlook this readily available information about them.

OBSERVER ASSUMPTIONS. The researcher often assumes that the subject is like himself. A behavior, therefore, may be interpreted on the basis of the observer's feelings. A hungry observer watching a child may assume that the child is putting away the puzzle because he knows it is almost time for lunch. In reality, of course, the child may not yet have developed such a concept of time and may simply be bored with the puzzle.

LIMITS OF THE HYPOTHESIS. Another obstacle to good observation is the tendency to look at too small or too large a piece of behavior. If we want to know something about a child's decision-making behavior, we would not need to record the minute details of his entire day. We would want to observe situations where he is in a position to make choices and decisions. One way of doing this would be to construct a laboratory setting that requires decision making, but here, too, we may run into difficulty. If a 5-year-old is placed in front of an apparatus which has 2 lights, 1 of which flashes in a random sequence, and he is asked over and over again to predict which light will flash next, his behavior may indicate very little about the decisions the child makes in the real world. Indeed, his reaction may be merely an example of what the child does when he is bored with an apparently trivial, meaningless task.

Thus far, we have confined our discussion of observation primarily to studies that take place in natural settings. Some of the best developmental theories have been the result of just such casual research. Recently, researchers have returned to natural settings, using video tape, film, and other recording devices to increase the precision of their observations. Nevertheless, these natural settings permit little control of individuals, events, and conditions and may provide rather imprecise measurement of behavior.

MAJOR CATEGORIES OF DEVELOPMENTAL RESEARCH

The settings that a researcher uses can range along a continuum from the most basic, controlled laboratory setting to the most applied naturalistic events (Gage, 1963). Precise observation is a key element throughout. But the degree of *control* of subjects, of events, and of conditions of the situation varies dramatically. The greater the researcher's control of the environmental situation, the more certain he can be about his findings. In experimental settings, the observer can control and manipulate these *independent variables,* which are the determining factors. In a laboratory study of children learning vocabulary, many variables can be manipulated—the amount of noise and distractions, the difficulty of the word list, the expectations and instructions of the teacher, the rewards or punishment, the pace of presentation, and so forth. The *dependent variables,* which are the resultant behavior such as rate of efficiency of learning or forgetting and symptoms of anxiety or anger, can be precisely measured. In naturalistic settings, the independent variables are controlled by selection only, not by manipulation. For example, the researcher can select for comparison high anxious and low anxious boys taught by strict or permissive teachers.

Just as naturalistic studies may suffer from lack of control and precision, so may experimental studies suffer from artificiality and from limited general applicability. It could be that a great deal of our knowledge of child development that is based on laboratory studies is applicable only to children in a closed cubicle with a stranger—that is, to children who have been deprived of their usual playmates and activities and who have been instructed to "play a game" in an unfamiliar setting.

Experimental Settings

A *longitudinal study* is a continuing observation of the same individual over an extended period of time. In a *cross-sectional study,* different individuals of different ages are observed at one time. While both

Longitudinal and Cross-sectional Studies

research methods have advantages and disadvantages, both are also very necessary to any study of human development.

Longitudinal studies have built-in controls. Individuals are compared with themselves at different points in time. A group of test subjects does not have to be sorted out again and again for matching variables. Such studies also have several drawbacks, however. Their subjects may fall ill, go away on vacation, move away, or simply discontinue their participation in the research. Some subjects, who are tested fairly often, get accustomed to test-taking and tend to do better on tests than those being examined for the first time. The studies require a great deal of time from both researchers and subjects. Also, researchers, like their subjects, may move to another part of the country and the subjects may not be willing to continue with someone new (Bayley, 1965).

Cross-sectional methods have the advantage of being quicker, cheaper, and more manageable than longitudinal studies. They do have some weaknesses of their own. They may not show the process of development of behavior over a period of time. Measurements taken from them may not be valid if subjects differ on important variables other than age, such as health, intelligence, and cultural or socio-economic background.

Self-reports and Projective Techniques

A researcher is likely to get quite different results in his work, depending upon whether he is directly observing the subject's behavior in actual situations, or is relying upon the subject's self-reports of behavior, thoughts, or feelings; and whether he is dealing with an imaginary situation.

Self-report techniques consist of interviews, survey or questionnaires in which the researcher asks questions designed to reveal the subject's feelings and behavior patterns. Sometimes the subject is asked to report information about himself as he is in the present or was in the past. At other times, he may be asked to reflect upon, or react to, statements or thoughts about himself, or to rate himself on some personality traits. In each case, he is expected to be as objective as possible.

Projective techniques require no such objectivity. Here the individual reacts to a somewhat ambiguous situation, picture, or task. The subject is asked to tell a story, interpret a picture, or guess the outcome of a situation. Since the task is ambiguous and there are no right answers, it is assumed that the individual will project his or her own feelings, attitudes, pressures, and needs into the situation. Rorschach inkblots are probably the most famous projective technique, with word association exercises running a close second. There are also sentence completion tests in which subjects are asked to finish a thought such as, "My father always. . . ." Pictures can be used in a variety of ways. Subjects can be asked to interpret, analyze, react to, arrange, or construct a story around a series of pictures.

Case Studies

Case studies are used frequently as descriptive, explanatory material. However, they are rarely used in research because they involve problems of subjectivity, uncontrolled variables, and relation to one specific individual. Generalizations and hypotheses cannot be made on the basis of the study of one person; cause and effect relationships cannot be established in a single individual.

In practical settings, however, such as medicine, education, social work, and clinical psychology, case studies provide an important tool for diagnosis and prescription. Case studies are excellent for providing a rich, clinical, descriptive picture of the evolving, integrated human being, but they should be used cautiously as a research tool.

Many special problems face researchers of nonverbal infants or young children. How can we know what an infant sees, thinks, understands, remembers, or expects? Solutions to some of these problems are sometimes surprisingly simple. Perhaps an example of research technique with infants will be helpful.

Special Research Problems

Collard and Rydberg (1972) wanted to know whether a 1-year-old infant discriminates between forms (spheres and cubes) and between colors. They knew that infants get bored with a familiar toy with which they have been playing for 5 to 10 minutes. They also knew that if they gave an infant a choice between the toy that he had been playing with for 6 minutes and a new toy, the 1-year-old would probably select the new toy. On the basis of this knowledge, they made toys that looked very similar, varying only in shape, color, or size.

Collard and Rydberg had the infants play with a series of simple toys—in this instance, 3 strings of small red spheres each differing in the size of beads—for 2 minutes apiece. Then they gave the infants a choice between a string of large red spheres and a string of large red cubes. Which one did the babies consider new? Did they discriminate spheres from cubes? Did they remember that they had just finished playing with round things, and did this matter to them? In this experiment, 16 out of 16 babies chose the new shape!

The goal of any science is *understanding*. The first step toward this end is careful description, followed by guarded generalization, cautious prediction, retesting, and more observation. This statement may make a scientific study appear to be a timid endeavor. It is intended, however, to serve only as a caution against conclusions based on incomplete or biased observation. Understanding can come only through honest, well-researched, logical conclusions.

UNDERSTANDING

The task of developmental psychology is to examine the influences which affect the physical, emotional, moral, and intellectual growth of human beings in order to arrive at an explanation of human behavior

SUMMARY

across the life span. The study of developmental psychology must be interdisciplinary with a cross-cultural as well as an historical perspective.

Human development is the change in the structure, thought, or behavior of a person as a function of both biological and environmental influences. Maturation is a biological process of the unfolding of hereditary potentials. Learning is the process of behaviorial change within the individual brought about by the influences of the environment. Heredity and environmental influences interact in shaping the behavior and development of the individual.

Observation is a key tool in forming basic assumptions about human development and behavior and also in testing these assumptions. To be valid, observation must be reliable, logical, and free from bias. In addition to the observation of subjects in both naturalistic and experimental settings, the use of longitudinal and cross-sectional studies, self-report data, and case studies can provide knowledge and understanding of human behavior.

REVIEW QUESTIONS

1. If you were asked to develop a profile on people who enter nursing and the paramedical professions, how would you proceed? What factors would you consider? What research techniques would you use? What considerations would you have to take into account in drawing your conclusions?

2. What ethical problems might you encounter when using some of the research techniques mentioned in this chapter? How could these be avoided?

3. If you were asked to study the behavior of infants or preverbal children, what type of behavior would you choose to study? What are some of the techniques you might use?

SUGGESTED READINGS

Kessen, W. *The child.* New York: Wiley, 1965. The child as viewed by important figures in the last two centuries. This book includes selections from Rousseau, Darwin, Baldwin, Freud, and Piaget.

Rogers, C. R. *On becoming a person.* Cambridge, Mass.: Riverside Press, 1961. In very readable style, Rogers presents a perceptive and hopeful model for personal growth throughout the life span.

Turnbull, C. *The mountain people.* New York: Simon & Schuster, 1972. An anthropologist's dramatic account of the survivors of a hunting and gathering people who were forced to alter their culture when their territory was declared a game preserve.

2

THEORIES OF HUMAN DEVELOPMENT: AN INTRODUCTION

What is the basic nature of man? Is he primarily rational and goal-oriented, or is he driven by passions? How does he learn—by discovery, by insight, or by small, sequential steps of increasing complexity? How is he motivated—by reward, by pain, by curiosity, or by inner drives?

An important reason for studying developmental psychology is to seek out answers to these questions, in order to acquire a better understanding of human behavior. Psychologists use theories to formulate their answers. Theories are attempts first to organize data; then to integrate assumptions based upon the data into a unified whole; and finally, with this body of information, to generate hypotheses which will explain human behavior and predict the future course of man's actions.

If you think about the questions raised above, you will probably realize that you have your own "theories" about the answers to them. You lean toward one explanation or another of a specific problem, and the assumptions implicit in your explanation probably have a lot to do with your thoughts about others. For instance, you may view juvenile delinquents either as responsible for their actions, or as victims of their conditioning. You may believe that a 6-year-old is able to decide for himself what he should study in school, or you may think children cannot be expected to know what they want. In other words, you probably have assumptions about both the degree to which an individual's behavior is his responsibility, and the degree to which the rationality of man can be relied upon to direct man's actions wisely.

Since we all have our own "theories," then why bother to spend a chapter discussing the theories advanced by others? Why not simply deal with people in the way that seems natural at the time, without worrying whether our actions follow one theory of behavior or another? One of the most important things we can get from a broad understanding of different theories is an ability to evaluate our own views. It is important for us to reexamine the assumptions behind our actions to see whether these assumptions make sense, whether they fit the circumstances, and what follows from these assumptions. An introduction to the major theories allows us to examine, evaluate, and discipline our intuitions and our own theories on human behavior.

Besides helping us understand our own ways of thinking, a knowledge of the major theories equips us with an eclecticism helpful in understanding human development. It is always worthwhile to be able to look at behavior through "different pairs of glasses," to step outside one's usual frame of reference in order to see the value of other explanations. To achieve the goal of understanding behavior requires looking from many different directions, while constantly reexamining our own assumptions in the light of other opinions and new data. A basic understanding of the theories of others can help us to gain this necessary perspective.

In this chapter we shall discuss some of the theories of developmental psychology. Many psychologists are eclectic, selecting from many theories those particular aspects that will help them in their work. Few of these psychologists have not been influenced by theories other than their own. The descriptions of the various theories given in this chapter, therefore, are not intended to label or pigeonhole psychologists, but are merely attempts to provide the basic outlines of some of the most popular beliefs.

LEARNING THEORIES

How does personality develop? For the past 40 or 50 years, the dominant American model for the answer to this question has been the explanation provided by the various learning theories. These include reinforcement theory, social learning theory, and several other learning theories.

Learning theories find the key to each man's nature in the way he is shaped by his environment. According to these theories, most behavior is acquired and it is acquired by learning. Learning is a complex process. It is not confined just to picking up grammar, the social niceties, or tennis skills; it also includes the acquiring of morality and of biases and the adopting of mannerisms such as nervous tics or stuttering. Since it covers so broad a spectrum of behavior, learning is not easy to define. We shall use the working definition proposed by Hilgard and Bower (1966) as the basis for our discussion:

> Learning is the process through which an activity originates or is changed through reacting to an encountered situation, provided that the characteristics of the change in activity cannot be explained on the basis of native response tendencies (instinct, for example), maturation, or temporary states such as fatigue or drugs. (p. 1)

Reactive Man

A basic assumption of learning theories is that man is a reactive, responsive individual. He is shaped and molded by the associations and rewards that he experiences. In other words, man is literally a function of his learning. The learning theorist's model of man is *mechanistic*. Man is viewed as a machine, set in motion by input (stimuli) and producing output (responses). There is little concern for analyzing the machine's structure, the human body, or changing the hardware, the mind itself.

The learning theorist's model of man is also *deterministic*. Everything in the individual's behavior, including his values, attitudes, and emotional responses, is believed to be determined by either his past or present environment. Therefore, such concepts as blame, respect, and dignity are considered irrelevant. According to the theory, since man is merely a product of his past learning history, he deserves neither credit nor blame for his actions. The title of a recent book by a modern learning theorist expresses this idea: B. F. Skinner's *Beyond Freedom and Dignity* (1971) implies that man's behavior is preprogrammed, beyond his control.

How did learning theorists come to this view of man as deterministic, mechanistic, and reactive? These underlying assumptions are, in part intentional, and in part a by-product of the learning theorist's experimental design, which studies man as the dependent variable and the environment as the independent variable. The theory builds its assumptions from an empirical base of data, studying man in the same way other scientists study biology or physics. It considers only the immediate stimulus environment in one situation and the individual's behavioral responses to that isolated event, avoiding any broader interpretations of his actions. In establishing such narrow limits for each activity, the learning theorist must assume that the behavior he sees is primarily a function of the immediate stimuli. Does this manner of looking at behavior unduly influence the observer to view the experiment in cause-and-effect terms?

The methodology of learning theorists is very painstaking. They do not start from a "grand design," as some other theorists do, and then devise experiments to test their hypotheses. Instead, they build their theory bit by bit, piece by piece, from simple experiments to more compex ones—an inductive approach. Theirs is a cautious and conservative strategy. It may be unsatisfying at first, because it does not tackle the more interesting, complex questions right at the start. Instead, it begins with a dog salivating, or a rat pressing bars, and then builds basic laws about animal behavior. For this reason, the theory is frustrating to those who are seeking an immediate explanation of an adolescent love affair, for example.

Gradually, learning theorists hope to be able to explain all of human behavior, and as experimenters gather evidence little by little, the theory is taking up more and more complex questions. Social learning theory, described later in this chapter, is just such an attempt to get at the more complex aspects of human behavior. But most learning theorists have not yet tried to offer a full explanation for much of life. Only within the last 15 years have learning theorists, particularly followers of Skinner, branched out to apply their principles to wide areas of human behavior.

Learning Process and Its Applications
While the methodology of learning theory is cautious, the theory has been amazingly productive in describing basic learning processes. Experimental research, generally carried on in laboratories and using animals, small children, and college students as subjects, has told us much about conditioning as a major process of learning.

CONDITIONING. Human behavior has long been recognized as falling into two general categories. Either we act in response to a stimulus (the pupils of the eye contract in bright light; an infant sucks if a finger is put into his mouth) or we act voluntarily (a child kicks a ball; a man scratches his knee). The terms *respondent* and *operant* are used to describe these two types of behavior. In respondent behavior, a stimulus or a set of conditions *elicits* a particular response; in operant behavior, the actor operates on the environment or *emits* an action.

Sometimes the same behavior may be both respondent and operant. While putting a finger into an infant's mouth elicits a sucking reaction by the baby, still the infant has some voluntary control over his own

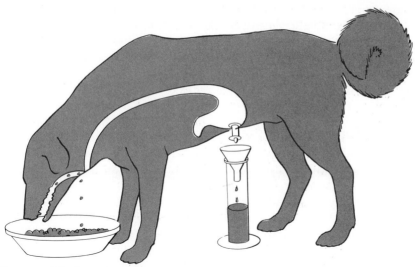

Drawing of Pavlov's dog demonstrating the classical conditioning reflex phenomenon. The apparatus under the dog is collecting and measuring his saliva.

sucking. He can begin it, stop it, slow it down, or speed it up at will. A knee jerk can be both respondent and operant, too. The patient's leg will respond to the doctor's knee tap with a kicking motion; but the patient can also kick his leg any other time he wants to.

The learning process of conditioning varies according to whether it is applied to respondent or operant behavior. *Classical conditioning* takes a respondent behavior and brings it under the control of a previously neutral stimulus. The experiments of Ivan Pavlov (1928) are among the most famous examples. Pavlov noted that dogs salivated when offered food. He began to ring a bell at the same time that he offered food to a dog, and he repeated the pairing of a neutral stimulus (the bell) with the food several times. Before long, the bell alone was enough to make the dog salivate, even when no food was within sight or smell. The bell had come to elicit the same response from the dog as the food had always produced. The bell had become a *conditioned stimulus.*

Emotional reactions are easily conditioned. A famous experiment on classical conditioning of fear was performed by John B. Watson, the originator of the behaviorist school of psychology from which learning theory developed. An 11-month-old infant named Albert was the subject of Watson and Rayner's experiment (1920). Albert was confronted with a white rat. At first, he showed no fear of the animal. But then the experimenters made a loud clanging noise every time the rat was shown to Albert, causing the baby to cry and crawl away. It did not take many pairings of the previously neutral stimulus of the rat with the unpleasant loud noise for Albert to respond with anxiety and fear to the rat alone. Soon Albert came to fear anything white and furry, even Santa Claus's beard.

Albert's case is a dramatic example of conditioning, but we can see clear parallels in children's everyday lives. Doctors' white uniforms or medicinal smells may arouse fear in children because of their association with unpleasant stimulation such as painful injections. Positive emotional reactions can be conditioned just like negative ones, too. Reactions of relaxation or pleasure are easily associated with previously neutral stimuli, like the old song which brings back all the memories of a sunny day at the beach or the excitement of a high school dance.

If a person comes to associate a previously neutral stimulus, such as Albert's rat, with an unpleasant emotional state, what can be done to reverse this conditioned response? In *counterconditioning*, the subject is gradually introduced to the once neutral stimulus in the presence of a strong and opposite conditioning stimulus (such as the caged rat introduced at a distance at a banquet). This soon reverses the conditioned negative response pattern.

Wolpe, Salter, and Reyna (1964) have used counterconditioning to treat common phobias such as fear of flying or driving, fear of authority figures, and fear of hospitals, where the conditioned stimuli are such things as height, uniforms, hospital smells, and "the boss." The most common counterconditioning technique is *relaxation* training, or *desensitization*. The client is taught deep relaxation, and in this state he is told to imagine himself approaching the feared situation. Each time the client reports tension, he is immediately instructed to stop the image and return to relaxation. With repeated pairing, a new response of relaxation replaces the old anxiety response, first to the image and finally to the real event or object. Two processes work together in counterconditioning. The old response is gradually extinguished because it is not actively reinforced. And in the meantime, the client is learning a new, competing response through the process of classical conditioning.

OPERANT CONDITIONING. All the examples we have mentioned above deal primarily with classical conditioning and respondent behavior (although they also include some operant behavior, as when Albert crawled away from the white rat). But operant or voluntary behavior may also be learned by conditioning. In fact, most cases probably include elements of both classical and operant conditioning. We shall discuss the two types of conditioning separately to enable us to examine both processes carefully.

The important difference between classical conditioning and *operant conditioning* is that in the latter, behavior cannot be elicited automatically. The behavior must occur before it can be strengthened by conditioning. In operant conditioning, what is rewarded or reinforced is learned. Since the behavior does not happen automatically, there is the problem of getting it to occur the first time before it can be rewarded. If a child comes into the house and throws his coat on the floor every day, his mother cannot reward him for hanging up the coat until he does it himself.

Edward Thorndike (1911) conducted experiments on operant conditioning with cats. The cats learned to manipulate a latch to open a door to get food. Thorndike described the learning phenomenon with what he called the *law of effect:* an act may be altered in its strength by its consequences. The cats' act of pressing the latch so that the door opened first occurred by chance. But when this act was reinforced by being paired with the reward of food, it was strengthened until the cats soon learned to open the door at will.

In this experiment, Thorndike used a *positive reinforcement* or reward to strengthen the original desired action. While he and many other experimenters used food as the inducement, positive reinforcements may also be a nod of approval, a token gift, or any number of things. Operant behavior can also be taught by avoidance conditioning, where the reinforcement consists of the ending of an unpleasant stimulus. For example, a bright light can be turned off, a loud noise can be stopped, or an angry parent can be quieted.

How can operant conditioning be used to teach a complex act? Very often, the final behavior must be built bit by bit. In *shaping,* the individual is rewarded for behavior that comes closer and closer to the desired act. This shaping through *successive approximation* to the desired act can make it possible to condition quite complex tasks. For example, to help a child learn to dress himself, a parent could begin by putting the child's socks on part way, and letting him finish the job. Each succeeding time, the child would do a little more for himself until he could finally complete the activity alone. Skinner used shaping in applying teaching machines to education (Skinner, 1968). With the

A first grader is shown using a computerized teaching machine. She receives instructions from the computer, types out the question, and receives the answers. This teaching machine is based on B. F. Skinner's concept of operant conditioning. (*Paolo Koch, Rapho/ Photo Researchers.*)

machines, the student learns in small, incremental steps, starting with simple problem solving and building up to more complex tasks. The desired behavior or answer is reinforced at each step by feedback from the machine and by the appearance of a new problem to solve. Eventually, the student succeeds in mastering a fairly complex problem.

One application of operant conditioning which has become a fairly popular way of shaping behavior in school situations is called a *token economy*. Here, a secondary reinforcer or token takes on the significance of an immediate reward, and it is used to encourage a specific behavior (O'Leary & Drabman, 1971). In a typical example of a token economy in a classroom, a disruptive child is given a poker chip for remaining quiet for a certain period of time. He understands that when he has earned a certain number of chips, he can trade them in for a toy, a candy, or some other reward. Usually, the child is persuaded to change his behavior and thus the method is successful.

Observational Learning and Social Learning Theory

Learning theory can be applied in more ways than just the direct conditioning of the subject. In an important extension of learning theory, social learning theorists have applied it to vicarious or *observational learning*. They demonstrate that much of what can be learned directly can also be learned by watching another person's behavior and its consequences (Bandura, 1969; Bandura & Walters, 1963). Modeling, identification, copying, and role playing are a few of the terms used to describe the process when one person learns by watching the results of another's act.

Learning theorists are particularly interested in observational learning as the area where learning theory can be applied to more complicated areas of human behavior. *Social learning theory* investigates the way people use models to learn social traits such as aggression, dependency, generosity, and indifference. It also studies how individuals learn to eat, walk, and speak in socially acceptable ways.

As an example of social learning theory, Bandura, Ross, and Ross (1963c) conducted an experiment in which children watched various levels of aggressive behavior in films. One group of children saw the aggressive behavior rewarded; another saw it punished; a third group saw a film of nonaggressive behavior play; and a fourth group saw no film at all. The children who saw aggression rewarded were significantly more aggressive in their own play, while those who saw the model punished were less aggressive. An uneasy sidelight of these findings is the question of how much children learn from the violent behavior they see on modern television programs.

A Cumulative Theory of Development

All learning must occur within the framework of a person's biological development. For example, a child 2 years of age is biologically unable to write his name or to assume responsibility for his infant brother while his mother goes out. Gagné (1965) describes a *cumulative theory of learning*, which is an attempt by learning theorists to take into account both long-term development and short-term learning processes. He sees learning as a cumulative procedure in which complex principles are gradually built up by the adding together of several simpler ideas, according to the learner's skills, his memory of what he has already learned, and his ability to generalize and apply what he learns to other situations.

Learning theories have been remarkably productive in generating insights into the reasons why people behave the way they do. The theories' emphasis on measuring empirical data has resulted in a great deal of important research, with hard data to support the findings. Learning theories have the advantage of being easy to test in the laboratory, or even in the classroom or the home. Overall, the learning theorists have made many contributions to our understanding of behavior, and we shall be looking at their approaches to development throughout this book.

An Evaluation of Learning Theories

But while learning theories are very productive within empirically testable areas, the types of behavior which lend themselves to the theories' methods of experimentation are somewhat limited. Learning theory principles are best applied to specific behaviors rather than to whole areas of development. The theories have difficulty explaining broad complexes of behavior such as adult moral decisions, scientific thoughts, or psychotic actions. They also cannot account for novel responses or for differences between individuals, and they are unable to analyze successfully emotional experiences such as artistic creativity, joy, or love.

The learning theories' empirical approach builds fact on fact slowly and cumulatively. Despite recent applications of social learning theory to classroom learning, parent education, and psychotherapy, there are still many questions which learning theorists are unable to answer—and which many psychologists believe may never be explained in terms of conditioned learning.

start c testing

The empirical approach of the learning theorists is considered by some psychologists to be a "typically American" practice. In contrast to it is the comprehensive theory approach of the "workers of a grand design." Jean Piaget, a Swiss, typifies many Europeans (and some Americans, too) in beginning with a complex integrative theory, then later testing its parts.

COGNITIVE THEORIES

start c theory

Cognitive theorists have appeared relatively recently on the American psychological scene, but their roots in European tradition are very old. The rationalist tradition manifests a respect for the mind and for mental organizing principles. Learning theorists such as Watson advised psychologists to ignore these mental concepts because they could not be scientifically observed. Though by no means ignoring behavior, the cognitive theorists have sparked a renewed interest in the mind. They have encouraged research to determine what is in the mind and how the mind develops. Piaget was originally a biologist, and he brought back to psychology the use of a biological model. To Piaget, the mind, like any other living structure, does not simply respond to stimuli; it grows, changes, and adapts to its world. The term *structuralists* (Gardner, 1973b) fits Piaget and the other cognitive psychologists because they are concerned with the structure of thought. Key figures among the cognitive theorists are Werner, Piaget, and Bruner, but in this section we will have room to discuss only Piaget, a Swiss, and Bruner, an American.

Rational Man In contrast to the behaviorists or learning theorists, cognitive theorists see man as active, alert, intelligent, and competent. For them, man does not merely receive information; he also processes it. Thus he is a thinker and a creator of his own reality, with intrinsic or innate motivation toward mastering problems. Man is curious; he discovers. He does not merely reflect relationships—he can himself create them. When he takes in stimuli, man does not merely respond to them but gives them structure and meaning. Many psychologists see in the cognitive theory a useful corrective to the learning theorists' idea of man as a direct product of his environment.

Piaget Piaget has been one of the most influential and prolific of twentieth-century psychologists. As a young man, his two main interests were biology and epistemology, a branch of philosophy that seeks to define human knowledge. In his lifelong effort to understand human knowledge, Piaget has used psychology to attempt to bridge the gap between biology and philosophy.

In his early years, Piaget worked with the Binet intelligence (IQ) tests. While testing children, he became less interested in their right answers than in patterns he found in their wrong answers, which seemed to be a clue to the way thought processes develop in children. He theorized that the differences between children and adults were not confined to how much they knew, but the *way* they knew. There were qualitative as well as quantitative differences in the thinking of children and adults.

To test his theory, Piaget devised one of his most famous experiments. He showed a child two identical glasses, each containing the same amount of liquid. After the child agreed that the amount of liquid in each glass was the same, Piaget poured the liquid from one of the glasses into a tall, narrow glass container. He then asked the child how much liquid was in the tall glass container—was it more or less than in the original glass, or was it the same amount? Most children aged 6, 7, or older answered that the amount was the same. But children under 6 said that the tall glass held more. Even when young children watched the same liquid being poured back and forth between the original glass and the tall glass, they said that the tall glass held more. This experiment has been tried with children of many cultures and nationalities, and the results are always the same.

Piaget reasons that until they reach a certain age, children form judgments based more upon perceptual than upon logical processes. In other words, they believe what their eyes tell them. To the younger children the liquid looked like more in the tall glass, so it was more. Children 7 years or older, on the other hand, barely glanced at the glasses. They knew that the amount of liquid remained the same, regardless of the size or shape of the glass it was in. (Piaget calls this the *principle of conservation*.) They did not base their judgments solely on perception; instead they used logic. Their knowledge came from within themselves, just as much as from outside sources.

THE ACTIVE MIND. To Piaget, the mind is not a blank slate on which knowledge can be written, nor a mirror which reflects what it perceives. If the information, perception, or experience presented to a person fits with a structure in his mind, then that information, perception, or experience is "understood." If it does not fit, the mind rejects it (or, if the mind is ready to change, it changes itself to accommodate the information or experience). Piaget uses the word *schema* (the plural is *schemata*) to designate what we call structure here. Schemata are ways of processing information, and they change as we grow. An infant uses a mouthing schema to explore any objects that can be grasped and brought to the mouth. As he grows and discovers more and more objects that do not fit this schema, the infant's way of processing information changes to another schema: he learns to explore with his hands.

A conservation experiment. A child is shown liquid from two identical glasses poured into a short, wide glass and a tall, narrow glass. When asked which has more or less, children under 6 say that the tall glass holds more. (*Sam Falk, The New York Times.*)

Schemata are ways of processing information. Here an infant uses an action schema to find out about the world. (*Suzanne Szasz.*)

Piaget proposes a biological model to describe the process by which we adapt to the world. An animal that is eating does two things. He accommodates to the food, changing his digestive system to produce enzymes and start the muscular activity of peristalsis. He also assimilates the food, making it part of himself. Human beings gain intelligence, says Piaget, in the same way. We adjust our schemata to *accommodate* new information, but at the same time we *assimilate* this learning into the mind's structure. On seeing a new object for the first time, we try to fit it into what we know. Is it a weapon? A grooming tool? A cooking implement? If it does not fit our existing concepts (if we cannot assimilate it), we may have to change our concepts or form a new concept (accommodation).

The mind always works in this way to find a "balance" between assimilation and accommodation, to eliminate inconsistencies or gaps between reality and the mind's picture of reality. This process, which is called *equilibration,* is basic to human adaptation and, indeed, to all biological adaptation.

STAGES OF MENTAL DEVELOPMENT. As the human being develops and his structural abilities for organizing new information become greater, he is able to use more complex schemata to understand the outside world. Piaget sees this development as occurring in four steps (see Figure 1). The schemata that infants use are comparatively few and they all involve action. The infant period of learning is therefore called *sensorimotor,* because infant intelligence uses the senses and bodily motion in its equilibration. A second stage begins about the time the child starts to talk. This is the *preoperational* period (from about 2 to 7 years of age). It is the time when, among other things, the child begins to develop symbolic images. He learns that words are symbols for objects. At the beginning of this stage especially, a child will take names so seriously that he cannot separate their literal meanings from the things they represent or differentiate images from objects. If he decides that a wad of paper is the cake to be served at his tea party, and his mother unwarily throws his paper "cake" in the garbage, he will be just as upset as a bride would be if someone threw away her wedding cake. But by the end of this period, the child has learned that language is really quite arbitrary and that a name could just as easily represent one object as another.

In the next stage of *concrete operations* (about ages 7 to 11), the child begins to be able to think with some logic. He can classify things and deal with a hierarchy of classifications. A preoperational child, for example, cannot understand that a person can be both a Democrat and an American: he can deal with only one classification at a time. But a 7-year-old understands that Democrats are a smaller group within the larger group of Americans. The concrete operational child still has several hurdles to go over before he thinks like an adult; the final and most important stage is the period of *formal operations* (beginning at ages 12 to 15 years). After this point, the adolescent can imagine things contrary to fact; think realistically about the future; build ideals; and grasp metaphors which younger children cannot comprehend. Our minds do not stop growing after the age of 15, but there are no more major developmental steps.

SUMMARY OF PIAGET'S THEORIES. For Piaget, intelligence is a biological adaptation. It evolves gradually in qualitatively different steps, as the result of countless assimilations and accommodations, while the individual attempts to reach new balances. The mind is active, not passive. Piaget's theory stresses interaction between the biological capacities of each man and the materials he encounters in his environment. We all develop as a result of this interaction. Can the stages of development be speeded up so that, for example, a bright 5-year-old can be taught concrete operations? Piaget calls this the "American question" because he is asked it each time he visits here. His answer is that even if this is possible, its long-run value is doubtful. Instead, he stresses the importance of giving each child enough learning materials appropriate to each stage as he is growing, so that no areas of the mind are left undeveloped.

Figure 1 A comparison of Piaget's and Erikson's stages of life span development.

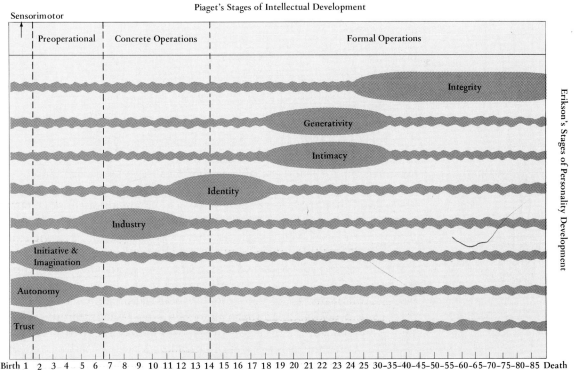

THEORIES OF HUMAN DEVELOPMENT: AN INTRODUCTION   35

Bruner   Like Piaget, Jerome Bruner has been a prolific cognitive theorist. Most recently, his subjects have been infants and children. While Piaget has shown little interest in applying his theories, Bruner has applied cognitive theory to education, and he has had both a direct and an indirect influence on school curricula. Bruner is also fascinated with the processes of intuition, creativity, and aesthetics. A lesser known book of his, *On Knowing: Essays for the Left Hand* (1965b), investigates the kind of knowing expressed in poetry, art, and myth as opposed to rational, problem-solving thought. Throughout his career, Bruner has sought to integrate two images of man: the artist and the scientist.

Bruner has been influenced greatly by Piaget, however, and the similarities between their two theories are basic ones. Both men are interested in biology and epistemology. Both see cognitive structures as changing qualitatively as a child develops. And both see the mind developing in a few major stages, with growth involving the movement from a state where the immediate and apparent absorb the child's attention to a state where his mind can think beyond appearances (Bruner, 1973).

Bruner's three stages of development correspond roughly to Piaget's first three periods. In the *enactive* stage, like Piaget's sensorimotor stage, the infant learns through action. The *iconic* stage, akin to Piaget's preoperational stage, involves the development and use of imagery. And in Bruner's *symbolic* stage, the child uses language to relate the real and the abstract.

An important, largely unresolved difference between Bruner and Piaget is the role that language plays in this third stage of growth. Bruner has found that the children in the operational stage are those who, in the example of the experiment with glasses of liquid, can use language to explain why the liquid is the same amount in differently shaped glasses. To Piaget, language skill is not the causative factor in reaching concrete operations; for him, the thought comes first, then the language. To Bruner, the 7-year-old's problem-solving skills are partly the result of verbal formulations that enable him to overcome incorrect sensory evidence in experiments like this one (Elkind, 1968).

An Evaluation of Cognitive Theories   Whatever their disagreements in other areas, Bruner, Piaget, and other cognitive theorists agree in rejecting mechanistic learning theory. They find it hard to believe that between a person and his understanding of a problem there is merely a reward of praise or candy. They feel that when man solves a problem, he is motivated by his own basic competence, not by a mere stimulus-response reaction (Bruner, 1971).

Cognitive theories give man a respect for his rationality that is missing from the mechanistic model of learning theory. They see the human being of all ages as an integrated person who can plan and think through a problem. In addition, they allow us to account for the role that understanding, beliefs, attitudes, and values seem to play in so much of behavior. And many psychologists feel that the cognitive theories, in dealing with language and thought, take up where the learning theories leave off.

Cognitive theories have been widely applied to education. They ← *mabaorat.* have been especially useful in helping educators to plan the curriculum to fit children's stages of development. The theories have also made it possible to determine when a child is ready for a certain subject and to select the best way of approaching any subject at each age. The teaching of mathematics and science in particular has benefited from a new understanding of the abilities of elementary school children during the stage of concrete operations. For example, educators have learned much from the seeming failure of the "new math" to improve children's grasp of the subject (Elkind, 1968). We now realize that some of these programs wrongly assumed that if children in the concrete operational stage were given a new vocabulary for dealing with numbers, they would understand mathematical concepts more easily. Instead of emphasizing symbols to describe concepts, the teaching methods for children of this age should deal more with concrete objects like blocks. Since the child is able physically to manipulate these objects, he can relate to them far more easily than to abstract verbal symbols.

A persistent controversy among cognitive theorists concerns the role of language skills in the development of thought. It is clear that language skills are a help in school. While disadvantaged children learn concrete operations at the same age as other children, they may be unable to show their understanding at school because they lack an adequate vocabulary. In the same way, middle-class children may be so articulate that their teachers mistakenly believe these children understand more than they actually do. Or is the relationship of language to thought more basic than that? Perhaps the best way to help the disadvantaged child may be to provide greater language experience (Elkind, 1968).

Since cognitive theories are concerned mainly with intellectual development, thus far they have been unable to explain all of human behavior. Some important areas still to be investigated include social, emotional, and personality development, although Spivak and Shure (1973) have made a beginning in this direction. While cognitive theorists have looked chiefly at the development of perceptual abilities, language, and complex thought, they have not yet explored the individual's potentialties for dependence, nurturance, aggression, and sexuality. Psychoanalytic theory has traditionally been concerned with these areas, studying emotions and their relation to personality development. It is to this tradition that we will now turn.

THE PSYCHOANALYTIC TRADITION

The theories of Sigmund Freud, the neo-Freudians, and the ego psychologists form what we call the psychoanalytic tradition. The source of data for these theories has been primarily clinical case study material. Freud's notion of man is a deterministic one, resembling the view of the learning theorists, but it emphasizes the determinism of innate drives which are by and large beyond man's control. According to psychoanalytic theory, man is a driven creature, constantly trying to redirect or channel the potent forces within him. These forces, which are evident from childhood, are transformed as man develops various forms of behavior. Modern psychologistsof the psychoanalytic tradition, such as Erik Erikson, no longer see animal drives as the sole basis for man's actions, but they still draw heavily from the traditions of Freud and the neo-Freudians.

Freud

Freud lived during the Victorian era, and in many ways his theory was a reaction against his time. His concern was man's emotional life, which was kept well hidden in the society in which Freud lived. Freud emphasized the unconscious as a determinant of behavior. He believed that the biological or animal drives, such as sex and aggression, were the primary forces behind human behavior. This assertion that man was biologically directed, along with Freud's systematic study of man as an animal, was important historically in opening the way for the scientific study of man in modern psychology. Much of Freud's theory looked to childhood for clues about the underlying nature of man.

According to Freud, the development of the personality takes place in several *psychosexual stages*. The first three stages occur before puberty, and they are marked by the child's focus of sensual pleasure in different areas of his body, called *erogenous zones*. In early infancy or the *oral stage*, the child's mouth is the most pleasurable area of sensual stimulation. He loves to suck things, to mouth toys. Later, during the *anal stage*, the release of tension associated with defecation becomes a central focus for self-stimulation. And during the *phallic stage* (ages 3 to 5), the child becomes aware of the pleasurable feelings he can provide himself by manipulation of the genitals, or masturbation. The way in which the child's parents react to these natural stages will profoundly affect the child's adult personality. For example, too harsh treatment of mistakes in toilet training during the anal stage may produce a compulsively neat, over-controlled adult.

The oral, anal, and phallic stages are part of the *pregenital period*, in which the child's sexual or sensual instincts are not yet directed toward reproduction. After a period of sexual latency from the age of 6 or so, the child enters the *genital period* with the onset of puberty. This longest stage of development does not center on self-stimulation as much as on directed sexual activity, socialization, and choosing a way of life. But it is profoundly shaped by the developments of the pregenital stage, and it still satisfies many pregenital impulses in sublimated or muted form.

Freud's theory is far more complex than the short summary we have been able to provide here. But instead of dwelling too heavily on Freud, it is much more worthwhile to spend some time with the neo-Freudians, who have had a far greater influence on modern psychology. One of the most interesting and important of the neo-Freudians is Erik Erikson.

Freud emphasized the unconscious in humans as a determinant of their behavior. A woodcut interpretation by Jean Cocteau. (*The Bettmann Archive.*)

Erikson's theory of personality development has much in common Erikson with Freud's, but it is marked by some important differences. Erikson sees the development of the individual as occurring in several stages, many of which correspond to those of Freud. But his model is *psychosocial*, not psychosexual as is Freud's. Erikson's stages expand upon the sexual forces within the individual and the way in which these forces are treated by the parents. In addition, Erikson sees the stages as periods in each person's life when his capacities or experience dictate that he must make a major adjustment to his social environment and to himself. While the attitude of his parents will affect the way the individual handles these conflicts, his social milieu is extremely important too (a good example is the "identity crisis" of many modern American Indians who are confused about which society they belong to). Erikson's model expands upon Freud's in another important way. Erikson's eight stages of development encompass all ages of human life. He sees personality formation as an ongoing process throughout childhood, adulthood, and even old age.

Erikson's book *Childhood and Society* (1963) presents his model of the eight stages of man. In Erikson's view, every man experiences eight crises or conflicts in development. The adjustments a person makes at each stage are not irreversible. For example, a child who was denied affection in infancy can grow to normal adulthood provided he is given the proper sort of extra attention at later stages of his development. But his adjustments to conflicts do play an important part in the development of that individual's personality. The resolution of these conflicts is cumulative—that is, a person's manner of adjustment at each stage of development leads him to a somewhat different way of handling the next conflict.

According to Erikson, there are different points in the life cycle where specific developmental conflicts are paramount. Figure 1 illustrates the development of personality in Erikson's eight stages almost as several strands of a rope. Each strand bulges at a particular period where one developmental task or conflict is of greater significance than the others are. The figure shows that while each of Erikson's conflicts is critical at only one stage, it is present throughout life, too. For example, adjustments to intimacy are especially important in early adulthood. But even young children have needs related to intimacy, and the elderly often suffer marked limitation in satisfaction of intimacy needs.

Erikson's eight stages may be described as points where each person's adjustment will lean toward one of two opposite poles. The first stage corresponds roughly in time to Piaget's sensorimotor stage and to Freud's oral stage. It centers on the formation of a basic sense of *trust* (or the opposite pole, *mistrust*) in the environment. If the infant's needs are met, if he receives attention and affection, his later outlook on the world will probably reflect a foundation of trust formed during this period. Needless to say, the parents play a major role in molding the infant's outlook at this period, just as they do in Freudian theory. But at later stages, when the child's life is no longer centered in the home, Erikson gives the social environment, and the individual himself, the more important roles.

In the second stage, the 1- to 3-year-old child is faced with another important step: the development of either a sense of *autonomy* or a sense of *doubt* with which he will face his world. The child's new motor skills, as well as his mental accomplishments and his knowledge of himself as a separate being, cause him to form basic feelings about his own abilities to do things for himself. The parents are crucial in this resolution, too. If they do everything for the child, prevent his explorations, or impose too many punishments, he may leave this stage doubting his own abilities.

The 4- to 5-year-old faces the task of building a sense of *initiative* (or *guilt*, if the initiative is not supported). He has reached the point where he can now decide on many of his activities for himself. His growing intellectual initiative is also shown in the endless questions he asks and in his creation of a make-believe world. How others react to these advances will influence his later feelings of pride or of guilt in self-initiated activities.

During ages 6 to 11, the elementary school years, the child develops abilities in deductive reasoning and in playing games according to rules. *Industry* indicates the child's interest in seeing how things work. *Inferiority* indicates that his skills and abilities are inadequate or hopeless. Children who are encouraged to make things, to complete projects, to establish friendships, and to discover new interests for themselves are more likely to leave this period enjoying their productivity. But if they meet with no success, their interest in schoolwork, sports, projects, or even friendships may suffer.

From about ages 12 to 18, the adolescent faces the task of sorting out his own *ego identity*; his failure to do so results in *role confusion*. Unlike Freud, Erikson sees this stage as centered on more than the emergence of sexuality, for the adolescent's mental maturity gives him a new interest in looking at his world (characterized particularly by the "youthful idealism" which often appears at this age). If he can discern his self-image from a confusing array of roles as son, friend, student, and sexual being, he will emerge with a fairly solid feeling of an integrated identity. At this stage, the individual begins to take a primary role in resolving his own conflicts, and the social milieu plays as important a part in his development as the primary family does.

Young adulthood covers the years of courtship and early family life. The adjustment to be made at this stage—largely overlooked by classical psychoanalysts—involves the dimensions of *intimacy* and *isolation*. The intimacy which Erikson talks about concerns more than sexual intimacy. It is the ability to share one's self with another person of either sex without fearing the loss of one's own identity. A person's success in establishing this dimension will be affected by his resolutions in the five previous stages; but here, too, the surrounding social conditions will play an important role.

Middle age brings the choice between preoccupation with self—

In Erikson's view, if children can master an experience in miniature, they can transfer that sense of control to the environment. Here, a hospital pediatric recreation director applies that concept to help children cope with hospitalization. (*UPI*.)

with one's own health, needs, and comfort—and concern for others. These dimensions are called *generativity* and *self-absorption*. This is the stage when the family unit begins to disperse. Parents find themselves with more freedom for their own concerns. The choice between using this new freedom for one's own interests or for outside involvements forms the seventh developmental task.

Old age is the time when the individual looks back on his life. If he is satisfied that it has had meaning, his outlook has *integrity*. If he sees his life as a series of misdirected energies and lost chances, he *despairs*. In this stage, the adjustment each person faces is his own. His final resolution is the cumulative product of all his previous resolutions.

An Evaluation of the Psychoanalytic Tradition

While the psychoanalytic tradition is often thought of in historical terms, it continues to make important contributions to the study of human behavior. Its basic strength lies in the richness of its holistic approach: its willingness to look at the whole individual—including both his conscious and unconscious mental activities—and to deal quite specifically with his emotions. Its emphasis on unconscious processes allows it to explore important areas of human behavior which many other traditions barely touch. It is also a rich theory for dealing with interpersonal relationships, particularly the relationships of childhood and those in the primary family unit.

The basic weakness of psychoanalytic theory is inseparable from its strength. While the theory explores the depths of personality, it is precisely this area which is almost impossible to define or to validate by experiment. The theory must draw much of its data from case studies of adults, where childhood is reconstructed subjectively by the patient. The result is a theory which is often vague, unscientific, and difficult to test.

HUMANISTIC PSYCHOLOGY AND THE SELF THEORIES

Humanistic psychology has been called the "third force" in psychology (Maslow, 1968), for it reacts against both the environmental determinism of learning theory and the Freudian determinism of the instincts. Humanistic psychology and the related "self" theories (which center on the individual's self-concept, or perception of his own identity) confront deterministic learning and psychoanalytic theories. They ask the question, Why is it that persons who deny human freedom continue to make choices in everyday life? (Severin, 1974). The stated aim of these theories is to form a picture of man which is as close as possible to our own human experience: a man who is more than the sum of his parts and more than a bundle of stimulus-response patterns or animal drives.

Humanistic psychology provides a holistic personality theory with close ties to existential philosophy. It seeks to maximize man's potential, to rescue the will from the drives of the instincts as well as from the stimuli of the environment. It maintains that man can make choices about his own life. He can, if he wishes, be spontaneous, self-determining, creative. In this sense, humanistic psychology sees life as fuller, more complicated, and more hopeful than do other theories.

Man is qualitatively different from other animals, for he can use symbols and think in abstract terms. For this reason, humanistic psychologists say that experiments with animals cannot tell us much about man. A rat in a maze cannot conceptualize his problem as a human would. Man in a maze will put many more processes—logic, self-reflection, response to a challenge—into play than could any rat.

Humanistic psychologists emphasize consciousness, as much as unconsciousness, as a basic human process. They reject the sharp dichotomy between subject and object in psychology. In their view, the psychologist must recognize himself as both subject and object of his study. Man experiences himself, as well as others, as spontaneously self-determining and creatively striving toward goals (Severin, 1974). This optimism of the humanistic psychologists is in marked contrast to most other theoretical approaches.

An important psychologist of the humanistic school is Abraham Maslow. His theory of self, proposed in 1954, stresses man's need to develop his full potentialities. This need for *self-actualization* is an innate force, but it only comes into action in the well-integrated person whose "lower needs," such as safety, love, food, and shelter, have already been satisfied. For example, a farmer faced with a crop failure and a family of eight to feed will spend little time in self-expression through painting. Maslow sees the drive for self-actualization as relatively recent in man's evolution; the more basic needs have historically occupied most of mankind's energies. Even today, very few people have successfully developed this self-actualization value.

Another humanistic psychologist, Carl Rogers, approaches man's attempts to become fully functioning from a different angle. Rogers is concerned with the problem of helping people to realize their own potential. He has constructed a model which he believes lays out the conditions needed for positive personality growth. The model is drawn from Rogers' own experience as a counselor and therapist, but it is intended as well to apply to lifelong growth in real life, outside the therapist's office. These conditions are the characteristics basic to any positive interpersonal relationship. They include such qualities as the therapist's unconditional willingness to accept and like the client just as he is; the therapist's genuine, total involvement in the relationship; and his empathetic understanding of the client's problems. Rogers's model is important as an attempt to set an interpersonal climate for maximal personality growth.

Without the everyday pressures of "lower needs," the self-actualized individual is more free to express himself. (*George Daniell, Photo Researchers.*)

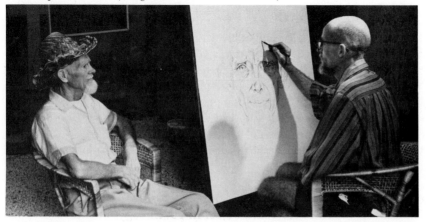

An Evaluation of Humanistic Psychology

Humanistic psychology, although a comparatively recent approach to human development, is beginning to have an impact in several ways. It acts as a spur to other developmental psychology approaches, for it stresses the importance of keeping in touch with real life in all its richness. It has had considerable impact on the counseling of adults, but comparatively little, so far, on child development. It has begun to influence education in the direction of "humanizing" the more traditional relationships within the schools.

As a developmental psychology, though, humanistic theory has yet to mature fully. While study has been done in the field of self theory, research in many other areas is just starting. There is little solid evidence of how the self-fulfilling, self-actualizing person develops, and much skepticism has been heard from "hardheaded" researchers. But these gaps and the initial skepticism may be a result of the theory's comparatively recent appearance. The fact remains that humanistic psychology is an active and growing approach.

ETHOLOGY

Ethology, like humanistic psychology, is a relatively new force in developmental psychology. But here the resemblance between the two subjects ends. Ethology is a branch of biology which studies patterns of behavior in animals. It has stimulated among psychologists a renewed interest in the biological characteristics which man has in common with animals. A prime concern of ethology is the importance of studying both man and animals in their natural settings. Just as ethologists choose to study the social relationships of baboons in the wild instead of in a wire cage, so they also insist upon observing children at play during a school recess, not in a contrived laboratory setting.

The ethologist applies the same theoretical principles to the study of the behavior of both men and animals. He sees many similarities between animal and human behavior; and he believes that a similar evolutionary experience has preserved certain behavior traits in man which are common to animals, too. The ethologist also proposes that like other animals, human beings may have inherited behavior patterns involving sexual behavior, aggression, and social responses—patterns in man which are much older than his culture. This tenet of ethology bears a resemblance to psychoanalytic drive theory, but there is an important difference. The psychoanalyst sees human drives as remnants of archaic, biological drives that must be restrained if civilization is not to be destroyed. The ethologist says that sexual and aggressive behavior patterns may be an integral part of civilization itself. Perhaps the successful civilization is the one that does not attempt to restrict this biological heritage (Hess, 1970).

Ethology adds another important innovation. Most developmental psychologists look at situational and historical causes of behavior. The ethologist sees these, but he considers an adaptive cause as well: the function of the behavior for the preservation of the individual or the species. He also sees an evolutionary cause. For example, a baby cries. The situational cause may be that he is in pain. The historical cause may be that he has been rewarded by care when he cried in the past. The functional or adaptive cause is to alert the mother and "trigger" her nurturance. Crying is an innate behavior pattern directed toward the specific target of nurturance. Finally, the evolutionary cause is the immobility of the human infant which makes crying, rather than running to the mother, a dominant response (Hess, 1970).

Ethology represents an interesting new way of looking at man which is making its mark on psychology. Ethological methods of observation have already been applied to man, as in one naturalistic study of the differences between boys and girls at play during recess (Omark & Edelman, 1969). A growing interest in the methods and principles of ethology suggests that its influence will increase during the coming years.

We study contrasting psychological theories in order to understand human behavior and to establish a basis for integrating facts and understanding new research.

The most widely studied learning theories view man as a function of his experiences and consider development to be a cumulative increase in knowledge and behavioral capabilities. Their major learning processes are conditioning (classical and operant) and observational learning.

Cognitive theories view man as constructive and rational. Piaget and Bruner, the major proponents of these theories, view development of the mind as biological adaptation. For them, the mind is not a blank

An ethologist could make lengthy naturalistic observations of patterns of nurturance, mating, and dominance in a complex social setting such as the family. (*Ken Heyman*.)

slate; it absorbs and processes information according to the existing *schema*. Cognitive theorists feel that learning occurs by active exploration and discovery, with a resulting adaptation.

Psychoanalytic theory maintains a holistic perspective. Freud recognized the importance of childhood experience and the unconscious as determinants of adult behavior. Erikson proposed a developmental view where Freud's psychosexual stages merge with culture's developmental tasks.

Humanistic psychology is a reaction to the pessimistic determinism of environment and innate drives. It seeks to maximize man's potential, achieve self-actualization of the individual, and reaffirm for man some control over his own life.

Ethology is a holistic theory which looks at the individual in context and in a naturalistic setting. In addition to seeking historical and situational explanations of man's behavior, ethology is concerned with adaptive and evolutionary causes.

REVIEW QUESTIONS

1. Name two theories of human development which emphasize the human being's feelings and his way of relating to society and other people. Explain each theory.

2. How would you countercondition the child who hated and feared school?

3. One of the experiments used by cognitive theorists involved two balls of clay. Children were shown both balls and they agreed that the balls were the same size. One ball was then rolled into a sausage shape, and the children were asked if the sausage-shaped piece then contained more, less, or the same amount of clay. How do you think 4-year-olds answered the question? Eight-year-olds? Give Piaget's explanation of the reason why the children responded as they did.

SUGGESTED READINGS

Bruner, J. *The relevance of education.* New York: Norton, 1971. This popular cognitive theorist applies some of his psychological insights to the field of education.

Keller, F. S. *Learning: Reinforcement theory* (2nd ed.). New York: Random House, 1969. A brief, concise description of the basic principles of learning by reinforcement theory.

Lorenz, K. *King Solomon's ring.* New York: Crowell, 1952. Lorenz, a popular ethologist, provides fascinating descriptions of the ways and habits of various animals and birds. His accounts are humorous, affectionate, and provocative.

Skinner, B. F. *Walden II.* New York: Macmillan, 1948. This popular novel describes a community based on the principles of operant conditioning.

3

PHYSICAL AND BIOLOGICAL ASPECTS OF DEVELOPMENT

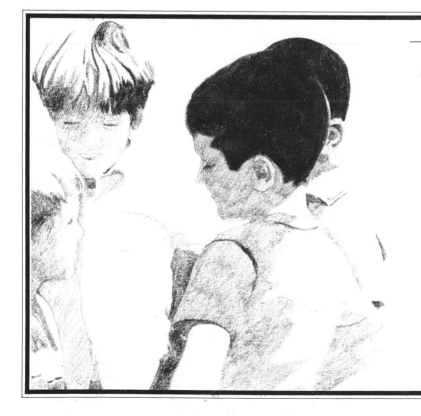

Human development is an integrated phenomenon which involves a person's body, his mind, and his emotions. In considering the various aspects of the development process, then, we shall divide our discussion into three broad areas: physical development, cognitive development, and socioemotional development. This approach, while it allows us to focus on one aspect at a time, tends to de-emphasize the fact that all of the aspects are tightly interrelated. It is important to remember that in real life, such arbitrary divisions as we are making simply do not exist.

Bearing in mind that every individual, at every stage of his life, is an integrated and whole person, we shall begin to describe some elements of this complex growth process. In this chapter, we shall discuss a few of the general characteristics of physical and biological development as they occur over the total life span. This general treatment of the topic will lay the groundwork for later chapters that focus on physical development at particular stages. Our approach in this chapter will thus be selective and we shall confine our discussion to representative aspects of physical development, as a means of approaching some of the underlying concepts. In a similar way, Chapter 4 will establish an overview for cognitive development, and Chapter 5 will provide an overview for social and emotional development.

PHYSICAL GROWTH AND MATURATION

Two important kinds of changes can be traced in the development of every individual. The first, and most apparent, is physical growth, revealed in the dramatic increase in size as the individual progresses from infant to toddler, then to child, and on to adolescent. Inseparable from this physical growth is a process of maturation by which the individual becomes a more complex organism and learns more and more refined skills. An infant is not just a miniature adult, for he differs from the adult in a number of significant ways. The inability of a 2-year-old child to write has little to do with his relatively small size. Rather, he is unable to write because he has not yet acquired the requisite skills, which involve motor coordination, powers of reasoning, attention to detail, and the ability to interpret written symbols.

Qualitative and Quantitative Changes

Growth may be described as *quantitative* in that a child experiences an increase in size. Growth is also *qualitative* in that the child's body systems undergo substantial changes in structure and function. An infant's digestive system, for example, gradually develops into a more complex, functioning organ. The newborn is able to digest only milk; but as he grows older his system changes structurally so that it can assimilate a more varied diet. Along with this kind of biological change, similar qualitative changes take place in the areas of cognition and emotional development. A growing child acquires a capacity for more complex reasoning, as he also begins to experience a wider range of human emotion (Breckenridge & Vincent, 1955).

The Order and Tempo of Growth

Growth is an orderly and predictable process which allows us to pinpoint with relative accuracy how and when developmental changes will occur. Each child is distinct and individual, but nonetheless each child progresses through an orderly sequence of experiences. He sits before he stands, he stands before he walks, he babbles before he talks, and he learns to draw a circle before he draws a square (Gesell, 1940).

The overall process of growth is also continuous. As a child develops he adds to the skills he has already acquired, and his new skills in turn become the basis for further achievements. Thus, most stages of development depend upon what has gone before and influence what will occur later. In a few instances, changes in growth can be discontinuous as well, since they involve the abandonment of some previous development. During the prenatal stage, for example, a yolk sac develops to nourish the embryo but a few weeks later, when the sac has served its function, it disintegrates and disappears. Similarly, an infant 9 or 10 months old first learns to creep and crawl, and he later abandons this skill when he learns to walk.

While growth is orderly and continuous, the tempo at which it proceeds is uneven and differential. Individual development usually takes place in spurts, with various parts of the body developing at different rates. Figure 2 shows the different rates of growth for four principal areas of the body.

The general body develops rapidly during the preschool years, slows

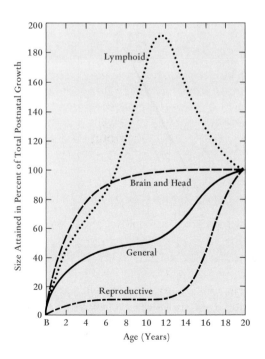

Figure 2 Patterns of growth of various parts of the body. The lymphoid system includes the lymph nodes and thymus. The brain and head include the brain, spinal cord, and optic parts. The general type is the body as a whole, and specifically the kidneys, respiratory and digestive organs, and the aortic and pulmonary parts of the heart. The reproductive system includes the prostate, Fallopian tubes, testes, and ovaries. (*Taken from Tanner, J. M.* Growth at adolescence *(2nd ed.). Oxford: Blackwell Scientific Publications, 1962. Redrawn from Scammon, R. E. The measurement of the body in childhood. In J. A Harris, C. M. Jackson, D. G. Paterson, & R. E. Scammon (Eds.).* The measurement of man. *Minneapolis: University of Minnesota Press, 1930.*)

down during the middle school years, increases rapidly during adolescence, and then tapers off. The lymphoid system shows a growth curve that rises rapidly just before adolescence and then decreases sharply during the teen years. Reproductive capacity develops very slowly at first but then grows very rapidly during middle to late adolescence. The brain and head mature dramatically during the preschool years, and then development slows to a gradual development into adulthood (Tanner, 1970).

All of these differential growth rates produce different body shapes and proportions at different periods of time. The size of the head is one salient illustration of this. At 2 months after conception, the head is nearly one-half the length of the body; by the time of birth, it has decreased to one-fourth the length of the body. It then continues to decrease in proportion during childhood, even though it continues to grow in size. By adulthood, the size of the head is not much more than one-eighth the total body length. This shift in proportion occurs because the rate of growth of the head is slower than that of the rest of the body (see Figure 3).

The growth of teeth and the development of fine motor coordination also show how different the rates for two body systems can be. When the child is between the ages of 2 and 6, the teeth show relatively little

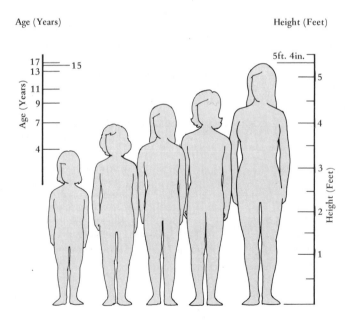

Figure 3 A girl's growth from early childhood to adulthood. (*Reprinted from Bayer, L. M., & Bayley, N.* Growth diagnosis. *By permission of The University of Chicago Press, Chicago, Copyright © 1959.*)

growth. The first set of teeth is complete at age 2, and the permanent set does not begin to erupt until age 6. During the same age interval, fine motor coordination develops smoothly and with relative rapidity. Gesell, Ilg, and Ames (1940) described how children handle small cubes at various ages. At age 2 the child can build a tower of six or seven cubes. At age 2½ he can build a tower of ten cubes. At 3½ years he can build a bridge between two towers, and at age 4 he uses one cube as a gate. At age 5 he uses the cubes to build two steps, and at age 6 he can build three steps. Thus, while the teeth have shown very little change, cognition and motor coordination have developed at a fast pace.

As we have just seen, the sequence of growth is an orderly and predictable phenomenon, since all of us experience the stages of development in more or less the same succession. However, children vary a great deal in the pace of their growth. Most of them maintain a fairly consistent growth rate, one that is established at birth and continues throughout development. Thus, the child who develops more slowly than his peers will probably continue this slower rate throughout his life (Haimowitz, 1973). Differing individual growth rates are perhaps most easily seen during adolescence. The photograph points up how wide the variations can be.

In an effort to discover if different growth rates affected personality, Jones and Bayley (1950) studied two groups of boys during adolescence. One group consisted of early maturers, the other of later maturers. The authors found that the boys whose physical maturity was rapid were usually treated by adults and by other children as more mature. These early maturers had relatively little need to strive for status, were successful as athletes, and were often chosen as student leaders. A fair proportion of the later-maturing boys strove for attention, often in inappropriate ways and probably, the authors concluded, as a means of compensating for their physical disadvantages. The authors did not find that their bodily immaturity *caused* the boys' psychological characteristics. Rather, they pointed out that our culture treats adolescents in a way that implies certain disadvantages for slow-maturing boys.

One further point to be mentioned here concerns those children whose rate of maturity has been adversely affected by poor nutrition, by illness, or by neglect. J. M. Tanner has shown that each individual has a target growth which is "governed by the control systems of [his] genetical constitution and powered by energy absorbed from the natural environment" (1963, p. 818). If the body is prevented from reaching its target growth at any particular period—and provided the period is not too long—once the adverse condition is corrected the body is able to speed up its maturation so that at some succeeding time it is again on target. Thus, once a proper diet is introduced, or an illness conquered, or a climate of genuine affection established, children whose natural growth has been retarded will frequently step up their rates of

Individuality of Pace of Growth

There is a marked difference in the growth pattern of these 12-year-olds. (*Alice Kandell, Rapho/Photo Researchers.*)

development. They reestablish their individual tempos, sometimes showing remarkable developments within short periods of time (Haimowitz, 1973). The mechanism by which the human organism knows when to stop "catching up" remains wholly mysterious.

Aging We have seen how "growing up" involves quantitative and qualitative change, how the orderly process of development can proceed at an uneven tempo, and how the various bodily systems develop at different rates. These same developmental characteristics continue to operate in the period of old age, in the stage of life termed *senescence*.

Just as growth in adolescence is more than a matter of chronological age, decline in senescence differs from one individual to the next (Marshall, 1973). There is considerable variability in the rate and style of aging so that a group of 65-year-olds will show a diversity of development that is comparable to the diversity seen in any group of adolescents. If this variability were fully understood, we would begin to question the policy of legislating for the aged on the basis of chronological age.

Identical twins show similar physical characteristics throughout their lives. Here are two women at the ages of 12, 17, 67, and 91. (*Reprinted from Kollmann, F. J., & Jarvik, L. F. Individual differences in constitution and genetic background. In J. Birren (Ed.).* Handbook of aging and the individual. *By permission of the University of Chicago Press, Chicago, Copyright © 1959, pp. 216-263.*

Studies of identical twins bear out the belief that many aspects of aging are determined by innate biological mechanisms. (Identical twins are those having the same heredity, unlike fraternal twins who are no more alike than any two brothers and sisters.) We are familiar with the similarities of twins in the early part of life, but it is sometimes eerie to see the physical likeness continue through middle age and senescence, even when the twins have been separated for many decades. Obesity, baldness, and patterns of facial wrinkles are dramatically alike in aging identical twins. Furthermore, although fraternal twins have very different life spans, identical twins who die of natural causes often die at almost the same age (Kallmann & Sander, 1949).

AGES AND STAGES

Developmental psychologists have carefully studied the characteristics of the infant, the child, and the adolescent at various ages. Arnold Gesell and his colleagues studied hundreds of children over a period of time and reported their results in a series of books: *The First Five Years of Life* (1940), *The Child from Five to Ten* (1946), and *Youth: The Years from Ten to Sixteen* (1956). Gesell compared children to determine the ages at which they were able to perform such actions as walking, running, picking up a small pellet, cutting with scissors, managing a pencil, or drawing the figure of a man. From the resulting data, he then determined the capabilities of the "average" child at various ages. At 15 months, for example, the average child is able to walk; at 18 months, he can walk fast and run stiffly; at 21 months, he is able to kick a large ball.

Gesell felt that learning is not primarily conditioned by the environment but that, given a normal environment, learning depends heavily upon maturation. He believed that knowing the age of a child made it possible to predict not only the child's approximate height and weight (Gesell studied those, too) but also what the child knew and what he was able to do. Gesell went beyond the study of physical and cognitive growth to examine personality as a function of maturation. He saw growth occurring in a pattern of spirals, with the child at one age exhibiting expansive, outgoing, vigorous behavior which, in the next age, became consolidated and better controlled. This age of smoother growth would last until the child was ready for the next spurt of maturation. Based on the norms established by Gesell, many people have tended to equate chronological age with the developmental stage. This hasty reading of Gesell's ideas has produced such oversimplified concepts as "the terrible twos," "the trusting threes," and "the frustrating fours."

There are several weaknesses to Gesell's system. First, it determined when developmental phenomena occur but did not explain why they occur. It implied that maturation *caused* changes in behavior but gave no evidence that it did. Second, the children studied by Gesell came from one socioeconomic class within one community (they were

MOTOR DEVELOPMENT IN THE EARLY YEARS. (*Suzanne Szasz.*)

middle-class white children in New Haven, Connecticut), but Gesell paid little attention to the way in which their similar environments may have influenced their similar behaviors. And third, there is the danger of taking his "normative" behavior too seriously. Gesell described the 4-year-old child as tending "to go out of bounds" in many ways—socially, verbally, and in his motor activity (Gesell, 1940, p. 337). The parents of a 4-year-old who does not attempt to exceed restrictions may begin to wonder if there is something wrong with her. Nevertheless, though the theory is thin on explanations for the behavioral stages described, and though it contains certain other weaknesses, Gesell's contribution remains a substantial one. He succeeded in describing the developmental patterns of a specific group of children within a certain culture.

ETHOLOGY

Gesell's approach to psychology is a biological one in that it sees development as depending upon the unfolding of innate capacities. For many years, his emphasis on the interrelation of biology and psychology was exceptional, since most American psychologists focused on learning and on the effects of different kinds of environments. Recently, however, ethologists have begun to concern themselves with this interrelationship, and their approach is based on biology even more firmly than were Gesell's theories.

Since ethology sees human behavior in the context of evolution (see Chapter 2), it regards man as sharing many patterns of behavior with other species. Although man differs from the other animals in his capacity for language and abstract thought, he is similar to them in such areas as courtship patterns or assertion of territorial rights. In Chapter 2, for example, we considered some of the ethological implications of a baby's crying, and we discussed how the crying was an innate behavior directed toward nurturance. Several ethologists have compared this infant behavior with the "following" behavior of young chicks and ducks. The chick follows its mother to "trigger" her nurturance; the infant, who is incapable of moving about so freely, cries to trigger a similar nurturance (Hess, 1970).

Other psychologists have discussed human aggression as a learned behavior and have considered how changes in childrearing or in education might prevent its development. The ethologist, however, points out that aggression exists in all animals in which individual members are capable of forming bonds. He claims that aggression is an innate human behavior and that no change in man's environment can do away with it. A man may be angry even when his survival is not threatened, just as a cat will hunt even when he is not hungry. If you remove one stimulus for the man's anger, another stimulus will trigger the emotion. Ethologists point out that many societies encourage the release of aggression in ritual and sports, as if society, like the individual, were influenced by its biological heritage.

CONSTITUTION AND BEHAVIOR

The notion that a person's anatomy and physiology affect his behavior can be traced as far back as the Greco-Roman era. According to an ancient belief that persisted until the beginning of the modern age, there were four basic human temperaments, each of which was determined by the predominance of a particular body fluid. Thus, a person's general disposition toward cheerfulness, apathy, irascibility, or melancholy was seen to depend on the nature of his chemical makeup. Modern theorizers have discarded the idea of the four temperaments, but they have periodically focused on the *body type* as one of the fundamental biological facts that influence human behavior.

Body Type

W. H. Sheldon (1942) proposed three basic body types—endomorph, mesomorph, and ectomorph—and he described the personality traits that he found most usually associated with each of them. The *endomorph* is the person with a round, soft body, whom Sheldon characterized as affectionate, sociable, and fond of comfort. The *mesomorph* has a body with more than average musculature and tends to prefer vigorous physical activity. The *ectomorph* is tall, thin, and fragile, and frequently tends toward a thoughtful and sensitive disposition. Although it is rare for an individual to fit any one of these categories exactly, Sheldon found a good deal of correspondence between a person's body type and his predominant personality style.

A few studies have investigated this idea further. Glueck and Glueck (1950) used physical and personality measurements to determine whether any one of these body types could be associated with juvenile delinquency. They found that the proportion of mesomorphic individuals was higher among their delinquent group than among their "normal" control population. We cannot, of course, infer that a muscular body *causes* delinquency. It is possible that children who grow up muscular and vigorous, as opposed to those who are obese or thin, experience success in adopting an outgoing, active and aggressive attitude toward their environment. Moreover, the aggressive and vigorous individual who is also antisocial is much more noticeable and thus much more quickly labeled as "delinquent" than the quiet, withdrawn, and passive youngster who is just as antisocial.

In a related study, R. N. Walker (1963) set out to compare the body builds of a large group of nursery school children with the parents' ratings of each child's personality. First, he determined whether each child in the sample was predominately an endomorph, a mesomorph, or an ectomorph. Then, he submitted to the parents of each child a checklist on which the parents indicated those traits most characteristic of the child's behavior. When Walker compared the body type of each child with the parental observations, he found that a child's physique was indeed related to the way in which his parents perceived him. Walker further suggested that there were many reasons for this physique-behavior association and that these involved a complex interaction between biological and social factors.

In addition to body type, sheer physical size can affect both the way in which a person is treated and the way in which he experiences his environment. Underlying many of our attitudes toward height seems to be the notion that a greater-than-average height is related to power, which in turn is related to masculinity. Conversely, short stature is assumed to be related to accommodation, which in turn is related to femininity. Therefore, it is usually considered an advantage for a male to be taller than his peers, but a cause of concern for a female to be taller than her peer group.

Size affects not only others' expectations of us but also our experiences with our environment. Standing among a team of professional basketball players can give us some idea of the sensations that shorter people experience daily. Since height is relational in this sense, the tall child in a small family perceives his environment in a different way than does the tall child in a tall family. Furthermore, a person's relation to his environment can be substantially altered by such changes as a sudden spurt in growth or a move to a new neighborhood in which individuals are of a somewhat different size.

The term *learning disability* is highly controversial because it is used to identify the difficulties of a broad category of children who often have no more in common than the label itself. In our school systems today, children are described as learning disabled when they require special attention in the classroom setting—that is, when they have trouble learning to read, to write, or to spell and seem to need an inordinate amount of instruction. In the absence of any readily apparent physical abnormality (such as blindness, deafness, or a disease like cerebral palsy) that would result in a sensory defect, these children are described as having learning disabilities.

In a very real sense, then, we use the term for children who have difficulty in learning, but whose medical history offers few clues to explain the condition. Various theories have related learning disabilities to minor perceptual disorders, to psychological blocks, to emotional problems, or to minor organic problems. Of interest to us here are those theories which attribute disruptive behavior and disabilities to biological factors.

SYMPTOMS. P. H. Wender (1971) has described one set of learning disabilities which arise from minimal brain damage or *minimal brain dysfunction*. Children with this type of learning disability demonstrate difficulties in one or more of the following areas:

> motor activity and coordination; attention and cognitive functions; interpersonal relations, particularly with respect to dependence and independence or with responsiveness to social influence; emotionality (Wender, 1971, p. 12).

In Wender's view, these behavioral symptoms are of organic origin and can be attributed to a minor dysfunction of the brain. Precisely because the brain dysfunction he describes is minimal, it is difficult to diagnose. Thus there is often a suspicion of brain damage in children showing the above symptoms, but rarely much hard evidence of it.

Another of the more common behavioral symptoms discussed in the literature is *hyperactivity*, which is usually defined as a tendency toward a high activity level accompanied by some type of impaired coordination. Hyperactive children are described as restless, driven into everything, always moving. Their short attention span makes it difficult for them to stay at one task long enough for them to learn. The issue of hyperactivity has generated considerable controversy, and the professionals have in no way reached agreement on its definition, its causes, or its treatment.

CAUSES. For each of the symptoms in the broad category of learning disabilities there are a variety of possible causes. Just as people experience headaches for any number of reasons, a symptom such as hyperactivity may arise from one of several conditions. Some of the causes of learning disabilities that have been suggested in the literature include organic brain damage; genetic transmission; interuterine abnormality; deficiencies during the prenatal period; and lack of oxygen during fetal development, during childbirth, or during early infancy. A large proportion of children showing symptoms of learning disabilities are known to have experienced some sort of irregularity at birth (one of the more frequent being prematurity). Thus, the delineation of the causes of learning disabilities becomes a matter of locating for each child the source of his individual behavioral symptoms.

TREATMENT. Similar uncertainties pervade discussions of the treatment of learning disabilities. Two types are generally suggested: drug treatment and educational or home management. A somewhat less popular mode of treatment is psychotherapy. The history of drug treatment provides an interesting example of the inadvertency with which we sometimes learn about the causes of certain behavior patterns.

Several years ago, it was discovered that some children who displayed symptoms of hyperactivity responded to a drug called *Ritalin*, a stimulant in the amphetamine family. These children, who had been unaffected by tranquilizers or depressants, actually calmed down in response to this drug, which ordinarily stimulates normal adults. This unusual response gave rise to the hypothesis that these children were in fact *understimulated*, that they required more than average stimulation before they could respond effectively. Hence, their high activity level was an attempt to experience more stimulation from the environment. Ritalin lowered the children's threshold of sensitivity and calmed them, since they no longer needed to seek as much external stimulation. Although this drug has proven effective with some children, the precise mechanisms by which it operates remain open to further research.

The second kind of treatment is educational management, both at home and at school. In most cases, this involves an attempt to restructure the environment by simplifying it, reducing distractions, making expectations more definitive, and, in general, reducing confusion.

THE STUDY OF LEARNING DISABILITIES. Because so many questions about learning disabilities remain unanswered, the student studying these difficulties should approach them with a healthy amount of skepticism. He should evaluate carefully each diagnosis, each proposed program, and each suggested theory. On a basic level, he might even begin to question whether learning disabilities are, in fact, disabilities at all. Is it possible that they are sometimes minor variations in the normal pattern, or that they constitute little more than a lag in development? Perhaps if we revised our concept of "normal," some of these variations would cease to be anomalous.

Because this area of human development includes so much controversy and so many unanswered questions, it possesses a very rich potential for future research. It is possible that, as we learn more about specific learning disabilities, we will begin to comprehend more clearly the development of the normal child. For example, the more we find out about some of the perceptual disorders common among the learning disabled, the more we will understand about perceptual development in normal children.

Disease and Physical Handicaps

The frequency and type of diseases that appear at different periods in the life span, often follow a fairly predictable pattern. Not all people experience the same diseases at the same point in their lives, but it is nonetheless possible to offer certain generalizations about the occurrence of illness at various age levels.

Infants and preschool children have a relatively high incidence of illness and are particularly susceptible to respiratory diseases. At age 4, for example, both girls and boys have an average of four respiratory diseases during the year (Valadian, Stuart, & Reed, 1961). Frequency of illness declines during the school years, though respiratory illnesses continue to be the major annoyances. This is also the time when children become exposed to communicable diseases such as measles, chicken pox, and mumps. Fortunately, in our country today, these diseases are much less threatening than they once were. In adolescence, the frequency of disease continues to decrease, though some individuals experience spurts of illness during this time. Venereal disease becomes a serious threat during adolescence, and the incidence of both gonorrhea and syphilis has increased to epidemic proportions among teenagers in recent years. Acne often appears at this age level, and although it does not pose a serious threat to the adolescent's health, it can become an uncomfortable psychological burden.

Incidence of illness remains fairly low in early and middle adulthood, though heart disease becomes more frequent in males aged 25 to 44. This higher incidence of heart disease may be attributable to greater amounts of cholesterol in the blood, to excessive smoking, or to high blood pressure. From age 45 onward, illnesses become more frequent, with cardiovascular ailments such as coronary heart disease, cerebral hemorrhages, strokes, and hypertension being the most common (Jones, Shainbergh, & Byer, 1974). Various forms of cancer also become more prominent at this time, as do emphysema, pneumonia, and diabetes. The variety of illnesses that affect people over the age of 65 appears to be related to the extension of the average life span, which permits degenerative diseases the extra years they require to develop.

Physical handicaps represent a further category of constitutional factors that can influence behavior and development. The handicapped child, for instance, often experiences the world differently than does the child who is healthy, vigorous, and fully functioning. In addition to the physical discomfort that is directly related to his disability, the handicapped child often misses out on the normal activities of everyday life. Recently, however, we seem to have become more aware of the difficulties of being handicapped. Many school systems are now equipped with special ramps (instead of flights of stairs) so that students in wheelchairs can get about with far more ease. And a number of museums have instituted special programs that allow blind children to experience through their fingertips the shape and texture of sculptured objects. In a setting that offers the handicapped child this kind of opportunity, the socialization processes available to him may resemble closely those of the normal child (Goodman, Richardson, Dornbusch, & Hastorf, 1963).

Implicit in this supportive environment is a concept of "handicap" that accepts the disability fully and attempts to adjust to it. As with other aspects of development, this forthright approach can provide incalculable benefits for the handicapped child or the child with a chronic illness such as asthma or diabetes. Indeed, the way in which a disability is handled often has a much greater impact on the individual's self-confidence, his sense of independence, and his feelings of competence than the particular disability itself. In an environment in which children must be active and aggressive, for example, physical disabilities that prevent such behavior are often more of a handicap than they would be if the demands were less intense.

NUTRITION   In the developed countries of the world, the rate of a child's growth and maturation has increased over the last 50 years. Today children mature earlier, become taller and stronger, and live longer. Improved nutrition—resulting both from increased knowledge and education about proper diet and from modern methods of transporting food—is usually considered the most important single factor in this increased growth rate. This point has recently been driven home by the proliferation of popularized nutrition books whose theses have been that "you are what you eat."

Despite certain advances in the area of nutrition, there is widespread evidence that malnutrition continues to affect the lives of a great many people, and particularly children, even within the United States (Birch & Gussow, 1970). Ours may be the best-fed nation in the world, but many of its population still suffer from nutritional deficiencies. R. H. Hutcheson, Jr. (1968) found that, among 1-year-olds from poor families in Tennessee, 20 percent of the group studied suffered from severe anemia (caused by a lack of iron), and another 30 percent experienced lesser degrees of the same deficiency. In poor areas in Alabama and Mississippi, anemia rates as high as 80 percent have been found among preschool children.

Two kinds of malnutrition can generally be distinguished. One results from an insufficiency of the total quantity of food, and the other results from an insufficiency of certain kinds of nutrients. The latter is the type most prevalent in the United States, since even persons who can afford a good diet often consume too many "empty calories" in the form of foods high in carbohydrates but low in protein, vitamins, and minerals. In impoverished areas, both kinds of malnutrition usually exist. Many people receive too few calories, cannot afford to buy animal protein, and receive inadequate amounts of protein from other sources. Vitamins A and C, and the mineral iron, are most likely to be lacking in poor diets.

Children are particularly vulnerable to malnutrition in the first 5 years of life, for a variety of reasons. They are not yet able to feed themselves, and they can digest only a small quantity of food at one time. Moreover, there are insufficient foods available in a form that is palatable to young stomachs. The finger food usually given to young children is especially high in carbohydrates and low in many required nutrients. Dry cereals, cookies, crackers, pretzels, and potato chips are representative of this kind of high-carbohydrate snack food that is often given to children instead of more nutritious food. As a result, many of these children have some degree of protein deficiency. Proper diet at this age level is crucial, since malnutrition during the first 5 years can result in a permanent depression of the growth cycle (Cravioto & Robles, 1965). Among the areas of development most directly affected are the brain and the nervous system. Although depressions of the growth cycle can be reversed if the period of malnutrition is not too lengthy, the poverty-level child is rarely given such a "second chance."

Children being fed a protein-rich diet to remedy deficiencies at a research institute in Lwiro, Zaire. (*UPI.*)

THE BIOLOGY OF POVERTY

Poverty, by definition, denotes a state of privation in which individuals lack the necessities or the minimal amenities of life. On an obvious level, poverty can affect a person's life by imposing serious constraints such as educational disadvantage, lack of job opportunity, or overcrowded living conditions. Far more subtle, but equally detrimental, are the effects of poverty on an individual's physical development and, ultimately, on his behavior.

In this chapter, we have examined some of the numerous aspects of physical development and we have seen how these aspects influence

Poverty can affect a person's life by imposing serious constraints such as educational disadvantage and overcrowded and unsanitary living conditions. (*Alinari-Scala.*)

the direction of a person's behavior. Here, we will view our subject in a wider context, by considering the ways in which a person's development can, in turn, be influenced by certain factors directly related to poverty. In other words, where we earlier discussed how behavior was influenced by biology, we will now add a further level to our considerations and examine how the biology-behavior interaction is affected by the factor of poverty. To do this, we must understand the ways in which the complex sociocultural factors characteristic of poverty affect the general health, the nutrition, and the growth and development of the individual. Then, in turn, we can see how these factors affect the individual's behavior.

For many people, poverty is not a sudden circumstance but a lifelong condition that produces permanent biological and psychological effects. These negative effects are difficult to separate from one another, as they are caused most often by a multiplicity of factors. For one thing, impoverished mothers experience more difficulty in childbirth; they have a much higher incidence of stillbirth, of complications during birth, of prematurity, and of low birth-weight babies. Their infants are more vulnerable to disease and show a higher rate of birth defects. Although both mother and child run higher risks during the birth process, there is no single cause for this occurrence. Lower levels of nutrition, inadequate health care, the extreme age of the mother (on either end of the scale), and the tendency of poverty mothers to bear more children than their affluent counterparts—all contribute to the increased risks.

Just as the impoverished child is more vulnerable at birth, so also he continues to develop at a disadvantage. Inadequate nutrition during the early years can result in a smaller individual with an underdeveloped skeletal system. If the period of malnutrition is prolonged—as it is only too often—the child will no longer be able to "catch up" and to restore his physical development to its target growth. Studies of underdeveloped countries that have experienced long periods of drought or starvation have indicated this danger quite clearly.

In addition to their effects on physical growth, poor health and poor nutrition can cause a person to suffer an overall lack of energy, with a tendency to become discouraged easily and to be unable to cope with stressful situations. These conditions can affect an individual's adaptability to daily life situations, as well as the level of his performance in the classroom. The tearful, frustrated child who has little patience with mastering the basics of reading may well be demonstrating the ultimate effects of the biology of poverty.

SUMMARY

Physical growth is one aspect of the process of human development and involves qualitative and quantitative change. While the growth process is orderly and continuous, the tempo at which it proceeds is uneven and differential. Moreover, children vary a great deal in the pace of their growth. The evidence seems to be that aging is also continuous and orderly, with different body systems declining at different rates.

How a child matures has consequences for his personality. Gesell believed that certain stages of maturity were associated with certain personality traits. Because he studied a limited socioeconomic group, it is not known how widely his norms can be applied. By comparing the behavior of animals with that of human beings, ethologists have begun to examine the interrelation between biology and psychology. Other aspects of this interrelation are the connections between physique and personality (Sheldon, 1942) and between body size and personality.

The presence of a learning disability or a physical handicap can also affect a child's personality. The term *learning disability* remains controversial because numerous questions exist about its application, its symptoms, its causes, and its treatment.

We closed our discussion with a consideration of the effects of nutrition on physical growth and an examination of the ways in which a person's overall development can be influenced by factors directly related to poverty.

1. Drawing upon your own experience, give an example of how the chronological age at which a boy or girl begins adolescence can affect his or her personality.

2. Compare or contrast the growth rates of any two systems of the human body.

3. Discuss the biological factors that are known to affect the learning ability of children. Discuss a biological factor that has been thought to account for learning disabilities.

SUGGESTED READINGS

Birch, H. G., & Gussow, J. D. *Disadvantaged children: Health, nutrition and school failure.* New York: Harcourt Brace Jovanovich, 1970. The social and psychological consequences of poor health or poor nutrition, particularly among people in poverty areas, are presented in a clear, provocative, and well-documented fashion.

McCarthy, J. J., & McCarthy, J. F. *Learning disabilities.* Boston: Allyn & Bacon, 1969. A review of the major categories of learning disabilities, assessment procedures, and educational strategies.

Pelcovits, J. Nutrition for older Americans. *Journal of the American Dietetic Association,* 1971, *58*, 17–21. A discussion of the nutritional problems experienced by the aged and ways of improving these conditions.

4

COGNITIVE ASPECTS OF DEVELOPMENT

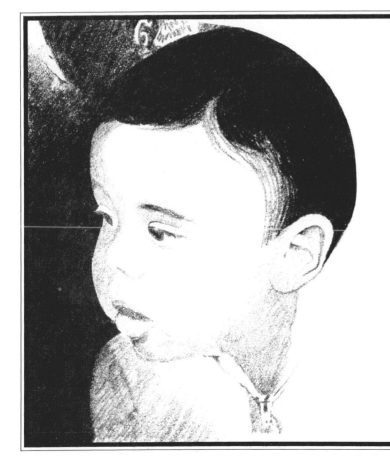

Cognition is the process by which we come to perceive, know, or understand something. Learning a new word, solving an equation, and memorizing the conjugation of a verb are all examples of cognitive activity. Cognitive development refers to the growth, refinement, and, in some aspects, decline of this intellectual capacity. The mind is not a cupboard with a fixed number of drawers and slots; it grows and changes in response to a variety of biological changes and life situations. This growth occurs at different rates and assumes dramatically different forms in infancy, childhood, adolescence, and adulthood.

Cognition is composed of many different kinds of processes—perception, memory, problem solving, and the relationship of one piece of information to another. Such cognitive processes include generating hypotheses, analysis, synthesis, inductive and deductive reasoning, evaluation of one's own thoughts, and less directed kinds of thought, such as free association.

Even on this initial level of definition, however, psychologists have debated whether to include certain processes, particularly sensation and perception. *Sensation* refers to the stimulation of the sense organs by physical or chemical energies. *Perception* is the process of extracting meaningful information from sensory stimulation. For example, a sound of a certain pitch and frequency stimulates the auditory nerve (sensation); the mind identifies the sound as a train whistle, or an owl's hoot, or the moaning of the wind (perception).

Formerly, psychologists analyzed sensation and perception as part of a physiological process. Perception was viewed as a passive, receptive function. Today, largely owing to the influence of Gibson, Bruner, and others, most psychologists have revised their concept of perception, emphasizing its active, selective nature—the way in which the mind grasps and immediately interprets certain external data, while tuning out other information. Following this view, we shall treat perception as a cognitive process in this chapter.

COGNITIVE DEVELOPMENT OVER THE LIFE SPAN

The most fascinating, complex, and rapid changes in cognition occur before adulthood. These changes are sequential and irreversible; they succeed each other in a fixed order, irrevocably replacing the previous intellectual framework. Most cognitive development during childhood and adolescence is a product of the joint interaction of environment, or learning, and the maturation of the nervous system. Because biological growth plays such an important role, it is not surprising that remarkably uniform patterns of mental development are observed during this period, although there is wide individual variation. In this chapter we shall consider the various stage theories of cognitive development, in particular the pioneering work of Jean Piaget.

Previously, many psychologists believed that cognitive skills peaked in a person's late twenties and that the rest of adult life was marked by general intellectual decline. Today, this model has been modified to a much more dynamic (and optimistic) concept of maturity. Although there is controversy as to the exact time in the life span when intellectual growth begins to slacken off and some functions start to deteriorate, most psychologists (Bayley, 1966; Jones, 1959; Kimmel, 1974) agree that some cognitive abilities continue to develop during maturity.

Adult cognitive development tends to be less dramatic and more diverse than childhood development, because adult cognitive development is much less a function of maturational complexity and much more a function of life experience.

The growth experiences that many adults face may be programmed encounters such as adult education or psychotherapy, or unprogrammed events such as marriage, parenthood, and occupational tasks. In either case, the conflicts and challenges are likely to center on social-interpersonal issues. Consequently, adult cognitive changes tend to involve value judgments and theories about oneself and the human condition (Flavell, 1970). In contrast, children spend much more time trying to understand natural phenomena in the real world, and their cognitive development involves more construction of basic logical models. Another point of difference between cognitive development in adults and in children is the selective application of new skills. Adults may learn to use one type of cognitive processing for scientific work and a somewhat different one for interpersonal relations. Children, on the other hand, tend to process all information through the same cognitive models.

In elderly people, the pattern of cognitive change is complex; some abilities remain relatively unimpaired, while others deteriorate. The picture is complicated by the physiological processes common to aging,

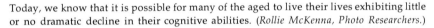

Today, we know that it is possible for many of the aged to live their lives exhibiting little or no dramatic decline in their cognitive abilities. (*Rollie McKenna, Photo Researchers.*)

most notably the general slowdown of the functions of the central nervous system, including reaction time. Early research on aging indicated a classic pattern of general mental decline, but this may have been because test scores depended heavily upon performance of physical tasks under time pressure. In some tests where speed was not a factor—for example, vocabulary tests that were administered verbally—little or no mental decline was shown by elderly persons (Kimmel, 1974; Flavell, 1970).

One important cognitive change in the elderly that is indicated is decreased problem-solving ability in problems where past experience is irrelevant. Stored information, on the other hand, is relatively unaffected. Thus, elderly people may do poorly on new tasks like IQ tests or filling out Medicaid forms, even though they perform their ordinary intellectual functions as effectively as ever. Furthermore, older people tend to compensate for their decreased problem-solving ability by choosing tasks where accumulated knowledge is important; thus they may accomplish as much or more than a younger person (Kimmel, 1974).

General health is a critical factor here, because disease aggravates the slowdown of the central nervous system and may affect motivation, compensatory strategies, and other noncognitive processes that become increasingly important in old age. Kimmel (1974) concludes that the elderly population may consist of two markedly different groups: the healthy (exhibiting little or no intellectual decline) and those in poor health (showing dramatic decline). This may be one explanation for the data of large mixed samples indicating relatively uniform and steady decline in intellectual functioning for all elderly people.

PERCEPTUAL DEVELOPMENT
Perception as Part of Cognition

Cognitive change at any point in the life span is affected, to some degree, by perceptual development. Perception, which is the process of extracting *meaningful* information from an external sensation, is one of the major aspects of cognition. Understanding a certain fact or problem may be achieved without perception—for example, when information is recalled from memory—but often perception is the first process involved in cognition. We take in information from the outside world before we act on it.

As a child grows, much of his development of intelligence or cognition comes first from the organization of the perceptual processes. The child receives millions of stimuli through his sense organs and he needs to categorize these stimuli in order to give significance to the information they bring him. He begins doing this from the time of birth (if not before), with one of the first distinctions being the familiar versus the strange. Later he will refine these crude divisions into a vast number of more narrowly drawn definitions.

The infant does not categorize every piece of information he receives, only those pieces for which he has some preference. A baby will attend to some kinds of stimulation but ignore others. This selection process begins at birth, when infants display distinct preferences for certain kinds of sights and sounds. For example, an infant may block out very loud sounds, such as a rattling dump truck, but respond to the sound of soft footsteps as his mother checks to see if he is asleep.

Perception is an essential foundation for other, more complex aspects of cognitive development. For example, an individual's eye-hand coordination depends, among other things, on his ability to identify the object he wants to touch with his hand and then to judge the distance between his hand and the object. It takes an infant a long time to develop this kind of perceptual-motor coordination. He can visually follow the movement of an object within the first week of life. He reacts to it with general excitation of the body, including squirming, waving, and kicking. Sometimes the infant may clench his fists as if he wants to reach out and grab the object. Nevertheless, it may take as much as 4 to 5 months before he can successfully coordinate the act of perceiving an object and the act of grasping it. If early perceptual development is flawed, other cognitive processes will also be impaired.

Not all healthy individuals, whether infants or adults, reflect natural phenomena the same way. Human perception is not a standard mechanism merely reflecting images, like a camera; it involves an enormous variety of individual differences. People see things from their own vantage point in space, and in terms of their own values, education, and moral standards. Thus, some stimuli are more noticeable to certain individuals than to others; that is, the stimuli appear more prominent to those individuals and attract their attention more readily. For example, one person smells smoke some minutes before others in the same room do; another person hears the fire engine before anyone else does. Developmentally, some characteristics of the physical world are uniformly more noticeable than others for persons at a certain age level, but within any one age group there will always be a wide range of perceptual ability.

One outstanding quality of child perception at an early age is egocentrism. *Egocentrism* in this context means concentration upon one's own perceptions, and, conversely, the failure to distinguish between one's own perceptions and those of other people. Children cannot adequately make this differentiation between self and non-self; they assume that everybody's outlook is the same as theirs. The egocentrism of a young child may be very literal and refer to a physical vantage point. Piaget made an interesting study (Piaget, 1954) that demonstrates this quality graphically. In the test, a child is seated in front of a plaster model of a mountain range and is shown several pictures of the mountain range, each taken from a different angle. He is asked to select the picture that shows his view of the mountain range. Most children can quite easily pick out the picture that matches their particular view. Then the child is asked to pick out the picture that matches what a doll sees when it is sitting in another chair facing the mountain range from a different angle. The preschool child is literally unable to cast himself

One of Piaget's experiments on preoperational thought. The child is asked to pick out the picture that matches what the small doll sees which is facing the mountain range from a different angle. A young child is egocentric and cannot imagine the perspective that the doll has on the range. (*Sam Falk, The New York Times.*)

in the physical position of the doll and imagine the doll's perspective of this object. He assumes that his perspective is the only one there is.

Gradually, during childhood and adolescence, a person's egocentrism of thought and perception becomes less bound to the physical aspects of perception and more dependent on the attitudes, values, and cultural meanings with which he interprets the perceptual world. A form of egocentric thought often found among adults is *ethnocentrism*, a belief that one's own race, tribe, or group is superior to others. It is a point of view restricted by cultural or ethnic perspectives that prevents an individual from intellectually "walking around" something in order to consider it according to another culture's beliefs or value system (see Chapter 8).

Developmental Changes in Perception

Most changes in perceptual development take place in infancy and early childhood; the selectivity and organization of the perceptual world become more complex. Starting with the basic division between familiar and strange, the infant gradually progresses to a highly sophisticated framework that includes selection and differentiation based on size, temperature, taste, age, gender, and so on.

However, perceptual ability continues to develop, in a less dramatic way, throughout life. Initially there is a growing efficiency and systematic approach in conducting a perceptual search. The older child learns progressively to focus his attention over a period of time. His concentration span increases and he spends less time on irrelevant information. Later, the selectivity of attention changes. Because an older child has developed a cognitive framework which is much more complex than that of a younger child, he attends to smaller clues, attaching significance to a piece of information that a younger child might ignore. For example, the older child might see a bag made of white, shiny paper and understand that it comes from the bakery. Or he sees his mother's foot tapping and understands that she is impatient.

Eleanor Gibson (1969) contends that much of perceptual learning and development is a process of *differentiation*; that is, what is learned are the distinctive features of an object and its variance from similar objects. She sees this process as primarily one of filtering and abstraction, rather than simple association. For example, as the child gets older he is better able to identify pictures or simple schematic drawings of things. This is because he can now discriminate between the distinctive features of an object and hence is able to recognize the simplified picture of it. He filters out irrelevant or variable aspects and focuses on the distinguishing or invariant aspects of the object, at least to the point of being able to categorize that object.

The selectivity and richness of meaning attached to perceptions continue to expand in individual ways. Throughout adulthood, an individual's perceptions reflect more and more the uniqueness of his own experiences.

INTELLIGENCE AND INTELLIGENCE TESTING

There are many controversies in the relatively new field of developmental psychology, but perhaps none arouses the ire of theorists or stirs popular passions more than the concepts of intelligence and intelligence testing. The academic debate has spilled out of seminars and into the public spotlight, largely because of the wide implications of intelligence test scores for determining educational and social opportunities. A label attached to a young child can affect the extent and quality of his education, the kind of job he will have as an adult, and the regard he has for his own abilities. These tests are administered more widely and taken more seriously in the United States than anywhere else; certainly Europeans are puzzled by this national obsession of ours. Emphasis on testing, particularly at the elementary and secondary school levels, has resulted in the grouping and implicit rating of students solely on the basis of their test performances. And the significance of the categorization is not lost on the children.

Why is it that we hold intelligence tests in such high regard? What is it that we are trying to measure, after all? In this section we shall explore the concept of intelligence, beginning with some early attempts to measure and, thus, define it.

These 3,000 college freshmen are taking an intelligence test which could greatly influence their academic future. *(DPI.)*

The History of Intelligence Testing

The first comprehensive intelligence test was the fruit of a study commissioned by the French government in the late nineteenth century. In order to cut their budget, education officials commissioned Alfred Binet, a French psychologist, to devise a method of identifying those children who would not profit from a public education. Binet needed some kind of scale that would yield an index on the educability of these problem learners, and it was this research problem that spawned the first overall intelligence test. Binet's concept of intelligence focused on such complex intellectual processes as judgment, reasoning, memory, and comprehension. He tailored his research plan accordingly, using test items of problem solving, word definition, and analysis to measure these capacities. His test stemmed from the theoretical position that intelligence grows and changes, rather than remains static. Therefore, test questions had to be carefully graded in order of difficulty. A good test item was one that differentiated between older and younger children. If more than half of the 5-year-olds were able to define the word "ball" and somewhat less than half of the 4-year-olds were unable to do so, then the definition of ball was felt to be a good item for 5-year-olds. (Binet & Simon, 1905; 1916). This form of gradation was a landmark in the testing movement.

By 1916 an English version of the test, refined by Terman and Stanford University, was widely used in the United States. However, Binet was not responsible for introducing the IQ, or intelligence quotient; this was an American innovation. It represents a fixed mathematical relationship between some of Binet's statistics. An *intelligence quotient* is the ratio between an individual's mental and chronological ages. It is computed by taking the mental age (MA), dividing by the chronological age (CA), and multiplying the result by 100 (to eliminate any decimals). Binet and his colleagues were interested in the difference between mental and chronological ages, but they never attached any significance to the ratio of the two. Nevertheless, the IQ won wide acceptance in the United States through the 1950s. Many American psychologists reasoned that the ratio remained constant over the lifetime of an individual—that although mental and chronological ages increased, the ratio between them remained quite stable. Today, except for a few unpopular tests, the ratio IQ has fallen into disuse in favor of an IQ based on deviations from the average score.

The development of sophisticated models for testing and measuring the quality called intelligence stimulated renewed inquiry, both popular and scientific, into the nature of the phenomenon itself. Briefly, we shall consider some of the highlights of this ongoing debate.

The Nature of Intelligence

THEORETICAL AND OPERATIONAL DEFINITIONS OF INTELLIGENCE. A *theoretical* definition of intelligence is based upon those intellectual activities that comprise intelligence. Binet's theoretical definition included judgment, reasoning, and the ability to adapt to the environment, but excluded sensory and motor functions. It was necessary for him to define intelligence this way in order to devise his test. However, the operations or behaviors that are actually measured are referred to as the operational definition. Thus, the *operational* definition of intelligence is based on those skills measured by the intelligence test. This may sound circular, but the distinction is quite useful in facilitating communication among psychologists, educators, and others. Intelligence as defined by the Stanford-Binet test means exactly the same thing to two different people. No theoretical definition can hope to achieve this degree of precision and succinctness.

FIXED AND MODIFIED MODELS OF INTELLIGENCE. For a long time, the dominant view among psychologists was that the intelligence of an individual remains constant throughout his life because it is an innate quality, determined largely by heredity. Early empirical data supported this view, including findings that test performance improves with age, that the average IQ is constant from one age to another, and that test scores correlate with academic grades and teacher evaluations. Subsequent research, however, somewhat contradicts the theory of fixed intelligence and instead emphasizes the roles of environment and experience. The evidence comes from three sources in particular: studies of identical twins raised apart, repeated testing of the same subjects over time, and studies on the effects of training. Some of the results suggest that the evidence for fixed intelligence was gathered in studies that were methodologically flawed or incomplete. Today, most psychologists agree that individual IQs are modifiable and are often influenced by a person's experience. For example, it is not unusual for children to show a 10 to 15 point spurt in IQ after 6 months in a Head Start program. If there is such a phenomenon as fixed intelligence (an hypothesis that is somewhat dubious), it cannot be demonstrated with any of the testing techniques at our disposal today (Hunt, 1961).

GENERAL AND SPECIFIC ABILITIES. Several early theorists, most notably Spearman (1904), believed that intelligence was a single kind of general attribute or ability to learn. He drew this conclusion from the correlation he noticed among the various Binet-type tests (Hunt, 1961). Other theorists contend that intelligence is a composite or combined result of different kinds of abilities. The same individual may have a good memory and the ability to perceive similarities, but do poorly on tasks involving spatial relationships. Thurstone (1938) concluded that there were seven primary abilities—perceptual speed, word comprehension, word fluency, space, numbers, memory, and induction. More recently, Guilford (1959) has suggested a more complex scheme composed of at least three structural dimensions: operations, contents, and products. An operation applied to a certain kind of content may result in a number of different products. This concept of the intellect is that of an agency with different strategies for dealing with different kinds of information.

Intelligence tests have generally adopted a definition based on a composite of several abilities. For example, the Wechsler Intelligence Scale for Children (1974) has subtests yielding separate scores for information, comprehension, mathematics, vocabulary, digit span, and picture arrangement, as well as other tasks. The current version of the Stanford-Binet test (1960), on the other hand, results in only one composite score indicating a general intelligence level, even though it contains diverse items designed to measure different skills and abilities.

INNATE AND LEARNED INTELLECTUAL ABILITIES. The nature versus nurture controversy, like the volatile testing issue, is still sparking academic and popular fireworks. Arthur Jensen (1969) is one of the most vigorous proponents of the theory that intellectual capacity is largely determined by heredity. He contends that 80 percent of what is measured on tests is a result of genetic inheritance. Thus, in Jensen's view, only 20 percent of the variability in the intelligence of a given population is caused by experience.

Jensen's conclusions are framed in terms of populations, not individuals. The variability he measures is a total of the individual differences that exist among all members of any given group or population. He does not measure single individuals or circumstances, such as intellectually mediocre children reared by highly intelligent parents, or a genius reared by parents with limited mental powers. The question, as he sees it, is not an either-or choice between genetic inheritance and environment, but rather a problem of degree. What proportion of the variability in a population is attributable to heredity? Jensen is a respected academician, trained in statistics, biology, and genetics, and he presents a forceful case for the preponderant influence of genetics. However, Jensen has had to collect his statistics from a variety of poor studies based on various kinds of individual and group intelligence tests, each of which has a number of built-in biases and shortcomings. Thus, his data are not conclusive. Most psychologists agree with Jensen that the issue is one of degree. Many of them, however, are strongly convinced that Jensen's theories drastically underrate the impact of training and environment (Kagan, 1969; Williams, 1974). The debate remains open, unresolved, and heated.

Generally, intelligence tests fall into two categories: group tests and individual tests. The group tests are written paper-and-pencil tests easily administered to whole classrooms. Individual tests are usually given by a school psychologist, a psychometrician, a staff member in a diagnostic clinic, or another testing specialist.

Intelligence Testing of Infants and Children

THE STANFORD-BINET TEST. The Stanford-Binet test is still considered the standard intelligence test and has served as a model for many others. It is administered individually to children ranging in age from 2

A preschool child taking the Stanford-Binet Test is asked to do tasks like identifying pictures and stringing beads. (*Sheila A. Farr.*)

years to adolescence, with a few generalized levels designed to accommodate adult intelligence. The items for preschool-aged children are somewhat different in nature from those designed for older children. The preschooler or retarded child is asked to do tasks such as identifying pictures, stringing beads, and folding paper. Items for older children involve answering more direct questions, such as defining words, explaining proverbs, or solving arithmetic and verbal problems. For example, 8-year-olds are expected to be able to name the days of the week, specifying which day comes after Tuesday, Thursday, and Friday (Terman & Merrill, 1960). The Stanford-Binet test does not depend on literacy and requires very little in terms of formal educational knowledge, such as mathematics or science. It is a highly verbal test, administered orally, and an individual must possess a fair verbal ability to be able to complete it. The Stanford-Binet test yields one comprehensive score or IQ. The IQ is not computed with the old formulation of MA (mental age) over CA (chronological age) multiplied by 100; instead it is derived from a statistical table comparing an individual's score with scores of other individuals of the same age. This is called a *deviation IQ*. An average score is 100. The scores of 66 percent of the population fall between 84 and 116. The farther a score is from the average, the fewer people there are at that scoring level. For example, people who score above 136 are in the top 1 percent. People who score below 64 are in the bottom 1 percent.

THE WECHSLER TESTS. David Wechsler and his associates have developed a number of intelligence scales. Currently in use are the Wechsler Adult Intelligence Scale (WAIS) (1955), the Wechsler Intelligence Scale for Children—revised (WISC-R) (1974), and the Wechsler Preschool and Primary Scale of Intelligence (WPPSI) (1967). Each of the scales operates on the premise that intelligence is composed of a number of abilities, each of which is measurable in distinct subtests. Each scale is divided into a verbal half and a performance half, which in turn are composed of five or six subtests. Subtests in the WISC include, among others, "object assembly," which involves putting puzzles together; "picture completion," which involves picking out the missing details in a picture; and vocabulary and general information questions. The test is individually administered, so that the examiner can observe a number of other kinds of behavior at the same time. Like the Stanford-Binet test, the Wechsler tests use a deviation IQ with an average score of 100.

INFANT INTELLIGENCE TESTS. Several tests have been devised to measure an infant's general development during the first 2 years of life. Among them are Arnold Gesell's recently revised scales based on developmental schedules (Knobloch & Pasamanick, 1974) and Nancy Bayley's Scales of Infant Development (1969). All of these scales measure a combination of sensory capacities, motor development, and some cognitive and social behaviors. Typical items on the Bayley scales include response to the sound of a rattle, interest in playing games, and ability to throw a ball. Clearly, these items have little in common with those used in tests for older children and adults, a necessary result of the fact that infants exhibit a rather narrow range of behavior. The most striking difference is the scarcity of verbal items in the infant tests. Not surprisingly, these infant scales are not very helpful in predicting performance on later intelligence tests (Stott & Ball, 1965). Many researchers had hoped that infant scales would reveal some factors closely related to later intellectual development, a finding that would bolster the concept of innate, fixed intelligence. Today, however, largely owing to the influence of Piaget, most psychologists agree that mental activity in infants is somehow qualitatively different from the activity observed in later years, and that mere biological maturation is not enough to account for intellectual growth. Infant intelligence tests do, however, serve a useful function for the childcare worker who needs an index of a baby's responsiveness and general developmental progress.

Since we have characterized the operational definition of intelligence as "that which is measured by the intelligence tests," we need to know exactly what a test like the Stanford-Binet is measuring. The degree to which a test successfully measures a given subject or phenomenon is called its *validity*. The *construct validity* of a test involves how well the data generated by the test enables us to draw conclusions about the nature of the particular construct with which we are working. For example, looking at the Stanford-Binet test, what conclusions can we draw about the construct of intelligence? What is the construct that is being measured?

Construct Validity of the Stanford-Binet Test

First, the Stanford-Binet is a test of current, not innate, ability. Response to test items depends on skills that have already been developed. For example, the child taking the test must be able to speak English. If he cannot, the Stanford-Binet test can only indicate that fact. It cannot predict whether the child will ever be able to learn English. In other words, the Stanford-Binet test is a rather general achievement test, indicating the level of general skills attained to date.

Second, whatever the Stanford-Binet test measures is somehow involved in academic performance as it is currently evaluated in our educational system. The test is an accurate tool for predicting achievement in many elementary and secondary school systems. Of course, this is not true for all children or for all schools, but on the average, children who do well on the Stanford-Binet test tend to do well in grade school and high school.

Third, the Stanford-Binet test measures different skills at different ages. The tasks required of the preschooler have very little in common with those put to the 8-year-old or the 12-year-old. Hence, there may be little correlation between a child's early scores and his scores at a later age. The variation is attributable to the change in the individual between tests, as well as to changes in the test items.

Fourth, the Stanford-Binet test is heavily oriented to verbal tasks. Children with good verbal abilities will generally perform better than children with poorer verbal skills. Those children with mixed language backgrounds or limited vocabularies are generally at a disadvantage.

Cultural Bias of Tests From the layman's point of view, recent criticism of the validity of intelligence tests has focused more on cultural bias than on any other aspect. Minority groups resent being measured by, and consequently scoring lower on, tests that assume wide exposure to the dominant white culture. To make their point, some black psychologists have created alternate tests that draw on black culture. One example of this is the "Chitling" test ("Summer Scholars at Work: Bridging the Intelligence Test Gap," 1968). The somewhat tongue-in-cheek conclusion drawn here is that most white children would not perform well because they are "culturally deprived" (see Table 1).

TABLE 1 SELECTED ITEMS FROM THE WECHSLER INTELLIGENCE SCALE FOR CHILDREN AND FROM THE "CHITLING" TEST

QUESTIONS SIMILAR TO THOSE IN WISC (1949)

1. Who wrote *Paradise Lost*?
2. What should you do if you see someone forget his book when he leaves his seat in a restaurant?
3. Why is copper often used in electrical wires?
4. How many nickels make a dime?
5. What is the advantage of keeping money in a bank?

REPRESENTATIVE QUESTIONS FROM THE "CHITLING" TEST*

1. Cheap chitlings (not the kind you purchase at a frozen-food counter) will taste rubbery unless they are cooked long enough. How soon can you quit cooking them to eat and enjoy them? (A) 45 minutes, (B) 2 hours, (C) 24 hours, (D) 1 week (on a low flame), (E) 1 hour.
2. If a pimp is uptight with a woman who gets state aid, what does he mean when he talks about "Mother's Day"? (A) second Sunday in May, (B) third Sunday in June, (C) first of every month, (D) none of these, (E) first and fifteenth of every month.
3. "Down-home" (the South) today, for the average "soul brother" who is picking cotton from sunup to sundown, what is the average earning (take-home) for one full day? (A) 75¢, (B) $1.65, (C) $3.50, (D) $5.00, (E) $12.00.
4. If you throw the dice and seven is showing on the top, what is facing down? (A) seven, (B) snake eyes, (C) boxcars, (D) little Joes, (E) eleven.
5. "Hully Gully" came from: (A) East Oakland, (B) Fillmore, (C) Watts, (D) Harlem, (E) Motor City.

*The correct answers to the "Chitling" Test are: (1) C; (2) E; (3) D; (4) A; and (5) C.
Source: Adapted from Wechsler, D. *Wechsler intelligence scale for children*. New York: Psychological Corporation, 1949; Summer scholars at work: Bridging the intelligence test gap. *Newsweek*, July 15, 1968, pp. 51–52.

It is impossible to estimate how much influence cultural bias exerts on test results; this depends on the test items, the age and socioeconomic background of the children being tested, and how the test is administered. One major study conducted in the Midwest (Liebert, Poulos, & Strauss, 1974) analyzed the items of eight intelligence tests for relevance to higher and lower social classes. Response to many of these questions showed a surprising relation to social status; for adolescent subjects, as many as 85 percent of the items were answered differently by children of different social backgrounds. Another group of researchers found that a white examiner generated substantial stress in black students and markedly impaired their test performances. Another conclusion drawn from the research is that minority groups have acquired low expectations of success in competition with whites. This noticeably lowers their scores, a sadly self-fulfilling prophecy.

Some psychologists have drawn a hypothetical profile of the minority or lower-class child that highlights cultural origins of poor performance, both on tests and in schools (Deutsch, Fishman, Kogan, North, & Whiteman, 1964). The characteristics of such a child include: less verbalization, greater fear of strangers, less self-confidence, less motivation toward scholastic achievement, lower intellectual competitiveness, greater likelihood of having a bilingual background, less exposure to intellectually stimulating materials both at home and elsewhere, and higher incidence of exposure to inferior schools. Given these obstacles, such a child often dislikes school and everything connected with it, and his approach to a test is often to get through a potentially uncomfortable situation as soon as possible—if necessary, by guessing, skipping, and making random responses. The successful child, on the other hand, is more likely to make his best efforts, since he wants to please his teachers and his parents and he is more aware of the significance of the test. There have been many attempts to create culturally fair tests, such as Raven's Standard Progressive Matrices (1958) which rely on abstract diagrams rather than verbal items. The Goodenough-Harris Drawing Test (Harris, 1963) is even less complex; the subject is merely asked to draw a picture of himself, a man, and a woman. Both these tests correlate well with other intelligence tests, but unfortunately both are also culture laden; the Raven Matrices reflect to some extent the subject's education, while the Goodenough-Harris depends upon the importance of representational art in the subject's culture. Other tests that have eliminated most cultural factors are poor predictors of academic performance (Liebert et al., 1974). So, for the moment, the established ethnocentric testing devices, with all their foibles, are the standards. At least, if we can remain aware of their shortcomings, we will not fall into the trap of according testing statistics more validity than they warrant.

Arthur Jensen (1969) disagrees with this interpretation of test results. He argues that the difference between average white and black IQs depends to a much greater extent on genetics than on cultural factors. His theory is based on these demonstrated facts: (1) the more closely two people are related, the more similarity their IQs exhibit, suggesting a genetic role in test performance; and (2) black children generally score lower on tests than whites. His conclusion is that the lower scores of black children are genetically determined. However, as Jerome Kagan (1969) points out in a reply to Jensen, genetic factors produce a range of qualities; for example, height is controlled by genetic factors. Furthermore, within the outer limits of heredity, environmental factors of health and nutrition determine how much of the genetic potential is realized.

Genetic limitations have their greatest impact on levels of mental proficiency that are very difficult to attain, such as musical or mathematical genius. Achievement of intermediate levels of school-related tasks may be much more dependent upon health, nutrition, and cultural familiarity than upon heredity. Furthermore, we should look to situational factors such as recent educational opportunities, fatigue, cultural bias of the test, and the way the test is administered. Jensen's theory is controversial to say the least, but a definitive affirmation or refutation of it awaits further research.

Intelligence Testing of Adults

Earlier, we discussed how the traditional theory of steadily declining intellect has been modified and updated to account for a host of experiential factors that accentuate individual differences. Some of the earlier conclusions of failing ability were the result of methodological errors in the research plan (Kimmel, 1974). For example, the best way to study aging would be to trace individuals over the course of their development. Instead, the early research took different groups of individuals at each age level and compared their scores (a cross-sectional study). The problem was that the samples were not strictly comparable: the younger people were of a different generation, with different life experiences, and were appreciably better educated than the older people. In fact, the difference in education was approximately the same as the (indicated) difference in intelligence test scores. Other studies have shown that adults with more education tend to do better on general intelligence tests than do the less educated. So the sampling technique was a major factor in the faulty conclusion of intellectual decline among the aging.

Another contaminant was the amount of disease or even impending death among the older people studied. An interesting study by Lieberman (reported in Kimmel, 1974) indicates that a dramatic drop in certain intellectual and physiological functions occurs during the year or two immediately preceding death. Certainly the older sample had more people experiencing this dramatic change than any other sample.

A third factor in testing adults is that intellectual decline varies among individuals and groups, depending somewhat on their original level of achievement. Longitudinal studies tracing the same individuals revealed that high scorers at an early age showed continued increases in test scores into old age; those with average scores showed increased verbal ability and the same level of nonverbal logical reasoning; and low scorers showed a decrease in general vocabulary and a decline in nonverbal reasoning (Botwinick, 1967).

Certainly, the evidence for the decline of intellectual functioning with advancing age is nowhere near as definitive as was once thought. In Chapter 21 we shall look at some specific abilities and the course of their decline among the aging. It is not true that all abilities, or even most abilities, decline in an aging population.

Intelligence testing at different age levels is only one way of looking at cognitive development over the life span. The testing has generated norms for average age groups but has shed little light on how intelligence develops from one age to another. This is due largely to the assumption of some researchers that mental growth is simply an accumulation of more information and more relationships. It will now be helpful for us to turn to the cognitive development theorists, who

Intelligence testing at different age levels is only one way of looking at cognitive development over the life span. Mental growth is an accumulation of more information and more relationships. (*Guy Gillette, Photo Researchers.*)

have tried to examine the nature of the mind at different points in time. Instead of conceiving of mental growth as a steadily additive process, many of the cognitive theorists analyze it as a process of qualitative changes, with developmental stages building on and modifying previous stages in an orderly, sequential way. Thus, infant strategies for coping intellectually with the world are quite different from those of the preschooler or the adolescent. The individual must pass through one stage before achieving a higher stage, and once the change to a higher stage is accomplished, it is irreversible.

STAGES IN COGNITIVE DEVELOPMENT
Piaget's Theory of Intellectual Development

In Chapter 2 we mentioned Jean Piaget, one of the weavers of a grand design large enough to encompass all human intellectual development. Few American theorists have attempted an analysis of such sweeping breadth. Piaget had a personal fascination with the unfolding of the human mind, a passion that fueled his natural talents as an observer of behavior. On the one hand his work focused on the interaction of heredity and environment, and on the other it dealt with the processes by which a child manipulated the environment to exercise and develop his intellect. As a cognitive theorist Piaget embraced the concept of development in stages that are sequential, irreversible, and qualitatively different. This does not mean that all skills have reached a certain level at the same time. A child may perform at an advanced stage with one kind of material yet show a lower stage of development with other material. Piaget's four major divisions of development are: (1) sensorimotor, (2) preoperational, (3) concrete operational, and (4) formal operational.

SENSORIMOTOR PERIOD. Piaget believes that intelligent behavior stems from the child's responsive interaction with the environment and from the perceptual organization that the child imposes on sensory data. The initial development of intelligence does not depend on language. It takes place through the complementary processes of assimilation and accommodation. Both of these processes relate to the way in which a child copes with new information and relates it to the categories already existing in his mind (see Chapter 2). Piaget refers to these general, all-purpose categories as schemata. Assimilation concerns the way a child incorporates new information into existing schemata. Accommodation, on the other hand, takes place when an element in the environment does not fit into existing schemata and the child is forced to modify the schemata. Piaget (1962) gives an example of assimilation in describing how he gave his child a pack of cigarettes to play with. Although the pack was unlike any previous toy the baby had seen, she treated it as a toy, mouthing it, banging it, and so on. The child incorporated, or assimilated, the pack of cigarettes into her toy-manipulation schemata. Through this dual process the ready-made, reflexive schemata of the newborn infant eventually develop into the mature logical powers of the adult.

The sensorimotor period is composed of six fairly discrete stages encompassing the first 18 months of life. Stage One (age 1 month) is primarily devoted to exercising the ready-made, reflexive schemata such as sucking, crying, and making fists. Stage Two (approximately age 2 and 3 months) involves acquired adaptation and primary circular reactions. *Acquired adaptation* is a change in behavior stimulated by the same recurring factor. For example, the baby is repeatedly put in a certain position before nursing; at some point in Stage Two she makes the association and shows sucking behavior when placed in the nursing position (Piaget, 1936/1952). *Primary circular reactions*, like thumb-sucking, may arise initially by accident. The response of sucking is biological and responsive. However, the child learns to repeat and control the initial occurrence of the thumb landing in the mouth. It is primary because it is biological and reflexive. It is circular because the initial event occurs by accident, but through repetition and elongation of the event the infant eventually achieves a degree of control of the reaction. Stage Three (approximately 4 to 8 months) is characterized by *secondary circular reactions* which are derived from, or composed of, combinations of primary reactions (Piaget, 1936/1952). For example, Lucienne, Piaget's child, learned to kick her legs (primary reaction). This shook the bassinet and a hanging doll. After noticing the moving doll, Lucienne learned to move her legs in order to move the doll (secondary reaction). Stage Four (about 9 to 12 months) is marked by the coordination of secondary schemata. The child borrows selectively from earlier secondary reactions to achieve a new result. To get a hanging toy, she pulls on its string. Previously, she would have pulled on the string only after attempting and failing to grasp it with her hands. Stage Five (approximately age 12 to 18 months) is characterized by *tertiary circular reactions.* The child is busy exploring and manipulating different means to the same end, or investigating one particular activity for a variety of results. Finally, in Stage Six (about 18 to 24 months) of the sensorimotor phase, the child invents new means, unlike any she has tried previously. For example, without any prior experience, she figures out how to open a box (Piaget, 1936/1952).

The primary accomplishment of the sensorimotor phase is something Piaget calls *object permanence.* This is an awareness that an object has an existence in time and space independent of one's own perception of it. For babies, "out of sight, out of mind" is literally true. If they cannot see something, it does not exist for them. Thus, a covered toy holds no interest, even if the child continues to hold on to it under the cover. Piaget (1936/1952) investigated search behavior to understand an infant's idea of permanence. Generally, full and complete search does not occur before an infant is 18 months of age. However, children usually develop a complete concept of their mothers' permanence before they apply the concept to other objects; the insight does not develop simultaneously toward all external objects.

PREOPERATIONAL PERIOD. This stage extends approximately from the age of 18 months to 7 years, although these limits are only rough guide-

A 9-month-old demonstrates the lack of object permanence. First he plays with the stuffed animal but when it is covered it holds no interest for him. (*Ray Ellis, Rapho/Photo Researchers.*)

lines. It is often subdivided into two parts, the preconceptual (2 to 4 years old) and the intuitive (5 to 7 years old). The intuitive is sometimes called the transitional stage because it leads directly into the next major stage.

The highlights of the preconceptual stage are the new use of symbols, symbolic play, and language. Symbols and symbolic play are qualitatively new because they mark the child's ability to think about something that is not immediately before him. Previously, intelligence was limited to the child's immediate environment. This development gives the mind greater flexibility. Similarly, words now have the power to communicate, even in the absence of the things they name. The child still has difficulty with major categories, however; he cannot distinguish between mental, physical, and social reality. He thinks that anything that moves is alive, even such things as the moon and clouds. He expects the inanimate world to obey his command, not realizing that physical law diverges from human moral law. These traits stem partly from the child's egocentricity, or his inability to clearly separate the realm of his existence and power from everything else (Brown, 1965).

The intuitive or transitional stage begins roughly at 5 years of age. It is closer than preconceptual thinking to adult thought in that during this stage children attempt to separate mental from physical reality and to understand mechanical causation apart from social norms. (Before, the child thought of everything as having been created by his parents or someone like them. Now he begins to grasp the force of other powers.) He is better at understanding multiple points of view and relational concepts than the preconceptual child. Still, his thought is characterized more by what he does not know than by what he does know. His comprehension of arrangements by size, numbers, and spatial classifications is incomplete. He is unable to perform mental operations or transformations of perceptual reality.

CONCRETE OPERATIONAL THOUGHT. This stage generally occurs between the ages of 7 and 11. At this point the child begins to exercise a rudimentary logic, although it is based on fairly concrete objects in the world. He realizes that thought may be at least as good a guide to a problem as perception. In the water-pouring problem discussed in Chapter 2, the child is able to conserve or retain the concept of a fixed volume of water while experiencing changing perceptions. He is increasingly able to think about things from points of view other than his own, although these thoughts do not rise to the level of abstractions. He can perform some operations on specific events or objects, but he cannot operate on his operations (Phillips, 1969; Inhelder & Piaget, 1958).

FORMAL OPERATIONS. Now the child has the basic equipment necessary to hypothesize all potential situations, independent of any perception. He can systematically test all possible hypotheses and reach conclusions. Sometimes the child will verbalize this process or write it out on paper, but he is nevertheless functioning in a formal, abstract manner. This concludes the most dramatic developments in cognition, although other forms of growth continue throughout adulthood, as we have seen.

Bruner and Others

Piaget is perhaps the most renowned cognitive theorist. But there are others, such as Jerome Bruner, who have articulated their own extensive theories, as well as those who specialize in one area of cognitive development.

Bruner proposes a stage theory composed of three modes of representation, somewhat parallel to Piaget's first three stages. The first mode is enactive; the child views things in terms of actions taken toward them. In this stage, if the object is not present, the child cannot comprehend it. The second mode is iconic; it depends on visual or sensory data, as well as on images that abbreviate the data to a simpler form. At the same time, the child needs the complementary functions of filling in, completing, and predicting. The third mode is symbolic, best exemplified by language. Bruner places heavy emphasis on symbolic representation because it frees the child from dependence on the immediate stimulus. He considers language especially effective as a teaching tool. In fact, Bruner's practical emphasis on educational technique and a theory of instruction is one of the major distinctions between his work and that of Piaget.

Other Aspects of Cognitive Growth

So far, our discussion has centered on directed forms of logical thinking and problem solving. We need to remember that there are entire realms of cognitive activity which we have not examined. For example, some kinds of creativity do depend on directed thought, but others utilize less structured processes like free association, remote association, divergent thinking, and imagination. There are many definitions of creativity but few theories about the development of creative thought. One recent book (Gardner, 1973a) points out an interesting parallel between aesthetic and cognitive development. It seems that both our appreciation of art, rhythm, and harmony and our ability to produce pleasing, artistic, and harmonious forms pass through developmental stages similar to those observed in cognition. Some psychologists also include the development of moral attitudes in cognitive development. Moral judgments may be characterized as cognitive, following particular stages of growth. We will give more consideration to this important issue in the section on adolescence, where much of this development takes place.

SUMMARY

Cognition is the mental process of knowing, recognizing, and understanding. Over the lifetime of any individual, this process will take on many different forms, growing at different rates in different directions and eventually suffering some decline. Development in the early part of life, as analyzed by cognitive theorists such as Piaget and Bruner, is strikingly similar from one child to another, with each person passing through the same sequence of irreversible and qualitatively different periods. After adolescence, biological maturation fades in importance as a uniform developmental factor, and individual differences in cognition are accentuated by divergent experiences.

Perception—the ability to select and attach significance to sensory data—is one of the major processes of cognition. In the young child, much of cognitive development initially springs from perceptual development. If perceptual development is impaired, other cognitive processes will not develop completely. There are wide variations in perceptual abilities, but people follow a similar developmental pattern.

Much of our knowledge of cognitive and intellectual functions has been influenced by the tests we use to measure them. Since Binet and Simon introduced their intelligence test, numerous scientists have devised hundreds of other tests in an attempt to discover the characteristics of intelligence. Three main issues in dispute have been: (1) whether intelligence is fixed or modifiable, (2) whether intelligence consists of one general ability or a configuration of different abilities, and (3) how much of intelligence is a function of heredity rather than of learning and experience. The two major tests, the Stanford-Binet test and the Wechsler scales, are valued for their ability to predict academic performance. Both tests contain cultural biases, however, and thus may not be accurate in measuring the abilities of minority children. No culture-free test with substantial predictive value has been designed to date, nor are there any tests for infants that accurately predict future performance.

Tests are useful for evaluating current ability at different ages, but they have little to tell us about how a mind grows from one level to another. The pioneering research of Piaget and Bruner has revealed an elaborate picture of the human mind interacting with its environment in particular ways, evolving from primarily reflex to a high degree of intellectual control and manipulation.

REVIEW QUESTIONS

1. Discuss the major factors in cognitive development. At what point in the life span does each have its greatest impact?

2. Outline several ways in which theoretical assumptions about the nature of intelligence affect a researcher's choice of test items and the conclusions that he draws from them.

3. Describe the major characteristics of Piaget's four stages of cognitive development. Can you picture yourself at each of these stages?

SUGGESTED READINGS

Brearley, M., & Hitchfield, E. *A guide to reading Piaget.* New York: Schocken Books, 1966. A clear, concise description of the major principles of Piaget's theory, with a number of applications of that theory particularly relevant to education.

Hunt, J. McV. *Intelligence and experience.* New York: Ronald Press, 1961. A detailed and competent discussion of the nature of intelligence, the intelligence test movement, and the relationship of intelligence and experience.

Piaget, J. *Language and thought of the child.* London: Routledge and Paul, 1932. One of Piaget's earlier books, it is readable, entertaining, and full of examples from his interviews with young children.

5

SOCIAL AND EMOTIONAL ASPECTS OF DEVELOPMENT

From the first cry to the final breath, life is a continuous process of social and emotional development. Infants are born into families; children go to school; adolescents begin to date; adults enter businesses; old people move to retirement communities. In all such new situations individuals learn to recognize and deal with the social expectations of the groups involved and to handle personal feelings and desires in socially acceptable—or not so acceptable—ways. They form new relationships and develop self-attitudes, beliefs, and values.

These actions are all part of the extremely complex processes of social and emotional development. The result of the successful working out of these processes in an individual is an integrated personality—a total being.

In the preceding two chapters we have been concerned with biological and intellectual development and have focused primarily on the

Socialization is a lifelong process by which individuals develop values, awareness of social expectations, and appropriate role behavior. In crowded subway cars people avoid looking directly at each other. (*Philip Teuscher.*)

discontinuity, or qualitatively different stages, of these processes. In contrast, when dealing with social and emotional development, we shall focus on the continuity of the process, since the balance of evidence seems to support this approach.

As David Elkind (1972) points out, adults often make the mistake of assuming that children's thought processes are similar to their own but that children's feelings are somewhat different from those of mature individuals. He cites the example of a woman who insists that her 4-year-old daughter watch "Sesame Street" on television, even though the child might prefer to do something else. This same woman would probably not consider trying to force her husband or friends to watch a program that she felt might be intellectually beneficial. Most adults would resent such tactics; many would rebel. But obviously, it has not occurred to the woman that her daughter is capable of a similar emotional reaction.

In actual fact, young children experience the full range of emotions. They may know intense anger, fear, and joy; their feelings are easily hurt; they resent being ordered around. While children may react in a far more direct and overt manner than adults, who generally learn to master tears and tantrums, their underlying emotions are roughly the same as those of mature individuals.

In certain respects, children's early relationships resemble those of adolescents and adults. One of the most appealing things about toddlers is the rather primitive way in which they caricature their elders. They exhibit strong shifts between dependence and independence, between crying for Mommy and insisting "I can do it myself." By the age of 2 they have many personality traits, such as impulsiveness or reflectiveness. Certainly, they have not yet acquired the subtleties of adult behavior, such as hypocrisy. But in their basic expression of emotions, formation of social relationships, and development of personality styles, young children bear a striking resemblance to adults.

SOCIALIZATION

Socialization is a lifelong process by which individuals develop attitudes, values, beliefs, knowledge, awareness of social expectations, and appropriate role behavior. Along the way they are influenced by certain important socialization agents: family members, peers, teachers, and bosses, to name just a few. Equally important are the life cycle milestones, or major events, that all people must deal with. After an almost entirely family-centered existence, children must suddenly adapt to a school environment where they have to come to terms with a new set of rules and expectations. This need to adapt, of course, applies to every new situation in life, whether it is moving to a new part of the country, entering college, getting married, having children, or going into a nursing home.

Sometimes socialization is almost automatic, and sometimes it takes a great deal of effort. But one way or another, people must become socialized to the immediate environment in which they find themselves, as well as to a larger social context such as a nation or a political party. But how do they become socialized? By what means do they learn to adapt to new and sometimes very different social situations? To fully comprehend the process, we must focus on the various social factors that influence behavior and on the gradual evolution and control of emotional reactions.

Socialization Processes

DIRECT REWARD AND PUNISHMENT. It is no secret that most people learn to behave according to what "pays." Reward patterns commonly produce or reinforce behavior patterns. Thus, children who receive attention when they whine are very likely to become chronic whiners.

A 3-year-old girl visiting her grandmother in a large city was awakened one night by the unaccustomed sound of a fire siren and began to cry. Her grandmother rushed in to comfort and reassure her, gave her candy, and stayed with her until she fell asleep. Since the grandmother's apartment was near a fire station, this situation repeated itself at least once a night for the duration of the little girl's stay. Her cries and protests became more frequent. Even as an adult, she puts up a fuss in reaction to sirens.

The effects of punishment, on the other hand, are not so easily interpreted. Clearly, punishment is a two-edged sword. While it seems to be fairly effective in suppressing a given type of behavior, it may cause various far-reaching side effects, some of which may be even less desirable than the original offense.

For instance, parents who use physical punishment to discipline their children are actually aggressive models. Their children may well learn to imitate the aggression, in addition to—or rather than—learning to stop the behavior that provoked the punishment. As Parke (1972) points out, there is significant evidence supporting a positive correlation between physical punishment by parents and aggressive behavior in children. But he is quick to warn that this aggression could be the result of the parents' encouraging aggressive behavior outside the home. It is not unusual for a father to be proud of his son's first "shiner" and to be more interested in "who won" the fight than in punishing the aggressive child. It is also possible that aggressive behavior is the *cause* and not the effect of physical punishment, that aggressive children force their parents to resort to spanking and slapping.

Another possible side effect of punishment is a secondary emotional response (Becker, 1964; Parke, 1972). Children may become frightened, or anxious, or angry, and then learn these emotional responses in reaction to the situation. Still another potential danger is suppression of the wrong response, or avoidance of the wrong part of the situation. For example, if the father is always the one who does the spanking, the child may learn to avoid the father rather than the situation that brought about the punishment. If this happens, the father will probably have less influence over the child's behavior than the mother. Sometimes, as in a classroom, children cannot escape from the punishing agent. If this situation continues, the children may become passive and withdrawn (Seligman, Maier, & Solomon, 1971) or they may adapt to the punishment itself, so that it no longer bothers them. Or children may learn a generalized dislike and anxiety toward all classroom situations.

Obviously, the potential side effects of punishment should always be considered, and whenever possible, the simpler—and therefore more successful—system of rewards should be used instead. This point is perhaps best illustrated by a study employing reward of an incompatible response (Brown & Elliott, 1965). A group of nursery school teachers were asked to ignore aggression and reward behavior that was incompatible with aggression. Encouraging such "good" behavior as cooperation and helpfulness led to a noticeable drop in classroom aggression.

Of course, punishment may be useful in certain situations. It can be a fairly effective means of controlling behavior, especially when appropriately combined with a system of rewards. But it must be closely related to the behavior that is being punished and should be carefully and consistently administered. In any event, the dangers of using punishment should always be weighed against the possible benefits.

MODELING. From early childhood, individuals observe the actions of those around them and copy whole behavior patterns, often down to the most minute detail. As many an embarrassed parent will testify, young children have a remarkable talent for capturing Mommy's or Daddy's actions, words, and mannerisms and mimicking them publicly. Modeling (or imitation) is also illustrated in adults by the customs and conventions that shape many of our thoughts and actions, and by the fads, fashions, and trends that regularly sweep this and every other country.

The influence of modeling on learning has been the subject of a great number of studies. The research has clearly shown that the introduction of a model greatly facilitates the acquisition of behavior patterns.

Certain models are more influential than others. To be effective, a model must possess certain characteristics that invite imitation. Three characteristics repeatedly identified in research are power, nurturance, and perceived similarity (Bandura, 1969). *Power* is the ability to control desirable resources and to exert influence over others. Studies involving a relatively powerful adult, a relatively powerless adult, and a child reveal that the child is more likely to imitate the powerful adult (Bandura, Ross, & Ross, 1963a).

Nurturance, or affectionate care and attention, also plays a part. Children tend to imitate the warm, rewarding, affectionate model rather than the cold, punitive, distant one. *Perceived similarity* with the model is still another significant factor in the effectiveness of modeling. Boys tend to model other boys or men; blacks tend to model other blacks; muscular, athletic children tend to imitate athletes; quite pen-

SOME EXAMPLES OF MODELING.

A little boy imitates his father driving a car. (*Philip Teuscher.*)

The trend of bicycle riding in recent years has become popular among adults. (*Jan Lukas, Rapho/Photo Researchers.*)

Children model their behavior after their heroes. (*Wide World.*)

sive children tend to select reserved or reflective models, and so forth.

Modeling appears to continue throughout the entire life span. We are constantly coming into contact with individuals we envy or admire and consciously or unconsciously copying their behavior. At the most basic level, a child develops a sexual identity by modeling; at a more frivolous level, a woman will buy a mini or a midi or a maxi simply because it is in fashion. But at any level, imitation is a process that is constantly shaping and augmenting our lives.

While conditioning and modeling are responsible for a large portion of social learning, there are certain complex behavioral phenomena, developing over time, that cannot be fully explained in these terms. Many theorists find the concept of identification useful in explaining the complex developmental patterns.

IDENTIFICATION. *Identification* is a relatively involved and somewhat confusing concept. It has been defined in a number of ways and used in a wide variety of theoretical contexts. In everyday conversation we may speak of identifying with a friend, with a social group, a cause, or an underdog. What we mean is that we feel closeness to that cause or group, we conform to it, live vicariously through it, join it, or empathize with it. Here, however, we shall use identification to mean the gradual process by which individuals adopt as their own the characteristics, attitudes, values, or beliefs of others. Most frequently, identification will be with a parent or other real model, but it may also occur with an idea or a fantasized model.

The concept of identification was introduced by Sigmund Freud to mean a rather specific set of processes of incorporating parts of another's thoughts, feelings, or behaviors. Since then, other theorists have expounded several types and descriptions of identification. Jerome Kagan (1958) has pulled together many of the psychoanalytic and social learning notions about identification and has grouped the related behavioral phenomena into four classes: imitation learning, prohibition learning, identification with the aggressor, and vicarious affective experience. According to Kagan, all these processes result in overt similarities between the individual and the model, but each category involves very different motives and rewards.

By *imitation learning*, Kagan means the initiation of certain socially acceptable responses by imitation of a model. Such imitation learning is often motivated by the desire to reproduce some of the beloved parent and is self-rewarding through association with the nurturant model. This aspect of identification is close to what we referred to in the last section as modeling.

Prohibition learning is the adoption of certain rules or prohibitions of the parents or other models. This type of learning is apparently motivated by the fear of punishment or loss of love and is reinforced by continued nurturance.

In *identification with the aggressor,* individuals adopt a threatening model's behavior in order to reduce anxiety over the prospect of aggression. The concept was first formulated by Anna Freud (1949). If one sees oneself as like the powerful, frightening father, or boss, or teacher, or tiger, the frightening figure is somehow not quite so scary.

Vicarious affective experience refers to the positive or negative feelings of the individual resulting from something positive or negative that has happened to the model. It is through this phenomenon that we may react with sincere joy to a loved one's achievement as if it were our own, or with sorrow to the grief of a friend.

Kagan's summary of identification processes (1958) involves only slightly more than the notion of modeling. Both identification and modeling describe the processes of acquisition of some of the attributes, motives, characteristics, and affective states of a model. In both identification and in modeling, the two major goals are power and love. Gradually the child models himself after the important, powerful, respected, loved, and similar people in his life. As he adopts their characteristics more and more, he sees himself as more powerful and worthy of love than the earlier helpless child. Theorists who emphasize identification, rather than modeling, as a key process stress internalizing attitudes and rules of behavior. They also emphasize the role of anxiety in motivating this process. In either case, identification or modeling is considered a key process in the development of sex roles and the development of conscience.

SELF-DISCOVERY. Reward and punishment, modeling, and identification are unquestionably important processes in the social and emotional development of an individual. But they cannot account for all the attitudes, values, beliefs, and behaviors that arise in the individual. There is a time when self-discovery becomes important, when an individual thinks about what he has learned through teaching, or by observing models, or through identifying with others. The individual develops a "theory" about himself and others and then matches his behavior to this thought.

| Aggression: An Example | At one time or another, even the meekest individual has experienced an overwhelming desire to hit someone. It is just such an urge that is socialized by all four processes we have just discussed.

In the course of development, the expression of emotion—in this case, anger—goes through a series of changes. The angry young child is very direct with his aggression: he screams and cries and kicks his feet. He does not hold in his feelings. Gradually, in some kind of socialization process, he learns some social judgments and some self-control. He also learns certain expectations as to when an angry outburst is appropriate, how much of an outburst is appropriate, and how the anger should be expressed. This appropriate expression of anger is learned in a number of ways. The first is through direct reward and punishment. Children who are rewarded for aggressive behavior are almost certain to make a habit of it. The reward may take the form of overt peer, or even parental, approval. Or it may be the satisfaction that comes from winning. Certainly, the child who loses every battle is not apt to keep on fighting.

Direct reward and punishment are only the beginning of socialization. A great deal of social learning takes place through observation and imitation of models. Modeling is particularly effective in increasing negative behavior such as aggression (Friedrich & Stein, 1973). However, it is also effective in increasing prosocial behavior such as self-control, sharing, and nurturance by children. Yarrow, Scott, and Waxler (1973) found that children who are cared for by nurturant caretakers demonstrate increased helping behavior both in school and in the home situation.

Even as individuals are observing and imitating available models, they are internalizing attitudes, values, and rules. These values become part of broader patterns of values such as independence, masculinity, femininity, and altruism. At first these networks are incorporated as total patterns. Later, individuals examine these networks of attitudes and values for consistency and evaluate each new situation in relation to these patterns. These later processes are identification and cognitive self-discovery.

DEVELOPMENT OF THE SELF

Most people spend a good deal of time thinking about themselves. This does not necessarily mean that they are selfish or inconsiderate. But individuals tend to interpret things subjectively, to see the world as it affects them personally. They may also worry about the way they affect others, about their appearance, their health, and their happiness. At another level they may worry about "who they are" and "where they are going." Such terms as *ego, identity,* and *self-fulfillment* have become little more than pseudopsychological jargon when used by the layperson, but the concepts they represent are very basic ones.

All these thoughts and worries seem to indicate personal attitudes toward the self. How do these attitudes develop? How are they maintained? While most psychologists recognize the importance of studying the subjective phenomena, many have questioned the value of a generalized self-concept. Some reject the idea as "unscientific"; others seem to feel it is just a matter of common sense and does not even warrant explanation. The theories of the self-concept are far too numerous and too complex to study here, but they contain certain basic ideas that may be helpful at this point.

Seymour Epstein (1973) seems to have brought together a great number of the ideas about the self. He has synthesized the salient characteristics that have been attributed to it and formulated an extremely plausible yet conservative theory. He sees the self as consisting of hierarchically organized and internally consistent concepts, as knowing and yet being known, as dynamic and yet essentially stable, unified but differentiated, necessary for organizing experience, and subject to collapse. In other words, Epstein asserts, the self-concept is actually a self-theory, "a theory that the individual has unwittingly constructed about himself as an experiencing, functioning individual"

(p. 407). This theory is seen as a "conceptual tool" for obtaining the optimal balance of pleasure and pain, maintaining self-esteem, and organizing all experience.

Development of Self-Awareness

Infants are initially unable to differentiate clearly between the self and the world around them. Gradually, however, they develop a body awareness; they begin to realize that their bodies are separate, are uniquely *theirs.* Much of infancy is devoted to making this distinction. A sudden movement catches a baby's eye and he discovers that the thing that is moving is his own hand, that it is part of him. Yet something that looks similar, only bigger, turns out to be his mother's hand. This hand is not always there and it does not hurt him if he pinches it, so he soon realizes that it is *not* part of him. Or, for example, an infant girl discovers her own voice. She figures out how to control the voice, how to cry louder if she does not get attention. Gradually she learns to make more and more complicated distinctions. By the age of about 10 months, she will probably know that an image in a mirror is not a new face but her own. And soon she will have a fairly good idea of what she looks like and how she compares with others.

Young children are always comparing themselves with their parents, peers, siblings, and even family pets. They know that they are smaller than their older brothers and sisters, darker or fairer, fatter or thinner. They love to talk about themselves, to point out the observations they have made about themselves.

Children also begin to develop personality awareness, a sense of psychological autonomy. Epstein (1973) speaks of "development of an inferred inner self" whereby children discover the existence of their own unique personalities, much as they have already discovered their bodies. All the processes of social learning enforce this sense of self until children begin to formulate a very real, integrated idea of "who they are."

As Erik Erikson points out, one of the major tasks of adolescence is putting together an identity (Elkind, 1970). Even as they are undergoing dramatic physiological changes, adolescents are maturing mentally, experiencing new feelings, and sorting out personal attitudes and values in terms of those around them, especially their peers. It is during this time that the intellect becomes capable of formulating philosophies and theories about the way things are and the way they ought to be. And with this new mental ability adolescents begin to develop a sense of "ego identity." Until this point a girl may have been an oldest child, an average student, a choir girl, a promising pianist, a champion swimmer, a best friend, and an archenemy. In her teens she begins to fit these jigsaw pieces together, and eventually she completes the puzzle and comes up with a total picture—a coherent, unified idea of the self. If for any reason she cannot fit the pieces together, her personality will remain fragmented and she will be a victim of "role confusion."

A self-concept will change with time. A healthy one grows fuller and more complex, while a weak or superficially formed one may fall apart

entirely. Erikson sees young adulthood—with its new-found independence and productivity—as a time for developing interpersonal relationships, for achieving the intimacy of love and true friendship. If
intimacy is not achieved, however, it can be a desolate time of isolation
and loneliness (Elkind, 1970). The emotional success or failure at this
and subsequent stages of life seems largely a function of the strength
and resilience of the self-image.

All individuals have both a public and a private self (Mead, 1934).
They have an outward side they share with others and a deeper, more
private side they may hide even from themselves. To a certain extent,

All individuals have an outward side they share with others and a deeper, more private
side they may even hide from themselves. Here, a community college student participates
in an encounter group. (*Al Kaplan, DPI.*)

this is healthy. Obviously, we cannot bare our innermost thoughts to everyone we meet. But sometimes the individual's perception of the inner self is a source of shame and great insecurity, and this may inhibit intimacy and stunt emotional growth.

The self-concept also includes both a real and an ideal self—that is, the self we believe we are and the self we think we ought to be (Mead, 1934). The individual who perceives these selves as similar is likely to have a strong, healthy self-concept and will probably be much better prepared to mature and adapt than the individual who sees the real self as vastly inferior to the ideal one.

Even the healthiest self-concepts must weather various identity crises. For example, the successful businessman who loses his job and the wife whose children have all left home may experience drastic changes in their self-concepts.

Other crises typically occur at women's menopause and "male menopause," at retirement, when a spouse dies, and when an elderly person enters a nursing home. Situations beyond our control, such as wars, financial depressions, and crippling accidents, can also precipitate identity crises.

Traditional sex roles can seriously inhibit the development of talents and the formation of healthy self-concepts. In fact, stereotyped sexual identity seems to be one of the major causes of some crises. Many men and women develop "masculine" and "feminine" public selves according to societal expectations. If their abilities and personality traits do not lend themselves to the acquisition of the proper image, these individuals will be doomed to frustration and failure. Even if they are successful, their private selves may be at great variance with their public images; and this variance can lead to violent internal conflict, seriously impairing their ability to share and to achieve intimacy. Individuals who devote their lives to being what they are not, or do not really want to be, are apt to suffer acutely when they realize the emptiness and futility of their masquerade. At best, rigid adherence to traditional sex roles may keep people from realizing their full potentials; at worst, it may lead to fragmented, unhealthy self-concepts.

According to Erikson, middle age is either a time of "generativity" or of self-absorption and stagnation (Elkind, 1970). That is, by this time individuals should be able to extend themselves beyond their immediate families and friends to a concern for the future and for society as a whole. If they fail to do this, they may become wrapped up in themselves and their personal well-being. The final years, in Erikson's opinion, are a time for reflection. If an elderly person can look back with pride and satisfaction, he or she will achieve a sense of "integrity." If not, old age will be a time of despair as the realization dawns that it is too late to correct the mistakes or begin again.

A Consistent Self-Concept
Even as the socialization processes are helping to develop the individual's self-concept, the self-concept is influencing socialization. Young children do not imitate everyone with whom they come into

contact, and they become increasingly discriminating as they grow older. As we have seen above, perceived similarity with the model is an important factor in imitation. For instance, a little girl who is tall for her age may pattern her behavior on that of a tall female teacher. Older children and adolescents tend to choose cultural heroes—famous athletes, politicians, movie stars, popular singers. They imitate these models not just because of their power, glamour, or status but because of some perceived similarity. At a very early age children possess attitudes, values, skills, and physical traits that will influence their choice of models. Although these attributes have not yet been fused into an integrated identity, they are very significant parts of a forming self-image.

The self-concept may be self-rewarding and self-punishing. When individuals behave in a way that is consistent with their self-image, they do not necessarily need a pat on the back from society; they feel pleased with themselves and are thus rewarded. Of course, it is often difficult to separate intrinsic and extrinsic rewards, for individuals do not exist in a vacuum. A boy who considers himself a good athlete will receive praise from his parents and peers after playing a good game, but he will also gain satisfaction from having performed in a way that is consistent with his self-image. And if he does well when he is practicing by himself, he will feel the same sort of pleasure.

Self-images can also be self-perpetuating and self-fulfilling. Individuals who perceive themselves as failures may unconsciously sabotage their own endeavors in order to maintain that image. Drastic change in an image—even for the better—can be very upsetting. An individual with buck teeth and an oversized nose may emerge from braces and plastic surgery in acute psychological distress despite a radically improved appearance. The reflection in the mirror is no longer consistent with the homely self-image, and the result may be a severe identity crisis.

A number of studies have been conducted to explore the consistency of behavior over a period of time. One such study (Kagan & Moss, 1960) clearly illustrates the long-term stability of certain behavior patterns, as well as the conditions that may interfere with this stability. A group of "normal" adults was interviewed and tested for signs of passive and dependent behavior. These same individuals had been studied intensively throughout their childhoods in a longitudinal study. The findings indicated that passive or dependent behavior was quite stable for women but not for men. The experimenters concluded that this difference in behavior had a great deal to do with sex-role identity and the socialization processes that contributed to it. Little girls are traditionally encouraged to be passive; in fact, aggression and independence are often considered "unfeminine." Little boys, on the other hand, are expected to be independent and are even condemned as "sissies" if they are too passive. However, early behavior that is not discouraged is extremely likely to perpetuate itself and remain stable throughout an entire lifetime. If, as adults, we come across our old report cards or letters to our parents from teachers or camp counselors, we may be amazed by the striking resemblance between the descriptions of our early behavior and our present personalities.

In a way, personality is like physical appearance. If we look at old photographs of ourselves, we will discover that we still look very much the same. Yet, of course we have changed. So it is with the self-concept. Like our bone structure, the basic elements of our self-concept begin to take shape while we are at a very early age, and they are likely to remain constant throughout our lives. But as we grow and mature physically, the healthy self-concept is expanding and adapting to new situations.

MOTIVATION
Just what sort of motivation energizes personality development? As in the case of so many other important questions, psychologists are far from any sort of agreement on an answer. For many years, behavioral psychologists explained all motivation in terms of basic physiological needs or drives, such as hunger, thirst, sleep, and sexual activity. All other needs were learned from these basic ones. But eventually this approach lost favor as it became more and more apparent that need satisfaction was not sufficient to explain such behavior as exploration, manipulation, and seeking challenge.

Competence Motivation
Among the more interesting and plausible motivational formulations is Robert White's concept of competence (1959). White asserts that beyond the basic physiological drives, there is an innate need to develop competence—that is, to achieve mastery over the environment. White uses the term *effectance* to designate the motivational aspect of competence and he characterizes the desired result as a "feeling of efficacy."

This is certainly a change from the idea of human beings at the mercy of the elements and their own bodily functions. The concept of competence involves "selective, directed, persistent" behavior in an attempt to provide oneself with positive stimulation and achieve the feeling of efficacy, or mastery. People seek novelty and challenge. Infants, of course, are very preoccupied with their physical needs. But after they are fed and diapered and comforted, they begin to look around for something to occupy them. They touch, watch, pull, suck, and in general show a tendency to develop skills that no one has taught them. Young children show extraordinary tenacity when they begin to learn to walk, and this cannot be explained entirely in terms of reward and punishment or modeling, although these processes may well enter in. Once they achieve a degree of success in pulling themselves to their feet, children will continue standing and trying to walk without apparent need for any reinforcement other than the satisfaction of increased efficacy.

Many early skills seem to "explode" after a somewhat tentative period of half-hearted attempts. Sometimes children will hesitantly try to write without any degree of success and suddenly "explode into writing," as Maria Montessori (1912) phrased it. They will form letters, words, and numbers, covering every available surface. This near obsession with mastering a newly discovered skill is internally motivated; the only apparent reward is the sense of achievement.

Later in life, motivation becomes a good deal more complex, and competence for its own sake may be more disguised. Yet, White asserts, effectance still contributes to adult interests. Adults, too, still seek challenge, novelty, new conquests, new creations—often without regard for clear reward, approval, or status gain. They sometimes tackle the environment simply because they want to test their capabilities and gain the satisfaction of conquering problems they have sought out themselves.

Maslow's Hierarchy of Needs

Another most helpful description of motivation is provided by Abraham Maslow's hierarchy of needs (1954). According to Maslow, needs, and therefore motivations, are hierarchically organized so that the lowest, or most basic, ones must be satisfied before the higher ones can even be considered. This hierarchy of needs is diagrammed in Figure 4.

The most basic needs are physiological survival needs. Like most animals, human beings must have nourishment, warmth, and rest if they are to survive at all. Next, the safety needs must be satisfied. Individuals must avoid danger on two levels: on one level to preserve

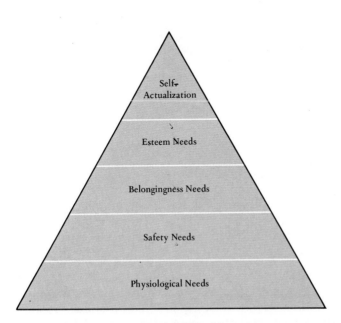

Figure 4 Maslow's Hierarchy of Needs. The stages, from the bottom, correspond to how crucial each need is for survival and how early it appears in the development of the individual. (*Adapted from A. H. Maslow,* Motivation and personality. *New York: Harper, 1954.*)

life, and on another to achieve a feeling of security. Such mechanisms as fear and avoidance, as well as anger and aggression, can be included in safety needs. Once these basic drives are taken care of, people are free to turn their attention to the more sophisticated "belongingness" needs. Human beings are social organisms and they need to be part of a group, to associate with others, and to love and be loved. Next higher on the pyramid are the esteem needs. This stage involves positive feedback of all sorts—from the confirmation of basic abilities to the achievement of prestige or even fame. Meeting these needs provides a sense of well-being and a degree of self-satisfaction. And finally, when people are fed, clothed, sheltered, established in society, and reasonably confident of their abilities, they are ready to tackle the problem of self-actualization, or fulfillment of their potentials.

The concept of self-actualization is an exciting one. It opens up whole new vistas for learning, promises enormous potential for personal growth, and opposes the pessimism of much of the rest of psychology.

Self-actualization is especially significant in terms of adult growth and psychotherapy. Certainly, psychotherapists have always believed in the possibility of continued learning during adulthood, but this has largely been seen as a healing process, a way of solving adjustment problems or mental illness. Maslow (1968), Rogers (1961), and other humanists have gone far beyond this view by proposing that individuals may strive toward a psychological ideal, not simply a "normal" mental state. They may develop to their full potential, discover capabilities they never even knew they had, and create for the sake of creativity.

Self-actualizing individuals are autonomous and able to think independently in the face of cultural and environmental stereotypes and limitations. They are able to form close interpersonal relationships with a select few persons and at the same time reach beyond the self to a concern for humanity in general (Maslow, 1968). According to Maslow, self-actualizing people have "peak experiences"—moments, or even extended periods, of joy from fulfillment and feelings of oneness with the universe. Ellis G. Olim (1968) speaks of human beings "as becoming," as being in a constant evolutionary state of psychological upward mobility. To foster such "becoming" requires a family environment relatively free of constraints, one that encourages experimentation, expressiveness, and spontaneity.

Man's need for self-fulfillment can never be completely satisfied, but the challenge in striving to achieve self-actualization is what enables sophisticated human beings to live life to the fullest.

In contrast to White and Maslow, many psychologists take a much more pessimistic view of human motivation. In several of their theories, anxiety plays a key role. In fact, most motivational theories must take account of anxiety in one way or another.

Anxiety   From the earliest moments of life children experience anxiety, and this emotion is an extremely powerful force in their development. When certain basic needs—such as for safety, acceptance, or security—are not satisfied, children have feelings of fear or apprehension without a clear idea of the cause. When they become fully aware of the expectations and prohibitions of their culture; when they feel hostility, anger, or jealousy; when they lose control and give vent to their rage—then, too, children suffer anxiety.

In fact, anxiety seems to be an inevitable human condition. Over a period of time we learn to cope with it, both consciously and unconsciously. Even as the drug industry is making record sales in tranquilizers and sleeping pills, we are developing a complex network of psychological responses, or defense mechanisms, to combat anxiety. In Chapter 13, we shall examine the development of a number of these defense mechanisms.

The Javanese culture instills in its people strong concepts of self-control and respect. Here, a woman and her children quietly wait for a Buddhist ceremony to begin. (*Josephus Daniels, Rapho/Photo Researchers.*)

At a very early age children begin to develop their own personal styles of coping with anxiety, and their characteristic approaches are greatly influenced by cultural and family patterns. Different ethnic and socioeconomic groups—and individual families within those groups—encourage particular ways of dealing with anxiety and with emotions in general. Some societies expect a high degree of control and frown on any emotional display, while others actually require it.

The Javanese culture is one that demands a remarkably high degree of control. Hildred Geertz (1959) observed the people of a town in central Java and has presented a fascinating sketch of the emotional climate of that island. The Javanese are seen as poised and fastidious, nearly obsessed with the desire to protect themselves from shock or confusion. Strong emotional displays are extremely distasteful to them. The key word in their behavior code is *equilibrium,* and their infants are treated accordingly. Babies are thought to be extremely vulnerable to shock and are swaddled, held continuously, and prevented from developing any degree of independence. Virtually no demands are made upon children until they are considered old enough to understand verbal instructions; but then they are strictly, though unemotionally, drilled in self-control and in a concept of "respect" which actually involves fear and shame as well as politeness.

When societies and families make their demands and prohibitions—whatever they may be—children begin to feel anxious about measuring up to them. This is especially true of sex roles. Dependency is generally allowed, and is often even encouraged, in girls, while aggression and assertiveness are expected in boys. Girls may therefore feel anxiety over their drives and ambitions and boys over their dependency and passivity. There are also sex-related differences in the way anxiety is handled. Generally, girls are more likely to suppress emotions and anxiety while boys resort to displacement and acting out. Therefore, anxiety may have dramatically different effects on the personality functioning of boys and girls (Sarason, Davidson, Lighthall, Waite, & Ruebush, 1960; Sarason, Hill, & Zimbardo, 1964).

RELATIONSHIPS
The Mutuality of
Relationships

Earlier in this chapter, we looked at some studies involving rewards and punishment and modeling. Some of this research has proved extremely effective in isolating the variables that contribute to the development of specific behaviors. However, the research cannot fully explain long-term social rules or expectations which are crucial in situations outside the laboratory. Obviously, life is not a laboratory situation. Social learning takes place within the context of social interaction and of significant interpersonal relationships. When children hit their brothers or sisters, they are not simply "aggressing at home;" they are behaving in a very human way within the context of the family. Parents have fairly well-established sets of values and social expectations which they

Adults and children have well-established sets of social values and expectations. These feelings are the basis of interpersonal relationships. (*Grete Mannheim, DPI.*)

try to instill in their children. Children, too, have certain expectations regarding those around them. They learn to anticipate treats or spankings from their parents, fights or games with their siblings, acceptance or rejection by their peers, and they are extremely sensitive to such indications of approval or disapproval. These mutual feelings and expectations are the basis of interpersonal relationships.

Children soon develop characteristic ways of feeling or of reacting to their own emotions within the context of these relationships. Later, as their range of experiences expands, these responses are extended, or transferred, to new relationships where they may or may not be appropriate. For instance, when children begin school, they may have a great deal of difficulty adapting to the expectations of the teacher and other pupils, especially if their own ethnic and socioeconomic backgrounds are significantly different from those of their fellow students. Children who are dependent or passive may find themselves surrounded by independent, aggressive schoolmates and a teacher who directly or indirectly encourages these latter behaviors. Or, of course, the reverse may be true and an active child may be put into a group of completely passive playmates.

Every time individuals encounter major new situations in life they must form new relationships. Adolescents have to learn to deal with members of the opposite sex in a new way. The 17- or 18-year-olds who go away to college may be leaving their families for the first time and living with students from very different ethnic and socioeconomic backgrounds. Similarly, leaving high school or college very often means entering a shop or an office environment, renting an apartment, and perhaps seeking out an entirely new set of friends. All these new relationships are greatly influenced by past experiences with others, but new learning and adaptation are always necessary.

Adult psychotherapy is an example of a novel relationship. The therapy situation involves learning to relate to another human being who has a new set of expectations quite different from any the client has previously encountered. Ideally, at any rate, the psychotherapist is nonjudgmental. He or she tries to avoid arbitrary standards that might cause guilt or create anxiety in the client. Yet, he or she expects disclosure of very personal, private thoughts and feelings. Many people entering into psychotherapy for the first time find it difficult to form a relationship at this intimate level, for past relationships color their expectations and behavior. But eventually, if the individual is able to adapt, this new situation becomes optimal for learning.

Attachment and Loss   In the course of a lifetime, most individuals are involved in a number of significant interpersonal relationships. The first, and undoubtedly the most influential, is the bond that immediately begins to grow up between the infant and the mother. This bond becomes firmly established by the time the child reaches the age of 8 or 9 months. Often termed *attachment,* this relationship is characterized by strong interdependence, intense mutual feelings, and vital emotional ties.

Attachment occurs through a characteristic series of events as the infant progresses from earliest awareness to the development of trust and confidence in the mother. Later, there is an equally characteristic sequence of steps away from the primary caretaker, or a *loss* of relationship. These first responses to attachment and loss lay the foundation for all later relationships, whether with peers, relatives, other adults, spouses, or lovers. As such, this infant-mother bond is called a *prototypical relationship*.

Although attachment and loss can take place at any point in life—an infant can lose the mother and suffer loss, and an elderly person can marry and gain attachment—there is an increasing need to cope with separation as time passes. The older we get, the more likely we are to lose family, friends, lovers, or spouses.

There have been a number of studies on separation of young children from their parents. James Robertson and John Bowlby (1952) observed and described preschool children who were hospitalized and separated from their families. The generalized loss reaction consists of protest, then despair and detachment, followed by reintegration. When they were first separated from their primary caretakers—usually their mothers—the children entered a *protest* phase, which lasted from a few hours to a week or more. At this stage, the children were extremely distressed and restless, appearing very angry and frustrated but obviously expecting their mothers' return. They often rejected alternate caretakers. After this initial protest, there was a phase of *despair*, characterized by inactivity, apathy, and withdrawal. This phase actually seemed to be a period of mourning, and the children's crying often changed from an angry howl either to a monotonous, mournful wail or to silent longing. Finally, there was a positive stage of *reintegration* and renewed relationships. The children began to take an interest in their surroundings and sought activity and companionship. This was a period of recovery and rebuilding.

There seem to be a number of variables that influence the length and intensity of the reaction to loss. A child between the ages of 18 months and 3 years tends to suffer more acutely than an older child. Other factors which affect the child's response are the exclusivity of his relationship with the primary caretaker, the length of separation, and the relative novelty of the environment. Some children move smoothly and rapidly through the various stages while others struggle through them slowly and painfully.

These phases of adaptation are prototypical of reactions to loss later in life. There is a remarkable similarity of response between a hospitalized 2-year-old separated from his mother and an elderly individual who has just lost his spouse.

A personality develops, not in isolated bits and pieces of rewards and punishments or imitations of models and heroes, but in the context of ongoing relationships. The nature of these relationships—their diversity, the way they are formed, the mutuality and depth of understanding and of trust they engender, and the ability of their participants to adapt to loss—all have profound effects on an individual's personality and self-concept. Relationships undergo stress and change, but there is the potential with each new relationship for greater self-awareness, self-control, and a more mature self-concept. Only under excessive conditions—excessive stress of loss, or an unusually shallow, unresponsive, or punitive relationship—is there a restricted self-concept. It may well be that there is much psychological truth in the saying, "Better to have loved and lost than never to have loved at all."

MORAL DEVELOPMENT

Somehow, children learn to be "good" or "bad." They learn to demonstrate kindness, moral judgment, and altruism or to show cruelty, insensitivity, and selfishness. The development of a conscience and of a consistent set of moral attitudes is a perfect illustration of the integration of social and emotional development with cognitive development. Conscience may be seen as a double concept involving self-control on the one hand and the reaction to loss of self-control on the other. Identification is one of the more popular concepts used to explain just how these two tendencies develop. In Chapter 13, we shall discuss the development of conscience through identification.

Lawrence Kohlberg (1963) has departed from the classic social learning views of moral development. He has rejected the notion that internal moral standards are acquired simply by internalization of cultural rules. He advocates a cognitive developmental interpretation which emphasizes the development of *moral judgment*. The progressive sequential growth of moral attitudes—rather than behaviors—is of central importance.

Kohlberg tested various groups of children and adolescents, presenting them with hypothetical moral dilemmas. From the results he was able to define six "developmental types of value-orientation," which he saw as stages within three distinct levels of moral development (see Table 2).

The first level of premoral development encompasses the two most primitive stages of moral judgment. The first stage, punishment and obedience orientation, is seen as externally motivated by punishment and characterized by obedience to rules to escape punishment. At this stage, individuals have no concept of having a right; rather, they equate the principle with "being right" or obeying authority. Outward acts constitute goodness and the major concern is with consequence, not intention.

Naïve instrumental hedonism is the second stage. Here, the motivation is manipulation of goods and rewards, and the central element is conformity for the sake of getting something or having favors returned. Individuals at this stage believe that they are free to do whatever they want with themselves and their possessions, regardless of how their actions affect others. Although still a primitive form of morality, the

TABLE 2 KOHLBERG'S STAGES OF MORAL DEVELOPMENT

STAGE	ILLUSTRATIVE BEHAVIOR
LEVEL I. PREMORAL	
Stage 1. Punishment and obedience orientation	Obeys rules in order to avoid punishment
Stage 2. Naïve instrumental hedonism	Conforms to obtain rewards, to have favors returned
LEVEL II. MORALITY OF CONVENTIONAL ROLE-CONFORMITY	
Stage 3. "Good-boy" morality of maintaining good relations, approval of others	Conforms to avoid disapproval, dislike by others
Stage 4. Authority maintaining morality	Conforms to avoid censure by legitimate authorities, with resultant guilt
LEVEL III. MORALITY OF SELF-ACCEPTED MORAL PRINCIPLES	
Stage 5. Morality of contract, of individual rights, and of democratically accepted law	Conforms to maintain the respect of the impartial spectator judging in terms of community welfare
Stage 6. Morality of individual principles of conscience	Conforms to avoid self-condemnation

Source: Kohlberg, L. The development of children's orientations toward a moral order. I. Sequence in the development of moral thought. *Vita Humana 6*, 11–33 (S. Karger Basel, 1963). (Adapted from Hilgard, E. R., Atkinson, R. C., & Atkinson, R. L. *Introduction to psychology* (5th ed.). New York: Harcourt Brace Jovanovich, 1971, 78.

central value of satisfying personal needs reflects an awareness of one's own interests.

Kohlberg's second level of conventional role-conformity is slightly more advanced than the first level, but nevertheless simplistic. At this level, moral stereotypes emerge and there is a greater degree of social awareness. The "good-boy" morality of stage three, which occurs at this level, is motivated by disapproval by others and is characterized by conformity to avoid this disapproval. Like the hedonist, the good boy believes in the rights of ownership, but he does not believe that these rights allow anyone to harm others. This view equates performance of expected roles with value, but in a superficial, stereotyped way it recognizes the importance of good intentions and helping others.

The central motive of authority maintaining morality, stage four, is censure by authorities; there is little interest in the opinions of peers. This stage is characterized by conformity for the sake of escaping official disapproval. Here, good is seen as respect for authority, and conscience is equated with avoidance of censure by authority figures.

The third and highest level, that of self-accepted moral principles, involves recognition of a conflict of interests and a rational attempt to choose between alternatives, even though neither choice may be "right" or "wrong." The fifth stage is morality of contract, of individual rights, and of democratically accepted law. This type of morality is motivated by social respect or disrespect; it is characterized by conformity to maintain respect on the basis of community welfare. At this stage, universal rights are acknowledged but the law is always the deciding factor.

The sixth and final stage, morality of individual principles of conscience, is motivated by conscience and is built around the desire to conform to avoid self-condemnation. At this stage, moral principles, rather than rigid cultural *do's* and *don't's*, determine values and the aim is justice and respect for others.

Age is seen by Kohlberg as a factor in progressing from one stage to the next. There is strong evidence of developmental sequence whereby a stage cannot be attained unless the one below it has first been achieved.

Moral development extends over long periods of time, especially adolescence and young adulthood, and many individuals may never reach the highest stages at all. Kohlberg's view emphasizes the significance of intellectual maturity and reasoning capacity in moral development. This cognitive developmental approach is closely related to self-theory, which assigns to individuals a major role in forming their own characters. Thus, we may not simply expect models and disciplinary techniques to provide moral guidance and training but must assume the responsibility for our own morality.

SUMMARY

Socialization is the complex, lifelong process by which individuals develop socially and emotionally and acquire the values, attitudes, and beliefs that form the integrated personality. Social learning theorists explain this process in terms of direct reward and punishment, modeling, and imitation. Other theorists emphasize identification and self-discovery.

Through socialization, children develop attitudes about the self. Later, as adolescents, they put together their individual identities, integrating all the specific behaviors and notions about the self into consistent but flexible self-concepts which will influence their subsequent behavior.

Human behavior is motivated by certain basic needs. In addition, individuals seek competency or mastery of their environment. Maslow proposes a hierarchy of needs, much like a pyramid. Lower-level needs must be satisfied before individuals can proceed to higher needs. At the top of the pyramid is the need for self-actualization, for developing the fullest potential.

When certain needs are not met or certain social demands are made, individuals experience anxiety—a feeling of fear or uneasiness without an identifiable cause.

All social learning takes place within the context of ongoing mutual relationships through a lifetime of attachments. Each relationship has its own expectations, course, and losses.

One important part of learning is the development of a set of moral principles, or a conscience, which in turn guides much of human behavior. Many theorists explain the development of conscience in terms of identification, but Kohlberg postulates a convincing hierarchy of moral levels as a cognitive developmental process.

1. How do individuals become socialized? Name the major processes involved in socialization and discuss each one briefly.

2. What is an identity crisis? What factors may cause such a crisis?

3. What are Kohlberg's six stages of moral development? How would you characterize each stage?

Axline, V. *Dibs: In search of self.* New York: Houghton Mifflin, 1964. A sensitive account of a child in therapy. Dibs emerges from isolation and loneliness as a sturdy, healthy personality.

Dennison, G. *The lives of children.* New York: Random House, 1969. A study of the lives of 23 children enrolled in a small private school on New York's Lower East Side. In this free, humane educational environment, the children emerge as struggling, learning, and growing personalities.

Erikson, E. *Childhood and society.* New York: Norton, 1963. This classic book presents Erikson's theory of the eight ages of man and some cross-cultural comparisons of psychosocial development throughout the life span.

PART II
THE BEGINNINGS OF HUMAN LIFE

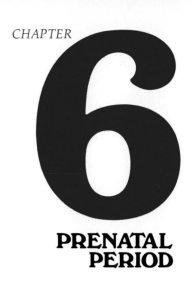

6

PRENATAL PERIOD

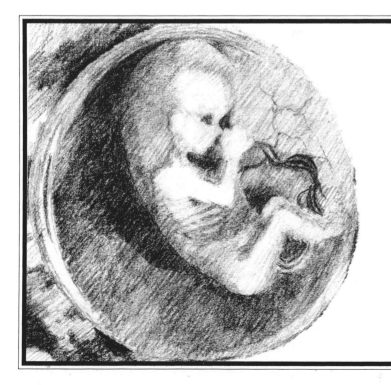

Ruth and Jim had been married for nine years when Ruth became pregnant for the first time. When she was three months pregnant, Ruth gave up her job and devoted her energies to decorating the nursery and studying child care and development. When her friends suggested that she might regret having given up her job so soon, Ruth explained, "Jim and I have wanted this baby for so long. I don't want to do anything now but make sure that life will be perfect for this child—and that includes taking care of myself during pregnancy and learning as much as I can about how to care for the baby when it arrives. Sure, I'll probably get bored from time to time during the months ahead, but it will all be worth it in the end."

Virginia had been hospitalized for a series of tests to determine the cause of her bouts of dizziness, poor coordination, nausea, and semiparalysis of joints in some fingers on one hand. The diagnosis was multiple sclerosis, a slowly progressive, ultimately fatal disease. (Based on the history of her complaints, the doctor thought that she had probably had the disease for five years or more.) A further diagnosis was pregnancy—her third. Virginia commented, "Abortion is out of the question. It's against our religion—although we don't usually practice our religion—and besides, you shouldn't just run away from life's problems. But my concern is, will the baby be all right? For six to eight weeks I've been so nauseous and lost so much weight. How will I manage when the baby comes? When I have these spells, I can barely stand up, and the dizziness lasts for weeks. In five to ten years at most, I'll be a complete invalid, I'm told. Also, what am I going to tell my other children? And when should I tell them? It's not fair to them or to the one on the way. I have very few years left. I can't believe it. This can't be happening to me."

TRANSITION: THE SOCIAL CONTEXT OF CONCEPTION

These excerpts from case studies show dramatically that from the moment of their conception children are a part of a social and psychological context. They do not begin life with a "clean slate." The expectations and anxieties, riches and deprivations, health and illnesses of the families into which they are born affect not only their life after birth but also their development during the prenatal period.

In the case of Ruth and Jim, everything possible is being done to ensure a "perfect" life for their baby. But what happens if that baby is born with a physical or mental defect that makes a normal life impossible? What happens if the parents' idea of perfection does not include a child who cries and keeps them awake throughout the night, or who has difficulty learning to read or to relate to others? A child born into a family that has unrealistic expectations for him enters life with burdens that will affect his development just as surely as the child born into a family that resents or is uneasy about his arrival.

Virginia's health will affect her child both during and after the pregnancy. Even her emotional stress may influence the child during the prenatal period. If she does not eat well because she is depressed, or if she skips appointments with her doctor because she just does not want to think about the impending birth, the baby may suffer.

A pregnant woman who is considering an abortion may pay little or no attention to her nutrition or general health. Some women who do not want a baby may refuse to see a doctor in the blind hope that "the problem" will go away if it is not confirmed by a professional. The poverty and cultural background of the mother can also have an effect upon a child during the prenatal period. Some women literally cannot afford to eat properly or to see a doctor during pregnancy, while others are constrained from seeking adequate care by superstition, family practices and tradition, or ignorance of healthy procedures.

During the prenatal period, the family is also making adjustments to the impending birth. Sometimes this involves stress and change in the family context; at other times there is dramatic upheaval that affects the emotional state or nutritional state of the mother. For example, a couple may marry because of the pregnancy of the woman. If one or both of the partners are unhappy about the forced marriage, the child may feel the effect. On the other hand, an existing family may have its problems aggravated by the impending birth of another child. The father may be out of work, the mother or another family member may be ill, or a couple may have decided that they simply do not want any more children. Any of these conditions will have an impact upon the expected child.

In this chapter we are concerned primarily with the biological and maturational processes during the prenatal period—the unfolding of the inherited potential. In addition, we will look at the precise environmental influences which may affect the developing fetus and the manner in which they interact with this unfolding maturational process.

CONCEPTION

Human development begins at the moment of conception. A one-celled fertilized egg that can hardly be seen carries all the genetic information needed to create a whole new organism. In Chapter 8 we will investigate the genetic blueprint contained in the chromosomes of the egg cell. Here, we will look at the process of fertilization that marks the beginning of the life cycle of a human being.

Union of Ovum and Sperm

About the tenth day after the beginning of the average woman's regular menstrual period, an *ovum*, or egg cell, that has developed in one of her two ovaries, is stimulated by hormones and enters a sudden period of growth that continues for three or four days. By the end of the thirteenth or fourteenth day of growth, the *luteinizing hormone* causes the follicle surrounding the ovum to break, and the ovum is released to begin its journey to one of two *Fallopian tubes.* This release of the ovum from the ovary is called *ovulation.*

In many women, then, ovulation occurs about the fourteenth day after the onset of menstruation. The mature ovum survives only for two or three days. A man's *sperm,* deposited in a woman's vagina during sexual intercourse, also survives for three days, at most. If a viable sperm, moving from the vagina through the uterus and up the Fallopian tube, reaches the ovum during the critical 48- to 72-hour period for maturity, fertilization of the ovum takes place. Otherwise, the ovum continues down the Fallopian tube to the uterus, where it disintegrates.

The sperm and ovum are single cells, each containing half of the hereditary potential of the individual. The union of the two cells to produce a human being is quite a remarkable achievement. Some 300 million spermatozoa are deposited in the vagina during intercourse, yet only one of these can fertilize the ovum. The sex and inherited traits of the child depend upon which of these millions of sperm cells survives to penetrate the ovum. For the sperm, the trip to the ovum is long and difficult. The microscopic sperm cell must work its way upward through a foot-long passage, through acidic fluids that can be lethal to it, through mucus and other obstacles, and finally arrive at the proper place at the proper time. Considering all this, it sometimes seems surprising that any of us are here!

A living human ovum at the moment of fertilization. At the top a sperm has penetrated the ovum. (*Dr. Landrum B. Shettles.*)

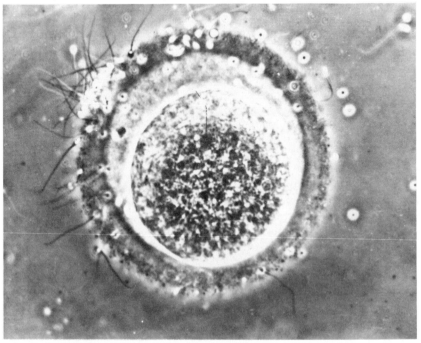

Monozygotic twins are genetically identical. (*Harvey Stein.*)

Fraternal or dizygotic twins are as different or as similar as other siblings. (*Harvey Stein.*)

After fertilization, the ovum proceeds down the Fallopian tube toward the uterus, where it begins to divide and develop. In some cases, however, the single cell first splits into two identical cells, which then develop into two individuals. In this instance, the result will be *identical* or *monozygotic twins.* Because they are created from the same cell, identical twins always are the same sex and share the same traits. In other cases, two separate ova unite with two separate sperm producing *fraternal* or *dizygotic twins.* The genetic traits inherited by fraternal twins can be as different or as similar as the inheritance of brothers or sisters. And fraternal twins may be of the same or opposite sex, since fertilization involves two different cells.

We can describe much of what happens in fertilization, and in the development of the fetus that follows, but there are still many things we do not fully understand about the outcome of fertilization. Researchers are working on some rather interesting questions. For example, for every 100 girls conceived there are approximately 160 boys conceived. Yet at birth there are only 105 boys born for every 100 girls. Researchers are concerned with why there are more successful male sperm than female sperm. We know, for instance, that the male sperm are shaped somewhat differently, have somewhat longer tails, swim faster, are more affected by the acid environment, and tend to live a shorter period of time than female sperm (Rosenfeld, 1974a). Scientists have not yet worked out all the factors so that we can, for instance, predict whether or not someone will have a boy baby or a girl baby. Similarly, we know that during the prenatal period, more boys die prior to birth than girls. But all the factors involved in this are not yet clear. There are other problems that intrigue the researcher. Why is it that one single sperm out of millions is able to penetrate the wall of the ovum? What stops the others? What prevents more than one sperm at a time from penetrating? Why is it that the ovum rejects all other sperm as soon as one has penetrated? These are just a few of the many challenging questions that are still to be answered about the process of fertilization.

PRENATAL DEVELOPMENT

After union with a sperm, the ovum enters the *germinal period,* a time of very rapid cell division, which lasts for about a week. This is followed by the *embryonic period* of about seven weeks, during which structural development of the fetus takes place. From the beginning of the third month until birth—a time known as the *fetal period*—the organs, muscles, and systems begin to function. Many of the processes that the organism will need in order to survive at birth are being developed at this time.

Germinal Period

Within hours after the sperm penetrates the ovum, the process of fetal development begins. The pronucleus of the ovum, containing 23 chromosomes, moves slowly to the center of the ovum where it joins with the pronucleus of the sperm, which also contains 23 chromosomes. The merger of the pronuclei of ovum and sperm produces a *zygote,* a fertilized egg cell, with 23 pairs of chromosomes, the number required to develop a human baby. (Half of each pair of chromosomes comes from one parent, the other half from the other parent.)

Once the zygote is formed, the process of cell division commences. The first *cleavage,* or cell division, produces two cells identical in makeup to the original zygote. The second cleavage, which takes place after about two days, produces four cells. A third cleavage then produces eight cells, and so on. By the end of four days there may be as many as 60 to 70 cells.

As the cells continue to divide, they form a ball which moves through the Fallopian tube toward the uterus. At this point, the solid mass of cells forms a hollow sphere, or *blastula,* around an accumulation of fluid. During the formation of the blastula, the cells begin *differentiation* (the separation into groups according to their future functions). Some of the cells move to one side of the hollow sphere and begin to develop into the embryo, while other cells develop into a protective covering for the embryo.

Near the end of the first week the fertilized ovum (blastula) completes its journey down the Fallopian tube and arrives in the uterus, which will be its home for the coming months. Within a few days the ovum becomes embedded in the uterine wall, in the process called *implantation.* Once the blastula has implanted itself, the developing organism enters the embryonic period.

STAGES OF PRENATAL DEVELOPMENT. (*Dr. Landrum B. Shettles.*)

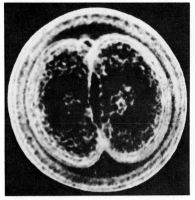

A two-cell organism 30 hours after fertilization.

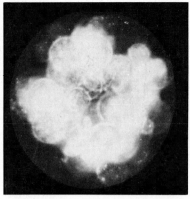

Three and one-half days into the germinal period. Four or more cleavages have taken place but there is not yet cell differentiation.

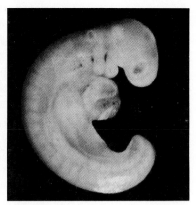

An embryo at 28 days.

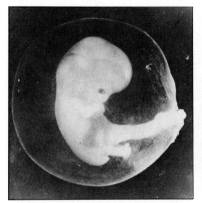

An 8-week-old embryo showing the development of the basic elements—arms, legs, fingers, organs.

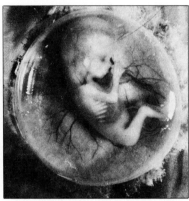

A 14-week-old fetus showing the placenta, amniotic sac, and umbilical cord.

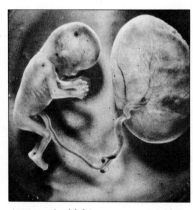

A 16-week-old fetus.

Embryonic Period

Generally, the embryonic period is considered to extend from the end of the first week to the end of the second month after conception. It is a crucial time when much that is essential to the baby's further prenatal development and future lifetime development occurs. During the embryonic period, all the tissues and structures that will house, nurture, and protect the embryo and the fetus for the remainder of the nine months begin to grow. In addition, there is the development, in form at least, of all the organs and features of the embryo itself. At the end of the embryonic period, this very tiny creature has arms, legs, fingers, toes, a face, a heart that beats, a brain and lungs, and all the other major organs.

The embryo develops within an *amniotic sac* filled with fluid and gains nourishment through an organ called the *placenta,* which develops specifically to assist the growth and progress of the new organism. The placenta is a disk-shaped mass of tissue on the wall of the uterus, formed partly from the tissue of the uterine wall and partly by the *chorion,* a layer of tissue that originates with the embryo.

The placenta begins to develop at the moment of implantation and continues to grow until about the seventh month of pregnancy. It is connected to the embryo by the umbilical cord, which is a rope of tissue containing two fetal arteries and one fetal vein. The placenta provides for an exchange of materials between mother and embryo, keeping out large particles of foreign matter but passing on nutrients. Thus, enzymes, vitamins, and even immunities to disease pass from the mother to the embryo through the placenta. At the same time, waste products pass from the embryo to the mother through this organ. Sugars, fats, and proteins pass through to the embryo; some bacteria and salts do not. It is important to note that the mother's blood system and the child's blood system do not mix. All of this exchange of nutrients occurs across cell membranes in the placenta.

Since the embryo receives its nutrients from the mother through the placenta, it is obvious that the diet and health of the mother will have an effect upon the developing child. Not so obvious, perhaps, is the effect that the fetus might have on the mother. The fetus draws from the mother's body whatever it needs to survive and grow. If the mother does not provide sufficient additional nourishment to cover the demands of this rapidly developing child, then her own physical system will suffer, as well as the baby.

Many of the miscarriages, or spontaneous abortions, that occur take place during the embryonic period. They are usually caused by inadequate development of the placenta or of the umbilical cord, or both.

During this period the embryo itself grows extremely rapidly. There are daily changes. Immediately after implantation, the embryo develops into three distinct layers. They are the *ectoderm* or outer layer, which becomes skin and the nervous system; the *medoderm* or middle layer, which becomes muscles, blood, and the excretory system; and the *endoderm* or inner layer, which becomes the digestive system, lungs, thyroid, thymus, glands, etc. And, again almost immediately, there is the development of the heart and of the *neural tube,* which is the beginning of the nervous system and brain. At the end of the fourth week of pregnancy and only three weeks into the embryonic period, the heart is beating; the nervous system, in its somewhat primitive form, is functioning; and both are monitoring the development of the rest of the embryo. And all of this occurs often before the mother is even aware that she is pregnant.

During the second month, there is very rapid development of all the structures we recognize as human. The arms and legs unfold out of small buds on the sides of the trunk. The eyes are first visible, seemingly on the sides of the head, at about a month. The full face changes almost daily during the second month. The internal organs of lungs and digestive system and excretory system are being formed, although they are not yet functional.

In this embryonic period, two developmental trends can be observed. In the *cephalo-caudal trend,* development takes place in a head-to-tail direction (*cephalo* meaning head, *caudal* meaning tail). For example, the arms, which are near the head of the embryo, develop sooner than, or slightly in advance of, the legs and feet. In the *proximal-distal trend* (near-to-far growth principle), development takes place from a position close to the midline of the body out to areas that are distal, or far away from the midline. That is, organs in the trunk develop before the arms; arms develop before the hands; and hands develop before the fingers. Both growth principles apply to the child after birth as well as during the embryo stage, since continuing development takes place in a head-to-tail, near-to-far pattern.

Fetal Period

The fetal period lasts from the beginning of the third month until birth —or about seven months, given an average total *gestation period* of 266 days. It is during this period that the organs, limbs, muscles, and systems become functional. The fetus begins to kick, turn its feet, turn its head, and, eventually, turn its body. Even with its eyes sealed shut, the fetus begins to squint, frown, move its lips, open its mouth, swallow a little amniotic fluid, and make sucking motions.

The first body movements of the fetus are total, gross responses. Later the movements become more differentiated and more specific. Following the head-to-tail development trend, the reactions of the head of the fetus are integrated sooner than are those of the lower part of the body. For example, by the end of the third month the fetus will suck in response to the stroking of its mouth, and it will squint in reaction to the stroking of the eyelids (Hooker, 1952).

During the third month, the first external sign of sex differentiation becomes apparent. The penis and scrotum in the male and the beginnings of labia in the female can be detected, although the male organs develop sooner than do those of the female. At the same time the male fetus develops a prostate gland, *vas deferens,* and epididymis, and the female develops Fallopian tubes and ovaries.

The eyes, still set toward the sides of the head, develop their irises, and all of the nerves needed to connect the eye to the brain are now in place. Teeth form under the gums; ears begin to appear farther down on the sides of the head; fingernails and toenails form. The fetus develops a thyroid gland, a thymus gland, a pancreas, and kidneys. The liver begins to function and the lungs and stomach begin to respond. By the twelfth week, the vocal cords have developed, the taste buds have formed, and the ribs and vertebrae have begun to ossify (turn from cartilage to bone). The fetus, although unable to survive on its own, has acquired almost all of the systems and functions necessary for a human being. And at this point it is only about three inches long and weighs around half an ounce!

During the fourth to sixth months (second trimester), all the processes begun in the first three months (first trimester) are continued, with further differentiation and refinement of the reflexes. The body becomes longer and the head does not look as out of proportion as it did during the preceding month. The face develops lips and the heart muscle strengthens, beating from 120 to 160 times a minute. In the fifth month, the fetus acquires a strong hand grip and increases the amount and force of its movements. The mother will be able to feel an elbow, a knee, or the head, as the fetus moves around during waking periods.

During this time, the fetus is undergoing a process of cell replacement in the skin. Oil glands form and secrete a cheesy coating, called the *vernix caseosa,* that protects the skin from the amniotic fluid. The fetus also develops a hairy covering on its body and begins to grow eyebrows and eyelashes.

In the sixth month, the fetus grows to about 12 inches in length and weighs approximately $1\frac{1}{2}$ pounds. The eyes are completely formed and the eyelids can open. Bone formation progresses, hair on the head continues to grow, and the fetus begins to straighten out its posture so that the internal organs can shift into their proper positions.

By the third trimester, a healthy fetus might be able to survive outside the mother if it were placed in an incubator and given special care. At seven months, the fetus weighs around three pounds and its nervous system is mature enough to control breathing and swallowing. During this seventh month the brain develops rapidly, forming the tissues that localize the centers for all of the senses and motor activities.

Researchers have determined that the human organism does much more than just develop physically during the prenatal period. The fetus not only reacts to touch and sound, but is even thought to experience needs such as hunger and thirst. If this is true, the movements the fetus makes may be more than just random reflexes. Facial expressions of the fetus may indicate pleasure and displeasure, and the turning, kicking, and sucking actions that take place in the womb may be purposeful movements designed to make the fetus more comfortable (Carmichael, 1970).

By the eighth month, the fetus may weigh from 4 to 6 pounds and will measure from 17 to 18 inches in length. Fat layers now form under the skin in order to protect the fetus from the temperature change that it will encounter at birth. Although the survival rate for infants born after eight months is 70 percent, these babies do face risks (Rugh & Shettles, 1971). Breathing may still be difficult; initial weight loss may be greater than for full-term babies; and, if their fat layers have not fully formed, temperature control could be a problem. For these reasons, babies born at this developmental stage are usually placed in incubators and given the same type of care as are babies born at seven months.

During the ninth month, the fetus continues to grow and begins to turn to a head-down position in preparation for the trip through the birth canal. The vernix caseosa begins to fall away, and the hairy coating dissolves. Immunities to disease pass from the mother to the fetus, and supplement the fetus' own developing immune reactions. Approximately one to two weeks before birth, the baby "drops" as the uterus settles lower into the pelvic area. The weight gain of the fetus slows, the mother's muscles and uterus begin sporadic, painless contractions, the cells of the placenta begin to degenerate—all is ready for the birth.

Throughout this discussion we have used terms such as average, normal, and healthy. The development of the fetus was assumed to progress in a predetermined and predictable sequence, because all conditions were presumed to be normal. These ideal conditions would include a well-developed amniotic sac with a cushioning of amniotic fluid, a fully functioning placenta and umbilical cord, an adequate supply of oxygen and nutrients, and freedom from disease and toxic chemicals. What we have not considered is the effect on the fetus of any alteration in these conditions.

Every year in the United States, some 250,000 or more babies are born with birth defects. These defects range from gross anomalies that spell certain and almost immediate death for the newborn to minimal physical or mental defects that may have little impact upon the future development of the child. Although we might like to assume that birth defects

PRENATAL ENVIRONMENTAL INFLUENCES

A nurse provides medical treatment to an ill newborn. (*March of Dimes.*)

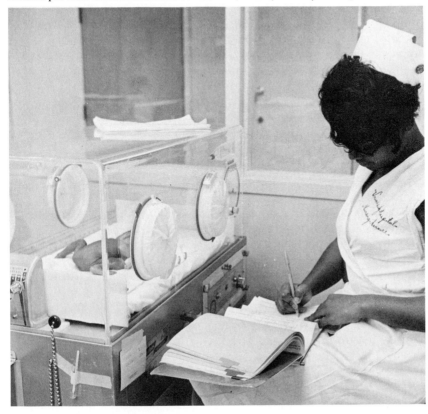

are problems that happen to someone else's babies and are probably caused by some inherited traits, the truth is that only a small proportion are the result of inherited factors. The majority of birth defects are caused by environmental influences during the prenatal period or during childbirth, or by the interaction of heredity and environmental influences.

The study of developmental anomalies is called *teratology*, which means the study of monsters. A teratogenic agent, or teratogen, is the specific agent that disturbs the development of the fetus—a virus or chemical, for example. Although the root meaning of the word teratology may be unpleasant, the subject itself is important because it investigates the reasons why things go wrong. In revealing the causes of abnormalities in infants, teratology also helps us to understand the normal process of development.

Processes of Environmental Influence

Perhaps the best way to begin an examination of prenatal environmental influences is to mention briefly those actions and events that do not influence the development of the fetus. Regardless of what old wives' tales may say, the mere thoughts of the mother do not affect the fetus. If a mother "thinks bad thoughts," her baby will not be born with some sort of psychic burden. If a pregnant mother is frightened by a snake, a spider, a bat, or some other creature, her child will not begin life with a personality defect or a birthmark. Grief, worry, or work experienced by the mother will not have an effect on the unborn child unless the stress on the mother leads to poor nutrition, illness, disregard for medical care, or ingestion of harmful drugs. For them to have an impact upon the unborn child, the mother's experiences must involve actions that will affect either the condition of the placenta or the substances that pass through the placenta to the child.

Chemicals, viruses, nutritional elements, drugs, and hormones can have an effect upon the fetus, because they are directly related to the growing organism through the placenta. Even the condition of the mother's nervous system might possibly affect the fetus. Short-term worries or fears are of no marked consequence. Yet prolonged and intense emotional stress in the mother may cause either chemical changes, as in secretions of the endocrine system, or muscle tensions which could affect the environment of the developing child (Montagu, 1950).

Critical and Sensitive Periods

The effects of many environmental conditions depend very dramatically upon the time of development. That is, the effects depend upon the point in the developmental sequence when the change in the environment occurs. This is true for most teratogens as well as for deficiency states such as malnutrition. Sensitive periods are those times when an organism is acutely receptive and responsive to certain influences. Critical periods are the *only* times when an organ, structure, or system is sensitive to a particular influence. Although most studies of both of these periods have been done on animals rather than on human beings, it is thought that the human goes through such developmental periods, both before and after birth.

The theory of prenatal critical periods is tragically illustrated by the story of the "thalidomide babies" (Taussig, 1962). During the late 1950s and early 1960s, a large number of children were born with seal-like arms and legs, large disfiguring birthmarks, and a strange variety of internal defects. Doctors and other researchers traced the disaster to the mother's ingestion of sedatives and sleeping tablets containing the drug thalidomide. In every case, the mother had taken the drug sometime between the thirtieth and fiftieth day after her last menstrual period, or 28 to 42 days after conception. In cases where the drug was taken only later in pregnancy, abnormalities did not appear. Evidence such as this has led researchers to believe that critical periods exist for the development of certain features and functions during which drugs and other agents and accidents can have a severe effect.

Unfortunately, most environmental effects on prenatal development have their maximal impact during the early period when a woman is often not even aware that she is pregnant. She is not worried about nutrition, nor is she particularly concerned about minor diseases such as rubella (German measles). She may not think about the potential effects of any drugs she may be taking. In short, the damage is often done before the woman knows that there is an embryo to worry about.

In embryological development, each organ or organ system seems to have a critical period, or a period of maximum sensitivity, when it is most responsive to the gross stimulating influences of the environment. Also, these are periods when the embryo is most vulnerable to disruptive or damaging elements in the environment. For example, rubella may cause blindness, heart defects, deafness, brain damage, or limb deformity in a fetus, depending upon the particular time in the developmental sequence when the mother contracts the disease. For most of these organ systems, the critical period and the more sensitive periods are during the first trimester of pregnancy (Greenberg, Pelliteri, & Barton, 1957; Sever, 1967).

Categories of Environmental Influence

The variety of factors that have been found to have an influence on prenatal development is impressive—even frightening. Drugs, diseases, nutrition, hormones, blood composition, and radiation all play a part in the development of the child.

DRUGS. In examining the effects of drugs taken during pregnancy, we must keep in mind that the effect of drugs on the mother may be quite different from their effect on the embryo or fetus (see Table 3). Certain developing structures are much more vulnerable to drugs than are structures that are already developed. Furthermore, some drugs may cross the placental barrier only to be trapped in the primitive system of the embryo. For example, the kidneys of the fetus may not be able to handle a drug as efficiently as the maternal system can. Instead of being passed on, the drug may accumulate in the system of the fetus. Just because a drug has been found safe for use by adults, it does not necessarily follow that it will be safe for the fetus that is sharing an environment with an adult.

TABLE 3 EFFECTS OF DRUGS ON THE FETUS OR THE NEWBORN

NAME OF DRUG	EFFECT ON THE FETUS OR NEWBORN
NARCOTICS:	
Morphine	Depression of fetal respiration. Decreased responsiveness of newborn.
Meperidine (Demerol)	
Heroin	Babies born to narcotic addicts develop withdrawal symptoms of hyperirritability, shrill crying, vomiting. Can be fatal.
Methadone	
BARBITURATES:	
Phenobarbital	All barbiturates and thiobarbiturates cross the placenta. In usual clinical doses they cause minimal fetal depression.
Amobarbital (Amytal)	
Secobarbital (Seconal)	Decreased responsiveness and poor sucking ability in early neonatal period.
Pentobarbital (Nembutal)	
LOCAL ANESTHETICS:	
Procaine (Novocaine)	Cross the placenta readily. May depress infant by direct drug effect or indirectly by causing maternal hypotension if used for regional anesthesia (spinal or epidural anesthesia).
Tetracaine (Pontacaine)	
TRANQUILIZERS:	
Chlorpromazine (Thorazine)	No definite untoward effect on fetus substantiated.
Meprobamate (Equanil, Miltown)	No untoward effect on human fetus substantiated.
Chlordiazepoxide (Librium)	No untoward effect demonstrated so far. Crosses placenta.
ANTIMICROBIAL AGENTS:	
Erythromycin	No untoward effect demonstrated so far.
Penicillin	No untoward effect.
Streptomycin	Hearing loss (very rare) in infants whose mothers have been treated for prolonged periods in early pregnancy.
Tetracycline (Achromycin)	Staining of deciduous teeth. Inconclusive association with congenital cataracts.
Chlortetracycline (Aureomycin)	
Oxytetracycline (Terramycin)	Potential for bone growth retardation but not proved to occur in utero.
STEROIDS:	
Cortisone	Possible relation to cleft palate. None definitely proven in humans.
Hydrocortisone	
ANTIHISTAMINES AND ANTIEMETICS:	
Dimenhydrinate (Dramamine)	No evidence of adverse effect in human beings.
MISCELLANEOUS:	
Ethyl Alcohol	No neonatal depression. May increase uterine contractions.
Salicylates (Aspirin)	No untoward effect in usual amounts. Salicylate poisoning may occur in neonate when mother takes overdose.
Smoking	Intrauterine growth retardation.

Source: Bowes, W. A., Jr. Obstetrical medication and infant outcome: A review of the literature. *Monographs of the Society for Research in Child Development*, 1970, *35 (4, Serial No. 137)*, 3–23.

In general, *narcotics* such as morphine and heroin cause depression of fetal respiration, decreased responsiveness of the newborn, and smaller babies. (The last effect may be due to malnutrition caused by the mothers' heavy use of narcotic drugs.) Also, babies born to narcotic addicts suffer withdrawal symptoms of hyperirritability, shrill crying, vomiting, shaking, and poor temperature control. The severity of these symptoms is proportionate to the extent of the mother's addiction, the amount of her doses, and the proximity of her last dose to the time of delivery (Burnham, 1972).

Barbiturates also seem to cross the placenta, although they do not have a major impact upon the fetus. At most, they appear to cause minor depression in the growing child. Regarding the use of barbiturates during pregnancy, however, the thalidomide story should be kept in mind. The sedative that contained this drug, as is the case with many drugs on the market, had not been tested with women in the early months of pregnancy!

There do not seem to be any marked or prolonged effects on the fetus caused by the mother's use of alcohol, except that the babies born to alcoholics often experience withdrawal symptoms and suffer from malnutrition.

Researchers have found that cigarette smoking during pregnancy increases the fetal heart rate (Simpson, 1957). Immediately after the mother has smoked a cigarette, the heart of the fetus beats faster; but whether this has any long-term harmful effects is not yet known. Also, babies born to heavy smokers tend to weigh less at birth and to have a greater incidence of prematurity than babies of nonsmokers. Since they are born before the end of nine months, they are thrust into the world before all their systems and functions may be ready for independence (Baird, 1964).

Another concern is the drugs and other agents whose influence on the fetus has not yet been determined. No one has investigated the long-range—or, in some cases, even the immediate—effects of hair sprays, food preservatives, certain cosmetics, insecticides, and polluted water and air upon the developing infant (Bowes, 1970).

DISEASES. If the expectant mother contracts rubella, syphilis, gonorrhea, poliomyelitis, or any of a number of diseases, she may suffer a miscarriage, or her baby may develop mental deficiency, certain forms of blindness, or deafness during the prenatal period. In addition, a chronic or latent condition of the mother, such as diabetes, may result in newborn respiratory problems or stillbirth. On the other hand, some diseases do not appear to affect the embryo or fetus. Certain kinds of bacteria do not cross the placental barrier, so that the fetus may get a virus cold from the mother, for example, but may *not* get a severe bacterial infection suffered by the mother (Montagu, 1950).

NUTRITION. Perhaps the single most important element in the prenatal environment is nutrition. As the following excerpt points out, the effects of lack of proper prenatal nutrition can extend throughout an individual's entire life span.

> . . . a fetus, malnourished in the womb, may never make up for the brain cells and structures that never came properly into being. Malnutrition both before *and* after birth virtually dooms a child to stunted brain development and therefore to considerably diminished mental capacity *for the rest of his life* (Rosenfeld, 1974b, p. 59).

In studies with rats, Stephen Zamenhof and others (1971) found that animals fed a diet low in protein had lower body weight, lower brain weight, and a smaller number of brain cells than those fed a protein-rich diet, and the effects were passed on to the next generation of offspring. Third-generation descendants of the original protein-deprived animals still showed reduced brain development. The social implications of such long-range findings—if the findings do, in fact, hold up for human beings—are enormous, considering the starvation rate in developing nations and social class deprivation in complex industrialized nations (Vore, 1973).

H. G. Birch and J. D. Gussow (1970) reported that carefully controlled "nourishment programs" for expectant mothers during wartime resulted in full-term, healthy babies, while starving expectant mothers often gave birth prematurely. When malnourished pregnant women carried their babies full term, their children often died shortly after birth.

Other researchers have found that mothers suffering from protein deficiency give birth to children whose neurological and psychological performances are reduced (Rosenbaum, Churchill, Shakhashiri, & Moody, 1969).

HORMONES. As we pointed out earlier, the hormone production of the mother can have an effect upon the fetus. A study done on the developing organism further supports this idea. When a male hormone (androgen) was injected into the bloodstream of the fetus of a genetic female, structural malformations of the reproductive organs resulted (Money and Ehrhardt, 1972).

RH FACTOR. The Rh factor is a component of the blood that is present in almost 85 percent of whites and nearly 100 percent of blacks. Its presence indicates a positive factor, its absence a negative factor. When the mother's blood is Rh negative and the baby's blood is Rh positive, the two types are incompatible. If there is some leakage of the Rh positive blood, the mother's body may build up antibodies to counteract the Rh factor in the baby's blood. This buildup does not usually happen rapidly enough to affect a first child; however, in subsequent pregnancies, the antibodies may leak back into the Rh positive fetus and damage its blood cells. There is no threat to the mother—only to the unborn child.

It is now possible to treat the Rh negative mother after the first Rh positive pregnancy to prevent the buildup of antibodies and hence to prevent blood incompatibility effects in later pregnancies (Freda, Gorman, & Pollack, 1966).

RADIATION. Excessive doses of radiation in early pregnancy either through the use of repeated X-rays, radium treatment during cancer, or radiation accidents (Hiroshima, for example) produce marked effects on prenatal development (Sternglass, 1963). Research is still going on to determine the effects of low-level radiation.

COMPOSITES OF ENVIRONMENTAL EFFECTS. The age of the mother can have an effect upon the prenatal development of the child. The incidence of prenatal defects or abnormalities is higher for first-time mothers over 35 years of age and for teenage mothers than for mothers between these ages. Although the precise reason for this is unclear, it is suspected that the hormonal balance and tissue development in the mother may play a role. Down's syndrome, or mongolism, occurs most often in children of mothers over age 35. Although doctors understand the structure of the abnormality (an incorrect number and pairing of chromosomes), they do not yet know why it occurs more frequently in this age group.

Among mothers of low social class and extreme poverty, malnutrition, generally poor health, increased rate of disease, and intense stress all increase the risk of prenatal damage to children (Birch & Gussow, 1970). The possible consequences of these factors, which we have discussed above, make clear the grave and widespread problems that arise from these social conditions.

NORMAL DEVELOPMENT. While we have mentioned some tragedies and pointed out many cautions in our discussion of the prenatal period, the vast majority of pregnancies in the United States result in full-term, healthy, fully developed babies. Thus, in most cases, the protective system of shielding in the uterus and the filtering system of the placenta work efficiently.

MATERNAL AND FAMILY ADJUSTMENT

Adjustment to parenthood is a major developmental task for adults, and particularly so with a first child. The new parents must make economic and social adjustments and often must reevaluate and modify existing relationships. Among the factors involved in this adjustment are the cultural attitudes of the family toward childrearing and the parents' original motivation for the pregnancy.

The motivations for childbearing vary considerably from culture to culture. In some societies children are valued as financial assets or as providers for the parents in their old age. Sometimes children represent someone to maintain the family traditions, or symbolize the fulfillment of the parents' personal needs. At other times, children are regarded

Today in Western cultures, women who work up until the time of delivery are viewed with fairly casual acceptance. (*Joel Gordon.*)

as a duty or a necessary burden. Some cultures accept children as inevitable, a "natural part of life about which one does not make conscious decisions." In the Hindu tradition of India, for example, women want to have children to guarantee them a good afterlife. Sons are needed to carry on the family name, to assist the father and follow in his footsteps, and finally to care for aged and ill parents. On the one hand, a daughter is a financial liability because her family must provide a dowry; on the other hand, custom requires that an Indian man have at least one daughter to give away in marriage (Whiting, 1963).

In all cultures, the pregnant woman must also adjust to the physical, psychological, and social changes that come with motherhood. There are profound bodily changes that occur and can hardly be ignored. Even before the fetus is large enough to create a change in the appearance of the woman, it may make itself felt through nausea, or in fullness or tingling of the breasts. The mother often suffers fatigue and emotional hypersensitivity during the early weeks of pregnancy, but in the middle stage of pregnancy, she frequently experiences a sense of heightened well-being. There is, in fact, increased capacity and functioning of some of the bodily systems such as the circulatory system. In the last stages of pregnancy, usually there is some physical discomfort and sometimes a feeling of emotional burden. Increased weight, reduced mobility, an altered sense of balance, and pressure on internal organs from the growing fetus are changes experienced by all women. In addition, other symptoms such as varicose veins, heartburn, frequent urination, or shortness of breath may contribute to the discomfort that some women feel. There is wide individual variation in the amount of discomfort, or fatigue, or burden experienced during the last few weeks. Some women find this final period of pregnancy much easier than others do.

All of these physical changes have an impact upon the psychological state of the pregnant woman. She must come to terms with a new body image and an altered self-concept and must deal with the reactions of those around her. Some women experience a feeling of uniqueness or distance from old friends, or a desire for protection. Some women regard their pregnancy with ambivalence—uncertain about giving up some career objectives or some educational plans, anxious about their ability to handle a child, fearful of producing a monster, uneasy about the financial burden, or simply uncomfortable with a markedly changed self-image. They may be eager to have the child, yet disappointed that they will have to share their time, energy, and husband with someone else (Jessner, Weigert, & Foy, 1970).

Societies vary in their attitudes toward, and acceptance of, the status of pregnancy. There have been times in history—and there are still some remnants of the attitude today—when pregnancy was considered an abnormal condition or an illness, something neither to be looked at nor discussed. A pregnant woman was confined and protected; she was certainly not out in public, or in school, or in an office carrying on a career. On the other hand, in many cultures, pregnancy is not only considered normal but is revered and accorded a special status as signifying the highest state of feminine fulfillment. In Western cultures today, there is a shift toward a more casual acceptance of pregnancy as "nothing very special." Often women are encouraged to continue to work and to perform all normal tasks up until the time of delivery. Some women experience little or no discomfort or fatigue or excessive conflict with this role. Others may choose to take discomfort and fatigue in stride and go on about their lives, minimizing the rather dramatic changes going on inside their bodies. Others may feel cheated that they are not treated as somewhat special. All of these conflicting social attitudes, both historical and present, coupled with the pregnant woman's personal needs and mixed emotions, contribute to a major period of adjustment for her. Certainly, none of these feelings will have any direct effect on the prenatal development of the child unless there is severe or prolonged emotional stress. However, their resolution or the resultant attitudes, feelings, and physical health of the parents will affect the atmosphere and environment that the child enters at birth.

SUMMARY

From the moment of conception the environment surrounding a child has an impact upon his immediate and future development. The attitude of the parents toward the child's arrival, their fears, beliefs, and expectations, and the mother's nutrition and general health, all affect the child's progress.

Once the sperm penetrates the ovum, the life span of the child has begun. After the initial cleavage cells divide rapidly, the blastula forms, and differentiation begins. Within the first two months after conception, the basic organs and limbs of the child are formed and the placenta begins its function of providing nutrients and protection.

Development takes place in a head-to-tail direction and from the midline of the body outward. With growth comes movement and function, as the fetus progresses toward the day when it will be able to exist independently. Generally, the fetus is unable to survive on its own until about the seventh month, and even then it will require the support and protection of an incubator.

Drugs, diseases, nutrition, hormones, the composition of the mother's blood, radiation, and social factors, all can influence the prenatal development of the child.

Pregnancy also has an effect upon the parents of the child. As new roles are required and as social, physical, cultural, and economic burdens arise because of the impending birth, the family must make adjustments and reevaluate self-concepts and relationships.

REVIEW QUESTIONS

1. How might an unwanted pregnancy affect the prenatal development of the child? How might it affect the mother? Take into consideration the social and emotional as well as physical factors.

2. Why might it be helpful for a nurse to know something about the effects of environmental influences during the prenatal period?

3. At what stage of development can a premature baby survive? Why not earlier?

SUGGESTED READINGS

Bettelheim, B. *Children of the dream.* New York: Macmillan, 1969. A sensitive description of the ideals, goals, and practices of collective childrearing in an Israeli kibbutz.

Rugh, R., & Shettles, L. *From conception to birth: The drama of life's beginnings.* New York: Harper & Row, 1971. The processes of prenatal development and childbirth are clearly and fully described in a manner appropriate for potential parents as well as for teachers and nurses.

Whiting, B. B. (Ed.). *Six cultures: Studies of childrearing.* New York: Wiley, 1963. An examination of six diverse cultures, focusing particularly on the issues, attitudes, and practices of childbearing and childrearing.

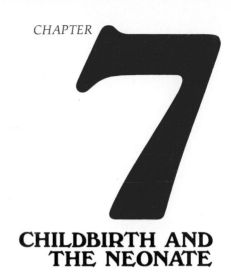

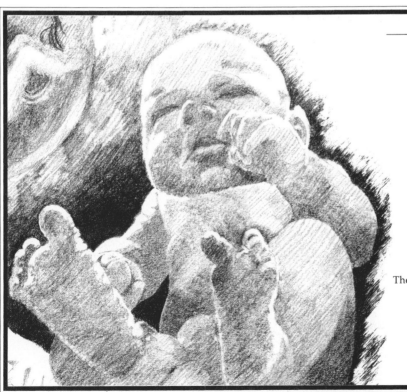

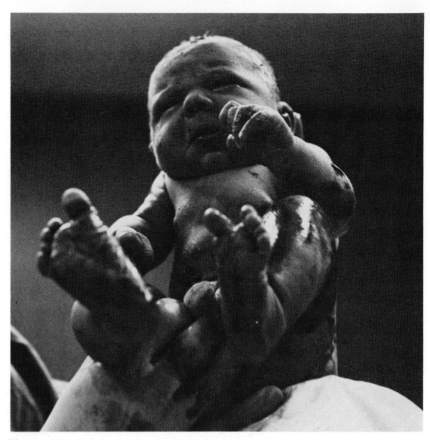

The moment of birth. (*Tom Myers, Photo Researchers.*)

Childbirth is viewed in widely different ways from one culture to another. Among the Jarara of South America, women give birth to their young in view of everyone (Gutierrez de Pineda, 1948). In the traditional Laotian culture, relatives and friends drop by to visit a woman in labor. They play musical instruments, tell jokes, and even make licentious comments in order to divert her attention (Reinach, 1901). In contrast, childbirth in many other cultures is kept hidden. The Cuna of Panama tell their children that babies are found in the forest between deer horns, and children never witness even the preparations for childbirth (Jelliffe, Jelliffe, Garcia, & de Barrios, 1961).

How is childbirth regarded in our own culture? In the United States and most Western countries, babies are usually born in a hospital, out of view of society. The reason for this is not the exaggerated modesty of the Cuna; rather, it is dictated by the knowledge that aseptic hospital conditions have greatly reduced the hazards of childbirth for both infant and mother. But the greater safety of the hospital has also had important side effects. The removal of childbirth from the family and community has meant the removal of a rich source of social support. The new mother especially, separated even from her husband except during hospital visiting hours, is apt to feel alone, exposed, and un-supported in a major event in her life. Although much has been written and said about the enforced isolation of mother and child at the time of birth, we still do not completely understand the long-range psycholog-ical effects of this sterile, hidden beginning of life on the mother, the infant, and the family.

Another side effect of segregating the new mother in a hospital has been that childbirth has come to be regarded as a mysterious process, with other family members having virtually no knowledge of it. Children grow up knowing little about the birth process except for secondhand reports. Even new parents are often surprised at the appearance of their newborn infant—the small, often wrinkled and red creature whose soft-boned head may be misshapen after a difficult passage through the birth canal.

Still a third side effect is widespread misunderstanding about the capabilities of the newborn. Can he see? Can he hear? Does he under-stand anything? Or is he merely a bundle of reflexes? Many of these questions are still unanswered. Only during the last fifteen years have there been imaginative studies of the perceptual capacities of the new-born, and even today we do not fully understand the infant's nature.

A discussion of childbirth must deal with three related topics—the birth process itself, the capacities of the newborn, and the psychological effects of the birth act on both the infant and the family. While modern science has provided answers to many of the mysteries surrounding childbirth, there is still much that we do not know about it. It is to the description of what we do know, and the questions whose answers we do not yet know, that we will now turn.

CHILDBIRTH

Pregnancy and childbirth are viewed in a variety of different ways from culture to culture. But in every society, the event of childbirth itself follows a universal biological timetable.

The Sequence of Childbirth

The process of childbirth is usually described as occurring in three stages: *labor, birth,* and *afterbirth.*

Labor, the first stage, takes the longest time and may last anywhere from 5 to 18 hours, with a mother's first labor usually taking longer than her successive labors. Labor is the period during which the cervix becomes dilated to allow for the passage of the baby's head. It begins with mild uterine contractions, generally spaced as much as 15 to 20 minutes apart. As labor progresses, the contractions increase both in frequency and in intensity until they finally occur 3 to 5 minutes apart. The muscular contractions of labor are involuntary and the mother can best help herself by relaxing during this period.

Some mothers experience false labor, especially with the first child. This is often difficult to distinguish from real labor, but one test which usually works is to have the expectant mother walk around. Real labor usually becomes more uncomfortable with simple exercise, while false labor tends to diminish.

During labor, two other events may happen—or they may not occur until just before birth. "Showing" is the release of a mucous plug covering the cervix. causing some bleeding. Also the amniotic sac or "bag of waters" which has enclosed the fetus may break and a rush of fluid may occur.

The second stage of childbirth is the birth of the baby. This stage may last from 30 minutes to 2 hours and, like labor, it tends to be longest for the first birth. Birth is usually distinguished as the period between the time the cervix has fully dilated until the time when the baby is completely free of the mother's body.

Generally, there are between 10 and 20 contractions during birth. These contractions occur regularly every 2 to 3 minutes, and are of greater intensity and longer duration than those occurring during labor, lasting about one minute each. While the mother should not attempt to help contractions during labor, she can now actively assist in the birth of the baby by bearing down with her abdominal muscles during contractions.

The first part of the baby to emerge is the head. It "crowns," or becomes visible, and emerges more and more with each contraction until the obstetrician is able to grasp it. The tissue of the mother's perineum (the region between the vagina and rectum) must stretch considerably to allow the baby's head to emerge. To enlarge the opening for the baby, often the doctor makes an incision, called an *episiotomy*, which will heal more neatly than a jagged tear. The obstetrician may use forceps to grasp the head and assist in the birth if complications arise at this point.

People in occupations which serve the public sometimes deliver babies in emergency situations. Here, Chicago cabdrivers are being instructed in childbirth procedures by a doctor. (*UPI.*)

In most normal births, the baby is born head first in a face-down position. After the head is free, the baby shifts around so that its body emerges with the least resistance. More difficult births occur when the baby is positioned in a *breech presentation* (buttocks first) or a *posterior presentation* (facing toward the mother's abdomen instead of toward her back). In each of these cases, the doctor usually must assist in the delivery to prevent injury to the infant or the mother.

The third stage of childbirth is the afterbirth, when the placenta and related tissues are expelled. This stage is virtually painless and generally occurs within 20 minutes after the delivery. Again, the mother can help the process by bearing down. After the expulsion, the doctor checks the placenta and umbilical cord for imperfections which might signal damage to the newborn.

"Natural" Childbirth

It has become common practice in our society to give the mother medication "to make childbirth easier." However, not all doctors encourage this practice. As we saw in Chapter 6, drugs can actually harm the baby. Some medications given to the mother during pregnancy can have either temporary or long-term effects on the infant, and even small amounts are able to slow down the newborn's respiration for a short time (Bowes, 1970). Some drugs can also slow the birth process and thus increase the danger of *anoxia* (lack of oxygen reaching the baby's brain for a prolonged spell).

The dangers of drugs are one reason why *"natural" childbirth* was first suggested by doctors such as Fernand Lamaze (1970) and Grantly Dick-Read (1953). This method has become increasingly popular in recent years. Basically "natural" childbirth (we put the word *natural* in quotes because here it means a good deal more than having babies naturally) involves three things: preparation, limited medication, and participation. To Dick-Read, the key was preparation. He explained that in Western society, all too often women anticipate childbirth with exaggerated fear and limited knowledge. Their fear creates tension, which causes unnecessary tightening of muscles and makes labor far more painful than it need be. Dick-Read argued that if the mother knows about the birth process—and knows how to help herself at each stage—she will be more relaxed during labor, the pain will be less, and she usually will not need medication.

How does "natural" childbirth work? The mother and often the father are well prepared for the event. They attend from six to eight classes where they learn about pregnancy and the stages of labor and where the expectant mother is taught exercises in relaxation, breathing, and muscle-strengthening. When the time comes for the baby to be born, the mother knows what breathing procedures will minimize the pain. She even knows the most effective way to push to help deliver her baby. Often, her husband can be with her during labor and at the delivery to lend moral support. During the actual birth, the mother is a full participant—awake, alert, and helping.

Is "natural" childbirth as successful as it sounds? Often it is. The infant has a quicker, safer delivery because the mother is able to help and because less drugs are used. The birth experience is also more rewarding for the parents. While most participating couples admit that "natural" childbirth is hard work, the overwhelming majority report that it is also one of life's most satisfying experiences.

Caesarean Section Most births, with or without medication, occur through the birth canal as described. However, in approximately 5 percent of the births, delivery through the birth canal may be unsafe. A fetus may be too large to pass through the mother's pelvis. The mother may experience excessive *toxemia* (a poisoning of the body due to a metabolic disturbance) or face the threat of hemorrhage. She may have a disorder such as diabetes or some other illness which may place immediate stress on the fetus. In all of these conditions, delivery by *Caesarean section* is advisable. This is a surgical procedure in which the baby and the placenta are removed from the uterus through an incision in the abdominal wall. After a woman has had one Caesarean delivery, it is recommended that future deliveries also be by this method.

Although a Caesarean section may be performed during labor, most predictable ones are arranged beforehand by appointment, as soon as the doctor feels the baby is ready to be born. This may create a problem due to inaccurate estimates of delivery dates. An estimated 5 to 10 percent of Caesarean sections are performed too early and result in premature births (Babson & Benson, 1966). But new techniques are improving both the accuracy of predictions and the safety of the operation. While they were once somewhat hazardous, Caesarean births are now only slightly riskier than normal births. However, the procedure is still an operation involving a prolonged recovery period and therefore it is not recommended just for convenience. Nevertheless, it is no longer uncommon for a mother to have four or even more babies safely by Caesarean section.

Midwifery *Midwifery* is the act of assisting at childbirth, carried out by a person who is not a doctor but has had special training in this skill. The practice of midwifery has had a long and distinguished career (Cutter & Viets, 1964), and it is now being revived as a valuable medical profession. (The profession even has its own journal.) The shortage of obstetricians has contributed to a new interest in midwifery and midwives are in great demand today. There are many more jobs than there are people trained to fill them, especially in areas where the shortage of doctors is most acute. Several new training programs for midwives have been set up to meet the demand. Most of these are hospital programs geared for nurses, and they usually provide a year or more of training in obstetrics and related subjects, such as nutrition and community health. At most hospitals, nurse-midwives take only those childbirth cases which are expected to have no complications, while obstetricians handle the more difficult births. Since nurse-midwives can give more time to each patient than can doctors, many mothers are happy to be assigned to their care.

Up to this point, we have been discussing childbirth as a biological process. But here we must stop and take a look at the most important part of childbirth—the new baby himself.

During the first month of his life, the new baby is known as a *neonate*. This first month is a very special period in the baby's life. It is distinguished from the rest of infancy because during this time the baby must adjust to leaving the closed, protected environment of his mother's womb and to living on his own in the outside world. The first month is a period of both recovery from the birth process and adjustment and perfection of vital functions, such as respiration, circulation, digestion, and temperature regulation.

The average full-term baby weighs between 5½ and 9½ pounds at birth and is between 19 and 22 inches long. The baby's skin may be covered with the *vernix caseosa*, which it developed in the fetal period. This coating is present especially in a Caesarean delivery where it has not had a chance to wipe off in the tight passage through the birth canal. The skin may also be covered with fine facial and body hair which will drop off during the first month. The newborn's head may be temporarily misshapen and elongated as a result of the process of *molding*. In molding, the soft bones of the head, which are connected only by tissue, are squeezed together in the birth canal. Also, the external breasts and genitals of both boys and girls may be enlarged. This enlargement, too, is a temporary situation, caused by the mother's female hormones which have passed to the baby before birth. The general appearance of the newborn may be a bit of a shock to new parents who expected to see the plump, smooth, 3- or 4-month-old infant shown in advertisements.

A Description of the Neonate

Despite his appearance, the neonate is a sturdy little creature who is already making the profound adjustment from having his mother do everything for him to functioning on his own as a separate being. Four critical areas of this adjustment are respiration, circulation of blood, digestion, and temperature regulation.

The Period of Adjustment

The birth cry traditionally symbolizes the beginning of the neonate's life. It also signals a major step in the child's development, for with the first breaths of air, the lungs are inflated for the first time and begin to work as the basic organ of the child's own respiratory system. The dramatic beginning of breathing takes only a few minutes. During the next few days, the neonate experiences periods of coughing and sneezing which often alarm the new mother but serve the important function of clearing mucus and amniotic fluid from the infant's airways. The onset of breathing marks a significant change in the neonate's circulatory system, too. The baby's heart no longer has to pump blood to the placenta for aeration. Instead, the blood now passes to the lungs to receive oxygen and eliminate carbon dioxide (Pratt, 1954; Vulliamy, 1973). A valve in the baby's heart closes to redirect the flow of blood along the changed route. The circulatory system is no longer fetal but is now entirely self-contained.

The shift from fetal to independent circulatory and respiratory systems begins immediately after birth but is not complete for several days. Lack of oxygen for more than a few minutes at birth may result in permanent brain damage to the infant.

The placenta has provided nourishment as well as oxygen for the infant. Therefore, with the cutting of the umbilical cord, the infant's own digestive system must begin to function. This change is a longer, more adaptive process than are the immediate and dramatic changes in respiration and circulation. Still another more gradual adjustment is that of the neonate's temperature regulation system. Before birth, the baby's skin never comes in contact with the air. After birth, the skin must constantly work to insulate the baby from sharp changes in external temperature. During the first few days of life, the baby must be warmly clothed. The neonate gradually accumulates a healthy layer of fat in the first weeks of life and soon becomes more able to stabilize his own body temperature.

The Apgar Score

All neonates are not equally equipped to adjust to the abrupt changes brought about by birth, and it is important to detect any problems at the earliest possible moment. Great advances have been made in this area in recent years. At one time, a baby was considered healthy if he merely "looked okay." Then, in 1953, Virginia Apgar devised a standard scoring system and hospitals were able to use objective tests to evaluate an infant's health (see Table 4). The Apgar test is used within the first 5 minutes after the baby's birth. It tests pulse, breathing, muscle tone, general reflex response, and color of skin (or mucous membranes, palms, and soles for nonwhite babies). A perfect Apgar score is 10 points, with a score of 7 or more considered normal. Scores below 7 generally show that some bodily processes are not functioning fully and require at least watching and perhaps special attention.

TABLE 4 APGAR SCORING SYSTEM OF INFANTS. A STANDARD OBJECTIVE TEST USED IN HOSPITALS TO EVALUATE A NEWBORN'S HEALTH.

	SCORES		
	0	*1*	*2*
Pulse	Absent	Less than 100	More than 100
Breathing	Absent	Slow, irregular	Strong cry
Muscle tone	Limp	Some flexion of extremities	Active motion
Reflex response	No response	Grimace	Vigorous cry
Color (For nonwhites, alternative tests of mucous membranes, palms, and soles are used.)	Blue, pale	Body pink, extremities blue	Completely pink

Source: Apgar, V. Proposal for a new method of evaluating the newborn infant. *Anesthesia and Analgesia*, 1953, 32, 260–267.

Many hospitals now use the Brazelton scoring system (Brazelton et al., in press), which is essentially an expansion and refinement of the Apgar test. With either test, a more complete follow-up is made later by a physician.

The Premature Infant

The condition of *prematurity* can pose problems for the newborn infant. There are two indicators of prematurity that are frequently confused. The first is gestation time. The infant who is born after a gestation period of less than 37 weeks is considered premature. The second indicator is low birth weight. The average weight of babies at birth is 7½ pounds. Generally, an infant weighing less than 5½ pounds is considered premature, or in need of special attention, even though only half of such infants have a gestational period of less than 37 weeks. Low birth-weight babies, even when full term, frequently have problems resulting from fetal malnutrition, for example. Therefore, both cutoff points of 5½ pounds and 37 weeks are used in classifying babies as premature (Babson & Benson, 1966).

Prematurity can occur for a number of reasons. The most common is a multiple birth, when two or more infants are born at the same time. Other causes include disease of the fetus, the effect of drugs upon the fetus, and malnutrition. Some diseases of the mother, such as diabetes, may lead the doctor to deliver the baby before full term.

Immediately after birth, the premature infant usually has greater difficulty in adjusting than does a full-term baby. His adaptation to the basic processes of circulation, respiration, and temperature control is more complicated. Among these, temperature control is an especially common problem. The premature infant has very few fat cells and thus he has little control over the cooling of his body. Therefore, newborns weighing less than 5½ pounds are usually put into incubators immediately after birth. Another common problem is feeding schedules. In their first few months, premature infants seem unable to catch up in weight and height with full-term infant babies. One reason may be that it seems almost impossible to match the nutritional conditions of the late fetal period to produce a growth rate outside of the uterus comparable to that inside.

The effects of prematurity may be felt long after infancy, too. Several studies have indicated that premature infants suffer more illnesses during their first three years of life, score lower on IQ tests, and are slightly more prone to behavioral problems than are full-term babies (Harper, Fischer, & Rider, 1959; Knobloch, Pasamanick, Harper, & Rider, 1959). Researchers have found a high rate of prematurity among children later diagnosed as being learning disabled, having reading problems, or being distractible or hyperactive. All such reports, however, must be very carefully interpreted. It cannot be concluded, for instance, that prematurity *causes* any of these defects. Although it is true that the baby's immature condition may make him less able to adjust to the shock of birth, prematurity has a more complex association with problems in later life than that. For example, conditions such as malnutrition, faulty development of the placenta, or crowding in the uterus, may result in a number of symptoms, only one of which is premature birth. In such case, the prematurity is a symptom of a disability or malfunction, not a cause of the defect. Again, we know that malnutrition accompanies prematurity. But as we saw in Chapter 6, malnutrition tends not to occur alone but in combination with other factors, such as social disadvantage, which also stack the cards against the newborn (Birch, 1968).

Problems of the premature child may also arise from the way he is treated during his first few weeks of life. He is kept in an incubator under aseptic conditions. He is heavily protected and, as a result, he has little of the normal contact of touching and closeness that most newborns experience. Few premature infants are breast-fed. Few are held even while being bottle-fed, and some are unable to suck at all. All of the social experiences of normal feeding, which establish an early mutuality between the mother and the full-term infant, are missing in the beginning life of the premature infant. Moreover, the isolation of the premature child may be further complicated as his parents become so accustomed to protecting him that they carry on an overly restrictive regime long after it is necessary.

Despite these findings, however, it should be stressed that the premature infant who later has problems of adjusting to his world is the exception these days—*not* the rule! The great majority of premature infants survive to normal childhood with little or no traces of their immature condition at birth.

The Competence of the Newborn

We already know that the newborn infant is sturdier than he looks and capable of adjusting to profound changes as he emerges from the birth canal. But there are many other fascinating questions about his nature of which we are just beginning to learn the full answers. What can he do? What can he hear? How much can he see? How does he learn? What are his preferences?

Until fifteen years ago, psychologists thought that the neonate was incapable of organized, self-directed behavior. It was common to read in psychological literature that an infant did not use the higher centers of the brain until he was almost a year old, or that the newborn saw light and shadow but not objects or patterns. Behavior in the first weeks of life was considered to be almost entirely reflexive. But recent experiments have shown that all these beliefs are false. We now know that neonates are organized beings capable of predictable responses and of complex mental activity. They have definite preferences and show a striking ability to learn (Stone, Smith, & Murphy, 1973).

The key to this new understanding of newborns lies in the way we look at them. Earlier studies were designed poorly and often the infant was placed in situations where he was least likely to respond. If a neonate is placed on his back in a cot and is covered up to his neck with a blanket, naturally he will do little more than cry, sleep, and suck (Prechtl & Beintema, 1965). But if the same infant is placed naked on his mother's skin in a warm room, he will display a much greater repertoire of behavior. He will root, crawl, grasp, and hold himself in positions which require the use of muscles to offset gravity. Recent studies are designed to let the infant respond to the fullest degree. This greater understanding of how to handle newborns, along with new techniques of observation, has led to a flurry of research in recent years. Some of the most important of these findings follow.

REFLEXES. The full-term infant confronts his world with a number of complex reflexes and combinations of reflexes. A few of these deserve special mention.

The *Moro reflex* is the newborn's startle reaction. Some have thought it to be a vestige of our ape ancestry (Dennis, 1934). When the newborn is startled, as by a loud sound, he reacts first by extending both arms to the side, with fingers outstretched as if to catch onto a tree branch for support. The arms are then gradually brought back to the midline. Another body reflex is the *tonic neck reflex*. It occurs when the baby's head is turned sharply to one side. He reacts by extending the arm and leg on the same side and flexing the arm and leg on the other side in a

SOME REFLEXES OF THE NEWBORN.

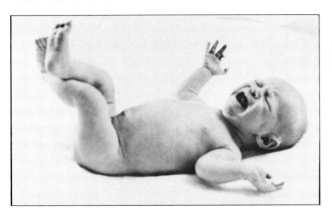

Moro reflex. (*Suzanne Szasz.*)

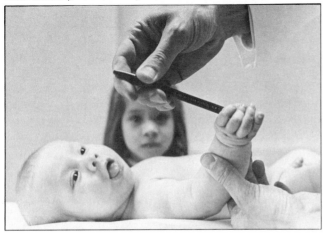

Grasp reflex. (*Photo Researchers.*)

Stepping reflex. (*Ray Ellis, Rapho/Photo Researchers.*)

king of fencing position. The *stepping reflex* occurs when the newborn baby is held vertically with his feet against a hard surface. He lifts one leg away from the surface, and if tilted slightly from one side to another, he appears to be walking. The *grasping reflex* is similar to both parents and nurses and it applies to the newborn's toes as well as his fingers. The baby will close his fingers over any object, such as a pencil or a parent's finger, placed on his palm. Some neonates can grasp with such strength that they can support their full weight for up to a minute (Taft & Cohen, 1967).

A very useful reflex of the mouth is the *rooting reflex*. When the baby's cheek is touched, he "roots," or moves his mouth toward the stimulus. This aids the baby in finding the nipple. A mother who is unfamiliar with this response may try to push the infant's head toward the nipple. Since the baby's reflex is toward, not away from, the stimulation, he will move toward the hand that pushes him and seem to reject the breast. The *sucking reflex*, like the rooting reflex, is clearly necessary for the infant's survival. Like some other reflexes, sucking begins in the uterus. Cases have been reported of babies born with thumbs already swollen from sucking. Sucking often persists for several years, while the rooting reflex disappears by the third or fourth month (Taft & Cohen, 1967).

The newborn's eyes are also capable of several reflex movements and motor patterns. The lids open and close in response to stimuli. The pupils widen in dim light and narrow in bright light; they also narrow when the infant is going to sleep and widen when he wakes. Even an infant only a few hours old is capable of following a slow-moving object, like a bright red ball, with his eyes (Brazelton, 1969).

Many other reflexes govern the behavior of the newborn. Some, like sneezing or coughing, are necessary for survival. Others seem to be leftovers from the behavior patterns of our more primitive ancestors. And still others seem to have no rhyme or reason at all.

LEARNING AND HABITUATION. Recent discoveries have shown that neonatal behavior consists of far more than reflexes. One of the first experimenters to explore the pattern and organization in the newborn's behavior was P. H. Wolff (1959). According to his observations, the neonatal state (regular or irregular sleeping, active or inactive waking) is the organizing factor in the newborn's behavior. Wolff found that when infants were sleeping or were in a state of alert inactivity, they responded to a stimulus with increased activity. When they were already active, however, they reacted to stimulation by becoming less active. This discovery helped experimenters to interpret infant behavior from the standpoint of the newborn—not from an adult viewpoint—and it clarified many earlier observations which seemed to show that infant responses were simply disorganized reflexes.

The methods of observing infants developed in recent years have been very productive. With these new techniques, we have learned that newborn babies can indeed learn some fairly complex responses. The newborn's ability to turn his head has been used in many learning experiments. Some of the most important were conducted by Papoušek (1961). In these experiments, newborns were taught to turn their heads to the left to obtain milk whenever they heard a bell. They also learned to turn their heads to the right, at the sound of a buzzer, for the same reward. Then, to complicate the problem, the bell and the buzzer were reversed. The infants quickly learned to turn their heads according to the rules of the new game.

Siqueland and Lipsitt (1966) used similar experiments involving head turning to show that even 1-day-old infants exhibited greater abilities to learn than any other primates. In their experiments, neonates were able to (1) discriminate between two sounds (a bell and a buzzer); (2) identify a different response for each sound; (3) discriminate between right and left head turns; and (4) detect the relationship among stimulus (bell or buzzer), response (head turn), and reinforcement (milk).

Since sucking is well developed in the neonate, this ability has also been used in studies of neonatal learning and visual preferences. Kalnins and Bruner (1973), in an expansion of an earlier study by Siqueland and DeLucia (1969), wished to determine whether infants could control sucking when the sucking was linked to rewards other than feeding. Pacifiers were wired to a laboratory slide projector. If the infants sucked, the slide came into focus; if they did not suck, the picture blurred. Bruner noted that the infants learned quickly to focus the picture and also adapted quickly if conditions were reversed— that is, they could learn to stop sucking to let the picture come into focus. In other words, the infants—some as young as three weeks old (Alexander, 1970)—not only coordinated sucking and looking but also effectively controlled the slide show. And their only reward was clear, rather than blurred, visual stimulation. Bruner concluded that the infants' ability to solve problems voluntarily had been greatly underestimated.

Papoušek's experiments involved more than the buzzers and bells discussed earlier. He also used lights to reveal a very important facet of newborn behavior (1961). Infants were taught to turn on a light by turning their heads to the left. An infant would turn his head several times during a short period in order to turn on the light. But then an interesting thing happened: the infant seemed to lose interest in the game. Papousek found that he could revive the infant's interest by reversing the problem, but the infant soon became bored again. Papousek's findings were important for two reasons. They supported Bruner's belief (1971) that competence, rather than immediate reward, motivates much of human learning. And they demonstrated a second learning phenomenon: *habituation*.

Infants habituate—that is, they become accustomed to certain kinds of stimuli and no longer respond to them. Habituation can be used to find out a number of things about the intellectual capacities of infants. For example, if a newborn hears a moderately loud sound, he first responds with a faster heartbeat, a change in breathing, and sometimes crying or general activity. If the sound continues, however, the infant soon habituates, or stops responding. But if the sound stimulus is changed by a small degree and the infant starts responding again, it is clear that he perceives the change and we know that he can discriminate small differences in pitch. This ability of newborns to habituate has been the basis of many experiments which have given us much information about the sensory capacities and perceptual skills of neonates.

SENSORY CAPACITIES. Can a neonate perceive small differences in forms, or is he incapable of seeing patterns at all? What does he perceive to be new or different? With experiments like the one described above, researchers have begun to find answers to questions such as these.

We know a good deal about the newborn's vision. We know that he will follow a light, such as a doctor s penlight, with his eyes. We know that there is some coordination of the eyes but not full convergence. We also know that the infant can focus on an object 7 to 10 inches from his face (Dennis, 1934). But it is not so clear just what the infant perceives—that is, how he puts together, or relates, what he sees. Does he see just bits and pieces of light and shading? Does he recognize objects, faces, and patterns?

Many recent breakthroughs in our understanding of infants' perception have resulted from some careful but relatively simple advances in methodology. One of the most important was developed by Robert Fantz (1958), whose astonishingly simple technique measures not only perception but also preference. To determine what stimuli are most attractive to infants, Fantz held two visual targets directly above a baby. He then noted which target was reflected most often in the corneas of the baby's eyes. By carefully recording, by camera or other means, exactly what the infant looked at and how long he watched it, Fantz established that the infant did not respond randomly at all.

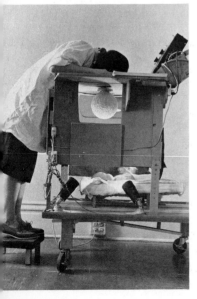

Fantz's "looking chamber" is used to test pattern discrimination in infants. The researcher records the fixation time for each object the infant observes. (*David Linton,* Scientific American, *May 1961, p. 66.*)

Fantz began his series of experiments with chicks, not human infants. He enclosed objects of various shapes in clear plastic so that no sense but vision could be used to distinguish between them. He then discovered that newly hatched chicks would peck at grain-shaped objects 10 times more often than at objects of any other shape. Fantz next experimented with primates. A young chimpanzee was placed on his back inside a "looking chamber" which was uniformly lighted and had the same color on the four walls and ceiling. Two test objects of different shapes were alternately shown on the ceiling, and the investigator measured the length of time the chimp watched each object. Fantz found that infant chimpanzees preferred round to square objects (1961).

The experiments with human infants were similar to those with the chicks and primates. Fantz found that the total time the infants looked at each one of a pair of objects differed sharply, and that babies preferred complex patterns to simple ones. When a bull's eye was shown at the same time as a striped pattern, the infants spent more time watching the bull's eye. They also preferred a checkerboard to simpler objects such as a square, a cross, a circle, or a triangle.

Fantz made an even more interesting discovery. He reasoned that infants would single out the human face just as the newly hatched chicks selected the grain. To prove this, he presented infants with a choice of three ovals shaped like human heads (see Figure 5). One was a stylized human face; another showed the same facial features but in a scrambled pattern; and the third had a solid dark patch at one end. Of 49 infants ranging in age from 4 days to 6 months, all showed a preference for the face (Fantz, 1961). Later studies have shown that the infant progresses from a preference for the facial outlines to the eye region and on to other features (Fantz, 1967; Gibson, 1969). The infant is quite selective.

Experiments with sound have shown that the infant distinguishes between pitches and has distinct preferences among them. Low-frequency sounds tend to arouse him to motor activity; sharp, high-pitched sounds often produce a freezing response. The newborn pays more attention to higher-pitched voices, like his mother's, than to lower voices (Brazelton, 1969). He notices even minor changes in the sounds, odors, and visual patterns around him.

The sense of touch is also important to the newborn—so important that it has been called the language or communication system for infants (Frank, 1966). When an infant is held or touched, he is receiving necessary information about his world. Touch often affects the infant as no other stimulation would. The simple action of pressing a baby's abdomen, or firmly holding his arm or leg, will often be enough to quiet him. Swaddling, or wrapping a baby snugly in blankets, has the same quieting effect (Brazelton, 1969).

What do all of these studies tell us? They seem to support the belief that the newborn comes into the world with capacities which have evolved in all animals over millions of years. They also indicate that with these capacities, the infant establishes order in his world, beginning with his very first look at that world. The young infant is selective about what he watches and listens to, and he shows clear preferences for complex stimuli, even within a few hours after birth. It is true that the methodology used in testing the newborn must be chosen carefully and the lighting or other stimuli must be subdued. But research shows that even a few hours after birth, the neonate looks at patterns, changes his preference after a few moments of looking at an object, and pays attention to changes and novelty in what he sees. He selectively tunes out both sights and sounds that are familiar or too simple, and he responds in different ways to different types of stimuli.

Figure 5 Fantz's experiment on pattern perception. Infants, ranging in age from 4 days to 6 months, spent the most time looking at the stylized human face and the least time looking at the plain colored and white oval. (*Fantz, R. L. The origin of form perception.* Scientific American, *May 1961, pp. 66–72.*)

The Individuality of Newborns

From the moment of birth, infants demonstrate their uniqueness and their variability. Mothers who have more than one child are sharply aware of differences in their children's personalities, even though all the children were "brought up" the same way. Many times, these differences can be noted even before a child is born. One fetus may kick actively, while another shifts position gently or cautiously.

How profound are these differences in temperamental styles of neonates? What does the newborn's behavior tell us about his future personality? What are the dynamics between the baby's personality and his mother's, and what is their effect? The individuality of the newborn has been the subject of many recent studies.

In trying to study newborn temperamental styles, researchers have used different criteria. One study compares the amount of time spent in deep sleep and light sleep, or in periods of waking activity and inactivity, postulating a relationship between states of activity and quietness in babies and the amount of time spent in each state (Stone et al., 1973). T. B. Brazelton (1969), using broad descriptions, identified three general temperamental types: the average baby, the active baby, and the quiet baby. Stella Chess (1967) identified nine criteria to differentiate neonatal behavior. These are activity level, biological regularity, positive-negative responses to new stimuli, adaptability, intensity of reaction, threshold of responsiveness, quality of mood (overall amount of pleasure versus displeasure displayed), distractibility, and attention span and persistence.

Chess used these nine criteria to study 136 children. Like Brazelton, she found that children could be divided into three basic types. She also determined that qualities seen as early as 2 or 3 months of age could be traced throughout childhood. The largest of Chess's three groups were the "easy children"—babies (and later children) who were biologically regular and rhythmical. The easy child has regular sleeping and eating schedules, accepts new food and new people, and is not easily frustrated. The "difficult children" form a smaller group. They withdraw from new stimuli and adapt slowly to change; their mood is often negative. A third type is the "slow-to-warm-up child." Children in this group withdraw from activities quietly, while the difficult child does so actively and noisily. Slow-to-warm-up children will show interest in new situations only if they are allowed to do so gradually, without pressure. Chess found no evidence that these temperamental types were influenced by parental behavior. On the contrary, a child's temperament seemed to be as much a part of him as the inherited color of his eyes.

However investigators report on their observations, all agree that widely different personality styles are apparent in children even at the time of birth, and that these differences increase over the first few months of life. The infant's temperament interacts markedly with his mother's, too. From the first days in the hospital, infant and mother are establishing a relationship based on the uniqueness of the individual child. The mother may learn very quickly how to soothe and quiet her child, and the neonate may easily adjust to the mother's manner of handling. On the other hand, there may be temperamental differences between mother and child so that the mother's handling, at least for the early weeks, may seem only to intensify the frustrations of both (Brazelton, 1969). Mild personality differences between mother and infant are probably fairly common, at least for brief periods of time. The development of mutuality, reciprocity, and what the neo-Freudians call the "symbiotic relationship" between infant and mother is certainly not automatic or instinctive.

During childbirth, both mother and child undergo very powerful experiences. Some writers have been interested in the effect of birth on the entire lifetime of a person. Others have investigated the mother's attitude—how her expectations affect the birth, and how she feels during birth.

THE PSYCHOLOGICAL SIGNIFICANCE OF CHILDBIRTH

Birth Trauma

There has been considerable conjecture by psychologists about the way the ordeal of birth affects the infant. One of the well-known theories is that of Otto Rank (1929). Rank was a follower of Freud and developed some of his own notions concerning the nature of birth from original ideas of Freud. In his theory, Rank proposed that the dramatic expulsion from the safe, all-satisfying uterine environment constitutes the first basic trauma of life. The traumatic birth event, he believed, is the chief cause of neurosis in human beings and constitutes the original and basic anxiety. One of the tasks of childhood is the working out of this anxiety, and adults who are unable to do so become neurotic.

According to Rank, anything that reminds the child of the womb arouses the anxiety the child first felt upon leaving it. To illustrate his theory, Rank gave the example of a child alone in a dark room at bedtime. The dark room and warm bed symbolize the security of the womb, but since the child is conscious of his separation from his mother, his anxiety can only be allayed by contact with her. Rank felt that adult phobias, such as fear of enclosed places, could result from the same unresolved anxiety.

Rank's theory is appealing to some, but it has also drawn much criticism. Certainly, birth is a dramatic physiological event. The transition from the calm security and warmth of the womb to the noisy, bright, outside world can be overwhelming. For the first time the neonate must exert effort to breathe, eat, even to regulate his own temperature and posture. All of the bodily processes must now work. Where formerly he was warm and enclosed, he is now naked and exposed. Unquestionably, he experiences drastic physical changes.

However, there is some doubt whether birth constitutes a psychological trauma as well. The belief that it is a psychological shock has been relatively popular from time to time, but the evidence is certainly not clear. It appears that in at least the initial day or two of the neonate's life, there is some reduced sensitivity to pain. Thus, the newborn may not experience birth as the painful event that the adult imagines. Furthermore, although the neonate has a complex system of reflexes and sensory capacities, he does not have the complex adult thought processes or memory patterns to enable him to attach much significance to this event or even to remember it. In sum, the question of the psychological significance of birth for the infant must remain unanswered, at least for now.

The Significance of Childbirth for the Mother

Another interesting question concerns the relationship between the mother's emotional attitude and the event of childbirth. Considerable research has been devoted to different facets of this question, but the results have been somewhat contradictory.

One study found that maternal anxiety was related to obstetrical complications (McDonald, Gynther, & Christakos, 1963), but a summary of several other studies (Grimm, 1967) found no such clear and consistent relationship. However, evidence did seem to indicate that the mother's attitudes—her level of fear, her expectations, her feelings about children and about sex, and her overall level of stability—affected both her emotional health during pregnancy and her psychological adjustment during labor and the delivery.

Was a definite correlation found between women who opted for "natural" childbirth and those who experienced short labors? While research has not pinpointed any overall connection between prepared childbirth and shorter, uncomplicated labors, one finding does emerge from almost all the studies made. Since a mother using "natural" childbirth requires less medication, she is more likely to have a spontaneous delivery and to produce a more alert, responsive newborn (Grimm, 1967). And women who have attended preparation courses generally have a more positive and less traumatic reaction to the experience of labor and childbirth. Certainly, many prepared mothers report that full awareness and a reduced use of drugs enhanced a dramatic, emotional, and self-fulfilling event.

Fathers and mothers practice the exercises together at a "natural" childbirth class. This exercise is designed to help in the last stages of delivery. (*UPI.*)

The women who select "natural" childbirth usually are fairly well educated and have relatively stable emotional backgrounds (Davis & Morrone, 1962; Grimm, 1967). Hence, it is difficult to tell whether "natural" childbirth has succeeded in producing "happy mothers" on its own or whether these mothers would have found childbirth a satisfying, self-fulfilling experience anyway. At any rate, the questions of why some women react positively to the birth process and why others do not are complicated ones which certainly deserve more research in the future.

SUMMARY

Childbirth occurs in three stages: labor, lasting from 5 to 18 hours; birth itself, which lasts from 30 minutes to 2 hours; and afterbirth, in which the placenta and related tissues are expelled from the uterus. "Natural" childbirth has become increasingly popular in this country because it allows the mother to participate in the experience of birth and enables her to deliver an undrugged, alert baby. Midwifery is a recently revised and popular profession.

The infant is called a neonate during the first month after birth. During this period, the infant recovers from the birth experience and adjusts the basic life processes of respiration, temperature regulation, circulation, and digestion. The premature infant has special adaptations to make after birth, and the effects of prematurity may last beyond infancy.

The neonate has a large repertoire of reflexes, including the Moro reflex (a startle reflex), the tonic neck reflex, the stepping reflex, and sucking, rooting, and grasping reflexes. Recent experiments have found that the older belief that infants were capable only of reflex actions is unfounded; a great deal of learning takes place during infancy, beginning with birth. Neonates are capable of sensory perception and can discriminate between different sounds, sights, smells, and touches. They are capable of pattern perception and have clear preferences for complex patterns and for the human face.

Individual differences in infant temperament are being increasingly recognized. Different temperamental styles of babies have been identified, such as average, quiet, and active, with these styles remaining somewhat consistent throughout childhood. We know that the event of childbirth has dramatic physiological effects on both mother and child, but we do not yet understand its full psychological impact on either.

REVIEW QUESTIONS

1. At the moment of birth, some fetal processes end and some infant processes begin. Explain some of the physiological processes that must undergo adjustment at this time.

2. What evidence has recent research provided to show that learning begins from the first days of life?

3. How may prematurity be connected with problems in later life? How is prematurity a cause, and how is it a symptom, of developmental problems?

4. What are the advantages of "natural" childbirth for both infant and mother? Is the research conclusive on the effectiveness of "natural" childbirth in producing easier deliveries?

SUGGESTED READINGS

Brazelton, T. B. *Infants and mothers: Differences in development.* New York: Dell, 1969. Three infant-mother pairs, all having quite different personalities and temperamental styles, are described just after childbirth and at selected periods during the children's first two years. Written in a highly readable fashion.

Dick-Read, G. *Childbirth without fear.* New York: Harper & Row, 1953. This is a classic presentation of the theory and practice of one approach to "natural" childbirth.

Spock, B. *Baby and child care.* New York: Pocket Books, 1957. This "bible" of child care in American society needs no introduction.

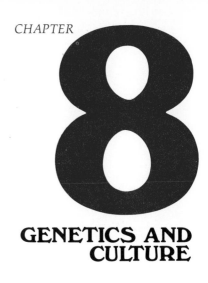

CHAPTER

8

GENETICS AND CULTURE

155

. . . their mark is on him, never to be changed—their taint is in him, never to be drawn out. Bone of their bone, blood of their blood, flesh of their flesh, by however various and remote a web, he is of them, they are in him, he is theirs. . . .

Although most of us do not view heredity with the emotionalism found in these words from Thomas Wolfe's *The Web and the Rock* (p. 62), we are aware—sometimes painfully—of the part that inherited characteristics play in our development. In addition to such outward characteristics as big feet or a stubby nose, dark skin or color blindness, our parents and their parents and grandparents also provide us with potential predispositions for various personality traits, learning styles, mental abilities, physical skills, and artistic talents. But the "mark" of family background, or the "web" of a person's origin, is very often not genetic at all. Instead, the very early network of attitudes, customs, beliefs, and expectations into which an individual is born has a subtle and profound impact on the ways in which that individual thinks and acts.

Some psychologists and biologists look very closely at innate factors to explain personality traits and mental capacities. Others consider the individual to be a blank slate upon which the environment carves its picture of the type of person that individual will become. But in a discussion of most personality traits, mental abilities, physical abilities, and behavioral styles, the question is not whether nature or nurture has the greater impact upon a person's development. Nor is the question a choice between heredity and environment, or between genetics and culture. The more important question is how genetics and culture interact in the shaping of an individual.

This chapter will deal first with the extreme determinants of human behavior—the genetic principles and processes—and then with the cultural influences. Finally, we shall show how these two pivotal forces interrelate as we examine the development of sex-role identity in the individual.

THE NEW GENETICS: PROMISE OR THREAT?

When Aldous Huxley's *Brave New World* appeared in 1932, the world that Huxley described seemed primarily fantasy. Particularly fanciful was the idea of controlling personality and intelligence by mass-producing babies in the laboratory. Yet today, both test-tube fertilization of an ovum and reimplantation of an embryo into the uterus have been successfully attempted. Furthermore, through a process called *cloning*, we can now duplicate a whole frog, for instance, from one of its *somatic*, or body, cells. Are we then very far away from knowledge that might permit the human duplication of Huxley's fiction?

Both the technology of genetics and our understanding of genetic determinants are advancing rapidly. Already 46 states have programs for the genetic screening of newborns. Hospitals throughout the country can now test for up to 60 genetic defects through the process of *amniocentesis,* involving the withdrawal and analysis of amniotic fluid between the thirteenth and the eighteenth weeks of pregnancy (Ausubel, Beckwith, & Janssen, 1974). Some of these defects can be treated if detected early enough. Other defects are incurable as yet, but sufficient information has been gained about them to enable parents to make intelligent decisions regarding prospective children. *Mapping* of several hundred individual genes for specific traits has been done on their respective chromosomes. Corrective *gene therapy,* which involves the manipulation of individual genes in order to correct or alter certain defects or traits, has not yet been successful. But new techniques will probably make such gene manipulation, at least in the case of single genes, a reality within the next few years. Genetic engineering is becoming possible. Positive treatment, as well as selective or restrictive breeding of human beings may be real options, should we wish to exercise them!

Genetic research is clearly an area in which knowledge is power. But what kinds of decisions are we to make with this knowledge? Shall we, as individuals or as a society, breed selectively? What traits should we eliminate? What kinds of disorders or disabilities are intolerable? What is an optimal or desirable human being? Should human beings be similar? Will relative uniformity eliminate the creative spark that has made man unique? Should every couple be free to procreate or to abort as they wish, despite genetic risks? And finally, who should provide the answers to these questions?

To bring decisions of this type down to a more personal level, consider the following situation.

Helen, pregnant with her first child, was 37 years old. Concerned about the higher risk of genetic defects in babies born to women in her age group, she asked her obstetrician about amniocentesis. During her fifteenth week of pregnancy, Helen entered a hospital where a sample of amniotic fluid was withdrawn through a long needle inserted in her abdomen. After the fetal cells were placed in a nutrient bath where they continued to grow and divide, Helen's doctor examined the cells under a microscope and discovered a chromosomal arrangement that indicated a mongoloid baby (Down's syndrome). Helen was told the diagnosis and was advised that there was no cure or treatment for this type of retardation. She was also assured that an abortion could safely be performed.

The decision in such a situation must take into account the attitudes and feelings of the persons involved, their religious and personal beliefs, and ethical considerations concerning the fetus. What are the couple's views about raising a handicapped child? Can they love and care for a mongoloid baby or would this infant be an intolerable burden for them? What if one parent, fully informed of the consequences, still wants this child and the other parent insists on terminating the pregnancy? Often the decision is not rendered easier by the genetic information; in fact, it may be much more difficult. But with increased genetic knowledge brought about by advances in medical technology, we as individuals, as scientists, and as a society have a solid base on which to make such decisions.

PRINCIPLES AND PROCESSES OF GENETICS

Cells, chromosomes, genes, DNA, and RNA are all relatively familiar terms. Nevertheless, a brief review of their significance may prove helpful before we look at the processes involved in inheritance.

Genes and Chromosomes

Life begins with a single fertilized cell (see Chapter 6). When that cell divides, and as further cell division and cell differentiation take place, each subsequent cell that is formed contains exactly the same number of genes and chromosomes as every other cell. Each human cell has 23 pairs of chromosomes—a total of 46 in all. As many as a few thousand genes may be strung out in chainlike fashion on a single chromosome. Estimates are that as many as 300,000 genes may be found in each of the millions of cells in the body (Winchester, 1971).

Genes are made up of *DNA* (deoxyribonucleic acid), a large molecule composed of carbon, hydrogen, oxygen, nitrogen, and phosphorus. It has been suggested that "the human body contains enough DNA to reach the moon and return 20,000 times if all of it were laid out in a line" (Rugh & Shettles, 1971, p. 199). The structure of DNA, as shown in the illustration, resembles a long spiral staircase. There are 2 long chains made up of alternating phosphates and sugars, with cross-links of 4 different nitrogen bases which pair together. However, the order in which these paired nitrogen bases appear varies, and it is this variation in order that makes one gene different from another. A single gene might be a chunk of this DNA stairway perhaps 2,000 steps long (Pfeiffer, 1964). Watson and Crick (1953) suggest that when a cell is ready to divide, a gene reproduces itself by an unwinding of this DNA staircase and a separation of the two long chains in a kind of unzipping action right down the middle of the paired bases. Each chain, then, attracts new material from the cell to synthesize a second chain and form a new DNA molecule. Occasionally there is a *mutation,* or an alteration in these long strings of nucleic acid. In most cases, this alteration may be maladaptive and the cell may die; but a small proportion of mutations survives and affects the organism.

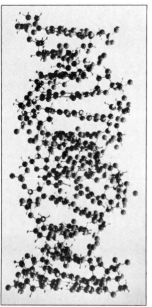

Model of a DNA molecule. (*Abbott Laboratories.*)

The DNA, then, contains the genetic code or blueprint to regulate the functioning and the development of the organism. DNA is the "what and when" of development, but it is locked in the nucleus of the cell. *RNA* (ribonucleic acid) is a substance formed from, and similar to, the DNA and acts as a messenger to the rest of the cell. RNA is the "how" of development. Shorter chains of RNA, patterned from the DNA, move freely within the cell and serve as catalysts for the formation of new tissue.

Since the genes carry the hereditary potential for all organisms, scientists have been eager to discover why and how genes give orders to certain cells. For example, what is happening to the DNA and RNA when a cell begins to multiply uncontrollably, as in a cancer? Genetic discoveries are being made at a tremendous pace. Geneticists have been working on the synthetic construction of the DNA molecule and exploring such things as the triggering mechanism that prompts the sending of a message to the cell (Translating genetic code, 1974). Working with a single bacterium, they have now constructed a DNA molecule which can be manipulated and exchanged from one organism to another. With this molecule, they are able to make basic changes in the composition of the bacterium and the results of these changes can be observed. It is interesting to speculate what new forms of bacteria or other organisms scientists may be able to produce in the future.

The chromosomes of an individual can be examined with a chart called a *karyotype*. A karyotype is prepared from a photograph of the chromosomes of a single cell of the person. The chromosomes are cut out of the photograph and are arranged in matched pairs according to length. These matched chromosomes are then numbered. The first 22 pairs, called *autosomes,* contain genes which determine a variety of physical and mental traits. The twenty-third pair contains the sex chromosomes. There are two X chromosomes in a normal female (XX) and an X and a Y chromosome in a normal male (XY). These sex chromosomes contain genes which control the development of the primary and secondary sexual characteristics and of various other sex-linked traits.

(Top) The chromosomes before they have been arranged to form the karyotype. (Bottom) A karyotype showing the chromosomes arranged according to type. Note that there are three number 21 chromosomes, indicating an individual afflicted with Down's syndrome. (*Dr. James L. German.*)

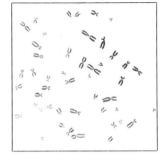

1	2	3	4	5	6	7	8
9	10	11	12	13	14	15	16
17	18	19	20	21	22	X	Y

Cell Division and Reproduction

In the process of *mitosis*, or ordinary cell division, cells divide and duplicate themselves exactly. There are a number of steps in this process. First, the DNA of each gene unzips and replicates itself. Then, each chromosome splits and reproduces the former chromosomal arrangement of the first cell. Thus, two new cells are formed, each containing 23 pairs of chromosomes exactly like those in the original cell.

In a reproductive cell, which may be either an ovum or a sperm, there are only 23 chromosomes, 1 from each pair. The process of cell division that creates these reproductive cells is called *meiosis*. The reproductive cells formed during meiosis have only one-half the genetic material of the parent cell. The rearranging of genes and chromosomes that results from meiosis might be compared to the shuffling and dealing of cards. The chance that any two siblings would receive the same assortment of chromosomes is about one in 281 trillion; and this figure does not allow for the fact that the individual genes on a chromosome often *cross over* to the opposite chromosome during cell division. Therefore, it is virtually impossible for the same combination of genes to occur twice.

Two living human sperms. The female sperm has a larger head than the male, which has a longer tail. (*Dr. Landrum B. Shettles.*)

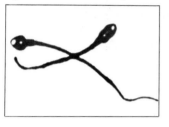

When fertilization of an ovum takes place, the sex of the resulting organism is determined by the sex chromosome carried by the sperm. One-half of the sperm carry an X chromosome; the other half carry a Y chromosome. The ovum, on the other hand, carries only the X chromosome. The male sperm are different from the female sperm. The female sperm have larger heads; the male sperm swim faster and have longer tails, among other characteristics. But it is clearly the male sperm that determines the sex of the child. Despite this biological fact, in some cultures the women are still blamed if they fail to produce sons!

Combinations of Genes

Nearly all of the tens of thousands of genes in an individual occur in pairs. Alternate forms of the same gene pair are called *alleles*. One gene in the pair is inherited from the mother. Some hereditary traits, such as eye color, are carried by a single gene pair. Other traits are carried by a pattern of several interacting gene pairs. For eye color, a child might inherit an allele for brown eyes (B) from the father and an allele for blue eyes (b) from the mother. The child's *genotype*, or gene pattern, for eye color would therefore be *Bb*. But how do these genes combine? Which eye color is expressed? In eye color, the allele for brown eyes (B) is *dominant* and that for blue eyes (b) is *recessive*. When a gene is dominant, the presence of that gene in a gene pair will cause that particular trait to be expressed. Thus, an individual with either the genotype *Bb* or *BB* will have brown eyes. The expressed trait, brown eyes, is called the *phenotype*.

In another example, let us assume that the father's genotype is *Bb* (brown eyes) and the mother has blue eyes (which must be a genotype of *bb*). All the children of these parents will inherit a recessive gene for blue eyes from the mother. However, from the father they may inherit either the dominant gene for brown eyes (B) or the recessive gene for blue eyes (b). Either possibility is equally likely. Therefore, all of the children will be either blue-eyed (*bb*) or brown-eyed (*Bb*). If we know

If we know the genotype of the parents, we can determine the probabilities of genotypes and phenotypes for their children. (*Alice Kandell, Rapho/Photo Researchers.*)

the genotype of the parents, we can determine all the possibilities of genotypes and phenotypes, and the probabilities of each, for their children.

However, most traits do not usually result from a single gene pair but from a combination of many gene pairs—with and without dominance —that interact in a number of ways. For the characteristic of height, for example, several genes or gene pairs seem to combine with others in an additive fashion to create larger or smaller people, with larger or smaller limbs and parts. Gene pairs may also interact in such a way that one gene pair either allows or inhibits the expression of another gene pair. A system of various types of interaction among genes and gene pairs is called a *polygenic system* of inheritance. Such systems frequently give rise to phenotypes that differ markedly from those of either parent.

CHROMOSOMAL ABNORMALITIES

The normal human organism needs all 46 chromosomes with their usual complement of gene pairs. Usually a gross chromosomal abnormality such as a missing or extra chromosome is lethal to the fetus. However, there are a few gross chromosomal abnormalities in which the individual does in fact survive and exhibits certain characteristic patterns. The most common is Down's syndrome, or mongolism, in which the individual has an extra chromosome numbered 21 which either floats freely in the cell nucleus or is situated on top of another chromosome in piggyback fashion. Another chromosomal abnormality is Klinefelter's syndrome in which the individual has an extra X chromosome, an XXY arrangement. This phenotype usually includes sterility, small external male sex organs, and mental retardation. Turner's syndrome results from an inactive or absent X chromosome, an XO arrangement. An individual with Turner's syndrome is usually an immature female who lacks reproductive organs, is abnormally short, and is mentally retarded. Recent popular attention has been focused on the XYY pattern. This chromosome arrangement results in a relatively normal-appearing male but one who often exhibits excessive

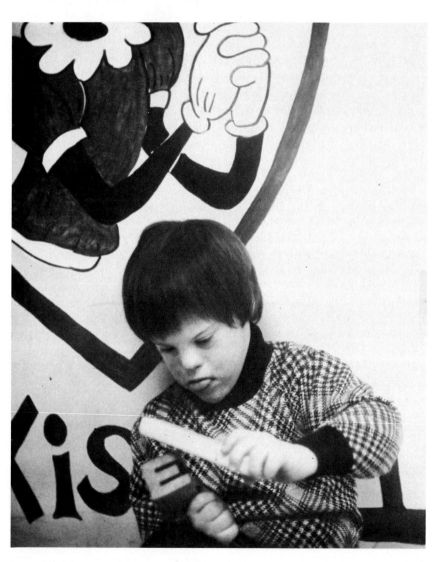

A seven-year-old boy with Down's syndrome. (*Burk Uzzle, Magnum.*)

aggressiveness or criminal behavior. There seems to be a much higher incidence of this chromosomal pattern among prison inmates than in the general population.

Sometimes a chromosome may break at some point along its length and the broken portion may be lost in later cell divisions. At other times, the broken portion may become attached to another chromosome. Some environmental effects, such as viral diseases or radiation, may trigger such breaks. There is also very limited evidence that chromosome breakage may be induced by LSD. Chromosome breakages early in the development of an organism sometimes have a very marked effect on the organism's later growth. Certain parts of the body may fail to develop at all. The effects of chromosomal breaks have not yet been fully determined.

The X and Y chromosomes form a rather unusual pair. Most of the genes on the X chromosome do not have pairs on the much shorter Y chromosome. These single genes are known as sex-linked genes, and the traits which are related to them are called *sex-linked traits.* **Sex-linked Inheritance**

Hemophilia, or bleeder's disease, is probably the most dramatic example of a sex-linked genetic abnormality. It is carried as a recessive gene on the X chromosome. Persons with hemophilia are deficient in a part of the blood plasma needed for normal clotting of the blood. A hemophiliac may bleed for hours from a small wound that would normally clot within five minutes, and internal bleeding is particularly dangerous for him.

Hemophilia was common among the royal families of Europe, and one of the most famous bearers of the disease was Queen Victoria of England. Since hemophilia is transmitted by a recessive gene, Victoria was not herself a bleeder, but merely a carrier of the defect. She had another gene in the chromosome pair that was dominant for normal clotting. Approximately half of her daughters were carriers as well, since they had inherited the recessive gene. About half of her sons were normal, having inherited the normal gene. The rest of her sons, however, inherited the recessive gene for hemophilia. Since there was no dominant gene on the Y chromosome they inherited from their father, this trait of hemophilia was expressed. A recessive trait is not expressed when it has a dominant allele. But since males have only one X chromosome, they express all the traits, dominant and recessive alike, appearing on that X chromosome for which there are no mates on the Y chromosome.

Another example of sex-linked inheritance is color blindness. A girl will be color-blind only if she receives the same gene from both parents. This means that her father must be color-blind and her mother must carry the gene of the defect. A boy will be color-blind if he inherits the one recessive gene, on the X chromosome, from his mother. He cannot inherit the trait from his father because he inherited only the Y chromosome from the father and none of the traits is expressed on the father's X chromosome. There are three or four different types of color blindness, some of which have different patterns of inheritance.

Other kinds of sex-related traits occur as a result of genes on other chromosomes. A beard is an example of a sex-related trait. Women do not normally have beards, yet they carry the genes necessary to produce them. Thus a son inherits traits from both his mother and his father that determine the type of beard he will grow. In fact, the dominant traits may be inherited through the mother and the beards of father and son may be completely different.

Non-sex-linked Traits The vast majority of inherited traits are carried not on the sex chromosomes but on the other 22 pairs. Many disorders are carried as single recessive genes. These include sickle-cell anemia, cystic fibrosis, and Tay-Sachs disease. For these disorders to be expressed, a child must inherit the recessive gene from both parents—that is, both parents must be carriers of the *non-sex-linked traits*. When both parents are carriers of such a disease, approximately 25 percent of the children will inherit the disorder, 50 percent will be carriers, and another 25 percent will not inherit the recessive genes at all. See the example of the inheritability of Tay-Sachs disease shown in Table 5.

TABLE 5   INHERITABILITY OF TAY-SACHS DISEASE WHEN BOTH PARENTS ARE CARRIERS

MOTHER CARRYING TAY-SACHS GENE

	T	t
t	TT normal child noncarrier	Tt normal child but carrier
T	Tt normal child but carrier	tt Tay-Sachs diseased child

FATHER CARRYING TAY-SACHS GENE

Note: If both parents carry the recessive gene, the possible genotypes are:
TT = 1 chance in 4 (25 percent) of a normal child who does not inherit the Tay-Sachs gene
Tt = 2 chances in 4 (50 percent) of a normal child but one who does carry the Tay-Sachs gene
tt = 1 chance in 4 (25 percent) of a child actually inheriting Tay-Sachs disease

T = normal gene
t = recessive gene for Tay-Sachs disease

An interesting characteristic of these particular disorders is that they occur almost solely within a specific nationality, race, or ethnic group. For example, Tay-Sachs disease occurs primarily among Eastern European Jews. Cystic fibrosis is most common among Caucasians. Sickle-cell anemia is found among Africans, American blacks, and some Mediterranean populations. A disorder called thalassemia is prevalent among Italians and other Eastern Mediterranean groups.

The discovery that one is carrying a so-called "bad gene" is a rather frightening experience. The possibility of transmitting the disease to future generations should be considered when a person who is a carrier is selecting a marriage partner or deciding whether or not to have children. However, most of us will never know what kind of bad genes we carry. All of us probably harbor between 5 and 8 potentially lethal genes at the very least, and many recessive and non-sex-linked genes will probably never be expressed. Still, we should obtain as much information as possible about our genetic inheritance and about a potential partner so that we can make intelligent and responsible decisions, should the need arise.

Some abnormalities are carried by dominant genes, rather than by a pairing of recessives. In other words, one gene inherited from one parent is sufficient for an occurrence of this type of trait. One such abnormality is Huntington's chorea, which is characterized by progressive dementia, random jerking movements, and a lopsided, staggering gait. The tragedy of this disorder is that it usually does not appear until the victim reaches middle age or later, after the childbearing years. A person with this disease, unaware that he is carrying the defective gene, may produce children who will inherit the dominant gene.

GENETIC COUNSELING

Once we know the dangers inherent in certain types of gene pairings and the tragic consequences of various chromosomal abnormalities, what can we do to avoid them? Even if we are aware that we all may carry some bad genes, how can that information be put to use? Genetic counseling can help us try to find some answers to these questions.

Using procedures designed to elicit information about chromosomal and genetic makeup, together with newfound knowledge about genetic possibilities, counselors help people evaluate the risks involved in childbearing (Hilton, Callahan, Harris, Condliffe, & Berkley, 1973). Genetic counselors do not provide answers to problems; rather, they put together various bits of information about a couple and come up with probabilities and risk factors that will enable the couple to make intelligent decisions for themselves.

To obtain data for an evaluation, a genetic counselor may use the techniques of chromosomal mapping (karyotyping) and amniocentesis, mentioned earlier in this chapter. In addition, a complete pedigree of the prospective parents, including a thorough description of the appearance of all forebears and the health history of all family members, is required. With this information, a counselor can calculate the risks to prospective children. For example, if a man's grandmother was diabetic and his wife's father was diabetic, both husband and wife might carry recessive genes for diabetes which, if paired in a fetus, could result in a diabetic child. If a wife had a hemophiliac father, she might produce a hemophiliac son or a carrier daughter, although her husband had no history of hemophilia in his family.

Often the genetic counselor will be able to do little more than point out the risks or the percentage possibilities of risk involved. At other times, however, the counselor can provide information of near certainty, as when amniocentesis reveals an abnormal chromosomal arrangement characteristic of mongolism.

A genetic counselor's function is not entirely a negative one, however. Frequently, a counselor can determine the factors causing abnormalities in earlier offspring and reassure parents or potential parents that the chances of another such accident are remote. Parents who give birth to a retarded child, for example, often worry about having another baby. A genetic counselor may be able to trace the defect back to a disease contracted by the mother during the baby's prenatal period, to a lack of oxygen for the fetus during childbirth, or to some other accident that is not related to the genetic potential available to subsequent offspring.

It is important to remember that while we can predict possibilities and potentialities based on knowledge of genetic makeup, we cannot predict the total development of any given individual. The expression of a child's innate potential depends in large measure upon the environmental influences surrounding him, both before and after birth. Prenatal environment is primarily physical and biological. At birth, however, the infant enters a social and cultural environment as well.

CULTURE AND SOCIALIZATION

Although we speak of a culture and of a social environment, we must keep in mind that these are not single, fixed entities. An individual's social environment is complex at the moment of birth and it changes over time. At birth the infant enters many social groups: a family, perhaps a tribe, a social class, a racial or ethnic unit, a religious group, and a community. Each of these social entities has some shared ideas, beliefs, assumptions, values, expectations, and "approrpriate" patterns of behavior. These shared expectations form the culture of the group. An infant enters a broad culture, such as the culture of twentieth-century man, and some subcultures at the same time. Every day, each individual must conform to a multitude of behavior patterns, for example, whether to eat roast beef or to breast feed in public, all of which are partially prescribed by the culture. The process of learning the various aspects of one's culture and adopting these beliefs and expectations as one's own is socialization. And socialization is a lifelong process.

Although there may well be some cultural universals—that is, aspects of behavior or values that appear in most, or all, cultural groups—we shall focus our attention here on cultural diversity and the rich variety of cultural patterns. In examining differences between cultures, however, many people find it difficult not to be a bit ethnocentric. *Ethnocentricity* is a tendency to assume that one's own beliefs, perceptions, and values are true, correct, and factual and that other people's beliefs are false, unusual, or downright bizarre. For example, the "primitive" man is often regarded as simple, unintelligent, even exotic, but quite "uncivilized"; or he may seem a kind of noble savage untainted by the evils of civilization and an industrialized society. Both of these oversimplifications can completely miss the complexity and the richness of distant cultures. But if it is difficult to be objective about distant cultures, it is even more difficult to suspend judgment on the cultural diversity close at hand. Thus, a visitor from abroad who speaks English with a pronounced accent may be accepted graciously, but a next door neighbor of foreign extraction who speaks with a similar accent may be treated with indifference or even hostility. It is difficult to be objective and avoid viewing the world from the perspective of our own particular cultural bias.

Alternate Family Styles

The type of family into which a child is born dramatically affects the expectations, roles, beliefs, and interrelationships that he will experience throughout his lifetime. For example, the *nuclear family* (parents and siblings) is often a somewhat isolated unit in Western society. Mothers, left alone with young children all day, may feel a sense of isolation. Conversely, young children often experience the exclusive attention of their parents for extended periods of time. In contrast, within an *extended family* (one having many relatives and several generations close by) children may be cared for by a variety of people—uncles, aunts, cousins, grandparents, or older siblings. In a third type of social structure, the *communal* social system found in Israel, Russia, or China or on a commune in the United States, the social interrelationships take yet another form. In all three types of family organization, the role of older brother, for instance, may involve very different responsibilities. Among several social systems, an individual's expectations, responsibilities, pride, respect, and duty may all have quite varied meanings.

West African girl carrying her sister in a back sling. (*Photo Researchers.*)

Although we might assume that the American and Western European concept of the nuclear family is the "normal" pattern, in fact this family style is unique (Stephens, 1963). The more common pattern in a large number of cultures throughout history—from Eskimo and Indian tribes to Pacific Island groups—has been the extended kin family. One of the distinct roles in some extended kin families is that of child nurse. Girls generally, but sometimes young boys, are pressed into service at age 4 or 5 as caretakers for still younger children. In Samoa, for example, older children are not only responsible for the safety and good behavior of younger children; they also are blamed for any misbehavior by the little ones. The caretaking child quickly learns to be a disciplinarian and to keep the younger children from disturbing the adults. Margaret Mead (1928) has reported that children may even develop rather monotonous and automatic ways of handling this responsibility. It is not unusual for older children to intersperse their conversations with frequent directives to the younger ones to "keep still" or "stop that noise," with these admonitions spoken rather mechanically and without much provocation from the little ones. In such a pattern of roles, responsibility and the giving and receiving of nurturance are learned early and are spread among a number of different individuals. The Samoan child's attitudes and expectations toward the mother, therefore, are quite different from those of a child in the nuclear family.

In the communal family styles of China, Russia, or Israel—and even in the communal experiments in the United States—the peer group is often an intensely powerful force in the socialization of the young child. Conformity and cooperation may be strong values and significant defiance from the group standards may be virtually nonexistent. In Chinese nurseries, reportedly high standards of self-discipline and responsibility for their classmates are expected from the children, and they receive a heavy indoctrination in national ideology as well. Yet, these children appear to be confident, energetic, animated, and enthusiastic, (Caldwell, 1974).

In the Russian vasli-sadi (nursery-kindergartens), children are trained in character development and, as in China, are indoctrinated in the values of the state. Urie Bronfenbrenner contrasts this kind of environment with the American preoccupation with instilling a thrust toward independence and autonomy in children. He hypothesizes that the rate of delinquency, failure, and lack of direction found among American youth may stem from such independence-oriented childhood training (Bronfenbrenner, 1968).

Some Israeli kibbutzim accept children into the children's houses as early as 3 days after birth (Rabkin & Rabkin, 1969). In these houses, the child is cared for, along with four to eight of his age mates, according to some mutually agreed upon childbearing values and practices. The child benefits from the care of the child-care specialist as well as from the individual relationship with his own parents which he enjoys during daily extended visiting periods. Although the concepts of private property and private enterprise are deemphasized within a kibbutz, there is a recognition of difference in individual potential and need. The peer group, with its members growing up in daily and intimate contact with each other, develops into a closely knit and supportive social group. Rather than being isolated from the rest of the community, the children growing up in the children's houses are, in fact, central to the functioning of the kibbutz (Spiro, 1954). Similarly, certain communal societies in the United States are gathered together to help their members implement their ideals and shared values. In fact, the very basis of some communes is an attempt by families to implement shared values by raising their children together in their chosen lifestyle (Berger, Hackett, & Millar, 1973.)

Childrearing Attitudes

Whatever the American culture of the seventies, probably the best way to view and understand it is to contrast it with some other models. For example, Whiting and Child (1953) collected some research on a number of different societies and concluded that American parents were less nurturant than 75 percent of all the other people in their cross-cultural sample. However, nurturance is a quality that is rather difficult to measure. Some other things are easier to measure, such as an infant's body contact with the mother. It is fairly simple to determine how often the child is carried by the mother, or how often he lies next to her or sucks at the breast. Stephens (1963) concluded that the American infant is downright deprived of sheer body contact, as compared with babies in a number of other cultures. In other societies, infants sleep next to their mothers for several years. They are put in various carrying devices, are carried around on the mothers' backs, and often are nursed for a couple of years. It is not uncommon among some groups for the last child in a family to be nursed for 4 or 5 years, or even longer. In these cultures as well as in our own, these practices simply reflect "the way it's done." The manner of treating infants is simply a commonly accepted pattern of expectations and behaviors, rarely questioned in some societies.

SEX-ROLE IDENTITY

There is no doubt that being born male or female has a profound effect on the growth and development of an individual's personality. Some would suggest that men and women are inherently and dramatically different in intellect, in personality, in adult adjustment, and in style, primarily because of the unfolding of their innate genetic patterns. The opposite point of view contends that men and women are different because of the way they are treated by their parents, by their teachers, and by their culture throughout their lifespans. However, whenever we ask such an either-or question—is either genetics or culture more important in determining sex-role identity?—we are probably asking the wrong question. Genetics and culture may set the outer limits of sex-role identity, but they also interact like two strands of a rope in forming the same personality or psychosexual identity. We need to look more closely at the interplay of these two influences during infancy, early childhood, adolescence, and beyond. Consider this rather dramatic example.

A child who was born a normal male and one of a set of identical twins underwent circumcision at age 7 months. Because of an accident during the surgical procedure, the child's penis was damaged to the point where it withered and fell off. Doctors recommended sex reassignment in which the genitalia would be reconstructed as that of a female and the child would be treated with female hormones. The parents agreed. They therefore changed the child's name, clothing, and hair style, and brought him up as a girl. By the time the twins were only 3 years old, the mother reported what appeared to be sex-based differences: the girl was quite conscious of her clothing and hair and was concerned with being neat, whereas the boy did not mind being untidy or having a dirty face. The girl asked for dolls and a doll house at Christmas time; the boy wanted cars and a garage (Money & Ehrhardt, 1972).

This girl's chromosomes are still male. She has received female hormonal treatment and her family has received counseling and instructions to raise this child "as a girl." This single, true case stimulates the imagination, but it actually proves very little. One set of parents and one set of childrearing practices are involved and it is unclear what effects are the result of hormonal therapy. But basing their conclusion on this and considerable other clinical data, Money and Ehrhardt suggest that much of the basis for an individual's sexual identity is acquired by the age of 3 years and is primarily a result of the different ways in which mothers and fathers treat boy and girl babies.

Male-Female Differences   Studies have shown that male babies, on the average, are slightly longer and heavier than female babies. The male infants also have a higher metabolism, on the average, and develop larger hearts and lungs than females (Hutt, 1972). Later, male children tend to lag behind females in physical development such as walking, talking, tooth cutting, and bone development. Puberty tends to come a year or two later in the average male than in the average female. Often, males have a shorter life span than females. At 85 years of age, for instance, women outnumber men almost two to one, and at age 100, there are five times as many women as men. Males are more prominent in business, industry, and the professions than are females. Men appear to excel in visual-spatial abilities and in mathematical skill, while women are superior in verbal abilities. Males generally display more aggressive behavior than their female counterparts (Maccoby & Jacklin, 1974).

Many of these differences between males and females appear to be biological and caused by genetics. However, many of the biological differences we have noted are measurements of the average male versus the average female. For instance, the range of variation in metabolism among males and females is far larger than the difference in metabolism between males and females—that is, many females have a higher metabolism than a sizable portion of the males. The differences among males themselves, on any of these dimensions, are far greater than the differences between the average male and the average female. Furthermore, some of the differences that seem, at first glance, to be of biological origin may or may not be so. Consider the multitude of reasons (wars, traffic accidents, risky occupations, or sports) that may partially account for the fact that women live longer, on the average, than men do.

Sex-Role Socialization   It is easy to recognize *sex-role stereotypes* in our culture. For example, girls are sweet and neat; boys are rough and tough. Girls like dolls; boys like cars and trucks. Girls help their mothers; boys work with their fathers. Girls cook and sew; boys build and fix. The list could go on and on. It is possible also to recognize deeper sex-role issues that affect the lives of men and women. Our culture restricts a man's right to express emotions. It tends to frown upon a woman who is aggressive or assertive, or is successful in a career or in certain intellectual pursuits.

The learning of the sex role begins in infancy. Kagan (1971) reports that mothers respond more physically to their boys and more verbally to their girls when the infants babble. These differences in the way boys and girls are treated are clearly detectable by the time a child is 6 months old, at least in Kagan's Boston area study. But in many cases it is not necessary to do a study. Many parents can report, on reflection, the differences in the way they act toward a 1-year-old boy versus a 1-year-old girl. The variance in treatment of boys and girls is not just a matter of pink and blue blankets. It is often hundreds of little things all day long—the way the child is held, how often the child is picked up, the way the child is talked to, the kinds of things that are said, the amount of help that the child is given, how the child is responded to when he cries. All these kinds of behaviors are often subtly influenced by whether or not the child is a boy or a girl. We become aware of these differences sometimes when we discover that we have mistakenly identified a child as a girl instead of a boy, and vice versa. Our surprise reaction in this kind of situation often tells us more about our

From an early age, children are stereotyped in sex roles. (*Alice Kandell, Rapho/Photo Researchers.*)

own attitudes and sex-role stereotypes than about the child himself.

From toddlerhood up to first grade, sex-role learning goes on in earnest. Much of the preschool child's play is imitative of the adult roles he sees around him. Playing house, cowboys and Indians, construction worker, Superman, Batman, doctor, nurse—all are examples of role playing. The child tries on the gestures, mannerisms, language, and actions of a variety of adult models. Yet the models he sees around him are not only the live models in his family and community, and perhaps in his school, but also the models in books and literature, in pictures, and on television. An analysis of a Lotto game distributed for 3- and 4-year-olds indicated some clearly stereotypical models. In this game, several adult careers for men and women were shown. Over 15 careers were pictured for boys, including truckdriver, fireman, doctor, lawyer, and businessman. For girls, only 3 careers were pictured— nurse, secretary, and ballet dancer. Yet, probably half of the children who played with this game were girls, and girls are just as busy trying on adult roles and fantasizing their future lives as are boys. Many of the toys marketed for preschool children are much more blatant bearers of sex-role stereotypes. The television commercials for toys such as G.I. Joe or Barbie doll demonstrate exaggerated masculine or feminine "appropriate" behaviors.

How are sex roles learned? It is generally accepted that there are three major processes by which an individual learns appropriate sex-role behavior, attitudes, values, and expectations (Maccoby & Jacklin, 1974; Mischel, 1970). First, a child learns through imitation of a chosen same-sex model. The same-sex parent is generally the most potent model in the early years, but the choice of model becomes much more complicated as the child gets older. Second, the child learns through praise and discouragement, or through reward and punishment for particular kinds of behavior. For example, parents usually actively encourage and reward "boy-like" behavior and discourage "feminine" behavior in their sons. And finally, sex roles are learned through self-socialization. The child develops a concept of what it is to be male or female. He then attempts to fit his own actions into this concept of behavior that he thinks is sex-appropriate. This monitoring of behavior by matching it with the self-concept becomes more and more important as the child grows older. However, the child's conception of appropriate male and female behavior is heavily dependent on the first two processes—that is, observing models and receiving praise or discouragement for his own actions.

Genetics and Culture: An Interaction

Although genes prescribe the physical blueprint for an individual's development, this development must be played out in a culture. Thus, the genes may set limits on the person's potentiality, but so may the environment. Genes may provide some of the cues in physical appearance that stimulate the social environment to respond to the individual in particular ways. Because human development is cumulative, all events, whether genetic or environmental in nature, have an effect on subsequent events within the individual's life span.

The important question in any discussion of heredity and environment is not which of these factors determines the behavior or physical growth of an individual, but rather, what is the nature of the interaction between the two.

The relatively recent advances in genetics have given rise to exciting, yet frightening, possibilities for mankind. As new discoveries are made about the nature of gene formation, we are faced with the prospect of being able to engineer human potential. If, through the manipulation of the formation of DNA, we are someday able to reconstruct and "improve" the genetic makeup of a human fetus, we will have come to terms with the issues of man's uniqueness and his right to procreate in his own image.

Although the pairing of genes from parents establishes a blueprint for a child's development, cultural influences have an impact on how and when—and even if—the genetic potential will be realized. The child's early socialization depends on the social structure of the family as well as the myriad of childrearing attitudes, customs, and practices he experiences. The formation of a sex-role identity demonstrates the cumulative interplay of genetics and culture in the development of a central aspect of the child's personality.

1. Construct a model illustrating the interrelationship of genetic potential, psychological development, and social and cultural influences during the growth of a child.

2. Discuss the differences between genotype and phenotype as they apply to eye color. How is the inheritance of brown eyes different from that of blue eyes?

3. After you have read this chapter, what advice would you give to a pregnant woman whose first child has cystic fibrosis?

Bronfenbrenner, U. *Two worlds of childhood: U.S. and USSR.* New York: Russell Sage Foundation, 1970. Bronfenbrenner suggests some weaknesses he observes in current American practices of childrearing by contrasting them with similar practices and expectations in the USSR.

Huxley, A. *Brave new world.* New York: Harper & Brothers, 1932. This fictional account of one future alternative explores moral issues brought about by advances in genetic technology.

Winchester, A. M. *Human genetics.* Columbus, Ohio: Merrill, 1971. A clear and readable discussion of the basic principles of genetics.

9

DEVELOPING COMPETENCIES

At the age of 12 months, Chris weighed 23 pounds and was 30 inches tall. He had been walking for a month but still resorted to creeping when he wanted to get somewhere in a hurry. And he was always in a hurry! He cried bitterly at any kind of restraint—his crib, his play-pen, the car seat, and even his mother's lap. From birth on, he was an active, restless, fussy child, given to irregular sleeping habits and long crying spells. He showed early, marked preferences for certain people, playthings, and foods, and at age 8 months he began to have temper tantrums when things did not go his way.

Billy weighed 22 pounds and was 29½ inches tall at the age of 12 months. Although he was able to pull himself upright at 7 months, he was not walking alone at 12 months and seemed to have no interest in doing so. He was a placid child, willing to sit in his play-pen or crib for as long as an hour provided someone remained close by to talk or sing to him or to play some sort of game. Although he would cry quickly and loudly if approached by a stranger, Billy showed few signs of ill temper, frustration, or anxiety in his day-to-day activities.

The two children described above are the same age and the same sex, but obviously they are quite different in their personality styles and developmental pace. While we might attribute the differences between them solely to family, environmental, and cultural disparities, in actual fact these two children are brothers, born to the same parents only a few years apart.

As we saw in Chapter 7, a neonate comes into the world with certain sensory and response capacities. The initial equipment he needs for functioning is present at birth, even though complex sensorimotor integration is just beginning to develop.

From birth to 2 years, the infant undergoes a dramatic transformation, changing into an individual aware of himself and the world around him. He learns to manipulate objects, himself, and other people. He learns to communicate. He begins to discriminate among people, places, things, tastes, sounds, and sights.

Although norms and averages of growth and behavior have been established for children at various ages and stages of development, essentially each child develops in his own way and, within limits, at his own pace. This individuality is apparent in the two brothers described above and becomes even more obvious as the children develop.

By 18 months, Chris had a vocabulary of 42 words and phrases. He enjoyed playing with small trucks and cars, lining them up meticulously and rearranging them endlessly. By 24 months he began to build rather complicated block structures and to draw human faces and figures when given a crayon and paper. He was a friendly child but seemed to seek out opportunity for solitary activity. He firmly resisted all attempts at toilet training.

Although Billy had access to the same kinds of toys that his brother had enjoyed, his preferences for types of toys and styles of play were quite different. Trucks and cars—the bigger the better—were for rolling into walls and furniture; blocks were for throwing. He, too, had a large vocabulary at an early age, and his favorite activity at 18 months was "chatting" with anyone who would listen and respond. He enjoyed drawing and putting puzzles together but only so long as someone watched him work. At 24 months he was quite interested in imitating his big brother's use of the bathroom.

We shall now look at some of the stages of development through which a child passes during the first 2 years of life. Although, as we saw in the descriptions of Chris and Billy, children vary greatly in what they do, when they do it, and how they do it, there are some broad developmental norms that we can examine.

AGES AND STAGES: AN OVERVIEW

As we examine the norms and averages for children at various ages, we should keep in mind that we are talking about the middle 50 percent of infants; we are not discussing those children who are nearer the two extremes of the development scale. But even in this middle group we find significant variations which may indicate healthy individuality among infants or represent differences in childrearing practices. The age-level descriptions that follow are not intended to serve as measuring sticks for infant progress, but rather to provide a backdrop against which we can examine infant behaviors and competencies.

Age 4 Months

PHYSICAL APPEARANCE. At the age of 4 months, a baby resembles the chubby, appealing child in magazine advertisements. He has nearly doubled in weight, from the 7 to 8 pounds at birth to somewhere between 12 and 15 pounds, and he has probably grown 4 or more inches in length. His skin has lost any evidence of paleness or redness, and his fine birth hair has been replaced by new hair.

At birth, the size of the child's head represents about one-fourth of the total length of his body. However, around the age of 4 months, the body begins to grow in length much more rapidly than does the head and these proportions change markedly. By age 12, for example, a child's head is only one-eighth the length of his body, and by age 25, the head is one-tenth of total body length.

Changes are also taking place in the infant's teeth and bones. In some children the first tooth erupts at 4 or 5 months, although the average age for this event is closer to 6 or 7 months. Many of the bones are not yet hard and heavily calcified but are still soft cartilage tissue and they tend to be pliable under stress. Muscles, however, may pull easily and be injured. Occasionally, well-meaning parents have discovered this when hoisting an infant up by the arms and swinging him in play (Stone, Smith, & Murphy, 1973).

Much to the delight of parents, the average baby is usually sleeping through the night by the age of 4 months. This sleep pattern sometimes begins as early as the second month, followed by a gradual settling down of the baby into the family daytime, as well as nighttime, routine.

For most infants in our culture, solid foods have been introduced by the age of 4 months. Some doctors recommend cereal as early as 6 weeks, followed by strained vegetables and fruits at around 3 months. Orange juice, egg yolk, strained meats, and whole milk, rather than infant formula, are often included in the 4-month-old's diet.

Infants vary widely in their reactions to new foods (Brazelton, 1969). Some eagerly accept almost anything that is put in their mouth, while others approach every new food cautiously.

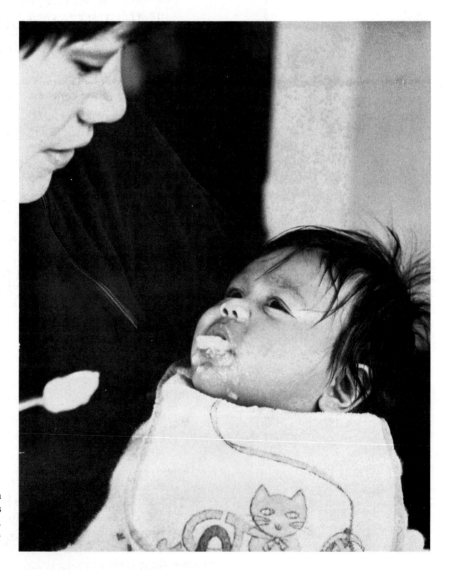

Some 4-month-olds approach the introduction of solid foods to their diet very cautiously. (*Alice Kandell, Rapho/Photo Researchers.*)

BEHAVIOR. When the 4-month-old is placed on his stomach, he can generally hold up his chest as well as his head. In a sitting position, he holds his head steady and observes very carefully everything that goes on around him. The average infant of this age can roll over from stomach to back and from back to stomach (Stone et al., 1973). Most 4-month-olds can reach and grasp an object (Frankenburg & Dodds, 1967).

Self-discovery usually begins about this time. The infant discovers his own hands and fingers and spends several minutes at a time watching them, studying their movements, bringing them together, grasping one hand with the other (Church, 1966). Some 4-month-old infants also discover their feet and manipulate them in much the same way as they do their hands and fingers (Brazelton, 1969). It is quite normal, however, for an infant to be 5 or even 6 months old before becoming aware of his feet, especially if he reaches this age during the winter when he is apt to be heavily bundled up (Stone et al., 1973).

At 4 months, nearly all babies smile, laugh, and coo quite selectively. They will react with a wide range of emotional responses to persons or events. Many babies also begin to engage in elementary social games at this age. Imitative sound play—mimicking an infant's vocalizations so that he continues to babble—is one such game that will probably amuse the infant longer than it will the average parent.

Age 8 Months

PHYSICAL APPEARANCE. At 8 months, the baby has gained another 4 or 5 pounds and has grown about 3 more inches in length, but his general appearance does not differ dramatically from that of the 4-month-old. He probably has at least one tooth and perhaps as many as two or three teeth. His hair is thicker and longer. By this time, too, the orientation of his legs is such that the soles of his feet no longer face each other.

DIET. Gradual changes in feeding schedules and diet occur between the ages of 4 and 8 months. In Western cultures, the 8-month-old is usually on a varied diet of solid foods and is probably beginning to make an effort to feed himself bits of food and crackers.

Very often an 8-month-old baby is being weaned or has been weaned from breast to bottle or even from bottle to cup. However, there is enormous variability in the weaning period within our own culture as well as between cultures. Some Western mothers may begin weaning babies from the breast at 3 or 4 months or even earlier. A few mothers may continue breast feeding for as long as 2 or 3 years. Although such extended breast feeding is infrequent in our culture, there are many other cultures in which normal breast feeding routinely continues for 2 or 3 years or even into middle childhood for the youngest child. In a report of cross-cultural practices, Stephens (1963) discusses a girl in Baiga, India, who was not weaned until her marriage at age 12 years!

BEHAVIOR. Most 8-month-olds can get themselves into a sitting posi-

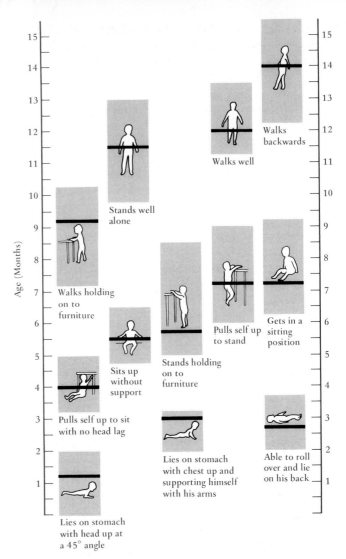

Figure 6 Examples of developmental tasks in infancy. The line across each box represents the median age at which the developmental task can be performed. (*Adapted from Frankenburg, W. K., & Dodds, J. B. The Denver developmental screening test.* Journal of Pediatrics, *1967, 71, 181.*)

tion, and nearly all babies of this age can sit without support once they are placed in position (Stone et al., 1973). If they are put on their feet, well over half of the 8-month-olds can stand while holding on to some support, and about half can pull themselves up into a standing position. A few may even begin to sidestep around the crib or playpen while holding on, and some babies may be walking, using furniture for support.

Although an occasional baby does take a few steps alone at this age, it is generally too early for free walking (Stone et al., 1973). There is wide variability in the age at which walking begins, depending upon both individual abilities and cultural factors (Hindley et al., 1966). It does appear, however, that norms for walking as well as for other motor development activities have accelerated over the years. Several decades ago, 15 months was thought to be the average age for walking (Gesell, 1940; Shirley, 1931). Now the period between 11 and 13 months is closer to the average (Frankenburg & Dodds, 1967).

Most babies of 8 months resort to crawling (with the body on the ground) or creeping (on hands and knees) to get around. Some use a method called "bear walking" in which hands and feet are employed, while others scoot in a sitting position. Whatever the style of movement, the 8-month-old is beginning to explore, and to get into things, over things, and under things.

The 8-month-old is also using his hands quite differently. Most babies of this age are able to pass objects from hand to hand and some are able to use the thumb and finger to grasp. They may delight in filling both hands and are usually able to bang two objects together—a feat that is often demonstrated joyfully and endlessly.

By 8 months, some infants begin to play social games. (*Alice Kandell, Rapho/Photo Researchers.*)

Many babies of 8 months begin to play social games such as peek-a-boo, bye-bye, and patty-cake, and most enjoy handing an item back and forth to an adult. Another quickly learned routine is that of dropping an object and watching someone pick it up and hand it back. This "game" is usually learned accidentally by both baby and adult, and the baby is often the first to catch on to the possibilities for fun.

At 7 or 8 months, an amiable baby may suddenly become quite shy with strangers, staring suspiciously at unfamiliar faces. If a stranger persists in his or her attentions or attempts to handle the baby, the infant may even burst into frightened tears.

An 8-month-old begins to pay more attention to speech, turning toward a voice and even imitating some speech sounds. Most infants of this age will say repeated sounds such as baba, or nana, or words like mama, dada, or bye-bye, although they usually will not know what the words mean. The sounds in an infant's babbling are much more complex and varied at 8 months than at 4 months.

Age 12 Months   PHYSICAL APPEARANCE. At 12 months, the average infant is about three times heavier than his birth weight and he has grown about 9 or 10 inches in length. Throughout this first year, girls tend to be slightly lighter in weight than boys.

DIET. Most growth charts developed over the past 15 years show a much more rapid weight gain and increase in length in infants and children than were shown in earlier times. The principal reason for this is the enormously improved nutrition of children in the Western world. From the time of conception through the first 3 to 4 years after birth, nutrition plays a crucial role in development.

Some studies indicate that part of any physical retardation caused by temporary poor nutrition may be made up later. However, severe protein deficiency or general malnutrition may cause permanent damage to the brain (Coursin, 1972; Dean, 1962; Wyden, 1971). According to Wyden (1971),

> . . . The rate of brain cell division decreases when a fetus is not given enough nourishment. A seriously malnourished fetus may have 20 percent fewer brain cells than normal fetuses. If a newborn baby is seriously undernourished during his first 6 months of life, cell division is also slowed down—also by as much as 20 percent. If an infant is malnourished both before and after birth, the brain may be 60 percent smaller.

Most researchers believe that overfeeding can produce problems just as well as underfeeding (Wyden, 1971). The fat cells that are formed during the first year of life stay in the body through adulthood; the obese baby may well develop into an obese adult.

Weaning is a crucial time for the onset of malnutrition. Particularly vulnerable is the 1-year-old who has already been weaned from the

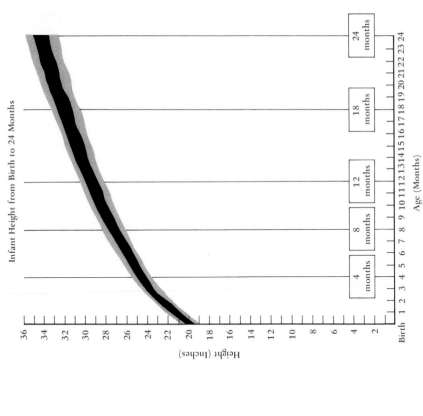

Infant Height from Birth to 24 Months

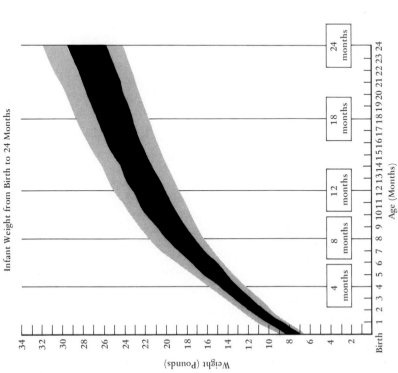

Infant Weight from Birth to 24 Months

Figure 7 The weight and height of about 50 percent of the infants at a given age will fall in the darkly shaded regions and about 15 percent will fall in each of the lightly shaded regions. Thus, on the average, 80 percent of all infants will have weights and heights somewhere in the shaded regions of the graphs. Note that as the infants age, there are greater differences in weight and height within the normal range of growth. (*From Watson, E. H., & Lowry, G. H. Growth and development of children (5th ed.). Chicago: Year Book Medical Publishers, 1967.*)

breast and whose family has insufficient money for milk and other nutritious foods. He may be surviving on a very poor diet in terms of general caloric intake as well as intake of protein, vitamins, and minerals. Many children of this age are filling up on "empty calories" in crackers and cookies. Even in homes where there is an adequate supply of varied food and milk, the year-old child may be unwilling to drink a sufficient amount of milk from a cup or to snack on cheese or meat rather than crackers. A parent who just assumes that a child is getting enough of the essential nutrients should remember that a 6-month-old needs twice as many calories and five times as much protein as an adult requires for each unit of body weight. A 2-year-old needs three times as much protein as the adult for each unit of body weight (Calder, 1966).

Many parents worry when children go through periods of refusing certain foods or eating one food to the exclusion of almost all others.

The 12-month-old actively manipulates his environment. (*Alice Kandell, Rapho/Photo Researchers.*)

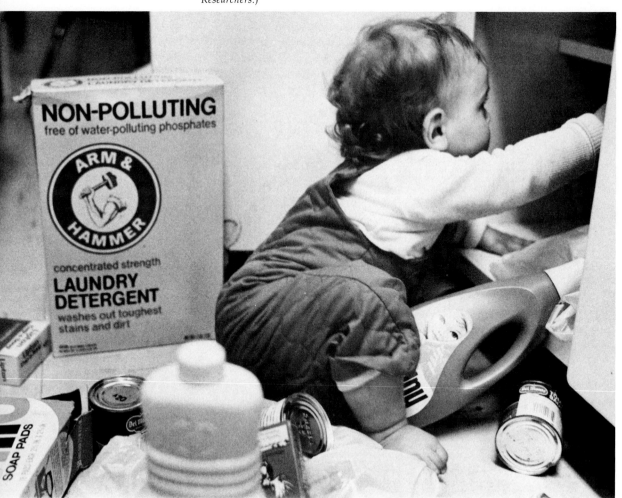

Studies have shown, however, that such short-term "binges" are normal and may be corrected voluntarily if adequate nutrients are easily available (Davis, 1939). It is the long-term limited diets that are the problem.

BEHAVIOR. At 12 months many babies are walking alone, although, as we mentioned earlier, there is great variability in this accomplishment. If they are not walking without support, most children of this age can walk while holding on to furniture and they are often able to stand alone in one place. Some can even stoop and then recover their balance.

The 12-month-old is actively manipulating the environment and is able to undo latches, open cabinets, pull toys, and twist lamp cords. His newly developed pincer grasp of thumb and forefinger allows him to pick up grass, hairs, cigarette butts, and dead insects. He can turn on the television set and the stove, and he can explore bottles of cleaning fluid, open windows, and electrical outlets. "No!" becomes an important word in the vocabulary of both child and parents.

The 12-month-old is often able to play games such as hide-and-seek; he can roll a ball back and forth with an adult and can throw small objects, making up in persistence what he lacks in aim. Many children of this age are beginning to feed themselves, using a spoon and holding and drinking from a cup.

As the year-old child becomes aware of himself as an individual separate from his mother, he begins to exercise choice and preference. He may suddenly and vehemently refuse a food that he has always liked; he may protest loudly at bedtime; or he may engage in a "battle of wills" with his mother over a formerly trouble-free event such as getting into his snowsuit or being placed in his high chair.

The 18-month-old is usually referred to as a toddler. Toddlerhood is an imprecisely defined stage of life where the child has a somewhat top-heavy, wide stance and walks with a gait that is not solidly balanced and smoothly coordinated. Viewed in terms of this description, most 18-month-olds are clearly toddlers.

Almost all children of this age are walking alone. However, some are not yet able to climb stairs; and many have considerable difficulty kicking a ball, for their balance is not reliable enough to permit them to free one foot for kicking. The child of this age also finds pedaling a tricycle or jumping nearly impossible.

The 18-month-old probably weighs between 22 and 27 pounds, an indication that the rate of weight increase has slowed down. The average length for this age is about 31 to 33 inches.

At 18 months a child may be stacking from two to four cubes or blocks to build a tower, and he can probably manage to scribble with crayon or pencil. When he walks, he generally likes to push or pull something with him or to carry something in his hands. He seldom drops down on all fours now, even though walking may actually take more effort and more time.

Age 18 Months

Older infants enjoy pulling wagons or toys. (*Alice Kandell, Rapho/Photo Researchers.*)

The 18-month-old has improved his ability to feed himself and may even be able partly to undress himself. (The ability to put clothes on generally comes later.) Many of his actions are imitative of those going on around him: "reading" a magazine, sweeping the floor, and chattering on a toy telephone. He has made great strides in language and probably has a vocabulary of several words and phrases.

Age 24 Months By his second birthday, the toddler has picked up another 2 or so inches and pounds. Again, the rate of gain is tapering off.

Since 2-year-olds are usually too young for most nursery schools and too old for regular monthly visits to the doctor, relatively little study has been made of this age group. These children are in private homes and are seen around neighborhoods, but they are generally out of range of most research psychologists. This is particularly unfortunate, since the 2-year-old is a fascinating creature, just beginning to break through into new skill areas and accomplishments.

The 2-year-old not only walks and runs, but he can usually pedal a tricycle, jump in place on two feet, balance briefly on one foot, and accomplish a not-too-bad overhand throw. He can climb steps and may even be able to come down again without assistance. He will crawl into, under, around, and over objects and furniture and will manipulate, carry, handle, push, or pull anything he sees. He will put things into and take them out of larger containers. He will pour water, mold clay, stretch the stretchable, and bend the bendable. He will transport items in carts or wagons or trucks. He will explore and test and probe.

Given a crayon or pencil, the 2-year-old may create "scribbles" and be fascinated briefly with the magical marks. He can stack from six to eight blocks or cubes to build towers and he can construct a three-block "bridge." His spontaneous block play shows matching of shapes and symmetry. If he is willing, he can take off most of his own clothing and can put on some items.

We now have an idea of what a baby can generally be expected to do at various stages during the first 2 years. What we do not know, however, is *why* an infant does what he does. What does he see and hear and what is he thinking? What prompts his movement from one stage of development to the next? What experiences and objects in his environment are significant to his future development? These are some of the concerns we shall now deal with in this chapter and later in Chapter 10.

A 2-year-old imitates activities she sees around her. (*Hanna Schreiber, Rapho Guillumette.*)

Through hard work and the use of imaginative research techniques, psychologists have discovered that the human infant is much more complex and has many more competencies than we had originally supposed. New technology has helped the researchers somewhat in their studies. Today it is possible to measure certain basic physiological reactions of a baby to the environment and to specific stimulation. Heart activity, brain wave activity, and electrical response of the skin can provide useful information. Researchers can also gather information from highly refined pictures of an infant's movements—for example, eye movement or hand manipulation. But new technology is only part of the answer. A good research plan or paradigm is even more important.

One such technique is the *surprise paradigm.* Human beings tend to register surprise—through facial expression, physical reaction, or vocal response—when something happens that they did not expect or, conversely, when something does not happen that they did expect. Researchers are able to determine an infant's surprise reaction by measuring changes in his breathing, heartbeat, and galvanic skin response, or simply by observing his expression or his bodily movement. Then they can design experiments to test very precisely what an infant expects and what events violate his expectations (Bower, 1974).

What has come out of these infant studies is the realization that infants are much more intelligent than we might have thought. As Pines (1970) has stated,

> It turns out that not only do infants notice many more details of their environment than adults ever suspected, but they actively invent rules or theories to explain what they perceive. . . . by the age of 2, the normal child has learned to speak, built himself a large framework of theories about the world, and taught himself various intricate skills which he can use in new combinations whenever the need arises—an extraordinary achievement. (pp. 72–73)

Perceptual Competence

There are rapid changes in the infant's visual capacity during the first 4 to 6 months. As described in Chapter 7, the newborn can follow a moving object, is able to show a clear preference for looking at certain patterns, and can discriminate between different shapes (Fantz, Ordy, & Udel, 1962). However, the newborn focuses his vision on objects rather close to him—usually about 10 to 20 inches away from his face—and has somewhat limited acuity. Distant objects are likely to be somewhat blurred. He probably perceives objects that are 20 feet away about as clearly as adults perceive objects that are 440 feet away. The infant's ability to focus on objects at varying distances improves rapidly and approaches adult performance by the time he is 3 or 4 months of age (Haynes, White, & Held, 1965). At the same time, the infant's visual acuity is becoming much sharper. The newborn may only be able to discriminate stripes that are ⅛ of an inch apart, whereas a 6-month-old infant can discriminate stripes ¹/₆₄ of an inch apart and 10 inches in front of him (Fantz et al., 1962). Although the newborn probably also has some color discrimination, there is a rapid increase in color discrimination and color preferences during the first 6 months. This is probably related to rather extensive cellular changes in the *fovea*—the area of the retina most highly packed with color sensitive cells (Mann, 1964). There are a number of other improvements in visual perception during the first 6 months. The infant becomes better able to control eye movements, and he can follow moving objects more consistently and for longer periods of time. He spends more time in scanning the visual environment; during the first month of life, only 5 to 10 percent of his time is spent in scanning, but nearly 35 percent of the time at 2½ months (White, 1971b). Infants are rather attracted to bright lights and to bright objects, provided they are not too bright. However, by 4 months they are able to see and to respond to objects of much less brightness than previously (Doris & Cooper, 1966).

DEPTH PERCEPTION. By the time the infant is about 2 months old, he begins to show a definite preference for three-dimensional figures rather than for flat, two-dimensional forms (Fantz, 1961). Infants as young as 1 or 2 months will dodge or blink in reaction to an inappropriately aimed object (Ball & Tronick, 1971). A more familiar experiment testing the infant's depth perception is the *visual cliff*. Gibson and Walk (1960) created a special box to simulate depth. On one side, a heavy piece of glass covered a solid surface. On the other side, the heavy glass was 2 to 3 feet above a floor, simulating the cliff effect. Infants 6 months or older refused to crawl across the surface which appeared to be a cliff. Younger infants who were not yet able to crawl showed some distress, as indicated by heart rate changes, when they were placed on the cliff side of the box (Campos, Langer, & Krowitz, 1970).

The "visual cliff" is used to test depth perception in infants. Even when coaxed by their mothers, infants will not crawl over the deep side of the visual cliff. (*From E. J. Gibson, & R. D. Walk,* Scientific American, *April 1960, p. 65. Photographer: William Vandivert. By permission.*)

These and many other experiments indicate that the infant's visual perception system matures very rapidly in the first 3 to 6 months of life. Furthermore, the infant's vision is selective; he prefers certain kinds of things and is less interested in other things. He prefers a certain amount of novelty, and after looking at an object for a while he will turn his gaze to something else. From the beginning, the infant is actively scanning and processing the information from the visual world. His developing perceptual system—be it visual, auditory, or tactile—provides a foundation for later integration and conceptual development.

Development of Sensorimotor Intelligence

As we saw in Chapter 4, Piaget viewed the development of infant intelligence as a series of adaptations as the infant acts upon the environment and then internalizes what he has learned. One of the ways in which the infant learns is by a reaction known as a circular response. First, something happens by accident and the infant perceives it in some way, by feeling, hearing, or seeing it. Then he prolongs, or repeats, or varies the discovered activity before he has full, conscious, voluntary control of the act. For example, the baby may happen to notice his hands in front of his face. Then, by moving his hands in front of his face he discovers he can change what he sees. Those are his hands; he can cause their motion. He can prolong the event, or repeat it, or start it again. The infant's early circular responses involve discovering his own body. Later circular responses concern how he can use his body or himself to change the environment, as in making a mobile move.

Another way in which the infant adapts and thus learns is by combining patterns of behavior. These patterns or schemata—such as mouthing, grasping, or reaching—are independent and rather broad at first. Bits and pieces of smaller schemata are eventually combined, integrated, and coordinated into a larger schema.

THE VISUALLY GUIDED REACH. Psychologists have been fascinated by infants' development of a seemingly simple ability to reach for and grasp objects in a fully coordinated manner. It takes several months to develop this skill. A newborn has grasping and sucking reflexes, and he can also look and scan. But he cannot put all these movements together. If a 1-month-old infant is shown a very attractive object, he will do one of a number of things. Often he will open and close his hands and move his arms in a random, seemingly excited fashion. Sometimes he will begin to move his mouth as if he is about to suck. Or he will look intently at the object. But he cannot coordinate these actions in order to reach out, grasp the object, and bring it to his mouth to suck on.

Researchers such as Jerome Bruner have taken detailed movies of infants at various ages on the way to developing this ability. Why the fascination with such a simple skill? First, successful reaching requires a number of different abilities. It requires accurate depth perception, voluntary control of grasping from early reflexes, arm control, and the organization of these behaviors in sequence (Bruner, 1969). Second, when the infant learns a visually guided reach, he is learning something about visual space and tactile space and the causes of events, even if only in a very primitive way. And third, the development of this relatively simple skill demonstrates a number of things that happen in the development of other abilities. For example, when the child develops a visually guided reach, he puts together a lot of bits and pieces of behavior. These pieces of behavior become *functionally subordinated* to the total pattern. At first the child has a looking schema, a grasping schema, and a mouthing schema, among others. He must focus his attention on each of these individual pieces. Later, they all become part of one act and the individual pieces or schemata are functionally subordinated to the total pattern. When he has first learned a visually guided reach, the child must focus considerable attention on the acts of reaching, grasping, and mouthing. Later, the reach itself becomes a means to an end and his attention can be on a larger task—building blocks, for instance. His reaching is now functionally subordinated to block building.

Even in the development of this simple skill, the environment makes a difference. If an infant is given very little to look at, to grasp, and to reach for, or if his hands are tucked under a blanket or into his sleeves, his visually guided reach will occur somewhat later than it would if he had been exposed to a free, highly stimulating environment (White, Castle, & Held, 1964). Although the child normally attains the visually guided reach at about 4 or 5 months, environmental stimulation may speed up the process so that the child achieves it as early as 2½ to 3 months.

OBJECT PERMANENCE. Another accomplishment of infancy is the development of *object permanence,* which is the assumption that objects continue to exist when they are out of sight or touch or lack some other perceptual contact. Piaget (1936/1952) successfully indicated that young infants have no such assumption. Memory has something to do with object permanence but not everything. There are a series of accomplishments in the development of a full concept of object permanence. First, there is the development of some recognition of familiar objects. As early as 2 months of age, an infant may show excitement or pleasure at the sight of his bottle or his mother, indicating some recognition.

The surprise paradigm has been used to study infants' development of object permanence. T. G. R. Bower (1971) carried out a series of experiments using this paradigm with infants ranging from 2 weeks to 18 months of age. He projected images of objects on a screen, and he discovered that 4-month-old infants were surprised and frustrated when they reached out for the objects and grasped only empty air. However, when the actual objects were dangled in front of the screen, the babies showed no surprise when they reached out and touched them. In other words, the infants expected what they saw to be something tangible, for they had already integrated visual and tactile information about objects.

Second, very young infants will follow a moving object that disappears behind a screen and then will visually move their eyes to the other end of the screen as if anticipating the reemergence of this object. Their visual tracking is excellent and well timed, and they are surprised if the object does not reappear. This experiment seems to indicate that the infants possess some degree of object permanence. However, an additional study indicated that infants 1 or 2 months old are not at all surprised or distressed if a completely different object comes out from behind the screen at the right time and place. Up to the age of 20 weeks, the babies will accept a wide variety of different objects emerging on the other side of the screen (Bower, 1971).

What about the development of the concept of person permanence? For example, is it true for infants that mother, too, can be "out of sight, out of mind"? Does the concept of mother as a separate entity that exists in some unique fashion develop more rapidly than the concept of other objects? In one experiment, Bower used an arrangement of mirrors to present infants with multiple images of their mothers. He found that infants less than 20 weeks old were not disturbed at seeing more than one mother; in fact, they were rather delighted. Older infants, however, seemed to have learned that they had only one mother and they became very disturbed by the multiple images.

Bower's multiple mothers experiment demonstrates that infants of less than 20 weeks are not disturbed by seeing more than one mother. However, older infants become quite disturbed by the sight of the multiple images. (*Dr. T. G. R. Bower,* Scientific American, *October 1971, p. 38.*)

Another series of experiments concerning object permanence involved searching for hidden objects (Gratch, 1972; Gratch & Landers, 1971; Piaget, 1954). Infants aged 6 months to 1 year enjoy a wide variety of hiding and finding games. They enjoy being hidden themselves— either by a blanket over their heads or by their hands placed over their eyes—and then discovering that the world reappears when their eyes are uncovered. They go through a predictable sequence of development in hunting for hidden objects. A very young infant does not hunt; he seems to forget an object once it is hidden. But from about 9 months on, most infants will begin to hunt. If the hidden object disappears, as through a trap door behind a screen, the infants will show surprise that it has vanished. If another toy replaces the first toy, 9- to 12-month-old infants will often show mild surprise but accept the new toy. Older infants, between 12 and 18 months of age, usually act somewhat puzzled and continue to search for the first toy. However, Piaget has demonstrated a number of rather strange irregularities in the 1-year-old's search for hidden objects. For example, if a toy is usually hidden in place A and the infant has experienced finding it in place A, he will often search for the toy again at A *even when he has just seen it hidden in place B* (Piaget, 1936/1952). It is as if the child has two memories—one memory of seeing the object hidden (the seeing memory) and another memory of finding it (the action memory). The action memory seems to be stronger than the seeing memory.

Many more experiments in object permanence have demonstrated the bits and pieces of temporal, spatial, and causal concepts that make up the full concept of object permanence. Most researchers believe that object permanence is not formed until the infant is about 18 months of age, with considerable individual variation. The level of locomotive ability is probably quite important, for when the child can crawl and walk, he can more actively pursue his own hypotheses and guesses. If a ball rolls away, he can follow it and find it. If mother is out of sight, he can go find her. He can more actively test the properties of the world around him. Person permanence probably develops slightly earlier than object permanence, but there are the same sets of mental representations, spatial relationships, and causal links that must fuse together into an organizational framework for comprehension of this sensorimotor world in which the child lives. Thus, a seemingly simple assumption —that is, that objects exist when they are out of sight or out of perceptual contact—has generated a series of studies on the nature of the development of the child's thought.

SYMBOLIC REPRESENTATION. Infants must learn to symbolize in some fashion and they begin to do so at an early age. They may smack their lips before the food or bottle reaches their mouths, or they may continue to make eating motions after feeding time is over. They may drop a rattle, yet continue to shake the hand that held it. They may wave bye-bye before they are able to say the word. These actions are the simplest forerunners of symbolic representation.

Imitation is an essential part of the process of symbolic representation. During the second half of the first year and the beginning of the second, children begin to imitate actions that represent ideas. For example, a child may communicate the notion of sleeping by putting his head down on his hands. Language, of course, is the ultimate symbolic system—a system whose common meanings must be learned through imitation.

There are a number of other cognitive developments that take place during the first year or two of life, but these examples should serve to indicate the essential characteristics of the infant's developing sensorimotor intelligence. He is selective; his sensory capacities are well developed; he engages in the sequential process of integration, coordination, and functional subordination of simpler schemata. His first thinking comes directly from action.

As we saw above in the discussion of the visually guided reach, the environment can have an impact upon the development of infants' competencies. Certain behaviors can be accelerated or retarded by the presence or absence of stimulation.

ENVIRONMENTAL STIMULATION AND INFANT COMPETENCIES

Deprivation Studies have shown that being deprived of normal experiences can have a marked and sometimes prolonged effect upon infants' development. Wayne Dennis (1960, 1973; Dennis & Najarian, 1957) found that institutionalized children were severely retarded in even such basic competencies as sitting, standing, and walking when they had no opportunity to practice these skills. And because of the almost total lack of stimulation in their environment, these children were also retarded in terms of language, social skills, and emotional expression.

> . . . as babies they lay on their backs in their cribs throughout the first year and often for much of the second year. . . . Many objects available to most children did not exist. . . . There were no building blocks, no sandboxes, no scooters, no tricycles, no climbing apparatus, no wagons, no teeter-totters, no swings, no chutes. There were no pets or other animals of any sort. . . . they had no opportunities to learn what these objects were. They never saw persons who lived in the outside world, except for rather rare visitors. (Dennis, 1973, pp. 22–23)

In a 15- and 20-year follow-up study, Dennis (1973) found that even those children who were adopted showed some developmental retardation in maturity. Those who remained in institutions showed marked retardation throughout life.

Normal versus Optimal Environments MOTIVATION. Studies have shown that the vast majority of infants seem to be motivated to develop their skills by self-rewarding experiences. For example, children show considerable persistence in learning to walk just for the sheer satisfaction of walking. But tasks seem to be learned not only because they are intrinsically motivated, but also because the environment responds. Infants learn to operate a mobile simply to see the mobile move; they practice motor skills to experience mastery in the task.

An important point here is the need for responsiveness in the environment. In a study which dramatized this need, three groups of infants were presented with three different types of responses (Watson & Ramey, 1972). Infants in the first group were given a mobile that they could control. The second group was given a stabile rather than a mobile. The third group was given a mobile, but the infants could not exercise any control over it. Later, when they were finally given an opportunity to control this mobile, the infants from the third group performed poorly, both immediately and 6 weeks later. They were not motivated to perform because they had learned that their behavior had no effect; the environment did not respond.

TIMING. A massively enriched environment is not necessarily the optimum environment for a child. Instead, a moderately enriched environment, in which stimulating objects are presented to an infant slightly ahead of the time when the infant would normally use those objects, appears to produce the greatest acceleration in development (White & Held, 1966). This point of timing is sometimes called "the match," since there has to be a match between the child's existing cognitive perceptual level and the environmental stimulation. A mild discrepancy between the child's perceptual level and the object—a slightly accelerated stimulation—is helpful in encouraging growth and development. If the discrepancy is too large, the child will become confused and ignore or reject the object.

VARIETY AND COMPLEXITY OF STIMULATION. Although some mothers (and most toy manufacturers) seem to think that a child requires a variety of colorful toys, researchers have found that a complex assortment of playthings is not crucial to a child's perceptual development (Yarrow, Rubenstein, Pedersen, & Jankowski, 1972). If the environment is responsive and stimulation is matched to the child's developmental level, then the child's environment contains the ingredients most vital to his sensorimotor and perceptual development.

THE CARETAKER. In thinking about the importance of the environment to the infant's development, we must not lose sight of the caretaking adult who structures this environment. Cognitive and perceptual stimulation can never really be separated from the stimulation a child receives from those who care for his needs. Indeed, cognitive stimulation most often occurs within the context of a relationship—a subject we shall explore fully in Chapter 10.

Mothers and fathers provide stimulation for their babies when they are feeding, diapering, bathing, and dressing them. Caretakers sing to their babies, talk to them, and play games with them. In much of their interaction with their infants, mothers demonstrate the relationships between objects as well as between people.

Unfortunately, the institutionally reared child who is given only perfunctory attention misses a great deal of this kind of stimulation. With the growing popularity of day-care centers, more and more mothers are turning their infants over to a caretaking situation. Some are excellent, responsive environments, some are not. A day-care center that appears to be a stimulating environment simply because it contains a large variety of expensive toys may be lacking the warm, human relationships that are crucial to a child's development.

SUMMARY

Although we can describe some developmental norms for various stages during the first 2 years of human life, we should not rely on these norms as an absolute standard for a specific child's progress. Within broad limits, human infants vary in when and how they do whatever they do.

Stimulated by the challenge of unraveling infant thought, researchers have devised imaginative methods to observe and understand the development of infants' perceptual competencies and sensorimotor intelligence. They have discovered that the human infant is much more perceptually skilled and competent than we had suspected some 15 or 20 years ago. Three key areas of research have concerned the development of the visually guided reach, object permanence, and symbolic representation.

Researchers have also found that the infant's development is greatly affected by the environment. If the environment is responsive to the child's needs and skills, and if stimulation is timed slightly ahead of a child's developmental level, an acceleration of the developmental process can be achieved with the normal child. When a child is deprived of stimulation and is subjected to an environment that is unresponsive, he will be retarded in his social and emotional development as well as in his perceptual development.

REVIEW QUESTIONS

1. Is the study of human infancy of any value to a person who does not intend to work with children? Explain your answer.

2. If you were asked to develop a test of infants' problem-solving ability, how would you go about it? What physical and perceptual skills of infants would you have to take into account?

3. If you were setting up an infant day-care center, what would be your requirements for the physical environment and for the people you would employ?

SUGGESTED READINGS

Church, J. *Three babies: Biographies of cognitive development.* New York: Random House, 1966. The life history of three babies is described by their mothers with notes and observations by Church.

Dittmann, L. L. (Ed.) *The infants we care for.* Washington, D.C.: National Association for the Education of Young Children, 1973. This paperback presentation sensitively presents the needs and potentialities of young infants. It is particularly appropriate for teachers and paraprofessionals in infant day-care centers.

Gordon, I. J. *Baby learning through baby play.* New York: St. Martins Press, 1970. One of several curriculum books for infant education. Ira Gordon is directing his suggestions for infant play and infant materials to parents and day-care workers.

CHAPTER

10

DEVELOPING RELATIONSHIPS

The environment of the human infant is full of expectations, norms, attitudes, beliefs, values, and ways of doing things. Family members are already aware of their relationships to the neonate; certain social expectations await him; and a cultural heritage, complete with value systems and standards for social development, has existed long before his birth. But the neonate has no concept of his relationship to those around him. He also has no awareness of himself as an individual or as an organism that can interact with his environment. He cannot recognize his image in a mirror. He does not know that his hands are part of him and that he is the agent responsible for their movement. He has no sense of trust or mistrust and no expectations concerning those who care for him. The newborn is not conscious of being male or female.

As we mentioned in Chapter 9, a dramatic series of changes takes place during the first 2 years of human life. The unaware neonate becomes a toddler—aware of being either a boy or a girl, with a beginning appreciation of what the sex designation means in terms of behavior and of others' expectations; aware of various family relationships; aware, in a very broad sense, of what is good and what is bad; aware of his environment and of the ways in which he can act upon it; aware of whether the world around him is responsive or unresponsive to his needs; aware of what he can do for himself and of his competence to seek help when necessary.

Babies come into the world with certain response styles. Some are more sensitive to light or to sudden loud sounds than others are; some react more quickly to discomfort than others do. Some infants are fussy; some are placid; some are active, assertive, and vigorous. But by age 2, the child has elaborated or restricted these basic response styles within a cultural context to produce what we call a personality.

In this chapter we shall look at the process of personality development as it occurs *within relationships*. We shall focus primarily upon first relationships—those that establish patterns for the development of future relationships and for the acquisition of basic attitudes, expectations, and behaviors.

ATTACHMENT

During the last decade, psychologists have applied the term *attachment* to the process of development of the first relationship. Attachment should be thought of as a long process, with some milestones or stages occurring in infancy but with no clean end point. In attachment, the child actively seeks a physical closeness with the person or object that satisfies his wants (Yarrow & Pedersen, 1972).

Attachment Behaviors

The hallmark of attachment is behavior that promotes proximity to or contact with the specific figure or figures to whom the person is attached. Such proximity and contact-promoting behaviors are termed "attachment behaviors." Included are signaling behavior (crying, smiling, vocalizing), orienting behavior such as looking, locomotions relative to another person (following, approaching), and active physical contact behavior (clambering up, embracing, clinging). These behaviors indicate attachment only when they are differentially directed to one or a few persons rather than to others. (Ainsworth, 1973, p. 2)

The important point here is that the infant must act in order for attachment to take place. The infant's initial behavior serves to elicit the mother's nurturant responses, which include not only feeding, diapering, and generally caring for the physical needs of the child, but also such acts as talking, smiling, touching, and nuzzling. The attachment process is a mutual system. The baby's behavior stimulates or releases particular behaviors in the mother, and the mother's behavior sets off responses in the baby.

Why does attachment occur? Is it a conditioned response, or is there an innate need for the establishment of a relationship? For a long while, developmental psychologists thought that a baby formed an attachment to his caretaker only because that person fulfilled the child's primary needs. They thought it a matter of secondary reinforcement in that the child *learned* to associate the caretaker's proximity with reduction of primary drives such as hunger (Sears, 1963). Research—conducted primarily with animals—now indicates, however, that this is only a small part of the picture.

We can probably understand the infant's first relationship with his caretaker better if we look at some of the relationships that other animals have with their mothers. This relationship has been studied very extensively in ducks and geese.

Imprinting

Imprinting refers to the process by which newly hatched birds form a relatively permanent bond with the parent in a comparatively brief period of time. Forty years ago Konrad Lorenz, an Austrian zoologist, observed that goslings began to follow their mother almost immediately after hatching. This bond between the goslings and the parent served a very important function in later protection of the goslings and in teaching them new behaviors. Interestingly enough, Dr. Lorenz also found that orphaned goslings, nurtured by him during the first 24 hours after they hatched, developed a pattern of following *him* rather than another goose. This pattern, too, appeared to be relatively permanent and sometimes annoyingly persistent. Some of Lorenz's graylag geese much preferred to spend the night in his bedroom rather than on the banks of the Danube River (Lorenz, 1952). It was about this time that Lorenz also discovered that graylag geese could not be housetrained!

There is a critical period for imprinting, before and after which this relatively permanent bond cannot be formed. It occurs when the gosling is strong enough to get up and move around, but before it has developed a strong fear of large moving objects. If imprinting is delayed too long, the gosling is either afraid of the model or it simply gives up trying and appears to be limp, tired, and listless.

The goslings, nurtured by Konrad Lorenz during the critical period for imprinting, follow him as they would their mother. (*Tom McAvoy, Time Life-Pictures © Time Inc.*)

It is possible to imprint baby birds to objects that are quite different from the mother. For instance, in a laboratory setting ducks have been imprinted to duck decoys, flashing lights, windup toys, milk bottles, or even to a checkerboard wall (Hess, 1972). However, the strength of this bond is somewhat variable and seems to be related to the activity of the duckling. If the duckling has had to exercise vigorously in the course of imprinting, then the bond is stronger. For example, if the bird experiences some degree of difficulty following the imprinting stimulus, the bond will be strengthened as will .the bird's peeping and vocalizing behaviors. It is also helpful for the imprinting stimulus to be a large moving object. The object should move enough to require some, but not too much, exercise by the baby bird. And if possible, the stimulus should respond with some kind of sound—clucking, or peeping, or humming, for example. Ethologists who study imprinting are concerned with the *triggering* or the *release* of particular kinds of behaviors in the presence of particular kinds of target stimuli. A large moving object, for instance, may be all that is necessary to release the behaviors of following and vocalizing and to begin the process of imprinting. In a natural setting, this triggering or releasing process is mutual. The mother's clucking tends to release peeping, visual scanning, and following behaviors in the duckling. Similarly, the duckling's peeping will trigger the mother's vocalizations (Hess, 1972).

And what does imprinting have to do with attachment behavior in human infants? Mostly it raises questions rather than provides answers. Are there particular aspects of the caretaker that trigger certain behaviors in the human infant? The human face, for instance, seems to trigger a smile. Human caretakers and infants engage in a great deal of mutual vocalization. The duckling vocalizes and follows and, as a result of his own behavior, develops a bond. Does the human infant's behavior function in somewhat the same way? The human infant can signal by crying, smiling, and vocalizing. He can visually scan and follow and later physically follow. He can cling to, grasp, and clamber upon an object. All these look like possible "imprinting" behaviors. Is there a critical period for imprinting in humans? If so, it is probably much, much longer than the period for birds. Most processes in human beings are not nearly so permanent or precise as those for other species. Nevertheless, there is evidence that a relatively long period exists during which this initial relationship needs to take place if normal development of the human being is to occur. Clearly, severe social deprivation of children during the first 3 years of life results in long-term emotional disturbances.

Attachment Behavior in Monkeys   Another important series of studies was done by Harry Harlow on social deprivation in monkeys. Certainly, monkeys are a species closer to humans than goslings are and thus they may tell us more about our own social development. This rather significant series of studies originally occurred somewhat by accident when Harlow was studying learning and concept development in monkeys.

When Harlow (1959) was setting up laboratory conditions which would permit the study of learning in monkeys, he decided that it would be best to rear each young monkey without its mother so that he would be able to control the total learning environment. The mother was an uncontrolled variable. She taught the baby certain skills, and she rewarded and punished certain behaviors. She also served as a model that the baby could imitate. Harlow wanted to get at the basic process of learning, and to do this he felt it necessary to remove the mother from the cage. In doing so, however, he stumbled upon a new and more exciting area of study.

Harlow found the separation of mother and infant extremely difficult. Once it was accomplished, he encountered other, more dramatic problems: some of the monkeys died, and the ones that survived demonstrated highly neurotic behavior. They were withdrawn, jumpy, easily frightened, reluctant to eat, and unwilling to engage in the exploratory, curious, playful behavior of the normal monkey. Many of them showed their disturbed emotional development through repetitive, self-stimulating behavior such as rocking, head-banging, or even self-mutilation.

When raised in cages with bare wire and cloth-covered surrogate mothers, Harlow's infant monkeys developed attachment bonds with their cloth surrogates and would not accept substitutes. (*Harry F. Harlow, University of Wisconsin Primate Laboratory.*)

Although the nutritional and other physical needs of the infant monkeys were being met, something critical for normal development was obviously lacking. When Harlow and his colleagues noticed that their neurotic monkeys would cling to a diaper or cloth pad placed in the cages, they systematically explored the effects of such tactile contact as the possible missing need (Harlow & Harlow, 1962). In one early experiment, infant monkeys were placed in individual cages. Each cage contained two surrogate mothers. One surrogate was bare wire, cylindrical in form and topped with a wooden head. The other was a similar form, covered with terrycloth. Half of the infant monkeys were fed on the bare wire surrogates, the other half were fed on the cloth forms. Regardless of which surrogate supplied their food, all the infant monkeys spent long hours each day clinging to and vocalizing to the cloth forms. When threatened or surprised in any way, they consistently clung to the cloth-covered surrogates before gaining the courage to explore the threat or the novelty. The infant monkeys developed bonds with their cloth surrogates and would not accept substitutes. The object which they looked at, clung to, and vocalized to was the object to which the attachment developed. The source of food seemed irrelevant.

One of the basic ingredients in developing a satisfactory surrogate seemed to be tactile contact and comfort. The baby monkeys needed something to cling to. However, was this sufficient? Certainly, baby monkeys who had surrogate mothers were less afraid of strange environments. After some initial clinging, they were able to branch out and explore strange objects and to gain a certain security from their surrogates. Furthermore, they did not develop the kinds of neurotic, self-stimulating, repetitive behaviors that the infant monkeys without any surrogates had developed. However, these surrogate-raised monkeys did not show completely normal behavior in adulthood. They had great difficulty in establishing relationships with peers, and in many

Peer contact among these infant monkeys at least partially makes up for the deprivation of the infant-mother attachment bond. Mutually responsive social interaction seems crucial for normal monkey development. (*Gordon Coster,* Scientific American, *November 1962, p. 44.*)

cases they did not establish any relationships at all. They could not play normally, nor could they engage in normal sexual behavior. For the most part they were extremely frightened of peer contact and sexual contact, and they proved to be horrendous mothers. After pregnancy by artificial insemination, they did not show normal nurturant behavior toward their own offspring. Despite Harlow's repeated attempts at "psychotherapy" with "normal" adult monkeys, most of these monkeys were unable to make up for the inadequate social bond formed during their first year.

More recent studies in this series have indicated that peer contact among infant monkeys at least partially makes up for the deprivation of the infant-adult attachment bond. Infant monkeys who are raised with surrogate mothers and have adequate opportunity to play with other such infant monkeys develop reasonably normal social behavior. Thus, it seems that mutually responsive social interaction is crucial for normal monkey development. One would suspect that humans, too, are a social species!

The Developmental Course of Attachment

In human infants, attachment occurs over a period of time. A child goes through stages of emotional and social growth which result in the firm establishment of this first relationship. Mary Ainsworth (1973) has charted the course of this development, taking her data from extensive observation of infants in this country as well as in Uganda.

SOCIAL RESPONSIVENESS. In the first 2 or 3 months of life, the infant uses signaling and orienting behaviors (crying, vocalizing, visual following) to establish contact with other human beings. However, his efforts are indiscriminative. He has not yet distinguished between primary caretakers and other people. He will react the same way toward any human face, whether by crying, smiling, or vocalizing. He has not yet discovered the differences in response and attention among the various human beings he has experienced. In a second phase, he begins to recognize familiar figures and to direct his attentions more toward his significant caretakers than toward strangers. This is an intellectual achievement marking the development of a schema for "mother" and a sensitivity to "discrepant" elements.

ACTIVE PROXIMITY SEEKING. At approximately 7 months of age the infant becomes capable of some form of locomotion. He can creep or crawl. In addition, he can hold out his arms to be picked up, cling to or clamber up on a person, and more effectively greet or call someone. Thus the child now has much more voluntary and active control over his attachment. He becomes the initiator in seeking proximity or contact. He can be much more sophisticated and effective in maintaining proximity or contact with the caretaker. It is much easier to conduct research on attachment when the infant has reached this stage of development. The child can actively demonstrate the strength of his attachment as well as his resistance to being separated from the caretaker.

PARTNERSHIP BEHAVIOR. Beyond infancy, the initial attachment continues to develop. Both Bowlby (1969) and Ainsworth (1973) suggest that a partnership begins to form when the child is about 3 years of age. The child becomes aware of his caretaker as a separate person who is important to him. He begins to acknowledge himself and the other person as acting and reacting in a relatively understandable environment. The child also tries to discern what it is that the other person wants, and he attempts to manipulate the other person's goals and modify his own needs in terms of this knowledge. In short, he is working out a partnership in which he and his caretaker can act and react satisfactorily. To a certain extent, the child can anticipate struggle and can precipitate conflict in order to test his own authority. He may know that a flat-out "No!" will elicit a predictable response, just as he is aware that a smile and a hug may pave the way to need fulfillment.

One of the landmarks of the progress of the attachment relationship is the appearance of stranger anxiety or separation anxiety in the child. Because the phenomenon occurs almost universally around the age of 28 weeks, some pediatricians and psychologists refer to it as 7-month anxiety. Babies who have been smiling, welcoming, friendly, outgoing, and accepting, suddenly become shy and fearful in the presence of

ATTACHMENT AND ANXIETY

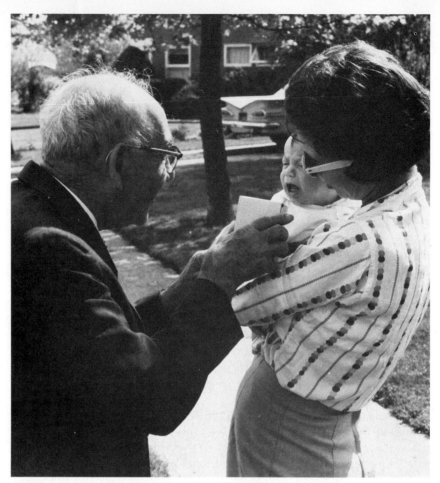

Fear of strangers or fear of separation from their parents often appears in children about the age of 7 months. (*Andrew Lewis Botwick, Monkmeyer.*)

strangers. No traumatic event is necessary; no experience of sudden or harsh separation need take place; no frightening encounter is a prerequisite. Children at this stage of attachment cry, cling, seek proximity to the mother, hang on, and only cautiously turn around to explore a stranger.

If no event is needed to bring on such anxiety, why does it occur, almost without fail, in most children at approximately the same age? Most psychologists see stranger or separation anxiety as a characteristic of the infant's intellectual development. As his cognitive processes mature, he develops schema for the familiar and notices discrepancies from the familiar. He can distinguish mother and father from stranger, and he is aware of the absence of the primary caretaker. When he detects a discrepancy from the known or the expected, he experiences anxiety (Ainsworth, 1967).

If, as we discussed above, the formation of an attachment relationship is an essential part of normal development, and if that relationship progresses through a series of predictable, nearly universal stages, what happens to the child for whom such a relationship does not occur or to the infant whose progress toward attachment is interrupted? What happens to the child who is brought up in an orphanage and is handled by numerous caretakers during the first few years? What happens to the infant who must spend a prolonged time in a hospital? And what about the child who has begun to establish a relationship and is suddenly separated from his primary caretaker?

In Chapter 9 we examined the effects of prolonged institutionalization on the development of cognitive and sensorimotor competencies in infants. Yet the more dramatic and devastating impact of such an environment involves the effect of social deprivation on emotional development. When an infant is cared for by a variety of different people, and when only his most basic physical needs are being met, he is unable to develop an attachment relationship. The mutual responses between child and primary caretaker do not occur consistently; the social interaction that permits expression of emotion is missing (Bowlby, 1960; Dennis, 1973; Spitz, 1966). The result is profound apathy, withdrawal, and generally depressed functioning, all of which have long-term consequences of inadequate personality development.

The child who has formed a full attachment relationship responds quite differently to separation from the primary caretaker than does the child who has never established such a relationship. The "attached" child goes through a series of rather dramatic stages of reaction to both brief or prolonged separation.

John Bowlby (1960) analyzes the separation reaction of hospitalized toddlers as consisting of three stages: protest, despair, and detachment. The first stage of the reaction, protest, is one in which the child refuses to accept separation from the attachment figure. He may cry, scream, kick, bang his head against his bed, and refuse to respond in any way to another person who tries to care for him.

During the second stage, which may come a few hours or even several days after the initial reaction, the child appears to lose all hope. He withdraws and becomes very quiet. If he cries, he does so in a monotonous and despairing tone. His movements and sounds lack the anger of the behavior shown during the first stage.

Eventually, the separated child begins to accept the attention of others around him and appears to have forgotten his misery. If he is visited by his mother, or primary caretaker, his attitude is one of detachment or even disinterest.

> A child living in an institution or hospital who has reached this state will no longer be upset when nurses change or leave. He will cease to show feelings when his parents come and go on visiting day; and it may cause them pain when they realize that, although he has an avid interest in the presents they bring, he has little interest in them as special people. He will appear cheerful and adapted to his unusual

situation and apparently easy and unafraid of anyone. But this socia-bility is superficial: he appears no longer to care for anyone. (Bowlby, 1960, p. 143)

When faced with the first two stages of a child's separation reaction, well-meaning adults often attempt to subdue what they see as inap-propriate behavior. By underestimating the complexity of a young child's emotional reaction, such adults do the child a disservice in their attempts to shortcut the separation response. Just as adults need time to work out their feelings of anger and grief when coming to terms with loss, so too do children need a period in which they can express their almost overwhelming reaction to separation from the most important person in their environment. Only through this expression can they reach a level of detachment that will permit them to survive emotionally in their new situation and eventually form new attachments.

CHILDREARING PATTERNS, ATTACHMENT, AND ANXIETY

Most children, in most cultures, form a basic attachment within the first year of life. Regardless of the cultural prescription for childrearing, most infants go through the phenomenon of undifferentiated social responsiveness and later move into an attachment relationship with a specific caretaking figure. Accompanying this developing relationship is a stranger or separation anxiety that occurs around the age of 7 or 8 months. Infants learn schemata for those things and people that are familiar, and discrepancies in familiar patterns produce anxiety. As we pointed out above, the development of these schemata and the con-sequent recognition of discrepancies are cognitive processes that are part of the formation of the attachment relationship rather than a result of it.

Although the various stages of development of the attachment relationship occur fairly consistently across cultures, the intensity of attachment and anxiety during this period varies according to character-istics of the childrearing practices and the relationship of parent and child.

Exclusivity

Infants who have a relatively exclusive relationship with a parent tend to show an intense stranger anxiety and separation anxiety. They also show these anxieties at an earlier age than do infants whose relation-ship with the caretaker has not been so exclusive (Ainsworth, 1967). If a child spends almost 24 hours a day with the parent, sleeping in the same room at night and being carried in a sling on the parent's back during the day, the intensity of the separation reaction is likely to be dramatic. On the other hand, the child who has experienced a number of different caretakers from birth on tends to accept strangers or separation with much less anxiety (Maccoby & Feldman, 1972).

This difference in reaction can be explained, at least in part, on the basis of the discrepancy hypothesis discussed above. If a child develops a schema for the familiar, then the infant whose immediate environment includes only the parent would find any other figure discrepant and therefore anxiety-producing. The infant to whom a variety of people are familiar, however, might be less anxious about seeing yet another face.

An interesting example of this phenomenon is found in the kibbutzim of Israel, where children are reared collectively and experience relatively limited time periods with their parents (Maccoby & Feldman, 1972; Spiro, 1965). Although these children do seek proximity in all the ways that American home-reared children do, and although they clearly view their parents as special persons, their attachment behaviors and anxiety reactions are somewhat less intense than those of children reared in the home. However, stranger and separation anxieties are not absent, and if a radically discrepant situation is created, the anxiety response is intense.

PATTERNS OF CHILD CARE.

A father kisses his 1-year-old goodnight in an Israeli kibbutz. (*UPI.*)
In this Tokyo family, the children may be attended to by a variety of relatives of different generations. (*UPI.*)
A Ugandan mother at work with her child. (*George Holton, Photo Researchers.*)

The Quality of Relationship	In her studies of children in Uganda, Mary Ainsworth (1967) found that children who showed the highest degree of attachment-separation behavior had a strongly responsive relationship with their mothers. Kibbutzim-reared children were also found to develop strong attachments when there was intense mother-child interaction (Spiro, 1965). The actual time mothers spend with their children is not by itself enough to stimulate strong attachment; it is the quality of the time spent that makes the difference.

Research on infant smiling provides a good example of the effect of the responsiveness of the environment on the development of attachment behavior (McCall, 1972; Watson, 1972). Both smiling and attempts at vocalization can be increased by the responsiveness of the caretaker (Rheingold, Gewirtz, & Ross, 1959). In one rather unpleasant experiment, it was shown that the amount of infant smiling can be decreased if the caretaker ignores the infant or simply looks at him and refuses to respond (Brackbill & Koltsova, 1967). While this kind of manipulation of human subjects is not recommended, the results of the study do serve to illustrate the importance of social responsiveness in the development of the human infant.

We have focused on smiling because it is one of the infant's first responses through which he can attempt the mutuality upon which attachment is built. It provides him with an opportunity to test his environment and find out whether it is responsive to him. He can act and elicit a response, or elicit no response. Whatever the case, he will have discovered something about the nature of those around him. The quality of the mother-child relationship begins to make itself felt through such early mutual behaviors.

CHILDREARING AND PERSONALITY DEVELOPMENT

Both parents and researchers often ask the wrong questions about childrearing. They ask very specific questions: whether to breast-feed or bottle-feed, when or how to wean a baby, whether to pick up a baby immediately when he cries or let him cry for a while, whether to allow thumb-sucking or blanket carrying, what to do about a temper tantrum, when to toilet train and how. If we look at each one of these specific practices all by itself, we tend to get rather mixed evidence. It is hard to interpret the answers. One must often conclude that it does not matter much whether a child sucks his thumb or not, or if he carries a blanket. Yet if we look cross-culturally at the widely divergent patterns of childrearing, such practices clearly do matter. These patterns make an enormous difference in terms of later personality development. The manner in which we convey our culture to our children, beginning at infancy, is not at all subtle. From their birth, we are working to convey to our infants attitudes and values about the nature of their bodies, the acceptability of self-stimulation, the degree of physical closeness that is desirable, the amount of dependency we will allow, and the goodness or badness of their behavior or of their basic nature as human beings.

These attitudes and values implemented in a myriad of childrearing practices have a very pervasive and potent effect on personality development.

It is in the context of these broad, cross-cultural, childrearing patterns that we shall look at specific childrearing practices. It is helpful, however, to look at three particular dimensions of childrearing practices, at least as they affect the infancy period. First, there are the initial two stages of Erikson's theory which were presented in Chapter 2. What is the infant learning about the basic trustworthiness of his social environment? Is the environment consistent and predictable? Is it responsive to his needs? Second, we should examine how the child's attempts at autonomy are met. When he begins to get up and move around, to do things for himself, to control his body, to try to control his environment —how are these needs satisfied? And third, during infancy, we can look at the set of childrearing practices as they affect the child's growing self-awareness. Children who are heavily swaddled during the first year or who are bound to a cradle board, for instance, do not experience the same kind of self-exploration of their bodies as do children who have relatively free movement. Children who have no access to a mirror do not discover their own image. But there are much more pervasive attitudes about the child's body and about himself that he is learning very early.

If we look cross-culturally at the kind of care given infants, we can see quite dramatic differences both in the approach and the result. One study, for example, suggests a difference between the attitude of the American mother toward her infant and that of the Japanese mother (Caudill & Weinstein, 1969). In general, the American mother tends to view the infant as passive and dependent, and her goal is to make him independent. The average Japanese mother, however, seems to view the child from the opposite direction. She sees the child as an independent organism who needs to be brought into a dependency relationship within the family.

Such differences in attitude often result in quite different childrearing practices. The American infant typically is put in a crib in his own room, while the Japanese infant usually shares a bedroom with the parents. The Japanese mother usually responds quickly when the baby cries and she feeds him on a self-demand schedule. The American mother tends to let her child cry for a short while in an effort to get him on a regular, more mature feeding schedule. The Japanese mother may feel the need to soothe and quiet her baby often, while the American mother may want to stimulate her baby to smile and vocalize. As a result of these different approaches, the Japanese baby quickly becomes less vocal and less active than the American baby.

FEEDING AND WEANING. One of the first decisions for any mother is whether to breast-feed or bottle-feed her infant. Over the past century, advocates of one position or the other have argued persuasively that one form of feeding was markedly superior to the other (Sunley, 1955;

Child Care and Nurturance

Wolfenstein, 1951). But the research evidence gives no clear indication that either breast-feeding or bottle-feeding is distinctly superior. There is a mutuality in breast-feeding that is hard to match in bottle-feeding. Also, there are certain antibodies for beginning immunity that seem to be transmitted from mother to child in breast-feeding. However, babies thrive under both feeding methods. No mother should feel guilty because she has selected one method rather than the other. The nutritional components of formulas and the breast milk of healthy, well-fed mothers are probably quite similar. The important question concerns how the selected feeding pattern fits into the total pattern of care for the infant. Feeding is one way of expressing both the physical and the psychological closeness between caretaker and child.

In some cultures, the transition period between the birth of the infant and the establishment of separation from the mother lasts for 3 or more years. Feeding is an integral part of the physical and psychological closeness in the prolonged relationship (Mead & Newton, 1967). Some children sleep close to their mothers, are carried around in a sling during most of the first year, and are breast-fed until the age of 3 (Goldberg, 1972). In other cultures—particularly in America—some infants experience an almost immediate separation from the mother: separate bed, separate room, early weaning. Somewhat in jest, Mead and Newton describe the transition period for some American babies as lasting less than a minute—until the umbilical cord is cut!

Weaning is the other side of the same pattern. When and how it is done may have a dramatic impact on the personality development of the child. In some cultures where weaning occurs quite late, the baby is actually separated from the mother (Goldberg, 1972). The baby is sent to spend time with another relative to help him break the physical bond with his mother. In other cultures, the weaning period may begin at 8 months or earlier but then extend for weeks or months or years, in a gradual process allowing the child some initiative (Sunley, 1955; Wolfenstein, 1951). Infants who experience close skin contact only during feeding may find weaning more traumatic than infants who have been fully clothed during feeding. The psychological significance of weaning depends on the degree of change it causes in the closeness of the parent-child relationship.

THUMB-SUCKING, BLANKETS, AND OTHER COMFORT DEVICES. Although considerable research has been devoted to thumb-sucking and other comfort devices, remarkably few definitive conclusions have been reached about them. Levy (1934; 1938) did a series of studies which indicated that puppies with very little sucking experience needed to suck and chew a wide variety of alternative objects. Conversely, puppies which were fed with a small nipple and had to suck hard to be fed did much less nonnutritive sucking. On the other hand, a study of human babies who were cup-fed from the beginning seemed to indicate that human infants without any sucking experience did not develop a need to suck. However, infants who did some sucking but had relatively little experience at it tended to need some additional sucking (Davis, Sears, Miller, & Brodbeck, 1948). For the most part, sucking experience seems to be a normal and natural need. Yet cross-culturally, parents have responded to this need in many different ways (Goldberg, 1972; Mead, 1955; Mead & Calas, 1955; Rebelsky, 1967). There have been historical periods when thumb-sucking was considered dirty and quite harmful to the child's general personality development. Elaborate devices, as well as simple sleeves, were used to cover the child's hands and to prevent thumb-sucking. Fortunately, this era of strong fear of pleasure or fear of sense exploration seems to be over. Some parents

Children use a wide variety of comfort devices and comfort behaviors which serve the purpose of providing familiar stimulation. (*Alice Kandell, Rapho/Photo Researchers.*)

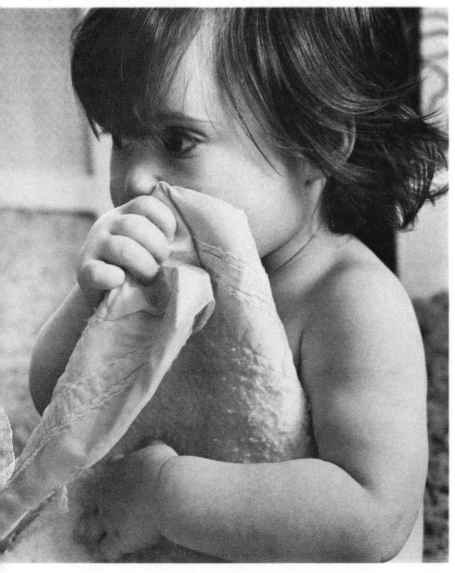

give their child a pacifier to suck on the assumption that the child can more easily give up the pacifier than he can give up his thumb! However, most children who use either thumbs or pacifiers give them up as regular comfort devices by the end of the preschool years. Children who are avid thumb-suckers or avid comfort seekers generally have other kinds of needs which are not being met. The evidence that thumb-sucking causes major damage to the dental arch is mixed. Most of this damage seems to occur with avid thumb-suckers who are still sucking at age 5, 6, or 7, when the second set of teeth emerges.

Children use a wide variety of comfort devices and comforting behaviors. Favorite blankets and toys, special feeling objects, twisting and rubbing their hair or their skin—all serve much the same purpose of providing familiar stimulation. Parental reactions to comfort devices are important because they directly convey certain values and attitudes. These reactions tell us the parents' attitudes about the child's body, their acceptance of the child's self-stimulation, the degree of closeness and dependency that they will allow. Furthermore, the child is learning from his parents' reactions whether he is good or bad, when he should feel anxious or guilty, and when he can feel comfortable and secure. He is learning a great deal more than merely whether or not he should suck his thumb or carry his blanket.

| Autonomy, Independence, and Discipline | By the time the human infant is 1 year old, he has learned the guidelines of acceptability, of his dependency needs, and his need for physical closeness through parental attitudes. But when the child is 2 years old, the parents must cope with a whole new set of issues. Again, their personalities, as well as their cultural background, will affect their attitudes and methods for dealing with the toddler. To appreciate the diversity of problems facing the parents of a toddler, let us consider the typical 2-year-old: |

He is in the process of exploring the qualities and possibilities of almost everything in his environment. He discovers the delight of pulling the toilet paper roll—endlessly. He uses pencil and crayon on walls, floors, and furniture. He enjoys picking up small things, from cigarette butts to crumbs to pebbles; many of these things will be given a taste test. He wedges his body into, under, or over any space that looks interesting. He picks up and carries around glass figurines as well as toys. He alternates between clinging dependence and daring exploration, often within the space of a 5-minute period. He walks and runs and climbs for the sheer feel of walking and running and climbing. He is docile and eager to please one minute and is presenting a challenge to authority and routine the next. He wants to feed and dress himself on one occasion and wants everything done for him on the next. He may rebel at bedtime, protest at bathtime, refuse to have his shoes or snowsuit put on, or reject a food he has always enjoyed. He learns to say "No!"

How do parents deal with the activity and challenge of the toddler?

How are limits set? And what about the seemingly constant attempts of the child to test the limits of authority? Should they be indulged? Is there a danger of producing a willful personality who is unresponsive to the needs and rights of others? If challenges are not permitted, is there a danger of producing a frustrated, anxious, or overly submissive personality? Some parents buy the latest book on childrearing and slavishly follow the instructions, even when those instructions blatantly disagree with their own beliefs or life-style. Other parents react to their children and the children's needs purely on the basis of their own child-hood memories—either thoughtlessly repeating or dogmatically rejecting the patterns of their own parents.

Probably there is no one best method of childrearing that can be used by every family everywhere. However, Burton White (1971) has produced a profile of what he thinks is one pattern of effective parenting. Effective mothers are not necessarily full-time caretakers. Many very good mothers have part-time jobs, and the rest are far too busy to spend long stretches of time in close direction of their children's activities. They generally allow, and even encourage, a great deal of childish exploration. They provide a safe environment, they set clear limits, and they do not always drop whatever they are doing to answer a child's request. Yet they provide a rich educational environment and many bits and pieces of learning.

Primarily, the effective mother acts as a consultant for the child's behavior and as an architect for the child's environment. She is available to explain a new phenomenon; to provide language for a new experience or object; to reinforce exploration and discovery; and to set limits designed to protect the child from physical harm and help him adjust to social requirements. At the same time, she provides an environment that is stimulating and evocative of both cognitive growth and physical development. Indeed, some researchers have found that the mother's reaction to, and interaction with, the child between the ages of 10 months and 1½ years will have a dramatic and lasting effect upon his cognitive and emotional development throughout childhood (Pines, 1971).

Burton White's profile of the effective mother presents only one pattern of middle-class American childrearing. It is a translation of some of the broad American cultural values into the actual behaviors of a parent as she interacts with her child. It is certainly not the only effective style. Nevertheless, it illustrates that important things are learned in this childrearing pattern. The child acquires a particular, active, exploratory learning style. He is developing a sense of confidence in approaching problems, a clarity in defining limits, an ability to depend on himself, and a sense of success and mastery in finding out about the world. These kinds of personality dimensions and learning approaches may affect his learning for a considerable period of time.

TOILET TRAINING. Although a great deal of the early research in developmental psychology focused upon the methods and effects of toilet training, recent studies view this issue as important only in the context of the total approach to childrearing. Toilet training is only one of a number of ways in which parents deal with children in terms of handling their own bodies, handling self-exploration, and handling needs for autonomy.

Parents who are severe and harsh in toilet training are usually just as severe in other areas which have to do with self-mastery and independence, such as feeding, dressing, and general exploration. The parent who demands of the child early and total mastery of bowel and bladder, and who regards "accidents" as intolerable and dirty, will probably view the child's breakage of household items, exploration of places and objects, and even self-feeding attempts in the same light.

Although some studies have shown that a child is ready for training between the ages of $1\frac{1}{2}$ and 2 years, the exact timing of such training is not necessarily crucial (Mead & Calas, 1955). Some children appear to be trained before $1\frac{1}{2}$ years; however, it is usually the mother who is trained to anticipate the child's functions and rush him to the bathroom at the appropriate time. Other children are not toilet trained until the age of 3. The important point is to encourage the child to achieve this kind of autonomy and independence when he is physically able to control his bladder and bowels, when he is able to communicate his needs, and when he is able to wait briefly after signaling his needs. Ideally, this should be done without threat of punishment and with as little fuss and bother as possible.

As with other routines such as going to bed, eating, and getting dressed, toilet habits will be used by many toddlers as a basis for testing limits of authority. The child who appears to be absolutely reliable in signaling his needs and producing in the bathroom may suddenly begin to have accidents. There may, of course, be a physical or emotional reason for this (teething, a cold, a sudden separation from mother), but in many cases it may be simply an attempt to demonstrate autonomy: "I control my own body and its functions, and I can withhold something that is very important to those around me!" The parent who reacts to such rebellion with alarm, confusion, or anger just confirms the child's conflict over power. The parent who reacts matter-of-factly will probably convince the child that deliberate accidents are not terribly impressive. Again, the parent's reaction to such occurrences will probably be consistent with reactions to the child's other attempts at autonomy and independence.

DISCIPLINE. How does a parent go about setting limits on a child's behavior? Some parents, afraid that any kind of control on the child's behavior will prevent creative exploration and independence, helplessly stand by while the 2-year-old does whatever he pleases whenever he wants. Discipline, when it comes, is often a harsh overreaction to the parents' own feelings of frustration. Other parents, determined not to "spoil" their child and convinced that their 2-year-old should act like a responsible little citizen, set so many limits on behavior that the child literally cannot do anything right.

Although it is easy, from this vantage point, to see the errors in these extremes, it is not quite so simple to provide a set of rules that will be effective for every occasion. For example, we could propose a rule that parents must encourage exploration and manipulation. But what do we do about the child whose favorite form of play is sticking pins into electrical outlets? Obviously, any such rule must be tempered with common sense; and guidelines must take into consideration the child's needs for safety as well as his needs for independence and creative experience. The child who is permitted to run, jump, and climb in the house may also be taught to walk quietly, holding someone's hand, or to submit to being picked up and held in public places.

The child who has developed a strong attachment relationship, and whose needs are met through loving interaction with an adult, is neither spoiled by too much attention nor frightened or threatened by the reasonable limits that are set. He is stronger and more confident because he has a trustworthy basic relationship from which he can venture forth into independence.

During the first year of life, the child is discovering himself and forming concepts about who and what he is. He discovers his voice and how to use it; he finds his hands and feet and gradually learns how to make them work in order to achieve certain goals; he learns to recognize his image in a mirror and enjoys testing and exploring his own responses. Through observing the behavior of those around him, he learns what his own behavior should be. Certain actions are expected and approved; certain other actions are punished or ignored. An awareness of sex role is beginning, and cultural expectations for fulfillment of the appropriate role are already being felt (Goldberg & Lewis, 1969).

Development of Self-Awareness

During the second year, the child's language has considerable self-reference. He knows his name and uses it, often describing his needs and feelings in the third person. The words "me" and "mine" are important in his vocabulary, and his concept of ownership is clearly and strongly acted out. Even in families in which sharing is emphasized and ownership is minimized, toddlers show fairly extensive evidence of a feeling of possessiveness. It may be that they need to establish a concept of ownership in order to round out their definition of self and all that it entails. Sharing and cooperation come more easily after toddlers are confident about what is theirs.

Self-awareness comes from self-exploration, from cognitive maturity, and from reflections about self. The toddler can often be heard talking to himself, admonishing himself ("No, Billy don't touch") and rewarding himself ("Me good boy!"). He incorporates cultural and social expectations into his self-reflections as well as into his behavior and begins to make judgments about himself and others in light of these expectations. If he is nurtured by consistent, loving interaction with the attachment figure in an environment that he can freely explore and begin to control, he becomes able to make valid predictions about the world around him. He can strive confidently and eagerly for independence, secure in the knowledge that he is an acceptable, competent individual.

SUMMARY Through studies of imprinting in birds and social deprivation in monkeys, researchers have found that the early establishment of a strong attachment relationship is essential to healthy personality development. In the human infant, this kind of relationship develops out of a series of social and emotional stages, culminating in the formation of a partnership. By the third year, the child begins to see the attachment figure as an individual separate from himself, with a point of view that may differ from his own.

The development of the attachment relationship is dependent upon interaction—that is, mutual response—between mother and child. Not only what a mother does, but also what the infant does, will affect the emotional growth of the child. The exclusivity and responsiveness of the relationship, together with the values and attitudes the mother brings to feeding, weaning, thumb-sucking, toilet training, and discipline, have a dramatic and lasting impact upon the personality development of the child.

Through a child's behavior and the emergence of language, a gradual growth toward self-awareness can be seen. He learns who he is and how he fits into his environment. He begins to make judgments about himself and the world, and the nature of those judgments is affected by the strength and quality of his attachment relationship.

REVIEW QUESTIONS 1. Why do psychologists depend so heavily on animal studies when investigating the development of the human infant? Would it make more sense to use human subjects for such investigations?

2. Review the sections of the chapter which discuss social deprivation and separation. How could this information be helpful to a person working in a hospital or a day-care center?

3. Examine one of the currently popular manuals on child care. Do you agree or disagree with the advice given for feeding, toilet training, and disciplining a child? Why?

SUGGESTED READINGS Bowlby, J. *Child care and the growth of love.* New York: Penguin. Bowlby collects many of the studies on the effects of institutionalization on infants. In very readable style he presents the needs of the infant for a stable and responsive relationship with a caretaking adult.

Keister, M. E. *The good life for infants and toddlers.* New York: Harper & Row, 1970. Mary Elizabeth Keister directed an ideal infant day-care center. The infants in this day-care facility developed as well as, and in many cases better than, control infants raised in families. Keister presents in sensible, readable style the important components of good day care.

Sidel, R. *Women and child care in China: A firsthand report.* New York: Hill and Wang, 1972. Ruth Sidel presents a glimpse of another style of collective childrearing. This book is attractively illustrated with numerous photographs.

PART IV:
AGES TWO TO SIX: THE PRESCHOOL CHILD

CHAPTER

11

LANGUAGE: THE BRIDGE FROM INFANCY

TOMMY: Sally broke the toy, didn't she?
MOTHER: Yes, dear, she did.
TOMMY: I don't break toys. I'm a good boy, amn't I?
MOTHER: "I'm a good boy, *aren't* I?
TOMMY: Nah. You're a *girl!*

Even newborn infants can communicate. It doesn't take long for them to discover how to let their parents know that they are hungry, wet, or bored. By the age of about 1 year, children begin to talk, and by age 4½ most have developed amazing verbal competence. Of course, their vocabulary is limited and their grammar far from perfect, but their unconscious grasp of language structure is truly remarkable. They not only know the words with which to designate things and communicate thoughts but also have a very sophisticated understanding of the rules governing the combinations and uses of these words.

The complexity and originality of the 4½-year-old's speech are perhaps best illustrated by the *tag question,* which is a direct statement followed by a tag, or request to confirm the statement: *Sally broke the toy, didn't she?* This apparently simple question actually involves a number of grammatical processes. In order to form the tag *didn't she,* Tommy had to understand several different rules. He had to know how to copy, or supply, the correct subject pronoun for *Sally,* how to supply the auxiliary verb (the proper form of *do*), how to negate that auxiliary verb, and how to invert the word order of the auxiliary verb and pronoun. Somewhat younger children may have the general idea of the tag question but may not yet be able to master all the grammatical processes. Thus, they might say, "Sally broke the toy, unh?"

Of course, young children do not speak with perfect grammar, but sometimes their errors can help us understand the inductive processes they use. Tommy has never heard his parents say "amn't I," and yet by following the rules he has formulated independently, he has arrived at this form. There is nothing wrong with his logic; the form just happens to be incorrect.

LANGUAGE
Aspects of Language

The acquisition of language is an extremely involved process. Perhaps better than any other single accomplishment it illustrates the incredible complexity and unlimited potential of the human organism, and for this reason it is a particularly fascinating area of psychological development. To fully understand the phenomenon, we should first be aware of the various elements involved in it.

Essentially, language can be broken down into four major aspects: phonemes, morphemes, syntax, and semantics. *Phonemes* are the smallest units, the basic sounds—vowel and consonant—that combine to form words. *Morphemes* are the minimal units of meaning—the basic words, prefixes, and suffixes. The sentence *Mommy warmed the bottles* can be divided into six morphemes: *Mommy, warm, ed, the, bottle,* and *s*. Those able to stand alone (*Mommy, warm, the, bottle*) are free morphemes; those that must be attached (the past-indicator *ed* and the plural *s*) are bound morphemes. Every language has a grammar—that is, a complicated set of rules for building words (*morphology*) as well as for combining words to form phrases and sentences (*syntax*). In English, however, grammar is primarily concerned with syntax and the two terms are often used interchangeably. *Semantics,* which refers to meanings, is the final—and broadest—aspect of language. Inherent definitions of words are only part of the picture; syntax also conveys meaning.

When children first begin to speak, they learn single words. But soon they combine these words, and even their earliest syntax—the way they form their first two-word utterances—has its own meaning. By studying children's developing speech we can learn a great deal about the development of their concepts. For example, when a little girl utters the simple phrase *Mommy's dress,* we may infer that she not only knows who Mommy is and what a dress is but has also grasped the possessive relationship. Even a younger child who has not yet mastered the possessive form *'s* may have the idea and attempt to convey it through word order, simply saying, "Mommy dress." That same child may point to her favorite party dress and say, "Mommy dress," meaning, "Mommy, I want to wear that dress" or "Mommy, dress me." By studying the speech of three young children between the ages of 19 and 21 months, Lois Bloom (1970) discovered simplified expression of the following grammatical relationships: subject-object (*Mommy pigtail*), genitive (*Kathryn sock*), attributive (*bread book*), subject-locative (*sweater chair*), and conjunctive (*umbrella boot*). Quite a repertoire for children under 2 years of age!

Children between the ages of 12 and 18 months form numerous con-

TABLE 6 EXAMPLES OF CHILDREN'S SIMPLIFIED EXPRESSIONS

SIMPLIFIED EXPRESSION	RELATIONSHIP	POSSIBLE ADULT TRANSLATION
Mommy pigtail	Subject-object	Mommy make me a pigtail
Kathryn sock	Genitive	Kathryn's sock
Bread book	Attributive	The book about making bread
Sweater chair	Subject-locative	The sweater is on the chair
Umbrella boot	Conjunctive	Take my umbrella and boots

Many children's simplified expressions may be ambiguous and have several possible expansions with the correct meaning depending on context. For example,
"Mommy pigtail" may mean "Mommy has a pigtail"
or "Mommy's pigtail"
or "Mommy make me a pigtail"
or "Mommy is making a pigtail."

Source: Bloom, L. *Language development: Form and function in emerging grammars.* Cambridge, Mass.: The M.I.T. Press, 1970, 54, 56, 60, and 61.

cepts about the world around them. When a toddler points to his bottle and says, "See bottle," he is acknowledging its existence. If his mother puts it away he may say, "All gone bottle" or "Where bottle?" indicating that he knows it exists even if he cannot see it. Similarly, when he is thirsty he may say, "More bottle," demonstrating the notion of recurrence. These abstract ideas of absence and recurrence are really very sophisticated. Although the child's syntax is not yet fully developed, it is expressive of a number of highly complex cognitive processes (Brown, 1973).

The Processes of Language Learning

Just how do human beings progress from crying to babbling to speaking the infinite forms of adult language? In recent years a great deal of research has been devoted to this question, both for its own sake and for the insight an answer might give into other areas of learning. There has been much controversy and little agreement as to precisely how the process works, but it is possible to divide the numerous theories into four major groups, each emphasizing one of four processes: imitation, reinforcement, innate language structure, and cognitive development. Probably all four theoretical approaches are at least partially valid.

IMITATION. It is evident that imitation plays a large part in language learning. Children's first words—usually simple labels—are obviously learned by hearing and imitating. In fact, most early vocabulary must be learned in this way; children cannot invent words and make themselves understood. But the development of syntax is not so easily explained. No doubt some phrases result from imitation, but such forms as *amn't I* and *all gone bottle* are clearly original. It is unlikely that children have heard their parents speak this way. Even when parents use baby talk or attempt to correct their children's errors, the children tend to adhere to their own consistent speech patterns for which there are no immediate models.

REINFORCEMENT. As we have seen in previous chapters, reinforcement is a powerful learning device, and this probably holds true for certain aspects of language acquisition. Certainly, children are influenced by their parents' reactions to their speech. Smiles, hugs, and increased attention will encourage learning to some extent. Also, when words produce favorable results, children are likely to repeat them. If an infant calls "Mommy" and she comes, or if he says "Cookie" and gets one, he will use these words again. But reinforcement does not seem sufficient to explain the acquisition of syntax. As we know, much of children's speech is original and has never been reinforced. Even if some forms are encouraged and others discouraged, it simply would not be possible to reinforce all correct forms and extinguish all incorrect ones. Also, especially when children first begin to talk, parents tend to reinforce any speech at all, however unintelligible or incorrect. Even when parents are more discriminating, they are likely to respond to content rather than form. If a child says, "I eated my peas," his parents will

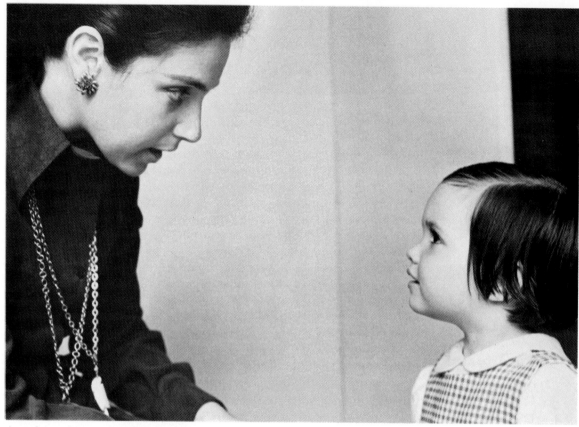

A mother and 3-year-old conversing. (*Alice Kandell, Rapho/Photo Researchers.*)

probably praise him—unless his statement is not true, in which case they will no doubt call his attention to the vegetables remaining on his plate.

INNATE LANGUAGE STRUCTURE. Linguist Noam Chomsky (1959) rejects reinforcement theory, maintaining that language is acquired through innate knowledge. He believes that at birth, every human being is equipped with an intrinsic mental structure for acquiring language. This language acquisition device (LAD) makes it possible for children to selectively process linguistic data from their environment and formulate a generative grammar, from which they create language. Thus, children hear people talk, they induce rules, and they form their own language according to those rules. This process follows a developmental sequence; children can assimilate certain data before others. But according to Chomsky, at least some of the basics of language are pre-programmed into the human organism.

This theory is not without merit. For one thing, it takes into account the incredible complexity of human language. For another, it points out the inadequacy of simple imitation and reinforcement theories.

However, Chomsky's argument does not really explain the process of language learning. In a sense, his argument is a circular one; he claims that we learn language because we are prewired to learn language.

COGNITIVE DEVELOPMENT. The fourth major theory of language acquisition explains the phenomenon in terms of developing concepts and relationships. This view is supported by the fact that basic grammatical structures are not present in earliest speech but develop progressively, leading the theorists to conclude that they depend on prior cognitive development (Bloom, 1970). Thus, a regular speech pattern will not emerge before the child has grasped the concept behind it. Between the ages of 1 and 4½, children are actively constructing their own grammar, gradually approaching the full grammar of the adults around them. But at any given time, children are capable of expressing only those concepts that they have mastered.

At the present, no one language acquisition theory seems adequate. But as we have seen above, all four points of view have some merit as complementary explanations for certain aspects of the language learning process.

THE COURSE OF
LANGUAGE
DEVELOPMENT
From Vocalization to
Words

Infants begin to vocalize at birth. At first their "language" is just an undifferentiated howl; but soon they develop a whole repertoire of cries, and at about 6 weeks they are making a variety of cooing sounds. By 6 months most babies are babbling—stringing together a wide range of sounds, drawing them out, cutting them off, and varying the pitch and rhythm. They are discovering their vocal cords, and they enjoy playing with the sounds of their own voices. Early variations appear to be random, but later there seems to be conscious control—purposeful repetition, elongation, and pausing—in a kind of self-imitating pseudo-talk known as *iteration*.

Most early vocalization consists of vowel sounds. But as early as the second month, infants form a number of consonants, as well as clicks, gurgles, grunts, and other sounds, some of which are extraneous to their parents' native language. The number of phonemes expands tremendously during the first year; but toward the end of that period there is a phonemic constriction as infants produce more often the sounds that appear in their native language and drop some of the extraneous ones.

During the second part of their child's first year, many parents hear something suspiciously like *ma-ma* or *da-da* and report that their precocious infant has spoken his first words. Usually, however, these are chance repetitions of sounds and have no real meaning. Around this time, the child's babbling takes on inflections and patterns very much like those of the parents. In fact, the babbling begins to sound so much like adult speech that we may strain to listen, thinking that perhaps it

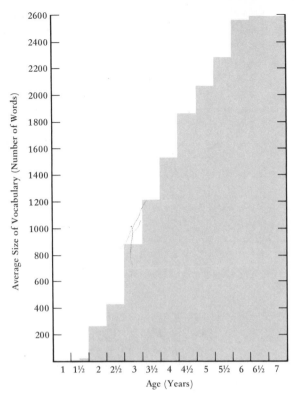

Figure 8 The average size of vocabulary of children from ages 1 to 7. (*Adapted from Smith, M. E. An investigation of the development of the sentence and the extent of vocabulary in young children.* University of Iowa Studies in Child Welfare, *1926, 3 (5), 268–269.*)

is coherent language. This highly developed babbling is what Arnold Gesell has termed *expressive jargon*.

Just how important is babbling? Is it necessary as practice for speaking? Learning theorists watch babbling closely because they feel that it is shaped in the same way as speech—through reinforcement—and so may be used by mothers to speed up their infants' language learning. The mothers can imitate the babbling and play mutual imitation games, generally encouraging their children to imitate them. The theory is that this tendency to imitate will be carried over to words. While it does seem likely that such verbal play will enhance babbling, there is little clear evidence that it is basic to speech. In fact, there is some rather convincing evidence to the contrary. R. Collard (1974) cites the case of an infant who was unable to babble during the second half of the first year because of a tracheal obstruction. The condition was repaired and the child began to speak meaningful, well-articulated words at the normal age, with very limited babbling practice.

Even while infants are babbling, they are acquiring a receptive vocabulary—that is, an understanding of certain words and commands. Cognitive theorists feel that this comprehension is extremely significant, since it is closely linked to the concept development they believe essential to language production. To support this belief, Bernard Friedlander (1970) cites P. Carlson and M. Anisfeld's inventory of a 2-year-old's speech. Here, Friedlander isolates numerous "indicators that the emerging regularities in the child's speech were based on his listening experience, combined with observation of nonverbal cues" (1970, p. 37). For example, when the boy's mother burned her finger and he heard his brother ask, "What did Mommy do?" he repeated, "Mommy do?" This was the first time he had used the phrase. Later his mother swatted a fly and he asked, "Mommy do?" He had generalized the form and retained it. Friedlander believes that this correct generalization was the result of substantial practice in listening and watching.

It seems likely that both babbling and receptive language are closely related to actual language production. But just how essential they are remains to be seen. The critical studies do not yet exist.

From Words to Sentences

Regardless of babbling and receptive prowess, most children utter their first words by the end of the first year. During the next 3 or 4 years they make tremendous progress, as single words give way to two-word, then three-word, then increasingly longer and more complex grammatical structures. This development follows a regular and predictable sequence, not just in English but in every language. Dan I. Slobin (1972) and his colleagues have studied language acquisition in many countries and have discovered patterns that are remarkably consistent from culture to culture.

Throughout the world, infants' first utterances are single words—most often nouns and usually names of the people, things, or animals in the immediate environment. In the beginning, all children are strictly limited to one word at a time; they simply do not have the ability to make combinations. Some psycholinguists feel that despite this linguistic restriction, children are perfectly capable of conceiving full sentences and their early utterances are actually *holophrastic speech*—single words meant to convey complex ideas. Thus, in different contexts, with different intonation and gestures, *mama* may mean "I want my mother" or "Mama, tie my shoe" or "There she is, my mama." Other psycholinguists warn against overinterpretation of brief utterances.

When 2-year-olds begin to combine words, they are limited to two-word utterances. They may say "Mommy see" and "See truck," but they are not capable of putting the phrases together to say, "Mommy see truck." It is almost as if there is an unwritten law that will not allow them to put three words together. Gradually, children increase the length of their utterances, but at each stage there seems to be a very firm constraint on the number of words, or thoughts, in a sentence. The result is what Roger Brown (1965) calls *telegraphic speech*. Like penny-pinching adults sending cables, children retain high-information words and omit less significant ones. The former, which Brown terms *contentives*, are the nouns, verbs, adjectives, and other words with high content; the latter, known as *functors*, are the inflections, auxiliary verbs, prepositions, and other words that serve primarily a grammatical function.

In recent years, psycholinguists have studied language development by recording and analyzing lengthy samples of a child's speech collected at daily or weekly intervals. The *corpus*, or body of speech collected, has provided valuable insight into syntactical structures, as well as into such simple quantitative dimensions as sentence length. A regular developmental sequence has emerged, making it possible for us to predict from a corpus the kinds of grammatical rules a child will and will not use at any given stage.

Among the first significant grammatical analyses was a study by M. D. S. Braine (1963), which identified a *pivot grammar* at the two-word phase. *Pivot words* are usually action words (go), prepositions (off), or possessives (my). They are few in number and occur frequently in combination with x-words, or open words, which are usually nouns. *See*, for example, is a pivot word that can combine with any number of open words to form two-word sentences: *See milk, See Mommy,* or *Mommy see.* Almost never do pivot words occur alone or with other pivots (McNeill, 1972). X-words, on the other hand, may be paired or used singly. These prohibitions and combinations are not random but result from children's giving considerable attention to meaning. The length restriction seems to be the primary thing that keeps children from expressing their complex grammatical notions in more adult-sounding forms.

Lois Bloom (1971) suggests that the pivot grammar is too superficial, that children's comprehension of syntax goes far beyond the relatively simple rules for juxtaposition of two words. *Mommy sock,* for example, is a combination of two x-words, but it may express two entirely different grammatical concepts: possession and subject-object. To classify the expression merely in terms of its pivotal surface structure is to miss the more meaningful implications.

Roger Brown (1973) has probably provided the most complex analyses of language acquisition. With Colin Fraser and Ursula Bellugi, he gathered an especially rich corpus from three young children, Adam, Eve, and Sarah. Focusing on cognitive and linguistic ability, Brown has discerned five distinct, increasingly complex developmental stages. He views development in terms of mean length of utterance (MLU) or the average length of the sentence the child produces, rather than age, since children learn at very different rates. Eve, for example, progressed nearly twice as fast as Adam and Sarah. Yet the sequence is the same for all children. Certain skills are apparently easier and are mastered earlier than others, and certain errors are peculiar to particular stages.

In the first phase, characterized by two-word utterances, children begin to express certain semantic roles: agent (who did it), patient (to whom), instrument (with what), location (where), and so forth. This

This is a wug.

Now there is another one.
There are two of them.
There are two_____.

Figure 9 Illustration of the method used in Jean Berko's experiment to test children's syntax. Nonsense nouns and verbs are used to avoid interference from memorization. (*From Bellugi, U., & Brown, R. (Eds.). The acquisition of language.* Monographs of the Society for Research in Child Development, *1964, 29 (1), 43–79.)*

is the period in which telegraphic speech and pivot and open words become evident. However, Brown goes beyond surface structure to focus on the meaning children are attempting to convey with word order and position—the concepts of existence, disappearance, and recurrence, as discussed above, and of possession, agency, and attribution.

In the second stage, characterized by slightly longer utterances, children pick up *inflections* for plural, tense, aspect, mood, and specificity, as well as prepositions, articles, and case markers. Jean Berko (1958) developed an ingenious technique for testing children on these concepts, using nonsense nouns and verbs to avoid interference from memorization. For example: "This is a wug. Now there is another one. There are two of them. There are two _____." The subjects, never having heard the word *wug,* had to supply the correct inflection by generalizing what they knew about plurals. The tests, which have since been given to children even younger than Berko's preschool and first-grade subjects, reveal a surprising grasp of rules for conjugating verbs and forming plurals and possessives. In fact, children tend to *overgeneralize.* They may learn certain irregular verbs by imitation—*gone,* for example. But later, when they grasp the rule for creating the regular past tense, they apply the rule to nearly every verb, forsaking the correct irregular (*gone*) for the more logical form (*goed*). While this is technically an error, it demonstrates the children's extraordinary capacity for generalizing a complex language principle.

In stage three, children learn to modify simple sentences—to create the negative and imperative forms, to ask yes-no questions, and in other ways to depart from the simple statements that characterize earlier phases. The negative provides an excellent example of the complexity of language learning and illustrates particularly well the child's ability to create original forms without depending on models. The basic negative concepts seem to exist quite early. At first, children tend to emphasize negation by putting the negative word at the beginning. Such concepts as nonexistence (*No pocket*), rejection (*No more*), and denial (*No dirty*) are there, but the skills of providing an auxiliary verb and embedding the negative form in the sentence have not yet been mastered. By stage three, however, children are perfectly comfortable with such sentences as *Paul didn't laugh, Donna won't let go,* and *It's not cold* (Klima & Bellugi, 1966). Often, in acquiring negation children go through a period of using double and triple negatives, throwing them in wherever possible to emphasize a point.

Another concept acquired at the third stage is that of active and passive voice. Brown, Fraser, and Bellugi (Bellugi, 1970) developed a test to determine children's understanding of these forms, giving the subjects toys to act out *The cat chases the dog* and *The dog chases the cat.* The 3-year-old subjects performed quite well in tests on such simple declarative sentences. However, when shown two pictures illustrating *The boy is washed by the girl* and *The girl is washed by the boy,* the children seldom identified the picture corresponding to the sentence they heard. Apparently, they had not yet mastered the passive concept. The more typical word order of agent-action-object predominated in comprehension.

A 3-year-old understands the concept of the active voice but not the concept of the passive voice. The child could correctly demonstrate the statement *The rabbit chases the dog* (active voice), but not the statement *The dog is chased by the rabbit* (passive voice). (*Alice Kandell, Rapho/Photo Researchers.*)

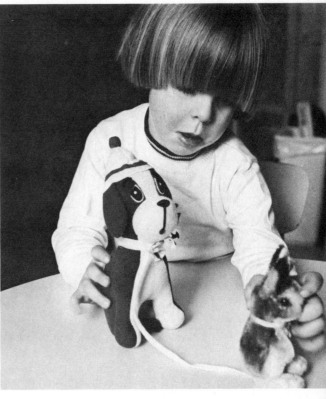

In stages four and five, children learn to deal with increasingly sophisticated structures, such as subordinate sentences and fragments within compound and complex sentences. By the age of 4½, children have an amazing grasp of syntax, but they still continue to learn for many years. Carol Chomsky (1969) tested subjects between the ages of 5 and 10 and found that children are actively acquiring syntax up to the age of 9 and even beyond. Such structures as *John asked Bill what to do* are learned very late; the subject of *do* was not clearly understood by some 10-year-olds. And of course, many adults—even well-spoken, well-educated ones—have great difficulty with certain constructions.

LANGUAGE AND CULTURE

We are all aware that socioeconomic and sociocultural influences leave their mark on children's evolving speech. Yet any study of the relationship between culture and language involves a great many issues—and a good deal of heated controversy. Central, perhaps, is the question of whether there is one "right" way to speak a language. Does nonstandard mean substandard? Are cultural differences necessarily deficits? And what of bilingual children—are they fortunate or handicapped? Should language conform to majority usage, or should it expand and adapt to accommodate variations?

These questions become crucial when we consider the role of parents and teachers in children's linguistic formation. Society must decide how to handle cultural differences—whether to encourage them or to intervene in favor of a standard approach.

Deficit and Difference Hypotheses

When we compare the language of poverty children with that of their middle-class schoolmates, we find obvious differences. But does this mean that many poor children are linguistically deficient? The deficit hypothesis asserts that this is in fact the case, as illustrated by the poverty cycle. Proponents of this theory believe that economic disadvantage retards children's development, which causes them to do poorly in school. Academic failure, in turn, precludes lucrative employment. Thus, it perpetuates the cycle by causing economic disadvantage. The language of the poor is viewed as underdeveloped, as substandard rather than merely nonstandard. The difference hypothesis, on the other hand, asserts that English, like most languages, has a variety of dialects, none of which is superior to any other. Speech variations are not seen as more or less sophisticated, as correct or incorrect, as acceptable or unacceptable (Williams, 1970b).

Recently, psychologists and linguists have begun to observe nonstandard English forms, and they have discovered that variations are not random errors but ordered, structured, syntactically consistent systems. One study, conducted in Washington, D.C., compared language performance of inner-city black children and lower-middle-income white children (Baratz, 1970). The subjects were presented with taped sentences in nonstandard Negro and standard English and asked to repeat them exactly. The white children did better in repeating the standard sentences, but the blacks were more successful with the nonstandard ones. Errors revealed that both groups consistently "translated" sentences outside their realm of experience to familiar forms. If nonstandard Negro English were not an ordered, structured system, such results would not have been possible.

Basil Bernstein (1966) has proposed a controversial set of distinctions between lower-class and middle-class speech. He typifies the lower-class "language code" as restricted and the middle-class as elaborated.

Restricted and Elaborated Language Codes

A kindergarten class copy symbols on their blackboards in a reading readiness group. *(Alice Kandell, Rapho/Photo Researchers.)*

These communication codes he views both as arising from and per-petuating certain social conditions. The strong communal bonds, rigid role system, and limited employment opportunities of a working-class environment create a restricted code, while the variety and flexibility of middle-class roles and opportunities promote an elaborated code.

According to Bernstein, *restricted* language is shorter, syntactically simpler, and less sophisticated than elaborated language. It does less explaining and depends more on context for its meaning. Under the restricted code, working-class mothers spend little time explaining rules and reasons when socializing and disciplining their children; they are less interested in abstracts, motivations, causes, and consequences than in the here-and-now. Middle-class mothers, on the other hand, use much more expanded, or *elaborated,* language with their children. They explain general rules and use more cause-and-effect statements, categorizations, and individualistic meanings, without limiting them-selves to the immediate situation. Since their grammar is more com-plex, they have a greater number of syntactic options to choose from and their speech is more flexible.

Because of these differences, Bernstein feels that working-class chil-dren are at a disadvantage in schools which are geared to an elaborated code. He hastens to add, however, that the lower classes are not incap-able of elaborated language; they simply do not use it very often and so are not accustomed to it.

Bernstein has been heavily criticized. William Labov (1970), for exam-ple, points out that many ideas about lower-class speech are based on inconclusive data. Typical studies automatically place the subjects at a disadvantage by testing them in middle-class situations with middle-class techniques. The subjects are defensive, and their responses are often inarticulate and brief, thus failing to reflect their true abilities. In an attempt to overcome these socioeconomic constraints, Labov con-ducted his interviews with Harlem children through a black interviewer who had been raised in Harlem and knew the subjects and their en-vironment very well. Even so, the standard interview technique pro-duced defensive behavior. One boy named Leon consistently answered questions with "Nope" and "Mmmm." In a second attempt, the inter-viewer tried to create a more relaxed atmosphere by taking along Leon's best friend, supplying potato chips, sitting on the floor, and using taboo words and topics. In the less threatening situation, the "non-verbal" Leon and his friend spoke eagerly and fluently, demonstrating a highly developed verbal capacity. Obviously, there is a gap between verbal performance and competence. What children do in a laboratory situation does not necessarily reflect what they *can* do.

Labov further argues that middle-class language may simply be verbose rather than useful. Further, he believes that Bernstein's elab-orated code may not be "flexible, detailed, and subtle" so much as "turgid, redundant, bombastic, and empty" (Labov, 1970, p. 164). Labov does agree that middle-class language is elaborated, but he does not find it superior. Here again, we see that while lower-class speech is dif-ferent, it may not be deficient.

Even difference theorists are aware that many poverty children are not doing well in school. Before they can learn, these children must first "translate" standard English into familiar dialect, while their middle-class schoolmates can concentrate on the curriculum (Baratz, 1970). Poverty children must also cope psychologically with the prevailing notion that their language is inferior and with the resulting rejection and alienation. Inner-city black children are condemned for their "bad English," "lazy pronunciation," and "poor grammar" (Seymour, 1971). It is this attitude as much as their nonstandard speech that handicaps them in school.

Black nonstandard English is as complex and structured as "legitimate" English. It has just as many grammatical rules. It is the native language of a sizable number of American schoolchildren. Unfortunately, most schools do not recognize a legitimate nonstandard dialect. Even if they do, they are not willing to let the minority pupils maintain their linguistic identity. Martin Joos (1964) suggests that when we correct speech from nonstandard to standard English, we remove education from the sphere of the real world. The social rules of the street or the home and the way ideas and feelings are expressed are "real." The rules of a classroom about how one behaves and even how one speaks seem make-believe, formal, arbitrary, or even incompatible with real life. By criticizing the "incorrect" forms and insisting on the "correct" ones, teachers often inhibit their pupils' desire to express themselves. Very intelligent students can perhaps adapt to the unreality and do well in school, although few can apply what they learn to life outside the classroom. Most children, however, reject the learning situation entirely, retreating to what they know to be valid. Joos believes that teachers can and must prevent this situation by teaching new usages without condemning the old ones and by making "the child's own resources available to him" (1964, p. 210).

Children in every culture learn that language can be used in various ways. They learn not only pronunciation, syntax, and vocabulary but also what to say, when, and to whom. They learn concepts about the world and ways to express them. Parental and societal values seem to play an important part in this learning.

In cultures where politeness is esteemed, for example, children learn polite forms of expression at a very early age. In Java, a child's first word may well be *njuwun,* "I humbly beg for it." A study of Puerto Rican and non-Puerto Rican middle-class children in New York revealed that the former are more oriented toward interpersonal relations and the latter toward problem solving (Hertzig, Birch, Thomas, & Mendez, 1968). Since language is closely linked with the respective values, the Puerto Rican children are at a disadvantage in New York schools, which place a high value on problem solving.

Another interesting study (Robinson & Rackstraw, 1972) examined the way in which lower-class and middle-class mothers answered their children's questions. The middle-class mothers avoided fewer questions, provided more extensive and accurate answers, and used fewer

Implications of Cultural Differences

Uses of Language

An elementary school in Nepal. (*Calogero Ciscio, Rapho/Photo Researchers.*)

checks on agreement. By conveying more information, they provided a cognitive base for their children's future learning. The lower-class mothers gave answers that conveyed little information but reinforced their own authority while apparently stifling their children's curiosity. In both cases, the mothers communicated their personal attitudes toward questioning. Middle-class children would probably realize that their questions are valued and might be expected to continue questioning in order to learn, to maintain contact with adults, and to strengthen relationships. Lower-class children would probably learn that questions annoy their mothers and net little or no information. Both groups of children would learn to use—or not to use—language to their benefit.

Olim, Hess, and Shipman (1965a, 1965b, 1967) have conducted a number of particularly interesting studies on maternal language style and its effects on children's cognitive development. The subjects were middle-class and lower-class black urban mothers and children. In one study, mothers were asked to instruct their children in various tasks.

CHILDREN LEARN LANGUAGE
IN SIMILAR WAYS.

A first-grade class in an Israeli kibbutz.
(*Louis Goldman, Rapho/Photo Researchers.*)

A nursery school in Boston, Massachusetts.
(*Lynn McLaren, Rapho/Photo Researchers.*)

As expected, the kinds of instructions varied dramatically along socio-economic lines. The lower-class mothers tended to be more controlling; they used more imperatives, rigid rules based on status orientation, and negative judgments. The middle-class mothers used more personal appeals, rational principles, and verbal directions, pointing out details, asking questions, and highlighting key dimensions. Not surprisingly, the middle-class children performed significantly better than the other subjects. While this could be partly due to the middle-class testing environment and tasks, it seems likely that certain types of language help children solve problems. The middle-class mothers provided verbal aid and encouraged curiosity and problem-solving endeavors; the imperatives and negative judgment of some lower-class mothers apparently inhibited their children's performances.

Language is used for different things in different families and cultures. In some cases it broadens the range of alternatives, highlighting causes and consequences, focusing on abstract qualities or potentials, drawing on both past and future. In other situations, language offers predetermined solutions, limiting alternative action and thoughts, focusing on the concrete, present situation. These different language styles create different kinds of concepts and attitudes.

As Ellis G. Olim (1970) points out, our increasingly technological society demands an ever greater degree of elaboration, complexity, and subtlety. Thus, it may become more and more difficult for the lower classes, socialized in a restricted code, to cope. Ironically, the explosion of scientific knowledge and accompanying emphasis on cognitive development have resulted in dehumanization and alienation among all people, regardless of socioeconomic level. Olim concludes that with the decline of job opportunities and increase of leisure time, our schools should emphasize development of human sensitivity as well as cognitive competence. If they do not, he predicts, all children may become culturally disadvantaged.

Anthropologist Martha Ward (1971) studied the linguistic development of six families living in Rosepoint, a rural Louisiana village, and found some rather dramatic examples of ways parental behavior affects children's language development. Using Bernstein's (1970) term, Ward labels these families *positional,* since their communication—particularly discipline—is based largely on emphasizing status, or position, within the family and community. The roles in the Rosepoint families are extremely rigid; children's status is determined by age and sex, and the children must behave accordingly. A rule is a rule, and there is no room for argument. *Person-oriented families,* on the other hand, would be more sensitive to individual differences, and roles would be flexible. Communication in such families involves arbitration, explanation, and rewards and punishment. Cause-and-effect statements (*If you don't go to school, then—*) are frequently used, helping the children to categorize the behaviors that will elicit certain consequences. In short, disciplinary language is used as a teaching device. In Rosepoint this is not the case. Cause-and-effect statements are almost never heard; punishment tends to be direct and often physical, and verbal controls are largely imperative (*Shut up, Stop that*). This linguistic behavior seems to have inhibited language development in the children, who appear very shy and rarely speak. But here again, of course, we must be careful about taking experimental data at face value.

Much communication in Rosepoint is nonverbal or extremely brief. This is especially true of affection and aggression, which are very closely linked in Rosepoint. Yet when language is used affectively, it takes a playful, almost poetic form which is rarely observable in more elaborated, middle-class language. This is just one more example of cultural differences—differences that convey attitudes, values, and expectations about the use of language.

It seems evident that language and intelligence are linked in some way. As we have indicated above, grammar may well be the result of cognitive development; certainly, there seems to be some relation between syntactic and intellectual development. And in studying socioeconomic differences in language, we have observed a correlation with certain cognitive abilities. But what is the nature of the linguistic-cognitive link? There are a great number of conflicting theories in this area.

Piaget feels that thought, at least in the early stages, develops from action, not from language, and that language follows as a symbolic expression of thought. L. S. Vygotsky (1962), on the other hand, has asserted that cognitive development is a function of linguistic development, that a child's intellectual growth is determined by his ability to use language. A. R. Luria (1961) directly opposes Piaget by suggesting that the child's activity is mediated through words. Certainly, language seems to play some kind of role in organizing activity, in focusing on specific aspects of the environment. And this tendency seems to increase as children grow older. Children use language in self-direction and self-instruction, identifying distinctive or common features of things with labels. As we have seen in the study of Olim et al. (1967), certain problem-solving tasks are made easier by instructions highlighting key features of the problems.

According to the Sapir-Whorf hypothesis of linguistic relativity, language shapes our concepts of reality. Thus, different languages, by expressing certain ideas more fully than others, create different world views. This may be a function of semantics or of syntax, or both. Roger Brown and Eric Lenneberg (1954) undertook a study to test a portion of the Sapir-Whorf hypothesis, attempting to correlate "codability" of lexical differences with the cognitive function of recognition. By showing various colors to groups of native-English-speaking students, the experimenters determined that the ability to perceive and remember colors is dependent upon the words and phrases used to label the

LANGUAGE AND INTELLIGENCE

colors. Colors that were easily and consistently named, or coded, when initially shown were more frequently recognized when seen later within a display containing numerous other colors.

Carol Feldman and Michael Shen (1969) have provided another interesting illustration of the relationship between language and thought. By testing the cognitive abilities of bilingual and monolingual 5-year-olds, the experimenters found that bilingualism, far from being the handicap it was once thought to be, provided certain advantages. The bilingual children performed significantly better than the monolinguals in tests for object constancy (recognizing a given object in altered circumstances), naming objects, and using the names in sentences.

It seems clear that languages differ in terms of meaning, emphasis, and basic structure, and these differences do seem to affect thought. But we cannot assume that this means one language is superior to another. Nor can we assume that thought does not develop independently of language. There is considerable evidence that cognitive development either precedes or accompanies linguistic development, at least during infancy and early childhood. Furthermore, studies involving deaf children with deficient language skills have shown that their cognitive performance compares very favorably with that of hearing subjects (Furth, 1971). The deaf children have developed many complex ideas without being linguistically able to express them. Verbal ability cannot, then, account entirely for the emergence of cognition. It seems safe to conclude that while language can facilitate many kinds of learning, the absence of certain linguistic structures does not necessarily prevent intellectual growth.

SUMMARY   By the age of 4½, children display remarkable verbal competence. Some theorists attribute this learning to imitation or reinforcement; others think it results from innate mechanisms; and still others feel it is a function of cognitive development. Probably all four theories have merit, but none alone seems adequate.

At about 6 months of age, infants learn to babble and understand some words. By the end of the first year, most begin to speak single words. Soon they progress to two-word utterances, then gradually build up to longer and more complex sentences. Though the rate of development differs, the sequence is universal. At each stage, speech is constrained by length restrictions and specific skills.

Cultural differences obviously affect language. The deficit theory claims that nonstandard forms are deficient. The difference theory maintains that they are different, legitimate dialects. Basil Bernstein's study of the speech of the lower and middle classes describes one dimension of their respective language codes as restricted and elaborated. Restricted speech is characterized by short, simple, rigid, context-

A deaf child without language skills will soon fall behind in cognitive performance. (*Hanna Schreiber, Rapho/Photo Researchers.*)

bound constructions, with attention to the concrete, the here-and-now. Elaborated speech is expanded, complex, flexible, universalistic, dealing with abstracts, with causes and effects. Our schools are geared to an elaborated code and to standard English. They refuse to accommodate variant forms, and the result is academic failure, inhibition, and alienation of minority students.

Language is a tool to use in social context. It reflects and instills the values, attitudes, and feelings of the family and society. Linguistic and cognitive development are closely linked, though the exact relationship is a matter of controversy. Some psychologists think that prior cognition is necessary for language; others feel language shapes thought. Probably, in the beginning cognitive skills are necessary; later, language may affect thought.

1. How do you think a child progresses from crying to babbling to speaking adult language? Consider the four theoretical explanations for this learning process discussed in this chapter and your own experiences with children.

2. Do you consider cultural differences to be a hindrance in learning to speak a language? As a teacher or social worker, would you encourage such differences or intervene to eliminate them among your students or cases? Explain and evaluate your answer in relation to the deficit and difference theories and the restricted and elaborated language codes.

3. How would you characterize a positional family? What effects might this orientation have on the language of the children?

SUGGESTED READINGS

Cazden, C. (Ed.). *Language in early childhood education.* Washington, D.C.: National Association for the Education of Young Children, 1972. Courtney Cazden has collected several studies and articles about language development during the preschool period. This is of particular interest to individuals working with young children in preschools.

Ward, M. C. *Them children: A study in language learning.* New York: Holt, Rinehart and Winston, 1971. In the style of an anthropologist, Martha Ward intensively studied the language learning of children in six families in a rural parish outside of New Orleans. She is particularly concerned with the cultural differences in the use of language.

Williams, F. (Ed.). *Language and poverty: Perspectives on a theme.* Chicago: Markham Publishing Company, 1970. A series of somewhat theoretical articles discusses the controversies and problems of social class and ethnic differences in language within United States society.

12

DEVELOPING THOUGHT AND ACTION

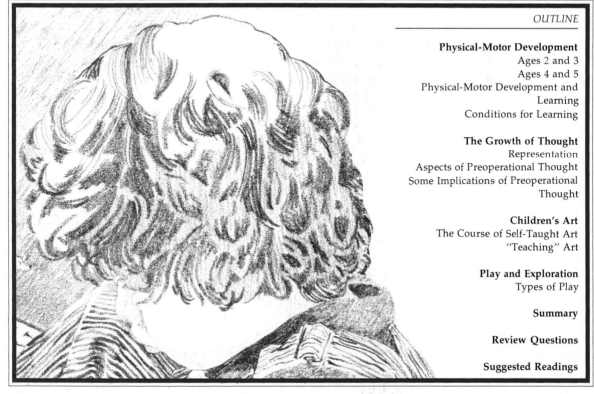

I like snow better than sun. I can build a fort out of snow, but what can I make out of sun?

Why do they put a pit in every cherry? We have to throw the pit away anyway.

Daddy, when I talked with you over the telephone, how did you manage to get into the receiver?

Once when two year old Eli felt offended, he threatened: "I'll make it dark, at once." And, closing his eyes, he was convinced that, as a result, the entire world was plunged into darkness.

(Chukovsky, 1963, pp. 21, 23, 30)

The preschool child, a relative newcomer in this world, demonstrates his thinking and some resulting misconceptions in both an amusing and a thought-provoking way. These comments of children, collected by Chukovsky, highlight not only the children's errors and hence their profound ignorance, but also the enormity of the task of developing the necessary thought processes for functioning in this world as a school-age child. A young child changes from a "magician," who can make things appear by turning his head and make them disappear by closing his eyes, to a concept-forming, linguistically competent realist (Fraiberg, 1959). He discovers what he can and cannot control; he tries to generalize from his experience; his reasoning changes from simple association to the beginnings of logic; and he acquires the language necessary to express his needs, thoughts, and fears.

The tales of children's attempts to deal with information that is beyond their comprehension are legion. One child assumed that the only logical way to end up with a baby in the tummy was to swallow one (Chukovsky, 1963). Another child, having been deluged with a full explanation of the process of conception, announced to his nursery school teacher that "Next time my daddy plants seeds, he is going to plant them in the cat so that she can have a baby in her tummy, too." The careful observer who looks beyond the humor in these conclusions will begin to appreciate the complexity and chaos of the information confronting the young child.

Just as we tend to underestimate cognitive tasks facing young children, we also underestimate their emotional and psychological capacities (Elkind, 1972). For example, we may assume that a child who cries and screams when the plug is pulled in the bathtub while he is being bathed is simply rebelling against being removed from an experience he enjoys. But instead of simply being "difficult," the child may be genuinely frightened of going down the drain with the water! His fear is as real to him and as unreasonable as an adult's fear of snakes, spiders, or heights. Just because the child lacks the language to describe the things that frighten him, adults tend to assume that there is a capricious basis for his reaction.

Adults sometimes demonstrate minimal recognition of a child's emotional sophistication as well as his need for information by "talking over his head" or by using excessively arbitrary techniques to control his behavior or encourage learning. Elkind (1972) suggests that we would rarely require an adult to watch an educational television program, to clean his plate, or to refrain from expressing anger because "it's not nice." Yet adults frequently act in just such an arbitrary fashion with children. A child may comply with these instructions because he is under pressure, but the attitudes and feelings he learns in these situations may not be quite what was intended. Merely following orders to watch a certain program or eat an unfamiliar food does not ensure that the child will automatically develop good taste in television program selection or a willingness to eat a wide variety of foods. Children are complex human beings simultaneously seeking information, searching for order and certainty, and discovering social and personal attitudes. It is impossible to nurture just their minds without nurturing the complex feelings and attitudes which accompany the learning process.

PHYSICAL-MOTOR DEVELOPMENT

It is totally arbitrary, and perhaps inappropriate, to try to separate physical, motor, and perceptual development from cognitive development in the preschool child. The child's understanding of the world depends upon the information he receives from his own body, his perceptions, his motor activity, and the way in which he experiences himself. Almost all that a child does from birth through the first few years is in some way laying the foundation not only for later physical-motor skills but for cognitive processes and for social and emotional development. Looking, touching, exploring, babbling, bouncing, scribbling —all form the basis for the performance of more complex developmental tasks. Much of what the preschool child does is sheer sensory exploration, whether it be making mud pies, swirling and turning in dance, crawling in different kinds of spaces, or hanging upside down. He explores places and objects to find out what they feel like, to see them, and to hear them. Yet this sensory exploration leads to concepts of up and down, swirling, straight, tight, loose, and so forth. For example, when a child is walking a balance beam, he is not only learning the gross motor coordination necessary to balance; he is also learning something about a cognitive concept (narrow) and emotional and social concepts (self-confidence). When a 2-year-old insists on one cookie for each hand, he is acquiring an action schema for the notion of two before he learns to deal with that number concept in a more abstract fashion.

Many aspects of development proceed from a physical-motor base. Some developmental sequences are continuous, as in the natural progression from scribbling to writing. Others seem somewhat discontinuous. For example, children may explore different textures and weaves of material quite randomly with their fingers and their eyes before they are ready to sort and classify, or compare and contrast, the materials. In similar fashion, they must sort and compare thoughts before they can deal with complex ideas. Some developmental sequences involve functional subordination. For example, a child's simple, random, fine-motor explorations with crayon and paper have value in and of themselves, at first. Later putting marks on paper becomes functionally subordinated to more complex skills such as writing, drawing, creating designs, or even carpentry. The roots of complex thought are not always obvious; nevertheless, a look at physical-motor development is a good starting point from which to seek out these roots.

Ages 2 and 3 Compared to an infant, the 2-year-old is an amazingly competent creature. He can walk, run, and manipulate objects. When we see him beside a 4- or 5-year-old, however, we recognize his limitations. The 2-year-old—and even the 3-year-old—is still rather short and a bit rounded. He walks with a wide stance and a body sway. While he can climb, push, pull, and hang by his hands, he has little endurance. He is inclined to use both arms or both legs when only one is required (Woodcock, 1941). Thus, when his mother offers him one cookie, he is likely to extend two hands; when he wants a shoe tied, he will offer both feet.

By the time a child is 3, his legs remain closer together during walking and running and he no longer needs to keep a constant check on what his feet are doing (Cratty, 1970). He runs, turns, and stops more smoothly than he did as a 2-year-old, although his ankles and wrists are not as flexible as they will be at ages 4 and 5 (Woodcock, 1941). The 3-year-old is more likely now to extend only one hand to receive one item, and he is beginning to show a preference for either the right or left hand.

Ages 4 and 5 The 4-year-old is able to vary the rhythm of his running. Many 4-year-olds can also skip in rather awkward fashion and can execute a running jump and a standing broad jump (Gesell, 1940). The average child of 4 is probably able to work a button through a buttonhole and can manipulate a pencil or crayon competently enough to draw lines, circles, and simple faces.

The 5-year-old skips smoothly, walks a balance beam confidently, can stand on one foot for several seconds, and imitates dance steps (Gesell, 1940). He manages buttons and zippers with ease and may be able to tie his shoelaces. He can throw a ball overhand and can catch a large ball that is thrown to him (Cratty, 1970).

While the 3-year-old may pull or push a doll carriage or a large truck for the fun of pushing it, the 4-year-old has *functionally subordinated* his pulling and pushing into a fantasy of doll play or a cars-and-trucks game. Where the 3-year-old daubs and smears paint with abandon and stacks blocks one on top of another, the 4-year-old makes a "painting" or uses blocks to build houses, castles, garages, bridges, or a farm. The 4-year-old is still exploring some physical-motor activities for their own sake—for example, he may accurately pour liquid into tiny cups or operate a syringe and a funnel—but much of his play is embedded in

A 2-year-old boy walking. (*Joel Gordon.*)

A 4-year-old skipping in the park. (*Joel Gordon.*)

A 4-year-old is more secure in her walking. (*Joel Gordon.*)

the acting out of complex roles or the purposeful construction of objects or games.

Physical-Motor Development and Learning

Part of every child's physical-motor development is not learning, it is simply growth: children get taller, their new teeth come in, their muscles grow in length. But a muscle skill is learned; the coordinated sequence is a function of practice. Much of physical-motor development is an interaction between growth and learning. Given ordinary practice, the 4- or 5-year-old has much greater strength and physical endurance, much more control and coordination, more self-direction and self-initiated movements than a younger child. But beyond this, many theorists differ on precisely what is learned as a result of physical-motor development. Many believe that from balancing his own body and from the symmetry of his two hands and two feet, a child learns some beginning foundations of equivalence in math, such as the balance between two items on either side of an equals sign in a math equation (Forman, 1972). Many others believe that the basic notions underlying speed, force, energy, numbers, time, and spatial relations are worked out physically in the preschool period long before the child is ready to deal with them intellectually. Some theorists (Kephart, 1960) believe that adequate motor experience for such concepts is essential before a child can later learn the related math and science concepts. Others have questioned this view, pointing out that many children with cerebral palsy or other severe physical handicaps eventually develop considerable facility with complex math and science concepts. Does a child need to learn to throw and bounce a ball before he understands about force and gravity and trajectories? Does a child need to explore many types of space with his body before he can acquire a thorough understanding of spatial relations? The evidence is unclear. Yet some preschool programs assume that many of these experiences are not only helpful but necessary to later thought.

Conditions for Learning

Children learn physical-motor skills in much the same way that they learn other tasks. As with intellectual development, there must be motivation, attention, activity, feedback, and readiness.

One of the strongest motives in motor skill acquisition is *competence motivation* (White, 1959). Children try things out solely to see if they can do them, to perfect their skill, to test their muscles and ability. Thus, they run, jump, climb, and skip for the pleasure and challenge of running, jumping, climbing, and skipping. This kind of motivation is *intrinsic;* it comes from within the child. However, *extrinsic* motivation can also play a part in skill development. Parental encouragement, peer competititon, and the need for identification can prompt a child to attempt, and then to perfect, a certain skill.

Learning is also enhanced by *attention.* If children focus on a task or attend to certain cues, they become aware of things that can be tried or improved. Sometimes a suggestion, or the model of another child, can draw attention to a key element of a task and stimulate learning.

Five-year-olds can dress themselves. (*Marion Faller, Monkmeyer.*)

Activity is also essential to motor development. A child cannot master stair climbing unless he engages in the act of climbing stairs; he cannot learn to throw a ball unless he has the opportunity to practice throwing. When young children are left alone, they often self-pace their own learning, providing their own schedule of practice. They imitate what they have seen others do, and they will repeat a task endlessly, if necessary. They stack up blocks and discover the possibilities for creating shapes. They pour water repeatedly from one container to another, exploring the concepts of full and empty, fast and slow, accurate and spilling, drops and streams of water. This self-designed and self-paced schedule of learning is often more effective than any adult programmed "lesson" (Karlson, 1972).

The course of learning motor skills is motivated by feedback. *Extrinsic feedback* comes in the form of rewards such as cookies, candy, or praise given for a task well done. The anticipation or promise of such rewards is the extrinsic motivation previously discussed. *Intrinsic feedback* is a very important trigger for skill development; a child finds that there are certain natural consequences to his actions, and these may be more potent than arbitrary extrinsic feedback. When climbing a jungle gym, he may derive pleasure from a feeling of tension in his muscles or from the experience of being up high and able to see things that cannot be seen from the ground. If he feels he has a wobbly perch, he will try to stabilize himself. The "wobble" is *intrinsic* to the task and is usually more effective in making the child aware of his need for safety than being told by an adult to be careful (*extrinsic*). Parents and teachers can help to point out the natural consequences of such a skill acquisition, but the learning process is most effective when the child himself has the experience.

Any new skill or learning generally requires *readiness*—certain prior learning or preliminary skills. As with activity, however, the child is often able to exercise some control over the process in that he can make self-judgments about his readiness to attend the new undertaking. Often a child's avoidance of a particular task may mean that in some ways he is not yet ready to accomplish it successfully.

THE GROWTH OF THOUGHT
The progression from the sensorimotor intelligence of infancy to the reasoning ability of middle childhood has many aspects. In Chapter 4, we looked at Piaget's developmental theory and briefly examined the preconceptual (2 to 4 years old) and the intuitive (5 to 7 years old) stages within the preoperational period. We also looked at Bruner's theory on the development of thought. Central to both theories is the development of symbolic representation during the preschool period.

Representation
The most dramatic cognitive difference between the infant and the 2- to 6-year-old child is in the use of symbols—that is, the use of acts, images, or words to represent events or experiences. For example, the 9- to 12-month-old infant who is given a set of keys will grab at them, pick them up, mouth them, or perhaps bang them together. He will explore them as objects. The 2-year-old, however, will demonstrate by his actions that to him these are car keys. He will imitate past events, roles, or actions, and his own actions symbolize events, uses, or wishes. By gesture in play, the preschooler may act out an extensive sequence that represents a car ride or a locked car. Given other props, he may act out a family dinner, a trip on the bus, a mean babysitter, or a fat relative. In Bruner's description of the development of thought, children progress through three modes of representation. The first is *enactive*, or representation by action, and occurs in the child's second

year. The second mode is *iconic* and refers to mental representation in the form of images. The third mode is *symbolic* and is best represented by the use of words. According to Bruner, during the preschool period the child increasingly comes to use words or other such symbols to represent events or experiences. Until he has developed an efficient system of representation such as words or symbols, the child is heavily limited to the present and, more specifically, to the immediate situation.

When children first begin to use words as symbols, they may use them in unique ways. They may use a single word for a very broad category; thus, the word *dog* may be applied to all animals. Or they may use a word metaphorically. The word *sweet,* for example, may be used not only for things that taste sweet but also for other kinds of situations that are pleasant. A color, for instance, may be labeled "sweet." The use of a particular symbol or word may be unique to an individual child. Once the child begins to use symbols, he is able to demonstrate more complicated thought processes (Piaget, 1950, 1951). He can demonstrate the similarities between objects or events by giving them the same label; he can indicate an awareness of the past and some expectations for the future; and he distinguishes between himself and the person with whom he is communicating. The acquisition and beginning use of symbols has been identified as the most dramatic cognitive accomplishment of the preconceptual or early preschool period.

Even with his development of representation, the preoperational child still has a long way to go before becoming a logical thinker. His thought processes are characterized by several limitations. First, they are *concrete*. The child cannot deal with abstractions; he is concerned with the here and now and very often with physical things which he can easily represent. Second, his thoughts are often *irreversible*. For him, events happen in one direction, and he cannot imagine how things would be if he turned them back to their original state. Thus, if he sees you roll a ball of clay into a sausage, for him the clay is now a sausage. He cannot imagine what it would look like if you rolled it back to its original shape—how large it would be, how smooth, and so on—at least not with any precision. Third, the preoperational child's thought is *egocentric*; he sees the world from his own perspective and cannot see it from anyone else's viewpoint. Fourth, the preoperational child's thought tends to be *centered on one aspect* or dimension of a problem at a time. He perceives one set of relationships and is unable simultaneously to think of another set. Fifth, he focuses on *present states* rather than on transformations. He makes judgments based on the way things look right now rather than on what has happened to them.

Several of these limitations of preoperational thought can be seen in one or another of Piaget's classic experiments on conservation. In one experiment, a preschool child is confronted with two identical balls of clay. While the child is looking, one ball of clay is transformed into another shape. Sometimes it is rolled into a sausage; at other times it is broken up into four or five little balls or flattened out into a pancake.

Aspects of Preoperational Thought

When the child is asked which contains more clay, the original ball or the pancake, he may select the ball because it's fatter or the pancake because it's all spread out. He does not say they are identical, even though he has watched the whole process. Clearly, the child focuses on the current state of the object rather than on the process of transformation. He centers on one dimension, either fatness or "spread-outness." His thinking is concrete, based on his direct experience in the here and now and not on some kind of logical operation. His view of the process is irreversible; he cannot imagine precisely what the size or shape of the clay would be if he rolled it back into a ball. He is incapable of compensating one dimension with another dimension; hence, he cannot say that this clay is fatter but it doesn't go out so far. He cannot think logically about the identity of the clay, and therefore he does not yet say it is all the same clay. He does not realize that if you do not add any or take any away, then you have the same amount. All these dimensions of his thought make him a nonconserver.

These several aspects of preoperational thought exist together in a conservation example. However, instances of one or another of these limitations can be found. Phillips (1969, p. 61) provides this example of irreversibility:

A 4-year-old subject is asked:
"Do you have a brother?" He says, "Yes."
"What's his name?" "Jim."
"Does Jim have a brother?" "No."
The relationship is one-way only; it is irreversible.

One final cognitive limitation of the preoperational child is a characteristic that Piaget (1951) calls *transductive reasoning*. The child comes to conclusions that adults view as totally illogical because he reasons from one specific here-and-now event to another (Phillips, 1969). He does not reason inductively, from the specific to the general. Nor does he reason deductively, from general principles to specific instances. He simply associates. For example, he sees the water go down the drain of the bathtub and disappear; since he and the water have been in the tub, he reasons that both he and the water could go down the drain. On the other hand, the preoperational child will often arrive at conclusions that appear to be quite logical. A 4-year-old girl who sees her dog run into the street and get hit by a car might well conclude that it is "bad" to go into the street. But Piaget (1951) warns that the validity of the conclusion does not necessarily mean that the reasoning took place on a mature, deductive level. The little girl's parents might assume that she now knows that it is bad to cross a street without looking; in reality, the child is probably just associating one event (dog runs into street) with another event (dog gets hurt). This same little girl might run into the street to retrieve a ball, because a ball rolling away and the desire to go after it are situations that bear no relationship to earlier events with her dog. "Just as an incorrect conclusion can sometimes reflect a deductive or inductive logical orientation, a correct conclusion can follow from a basically transductive one" (Flavell, 1963, p. 160).

CLASSIFICATION. The preoperational child also has a problem with *classification*—putting together those things or events that go together. A preschooler may put together a chair and table and then think about a child to sit in the chair; while thinking about a child, he may think about a child's hair; he then goes off to find a brush and comb; going into the bathroom to find those items, he comes upon a bar of soap, which leads him to think about playing in water; turning on the water reminds him that he is thirsty, and he goes off to find his mother who wonders what ever happened to the table-and-chair project that he was happily engaged in just 5 minutes earlier. He has difficulty sticking to one basis for classification.

The example above, of course, could result simply because a young child has a relatively short memory; he may forget on what particular basis he is putting things together before he finishes the problem or task. Other problems in classification arise, however, because of the confusing variety of bases on which things, events, and people can be classified. Use, color, texture, size, sound, and smell are criteria for classification that are readily apparent to an adult. But a child who has no trouble grouping together plates, forks, and cups on the basis of use may not immediately see the possibility of grouping plates according to size and cups according to color. One basis for classification may block another.

TIME, SPACE, AND SEQUENCE. A 3-year-old may be able to say, "Grandma will come to visit next week." Even a 2-year-old may use words that seem to indicate a knowledge of time and space: *later, tomorrow, last night, far away, next time*. A child of 2 or 3, however, has very little appreciation of what these terms mean. Noon may mean lunchtime, for example; but if lunchtime is delayed until 1:00 p.m., it is still noon to the young child. Afternoon is nap time, and if the nap is omitted, then afternoon does not come. Waking up from a nap, a child may not even know whether it is the same day. Concepts of weeks and months, minutes and hours, are quite difficult for a child to grasp. A date such as Wednesday, April 14, is an extraordinarily abstract concept.

With only limited notions of time, the young child has very little idea about cause-and-effect sequences. In fact, his beginning use of the words *cause* and *because* may have very little to do with the customary adult usage of these terms to indicate what came before and some relationship to what occurred later. The same is true of the word *why?*—the 4-year-old's favorite question. He may ask it endlessly, to the point where an adult thinks the child is deliberately being annoying.

CHILD: When is Daddy coming home?
MOTHER: Later.
CHILD: Why?
MOTHER: Because he has to work late.
CHILD: Why?
MOTHER: Because he has a very busy job.
CHILD: Why?

However, the child may be repeating the question in an attempt to understand what words such as *later, late,* and *busy* mean in terms of his environment. His mother's "because" statements, which appear quite logical and straightforward to an adult, only add to his confusion. What the child may be trying to say is that he is hungry and the family usually has dinner when his father comes home, or that he misses a favorite game with his father. Does this state of affairs mean that something is different about his feelings, or is something different about the family routine? Since he is not yet able to grasp concepts of cause and effect, or on-time and later, he is unable to ask the precise questions that will elicit the information he needs. He knows, however, that *why* will bring forth some sort of response.

Spatial relations are another set of concepts that must be developed during the preschool period. The meanings of words such as *in, out, to, from, near, far, over, under, up, down, inside,* and *outside* are first learned very directly with a child's own body (Weikart, Rogers, & Adcock, 1971). Weikart and associates suggest that the usual progression is for the child to learn a concept first with his body (crawling *under* a table) and then with objects (pushing a toy truck *under* a table). Later he learns to identify the concept in pictures ("See the boat go *under* the bridge!") and is able to verbalize it.

Sequences or series of any kind are also difficult for young children to manage. For example, when presented with six sticks of graduated length, a child can usually pick out the smallest or the longest. He may even be able to divide the sticks into piles, putting shorter sticks in one pile and longer sticks in the other. But a young child has considerable difficulty lining the sticks up in correct order like a staircase, because such a task requires a simultaneous judgment that each stick is longer than another one but at the same time is shorter than still another (Flavell, 1963).

Some Implications of Preoperational Thought

Knowledge of the preschool child's thought processes has some important implications for the ways in which we help children learn. As shown in Figure 10, rote learning of numbers will not automatically change the quantitative judgment of the preoperational child. Even though he can count 1, 2, 3, 4, 5, he continues to center on the length of the line rather than on the number of objects in that line; even though he watches the examiner remove one candy, he focuses on the state of the line rather than attending to the *transformation* that has taken place.

Plying a child with picture books about animals will not teach him to arrange the animals in a series according to size; telling him what time it is will not help him conceptualize temporal relations; describing similarities about vehicles will not lead him directly to an ability to classify; using words such as *in, out, up,* and *down* and correcting his use of them will not ensure his understanding of spatial relations. Most child development researchers conclude that children develop concepts of sequence, time, classification, and space through an interaction with the environment, using their bodies, handling objects, manipulating,

Figure 10 Piaget's experiment of the conservation of numbers. (*Adapted from Piaget, J. The child's conception of number. London: Routledge & Kegan Paul, 1952.*)

When shown the above arrangement of candies and asked whether one line has more or both lines are the same, the 4- or 5-year-old will generally answer that both lines contain the same number of candies.

Using the same candies, the examiner has pushed those in the lower row closer together, and he has removed one candy from the upper row but spread the line out so that it is longer. The child has watched this operation and has been told that he may eat the candies in the line that contains more. Even the preoperational child who can count will insist that the longer line has more, although he has gone through the exercise of counting off the candies in each line.

watching, and verbalizing. For example, a trip to the zoo might help a child identify and label various animals. He needs concrete objects or models to help him in seriation or classification (Weikart, Rogers, & Adcock, 1971). Later, he may be able to identify the animals in his picture books and then begin to represent certain of their characteristics through drawings or clay modeling.

Parents often find it exciting to teach a young child to count or to rattle off the alphabet, feeling that the demonstration of such "skills" is testimony to the child's mental acuity. Instead, such feats often indicate a child's rote memory and the parent's persistence, but not the child's understanding of quantities and the meanings of letters and words.

Most educators now recommend that to stimulate and facilitate his cognitive development, a child should be exposed to a wide variety of experiences and have a continuing opportunity to act on the concrete objects of his environment. Only in this way will he learn to conceptualize *how many, how much, what kind, where,* and *when.* Any plan for teaching the preschool child must proceed at the child's level, taking into consideration his cognitive skills and, most importantly, his limitations.

CHILDREN'S ART

As we have seen, it is difficult to take any one aspect of child development, such as concept formation or a motor skill, and isolate it from all other areas. Development is an integrated process; skills, both cognitive and motor, are interdependent. Nowhere, perhaps, is this more apparent than in children's art. Here we can see brought together fine motor coordination, eye-hand coordination, perceptual development, cognitive development, expression of feelings, and the acquisition of concepts. We can detect the development of motor skills through the ways in which children manipulate materials; we get clues to concept formation, self-image, and emotional development through the product that results from the use of art materials.

Although in this section we shall look at what children produce in their art forms, it is important to remember that it is the *process* of exploring with art media that is important in terms of development. Daubing, smearing, scribbling, and finally, more representational drawing—all are part of this developmental progression. As motor and cognitive skills develop, the child moves toward the ability to symbolize, and it is this movement toward symbolism that is illustrated through the process of art (Gardner, 1973a).

The Course of Self-Taught Art	From the moment a child takes a pencil or crayon in hand and begins to scribble, at about 18 months of age, he is working out patterns and forms that are essential to his later progress. Rhoda Kellogg (1970) has identified four stages of development from scribbling to picture making. During the *placement stage*, the child experiments with several basic scribbles, some of which are more difficult and advanced than others. He then explores various placements and organizations of marks on a page. He may confine his scribbles to the middle of a page, fill a page completely, fill in only the top or bottom half, or mark in a diagonal.

By the time the child is 2½ to 3 years old, he has usually mastered all of the basic scribbles and is ready to move on to the *shape stage*. Here he begins to draw circles, then more complex forms such as squares, rectangles, X's, and other outline forms. The child then moves to the *design stage* during which he combines some of the lines and shapes he has been drawing. He may draw a square with tiny circles inside it, or a circle with an X inside.

By the time he is 4 or 5, the child moves to the *pictorial stage* and begins to attempt representational shapes: houses, people, faces, animals.

At the same time that he is experimenting with drawing at his own self-teaching pace, the child may also be involved in manipulating various materials, providing his environment gives him access to them. Using paints, finger paints, clay, mud, sand, or even soapsuds, children do much more than just draw lines or paint pictures. They experiment with the shapes, colors, and textures of the materials, enjoying a total sensory experience of putting together what something looks like with what that something feels like. They learn about thickness and thinness, solid and liquid, what drips and what does not, what holds a shape, what happens when water is added, and so forth. In other words, they are learning concepts about the physical attributes of materials, and they are making associations between these materials and others.

A 2-year-old painting at the placement stage. (*Joel Gordon.*)

A chart depicting shape, design, and pictorial stages. (*Rhoda Kellogg, Child Art Collection, San Francisco.*)

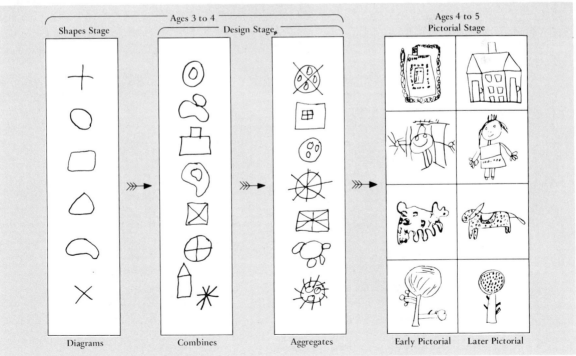

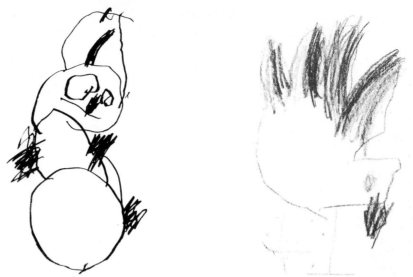

A 3-year-old's drawing of a snowman and a year later his drawing of a turkey. (*Patrick Riley, Lafayette, Indiana.*)

A 5-year-old painting at the pictorial stage. (*Joel Gordon.*)

The exploration and experimentation that occur in art and the gradual movement toward symbolic representation provide children with a foundation for the symbolic operations useful in later thought and, incidentally, for reading and acquiring number concepts. But art is not only symbolic representation of forms. It is also expression of mood and balance and harmony. Adults looking at children's art often focus on the representation of form ("What is it?") to the exclusion of the expression of other qualities of art.

There is evidence that providing models or specific instruction in art is confining, discouraging, and somewhat ineffective (Dewey, 1958; Dimondstein, 1974; Gardner, 1973a; Kellogg, 1970). When a child imitates a model, he experiences considerable disappointment because his rather awkward production never quite matches the precision or the clarity of the model. We do not have to tell the child this, nor can we fool him by false praise; his perception is too accurate. He knows when he has missed.

Furthermore, it does not seem to be helpful to be extremely evaluative. Adults often seem to be concerned about the accuracy of form or spatial relations or comparative size in a child's picture. Indeed, they are far too concerned with the final *product* rather than with the experience or *process* of art (Kellogg, 1970). Children's art, like adult art, is expressive of moods, ideas, and qualities, with emphasis on certain details at the expense of others. Formal accuracy is often irrelevant to what the child is experiencing. At some point, however, the child may want some sort of feedback from adults. He sometimes enjoys some verbal expression of his process or his product. A scary picture full of dark, heavy lines may be labeled "scary." Or an older child may enjoy talking about how he made it so scary or misty or fierce. If adults saw children's attempts at art as a means of communication or expression of ideas and images, of feelings and moods, of balance and harmony, rather than as photographs or accurate representations, the whole process could be mutually enjoyed. In fact, it is rather rich communication, including fantasies and images as well as realism.

PLAY AND EXPLORATION

Between the rituals and routines of the day—dressing and eating and getting ready for bed—the preschool child spends a good deal of time in what might be called play or exploration. Play is not easy to define. In fact, it is easier to say what it is not than what it is: Play is that which is not work, duty, or routine. It is usually entered into voluntarily, and it usually involves some kind of suspension of other activities and feelings in order that new activities and feelings can be taken on. It may be done all alone or with others; it may be imitative or ritualized; or it may be exploratory and full of variation. One of the major characteristics of play is that the process itself is important—the means is often more important than the end. The motivation is the interest aroused along the way; the final goal is usually somewhat secondary.

Types of Play Children's play can be separated into several types, each with its own characteristics and functions. In any play situation, however, there may be some overlap of types.

SOCIAL-AFFECTIVE PLAY. This is a simple kind of give-and-take of feelings and routines between two individuals, very often between an infant and a young child. Some of it is a kind of mutual stimulation, and some is a kind of teasing. It may even consist of bits and pieces of daily routines.

SENSORY PLEASURE. The aim of this kind of play is sensory experience: sounds, tastes, rhythms, odors, textures, movement. Throughout this type of activity, the preschool child learns about himself—his body and his senses—and about the various qualities of things in his environment. Climbing, swinging, rocking, handling objects, exploring among mother's perfumes and makeup, watching the patterns of light made by a prism—all these are forms of sensory play. Some of today's adolescents have rediscovered simultaneous multisensory exploration, or sensory bombardment intensifying brightness, loudness, rhythm, and pattern.

EXPLORATION. When a child plays with blocks, he may first explore the sensory properties of these objects; but soon he moves beyond that level to an exploration of the patterns and configurations of the blocks, the structures that can be built with them, which blocks fit on top of others, and what makes block structures stand up and fall down. The Montessori system of education, among others, capitalizes on this kind of investigation of materials—first a sensory exploration and then an exploration of principles of relationships. In that system, a great deal of information is self-taught through exploration.

SKILL DEVELOPMENT. The efficiency of learning a skill through play seems to be considerably better than learning a skill through instruction. Play is self-paced; the child repeats as much as he desires and then moves on to a variation of the skill when he feels that he is ready. Through play, a child develops his own style of coping with what often seems to be a confusing and frustrating environment (Murphy, 1962). As he masters skills through play, he gains a sense of control over his own body and over the environment with which he interacts.

DRAMATIC PLAY AND MODELING. One of the major types of play of the preschool child is a taking on of roles or of models: playing house, mimicking daddy going to work, pretending to be a fireman, a policeman, a truck driver. This play involves not only imitation of whole patterns of

Children discover that when they stack blocks a tall structure arises. (*Lew Merrim, Monkmeyer.*)

behavior but also considerable fantasy and novel ways of interaction. Through this imitative sort of play, the child is learning to understand various kinds of social relationships and certain aspects of his culture; he is learning sequences and notions of time.

GAMES, RITUALS, AND COMPETITIVE PLAY. As children get older, their play often involves rules and has a specific aim; they make decisions about taking turns, they set up guidelines about what is and what is not permitted, and they often create situations in which someone wins and someone else loses. Although the intricate rules of baseball and Monopoly are beyond the ability of the preschooler, he is beginning to cope with the ritual and rules of tag, hide-and-seek, Red Rover, and various war games. Such games require, and help to develop, cognitive skills such as learning rules, understanding the sequences of cause and effect, realizing the consequences of various actions, and learning to fit behavior to certain patterns and rules (Herron & Sutton-Smith, 1971).

SUMMARY   During the period that Piaget has labeled preoperational, the child makes enormous strides in the development of motor and cognitive skills. Compared to the infant, the preschooler appears to be a physical and mental giant; when compared to the older child, however, the 2- to 6-year-old is seen to have a number of cognitive limitations. His thought processes are concrete, irreversible, egocentric, and centered; he focuses on the present state rather than on a transformation; and his reasoning is transductive. He has difficulty with classification, time, sequence, and spatial relations.

For the purposes of discussion and investigation we can arbitrarily separate motor and cognitive development, but it must be remembered that development is an integrated process. This is most apparent, perhaps, in the process and product of children's art, where fine muscle control and eye-hand coordination are combined with perceptual and cognitive development. The child moves from one stage of artistic production to another as his motor and cognitive skills develop. A similar combination of skill development and use is also apparent in the types of play in which children engage. They progress from exploration and self-taught skills to more formal imitation and rule-governed play as their motor and cognitive skills increase.

REVIEW QUESTIONS

1. Children learn physical-motor skills in much the same way that they learn other tasks. Discuss the essential elements in motor skill acquisition.

2. What are some of the limitations in the thought processes of the preoperational child?

3. If you taught art to small children, what basic guidelines would you set to make experimentation in art more enjoyable for your class?

SUGGESTED READINGS

Chukovsky, K. *From two to five.* Berkeley, Calif.: University of California Press, 1963. In a light anecdote style, Chukovsky demonstrates the rather phenomenal development in thought and in personality during the preschool years.

Kellogg, R. *Analyzing children's art.* Palo Alto, Calif.: National Press Books, 1970. With many illustrations and diagrams, Rhoda Kellogg charts spontaneous artistic development from scribbles to representational form.

Weikart, D. P., Rogers, L., Adcock, C., & McClelland, D. *The cognitively oriented curriculum.* Urbana, Ill.: The University of Illinois Press, 1970. This demonstration project developed at the University of Illinois translates Piaget's cognitive theories into practical suggestions for preschool curriculum.

13

EMERGING PERSONALITY

In the new class of children entering public school, one little boy in particular impressed the teacher. He arrived at school each morning with neat, clean clothes and with his shoes shined. He was obedient and cooperative, and he followed directions well. He never argued or talked back or got into fistfights with the other children. Instead, he would politely state his rights if another child took something that belonged to him, without pressing his point. The teacher was delighted with this industrious "model" child.

One day, the little boy was occupied, as usual, somewhat apart from the other children at the playground. He was drawing in the dirt with a stick. A stray cat came into the playground and walked across the drawings the boy was making. The child stiffened and turned livid. Suddenly, he grabbed the cat by the tail and flung it against a tree trunk with all his might.

How can we explain such apparently unprovoked behavior? In his six years of existence, the little boy had learned well and intensely the appropriate behavior that was expected of him, and this knowledge had seen him through most situations. Yet he had not been able to find a reasonable way to cope with his unacceptable feelings and therefore he bottled them up inside himself. His "model" behavior provided no outlet for emotions he had learned to reject. The result was that the boy's otherwise calm behavior was interrupted periodically by such seemingly bizarre acts. While the case above is an extreme one, it illustrates the incredible thoroughness with which a young child can be trained to deal with his feelings. In this situation, the parental child-rearing practices had been strict and the results were unfortunate, to say the least. But the same process holds true in general for all young children. Between the ages of 2 and 6, the child develops dominant coping strategies, or methods of dealing with his feelings, that may last a lifetime. The processes of socialization—reward, punishment, modeling, identification, and self-discovery—all work to teach the child ways of behaving, as we saw in Chapter 5. In this chapter, we shall again be looking at these processes, using them to examine particular developmental issues and the child's unique strategies for adjusting to, and coping with, these issues.

How does the preschool child become socialized? Perhaps the easiest way to approach this question is to compare the 2-year-old with the 6-year-old and observe the dramatic growth of personality during these important four years.

The 2-year-old has all the basic emotions of the 6-year-old (or, for that matter, the adult) but his expression of these emotions is immediate, impulsive, and direct. He cannot wait to have his wants satisfied. A mother who has promised her child an ice-cream cone cannot afford the luxury of chatting with a friend she meets just outside the entrance to the ice-cream parlor. Her 2-year-old's impatient hounding will ruin her attempts at rational adult conversation. Expressions of dependence are direct and physical at this age, too. In a strange situation, the child will stay close to his mother, clinging to her clothing or returning often to her side to show her things. If separated from his mother, he may throw himself on the floor, howling with anger, protest, and grief. A 2-year-old's aggression is also direct and physical. The child may kick or bite instead of expressing himself verbally. He may grab a desired toy instead of asking for it.

In contrast, the 6-year-old is much more verbal and thoughtful. He takes a little longer to build his anger and he censors or controls his behavior. His coping patterns are also far more diverse than the 2-year-old's. He can displace his anger, kicking a door or a teddy bear, which cannot retaliate, rather than kicking his brother. Or he may have learned to hold his anger in, not expressing it outwardly at all. He may have developed a special assertive posture or even a specific fantasy which he uses to defend his rights or to see him through an unpleasant situation. Faced with the sudden loss of his mother, the 6-year-old is unlikely to howl and kick as the younger child would do. Instead, any sense of loss he feels may be talked out or expressed in a highly disguised form, perhaps emerging in art, or fantasy, or general grumpiness. In short, the 6-year-old has become quite refined in his abilities to cope and has developed his own distinct style. There are far more differences between individual 6-year-olds' methods of coping than there are between those of 2-year-olds. The personal styles of coping which are developed in these years are often the foundations of lifelong patterns of behavior.

DEVELOPMENTAL ISSUES AND COPING PATTERNS

Between the ages of 2 and 6, the child must learn to deal with a number of issues that will appear and reappear throughout his life. Some adults tend to underestimate the kinds of conflict and stress that children face in the preschool years. Children are presumed to be safe and secure within their families; their basic needs are met; and they do not have to face the problems of the outside world. Yet, most kinds of issues we deal with as adults, in both personal feelings and interpersonal tensions, are present in the preschool years too. And it is during these years that the child develops his own unique style of coping with these issues.

Children must learn to handle a whole host of feelings in these early years. Some are very good feelings, such as joy, affection, and sensuality. Others are not so pleasant: anger, fear, anxiety, jealousy, frustration, and hurt. All of these feelings are just as real to the 2-year-old as they are to the adult. The child must also find his own resolution to developmental conflicts. He must learn to deal with an awareness of his own dependence on other people. He must find a way of relating to authority figures—the people he sees as "the bosses" or those who are bigger than he is. And he must begin to deal with his own feelings of independence or autonomy—with his strong drives to do for himself, to master his physical and social environment, to be competent and successful.

A 3-year-old sometimes deals with a situation by crying. (*Chester Higgins Jr., Rapho/Photo Researchers*).

Handling Feelings   The sense of personal and cultural identity which the child forms between the ages of 2 and 6 is accompanied by many strong feelings which he must learn to integrate into his own personality structure. Finding outlets for powerful emotions such as fear, hostility, and jealousy which will be acceptable to both his parents and himself is no easy task. Children find many different solutions to this challenge, but they also experience conflict while doing so.

EXAMPLES OF SOCIAL
INTERACTION.

When you and a friend buy ice cream,
you can enjoy his choice too. (*Esaias
Baitel, Rapho/Photo Researchers.*)

A 6-year-old teaches his 4-year-old
sister to skate. (*Marilyn Schwartz
Rapho/Photo Researchers.*)

FEAR AND ANXIETY. One of the most important forces the child must learn to deal with is the tension caused by fear and anxiety. The two emotions are not synonymous: a fine but important distinction must be made between them. *Fear* generally has a specific source; for example, the child fears the fast cars in the street or the large tiger at the zoo. In contrast, *anxiety* has a more vague or generalized source. The anxious child experiences an overall feeling of apprehension but does not know its precise origin. A move to a new home in unfamiliar surroundings or a sudden change in parental expectations, such as the introduction of toilet training, may be the indirect cause of tensions which seem at first glance to be totally unrelated.

Anxiety and fear can have many causes. If he is very close to his parents, the young child may be anxious that they will leave him or stop loving him. Parents usually act in loving, accepting, and secure fashion. But sometimes—often as a means of punishment—they withdraw their love, attention, and protection. Love withdrawal is threatening and anxiety-producing to the child. Another source of anxiety is anticipated punishment. Parents are powerful people when viewed from the perspective of a 2-year-old who has no realistic idea of how far they will go in punishing him. Other sources of anxiety are situations of high predictability, or those where the child is faced with a puzzling or frustrating circumstance. For instance, if a child awakens in a strange place with no familiar faces in sight, he will be confused, frustrated, and anxious. Fear and anxiety are also often the result of the child's own imagination: he imagines that the birth of a new baby will cause his parents to reject him. Sometimes anxiety results from the child's awareness of his own unacceptable feelings: anger at a parent or teacher, jealousy of a sibling or friend, the desire to be held like a baby.

In Bali, children must resist constant teasing by adults and must never fight (Mead, 1955). The Ik child at 3 years can no longer expect care or nurturance from adults or older siblings (Turnbull, 1972). Such examples just exaggerate the usual control of feelings and resulting anxiety produced in the process of socialization.

Sometimes the source of a particular fear is easy to trace, like the fear of the nurse who gives shots at the doctor's office, or the fear inspired by the smell of a hospital or the sound of a dentist's drill. Other fears are not so easy to understand. Many children develop fear of the dark when it is time to go to bed at night. This type of fear is often related more to fantasies and dreams than to any real events in the child's life. But sometimes these fantasies stem directly from developmental conflicts with which the child is struggling at the moment. For example, imaginary tigers or ghosts are often part of the child's struggle with dependency and autonomy conflicts. In a classic study of children's fears (Jersild & Holmes, 1935), the authors found that younger children are most likely to be afraid of specific things such as strange people, objects, and noises, or of things that could happen to them, like falling. In contrast, children of age 5 or 6 show an increased fear of imaginary or abstract things—fantasized creatures, robbers, the dark, death, being alone, or being ridiculed.

Both fear and anxiety are patterns of psychological and physiological stress which are unpleasant to the person experiencing them, be he child or adult. They are potent emotions which we all try to avoid and minimize. But fear and anxiety are also normal human emotions which are necessary for human development. In fact, in some situations they are probably necessary for the organism's very survival, for they act as part of a physiological arousal system.

All children develop fears and anxieties. Some are helpful, such as a fear of fast-moving cars. Others—like a sudden aversion to the bathtub, for instance—are less helpful. How can children be aided in overcoming specific fears that serve no purpose? The most effective technique is a combination of helping the child to understand his fears and encouraging him gently and sympathetically as he attempts to confront and overcome them. Using force or ridicule or simply ignoring the fears generally has quite negative results.

DEFENSE MECHANISMS. The fears we have discussed above are difficult to study experimentally, for by the age of 5 or 6 many children have learned how to hide or disguise their feelings. We all feel anxious about different things—a result of our differences in cultural and family backgrounds and sex-role expectations. Despite personal differences in the causes of our anxieties, however, we all employ *defense mechanisms* (Freud called them "classical ego defenses") as strategies for reducing our tensions.

Withdrawal is a very common defense mechanism in young children. It is the most direct defense possible: if a situation looks as if it is too much to cope with, the child simply gets out of it or runs away from it.

Projection involves a distortion of reality. The child attributes his own undesirable thought or action to someone else. "He did it, not me" is a projective statement we have all heard and perhaps used—at one time or another. "He doesn't like me" may be more acceptable than "I don't like him." Projection is more complicated than withdrawal. In withdrawal, the child usually knows full well what he is trying to escape. In projection, the child may actually have become confused in his own mind about what really happened in order to defend himself against the feared event.

Displacement is the substitution of another person or object for the one that is actually the source of anger and, therefore, of anxiety or fear. For example, a child may be angry at his father, but he cannot admit this fully to himself because he also loves and depends upon his father. Therefore, he displaces this anger, aggression, and anxiety into an imaginary tiger or goblin which he thinks will eat him up.

Denial is the refusal to admit that a situation exists or that an event happened. A child may react to a potent situation, such as the loss of a pet dog, with the mechanism of denial, pretending that the pet is still living in the house, eating in the kitchen, and sleeping with him at night.

Repression is an extreme form of denial in which the child completely erases the feared event or circumstance from his awareness. He does not need to rely on fantasy, for he literally does not remember that the event ever occurred.

Regression is a return to a much earlier or more infantile behavior as a way of coping with a stressful situation. A 5-year-old child may suck his thumb or climb onto his mother's lap—behaviors he has given up for years—in order to reduce the tension of an anxious moment.

Sometimes a child's own thoughts or desires make him anxious and he reacts against them by exaggerating the opposite extreme of behavior. In such *reaction formation,* for example, he might want to be messy, but instead he is extraordinarily neat and clean. Or he would like to cling to his mother's skirts, but instead he shows an exaggerated independence and assertiveness.

Rationalization is a very common adult defense mechanism. Children take a little longer to learn it, for it requires knowledge of social rules and verbal skills. In rationalization, the child takes his unacceptable behavior or thoughts and makes them respectable by inventing a socially acceptable explanation for them. For example, he may say, "I had to hit my baby sister because she was being bad and had to be taught a lesson."

Most preschool children show several of the defense mechanisms we have mentioned. Very rarely does a child choose a single one and use it exclusively. Generally, younger children tend to show more withdrawal and denial; greater maturity is needed to manage reaction formation or rationalization. Some defense mechanisms are learned by observation of the behavior of parents or siblings; but most are learned directly, by the child's own experience of what defenses work best to reduce anxiety without causing other problems. The particular defense patterns each child adopts are learned very thoroughly during his preschool years and many will stay with him throughout his life.

ANGER, HOSTILITY, AND JEALOUSY. In our society, children are taught to inhibit angry, jealous, and hostile thoughts and actions to some degree. The child learns that these feelings are unacceptable in many situations. He may feel anxious whenever he has them and he will probably use some defense mechanisms to reduce this anxiety. The particular coping style he develops makes a difference in the ways he handles his feelings later on in life. For example, if he simply withdraws from a situation which causes unpleasant emotions, he does not distort the situation and he is likely to be able to deal with it realistically when he is a little older. On the other hand, if he uses one of the more extreme defense mechanisms of denial or repression to reduce his anxiety, he may be distorting his feelings so completely that he can no longer keep in touch with them to understand them. Well-learned defense mechanisms that markedly distort reality can be highly crippling later on; the child who uses them may become a good candidate for extensive therapy in adulthood.

There are other solutions for dealing with negative feelings besides the use of defense mechanisms. The child may recognize and perhaps verbalize some of his negative feelings. He can come to accept the feelings as a normal part of himself, yet learn to control or redirect his behavior. He may use anger to motivate increased striving, to overcome obstacles, or to positively assert his own or another's rights or concerns. In any case, the choice the child makes between accepting or rejecting his negative feelings and the ways in which he acts on them will have important consequences in later years.

AFFECTION AND JOY. In our culture, children face not only the problem of coping with negative feelings but also the task of learning to restrain positive emotions. There is a radical difference in the way the 2-year-old and 6-year-old deal with spontaneous feelings such as joy, affection, excitement, and playfulness. Just as the 2-year-old is direct in his expressions of anger, he is also likely to be very open in showing positive feelings by hugging, jumping up and down, or clapping his hands in excitement. But somewhere in the course of socialization during the preschool years, we manage to teach children to subdue such open expressions. Spontaneity, joy, and affection sometimes become embarrassing and are labeled babyish, and so children learn to control them. In addition, the child's culture may provide special circumstances—celebrations, rituals, games—which demand emotional expression that is in contrast to daily life. All these social norms the child must learn, even with respect to his good feelings. Yet, psychologists are just beginning to study these positive emotions!

SENSUALITY AND SEXUAL CURIOSITY. The 2-year-old is a very sensual creature. He derives a great deal of pleasure from the experience of his senses. He likes the feel of messy, gooey things; he is conscious of the softness or stiffness of clothes against his skin; he is fascinated with sounds, lights, tastes, and smells. While this sensuality was centered around his mouth in infancy, the toddler has a new awareness and fascination with the anal-genital area. Masturbation and sex-play are very common during the preschool period; and as children discover that such self-stimulation is pleasurable, they often gradually increase this behavior. They also develop a very active curiosity about their bodies and ask many sex-related questions.

The way in which the culture and the family react to this curiosity and sensuality as a natural part of development will have an important effect on the child, just as outside reactions affect the way a child handles his hostility and joy. In many historical periods, a mother was cautioned to prevent such sense exploration (Wolfenstein, 1951). The resulting anxiety and guilt engendered in the child led him to adopt the usual variety of defense mechanisms. A more recent study has looked at children's sensuality and sexual curiosity and at current parental reactions (Sears, Maccoby, & Levin, 1957). It found that at least half of the parents questioned reported some genital play in their preschool children and that the parents varied a great deal in the way they handled it. Some thought it was important to inhibit both the behavior of genital play and the feelings of curiosity and pleasure associated with the genital area. Other parents accepted both the behavior and the feelings as natural. While the conclusions are not clear, it seems certain that severe restriction of both the child's feelings and his sex-related behaviors may become a major source of anxiety, guilt, and conflict during his adolescence or adulthood.

Developmental Conflicts

The young child faces a major task in trying to fit his feelings into the structure of acceptability superimposed on him by the outside world, but this is not the only difficulty he must resolve during the early years. He goes through a number of developmental conflicts as he adjusts to changes in his needs during the course of his formative period. Dependency, autonomy, mastery, and competence are among the dominant issues for the preschool child.

DEPENDENCY. Dependency may be defined as any type of activity which demonstrates that one person derives satisfaction from other people (Hartup, 1963). Dependency is also a wish to be aided, nurtured, comforted, and protected by others, or to be emotionally close to or accepted by another person. Dependency is perfectly normal in people of every age, despite the connotation of weakness or inadequacy it often carries in the American culture. And it is necessary for the very survival of the infant or young child who must look to adults for the satisfaction of both his physical and psychological needs.

The young child and the infant show dependency by calling for attention and by seeking close physical contact. But a child of 4 or 5 has developed more indirect ways of showing his need for others. He is more verbal and seeks attention by asking questions, by offering to help, or by showing off. A study by Craig and Carney (1972) traced developmental trends in expressions of dependency by observing the ways that children at ages 2, 2½, and 3 maintained contact with their mothers in a strange situation. The 2-year-olds spent more time physically close to their mothers, staying in the same part of the room and looking up often to make sure that their mothers were still there. The 2½-year-olds and 3-year-olds did not stay as physically close to their mothers as did the younger children, nor did they check as often to see if their mothers had left the room. But the older the children, the more verbal contact they maintained rather than physical contact. All three age groups made a point of drawing attention to what they were doing, but the older children were inclined to demonstrate from afar. Other studies (Maccoby & Feldman, 1972) have shown similar patterns, finding that the amount of disturbance over separation from the mother declines from age 2 to 3, while "distal" attachment behavior, such as showing things to the mother from across the room, increases. In every study, there were found to be wide individual differences in each age group.

There is a popular tendency to think of dependence and independence as opposite types of behavior. But this is not necessarily the case for the young child. Because a child is very dependent at one age, it does not follow that he cannot be strongly independent at a later age. Children who have strong and satisfying dependency relationships in early years often become the most self-reliant adults (Sears, Rau, & Alpert, 1965). Even at a single point in time, many young children display both strong dependent and independent behaviors, especially when independence is measured in terms of self-reliance and achievement striving (Beller, 1955; Heathers, 1955). Children often act in dependent ways by showing affection and seeking attention, while at the same time they show independence by resisting distraction and initiating their own play activities.

Not too long ago, it was widely thought that to produce a strong, independent adult, parents had to start "independence training" early in the child's life by punishing babyish behaviors. Recent research seems to show exactly the opposite. Punishment of dependency may produce a fragile, isolated, and insecure individual. This is especially true when the punishment is inconsistent, as when a mother is doting one moment and punitive the next (Gerwirtz, 1954; Hartup, 1958; Sears et al., 1957). If a child is suddenly made to feel anxious or guilty about his dependent desires, he may become so uneasy that he disguises the desires by defense mechanisms. Instead of punishing dependency, parents may find a more reliable principle for guiding independence training to be that solid independence can have its grounds in a solid dependency. Praise for independent activity, coupled with a tolerance of dependent behavior, appears to be the most effective combination of tactics for encouraging both independence and the positive aspects of dependency.

AUTONOMY, MASTERY, AND COMPETENCE. Autonomy, mastery, and competence refer to slightly different drives (Erikson, 1963; Murphy, 1962; White, 1959). But they are all part of the same motivational and behavioral complex which plays an important part in determining our actions throughout our lives.

Probably everyone would agree that there is great satisfaction in being able to effect a desired change in one's environment, even if only by crayoning on a forbidden wall or retrieving a toy from a baby sister. And the 2-year-old is just as pleased with his creations and prizes as adults are with their accomplishments. Unfortunately, a youngster's autonomy needs often interfere with other people's plans. A young child's mastery over a white wall, or his discovery that he can improve the vacuum cleaner by filling its tubes with clay, does not always fit in with his mother's idea of how the house should be run. These variances of needs produce genuine conflicts between parent and child and within the child himself.

What happens when a child's attempts at mastery or autonomy meet with constant failure or frustration? What happens when he has little or no opportunity to try things on his own, or when his environment is so

chaotic that he cannot see the consequences of his acts? Every child has autonomy needs, needs to master his environment, and needs to feel competent and successful. If these needs are blocked, then the child will be affected. If he learns that his efforts at mastery are more trouble than they are worth, he may give up and adopt a passive outlook. Several studies have indicated that such children fail to develop an active, exploratory, self-confident approach to learning. White and Watts (1973) called this the development of learning competence. Beyond this, what happens to the child who is punished for his independence and for his autonomous attempts at mastery? Or the child who is frightened whenever he ventures off into new activities? When the child learns to feel anxious about his autonomy needs, he may learn to deny or minimize or disguise such needs. Such induced anxiety about autonomy may occur especially among young girls in our culture.

Some children undergo a particular restriction of their autonomy needs. The physically handicapped child, the child who experiences a prolonged illness, and even the child who is temporarily confined in a hospital—all may have little opportunity to test their skills in mastering the environment. Children who grow up in very dangerous surroundings and who are therefore restrained, or children living in small apartments or under the constant vigilance of adult caretakers, may also learn exaggerated passivity or exaggerated anxiety.

On the other hand, children can be taught to feel that autonomy needs are good and acceptable feelings. Parents can help a child find legitimate, harmless outlets where he can explore his powers at his own pace and safely learn the natural consequences of his actions. The child then has a chance to discover more about his autonomy needs and to learn to deal realistically with his powers.

Throughout the preschool years, the child is developing a very definite set of attitudes, beliefs, and concepts about himself in all of the areas we have examined above. Many of these ideas begin to emerge very early, at a nonverbal level. The child develops certain kinds of generalized attitudes about himself—a positive sense of well-being, or a feeling that he is "slow" or naughty. He may develop strong anxieties about some of his feelings and ideas but not about others. The child also develops a set of ideals during these years, and as he does, he learns to measure himself against what he thinks he should be. Often, his own self-evaluation is a direct reflection of what other people think of him. If Anne is told that she is a troublemaker, she may soon come to believe that she is, especially if the people who tell her so are important and close to her. These early attitudes eventually become basic elements of the individual's self-concept, but they are often very difficult to explore later on because they were partially learned at a nonverbal level.

The preschool child is fascinated with himself, and many of his activities and thoughts are centered on the task of learning all about

Self-Evaluation

Two 5-year-olds exploring their environment.
(*Alice Kandell, Rapho/Photo Researchers.*)

A 5-year-old shows off the space where her tooth was to her friends. (*Alice Kandell, Rapho/Photo Researchers.*)

himself. He frequently compares himself to other children, discovering that he is different from them in height, hair color, family background, likes, and dislikes. He compares himself to his parents, learning that he has common behaviors with them, and finding traits to imitate. And as part of his drive to find out about himself, he asks a variety of questions about where he came from, why his feet grow, whether he is good or bad, and so on.

As the child learns who and what he is and begins to evaluate himself as an active force in his world, he is putting together a form of cognitive theory about himself which helps to integrate his behaviors. Human beings are relatively consistent, acting in systematic ways and trying to bring their behaviors in line with their beliefs and attitudes. The strongest influences on the child's developing self-image are his parents, for they provide him with the definitions of right and wrong, the models of behavior, and the evaluations of his actions on which he bases his own ideas.

Up to this point, we have been discussing some of the most important areas of personality growth during the preschool years. Some basic questions in developmental psychology we have considered have concerned how, why, and from what sources each individual's personality derives its uniqueness. Now we shall look more closely at some recent research which is beginning to tell us just how significantly styles of parenting—the actions and attitudes of the parents—affect the child's personality development.

There are at least two ways of looking at styles of parenting. One is to observe quite specifically the particular behaviors and attitudes of the parents and the resulting behaviors of the children. If Johnny's parents have built their home life around the television set, Johnny is likely to do the same when he has his own home. This kind of analysis involves looking at three areas in which styles of parenting affect the child. First, the parents act as *models* whom the child can imitate and identify with. If parents shout and argue, the child is likely to shout and argue, too. Second, the parents in each family have specific *expectations* for their own children. One family may expect children to be quiet and reserved at the dinner table, while another encourages children to enter into lively discussions. And finally, parents control the whole area of *discipline*: what the child is disciplined for and the ways that discipline is carried out. Are children rewarded or punished? How are they rewarded or punished—by candy or praise, by physical punishment or scolding, or by deprivation of material pleasures or attention?

Many studies have dealt with these three specific parental behaviors and their effect on children's behavior; we shall look at some of their findings in the next section on aggression (Bandura, Ross, & Ross, 1961; Sears et al., 1957). But the problem with all such studies is that they are difficult to relate to real life, which is rarely so clear-cut. Parents do not always discipline their children consistently. They may be models of one kind of behavior in one situation and of quite different behavior in another situation. Or they may model a behavior like aggression, but at the same time expect their children *not* to be aggressive. Another, and different, way of looking at parenting helps to avoid many of the difficulties inherent in the type of study which separates behavior into such distinct categories. This method involves looking at broader dimensions of parent behavior and the combinations of these dimensions in each particular parent.

One of the best examples of this way of looking at parenting is the model developed by Becker (1964). Becker sees parent behavior as having three key dimensions. In his view, every parent's attitudes and actions fall somewhere along each of three continuums: restrictiveness vs. permissiveness, warmth vs. hostility, and anxious emotional involvement vs. calm detachment (see Figure 11). In its treatment of parental behaviors as dimensions instead of specific acts, Becker's model encompasses not only extremes of behavior exhibited by the

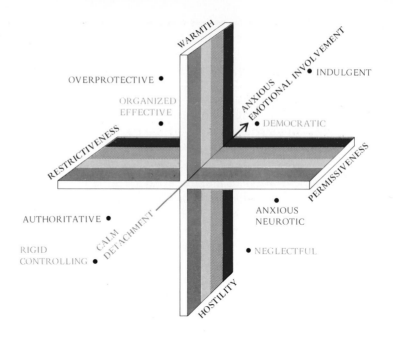

Figure 11 Becker's three dimensions of parenting styles. The three dimensions are indicated by the three axes. Styles of parenting which combine these dimensions fall in each quadrant according to the rough proportion of each quality. (Brown areas indicate high degrees of anxious emotional involvement.) The dots represent the actual positions of each quality. (*Adapted from Becker, W. C. Consequences of different kinds of parental discipline. In M. L. Hoffman & L. W. Hoffman (Eds.),* Review of child development research (Vol. 1). *New York: Russell Sage Foundation, 1964, 175.*)

openly hostile parent but also the actions of the great majority of parents who are not excessive at all in their behavior.

Becker's model also makes us aware of all the ways these three dimensions can interact with one another. For example, if we were to look only at their specific acts or attitudes, we might assume that two highly permissive mothers were raising their children in the same manner—an assumption which could be far from the truth, for it ignores the other two dimensions. The two mothers may both be highly permissive; both may even deal with their children in the same calm manner. But if one mother is warm while the other is coldly hostile, then there is quite a wide variation in their styles of parenting. One is democratic, the other is neglecting.

RESTRICTIVENESS, PERMISSIVENESS, AND OTHER DIMENSIONS. Recent research has given us important insights into the different effects of restrictiveness and permissiveness. The principal finding has been that restrictive parents usually tend to have children high in dependency, submissiveness, and compliance.

One longitudinal study done by the Fels Research Institute (Kagan & Moss, 1962) compared the effect of the mother's restrictiveness (defined by the degree to which the child was forced to adhere to the mother's standards and was punished for deviations from these standards) on children of different ages. It showed that early restrictiveness, on children ages 1 to 3, tended to have lasting inhibiting effects. Later restrictiveness, when children were ages 3 to 6, had fewer consistent effects. And restrictiveness from the ages of 6 to 10 seemed to have a pronounced opposite effect: the children, now old enough to sense the unfairness of the parent, reacted with hostility instead of submissiveness.

These same researchers also made some interesting findings about sex differences in children's reactions to restrictiveness (Kagan & Moss, 1960, 1962). They found that the long-term effects of childhood restrictiveness were much more stable in girls than in boys. Most dependent, passive girls remained this way as adults, as opposed to only a few dependent boys. Why the difference? The researchers found the answer in our cultural standards. Dependency is often expected of girls; therefore, this behavior is reinforced as they grow older. But boys are expected to be assertive, and so they soon learn to inhibit signs of dependency.

Although permissiveness is a polar opposite of restrictiveness, it does not necessarily produce independent children. In at least a few studies, *permissiveness* (defined as a noncontrolling, undemanding climate) was related to active, outgoing, creative, and successfully aggressive behavior in children (Baldwin, 1949; Watson, 1957). But the way that permissiveness interacts with the other dimensions is of crucial importance. Permissiveness in a climate of detached warmth (Becker's democratic parent) seems very likely to produce fairly positive characteristics. But when it is accompanied by high hostility (the neglecting parent), permissiveness is more likely to result in noncompliance and aggressiveness. Many studies of juvenile delinquents show that the delinquents' home environments have been exactly this combination of permissiveness and hostility (Bandura & Walters, 1959; Healy & Bronner, 1926; McCord, McCord, & Zola, 1959).

Although the way that anxious emotional involvement may interact with restrictiveness or permissiveness has not yet been the focus of a great deal of study, one important piece of research on maternal overprotection (Levy, 1943) has looked at the effects of both restrictiveness and permissiveness (overindulgence) when the two are combined with high warmth and high anxious emotional involvement. Some of the children studied were highly dominated, raised in a narrowly restrictive climate; others were indulged by overly permissive mothers. All of the children showed significant maladjustments, but these varied according to the degree of restrictiveness. Indulged, overprotected children generally showed tyrannical behavior, throwing tantrums when they did not get their way; dominated, overprotected children were timid, submissive, and withdrawn. Each group had trouble relating to other children.

AUTHORITATIVE, AUTHORITARIAN, AND PERMISSIVE PARENTS. Some very extensive research done by Baumrind (1972) looks at styles of parenting from a different angle. She finds three distinct patterns of parental authority as it combines with other dimensions of parenting. *Authoritative* parents, who combine high controls with warmth, receptivity, and encouragement of the child to do for himself, are likely to produce the most self-reliant, self-controlled, and self-satisfied children. *Authoritarian* parents—warm, more detached, and controlling—were more likely to have withdrawn, distrustful children who were less assertive and independent. And *permissive* parents, who combined few controls or demands with relatively high warmth, had the least self-reliant, explorative, and self-controlled children.

What conclusions can we draw from the vast amount of research on styles of parenting? None of the studies can provide a foolproof recipe for raising children to personal specifications. But they all do indicate the importance of the parents' role in the preschooler's development, and they give us a general idea of different ways in which parental styles as well as specific acts and expectations can influence the child's later standards, his anxieties, and his degree of self-reliance.

Fathers, Present and Absent

Although we have been considering styles of parenting throughout this chapter, most of our discussion has been concerned with styles of mothering. In our modern industrial society, where many fathers are away at work for all but a few hours each day, where there are many single-parent families, and where each family unit is usually isolated from the extended family, the mother often raises the children almost single-handedly.

What part does the father play in childrearing and how does his absence affect the child? These questions went largely unanswered (and unasked) until World War II, when many families expressed concern about what the father's going off to war meant to the young children left at home (Stolz, 1954). As a result, a good deal of research has delved into these questions in recent years, and it has begun to tell us just what role the father plays in the development of his children.

Studies have shown that a child is dramatically affected when there is no man in the house. For a boy, the effects of father absence are accentuated especially if this absence begins when he is very young (Ostrovsky, 1962). The young boy shows the effects of being fatherless very early. Because there is no male model to imitate and identify with, he must piece together an image of his sex role from male relatives, friends, or secondary sources—either his mother's interpretation of what men are like or the things he hears, reads, and sees around him. The result is usually a distorted image. This may have an effect on the boy's behavior, especially during the preschool years (Hetherington, 1966). In these early years, many fatherless boys exhibit less aggressive and more dependent behavior. For example, their doll-play is more characteristic of girls than of boys (Sears, P. S., 1951). As they grow older, this feminized behavior often disappears or is replaced by compensatory masculinity—an exaggerated effort to fit into the male role which often results in the sort of inappropriate hypermasculinity exhibited by

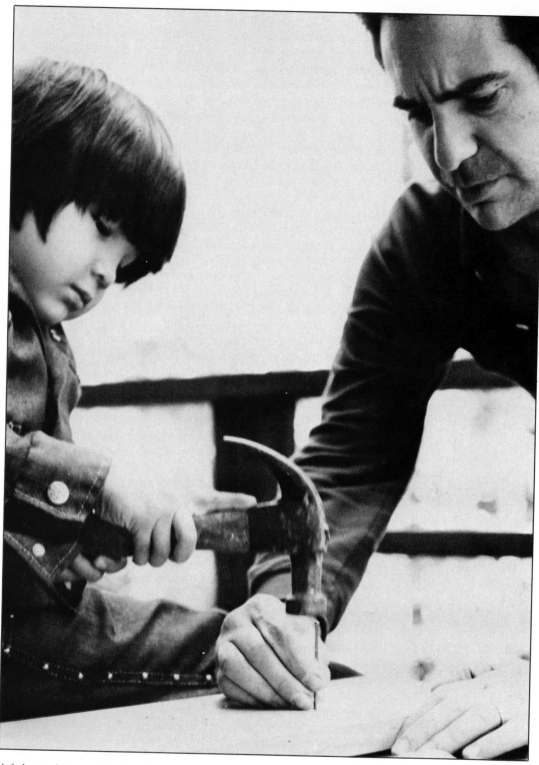
A father and son working together on a project. (*Alice Kandell, Rapho/Photo Researchers.*)

delinquent gangs (Hetherington & Deur, 1972; Miller, 1958). In fact, the high rate of delinquency in lower-income groups may be related to the large proportion of fatherless homes. Recent research has found another interesting side effect of father absence. Boys without fathers seem to show lower achievement orientation, performing poorly on IQ and achievement tests as compared to other groups (Santrock, 1972).

All of these side effects seem to reflect the absence of a male-role model. If another male, such as an older brother, a teacher, or even a mass-media hero, is available to act as a surrogate father, then a boy is much less likely to develop the tendencies described above. Other tests which extensively studied aspects of fatherhood may be equally important. The father's role in discipline seems important but perhaps exaggerated in literature. The need for two parents to provide two perspectives, two approaches, and two sets of needs and expectations may be underestimated as a positive preparation for a complex, social world with competing demands and expectations.

Usually, girls do not react as dramatically as boys to father absence during the preschool years. Girls are affected, but at a later age. The female child needs an opportunity to develop a rapport with adult males as a pattern for later affectional relationships. If her home life does not provide such experience, the fatherless girl is likely to have problems during middle childhood and adolescence. Often, she may develop one of two forms of maladjustment in relationships with boys and adult males (Heatherington & Deur, 1972). Fatherless girls tend to be either excessively shy, withdrawn, or intimidated at one extreme, or fascinated, seductive, and promiscuous at the other. Either way, their behavior reflects their lack of deep experience in relating to members of the opposite sex and, therefore, their lack of self-confidence and expressive social skills.

All of these findings suggest that the father plays an important role in the development of both boys and girls. We know that he helps in sex-typing, serving as a model for boys and providing a learning ground for girls in relationships with men. And we are beginning to see that his absence or presence can affect other areas of behavior, such as achievement striving. But fathers and mothers are not the only important people in the child's early development. Brothers and sisters also play a major part in socializing the youngster.

Siblings   Few children who grew up with brothers or sisters can deny that sibling relationships deeply influence the way children learn both to think of themselves and to relate to others. In families where parents are too busy to give attention to the children, siblings may even be the main socializing agents. Older siblings often act as models, and research suggests that children with older siblings of the same sex tend to show stronger sex-typed behavior than children whose older siblings are of a different sex (Koch, 1956b; Sutton-Smith & Rosenberg, 1970).

Sibling relationships provide a different kind of experience for the child than does parent-child interaction—they are like "living in the nude, psychologically speaking" (Bossard & Boll, 1960, p. 91). The down-to-earth openness with which brothers and sisters deal with each other gives siblings a chance (whether they want it or not) to experience the ups and downs of a human relationship on the most basic level. The question of what this means to the child has always fascinated storytellers. It has also produced a good deal of research, both popular and systemic, in recent years. But the conclusions—if they can be so designated—are far from decisive.

Most of these studies have dealt with birth order and the effect that being an older child, a younger child, or a middle child has upon later life. In general, oldest and only children have the most exclusive contact with parents, and the intensity of the relationship tends to produce greater anxiety, higher conformity, and increased achievement orientation (Sutton-Smith & Rosenberg, 1970). In the past century, there have been a disproportionately large number of firstborns who have achieved eminence in everything from *Who's Who* listings to National Merit Scholarships. In a similar way, later children's contact with parents is diluted by their simultaneous relationships with older siblings. This multiple relationship seems to produce lower anxiety and achievement orientation, but greater social orientation. Of course, all of these conclusions are general, tentative, and controversial—the effects of all relationships depend upon the individual personalities of the children and the parents. In any case, the subject of the effect of birth order upon a child's personality and achievement is a fascinating one which certainly needs further study.

AGGRESSION

In his early relationship with his parents and siblings, the child is learning to deal with other people and to handle his own emotions. Feelings of anger and hostility emerge in every area of interaction between people; therefore, one of the principal tasks in socializing the young child is to teach him to deal with such strong aggressive feelings.

While the layman often confuses aggression with assertive behavior, the two have separate meanings. *Aggression* refers to behavior where there is an intent to hurt or destroy. It may be verbal or physical. It may be directed at people—pulling their hair or biting, for instance. Or it may be displaced—directed toward things or objects like a punching bag. *Assertive behavior*, on the other hand, does not have the connotation of intent to hurt. One can assert one's own rights without trying to destroy the rights of others.

Considerable research has been devoted to aggressive behavior in an attempt to further define it, to find out how it originates, and to learn what factors control it. We shall look at some of the explanations psychologists have given for individuals' aggressive actions and we shall consider the effects that television has on aggressive behavior in children.

Frustration and Feelings   One explanation of why people act aggressively sees aggression as primarily a response to *frustration* (defined as the blocking of a goal). The frustration-aggression hypothesis is built from two observations: first, that frustration is one of the major sources of angry or hostile feelings, and second, that one of the dominant responses to frustration is often aggression (Dollard, Doob, Miller, Mowrer, 1939). When behaviorist experimenters set up tests to see if these observations were valid, they hypothesized the extreme—that frustration always led to aggression and aggression was always the result of some sort of frustration. Such an absolute is ideal for research, for it can be supported or refuted readily. A series of studies followed. One well-known study (Barker, Dembo, & Lewin, 1943) recorded children's behavior in a frustrating play situation. A number of attractive toys were given to a group of children and then removed to behind a screen—the toys were visible but the children could not reach them. The children reacted in a number of different ways to the frustration which they felt. Some were aggressive toward their peers or toward the investigators. Others tried to escape from the room or regressed to earlier behaviors like thumb-sucking. Interestingly, all of the children showed behavior that was substantially less creative under the frustrating circumstances than previously. The experiment revealed that aggression was by no means the only reaction or even the dominant reaction. Similarly, studies of aggression (Dollard & Miller, 1950) indicated that *sometimes*—but not always—aggression could be traced to frustration. Therefore, it was concluded that frustration often leads to emotional arousal, and this arousal often takes the form of anger or hostility. But we all respond to this anger in different ways, not always by aggression.

Modeling, Rewards, and Punishment   If aggression does not always follow from frustration, what other origins may it have? Some important studies during the last few years have dealt with two other influences on aggression: the effects of direct rewards and punishment and the observation of aggressive models. The processes of reinforcement and modeling were described in Chapter 5; however, we might examine them here as they relate to learning aggressive behavior. How effective are these processes? Research has shown that direct reward for aggression is an effective encouragement (Cowan & Walters, 1963; Lövaas, 1961). This positive reinforcement can be either of two things. It can be a reward, like a trinket or a nod of approval. Or it can be the intrinsic pleasure of success: if aggression works for the child, this in itself is a very potent reward. One study (Glueck & Glueck, 1956) suggests that a high proportion of juvenile delinquents are muscular mesomorphs whose body types have allowed them to succeed in acts of physical aggression—an experience which has acted as encouragement for even more aggressive behavior.

While the research indicates that rewards encourage aggression, the case for using punishment to discourage this behavior is not so clear-cut. True, if the child is punished for aggressive acts, he is very likely to inhibit this behavior—at least in the presence of the punisher. But he will probably rechannel the aggressive feelings and acts into other outlets instead. For instance, he may use less physically aggressive behavior, such as having fantasies, calling names, or tattling. Or he may direct his aggression toward inanimate objects, such as dolls. The parent who uses physical punishment to try to curb a child's aggression may actually be encouraging exactly the behavior he is trying to stop, for the parent is modeling aggression at the same time that he is punishing it.

Behavior can be learned as effectively by watching a model as by receiving rewards. It has been shown that aggressive behavior can be acquired merely by seeing someone else's aggression rewarded. One well-known series of experiments by Bandura, Ross, and Ross (1961) involved showing children films of aggressive behavior. One group of children watched an adult model display unusual physical and verbal aggression toward an inflated doll; another group saw an adult sitting quietly, ignoring the doll. Observations of the children's later play showed two things. First, the children were able to learn both specific new aggressive acts and a general aggressive attitude by watching the model. And second, watching a model's aggression being rewarded or punished may either loosen or strengthen inhibitions for previously learned behaviors (Bandura & Walters, 1963).

Experiments also showed that modeling occurs more completely when the model is perceived as powerful or in control, or when the viewer senses a similarity between himself and the model (thus, boys are more likely to imitate other boys than to imitate girls). When the model is perceived as nurturant, having a special relationship with the child, the process is even more effective. All these factors are often present in the child's parents, and they interact in different ways. For example, a girl may model herself after her father because he seems very powerful, because they have a strong nurturant relationship, or because people comment on their similar "tempers" or sense of humor!

Frustration, reward and punishment, and modeling all play a part in the aggressive behavior children learn, and all of these factors are present—and interact—in family life. They may work together: the child may be rewarded for nonaggressive actions and mildly punished for aggression. Or they may work against one another: the child may continuously be put in frustrating situations but be severely punished when he reacts aggressively. In any case, even the most careful parents cannot shelter a child completely from opportunities to imitate aggressive behavior, and many psychologists and sociologists feel that the omnipresent television in our society provides children with a sure model for learning aggression.

Television and Aggression

According to some recent research (Gerbner, 1972), children's cartoons have been among the most highly violent fare on television. We know that the presence of aggressive models increases the likelihood of aggression in the observer, and we know that a good many children spend hours in front of the TV screen each day, watching not only cartoons but

Television can have a strong influence on small children. (*Alice Kandell, Rapho/Photo Researchers.*)

also violent dramas such as "Batman." What effect is this exposure to television having on our youngsters?

There are two opposing answers to this question. According to one explanation, the viewing of violent acts on television has a cathartic effect (Feshbach & Singer, 1971). Television stimulates violent fantasy and this fantasy substitutes for overt aggressive acts. The idea is appealing but, unfortunately, the research is overwhelmingly against it (Liebert, Neale, & Davidson, 1973). Instead, the observation of TV violence has been shown to increase aggression in viewers (Friedrich & Stein, 1973; Leifer & Roberts, 1972). Television is a major socializing force in our society, and by exposing children to large amounts of violence treated casually on the screen, we are teaching them to think of aggression as both commonplace and an acceptable outlet for their own frustrations.

There are some moderating factors. Aggression shown on television does not have the same effect on all children. Those who are nonaggressive to begin with tend not to be affected by watching aggressive programming (Friedrich & Stein, 1973), while those who have little contact with real-life male models are more likely to be influenced by violent shows. A good deal of research supports the notion that there are many good effects of television, too, as a prosocial force. Well-constructed children's films or series can strengthen such positive qualities as rule obedience and task persistence in many children (Friedrich & Stein, 1973). In sum, the research seems to suggest that television is a potent socializer which can influence children's behavior in either positive or negative ways. Perhaps some planning should be used in exposing children to programs.

BUILDING A CONSCIENCE

In all the areas of development we have discussed in this chapter—learning to handle feelings, to cope with anxiety, and to control aggressive impulses—a basic process of socialization is taking place in the young child. This process is called *internalization*. The child is learning to make part of himself the values and moral standards of the society around him. The process is necessary for the maintenance of society, for if people never absorbed a morality, no law would be strong enough to control their whims. It is also desirable for the individual: tantrums, tears, and grabbing may be successful tactics for the 2-year-old, but such self-centered actions are inappropriate in an adult.

Internalization is necessary, but how does it happen? How is it that the toddler—who reacts with no feeling but fascination as he bangs his baby brother's head with a hairbrush—comes to develop both self-restraint and genuine feelings of remorse by the time he reaches the age of 5 or 6? The question of how we develop a conscience has stimulated a good deal of research in recent years.

Conscience may be defined as an internalized set of morals, values, and standards of behavior (Hoffman, 1970). As we saw in Chapter 5, some cognitive theorists contend that conscience is primarily a product of reasoning and develops hand in hand with the cognitive processes. But most psychologists think that the process is more complicated, for there are important forerunners to this rational set of standards even in the prelogical child. Mary says, "No, no, no!" as she goes ahead and crayons on the wall. She is following her whims, but she is also showing the beginnings of self-restraint by reciting the command, "No," to herself. In a few years, she will have developed enough self-control to arrest such impulses as soon as they reach her consciousness.

Identification

According to many theorists, the process by which we learn to internalize standards and controls is more complicated than reinforcement and punishment or modeling. It is an entirely different level of learning, for it involves the learning of not just one specific act but of a whole attitude and complex of behaviors. It is learning which has three special distinctions: it occurs very early in life; it seems to happen spontaneously; and it involves behaviors and attitudes which become basic parts of the individual's personality (Sears, Rau, & Alpert, 1965). This complex process is called *identification*, and it leads a child to think, feel, and behave as though another person's characteristics belonged to him.

Identification seems to begin like modeling, but it builds to a much broader scale. The toddler wants to be just like Daddy and he mimics all Daddy's actions. But as the child grows older, these simple imitated attitudes and patterns of behavior become deeply imbedded in his personality, until what was an exaggerated caricature at the age of 2 becomes a well-established set of expectations and behaviors at the age of 5. These acts and attitudes are well-learned, and the preschool child is often intensely moralistic. He knows the one right way things should be done, whether it be making a sandwich, looking both ways before crossing the street, or sharing candy.

IDENTIFICATION: HOW IT WORKS. The first explanation of identification as a learning process was conceptualized by Sigmund Freud (1923/1947). Freud thought there were two separate mechanisms of identification responsible for much of what we learn. One process, called *defensive identification*, he thought was rooted in the Oedipal stage of development. The child, who is strongly attracted to the parent of the opposite sex, finds himself competing with the same-sex parent. To resolve the competition, the child uses tactics that he already knows are successful: those of the same-sex parent. Sex-typing and other overall standards of behavior are thus learned as a result of the child's defensive attempts to compete for his parents' love. Some developmental psychologists feel limited by this defensive explanation of learning, principally because of its stress on the Oedipal theme. But many of Freud's notions about identification are basic to popular modern explanations of the way we internalize values and standards. A more complete description of types of identification is provided in Chapter 5.

Parents are almost invariably the models for identification, but the degree to which children identify varies significantly. Five key factors seem to be involved (Sears et al., 1965). An early, strong dependency in the child seems to heighten identification, as does high parental nurturance. Demanding parental standards of conduct increase identification, too. There also seems to be a correlation between the use of love-oriented techniques of discipline (withholding love rather than spanking or taking toys away) and the strength of identification. And finally, the clear presentation of models and the labeling of appropriate behavior (telling Johnny that Mommy is stepping on the match so that it won't start a forest fire) increase the child's discrimination of what behaviors he wants to imitate.

A number of theorists today feel that the complex process of identification is responsible for learning not only conscience but other generalized sets of attitudes and actions, too. For example, the process of sex-typing—the way we pick up attitudes about what we are as girls and boys, what we expect to be and to think as women and men—involves learning on a much broader range than simple modeling or reinforcement provides.

This notion has received some support from recent research. One study of 4-year-olds (Sears et al., 1965) used several different tests—for example, leaving a child alone for 20 minutes with candies he was not allowed to touch—to measure children's consciences. The findings linked conscience to sex-typing, for they showed that strength of conscience (as measured by resistance to temptation, guilt reaction, and adherence to rules) was higher in children who identified with a parent of the same sex and who showed well-developed sex-role behavior.

IDENTIFICATION: DOES IT WORK AS AN EXPLANATION? The fact that conscience and sex-typing seem to develop together lends some strength to the notion that one basic process, such as identification, probably accounts for the learning of broad complexes of behavior. Both conscience and sex-typing develop at a very early age, both depend upon parents' attitudes, and both are very basic parts of the child's and the adult's self-concept. Why shouldn't both be learned by the same process?

Other findings seem to support the idea of identification as the learning tool, too. Many of the studies on the development of prosocial behavior show that modeling, which is basically a very simplified and limited form of identification, is one of the most potent forces in the socialization of young children. When children have models to imitate, they learn behaviors much more quickly than if only rewards and punishments are used (Bandura, 1967). It seems likely that broad attitudes should be picked up in the same manner, by observing, ingesting, and digesting the standards of the most important models of all—the parents.

This last point is one of the keys to the argument against the notion of identification, too (Bandura, 1967). Many theorists feel that there is no real distinction between the processes of imitation and identification. In imitation, the viewer is learning either a simple or complex behavior from a model who may be either a loved one or a total stranger. In identification, complex attitudes and patterns of behavior are learned from selected significant models. These theorists view identification as no more than a special kind of modeling. In addition, the concept of identification is criticized because it cannot explain the selectivity of the learning process. Why do children adopt some of their parents' attitudes but not all of them? And how do they learn feelings like guilt or self-criticism, which are basic parts of conscience but which their parents are unlikely ever to exhibit in front of them (Hoffman, 1970). Defensive identification explains this better than either positive identification or modeling. The concept of identification is still a fairly amorphous one, yet perhaps it gives us a useful clue for understanding a little more about the early development of personality.

SUMMARY   The 6-year-old thinks and behaves in very different ways from the 2-year-old, for many important changes take place in the development of personality in these early years. While the 2-year-old is direct in his expression of emotion, the 6-year-old has developed more controlled, sophisticated coping strategies—methods of handling his feelings that will probably remain with him throughout his lifetime. Fear and anxiety are two stressful emotions which the child must find ways to reduce, and he often uses defense mechanisms to do this. Our culture demands that we learn self-restraint in other feelings, too, whether in unpleasant ones such as anger, hostility, and jealousy, or in pleasant ones of affection, joy, and sensuality.

Besides learning to deal with his emotions in these early years, the youngster is also beginning to resolve some developmental conflicts. He starts to deal with his dependence on others, and he develops basic ideas about his competence and autonomy. In fact, he forms a fairly thorough self-concept. In all of these areas, the child's self-image and coping strategies are greatly affected by his parents. Parents serve as important models for the child, and the dimensions of their attitudes and actions—their degree of restrictiveness, warmth, or detachment—have a crucial impact on the child.

One of the most important ways a child learns behavior and attitudes is by modeling. Studies show that aggressive behavior is directly learned by watching models. Some theorists think that identification, a process similar to modeling but on a broader scale, is responsible for the child's learning of basic attitudes and complexes of behavior such as conscience and sex-typing.

REVIEW QUESTIONS   1. Are defense mechanisms abnormal? What different effects might a child's early use of the defenses of denial and withdrawal have upon his later life?

2. Many theorists think we pick up our most basic attitudes by the process of identification. Do you think that identification is a satisfactory explanation for this type of broad learning? Why? How do identification and modeling differ?

3. What effects may television violence have on children? Are all children affected in the same way?

4. Explain the differences in the ways a 2-year-old and a 3-year-old deal with their feelings of dependency.

Fraiberg, S. *The magic years.* New York: Scribners, 1959. With great
sensitivity and a blend of practical observation and psychoanalytical
theory, Selma Fraiberg describes the evolving personality.

Ginott, H. G. *Between parent and child.* New York: Macmillan, 1965.
Ginott presents down-to-earth suggestions and examples for increasing honest communication and understanding between parents
and children.

Liebert, R. M., Neale, J. M., & Davidson, E. S. *The early window: Effects
of television on children and youth.* New York: Pergamon Press, 1973.
Liebert and his colleagues have drawn together considerable research
on the effects of television on children and youth and presented it in a
most readable and persuasive fashion.

PART V:
MIDDLE CHILDHOOD

14

THE SCHOOL BEGINNER: TRANSITION AND CHANGE

Tremendous change and growth complicate the journey of the school beginner as he steps out into the mainstream of society, on his own for the first time. Will you ever forget that first ride on the school bus, when the seats were so high your feet dangled above the floor and the fifth-graders seemed like giants? At school, there were new rules to follow, new adults to obey, new children to play and fight with, new games, and new problems. Most societies initially impose these changes on children somewhere between ages 5 and 7. Formal schooling begins in England at age 5, in Russia at age 7, and in the United States at age 6, often preceded by kindergarten. There seems to be a feeling, common to diverse cultures, that the 5- to 7-year-old has entered a new stage of responsibility, sometimes called the "age of reason." The transition may be marked by a ceremony in which the child receives symbolic gifts or is initiated into secret rituals. In the Middle Ages, the change was dramatically indicated by children's clothing; after the age of 6 or 7, the child was dressed like a miniature adult and was expected to act like a grown-up. Modern societies take a more general, less ritual-istic approach, easing the child into a series of age-graded tasks and responsibilities.

The fact that so many cultures have chosen this age period in which to begin the systematic socialization of their young is probably no historical accident. When a child is between 5 and 7 years of age, many of his cognitive, language, and perceptual-motor skills mature and interact in a way that makes certain kinds of learning easier and more efficient. Thus, cognitive theorists find a qualitative change in the think-ing process during this period. In Piagetian theory, for example, these years mark the transition from preoperational to concrete operational thought. Also, the child's thought becomes increasingly less intuitive and egocentric and more logical. For example, in verbal learning re-search, psychologists have noted greater use of language to direct thought and action at this age period. This process is called *verbal mediation* (Kendler & Kendler, 1959, 1962). And finally, there is a change in perceptual-motor maturity. A preschool child uses a crayon to make marks and squiggles, to explore dark and light colors, to contain spaces, or to fill spaces. The 5- to 7-year-old draws representational images of people, places, and objects. The older child has thus moved from the status of a mere onlooker to that of an active creator, symbolically ex-pressing feelings and experiences that have affected him in some way. By age 7 or 8, according to Gardner (1973a), the child has become aware of the essential function of the artist. Of course, this development is dependent upon increasingly refined motor skills, especially manual dexterity. The child may attempt to draw a happy portrait of his mother, but his clumsy fingers may produce nothing more than wild blobs of color. The 5- to 7-year-olds show progressively greater ability to manip-ulate pencils and scissors and to paint more effectively.

Several seemingly incidental changes also occur during this period. For example, there is the shift from *color dominance* to *form dominance*. In a widely used experiment, children are asked to find the pattern that most closely resembles the first object shown to them. While younger children overwhelmingly select on the basis of the same color, children 6 years and older increasingly choose on the basis of similar form. The accumulation of these small items of change constitutes a transition to a new period of development (White, 1965).

Children's effective learning of cultural demands should be coordinated carefully with their respective maturational levels in several areas. This coordination is particularly important if we make our cultural demands in the form of specific school lessons in which the children are carefully graded based on their age. If the tasks are either too simple or too complex for a child's cognitive perceptual-motor skills, his interests, or his past knowledge, he may become frustrated, bored, or inattentive. Learning programs proceed best when they capitalize on the optimal periods for developing various verbal, spatial, or numerical abilities or perceptual-motor coordination.

MATCHING CULTURAL DEMANDS AND DEVELOPMENTAL ABILITIES

Of course, the teacher or educational designer's task is complicated because there is no such creature as the "average" child. Children develop skills at varying rates. Thus, a very bright 6-year-old may read at a third-grade level, but he may be too immature emotionally to be able to participate in a reading group without disrupting it. Or, as happens quite often, his underdeveloped motor coordination may interfere with his writing ability and convince his teacher that he is a slow student, at least in his paperwork. The challenge of education is to work with each child and encourage the development of all his abilities. Every pupil has a unique configuration of talents and shortcomings, and his growth to more complex levels of achievement may occur in awkward fits and starts. Furthermore, growth in one aspect of behavior may cause disequilibrium and temporary setbacks in other areas. The course of learning, when individually paced, is rarely smooth and straight.

Educators have profound disagreements concerning the aims of education. Yet the child of 5, 6, or 7 years is abruptly confronted with one or another of these aims in his local elementary school. Kohlberg and Meyer (1972) suggest three types of educators: traditionalists, romantic humanists, and developmental progressivists. Traditionalists believe that their primary task is to transmit the accumulated knowledge, skills, and values of past generations. Romantic humanists stress spontaneous growth and self-actualization, to be achieved by the child's exploration of his own feelings and ideas. This humanistic school of thought tends to value emotional development, such as self-confidence and spontaneity, rather than formal academic achievement. The developmental progressivists, who take their philosophical premises from the work of John Dewey and incorporate much of Piagetian stage theory, argue that the educator's main function is to encourage

When the task matches the child's ability, he is not easily distracted. (*Mark Godfrey, Magnum Photos.*)

the child's natural cognitive development from one cognitive mode to another with activities appropriate for the specific age. Full development of each stage is felt to be more important than accelerating growth to the next highest stage. Kohlberg and Meyer obviously identify themselves with the third type of educator. The developmental progressivists' basic premise is that the demands of the educational task must be matched to the needs and abilities of the child at this particular stage of development.

CHANGING
THOUGHT
Qualitative Change

Most psychologists agree that there are qualitative changes in a child's thinking processes during the years from 5 to 7, although there are theoretical disputes about the nature and cause of the changes. Many of these changes appear at first to be isolated and incidental. We have already mentioned the average child's shift from color dominance to form dominance in matching-and-choosing tasks during this period. Other minor changes take place in the way that children explore the world around them. While the preschooler is often quite sensitive to tactual cues and likes to rub, pound, and poke new objects, the older child increasingly attends to visual and auditory stimuli. In one experiment where children were allowed to choose between activities—for example, they could choose either to mold putty or to use a kaleidoscope, or to look at slides rather than manipulate toys inside a dark box—older children chose visual and auditory tasks (Schopler, 1964). In direction and orientation problems, a large number of 6-year-olds developed a sense of personal left and right, although they still had difficulty ascertaining someone else's left and right. They also showed a notable decrease in form reversal mistakes by their ability to identify correctly a form or object that had been rotated or represented in mirror images (White, 1965).

Evidence of cognitive change may be indicated by the growing predictability of the adult IQ. While there is only a minimal correlation between a person's IQ at age 2 and his adult IQ, there is a highly significant correlation between the test scores he achieves as a 7-year-old and as an adult (Bayley, 1949). A dramatic change in predictability has occurred between ages 5 and 7. The evidence may result, in part, from the structure of the intelligence tests or it may reflect real changes in the 7-year-old's thought which are more consistent with adult intelligence.

One classic experiment highlights an important difference in the way preschoolers and older children learn. In this experiment, children are trained to choose the "correct object" in a situation in which there are two dimensions—large and small size versus square and circular form—and in which one end of one dimension is correct (for example, large always wins). (See Figure 12.) After the children successfully learn this first discrimination, the game is changed but the children are not told

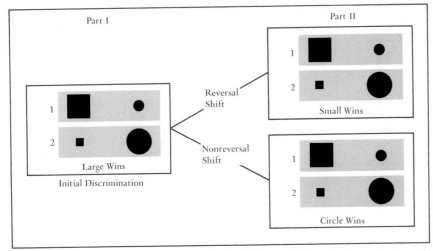

Figure 12 The Kendler discrimination task. A child is taught the rules for a win through repeated trials in Part I. In Part II, the items presented are the same but the rules for a win are changed by either a reversal or nonreversal (dimensional) shift. *(From Kendler, T. S. Development of mediating responses in children. In J. C. Wright & J. Kagan (Eds.), Basic cognitive processes in children.* Monographs of the Society for Research in Child Development, *1963, 28 [2, Serial No. 86].)*

that the rules have been switched. The change may be to the other end of the same dimension (large to small); this is called a *reversal shift.* Or it may be to one end of the other dimension of form; now either square or circular is correct. This is termed a *nonreversal shift.* The interesting result is that small children, rats, and monkeys generally find a nonreversal shift easier to learn, while bright kindergarteners and college students do better in learning reversal shifts. The Kendlers suggest that younger children and animals are operating on laws of reward and association; they have already been rewarded for one-half of the new task: choosing the large circle. In the nonreversal shift, they only have to learn to choose the small circle instead of the large square. Older children, on the other hand, seem to change easily to a new aspect of the same dimension, a conceptually more complex process. They have learned "size is important and large wins." Now they must change only the last rule (Kendler & Kendler, 1959, 1962).

Although psychologists dispute the fundamental causes underlying these cognitive changes, there is general agreement on two major principles. First, 7-year-olds increasingly resort to rule-controlled thought, although simple association remains an important part of their mental processes. Their thought tends to be deliberate and reflective, rather than impulsive, and they become more adept at using hypotheses and rules.

The second change involves the use of language. Many psychologists (Kendler, 1963; Mowbray & Luria, 1973), but not all, agree that language is increasingly interposed between thought and action. This process of verbal mediation involves the use of verbal links between the overt stimulus and the final response. (The child is thinking before he acts!) More and more, the child uses verbal labels and directions to himself to accentuate crucial aspects of a problem and arrive at a solution.

Precisely when verbal mediation comes into play is much debated, partly as a corollary to the question of whether language must precede the formulation of certain concepts. Some psychologists, including the Kendlers, argue that language is critical, while others, most notably Piaget, feel that a child must first develop certain concepts before he can attach and use the appropriate words meaningfully.

One researcher (Blank, 1974) suggests that verbal mediation occurs much earlier than the period from age 5 to age 7 indicated by the Kendlers' previously mentioned discrimination experiments. She argues that children as young as 3 years employ language when their other skills, such as pointing or mimicking, are of no avail in solving a problem. Since many experimental designs testing mediation present tasks that can be solved nonverbally—for instance, by pointing—the tests may not tap an existing ability to mediate. It is possible that younger children effectively mediate in some situations but not in others. For example, in discriminating time, 3- and 4-year-olds may rely heavily on verbalized labels or codes. The same age groups will not demonstrate as much verbalization in solving spatial problems, where they can discriminate between large and small with visual cues, by merely looking at the objects. At any rate, the debate on mediation and the role of language in cognitive development has clearly not been resolved.

| Piaget, Bruner, and Intuitive Thought | Piaget characterized the 4- to 7-year-old age span as the intuitive stage. The intuitive child relies more heavily on immediate perception and on his direct experience than on logical operations; he centers on one dimension or feature at a time (centering); he sees the world mostly from his own point of view (egocentricity); and he cannot reverse his thinking. Once the ball of clay has been rolled into a fat sausage, he cannot predict what size the clay will be when it is rolled back into a ball. His thinking tends to be static, based on the way things are now rather than on the transformations or changes that have taken place in the past or might take place in the future. Toward the end of the intuitive stage, the rigid, static, and irreversible qualities of intuitive thought begin to "thaw out," in Piaget's terminology, becoming more reversible and flexible (Flavell, 1963). Increasingly, the child is able to take notice of one, then another, facet of an object and reconcile differences between the two. The fact that a piece of clay now looks like a sausage is no longer inconsistent with the fact that it was formerly a ball or the possibility that it could be molded into a new shape, such as a cube. This emerging ability to go beyond the immediate self with mental leaps and bounds is the precursor of systematic reasoning in the "con- |

If a child finds reading a rewarding experience, she will continue to discover and explore. (*Leif Skoogfors, Woodfin Camp & Assoc.*)

crete" and "formal" stages. It may be very important at this time to engage the child's interest and enthusiasm in his new ability to perform mental acrobatics, to nurture love of learning and discovery as intrinsically rewarding and exciting things. The child who finds excitement in flexing his growing mental muscles will learn faster and more thoroughly than the child who feels only that he has "a job to do."

Since it is clear that certain changes are remolding and expanding the young mind during this period, we might ask ourselves about the possibilities of facilitating this growth. What are the roles of education in general and the teacher in particular? If these changes are seemingly inevitable and universal, should we make any effort at all to induce change, or should we let it bloom unaided? Perhaps all children are deprived of some crucial experiences; and if we uniformly enriched their lives, they would make the transition to concrete thought at age 3 or 4, instead of age 7 or 8.

Applied researchers have made interesting attempts to expedite the transition from preoperational thought to the concrete operational level. Their endeavors fly in the face of Piaget's assertion that cognitive development, in contrast to training, is primarily an integral organic process relatively immune to outside tampering.

Facilitating Change

Smedslund, for example, had some success in training preoperational children to produce the correct solutions to conservation problems modeled on Piaget's experiments with the differently shaped beakers of water (see Chapter 4). However, the children's ability to perform one concrete operational task did not generalize itself to other problems using the same principle (Smedslund, 1961).

Smedslund's techniques were noticeably more effective with 5- and 6-year-olds who were nearly ready to make such discoveries for themselves. Bruner and his colleagues also stress the importance of readiness or optimal periods, just prior to the natural transition, when training is most effective (Bruner, Olver, & Greenfield, 1966). This is not to say that attempts to induce cognitive change prematurely have been completely fruitless. Some recent experiments have instilled concrete thinking processes in 5- and 6-year-olds quite successfully, particularly in solving tasks of conservation, but were less successful with 3- and 4-year-olds (Siegler & Liebert, 1972a, 1972b). However, to get children to use concrete operational thought, it was first necessary to give them rather extensive training in a prerequisite set of rules. The educator might reasonably wonder whether it is really worth such arduous efforts to accelerate development by a year or so, rather than wait and allow the child the joy of making the discovery for himself.

Whether or not children can effectively be "jumped" from one cognitive level to another is still uncharted ground for both the psychologist and the teacher. However, it is clear that some teaching techniques facilitate growth and change in the way children think, while others do not. Unfortunately, too much of early education is devoted to rote memorization of letters, words, and numbers that pile up like dusty furniture in the attic. The child may be able to name each item successfully; but too often he fails to develop the mental muscles which would enable him to take the furniture out of the attic and put it in new and different positions for new and different purposes.

Bruner suggests several specific methods for aiding growth of the mind (Bruner et al., 1966). First, concrete objects are particularly useful for teaching 5- to 7-year-olds how to manipulate, compare, and contrast, so that they can discover the similarities, relationships, and irregularities. Furthermore, since the 5- to 7-year-old characteristically centers on one or another dimension of these physical objects, the teacher can stretch the child's horizons by calling his attention to another aspect with a simple demonstration. In the liquid conservation problem, for example, the teacher can show that the water in the tall, thin beaker will fill a standard 8-ounce measuring cup and so will the water in the short, wide beaker. Another important method is using language cues to highlight particular parts of the problem and focus the child's attention. For example, the teacher might say to the child, "You just told me that the beakers hold different amounts of water, but now it looks as if each one holds 8 ounces."

At the same time as we facilitate growth, we must maintain the child's interest in learning and problem solving. If a major problem that the child has is extrinsic to the learning process (such as trying to figure out what the teacher wants), he may lose interest in the problem itself. By the same token, if the child's main reward is something extrinsic, like praise from his teacher or a good grade, he may stop learning when he no longer receives a reward. When the child finds an intrinsic reward in the act of solving a problem, his interest in learning and his confidence in himself grow (Bruner, 1973).

When compared to informal education in the family or community, formal schools and instruction actually set up some obstacles to maximizing growth (Bruner, 1965a). In schools, we teach children by telling them, rather than by showing them. We remove the real-life, concrete context. The result is that children are left with an arid body of facts and no idea of how to use them in any situation other than the specific episode in class. We give them the rules and rote memory systems, but not necessarily the understanding. Although psychologists still have much to discover about the many possible ways of maximizing development, they do know that 5- to 7-year-olds learn by doing, by actively manipulating objects, and by solving problems within a situational context.

NEW CULTURAL DEMANDS

Most children enter some kind of school or group between the ages of 5 and 7, if they have not already done so before. The demands and expectations they encounter vary tremendously from one school or one culture to another, but all usually involve marked change from the earlier expectations placed on the children when they were at home, surrounded by their immediate families. New cultural demands come from many sources. Institutions such as schools operate under a complicated matrix of customs, roles, tasks, values, and expectations. New supervising adults, such as playground leaders and babysitters, may impose sets of their own rules and demands. Finally, the children in the new environment—both peers and slightly older, more experienced children—all place intense demands on the newcomer.

Diversity of Expectations

Regardless of whether the child enters into a formal school at age 3 or age 5, he must adapt to certain minimal changes immediately. Different people now supervise him; he is separated from his parent or former major caretaker and must develop trust in other people to look after his safety and satisfy his needs. At the same time, the child must become somewhat independent and learn to do certain things for himself. No longer can he sit down and yell, "Who will put on my boots?" It is time for him to put on his own boots. Even with a very favorable student-teacher ratio, children have to compete for adult attention and assistance. They must also learn to cooperate with others and develop a general understanding of the rules by which this cooperative society operates.

Beyond the general demands for autonomy and cooperation, the more formal schools operate with elaborate codes of behavior, the enforcement of which can consume an incredible proportion of teaching time. The child must listen when the teacher speaks, line up for recess, obtain permission before going to the bathroom, raise his hand before speaking, and so forth. Psychology students observing public school classrooms often perform an exercise which entails categorizing the teacher's activities such as the following: (1) teaching a fact or concept; (2) giving directions for a particular lesson; (3) stating general rules of appropriate classroom behavior; (4) correcting, disciplining, and praising children; and (5) miscellaneous. The results are quite revealing. It is not unusual, in a half-hour lesson, for a student to observe that somewhere between 70 percent and 90 percent of the teacher's comments fall into the third and fourth categories. The teacher may devote large amounts of time and energy to socializing the children to the highly particularized demands

A formal school classroom in Twin Falls, Idaho. (*Renee Burri, Magnum Photos.*)

An open classroom in New York City. (*Bruce Roberts, Rapho/Photo Researchers.*)

of this school, which may have only tenuous connections with real intellectual or social growth.

Of course, the character of the demands may differ radically, depending upon nationality, customs, and educational philosophy. For example, Bronfenbrenner (1970) describes, as he observed them, the extensive codes of behavior for school, home, and public places in the curriculum for Russian 7-year-olds:

> In school: All pupils are to arrive at school and in the classroom on time, wipe their feet upon entering, greet the teacher and all technical staff by name, give a general greeting to classmates and personal greeting by name to one's seatmate, keep one's things in order, obey all instructions of the teacher, learn rules of class conduct (standing when spoken to, proper position in listening, reading and writing)... (p. 28).

There are similarly detailed provisions for appropriate behavior toward parents and other adults, for execution of tasks at home such as washing dishes and shining shoes, and for behavior on public transportation. Contrast this kind of regimentation with an "open classroom," in which children sit, squat, or lie down anywhere they want in a decentralized room, select their work for the day, and mainly interact with the teacher and other children in small groups. Yet, there are rules in the open classroom too, even if unspoken. Children are expected to act independently, to ask questions, and to avoid disturbing others. This approach is based on the assumption that children are motivated to learn, and learn best, when they have a great deal of free choice of kinds of things to do. The teacher's task is to encourage each child to develop his own interests at his own pace (Gross & Gross, 1970).

Regardless of what kind of school the child enters, there is always a tremendous gap between behavior that was accepted and approved at home and the new demands thrust upon the child in the classroom. Certainly, the greater the gap, the more difficult the adaptation required. Recent educational critiques such as *Death at an Early Age* (Kozol, 1970) or *How Children Fail* (Holt, 1964) point out all too clearly the effect upon children of dramatic differences in environment. Preschool teachers and day-care workers are acutely aware of the tremendous variance in children's responses to new cultural demands; yet, sadly, the research literature on the adjustment reactions of 5-year-olds is rather scant (Read, 1971). And this is an age at which the child has just barely begun to internalize the rights and wrongs of family life. All of a sudden, we expect him to adapt readily to a whole new set of procedures. The success with which the child makes this transition depends upon external factors, such as family background and school environment, and also upon the variables of individual development. How well has the child previously coped with dependency, autonomy, the need to control aggression, and the promptings of conscience? His inner resources may be shaky; nevertheless, we require of the school beginner a flexibility that is rarely required of an adult.

Peers have some effect upon the socialization process as early as late infancy, but their most dramatic impact occurs later, during the formation of regular, structured groups like play groups or kindergarten.

LEVELS OF INTERACTION. Early studies on peer relations charted the development of different levels of interaction in young children. Mildred Parten (1932–33), in some seminal research, identified six levels: (1) *unoccupied behavior*; (2) *solitary play*; (3) *on-looker play*, where the child's interaction is limited to merely observing other children; (4) *parallel play*, where the child plays alongside another child and uses similar toys but does not interact in any other way; (5) *associated* or *associative play*, in which children share materials and interact somewhat, but not necessarily in one cooperative task with a single theme or goal; and (6) *cooperative play*, in which children engage in a single activity together, such as building one house with the same kind of blocks, or playing hide-and-go-seek with a commonly accepted set of rules.

Associated play occurs when children share materials and interact, somewhat, but not necessarily towards one cooperative goal. (*Tim Egan, Woodfin Camp & Assoc.*)

Cooperative play occurs when children engage in a single activity together. (*Alex Webb, Magnum Photos.*)

Different modes of play predominate at given age levels. Two-year-olds engage heavily in onlooker and parallel play. The 4- and 5-year-olds show increasing amounts of associative and cooperative play. In optimal surroundings, 5-, 6-, and 7-year-olds can develop relatively lengthy cooperative endeavors with much sharing of materials, the establishment of rules, mutual assistance, and variation of roles within the play.

MODELING AND REINFORCEMENT. Once children interact with each other, even if only as onlookers, peers become important both as models to be copied and as an audience or reinforcement for individual behavior. It is more fun to be silly if someone laughs at your antics. *Behavior contagion*, or copying, is already at work in nursery schools and day-care centers. Some school systems—the Russian and Chinese systems are outstanding examples (Sidel, 1972)—take particular note of the power of peers as reinforcement and models and use this power to help establish behavioral standards in classes. Other educators view copying as a nuisance or an irritant at best and try to suppress it. Since social pressure is clearly a major factor in child development, it seems more sensible somehow to incorporate it into classroom procedure. Some kinds of reinforcement are more effective than others. For example, one series of studies by Hartup (1964) indicates that occasional praise from a person who is not a friend is more encouraging to a child than identical praise from a friend. Similarly, praise coming from an older or younger child has more impact as reinforcement than praise from a child the same age as the one being praised.

PEER ROLES AND RELATIONSHIPS. Children must work out a number of interpersonal relationships in the course of maturing, and often it is easier to make these accommodations with peers than with adults. For example, the young child must experience dominant and submissive roles, alternately flexing power and accepting dependency in the appropriate situations. In an interdependent world, children need to modify rigidity and extremes of their behavior for the sake of mutual, cooperative responsibility for each other, and this is no easy task.

In learning to strike the delicate balance required in social relationships, young children often initially exaggerate the new roles of aggressor and victim, leader and conformist. Furthermore, during the course of a year in a single classroom, patterns of power and control tend to be established to the point where children can readily identify the toughest, the meanest, the smartest, and the most incompetent of their classmates. To give children a chance to try out a number of different roles over a period of time, teachers can strive for a flexible atmosphere and discourage pecking orders. One of the most successful techniques is changing the age mix of the group. With children younger than himself, a child can be the leader, the responsible one, the boss; and with the older children, he can experience submissive, dependent, and copying roles.

The child's reactions to the demands of schooling result from the complex interplay of all his resources: intellectual, perceptual, physical, motor, social, and emotional. Marked inadequacy or disequilibrium in one area may interfere with growth in others. For example, when children who speak only a foreign language enter a school where all subjects are taught in English, their initial capacity to process events at school intellectually is severely hampered. Some children learn English rapidly through this total immersion in the language, but others find the situation too difficult to cope with and fail to make a positive adaptation. Not only does language development suffer, but the repeated frustration and failure set a pattern for later adjustment to much of school and learning.

A second problem arising from the uneven development of skills involves the normative, age-graded structure of the schooling process. Teachers have particular expectations of the average 5-year-old or 7-year-old which few children are able to match in every respect. For example, reading readiness in the first grade requires sufficient perceptual maturity to identify letters and follow a left-to-right sequence, enough fine motor coordination to write letters, and the auditory ability

The Whole Child

to discriminate among phonetic sounds. In addition, however, to learn to read as part of a class, the child must also be able to sit attentively for long periods of time, follow directions, and inhibit irrelevant impulses. A child who is immature or unfamiliar with any one, or a combination, of these expectations may fail to learn to read in the specific manner in which the skill is taught. Teachers should be aware of the complexity of these potentially dysfunctional factors in analyzing the poor performance of an individual child.

SCHOOLS: GOALS AND FUNCTIONS OF EARLY EDUCATION
Why Early Education?

Many states require school attendance by age 7 and demand that each city and town provide school opportunities for children at a somewhat younger age, with attendance optional. Is there any clear advantage in mandatory schooling for, say, 3- and 4-year-olds? Educators are divided on this question, with both sides marshaling impressive arrays of experimental data, sociopolitical arguments, theoretical justifications, and more than a hint of plain old personal opinion. Opponents of early education feel that it places excessive demands on children who are too immature to cope with them and thus fall into early patterns of frustration and failure (Ames, 1971). The most important needs for the preschooler, these psychologists argue, are warmth, continuity, and security, and they feel it crucial that the child's environment be free of tasks that will be too taxing intellectually (Moore & Moore, 1972). The best place for early development, according to this view, is home, where the child is protected from mental and emotional problems that may disrupt his learning, motivation, and behavior.

Over in the other camp, extreme partisans in favor of early education rally under the famous maxim of Bruner, "Any subject can be taught effectively in some intellectually honest way to any child at any stage of development" (Bruner, 1960, p. 33). Other psychologists and educators pitch their tents on middle ground but generally feel that early education can stimulate intellectual, social, and motor development. Certainly, television programs of the type of "The Electric Company" and "Sesame Street" have demonstrated that a carefully designed presentational style can teach certain specific skills, such as numbers or letters, to millions of children simultaneously. Kindergarten and first-grade teachers generally agree that many of their students arrive at school better equipped, particularly in some of the rote memory tasks of learning numbers and letters, than children did even 5 years ago.

Nevertheless, the empirical data on different kinds of early education are extraordinarily confusing and have failed to resolve the question of what effects 2, 3, or 4 years of training before first grade can have on a child. In evaluating nursery schools, the problem is what to measure. Early nursery schools emphasized social and emotional development, with the children spending a great deal of time in free play, sociodramatic play, in the doll corner, and in the playground. The studies are contradictory at best, with some indicating increased independence and self-direction in children after attendance at nursery schools and others producing evidence of greater difficulty (as rated by the teacher) in following teacher directions and conforming to school rules. This latter phenomenon may stem from inconsistent expectations of the pre-school and primary school; alternatively, it may be partially attributable to the fact that some children are sent to nursery school precisely because they have poor self-control and nursery school is intended to be therapeutic (Evans, 1975).

Similar problems exist in evaluating kindergarten programs, because different curricula yield different results. Children in a classroom traditionally oriented to personal and social behavior seem to be more cooperative and friendly than children in a cognitively structured program; and children in a "creative-aesthetic" curriculum have been rated as more enthusiastic and aggressive than children in other programs or in no program at all (Evans, 1975).

The Head Start movement generated much more controversy and some thorough and complete evaluative research. As a major national economic investment, it involved considerable preparation as well as follow-up analysis. Head Start was begun with tremendous optimism that it would remedy basic problems in the social order by providing early intervention with individual children. The hope and the promise were only partly fulfilled, as indicated by the first major evaluative report, the Westinghouse Study (Westinghouse Learning Corporation, 1969). On intellectual measure, most Head Starters showed gains of as much as 12 points in IQ scores in the first 3 or 4 months of the program. However, long-term studies indicated that most of this initial progress was lost 2 years later when the children enrolled in regular school programs. There are several possible explanations for these disappointing data: (1) the changes were in fact short-lived; (2) the most important gains (in self-confidence and motivation) were not measured by the cognitive follow-up tests; (3) the formal school program was so inconsistent with Head Start activities that the early learning did not help; (4) the Westinghouse Study clumped together Head Start programs of vastly different quality, thus masking the fact that some excellent Head Start programs produced real and long-term gains, while inadequate programs may have actually instilled failure. Some later studies suggest that the last hypothesis is the strongest of the four (Horowitz and Paden, 1973).

The theoretical rationale for early education is much more encouraging. A great deal of the child research that we have surveyed in the last three chapters suggests that basic patterns of motivation, learning, and self-image are laid down in this early period. And a responsive environment is a crucial part of this picture—an environment which changes in response to the child's actions. Children learn by observing the consequences of their acts, by putting objects into new forms, by getting feedback from those around them. Whether at home or in school, the child's surroundings are a powerful force that can enhance or retard his growth. Positive and negative experiences can happen with equal regularity in both places.

Approaches to Early Education

MONTESSORI SCHOOLS. Although most Montessori schools in the United States tend to be expensive private schools, Dr. Maria Montessori, an energetic and innovative Italian physician, first began her experimental educational methods with retarded children, followed by socially disadvantaged children from the tenements of Rome. She believed that children who came from a chaotic and unpredictable home life needed a great deal of experience with materials that emphasized the sequence, order, and regularity in life. The Montessori approach features a *prepared environment* and signed, self-correcting materials. The child must arrange in sequence a set of graduated cylinders, weights, or smooth-to-rough textured pieces of cloth. Working in an age-mixed classroom with other children from 3 to 7, the child selects his own task and returns his materials to the shelf when he is finished with them. He also learns practical tasks such as washing dishes, making soup, gardening, and painting a real wall. The whole atmosphere in a Montessori school is one of quiet busyness and confident accomplishment. The curriculum is aimed at developing motor and sensory skills, as well as the ability to order and classify materials. These are felt to be the basic forerunners of more complex tasks such as reading and understanding mathematics. Many recent educational techniques selectively incorporate some of the Montessori methods, particularly self-teaching materials, individually paced progress, real-life tasks, and the relative absence of either praise or criticism.

FORMAL DIDACTIC EDUCATION. The formal approach, which uses carefully structured lessons to inculcate a particular set of skills, is best typified by the Bereiter and Engelmann program (Bereiter & Engelmann, 1966) designed specifically for disadvantaged children. In devising a sequence of lessons to teach the requisite skills in a gradual, sequential order (later known as the Distar program), the two psychologists divided the children into homogeneous small groups of approximately five members. The major part of the program has the teacher ask a question or give a sentence and the children respond by answering the question or repeating the sentence in unison. The children are also actively involved in individual interchange with the teacher, with immediate feedback and warm praise for success. Positive reinforcement is relied upon quite heavily. Lessons are taught in 20-minute drill periods. Little time is allowed for free play between periods because the play distracts from the major aim of the school, which is the learning of specific facts, principles, and skills.

Research indicates that the children do learn the specific behavioral objectives quickly and well. However, long-term results show less than complete transfer of the learned skills into public school experience. Again, there are several hypotheses which attempt to explain this phenomenon: (1) the schools that these disadvantaged children entered

Concrete experiences form the foundation for later abstract mathematics. (*Nancy Hayes, Monkmeyer.*)

were so stifling, socially and intellectually, that they could not encourage success in even the brightest, most motivated child; (2) the difference in expectations between the Distar preparation and the public school was so great that the particular behaviors could not be sustained; (3) the children became overly dependent upon the extrinsic rewards of praise, hugs, and smiles and failed to derive any intrinsic pleasure from the learning and problem-solving process. At any rate, children in these programs display marked initial success, with kindergartners often reading on a second-grade level. Usually the early advantage does not disappear until about the fourth grade.

OPEN EDUCATION. Open education is an eclectic movement drawing from such diverse theoretical sources as Piaget, John Dewey (1961), and Susan Isaacs (1930). It does not simply adopt a laissez-faire, anything-goes attitude, and it does not mean merely a large open space with lots of children and lots of different activities. Good open education, as exemplified by the British Infant School, requires extensive planning and preparation before the children burst into the classroom.

The British Infant School was designed to facilitate the transition of children into the formal English educational structure (Plowden, 1967). Some of its more salient characteristics are:

1. The integrated day. Instead of having their class time split up into discrete periods for each subject, children engage in ongoing projects that involve the use of several different skills simultaneously. For example, setting up a mock business office may entail a field trip for observation, a written report, group discussion, and some art work or other visual aids.

2. Vertical groupings. Children of different ages are put together in the same classroom. Over the course of several years, a child may develop from the youngest, following and learning from others, to a position of leadership and responsibility.

3. Child input in decision making. Children in open classrooms may often choose from a great variety of activities, deciding how they want to participate and for how long. Great respect is accorded to the child's ability to make responsible decisions. Coercive motivations, such as reward and punishment, are minimized.

The achievement of the British school is impressive, with children equaling or excelling the performance of students in more traditional programs. But the school's curriculum planning is extensive and community support is strong. Some open classrooms in other educational systems produce nothing but chaos; the difference seems to lie in the skill and forethought of the planners and teachers.

Compensatory Education

There is a fairly strong theoretical argument for using the preschool period as an antidote to social disadvantage (Hunt, 1964). We know that intelligence is not fixed or predetermined, that early experience has important consequences for later development, and that learning can be motivated by curiosity and exploration. Still, other problems arise when we attempt to use education to offset social, political, and economic inequities.

First, some of the disadvantages of the poor are not experimental at all; they are biological and physical. Poverty not only reduces the opportunities available to the poor, it also limits nutrition, health care, and, consequently, the physical growth of the organism. (See Chapter 3.)

Second, labeling any particular population group as socially or culturally disadvantaged is prone to degenerating into ethnocentrism, racism, or class snobbery. Certainly, in the last 10 years, we have gained a greater respect for cultural pluralism, for accepting cultural differences without concluding that there is an accompanying cultural deficit (Cole & Bruner, 1971).

There are many kinds of compensatory education programs. Some involve home intervention: training mothers to stimulate and encourage their children in daily interactions around the house (Gray & Klaus, 1970; Karnes, Studley, Wright, & Hodgins, 1968). Some, like the Bereiter-Engleman approach, set specific cognitive objectives, while programs like Head Start aim at broader development. Some more recent Head Start programs involve activities for both parents and their children under age 3.

In evaluating compensatory education, we can draw some general conclusions. First, small pilot programs with a heavy infusion of professional skill, like those we have just mentioned, have brought dramatic changes in the physical, social, emotional, and aesthetic behavior and development of children. Second, large and less well supervised programs, such as some Head Start and day-care projects, yield mixed results. Great success has been achieved in nutrition and the general health of children, but the cognitive changes do not persist over long periods of time. Third, programs need to be tailored to the needs of individual children or groups of children. Clearly, some children from certain backgrounds thrive on one kind of early education, while other children with different backgrounds and experiences make greater strides in other educational settings. The challenge remains to identify the crucial variable so that we can predict which child will perform best in, or benefit most from, which program.

SUMMARY

The inner and outer worlds of the 5- to 7-year-old are undergoing complex and interrelated changes. He is moving into the concrete operational stage of thought with a marked increase in verbal mediation, as well as new levels of perceptual-motor, social, and emotional maturity. All of these internal changes, which are related but do not necessarily develop concurrently with each other, take place at a time when the child is thrust into the new environment of school and is confronted with a host of new demands from both adults and peers.

He may make this transition smoothly, or he may encounter severe learning and behavior problems, again depending on the internal and external variables. One crucial factor seems to be how wide the difference is between behavior that was expected and encouraged at home and behavior demanded in school. Different modes of early education seek either to complement or to counteract learning begun at home; and although they aspire to rather different pedagogical goals, all modern approaches tend to agree on at least a few principles. These principles are: the more actively involved the child is, the more the learning is tied to real surroundings, and the more his educational environment responds to him, then the faster and easier the child will learn. The aim of all educational methods today, no matter how diverse, is to capture and foster the intrinsic pleasure in problem solving that is one of our most precious attributes as human beings, and to do this at an early age.

1. Compare the relationship between the personal traits that different societies value in their members and the educational techniques used to instill those traits in young children.

2. What do you consider the most important characteristics to be nurtured in the 5- to 7-year-old? What is the best way to encourage development of these traits? Are your answers based more on your own educational philosophy, on experimental data, on your own experience as a child, or on your experience as an adult dealing with children?

3. What are the advantages and disadvantages of concentrating on the holistic development of the child, as opposed to concentrating on particular skills or traits?

4. In what ways do parents and teachers complement each other in encouraging child development? On what issues are they liable to disagree?

SUGGESTED READINGS

Bereiter, C., & Engelmann, S. *Teaching disadvantaged children in the preschool*. Englewood Cliffs, N.J.: Prentice-Hall, 1966. Bereiter and Engelmann present what may become a classic example of a didactic, structured, carefully sequenced educational approach for young children.

Holt, J. *How children fail*. New York: Dell Publishing Company, 1964. This selection is one of a series of insightful educational critiques written in the last decade.

Montessori, M. *The Montessori method*. New York: Schocken Books, 1964. The Montessori approach to education has withstood the test of several decades, several socioeconomic levels, and several ethnic and cultural groups. It deserves study as a unique and well integrated approach to early education.

Postman, R., & Weingarten, C. *The school book*. New York: Delacorte, 1973. In this highly entertaining book, the authors present a number of serious issues that divide various educational approaches, define terms, and present major figures in education with capsule sketches. As such, it is a good introduction to the major educational controversies today.

CHAPTER

15

COMPETENCIES AND SCHOOL TASKS

For most children, middle childhood is a time for settling down, for developing more fully those patterns that have already been set. It is a period for learning new skills and refining the old ones, whether those skills be reading and writing, or playing basketball, dancing, roller skating, and jumping rope. The child's focus is on testing himself, on meeting his own challenges as well as those imposed by the environment. The child who is successful in these tasks will probably grow even more capable and self-assured; the one who is unsuccessful is more likely to develop the opposite—a feeling of inferiority, or a lessened sense of self.

Erikson has referred to middle childhood as the period of *industry*. The description captures the spirit of that time of life, for the word *industry* is derived from a Latin term meaning "to build." In this chapter we shall look at some of the building children do in the area of developing competencies, both physical and intellectual. In so doing, we shall see how the manner in which schools use tests, treat creativity, and shape their curricula can have significant effects on children's development. Finally, we shall examine how a child's approach to school, his level of anxiety, and his incentive to achieve combine in a complex set of motivations that can spell success or failure.

The development of competencies, industry, or direct mastery of the environment is only part of the motivation in this period of the child's life. Peer pressures and expectations also become increasingly important. The child needs to "appear" competent and capable to achieve some status within his age group. In order to "belong" to the group, he must meet some of the goals and expectations of his peers and fulfill certain social roles. Thus, the social context of learning has greater significance.

COPING WITH PHYSICAL CHALLENGES

Surely one of the first things that impresses any observer of school-age children is their high activity level. What function does all this activity serve? Far from being a waste of time, the games and sports in which children continually engage provide them the opportunity to develop strength, coordination, agility, and flexibility. Thus, at any given time in a neighborhood or playground, children can be seen testing their reflexes and balance by riding their bicycles through homemade obstacle courses; improving their hand-to-eye coordination and strength in games of handball, stickball, and basketball; and increasing their flexibility and agility by climbing trees or attempting feats of daring. Taking part in fads such as riding skateboards, learning the latest dance moves, practicing Kung Fu, or imitating the exploits of TV heroes—all can help a child improve his physical-motor development.

The rapid spurt of physical growth visible in the preschool child begins to slow down as he reaches middle childhood and does not pick up again until adolescence. Thus, aside from the somewhat start-

DEVELOPMENT OF MOTOR SKILLS
IN MIDDLE CHILDHOOD.

(Ellen Pines, Woodfin Camp & Assoc.)

(Ellen Pines, Woodfin Camp & Assoc.)

(Alex Webb, Magnum Photos.)

ling change when the toothless smile of a 6-year-old becomes the disproportionately large-toothed grin of an 8-year-old, the majority of bodily changes that occur in this period are gradual and continuous. Motor skills, too, develop continuously and cumulatively. In such basic motor skills as running, jumping, throwing, and catching the child advances in strength, coordination, balance, agility, precision, and flexibility over the months and years. For example, while a 7-year-old boy can throw a ball approximately 34 feet, he will probably be able to throw it twice that distance by the time he is 10 and triple that distance when he is 12—and he will greatly improve his accuracy, as well. Similar progress in athletic ability holds true for girls, although the average distances of their throws are less (Keogh, 1965).

There are numerous studies that demonstrate children's progressions in each aspect of motor development. In one such study of increasing precision, for instance, children were asked to try to intercept a ball swinging in front of them on a string. The 6-year-olds succeeded in touching the ball an average of one out of every five times. The 8-year-olds, however, succeeded approximately three out of every five times, and the 8½- to 11-year-olds were generally able to intercept the ball four out of five times (Cratty, 1970). Similar "experiments" are repeated daily by anyone who teaches children to bat a ball or play tennis or shoot baskets!

In our increasingly urban and industrialized society, it is becoming apparent that we must set aside areas and create opportunities for children to develop gross motor skills. One somewhat different approach created to meet the child's needs for physical activity is the adventure playground.

Adventure Playgrounds   Without the usual slides, swings, and baseball diamonds, but with mounds of dirt, trees, and conspicuous lack of clean cement, adventure playgrounds often are rather untidy looking places. In contrast to many public parks and playgrounds which contain equipment designed primarily for preschool children, the adventure playground is geared toward the abilities and needs of the elementary school child. It may contain lumber and tools, and a carpenter may even be on hand to teach the children to build such things as clubhouses and hutches for animals. It may have piles of earth and sand that can be moved around and shaped into different kinds of formations. Or there may be streams of running water and space for gardens where children can plant their own vegetables and flowers. Adventure playgrounds, in other words, are places where school-age children can do real things with real materials and develop valuable skills while doing so (Stone, 1970).

The environment in which a child grows has a major effect not only on the kinds of physical-motor skills he develops but on the kinds of interrelationships he forms as well. In this context, we can see that the freedom and opportunities for growth available in an adventure playground are quite different from those offered by a Little League field or some other organized recreational area, such as a town swimming

An adventure playground. (*Nancy Rudolph.*)

pool or ice-skating rink. Instead of being on a "team" with a group of other children, the child in an adventure playground is able to participate in activities on his own terms and at his own level. Thus, even the fat or awkward child has an equal chance to succeed. Furthermore, owing to the nature of the activities available, the stress on competition usually found in team sports is replaced by an equally strong emphasis on cooperation. By building something together, whether it be a clubhouse or a garden, a rabbit hutch or a sculpture, a dam across a stream or a sandpit for toddlers, school-age children learn both the value of shared efforts and a sense of respect for a product those efforts produce. Finally, by being provided with the opportunity to build things alone and to create something unique, they may enjoy the excitement of self-expression and independence.

Adventure playgrounds are one example of the kind of environment communities can provide to foster the development of certain physical-motor skills and social attitudes. Numerous other possibilities exist, each environment with its own potentials for physical and social development. But what about the place in which school-age children already spend approximately half of their waking hours—the school itself?

The School Environment
When we think of a child attending school, we generally are concerned with the effect the school has upon the child's intellect, his associations with his peers, or his relationship to authority. All too often we forget that the child has a body equipped with certain needs and skills, a body that also goes to school every day. The environment in which the child finds himself 5 days a week, 9 months a year, can be carefully planned to meet these needs or it can be a source of considerable stress and strain. In either case, the influence it will have on his future development will be significant.

The effect of the standard way in which American schools are set up was aptly summarized by one first-grader on her return home from her first day in school. When asked how she had liked her new school, she replied, "Oh, you mean sit-down school?" Instead of responding to the new children or the different teacher and time schedule, the child had reacted to the sense of being confined to a desk and chair for a whole day. Most adults do not like to be confined to a desk and a chair for several hours a day, and those who are so restricted often have a padded office chair rather than the straight-backed wooden type customarily used in elementary schools. The 6-year-old child is still learning with his body, is still integrating physical bodily knowledge with intellectual knowledge, and is still expressing himself physically whether by artistic expression, emotional expression, or intellectual expression. It is rather artificial to divorce the body from the mind and personality and to use it only in gym class and at recess.

There are many ways in which a school can be sensitive to a child's physical needs. In a math class, for instance, the children could first measure a corridor in yards and feet, or in meters and centimeters, and then measure it again in terms of their own footsteps or body lengths or the time it takes them to walk the length of it. In this way, their knowledge would become both abstract and concrete, both general and personalized. Alternately, more attention could be paid to the inherent value of physical expression. A number of English primary schools, for example, set aside a special period for movement expression and movement exploration. In these classes, the children are encouraged to dance and to use their bodies to express themselves in individual and collective movement (Evans, 1975). One of the many advantages to such expressive classes is that every child, regardless of his coordination or shape, can experience success.

It is also possible to design school space in such a way that children are given regular opportunities for challenge and self-expression. Indeed, throughout the fair amount of literature on how best to design schools, nowhere is it said that children learn best by sitting in straight-backed chairs for long periods of time or that lying on the floor interferes with learning. Quite to the contrary, studies cited previously indicate the limits of passive, receptive learning. A new elementary school in Massachusetts may be an example of the kind of design we shall be seeing more of in the future. In addition to desks and tables, the classrooms in this school have cubicles and caves built into the walls at varying heights. Each nook is large enough for one or two children and is furnished with rugs and an occasional pillow. The cubicles are special places to which the children can retreat with their own books or study problems or in which they can hold problem-solving discussions with one another. These quiet, busy classrooms provide a relaxed atmosphere and promote good achievement.

Clearly, a school's design can limit, challenge, stimulate, ignore, or interfere with the child's physical-motor development as well as his cognitive development.

A significant segment of the intellectual development of the school-age child occurs in the formal school setting. Formal instruction usually leads to the need to measure, observe, or generally account for the presumed knowledge of skills being developed.

TESTS, INTELLIGENT AND OTHERWISE
Why Tests?

In the last 40 years, we have seen the United States experience an absolute mania for testing. We have IQ tests, achievement tests, psychological tests, career aptitude tests. School files are filled with test scores of varying degrees of accuracy and significance. The rationale behind all this testing activity is that schools need to assess student abilities in order to draw up efficient educational programs. But all too often the scores have been misused. People employ them as a means for sorting and labeling others, for eliminating certain people from certain kinds of educational opportunities, or for requiring certain kinds of educational sequences. And almost as frequently, the test results are not used at all. More than one child has experienced the frustration of entering the first grade with reading test scores at the third-grade level, only to be assigned to a class in reading readiness for 6 months because he or she "has not had that subject yet."

In an approach known as *diagnostic-prescriptive teaching,* however, tests and informal assessment can be a vital aid to education. The idea behind this kind of teaching is that if educators know precisely what an individual child can do, they will be better able to prescribe the next step for him or for her. The diagnosis is not a generalized label but a specific observed behavior or skill. The child is assessed for what he *can* do. The tester is not calling the student "superior" or "mildly retarded" or "a slow learner"; he is simply diagnosing the child's particular skills and abilities. The tests that are used, when indeed formal tests are used, for this kind of diagnosis are called *criterion-referenced tests* (Glaser, 1963).

Because criterion-referenced tests focus on an individual's achievements, they differ quite radically from the more familiar *norm-referenced* tests, which are concerned with how one person's score compares with the scores of others (Glaser, 1963). Most standard IQ tests, achievement tests, and scholastic aptitude tests are norm-referenced. They compare one child's score on a series of items with the scores of a large number of other children. In other words, where criterion-referenced tests aim at describing a child's accuracy and speed in several specific math skills, norm-referenced tests seek to find out such things as whether a child is performing at a level that is higher or lower than the norm for his grade or age.

An increasing number of educators are growing impatient with norm-referenced tests because the tests tend to label a student without giving the teacher any specific information on what to teach him or on what the student's basic problem may be. For instance, such a test may identify a child as being in the bottom 10 percent of his class in arithmetic skills, but it will say nothing about why he is there or what specific skills he needs to acquire in order to progress. Also, the test reveals nothing about such factors as the child's pattern of attention, his level of anxiety when he faces a math question, or any one of a number of things the teacher may need to know in order to help him. All the test does is label the child, in a general way, as a problem student.

Use of Tests   It is not difficult to imagine the effect that being labeled "below average" or a "slow learner" must have on a child's self-image. What is often overlooked, however, is the effect that such labeling of students may have on the administrators of the tests—the teachers. Just this situation is the subject of *Pygmalion in the Classroom* by Rosenthal and Jacobson (1968). The authors assert that test results can lead to a *self-fulfilling prophecy* whereby teacher expectations based on test scores become confirmed by student performance. In their study, a few children selected at random in several classes were reported to teachers as having previously undetected high ability and the potential for an academic spurt. The children thus identified did, in fact, show better achievement during the year than their classmates. Presumably, the teachers acted differently toward these children and helped them to fulfill the expectations.

Some investigators have strongly criticized the Rosenthal and Jacobson study, pointing to methodological flaws and the failure of subsequent research to fully replicate its results (Fleming & Anttonen, 1971). But it is equally dangerous to underestimate the complexity of the student-teacher relationship and the effect that labels can have on children's performances. Labels do persist, and children do tend to live up to them, whether they be "class clown," "good girl," "underachiever," or "bright." And insofar as a teacher's expectancies affect his behavior toward a child, those expectancies will affect the child's learning. In the context of the use of tests, the point to be made here is that no one benefits if teachers use tests merely to form generalizations about their students and attach labels to them.

In our test-ridden society, we often seem to overlook the fact that there are times when tests need not be used at all. Quite often, teachers and parents can learn a good deal about how they should proceed by informally observing what children do and say. To return to the initial example, it should not have been difficult for the teacher to discover that the child did not need a reading readiness program. A number of the skills developed in that type of program, such as the abilities to read from left to right on the page and to make certain visual and auditory discriminations, can easily be discerned through simple observation. By merely giving the child a book and listening to her while she read, the teacher probably could have ascertained which skills the child had still to learn.

The issues of what kind of test to give and how the results should be used are related to educational priorities and the way the learning process is viewed. With these thoughts in mind, a number of theorists have asserted that the American educational system has focused too narrowly on the broad composite known as "intelligence" and has failed to make a meaningful effort to teach or assess a number of equally important abilities. For instance, B. S. Bloom and D. R. Krathwohl (1956) have listed six different cognitive abilities, only the first two of which are treated with any regularity in the schools. Beginning with the least complex, their six categories are as follows:

What to Test: Beyond Acquisition of Knowledge

1. *Knowledge of facts and principles* refers to the simple recall of facts and principles. Because common knowledge often involves the rote memorization of such items as dates, names, vocabulary, and definitions, it is very easy to teach and test. Perhaps it is because of its "convenience" that this cognitive category has long been the focus of American education.
2. *Comprehension* entails the understanding of facts and ideas. Unfortunately, tests that are successful in measuring recall of facts or principles are often unsuccessful in assessing how well the student actually understands the material.
3. *Application* refers to the need to know not only the rules and principles of basic procedures, but how and when to use them in new situations. This intellectual task is less frequently taught and measured than are the previous two.
4. *Analysis* involves breaking down a concept, idea, system, or message into its parts and seeing the relationship between these parts. This task may be taught in reading comprehension, math, or science classes. However, often the final product of that analysis is taught rather than the analytical process.
5. *Synthesis* refers to putting together information or ideas, integrating or relating the parts of a whole.
6. *Evaluation* is somewhat controversial in education. Basically, evaluation entails judging the value of a piece of information, a theory, or a plan in terms of some criterion or standard.

Most testing—and most teaching—focuses on category 1, with occasional attention given to category 2. Very rarely do teachers give tests that require the student to use the thinking abilities listed in categories 3 through 6. Indeed, many teachers go out of their way to avoid category 6, even though without evaluation much information becomes hollow and superficial.

Other researchers contend that in a world where new problems arise and "facts" change every day, it is increasingly important that children be taught the skills necessary to deal with the unknown as well as the known. The schools should teach children not *what* to think but *how* to think. As means for meeting this goal, the researchers point to a series of lessons that have been shown to be successful in teaching children such problem-solving skills as how to generate new ideas, how to look at an issue in a new way, and how to identify the important aspects of a problem (Olton & Crutchfield, 1969). It is these skills, they claim, not the facts and principles generally taught and measured, that should be the focus of a child's education.

Often schools will ignore an ability or skill because it is not particularly valued in the elementary school setting. We rarely measure sense of humor, for instance. At other times, skills are ignored because they are awkward to define in terms of the precise behavior they entail. Lacking such a behavioral definition, a teacher can have difficulty measuring a student's degree of competency. For instance, how should one go about measuring a child's ability to enjoy classical music or appreciate great art?

The tendency of schools to concentrate on those abilities that can be measured reflects the growing popularity of *behavioral objectives*. These objectives describe the kinds of knowledge and skills that can be expected of a student after a specified amount of instruction. The rationale behind behavioral objectives is that schools should be accountable for what they teach. At the end of the school year, they should be able to demonstrate in a tangible way what their students have learned. Valuable as this approach is, an overconcern with accountability may result in the major part of a child's school day being spent acquiring those competencies that can be easily measured and accounted for. The obvious result is that the less objective competencies, ways of thinking, and traits are given much less emphasis. How does one objectively measure kindness, courage, curiosity, sensitivity to others' feelings, or openness to new experience?

Of all the competencies developing in a school-age child, perhaps the most elusive is creativity. What happens within and around certain people that makes them more creative than others? How are they different from less creative people? How are creative people similar to each other? Indeed, what is creativity?

CREATIVITY AND PRODUCTIVE THOUGHT

An indication of the complexity of creativity is the number of approaches that have been used in attempts to answer the preceding questions. Some investigators have sought the answers in the products of creative individuals; others have focused on the creative process itself; and still others have concentrated on the personality attributes of creative people (Golann, 1963). The number of studies performed is far too large for us to examine each one here. Nevertheless, it is worth noting some of the major contributions to research on creativity and how they pertain to the school-age child.

In examining the processes of creativity and productive thinking—or thought that results in new ideas or solutions to a problem—J. P. Guilford (1967a) differentiates between two modes of thought: *convergent* and *divergent*. In convergent thinking, an individual seeks to find the "right" answer by reproducing or integrating established information. In divergent thinking, however, a person recombines and revises established ideas and procedures to arrive at new ones. It is this latter mode of thought, Guilford points out, that is most often associated with innovation and creativity.

Michael Wallach and Nathan Kogan (1965) have suggested that one of the vital elements in creativity is *associative flow*—or *ideational fluency*, as it is sometimes called. Similar to the concept of divergent thinking, associative flow refers to a process whereby individuals think of numerous and unique ways of associating objects and ideas. According to Wallach and Kogan, the basis for the creative process is the combination of this associative flow with a playful, permissive attitude (which in turn allows for more novel associations).

Divergent thinking and ideational fluency work in direct opposition to what psychologists refer to as *functional fixedness* (Duncker, 1945). As originally stated, functional fixedness was meant to describe the phenomenon that occurs when a person's experience in using a particular object in a particular way makes it difficult for him to consider the object for different kinds of functions. According to this notion, if a person learned that hammers are for pounding nails, this fixed conceptualization of hammers could interfere with his being able to use them for alternate purposes. Subsequent investigations into the influence of functional fixedness have shown that it does indeed impair creative problem solving (Birch & Rabinowitz, 1951). The implications such findings have for education are quite clear: by teaching one procedure and emphasizing *the* correct answer, the schools could in fact be teaching rigidity and limiting creative exploration.

Among the most controversial issues in the study of creativity and creative people is the extent to which creativity can be said to relate to intelligence. According to Wallach and Kogan, the two attributes are independent, and to understand a child's growth and behavior one must consider both of them. Furthermore, the authors claim, it is the relative level of creativity to intelligence that is particularly important in shaping the child's personality. Wallach and Kogan found, for instance, that children high in both creativity and intelligence showed the most self-confidence and displayed the highest levels of attention and concentration for school tasks; however, they also tended to be disruptive and engage in attention-getting behavior. The children high in creativity but low in intelligence were in many ways at the greatest disadvantage. They were the least self-confident, most cautious, and engaged in a great deal of disruptive behavior. By contrast, the children low in both creativity and intelligence exhibited greater self-confidence and less hesitation. Finally, the students high in intelligence but low in creativity showed high self-confidence, high attention spans, and were the least likely of all the groups to seek attention through disruptive behavior (Wallach & Kogan, 1965). As might be suspected, researchers have found that teachers tend to prefer those students who are highly intelligent but not particularly creative (Getzels & Jackson, 1962; Torrance, 1962).

One study that is particularly revealing of how schools approach creative growth compares those characteristics that seem to be typical of creative individuals with those that teachers feel typify the ideal student. Not surprisingly, the lists do not agree. For example, the teachers ranked "consideration of others" as the most important attribute of the ideal student. However, creative people often become so intensely involved in solving a problem that they are unaware of the needs of the people around them. And although the teachers ranked "independence in thinking" second, other aspects necessary to the creative process, such as "independence in judgment" and "being courageous," were relegated to much lower positions.

Particularly interesting is the number of characteristics that are prevalent among creative individuals but are also among those most frequently punished or discouraged by teachers. Teachers often punish playful or regressive conduct, for instance, yet this kind of behavior appears to be a vital part of the creative process. Similarly, because the very nature of creativity entails challenging the existing order, creative children are liable to disturb the classroom organization, a behavior ranked lowest or next-to-lowest in desirability by almost all of the teachers surveyed (Torrance, 1963).

These discrepancies raise a number of questions about the aim of education. As we have seen, creativity can even be chaotic at times. And there is no question that children who are obedient, cooperative, and directed in their thought are easier to manage in the classroom. But one might well ask how important this "manageability" is when compared to the importance of creativity and original problem solving. It is only when clearer priorities for desirable characteristics are set that steps can be taken toward restructuring educational programs and the classroom environment.

CURRICULUM AND DEVELOPMENT

Ideally, schools are set up to maximize human development, to help individuals reach their full intellectual, physical, and social potential. To attain these goals, each school devises its own curriculum, an educational plan complete with objectives, activities, methods, and means of evaluating success. Thus, nothing should fit together more logically than the curriculum and the development of the individual child. In the eyes of an increasing number of people, however, this ideal is rarely realized. Indeed, several critics feel that the mismatch between students and the curriculum they are offered is so great that the most viable solution to the problem is simply to get rid of schools altogether (Goodman, 1960; Illich, 1972).

But given that schools do exist and that it is possible to make them effective places for educating the young, what kinds of changes need to be made? What do we know about the development of competencies that might help us create an effective curriculum?

Much of the research generated from Piagetian theory indicates that certain kinds of mathematical knowledge are considerably easier for children to acquire than other kinds. It has been pointed out that 6-year-olds can master many of the abstract aspects of set theory and topological analysis relatively quickly. Nevertheless, because the adult world only recently discovered these areas of mathematics, educators have erroneously assumed that the concepts would be too advanced for

From Sets to Subtraction

A 9-year-old learning to group by tens using pencils. (*Nancy Hayes, Monkmeyer.*)

Two 8-year-olds using a Montessori multiplication board. (*Nancy Hayes, Monkmeyer.*)

children. Therefore, they have tended to concentrate on such areas as subtraction, multiplication, and division. As it turns out, however, these latter, seemingly "simple," concepts are rather difficult for children to grasp.

It is only within the last 20 years or so that math curricula have begun to reflect sensitivity to such aspects of children's development. Had schools been concentrating on how children actually think, rather than on whether they were producing the "right" answers or not, it is highly probable that more effective math programs could have been developed long ago.

From Decoding to Reading

Reading is an incredibly complex task. It is much more than just decoding, or "translating," written words into spoken language. It is the process by which a person gets information from a written page. But the transition from decoding sentences to understanding them takes place only after a good deal of work.

Part of a child's difficulty in learning to read is the tremendous burden that is placed on his memory. The beginning reader must constantly keep in mind a vast array of symbols and rules. This burden is increased by the beginner's slowness. This forces him to concentrate in order to remember what has gone before in the sentence or story at the same time that he is trying to remember and recognize letters, sounds, and words. It is only after much practice that many of the rules become automatic and a child's speed advances to the point where he can focus on comprehension rather than on word identification (Smith, 1971).

Several studies have shown that it is possible to teach a child to read as early as age 2 or 3. Indeed, the individual skills necessary for reading are not all that difficult to acquire. It has been demonstrated, for instance, that 1- and 2-year-olds have sufficient visual discriminatory powers to identify letters and words, and that most 3- and 4-year-olds can manage auditory discrimination of letters, provided that is all they have to do (Doman, 1964).

One of the most impressive techniques for teaching young children to read was devised by Omar Khayyam Moore. In Moore's program, nursery school children learned to read by using a computerized "talking" typewriter that would tell them what they were typing and assist them in reading and spelling. The children were allowed to spend as much time at the typewriter as they wanted and were able to learn at their own pace (Moore & Anderson, 1968). Purely phonetic techniques, such as an *initial teaching alphabet*, also have been shown to work well with 4- and 5-year-olds.

If such programs have proved to be effective with young children, why have educators had such difficulty teaching children to read at age 6? Why are there entire school systems in which the majority of children are 2 years behind in reading level? It appears that a large part of the answer to these questions lies in the classroom situation itself. While reading instruction programs for children under 5 are almost always individualized, with each child working at his own speed, most programs for 6-year-olds are geared to the classroom group, not to the individual child. If a student misses a week in the classroom situation, the instruction he will receive upon his return to the group will generally not reflect the fact that he has been gone. Also, there are children who daydream, or are worried about problems at home, or skip several workbook pages, or are bored by the slow pace. It is virtually impossible, in other words, for a classroom-sequenced program to be appropriate for *all* of the children involved. Furthermore, some children are "optimally" ready for a phonetic approach, while others need broader language experience or perceptual training. Do teachers take the time to make a precise diagnosis of a child's ability prior to assigning him to an instructional group or a specific reading approach?

As many teachers can attest, an 8-year-old who has never been exposed to reading is a sheer delight to teach. A 6-month tutoring program for such a child is generally extremely successful and gratifying to both child and tutor. However, most 8-year-olds who cannot read will never experience such success. Although they have not been able to master the task, they *have* been learning something in 2 years of reading instruction. They have learned frustration, confusion, faulty habits, and a sense of failure and inadequacy. In such a situation, it is remarkably difficult to wipe the slate clean and start anew. In fact, in a study that followed a large group of children from kindergarten through the twelfth grade, it was found that students who had developed reading problems in the early grades got progressively worse and fell into a pattern of scholastic failure, despite general ability. At the same time, the children who were good readers in the second grade proved to be the better readers in the sixth and ninth grades (Kraus, 1973).

Obviously, the initial steps taken in teaching a child to read are of primary importance. Since the present system of teaching reading does not seem to be working at maximum effect, what are some of the factors that might be considered in shaping a curriculum to better match the needs of the developing child? One of the first things that should be taken into consideration is children's need to experience success, not failure. Certainly, the notion of shaping pertains here, as any complex skill must be built up in gradual, sequential steps, allowing the child to succeed in the small steps along the way.

Early reading is decoding and word play. Children need to develop a heightened awareness of the auditory and visual distinctiveness of letters and words, and this activity should be fun. It should whet the child's appetite, as the repeated sounds typically present in the Dr. Seuss books do.

It is equally important to teach children words that are relevant to their own experience. All too often schools neglect this aspect of teaching, especially with children who have a mixed language background. In a book called *Teacher*, Sylvia Ashton-Warner (1971) outlines her "organic reading" approach, in which the children learn a new word with a personal meaning each day. The author found that children like to learn long and potent words, angry and loving words, sex and death words, words about ghosts and monsters. In short, the children showed a preference for words expressing strong feelings—a direct contrast to the rather tame and boring words most children are forced to learn, such as *look, see, dog, cat, baby*.

Finally, once a child has learned to read sentences and paragraphs, it is important that he be given something meaningful and exciting to read. Again, the material should have personal importance for him and should not avoid ideas, or complex plots, or messy feelings.

As may be seen, the developmental principles involved in devising an effective reading curriculum are somewhat different from those that must be considered in shaping a math curriculum. For mathematics we must consider what the child is capable of understanding. For reading, however, we must take into account the complexity of the overall task itself. The problem is not that a 6-year-old child is incapable of learning to read; on the contrary, in some ways he has been ready for a long time. Rather, the problem is that reading is much more complicated than we think. It is a skill that makes particularly great demands on the child's mind. In teaching reading, therefore, we need to follow all the principles we know that can help children develop complex bodies of information.

A number of attempts have been made to apply developmental principles to social studies programs, all with quite different results. One of the most interesting of these attempts was developed by Jerome Bruner (1966) for fifth graders. Entitled "Man, a Course of Study," the program explores three basic questions: What is human about human beings? How did they get that way? How can they be made more so? In the process of answering these questions, the children are exposed to some of the ideas of the best minds in anthropology, philosophy, and sociology. Bruner's position is that if the specific developmental capacities of the child for whom a course is intended are kept in mind, the child can be taught almost anything in an intellectually honest fashion.

Social Studies

To provoke further thought, children can be shown films of other cultures. (*G. Arvid Peterson, Photo Researchers.*)

Bruner's course teaches much more than just facts and principles. By encouraging children to participate and use their minds in creative, productive ways, the program also helps them learn a number of different thought processes, such as divergent and convergent thinking, analysis, synthesis, application, and evaluation. The course is divided into five areas of study: language, toolmaking, social organization, childrearing, and world view. In each of these areas, the children are given considerable concrete experience—often through the use of games—and are continually asked to compare their own lives and communities with those in other parts of the world. In the social organization section, for example, they are informed that although societies are structured, the structures can, and do, vary. To provoke further thought, they are shown films of other cultures and are encouraged to participate in games designed to make them aware of the elements involved in the shaping of a society's social organization. In a game called "hunting," which is based on the Kalahari Bushmen, the children deal with such issues as the allocation of resources, the implications of the division of labor, and planning where and what to hunt (Bruner, 1966). Such a program obviously differs quite radically in its goals and results from those that stress the simple memorization of places, names, and dates.

Behind all of these studies and experiments is the belief that it is desirable to help children maximize their potential and that given the proper conditions, any child can achieve. It is appropriate, therefore, to conclude by considering just what it means to achieve and why some children seem to be more successful at achieving than others.

ACHIEVEMENT AND ANXIETY

The educational literature is replete with biting critiques of our school systems. Although such books as *How Children Fail* (Holt, 1964), *36 Children* (Kohl, 1968), and *Death at an Early Age* (Kozol, 1970) differ in their specifics, they all agree in their conclusions: the majority of our schools are overwhelming failures. Instead of being places of intellectual excitement where children learn to be independent and productive in their thought, schools are places that stifle curiosity and breed conformity and mediocrity through their emphasis on discipline and "right" answer teaching. More often than not, schools are simply boring. These books claim that in this environment, it is not surprising that so many students are frustrated and unhappy in school. This unfortunate situation is summarized in the words of one 9-year-old student:

> In school we waste time until it's over. I do what I have to. I don't like the place. I feel like falling off all day, just putting my head down and saying good-bye to everyone until three. We're out then, and we sure wake up. (Coles, 1968, p. 1322)

Obviously, students do not succeed or fail in a vacuum. They are continually influencing and being influenced by the people and objects that form their world. Before looking at why some children achieve much more than others, we shall examine the values of the environment in which they are operating.

David McClelland, one of the major forces in the research on achievement, has defined achievement motivation as the drive toward success in competition with a standard of excellence (1955). Several researchers, including McClelland, have extended this notion of achievement motivation, or "need" achievement, to the study of cultures. They compared several periods of history in several different countries. Clearly achievement motivation is a *cultural* value. In some cultures, they found it expressed more strongly at certain times than at others, in literature, childbearing, education, and adult behavior. Within any given society at any time, some groups consider achievement motivation to be more important than other groups do (deCharms & Moeller, 1962; McClelland, 1955).

Achievement of What? For What?

Other studies have focused even more closely on the effect that culture has on an individual's achievement motivation and its measurement. For instance, Martin Maehr (1974) has pointed out that because societies have different goals, values, and regulations, the only valid way to measure whether or not a given behavior is achievement-oriented is on the society's own terms.

An implication of these findings is that in a school where the students have varied backgrounds, some children may have a strong pattern for achievement motivation and others may not. Futhermore, some of the children who do not seem to be motivated may simply be channeling their need for achievement into areas different from those generally sanctioned or measured by the school.

Numerous investigators have outlined the personality differences between high-achieving and low-achieving children. The high-achieving child is academically oriented, is independent yet compliant with authority, has high self-esteem, can delay gratification of wishes, and has a relatively high, yet well-controlled, level of anxiety (Sontag, Baker, & Nelson, 1958; Taylor, 1964). Parents seem to play a significant role in the development of these characteristics in a child. Generally, the parents of high-achieving students have lofty expectations and standards for their children. They tend to be more involved with their children than are parents of low-achievers and they demonstrate warmth and approval when their children are successful. However, when their children are not achieving, the parents' behavior is often characterized by rejection and hostility. Parents of high-achievers also appear to be more competitive themselves. They are often described by their children as being overprotective and pushing for success (Haggard, 1957; Rosen & d'Andrade, 1959).

Personality and Achievement

Some researchers consider need achievement—in tests and test-like situations—to consist of two kinds of motivation: the drive to succeed and the drive to avoid failure (Atkinson & Feather, 1966). As might be expected, the two kinds of drives have somewhat different patterns. The fear of failure, for instance, involves much more anxiety and often underlies the choosing of either very easy tasks or tasks that are so difficult that no one could be expected to succeed in them. This kind of motivation tends to result in high success on rote memory tasks, on speed of performance in familiar tasks (such as repeating multiplication tables), and on single solution, convergent-thinking types of problems. By contrast, the more positive drive toward success, because it entails less anxiety, tends to allow for more creativity, more productive thinking, more expansive original solutions, and higher performance on certain kinds of intellectual tasks.

Anxiety It is apparent from a number of studies that very high levels of anxiety are crippling and interfere with a wide variety of tasks, particularly the more complex ones (Castaneda, 1956). High levels of anxiety also tend to interfere with new learning and with performance on such tasks as creative writing tests and ad lib discussions. As previously mentioned, however, anxiety may not dramatically affect the performance of well-practiced, already learned material. Still, children who are highly anxious do not perform well on school tests or on standardized tests of intelligence and achievement (Sarason et al., 1960; Ruebush, 1963). These findings tie in closely with the previous discussion on the use and interpretation of intelligence tests, because a low score on such a test may be more a function of a child's anxiety than a function of his intelligence.

The evidence on the effect of very low levels of anxiety on learning and performance is contradictory. Some researchers contend that the lower the level of anxiety, the better the performance, or at least the better the learning (Neill, 1960). The more open a child is to new learning, they claim, the more free he will be to explore and associate new material in productive ways. These conclusions seem to be validated by Atkinson and Feather's conception of the fear of failure and by other research indicating that very anxious children tend to be much more cautious than less anxious children (Ruebush, 1960).

On the other side of the argument are researchers who contend that a moderate level of anxiety is necessary to spur motivation. They point to research with animals that suggests a certain amount of stress is required for the animals to learn new material at anything more than a very slow pace. To keep this argument in perspective, however, think back to the defense mechanisms discussed in Chapter 13. Because anxiety is unpleasant, it is very possible that when it is present in moderate or high levels, children will resort to a variety of defense mechanisms, some of which may facilitate learning but many of which may impede and retard learning.

The influence of anxiety on children in a classroom situation is highlighted in a study which measured the relative success of third-grade students in programs using one of the two most prevalent methods of teaching reading. In one of these methods—the "whole-word" approach—children develop a "sight" vocabulary by learning to recognize entire words rather than the smaller phonemes that make up the words. This approach often involves trial-and-error guessing and seldom uses systematic drills. By contrast, the "phonic" method entails a system of precisely defined rules and numerous drills. As might be expected, the anxious children who were taught to read by the unstructured, whole-word approach performed at a much lower level than did anxious children who were taught according to the more disciplined phonic approach (Grimes & Allinsmith, 1961). The authors suggested that an effective reading program would be one that took such personality variables into account.

The results of the Grimes and Allinsmith study can be seen as a reinforcement of the primary thesis in this chapter: Each child sitting in a classroom has his own needs and abilities; and if schools are to be effective places for growth, they must recognize these aspects of a child's existence and structure the environment accordingly.

SUMMARY

Middle childhood is a time during which children settle down and more fully develop the patterns that are already set. It is also a period of developing skills and of increasing motivation to meet some of the goals of peers.

In such places as adventure playgrounds, children can develop their skills and at the same time foster certain social patterns. The school environment can be structured in such a way that it either meets children's physical needs or restricts their physical experience.

All too often tests are used to label children. Norm-referenced tests, which compare one child's performance with the scores of other children, are used in this way. In diagnostic-prescriptive teaching, however, the focus is on meeting each child's individual needs. The tests generally used in this kind of teaching are the criterion-referenced type which do not compare children but merely describe their particular skills and abilities.

Recently, schools have tended to structure education through the use of behavioral objectives. Although this approach provides accountability, there is a danger of focusing too exclusively on those types of learning that can easily be specified behaviorally.

Creativity, which is believed by some researchers to result from the combination of divergent thinking, associative flow, and a playful attitude, also is often overlooked, or even stifled, in the classroom. Indeed, it appears that many of the qualities characteristic of creative children are qualities that teachers least prefer.

Educators are becoming increasingly aware that the school curriculum must be shaped to meet students' developmental needs. Particularly important in this regard is the need to individualize instruction as much as possible and to realize that different kinds of tasks require the application of different developmental principles.

Far from being something that exists in all people at all times in a single form, achievement motivation is a relative value. Children differ in their need to achieve, and the difference seems to be largely the result of parental influences. Anxiety over achievement also seems to be an important factor in a child's behavior—a factor that should be taken into consideration in the shaping of learning programs.

REVIEW QUESTIONS

1. What are some of the dangers in using norm-referenced tests? What do these tests *not* tell a teacher about students?

2. What elements are believed to be characteristic of creative people and creative thought? What factors tend to inhibit productive thought?

3. How might hospital buildings and schedules be designed to accommodate the physical-motor needs of children?

SUGGESTED READINGS

In the last decade, several sensitive, insightful teachers have written compelling portrayals of what really happens in the dynamics of a classroom. Each of the following is an excellent description of classroom life in a multiethnic, mixed socioeconomic setting.

Ashton-Warner, S. *Teacher*. New York: Bantam Books, 1971.
Dennison, G. *The lives of children*. New York: Random House, 1970.
Kohl, H. *36 children*. New York: Norton, 1968.
Kozol, J. *Death at an early age*. New York: Bantam Books, 1970.

16

PERSONALITY DEVELOPMENT WITHIN THE CULTURE OF CHILDHOOD

Ten-year-old Michael is playing ball with his friends when his father comes home from work. The boys are very intent upon their game; they communicate with each other through a shorthand of language and gestures. Michael's father remembers how he used to play ball with his friends in just the same way, and approaches the group and asks if he can join the game. As soon as he does, the natural, smooth equilibrium of the group disappears. The boys are no longer at ease with each other or with the game. Michael's father had hoped to recapture his childhood, but instead, he feels out of place. And indeed he should, for in a sense he is a foreigner in another culture.

It may seem a bit dramatic to say that children belong to a culture different from that of adults, but in many ways the statement is true. The world of the preadolescent child is not the same as the world in which adults live. The child's world has distinctive beliefs and values; it has rigid rules; and it often uses a distinctive language.

There are many points in their development where children seem to caricature adults. We have already seen how the 2-year-old reflects his parents' independence in his own fierce assertiveness. The culture of middle childhood also produces a caricature, as the child between the ages of 6 and 12 takes certain adult patterns of behavior and exaggerates them. Rituals, chants, rules, games, and traditions—all play very important parts in middle childhood. The child's world is one of almost superstitious attention to rituals, such as not stepping on sidewalk cracks for fear of breaking someone's back. It is a world of compulsive and compulsory accuracy. Rhymes must be said just so, and rigid rules dictate the one right way to play each game. Peer relationships are very important to the child; he may be intensely idealistic, making life-long pledges in private clubs and "blood brother" fraternities. The stunts, taunts, prescribed games, and customs of middle childhood are adopted automatically and unthinkingly by each child. These games and customs have been transmitted arbitrarily from older to younger children for countless generations in almost every culture (Opie & Opie, 1959). And although these traditions belong to the world of childhood, most of us still retain vestiges of them. We may still feel indignant if someone performs the "wrong" version of a cherished yo-yo trick; we may even argue heatedly about the proper word sequences in a tongue twister.

How is this culture able to remain so constant from century to century? (Many childish chants can be traced to medieval times, and some games, such as jacks, go back to the Roman era.) What is the purpose of the rigidly structured world of the 8-year-old? Children seem to derive potency from mastering the bits and pieces of a culture, from learning how to do things correctly. Perhaps the rituals and rules of middle childhood are practice for adulthood, exercises in learning the very complex and detailed behavioral expectations of adult society. Perhaps they are a form of security, a familiar framework of rules that allows the child to feel both at home and competent in an otherwise bewildering world. We still are not certain of the exact purpose these traditions of middle childhood serve. Nevertheless, the phenomenon

(Mimi Forsyth, Monkmeyer.)

DEVELOPMENT OF SOCIAL SKILLS
IN MIDDLE CHILDHOOD.

(Jerome Wexler, Photo Researchers.)   (Edward P. Lincoln, Photo Researchers.)

of a special subculture of childhood is one which we can find in almost every society. And a closer look at the child from age 6 to age 12 may help us to understand the world in which he lives.

AN OVERVIEW: AGES 6 TO 12

Middle childhood is the time before adolescence when the child is adjusting to the new environment of school, is forming close ties with people outside the home, and is developing work and play habits along with many new interests. During this time, the child experiences many developmental challenges and conflicts which prepare him for adolescence and adulthood.

These developmental steps are taken one at a time, and as Table 7 shows, each year brings with it particular patterns of behavior (Elkind, 1971). Of course, each child takes an individual approach to the challenges of his age. Not every 8-year-old is outgoing, nor is every 10-year-old stable and comfortable with himself and his family. But, in general, the developmental trend follows the overall pattern shown in the chart. The beginning of middle childhood is characterized by a restlessness and by poor family relationships. This active period is followed by a lull in which the child seems to be catching his breath, digesting the changes of the past year and preparing for the next important steps. Another period of high tension, restlessness, and poor home relationships follows. This, in turn, is followed by another lull—the calm before the "great storm" of adolescence. This pendulum motion seems to characterize the years of middle childhood for may children.

The pendulum picture of the 6- to 12-year-old's development gives us an overview of the social and emotional adjustments he must make and of the tensions these adjustments cause him. If we look more closely at children's games, we acquire another perspective. Children's games provide a good picture of the broad steps the child is taking in developing the social and psychological attitudes our society demands: attitudes such as cooperation, fairness, competitiveness, and respect for rules and authority (Piaget, 1932/1965; Sutton-Smith, 1958). While the preschooler's play is self-centered—he often ignores or is annoyed by the presence of playmates—the 6- to 9-year-old's play shows a developing spirit of cooperation and respect for authority. Most games played during the early part of middle childhood are central person ones such as "Simon Says," which many children play together under a very rigid authority pattern, with one player opposing the rest. Rules are very strict; there is only one "right way" to play each game.

Later on, the child begins to realize the arbitrariness of strict rules. He understands that rules—whether in games or in any other area of life—are made by people. They are not preordained or immutable; they can be changed (Piaget, 1932/1965). From age 9 to age 12, children prefer games that deemphasize sheer ritual; they stress democracy and competition. Late middle childhood games usually have fairly complex regulations which are designed to ensure each player equal treatment.

TABLE 7 AGE PROFILES FOR MIDDLE CHILDHOOD

AGE	OUTSTANDING CHARACTERISTICS	SELF-CONCEPT	SOCIAL AND FAMILY RELATIONSHIPS	WORK HABITS
6	High physical activity; boisterous, self-centered.	Begins differentiation of self by alternately opposing, then making overtures toward, parents.	Verbally aggressive but sensitive about being called names; dawdles, but is impatient with others. Has difficulty relating to parents and siblings; forms erratic friendships.	Works and plans in spurts. Does not know when to stop; tires easily.
7	Greater mental activity; almost brooding as compared to 6-year-old.	Less self-centered; more concerned with others' reactions to him. Sensitive; often ashamed of self.	More polite; likes to help at home. Has close peer friendships.	Persistent and careful with work. Better perspective of how much he can do.
8	New outgoingness; avid curiosity; not as comfortable with his world as when younger.	Critical and self-evaluative; demanding and critical of others, too. Likes to compare self with others.	General backsliding in home relationships. Highly critical of parents; poor sibling relationships. Peer friendships within same sex very important.	Social interests may interfere with schoolwork. Self-criticism may discourage work ("I can't spell").
9	Outgoing; curious; very involved in personal interests; self-confident.	Still self-evaluating but more at ease with self. Can admit mistakes without feeling threatened.	Better relationships at home as he becomes less critical. Very close peer friendships.	Very persistent, self-absorbed. Academic achievement very important.
10	Stable; at ease with the world. Sex differences emerging.	Less self-evaluative, more self-satisfied.	Likes almost everyone in family. Closer peer friendships, with sex differentiation (boys in larger groups; girls in small groups). Likes organized clubs.	Likes school; has responsible work habits.
11	High physical activity (also big appetite); intense curiosity; no longer quite at ease with self and others.	New doubts and tensions as adolescence approaches. Moody, sensitive, full of self-doubt.	Challenges parents and all adults. Conflicts with siblings. Peer friendships very important.	Personal and social interests overwhelming; often has difficulty sustaining interest in schoolwork.
12	Outgoing; open; beginning to see self as no longer a child.	Less self-centered; capable of some self-criticism. Shows a need to define self.	Participates less in family activities; friends more important.	Difficult in school. More interested in expressing self than in working with others.

Source: Adapted from Elkind, D. *A sympathetic understanding of the child six to sixteen.* Boston: Allyn & Bacon, 1971, pp. 64–89, 129–131.

As competition becomes more and more important, children become interested in sports which teach them to win within the rules.

A look at Table 7 shows us the pendulum of challenges and conflicts in the lives of 6- to 12-year-olds; observing children's games tells us a lot about how children's social skills advance during the middle childhood years. From both perspectives, we can see that the middle childhood years are a time of important psychological growth. A significant part of this growth is the gradual move away from the family, toward independence and close peer friendships. As we shall see in the next section, peer ties are very important agents of socialization during this time.

PEER INFLUENCES ON PERSONALITY
Siblings

The first, and probably the closest, peer group affecting a child's personality development is the sibling group—brothers and sisters in his own family. The relationships between brothers and sisters are intense ones, especially when the children are close in age. But even when children are spaced farther apart, they are directly affected by the experience of living with others who are both equals (as other children in the same family) and unequals (either more or less competent or powerful).

What influence do brothers and sisters have on each other? And how does birth order, or *sibling status,* affect each child's personality? Countless pieces of fiction have been written about the experience of having or not having siblings; the special status of the firstborn; the uniqueness of the only child; the many special behavior patterns of the middle child; the dependency of the youngest child; and the "Cinderella syndrome" of a youngest child with older stepsiblings. In contrast to the fictional literature, psychological findings on siblings seem rather thin and full of qualifications. It is difficult to generalize about sibling status, because we must first know whether the other siblings are brothers or sisters, how many there are, and how far apart they are. Many variables must be considered before any conclusions can be reached.

In general, the firstborn child tends to be more achievement-oriented than his siblings. He is the one most likely to achieve eminence in academic and scientific areas and in business (Sutton-Smith, 1958). The same is true for the only child, who is really a special case of the firstborn; he is just never dethroned by later siblings. Second and third children seem to be higher in social skills and more able to get along well with friends outside the family. There is some evidence that later children are more achievement-oriented in athletics than firstborns (Chen & Cobb, 1960).

Why are firstborn children more likely to achieve eminence, and why do later children tend to have greater social skills? Firstborns are only children for several months or years. Their parents give them exclusive attention and provide sophisticated behavior models. Parents also tend to be more anxious about the firstborn's achievements—whether he is late in walking, whether he is too aggressive, whether he is slow in school. One result of this attention is that firstborn children are likely to speak earlier (Koch, 1956a). They are also apt to be more adult-oriented, to be more conscientious, and to have more achievement anxiety (McArthur, 1956).

Later-born children have an easier life than firstborns in some ways. Their parents are more relaxed; they have been through all the worries of childrearing before, so they know that a baby will walk eventually, or that he will outgrow the habit of pulling other children's hair (McArthur, 1956; Sears, 1950). But parents cannot give exclusive attention to more than one child. As a result, the younger children do not have the same benefit of direct tutelage from experienced adults. Instead, much of their learning comes from observing the unpredictable and less sophisticated models of their siblings. Therefore, while younger children may talk later and be less achievement-oriented, they tend to be more at ease with other children and more comfortable in social situations (Bossard & Boll, 1955; McArthur, 1956; Sears, 1950).

All of these effects are greatly modified by other factors besides birth order. For example, if the family has six or seven children, many of the differences associated with sibling status seem to disappear. But large families have other side effects upon their members. All children need to establish distinct identities for themselves. If an older sibling is adult-oriented and studious, a younger child may be inclined to develop boisterous ways. In a large family, the task of establishing an identity can be quite difficult. What status is there, for instance, in being the fourth out of five girls? In order to carve out a niche for herself which is sufficiently different from her sisters', the fourth girl may take on a masculine role, or an exaggerated nurturant role toward the youngest sister.

Another important factor, in addition to the size of the family and the personalities of the other siblings, is the sex of the siblings. If they are of the same sex, siblings tend to compete much more intensely than if they are of the opposite sex, especially when they are close in age. Older siblings of the same sex also act as powerful models, hence they provide strong reinforcement in sex-typing. And finally, the spacing between siblings is an important modifier of the effect of sibling status. The closer the spacing, the more intense is the influence of the sibling relationship (Sutton-Smith & Rosenberg, 1970).

In any case, each child in the family is faced with the task of forming his own self-concept. His sibling status, the number of children in his family, the sex of the siblings, their closeness in years, and their individual personalities—all will have a great influence on the personality the child develops. However, while sibling relationships may be the most intense peer influences affecting a child, they are not the only important ones. Middle childhood is a time of movement away from the family, and friendships outside the home play an increasingly important role in molding children's attitudes and behaviors.

Friendship Pairs   Friendship patterns shift during childhood (Piaget, 1932/1965). The "egocentric" pattern typical of the preschool years changes in the early part of middle childhood when children begin to form close relationships, usually with one best friend. These friendship ties are very strong while they last, but they tend to be erratic and short-lived. In later middle childhood and adolescence, groups of friends become more stable; they also become larger, with several boys or girls regularly sharing activities.

What functions do the close friendships of middle childhood serve? Friendship pairs satisfy certain needs in each child. One friend may take a clear role of dominance, while the other is submissive. In another friendship pair, the relationship may be egalitarian, with neither member playing a clear or consistent role. The pattern depends upon the dominance, dependency, and autonomy needs of each child. Generally, the more stable and satisfying friendships allow for some flexibility in roles to fulfill each child's needs.

A friendship pair may also act as a vehicle of self-expression for a child. For this reason, children often choose friends whose personalities are quite different from their own. An outgoing, expressive child may choose a more reserved or conscientious child as a close friend. The relationship gives each a maximum of self-expression with a minimum of competition, and the pair, as a unit, demonstrates more personality traits than either child alone could muster (Hartup, 1970a; 1970b). Of course, friends are rarely complete opposites. Friendship pairs that last over a long period of time usually have many shared values, attitudes, and expectations both for each other and for outsiders.

The friendship pair also serves other functions. It provides a structure for the child's activity in ritualized games and in other pastimes. It serves to form, reinforce, and solidify group norms and attitudes and values. It intensifies exclusivity, and it provides a practice ground for both in-group and out-group competition (Hartup, 1970a). All of these functions are served by larger peer groups as well, and the friendship pair is only a special instance of the peer group. A great deal of research has looked at children's peer groups, and we have learned much about how these large groups form, about their structure and function, and about the ways in which the groups influence their members.

The Peer Group   What is a peer group? Is it any aggregation of children of about the same age, or can it consist only of close friends? How many members can it have—2, 5, or 25? The peer group is a pretty elusive concept in lay usage; it is important that we define what it is and answer the questions we have raised before we continue our discussion.

A peer group is not just any gathering of children. Its size is somewhat limited by the qualification that all of its members interact with one another. In addition, a peer group is relatively stable; it lasts over a period of time. Its members share many values; and there are common norms which govern the members' interaction and influence each child. And finally, some degree of status differentiation governs the group's

Girl Scouts work on an environmental project. (*Girl Scouts of America.*)

interaction: there is at least a temporary division into leaders and followers. Therefore, when we speak of a peer group, we are not talking
about just any "bunch of kids." We are referring to *a relatively stable
aggregation of two or more children who interact together, who share norms
and goals, and who have developed some division of roles and status which
governs their interaction* (Hartup, 1970b).

DEVELOPMENTAL TRENDS IN PEER GROUPS. Peer groups are important
throughout middle childhood, but there is a general shift in both their
overall structure and their meaning to the child during this 6-year span.

In the early years of middle childhood, peer groups are relatively
informal. They are usually formed by the children themselves, they
have very few operating rules, and there is a rapid turnover in membership. It is true that many of the group's activities, such as playing
hopscotch, jumping rope, or shooting marbles, may be played according to precise rules. But the organization of the group itself is quite
flexible.

The group takes on a more intense meaning for its members when they reach age 10 or 12, and its structure also solidifies. Group conformity becomes extremely important to the child, who may also be showing an almost compulsive reverence for rules and norms in all areas of social interaction. Peer pressures assume a coercive influence on the child. Groups also develop a more formal structure. They may have special membership requirements, club meetings, and initiation ceremonies. Some groups, such as the Boy Scouts or the Campfire Girls, are organized from the outside by adults. At this time, sex cleavages become very important, too. Groups are now almost always composed entirely of boys or entirely of girls, with different interests and activities for each sex. These strict attitudes about rules, conformity, and sex differentiation are common to children's interaction throughout the late part of middle childhood, and they are usually not relaxed until the children reach later adolescence.

GROUP FORMATION. Children are constantly being thrown together by circumstances—in school, in camps, in neighborhoods. In each case, it usually takes very little time for groups to form, for relationships to develop a differentiation of roles, for common values and interests to emerge, for mutual influences and expectations to grow, and for a feeling of tradition to take shape. The process is almost universal, and some interesting studies have recorded exactly how it happens.

Some researchers were curious about the way groups form. To find out, they set up naturalistic experiments to test three hypotheses (Sherif & Sherif, 1953; Sherif et al., 1961). First, they theorized that when a number of children are brought together in circumstances where they share both physical closeness and a common goal, a hierarchy of roles will form. Second, the individual members of the group will discover shared values and attitudes. And third, if two groups are brought together in competitive circumstances, intergroup hostility will develop.

The first study, called the "Red Rover" study, took place in three phases. In the first phase, fifth-grade boys with similar backgrounds were sent to summer camp (Sherif & Sherif, 1953). They lived in two separate groups for a few days and were watched carefully as they began to form friendships. Just as these budding friendships were beginning to solidify, the experimenters split up the friends by dividing the groups along new lines. Stage two of the study lasted for 5 days. The observers saw that in-group friendships soon formed in the new groups, and a clear hierarchy of leadership—not necessarily related to popularity—emerged very quickly. Group names were chosen (the "Red Devils" and the "Bulldogs") and group rules and norms were developed.

In stage three, the two groups were brought into direct competition in games that were rigged so that one group was almost never allowed to win. At first, the competition resulted in the quick development of animosity and even open hostility between the groups, with powerful feelings of in-group exclusivity. But the frustrated group's structure soon fell apart. Leadership disintegrated and intragroup disharmony developed.

The second study, sometimes called the "Robber's Cave" experiment (Sherif et al., 1961), duplicated the circumstances and findings of the first study, with one important change. The competition between the groups was now equal. The results showed some interesting things about group structure. The introduction of equal competition intensified in-group solidarity in both groups, reinforcing norms and expectations. Feelings of exclusivity and out-group hostility were also intensified, just as the experimenters had hypothesized. Another interesting thing happened. The hierarchical structures of both groups changed. Leadership shifted as the boys who did best in the current competition rose to new leadership positions. In other words, group roles were shown to be related quite strongly to group goals. When the goals changed, so did the leaders.

In both of these studies, the experimenters had created openly hostile situations, and in each case they tried to "undo the damage" before the boys were sent home from camp. In the highly frustrating "Red Rover" study, the hostility was never completely erased; but in the second case, the experimenters were able to keep the situation more under control. They theorized that if the two groups were brought together with a common goal, the hostility would break down. And this indeed happened when both groups were forced to cooperate on a camp project involving fixing the food truck so that both groups could eat.

Neighborhood children preparing to go on a camping trip. (*Steve Eagle, Nancy Palmer Photo Agency.*)

Why are these studies worth describing? They were conducted in naturalistic settings, the kinds of situations which are common to almost every child's experience. And they tell us a lot about groups. As the experimenters theorized, groups formed quickly from the aggregations of children, and status differentiation seemed to happen almost automatically. Group members found common values and shared norms; they even gave their groups names. And when groups were put into continuing competition against one another, feelings of exclusivity and hostility quickly developed. When the groups were required to cooperate, hostility was reduced. These findings are typical of the way groups form and compete in classrooms, in athletic competitions, in neighborhood or ethnic rivalries.

STATUS WITHIN THE PEER GROUP. If we watch a group of children during lunchtime or recess, we shall see evidence of a natural selection of group roles that always takes place. One girl is surrounded by children eager to get her attention. Another stays off in the corner, ignored by the others. Three boys play together in a tight group. This kind of division happens in every group of children, as we saw in the "Red Rover" and "Robber's Cave" studies. Many researchers have used very sophisticated techniques to study group roles in order to find out more about status differentiation and its effect on group behavior.

One type of research method makes use of *sociometric techniques,* which are any measurements designed to discern and measure the dynamic organization of a group (Moreno, 1934). The major technique for studying social status in a group is the *sociogram* (see Figure 13). It is a relatively simple map of the network of relationships within a group (Moreno, 1934). The data used to draw the sociogram are obtained from questions asked of each member. Usually, children are asked three simple preference questions about other members of the group. The questions might be, "Which three classmates would you choose to work with you on a social studies project?" "Which three classmates would you prefer to go to a party with?" "Which three classmates would you pick as teammates in a game of kickball?" Each question involves a different kind of skill, so the choices are unlikely to be based solely on popularity. This means that although Jerry is fairly isolated from the group in a sports sociogram, his reputation as a bright scholar may result in a more central position for him in a work project sociogram. Of course, not every quiet child is a scholar, and some children are always chosen more than others. The sociogram shows a disproportionate number of arrows drawn toward the popular children, and because of their appearance these children are called *stars* (for example, Jack in Figure 13 is a star). Infrequently chosen children are called *social isolates* (Harlan or Henry in Figure 13).

The sociogram points out the relative popularity of each group member; it also provides a clear picture of subgroups within the group. For example, our diagram shows that Dan, Paul, and George have formed a sort of mutual admiration society, choosing each other as companions for this activity. This relationship, called a *triangle,* may have a strong

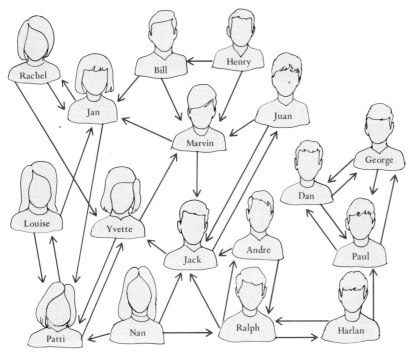

Figure 13 A sociogram is used to research the social status within a peer group. Here, members of a sixth-grade class have indicated their choices of classmates as companions on a special school trip.

influence on the structure of the whole group, especially if one of these boys is fairly popular.

The sociogram provides a clear picture of the network of relationships in a group. But it does not give us a very good measure of the dimensions of these relationships or their intensity. Much more detailed techniques are able to do this, and one of these is the *Syracuse Scale of Social Relations* (Gardner & Thompson, 1958). In the Syracuse Scale, each child is asked to construct his own intensity scale on a dimension of a relationship. The scale is begun with the child selecting the two most extreme individuals he can identify on a single dimension. For example, he might be asked, "If you had a very personal and important secret and you were allowed to share it with only one person, whom would you choose to tell it to?" The child answers with his favorite choice, his last choice, and someone just about in the middle. Then the child names two more reference points halfway between the extremes and the midpoint. Next, the child is asked to arrange the members of his group along his personal scale of "trust." This question we have asked measures trust, but other questions might measure dependence, or admiration, or any other feeling. The answers let us see the intensity of feeling the group members have for one another. They let us get away from the simple "yes and no" answers and into the level of understanding, trust, or rapport among group members.

Sociograms and scales such as the Syracuse Scale tell us a great deal about the nature of groups. They also have wide practical applications. Two sociograms done 5 months apart can show whether a new class seating arrangement has improved the cooperation in a class, or whether the reorganization of a team has broken up a stagnant central triangle and brought more boys into the group's activities.

We have seen that each peer group has some members who are popular and others who are not. A few factors often seem to contribute to this status differentiation. In general, peer acceptance is often related to an individual's good overall adjustment—to enthusiasm and active participation, to cooperation with group routines, to sensitivity to social overtures. This kind of attunement (or lack of it) tends to reinforce itself in a circular pattern (Glidewell et al., 1966). Well-liked children's good adjustment is bolstered by their popularity, and awkward children become even more ill-at-ease when they are ignored or rejected by the group.

A second factor influencing popularity or leadership is intelligence. In general, popular children have fairly high IQs (Roff & Sells, 1965). Often the slow learners are made fun of or ignored by their classmates. A third factor contributing to group status is athletic ability. This is particularly important in settings such as summer camp or playgrounds, where the whole group is involved in sports. Children less likely to be popular usually have "undesirable" traits, such as high anxiety, excessive dependency on the teacher, rebelliousness, or a physical problem like obesity. All of these traits tend to reduce the child's level of conformity to group standards—a behavior which, we have seen, is very important during the middle childhood years. How insistent is the pressure to conform to group standards, and who are the children who are influenced most by group membership?

PEER GROUP INFLUENCE ON THE INDIVIDUAL. Conformity itself is a normal and healthy behavior, and in many ways it is quite desirable. Children conform to the expected norms of a peer group as well as to adult expectations. But sometimes children can be excessively conforming to group norms, regardless of whether or not the group's standards are helpful to the child, to the group itself, or to others.

Which children are most strongly influenced by group pressures? It is dangerous to generalize in answering a question like this, but there are a few characteristics which appear to be common to the conformers. High-conforming children seem to have a low "ego strength," a feeling of inferiority (Hartup, 1970a). They have a relatively high social sensitivity and tend to be more dependent or anxious than other children. In many studies, girls are often more conforming to peer pressure than boys; however, this is not always the case. If the norms are highly sex-typed, then boys may be more conforming. For example, certain standards of physical toughness are almost compulsory for boys. Firstborns tend to be higher in conformity than are later-born children (Becker, Lerner, & Carroll, 1966).

Which children feel least pressure to conform? As with the children most influenced by group membership, their characteristics are hard to

By the age of 10 or 11, children show an almost compulsive reverence for game rules and organization. (*Burk Uzzle, Magnum Photos.*)

pinpoint. In some cases their traits are the opposite of those of the high-conforming children. Yet some children seem to be under pressure *not* to conform. One trait that does seem to be common among nonconformers is hyperaggression. There are some hyperaggressive youngsters who are unusually rigid and less susceptible to group pressure than are most children.

None of the traits that seem to be connected with high conformity works alone; all of them are influenced by a great number of other factors which we still do not fully understand. But we do know that conformity is especially important to all children during the middle childhood years. Children feel the need to belong; they need to feel accepted; they need to feel that they are part of a social setting larger than themselves. This need is especially strong during middle childhood because this is the time when they are moving away from the security of family life.

The need for social intimacy and acceptance is very strong, but it is juxtaposed with another need which is just as strong during the middle childhood years. This is the need for autonomy or mastery. Each child has a strong need to find order in disorder. He tries to achieve some degree of mastery or understanding or control over his social and physical environment, to understand its rules and limits, and to find his place within these limits. For this reason, he becomes very involved in making and learning rules and rituals.

This juxtaposition of two needs, autonomy and intimacy, is important at several points in each individual's development. It is especially strong in the 1½-year-old who is just beginning to learn how many things he can do for himself. During middle childhood, these two opposing needs are again paramount. But the particular balance that the child now finds as a solution to these needs is different from the solution of the 1½-year-old. For the child age 6 to 12, the peer group often satisfies both the need for acceptance and the need for autonomy.

PREJUDICE AND MINORITY GROUP STATUS

What happens to the child when, as he moves away from his family during middle childhood, he finds that the norms of the broader culture are different from those at home? This experience probably happens to most children to some extent—as they learn that their friends don't like spinach or don't go to church. But it can be an important crisis for the child of a small minority group who must often find a way to reconcile the unpleasant stereotypes and prejudices he now encounters with his own self-image.

Prejudice may be defined as "the negative attitudes directed toward members of social groups who are perceived by themselves and others in terms of racial, religious, national, or cultural-linguistic attributes" (Proshansky, 1966, p. 311). It is unpleasant, but it has always been a part of mankind (Coles, 1967).

We tend to think of prejudice as an adult attitude, but racial awareness actually begins to develop very early, even by age 4. Studies of both Jewish (Radke, Trager, & Davis, 1949) and black children (Goodman, 1952) show that ethnic awareness often appears earlier in the minority group child. And the minority child, especially a black child, often directs the prejudices he learns against others of his own group. In the late 1940s and the 1950s, studies showed that black children in nursery schools preferred white dolls to black dolls (Clark & Clark, 1947; Goodman, 1952). In addition, more black children of this age expressed hostility toward their own race than toward white persons. No such self-deprecation was observed for white children. Of course, minority group attitudes have changed a great deal since the 1950s, with ethnic pride growing in many groups. But although the studies cited above are somewhat dated, the influence of majority group prejudices and stereotypes on the minority child is still great, and the tendency still exists for very young black children, for example, to prefer things white to things black.

When a child is between the ages of 5 and 8, his racial and ethnic attitudes become more sophisticated and often more stereotyped. The preference of black children for white persons decreases with age (Clark & Clark, 1947; Radke & Trager, 1950). In turn, white children's tendency to reject blacks increases as they get older, as does their tendency to reject Jews (Radke et al., 1949). These early prejudices are often reinforced by the peer group in middle childhood, where the norms and values of the dominant members influence everyone in the group.

Racial and ethnic stereotypes are expanded and sometimes elaborated in groups with name-calling, chants, or jokes.

The racial and ethnic attitudes of middle childhood can develop into later prejudices in children of both the majority and the minority cultures. One very extensive study (Frenkel-Brunswik, 1948) showed that individual characteristics have a lot to do with the degree of prejudice which children eventually develop. Certain personality traits are likely to lend themselves to high levels of prejudice later on in life. The authoritarian child—the one who wants either to look up to his friends or look down to them, and who sees all his relationships in leader-follower terms—is liable to develop prejudices. Children who divide the world into rigid dichotomies of good and bad, with little tolerance for ambiguity, also tend to be high on prejudice. And children who show the most prejudice often have parents who are strict enforcers of discipline and place a high value on moralism and conformity.

Prejudice develops in both the majority and minority groups. But it creates special problems for the minority group child. For example, the black child who must learn to incorporate negative stereotypes of his race into his own self-image is put under quite a strain. The result is that he shows insecurity, anxiety, and lower self-esteem than the white child (Boyd, 1952; Deutsch, 1960; Palermo, 1959).

The minority child's ethnic awareness is often accelerated by his peer group membership. His needs for acceptance, belonging, and intimacy require that he establish ties with the wider culture through peer group membership. If he is a member of a small minority, that group will have norms that differ widely from his own. A lower-class black child truly belongs to a culture different from that of the white child in America (Rainwater, 1966). The degree of acceptance the black child finds in the larger group often depends upon his ability to conform to its norms. Many minority children, of course, join neighborhood peer groups that include other minority children. This makes adjustment easier during middle childhood, and it tends both to improve self-esteem and to increase in-group solidarity and out-group hostility. But each minority child eventually faces the problem of integrating society's image of him as a black, a Jew, a Pole, or an Indian with his own self-concept. And this can be the cause of conflict, anxiety, or anger at any age.

DELINQUENCY

Peer pressure to conform acts as an important socializer. But sometimes the norms of the peer group are quite different from those of society as a whole. Delinquent gangs have received much attention in the past few decades. Movies and shows such as *The Wild One* and *West Side Story* depict peer groups which are very small subcultures that set themselves apart from the larger culture. They are tightly organized groups whose members engage in acts that are against society but which are sanctioned by the peer group.

In the delinquent gang, individuals have group support for their actions even though they do not have society's support. But groups or gangs constitute just one type of delinquency. Individual delinquency consists of the aggressive acts of a single child against society or against particular people. The individual delinquent receives little or no support from peers, and his aggressive acts are usually the product of neuroses (Kessler, 1966).

Who Are Delinquents?

In recent years, arrests of persons under the age of 18 have increased at a faster rate than other arrests. In the 1960s and 1970s more than half of the people arrested in the United States for larceny, auto theft, burglary, vandalism, and arson have been juveniles. Who are the children who become delinquents, and what are the factors that lead them to commit acts against society?

Many, if not most, children engage in some kind of behavior which could be called delinquent at some point in their lives. Shoplifting, for example, is common as are minor acts of vandalism. Whether or not the child is labeled a delinquent has much to do with whether he is caught (and how often he is caught), with the social status of his family, and with the status of the victim. Nevertheless, sociological data provide at least a tentative answer to the question of which children are most likely to be brought to the attention of the courts for delinquent behavior.

THE SOCIOLOGIST'S ANSWER. Statistically, delinquency rates are highest in poor urban areas. Highest delinquency rates occur among ethnic groups which have recently been assimilated into urban life, either from other cultures or from the rural areas of our own country. There also seems to be a connection between broken homes and delinquency, for the lack of a male model seems to contribute to children's role confusion. Boy delinquents outnumber girl delinquents by over 4 to 1.

Sociologists have advanced many theories to explain this bunching of delinquency in poor urban subcultures. These theories are widely different, and we cannot hope to explain all of them. Therefore, we have singled out a few which are especially interesting although not necessarily representative or valid. According to the "functional" theory (Miller, 1958), delinquent gangs adhere to the norms which will best prepare their members for later lives as, for instance, longshoremen or blue-collar laborers. Gang emphasis on toughness and autonomy, on "street" smartness, on excitement and trouble, and the belief in the power of fate or luck—all are important norms of the lower-class culture, and therefore they are basic to gang values too. Many other theories do not view delinquent gangs as serving any preparatory function (Cloward & Ohlin, 1960; Cohen, 1955; Merton, 1957). Instead, they explain delinquency as a purposeless lashing out at society—a result of the frustration of the overcrowded, powerless lower classes who are confronted with the American dream but are not allowed to reach it.

THE PSYCHOLOGIST'S ANSWER. The sociological statistics and theories help to link delinquency to environmental factors, but they do not ex-

A delinquent may have group support for his activities even though he does not have society's support. (*Bob Adelman, Magnum Photos.*)

plain individual psychological factors. Why is it that most poor immigrant children in the cities are not delinquents? Why *are* many affluent children delinquents? To answer questions like these, we must look more closely at the individual psychological variables that cause different people to act differently within the same sociological conditions (Bandura & Walters, 1959). Individuals are not delinquent because they are poor, or black, or city dwellers. They may be delinquent because, as individuals, they have repeatedly been unable or unwilling to adjust to society or to develop adequate impulse controls or outlets for anger or frustration.

Kessler's theory (1966) has identified four areas of developmental problems that delinquents seem to have. These are: (1) high aggression as a response to personal or social problems; (2) an inability to identify with weak victims (part of an unwillingness to admit one's own weaknesses); (3) a defective conscience or superego; and (4) a "weakness of ego"—an inability to deal with personal disruptions and a poor perception of reality.

To answer the question of who becomes a delinquent, we must combine both the sociologist's and the psychologist's answers. Like the other patterns we have talked about in this chapter, delinquency is simply another form of adjustment to the social and psychological realities of middle childhood. It satisfies certain special needs for self-esteem, providing a sense of both autonomy and acceptance within the social context of a peer group. The kinds of personality disturbances we have discussed above seem to predispose certain children to delinquent behavior. When other conditions are right—when the social situation is highly frustrating, or when it seems to model or reward delinquency—then the chances are high that a child will become a delinquent.

PERSONALITY AND SELF-ESTEEM
Throughout this chapter, we have been looking closely at personality growth within the social structure during middle childhood. While we have ranged over widely different areas as we have talked about peer groups, status, conformity, delinquency, and prejudice, an important thread has been central to each part of our discussion. That is each child's need to maintain a sense of self-esteem as he moves away from the security of early childhood into the world outside the family.

The way a child learns to think of himself during these years depends in large measure upon what his friends think of him. The child who starts off with advantages of intelligence, high social skills, and self-confidence is liable to find that these good points are reinforced by his popularity in peer groups, and so his self-esteem grows. The boy in the delinquent gang may find that the tougher he acts, the more the group thinks of him. His "mean" self-image is encouraged by his peers. The inability to get along with peers is also reinforced by group experiences. The child who starts out with a few strikes against him—who is sickly, or not very smart, or comes from a different ethnic background—finds it harder to conform to group standards or norms. He may be anxious or awkward, and when the group fails to respond positively to him, he becomes more anxious and his self-esteem suffers.

This circular process (Glidewell et al., 1966) is very important in the development of the child's self-image. His personal successes or failures in different situations in the group can lead him to see himself as a leader, a loner, a criminal, as well-adjusted, or as maladjusted. Fortunately, it need not be a closed circle, and many children who start off with social handicaps discover that they are good at things that other children cannot do. But peer groups play a very important role in the culture of middle childhood, and they are almost bound to have an influence on each child's feeling of self-esteem.

SUMMARY
The "culture of childhood" is characterized by a reverence for rules, a love of ritual, and close relationships with peers. Between the ages of 6 and 12, the child is moving away from the security of the family, and so this is a time of learning—learning society's attitudes, rules, and expectations; learning to relate to others; learning about himself.

Both friendship pairs and peer groups provide important "practice grounds" for later social relationships. Peer groups may be either formal or informal. They develop naturally as children are in contact with each other over a period of time. They are characterized by common norms and values and by a relatively stable division of roles. Sociograms and scales such as the Syracuse Scale can be used to define and measure the way group members interact. Peer groups satisfy two important needs: autonomy, or the need to feel in control of oneself in social situations; and intimacy, or the need for acceptance. Some children need to feel accepted more than others, and they may be excessively conforming to group standards.

Some special problems may develop during the middle childhood years. Ethnic and racial awareness is present even in the preschool years, but certain personality traits make some children tend to develop definite prejudices as this awareness is reinforced during middle childhood. Ethnic stereotypes and differences in norms can make it very difficult for the minority child to conform to peer expectations. Another problem which starts to emerge in middle childhood is delinquency. A combination of sociological and psychological factors causes some children to act aggressively against society. In delinquent gangs, these acts conform to group norms. But some delinquents act alone, with no support for their actions. Peer groups, prejudice, and delinquency are widely divergent ways in which different children react to the frustrations and successes they experience during middle childhood.

REVIEW QUESTIONS

1. What is meant by the "culture of childhood," and what purpose does it seem to serve?
2. What social and psychological benefits, if any, do you think delinquent gangs provide for their members?
3. What is a peer group? Why is it so important during the middle childhood years?

SUGGESTED READINGS

Baruch, D. W. *One little boy.* New York: Dell, 1952. This still-popular narrative captures the spirit and personality of a child without resorting to the dryness of a clinical case study.

Coles, R. *Children of crisis.* Boston: Little, Brown, 1967. Through extensive interviews with children, their families, and school and community personnel, the author explores the initial racial integration in the schools of New Orleans.

Redl, F., & Wineman, D. *Children who hate.* New York: Free Press, 1951.
———. *Controls from within: Techniques for the treatment of the aggressive child.* New York: Free Press, 1952. Together these two books describe a small group of aggressive and delinquent children as they are before treatment and as they progress in a treatment program designed to develop "controls from within."

PART VI
ADOLESCENCE AND YOUTH

17

ADOLESCENCE: A DEVELOPMENTAL PERIOD

THE PHENOMENON OF MODERN ADOLESCENCE
In primitive societies, life expectancy was short and technology was rudimentary. Consequently, the simple skills needed in adult life did not require a prolonged period of education. Thus, the transition from childhood to adult status tended to be rather abrupt, usually occurring at the biological watershed of puberty and often attended by some symbolic ceremony, name change, or challenge. These symbolic events are known in anthropology as *rites de passage,* or "transition rituals." After reaching physical maturity and undergoing a *rite de passage,* a young person might be given a year or two of social apprenticeship to help him adjust to his new physical stature and his new status as a mature and responsible adult. Then, his youth was definitely over.

Our concept of adolescence as a developmental period all its own, with unique tasks, stresses, and solutions, is really a rather modern phenomenon. The idea of adolescence can be traced to Rousseau's *Émile,* the eighteenth-century classic that glorified and romanticized the innocence and educational potential of youth's "salad days"; but prolonged adolescence as a social phenomenon is described by some as an American innovation. An illuminating analysis by David Bakan (1971) attributes the development of adolescence to the economic, social, and political needs of post–Civil War America.

According to Bakan, in the late nineteenth century the United States rushed headlong into intense industrialization and urbanization. It absorbed millions of immigrants who had little formal education and were unacquainted with American institutions. New, technologically complex jobs demanded specialized training; and democratic institutions based upon popular participation by a literate citizenry required thorough assimilation of all American children, especially those of foreign parentage. The need for reliable workers in dangerous jobs who could adjust to bureaucratic subordination radically altered the opportunities available to adolescents. Although physically mature, the adolescents were *technologically* immature. Furthermore, they were part of a new labor surplus. There was a great impetus to create a new space in society for this age group, with new rules and roles.

The creation of a new space for adolescents in society was effected by (1) compulsory education, which both drilled students in necessary skills and subordinated them to the authority of school officials rather than that of their parents; (2) child labor legislation, which was enacted partly for humanitarian reasons and partly to keep children out of a tight job market; and (3) juvenile delinquency legislation, which was supposed to give law enforcement officials greater flexibility, leniency, and discretion in dealing with youthful offenders, but in fact has resulted in *fewer* constitutional rights for minors. Whether or not one agrees with Bakan's analysis, certainly many of the developmental tasks of adolescence—making career choices, preparing for an adult life of work and intimacy, and finding one's identity—are vastly complicated by the demands and anonymity of our complex society.

The psychological demands that the modern adolescent must meet in this new time slot are staggering. Blos (1971) has prepared a rather traditional, Freudian description of adolescent conflicts between intensified sexual drives and increased demands for ego dominance. He concludes that the demands of modern society for greater ego control and more highly developed cognitive functions have made prolonged adolescence a socially necessary condition that aggravates the biological and psychological upheavals characteristic of this period.

Furthermore, these adjustments become increasingly difficult in a world facing such global crises as hunger, pollution, and war, and crises of social disorganization, overcrowding, poverty, and ideological ferment. Formerly, young people could look to adults and a body of tradition for answers to their questions; today, youth sees only uncertainty and social disorganization in the world. In the midst of this chaos, the adolescent must come to grips with intellectual and physical maturity and incumbent psychological stress. In this chapter we shall examine the adolescent dilemma with all its problems, pressures, and distortions.

In the next chapter we shall turn to the variety of solutions devised to conquer these conflicts, some alternatives available to the young person, and the motives that result in the choice of one approach or another. This bundle of decisions amounts to a more or less coherent

Four students pose for their high school graduation picture in the early 1900s. (*The Bettman Archive.*)

The modern adolescent is expected to make many psychological adjustments. (*Christa Armstrong, Rapho/Photo Researchers.*)

life-style, but only after a very complex and difficult integration of roles, values, and experiences has been achieved. Today, we must undergo not one, but many *rites de passage,* all designed not actually to secure any particular niche in the adult world, but to produce an individual who can continually make choices and scramble to stay in tune with a world in flux (Winder & Angus, 1968).

SEXUAL MATURITY   Physiologically, adolescence ranks with the fetal period and the first two years of life for sheer magnitude of body change. However, unlike the infant in the earlier period, the adolescent has the pain and pleasure of observing the whole process: he watches himself with alternating feelings of fascination, charm, and horror as the bodily changes occur. Surprised, embarrassed, and uncertain, the adolescent constantly judges himself in comparison with others and continually revises his self-image. Both sexes anxiously monitor their development, or lack of it, with knowledge and misconception, pride and fear, hope and trepidation. Always, there is comparison of oneself with the prevailing ideal, and the ability to reconcile differences between the two is crucial for the adolescent as a spectator of his own transformation.

Biological Changes   The biological hallmarks of adolescence are a marked increase in the rate of growth and body size, rapid development of the reproductive organs, and the appearance of secondary sex characteristics. Some of the changes occur universally in boys and girls, but most of them are sex specific. The changes are precipitated by *hormones*. These are the chemical products of various endocrine glands which are located in different parts of the body but interact in a complex fashion. The hormones affecting adolescent growth may be newly produced and secreted, or they may have previously been present in the body in traces but now are manufactured in unprecedented quantities (Tanner, 1971). Each hormone is designed to influence a certain set of targets or receptors, but these receptors are not necessarily located in the same organ or type of tissue. For example, testosterone affects areas as diverse as facial skin, areas of the brain, cells in the penis, and cartilage in the shoulder joints (Tanner, 1971). The target tissues have the ability to respond selectively to only some of the hormones circulating in the bloodstream; for instance, the uterus selectively responds to two sex hormones, estrogen and progesterone (Garrison, 1973).

The secretions of the endocrine glands are intricately related in an extremely delicate and complex balance, the maintenance of which is essential to normal growth and functioning. Since a full description of endocrinological dynamics is beyond the scope of this discussion, we shall focus on the pituitary gland, sometimes known as the "master gland." Located on the underside of the brain, the pituitary produces several varieties of hormones, two of the most important of which are the growth hormone (somatotrophin) and some secondary hormones (Garrison, 1973). These secondary hormones stimulate and regulate the functioning of a number of other glands, including the testes, or sex glands. The testes have two jobs: to produce gametes (sperm or eggs), and to secrete the sex hormones vital to development of the reproductive organs. Secretions of both the pituitary gland and the testes have emotional as well as physiological impact upon the developing young person, and they are one important source of stress among adolescents.

The two sexes develop at different rates, with girls rather uniformly experiencing extensive bodily changes two years before boys (Tanner,

Puberty Growth Rates in Girls

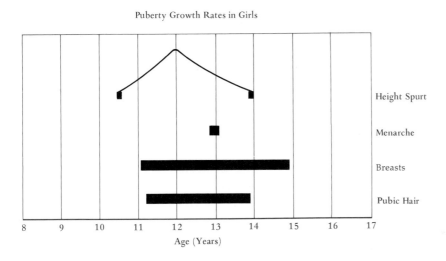

Puberty Growth Rates in Boys

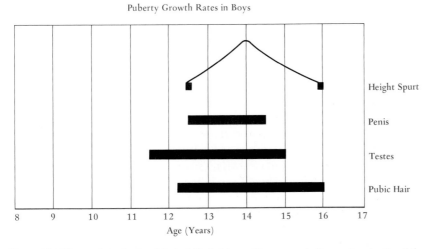

Figure 14 The peak in the bar labeled "height spurt" represents the peak velocity of the spurt. The bars represent the average beginning and completion of the events of puberty. *(From Tanner, J. M. Growing up.* Scientific American, *September 1973, p. 40.)*

1971). Moreover, there is a great deal of variation in rate of development between members of the same sex; some late-maturing boys may not have begun any change at all, while others who are the same chronological age will have completed a whole stage of development. Nevertheless, once the sequence of sexual maturation has begun, it progresses in fairly predictable order. (Interestingly, the commencement of these biological changes is occurring at an earlier point in each generation, a phenomenon which is probably the result of several diverse and external factors, such as nutrition and general socioeconomic conditions.) Keeping in mind the differences found from one individual to the next, let us look at the general schedule of the changes that characterize physical adolescence.

Most prominent is the spurt in growth and the *rate* of growth that reaches its zenith in girls at age 12 and in boys at 14 (Tanner, 1971). The body is getting larger at a speed equaled only in the 2-year-old child. Both bones and muscles are developing, triggered by the same set of hormones, but different parts of the body develop at varying rates, following an interesting, often comical, order. The extremities—hands, feet, and head—are first to reach adult size; the gangly, ill-proportioned physique that often results at this time is the caricature of the adolescent. In terms of growth rate, leg length peaks first, followed by general body width and, lastly, full shoulder growth. During this period, there is a corresponding loss of fat; the loss is more marked in boys than in girls. Fat accumulation resumes at the end of the growth spurt. Since their glands are producing the male sex hormone, testosterone, boys also develop more red cells and hemoglobin than girls at this time; the extensive red cell production may be one factor (although certainly not the only one) in boys' superior athletic ability at this stage. When we think of the adolescent boy, we cannot help but call to mind the awkwardly cracking voice. However, this actual voice change takes place relatively late in adolescence; and since it often occurs gradually, it is not very significant as a developmental guidepost in puberty (Tanner, 1971).

In addition to the growth spurt, the second major biological change is development of the reproductive system. In males, the first indication of puberty is accelerating growth of the testes and scrotum. Approximately one year later, spurts in height and penis growth occur, with concurrent development of the seminal vesicles and the prostate gland. In the interim between testical and penile development, pubic hair begins to appear, but it does not attain full growth until after the completion of genital development. Another change encountered in this period is the stepped-up activity of sebaceous and sweat glands in the skin, which results in distinctive new body odors and common skin problems (Tanner, 1971).

In girls, the "breast bud" is usually, but not always, the first signal that puberty has begun. There is simultaneous development of the uterus and vagina, with enlargement of the labia and clitoris. *Menarche* (the first menstruation), although perhaps the most dramatic and symbolic sign of the girl's changing status, occurs late in female adolescence, well after the peak of the growth spurt. The early menstrual cycles may vary tremendously from one girl to another, and from one month to another for any one girl. They are often irregular and *anovulatory* (no egg is shed) (Tanner, 1971).

The young teenager is frequently fascinated with, and critically appraising of, his or her body. Is it the right shape, the right size? Is he or she coordinated, or a klutz? How does he or she compare to the ideal? Sociologically, adolescents can be considered a marginal group, either between cultures or on the fringe of a dominant culture; and typically, such groups tend to exhibit an intensified need for conformity. For this reason, teenagers can be more intolerant of deviation, whether it be a deviation in body type, such as extreme obesity, or a deviation in timing, like the late bloomer. The mass media manipulate this tendency by marketing stereotyped images of attractive, exuberant youths who glide through adolescence without pimples, braces, or a cracking voice. Because adolescents are often extremely sensitive and perceptive about their own physical appearance and that of their friends, the discrepancies between their less-than-perfect self-images and the glossy ideals they are supposed to emulate can be a real source of anxiety.

BODY TYPE AND PHYSICAL APPEARANCE. Long before adolescence, children are aware of different body types and ideals, and they have a fairly clear image of their own body types, skills, and proportions. But in adolescence, body type receives renewed scrutiny (Dwyer & Mayer, 1968–69). Many young people subject themselves to intense dieting, either to counteract overweight or to achieve idealized body proportions. Others embark on rigorous regimens of physical fitness and strength training, weight lifting, athletics, or dancing. There are interesting differences in the changes sought by the two sexes (Frazier & Lisonbee, 1950). Girls want very specific changes: "I would make my ears lie back," or "I would make my forehead lower." Boys have greater difficulty articulating their dissatisfactions so precisely. A typical boy's response is, "I would make myself look handsome and not fat. I would have wavy black hair. I would change my whole physical appearance so that I would be handsome with a good build." In general, girls worry about being heavy, while boys are concerned with being thin in the upper arms and chest. Girls think of themselves as too tall; boys worry about being too short. Almost half of all adolescents worry about pimples and blackheads.

These three areas—height, weight, and complexion—are the major sources of concern, with two thirds of a sample of tenth graders seeking one or more physical changes in themselves (Frazier & Lisonbee, 1950). This high percentage indicates the tight grip that cultural ideals, such as thin female physiques, can have upon members of a certain society. There are many perfectly normal, even lean, adolescents who are medically healthy but who consider themselves obese and wish to lose weight

Body Image and Adjustment

(Sybil Shackman, Monkmeyer.)

ADOLESCENTS STRIVE TOWARD AN IDEAL.

(Peter Martens, Nancy Palmer Photo Agency.)　　　(David S. Strickler, Monkmeyer.)

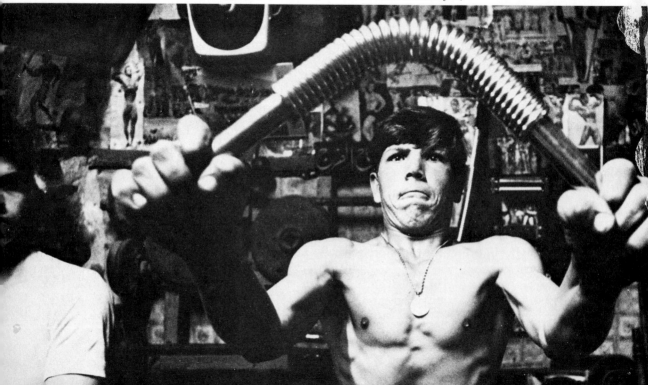

(Dwyer & Mayer, 1968–69). In other cultures, such thinness is considered unhealthy or indicative of poor family circumstances.

A study in *Psychology Today* indicates considerably greater acceptance of general physical appearance by older adolescents and young adults than by younger people (Berscheid, Walster, & Bohrnstedt, 1973). These findings may be partly the result of changed attitudes today and partly the result of using a voluntary sample of people who could be somewhat biased toward optimistic, self-satisfied individuals. Nevertheless, self-consciousness over body image generally recedes into the background as the young person approaches maturity.

EARLY AND LATE MATURERS. Timing in maturation, whether the development is late or early, has engrossed researchers almost as much as adolescents themselves (Mussen & Jones, 1957). Investigators have discovered that the social onus of ill-timed maturation falls more heavily upon late-maturing boys than upon early-maturing males or females (Hamechek, 1973). It should be remembered that, on the average, girls mature two years earlier than boys. Thus, in a manner of speaking, the late-maturing boy is the last to come of age. He may be at a disadvantage in athletics, since he is smaller and somewhat weaker, and he is generally treated as a younger, more immature individual. Sometimes his response is a self-fulfilling prophecy of less mature behavior. For example, the boy may overcompensate and become aggressive. At any rate, late-blooming boys have a much more difficult adjustment than early-maturing males, who tend to accrue all kinds of social and athletic prestige among their peers.

In contrast, the early-maturing girl may be at a slight disadvantage in comparison with slower females. She is taller and stands out like a giraffe in the elementary grades. She has fewer chances to discuss with her peers the particular changes she is undergoing, and there is no particular prestige value attached to her precocious development (Hamachek, 1973). The incidence of the effect of developmental variation in girls is mixed; but at any rate, the experience is clearly not as traumatic for most girls as it is for boys.

Sexual Identity

The formation of sexual identity is only one part of the reformulation of identity in adolescence. Furthermore, the reformulation is more a crystallization and refinement of previous experience than a whole new task. In Chapter 8 we saw how sex roles and sex-role stereotypes have been forged long before adolescence, with the crucial period being the preschool years. Nevertheless, adolescence and all the biological changes of physical maturation bring renewed interest in sexuality and sexual identity, accentuating the problem of integrating sexual drives with other aspects of behavior.

Let us consider male and female development separately, since a number of factors cause marked divergence in the behavior of boys and girls.

High hormonal inputs make boys more sensitive to genital arousal

(Simon & Gagnon, 1969). Masturbation, rather than romantic fantasy, is the major sexual activity for boys; and although it is extremely positive and gratifying, it may lead to a capacity for emotionally detached sex activity, a salient feature of our society. Class differences are an important factor in adolescent male sexuality (though not as prominent in female development). The ability to develop a rich fantasy life during masturbation (which depends partly upon adept manipulation of symbols) is more prominent in the upper classes. Guilt over the "unmanliness" of masturbation is of greater concern to the lower-class male, who has fewer opportunities to win social approval from peers. Males of all classes get little training in the way to link up sexual feelings with emotional relationships; this remains an area of female prowess (Simon & Gagnon, 1969).

American girls are not encouraged to be sexual; rather, they receive early training in evaluating themselves, and boys, as desirable mates. It has been suggested that dating and courtship are the processes in which each sex swaps its garnered expertise and trains the other in desires and expectations (Simon & Gagnon, 1969). It is important to note that class differences in sexuality are relatively unimportant among females, owing to the traditionally limited range of roles available to women. Some researchers (Angrist, 1969) stress the importance of flexibility and contingency planning in female sexual development. In our society, femininity connotes passivity, deference, and the ability to fit in. A girl must remain flexible enough to fit the value systems of potential spouses. But since marriage is not guaranteed, she must also acquire skills to support herself in the event of divorce, widowhood, economic need for a second income, or an independent single life.

Besides the male/female difference, other circumstances such as ethnic background and prevailing sexual norms can systematically alter adolescent sexuality within society. For example, one study indicates that although white girls are consistently more heterosexually oriented than white boys of the same age, black boys indicate heterosexual proclivities on a par with their black female peers. Twelve-year-old black boys seem to be more heterosexually oriented than their white male counterparts, although this may be more a result of class than racial background (Broderick, 1965). In fact, the degree of sexuality for both sexes is highly dependent upon the prevailing norms. Some societies preserve sexuality exclusively for reproduction. Others view such abstinence as a crime against nature! Biology, it seems, is highly modifiable!

Furthermore, the freer social climate of the United States in the 1970s encourages more social interaction between the sexes. One comparative study (Kuhlen & Houlihan, 1965) indicates that adolescents chose peers of the opposite sex as companions for various activities significantly more often in 1963 than a generation earlier, in 1942. The rate of change in heterosexual patterns seems to be accelerating as well.

Another variable is the amount of accurate information on sexuality possessed by the adolescent. There seems to be relatively little relation-

Today, adolescents often choose peers of the opposite sex as companions. (*Hella Hammid, Rapho/Photo Researchers.*)

ship between what teenagers *think* they know and what in fact they *do* know. Nevertheless, the preparation they receive does have an impact upon their adjustment, particularly with respect to menarche and to nocturnal emissions ("wet dreams"). Teenagers who were prepared for the physical and psychological experiences they were about to undergo showed much less anxiety and fear than those who were less prepared, and they had considerably more opportunity for positive, self-confident attitudes toward their own bodies and body functions (McCreary-Juhasz, 1967).

Much of the research on adolescent change has focused on how the adolescent feels, revolts, or adorns himself; there is a marked lack of study on adolescent cognitive change. Nevertheless, there are important developments taking place at this period, not only in capacity and

INTELLECTUAL MATURITY AND COMPETENCE

style of thought, but also in awareness, imagination, judgment, and insight. Furthermore, the adolescent uses his expanded mental powers to examine a wide new range of issues and problems.

Formal Operational Thought

In Piaget's developmental theory, the hallmark of adolescent cognitive change is the development of formal operational thought (even though it does not occur fully in all individuals). The adolescent becomes capable of reasoning with alternate hypotheses, musing over the possible and probable as well as the real and concrete (Gallagher, 1973). Formal operational thought can be characterized as a "second-order" process. The first order of thinking is discovering and articulating relationships between objects. The second order involves thinking about one's thoughts, looking for relationships between relationships, and fluidly maneuvering between reality and possibility (Inhelder & Piaget, 1958). The three major characteristics of adolescent thought are: (1) the capacity to combine all variables and come up with a solution to a problem; (2) the ability to conjecture the effect of one variable upon another; and (3) the facility to combine and separate variables in a hypothetical-deductive fashion ("if X is present, Y will occur") (Gallagher, 1973).

A classic demonstration of formal operational thought is called "combination of colorless liquids," in which the subject is presented with four numbered flasks containing four different colorless, odorless liquids. He is also presented with a small bottle of potassium chloride, a dropper, and two unmarked glasses. One glass contains a mixture of liquids 1 and 3, the other holds liquid 2. While the subject watches, the experimenter adds a few drops of potassium chloride to the liquid in the two unmarked glasses; the first liquid turns yellow, the second one does not. The subject is then asked to reproduce the yellow color by using the four numbered liquids. All he knows is that there is something about potassium chloride that will produce a yellow color under certain circumstances; he does not know whether the correct circumstance is the addition of liquid 1, 2, 3, or 4, or (and here is the key) a combination of two or more liquids. The adolescent who can use formal reasoning will systematically explore the liquids one at a time, then in combination, until he achieves the reward of a flask of yellow liquid (Inhelder & Piaget, 1958).

The development of this kind of abstract thought results from the joint operation of maturation, experience with the physical environment, and social transmission or education. It does not appear fully in all adolescents, nor does it function equally in all areas of problem solving.

Qualitative Changes in Style of Thought

Adolescents typically demonstrate an increased self-awareness and the ability to generate more possible alternatives, to speculate, and to intellectually walk around a problem (Peel, 1965).

There is also a peculiar kind of adolescent egocentrism that is a product of interaction between the adolescent's ability to cognize, or take account of, other people's thoughts, and his preoccupation with

The adolescent in today's cultural world. (*Paolo Koch, Rapho/Photo Researchers.*)

his own complex metamorphosis. He assumes that other people are as fascinated by him and his behavior as he is himself. He fails to distinguish between objects of concern to himself and the subjective attitude of others. As a result, he tends to anticipate the reactions of others, assuming that they are either as approving or critical of him as he is of himself. Thus, many of his social contacts will have a totally different meaning for him than they do, in fact, for the other people involved. At the same time that he fails to differentiate the feelings of others, the adolescent overdifferentiates his own feelings, believing that they are unique unto himself. Only he has known such agony or such rapture, he thinks. This egocentrism begins to recede when the adolescent reaches the age of 15 or 16, as he replaces real audiences with imaginary audiences (Elkind, 1967).

Some creative adolescents exhibit capacities for unusual ways of thinking that are different from the cognitive modes employed by the typical highly intelligent adolescent (as defined by high IQ scores). Creative individuals have the knack of restructuring forms and stereotypes in new and unexpected ways, of roaming divergently and randomly over myriad possibilities rather than articulating logical, linear models and explanations. Teenagers with high IQs but low creativity, on the other hand, focus on a search for the "right" or "customary" solution through channeled, convergent thinking. Educational institutions, and society in general, tend to reward the high IQ model, the convergent thinker, over the highly creative, unconventional, and divergent type, thus stifling a great deal of creative human energy (Getzels & Jackson, 1959).

Scope of Intellectual Activity

Cognitive changes in the adolescent period lack the dramatic quality of earlier stages, but there is an important broadening of the scope of the intellect. The emphasis shifts from learning new techniques of processing information to mastering an expanded body of information. Particularly during middle and later adolescence, there is increasing concern with social and political issues, as well as mathematical, scientific, and aesthetic problems and possibilities. The adolescent begins to develop holistic concepts of society and its institutional forms, along with ethical principles that go beyond those he has experienced in particular interpersonal relationships (Coleman, 1973).

Internally, this rational processing of issues is employed in a renewed effort for internal consistency, as the individual evaluates what he has been in the past and plans what he hopes to become in the future. Some of the swings and extremes of behavior during adolescence are a result of the young person's taking new stock of himself intellectually and rationally. He wants to restructure his behavior, thoughts, and attitudes, either in the direction of greater self-consistency or toward greater conformity with a group norm, a new and individualized image, or some other cognitive model.

Academically, the adolescent is an efficient learner in a number of areas. Many of the abilities and skills measured on standardized tests reach optimal or near optimal functioning during adolescence. Only a few abilities, such as vocabulary and general information, continue to improve well into adulthood. Other abilities, such as sheer memory functions, have already peaked at age 10 or 12.

ADOLESCENCE AS A CULTURAL PHENOMENON

What are the parameters of the cultural box into which we stuff the awkward youth? Earlier in this chapter, we described the advent of adolescence as a response to the political, economic, and social needs of late nineteenth-century America. Some social commentators like Erik Erikson (1959) view the period of adolescence as a psychosocial moratorium in which the individual is allowed to explore and experiment before settling into a social niche. Others take a more negative view, emphasizing the restricted legal rights and rigidly proscribed roles of students (Farber, 1970). What are some of the central issues around which the debate swirls?

We separate adolescents from younger children, thus depriving them of opportunities to guide and tutor those younger than themselves. The isolation is not total; adolescents often babysit or take care of younger siblings. Still, such responsibilities are institutionally separated from teenagers' primary identity as high school students (Coleman et al, 1974). Adolescents are also segregated from the adult world, isolated in classrooms with their peers. They engage in no apprenticeships; they do not learn meaningful work while living side by side with more experienced models in responsible positions. Instead, the adolescent is separated for long hours every day from the major activities, customs, and responsibilities of the rest of society. Supposedly, this is a period of preparation and transition; too often, it is limbo.

Age Segregation

Adolescents experience prolonged dependency in an industrialized society where increasingly complex jobs go to adults first. Even the jobs that are available for adolescents are not intrinsically rewarding, and they may indeed be only a small part of a long process that ultimately produces an extravagantly wasteful and perhaps useless item (Goodman, 1960). This situation has the effect of prolonging the adolescent's financial dependence upon others, delaying the opportunity for him to fully utilize his capabilities, and increasing his frustration and restlessness. Such enforced dependency also causes the adolescent to feel anger toward the source of the dependency, usually his parents.

Prolonged Dependency

The mass media provide a flood of immediate information during some of the most pressing global crises. Yet, there are few effective channels through which the adolescent, or anyone else, can respond to, or take action to correct, these problems. There is high stimulus input, but no machinery for manipulating the stimuli. This is the antithesis of the responsive environment that is most conducive to human growth. Individuals must be able to act in their environment, perceive the consequences of their actions, and feel some degree of power to effect change around them. Infants need a responsive environment in order to learn their own capabilities, and they are not unique in this respect. Both the world and the immediate environment of the child and adolescent are expanded in quantum leaps by the mass media, but the environment is not a responsive one. There is no way to alter events on television, the music on radio, or the action on the movie screen. The only choice is to passively accept the stimulus or terminate it. (Some classroom environments are not much more responsive. The lecture presentation style simply perpetuates the passive, dependent, "sponge" theory of learning. All too often, students just tune out the lecturer).

A Mass Media Society

Growing Anonymity   Modern high schools are increasingly depersonalized institutions. In *The Vanishing Adolescent,* Edgar Friedenberg (1959) analyzed this depersonalization as a result of the melting pot function of the schools in America. Since the primary commitments of the schools are to equalize social and economic opportunities for disparate social groups and to prepare these groups to strive against each other in society, there is little to be gained from encouraging each child to explore and pursue his own inner life. Instead, the children are pressured toward conformity and reduced individuality.

A World of Chaos   Today's parents struggle to raise their children in a world they barely understand themselves. Certainly, the world is very different from the one that the parent generation experienced as adolescents during the post–World War II era. Then, the emphasis was on return to normality and passionate devotion to the security of family life. The drives for stability and predictable advancement poorly equipped today's parents to deal with the contemporary crisis-ridden, volatile world (Conger, 1971). Inevitably, adult authority has declined, both individually and collectively. Parents are unable to respond to their children's questions with answers drawn from tradition, because tradition is no longer a motivating social force. Parents have lost their authority as ambassadors from adult society, because adult society is not a cohesive entity. Americans of all ages are bitterly and openly divided on everything from the broadest social issues to the most intimate questions of morality.

Community stability and interdependence have been severely undermined by the new American nomadism. In the last 10 years, one of every two American families has moved every 5 years. For example, businessmen must agree to "relocate" as their work demands, and agricultural workers are forced out of their jobs and into urban ghettos by automated agribusiness (Conger, 1971).

The technological explosion has altered the quality of life drastically. The body of technical knowledge has grown faster than we are capable of absorbing or even adapting to it. Toffler, in *Future Shock* (1970), estimated that for the child born in the early 1970s, cumulative world knowledge will have quadrupled by the time he graduates from college. By the time he reaches age 50, 97 percent of everything known in the world will have been learned since his birth!

The problems to be solved by today's adolescents are of comparable magnitude. If not resolved, they have the potential for threatening the very existence of our social order. The older generation does not realize that much of the cycle of generational similarity has stopped; its members strive in vain for a return to the "good old days." This return is impossible. Indeed, society changes so rapidly that, like Alice in Wonderland, its members can hardly keep in step with the present (Adams, 1973).

The sheer complexity and chaos of today's world aggravate the task of adolescent adjustment. The adolescent must seek answers in new ways

Adolescents demonstrating to improve their surroundings. (*Howard Petrick, Nancy Palmer Photo Agency.*)

different from those used by adults. He seeks meaning in a society increasingly devoid of meaning. He wants commitment and involvement in a world that often seems to him like a machine rolling on, irrespective of him and his endeavors. The type of involvement he seeks depends somewhat upon his socioeconomic background. Some poor and/or minority group member may strive for upward mobility, but the bottom line is day-to-day survival. If he receives a decent education, he will probably work ambitiously at his career. If he remains economically marginal, he may fall into disillusionment, drug use, or crime. At any rate, the poverty youth's energies may be channeled toward garnering a larger share of the society as it exists. For him, social concern with issues such as ecology and overpopulation seems only indirectly related to his own future. He sets his sights on individual goals; he cannot afford to worry about society at large (Adams, 1973).

Middle-class youths, on the other hand, can afford the luxury of involvement in social and political issues; they are not confronted with daily needs to obtain enough food, shelter, or education. But they, too, have difficulty finding meaningful involvement. A small number become activists, with a long-time commitment to social change. Whether this type of youth will be able in the future to regenerate the rich ferment of the 1960s on campuses and elsewhere remains to be seen. A larger number of adolescents turn to the counterculture for new values and for institutions more responsive to human needs. In Chapter 18, we shall evaluate some of the successes and failures of adolescent innovations in life-style; but for now, it is important to remember that the experience of growing up in a chaotic world will inevitably affect their style and the vigor of their leadership when (and if) today's adolescents move into positions of responsibility.

ADOLESCENCE: CRISIS OR NOT?

The popular notion of adolescence is one of storm and stress, a dramatic upheaval and reorganization. The Freudians argue that the inputs of biological maturation and sexual drive pose an enormous number of conflicts between the adolescent and his family, the adolescent and his peers, and the adolescent and himself. Engaged in a struggle to liberate himself from parental dominance but uncertain as to how to take advantage of his new freedom, the adolescent is confused, unpredictable, even irresponsible.

On the other hand, some psychologists, such as Bandura (1964), argue that the turmoil is more apparent than real, and they support this conclusion with data drawn from interviews with adolescent boys from middle-class families. Bandura found that by the time the boys had reached adolescence, they had already so thoroughly internalized their parents' values and standards of behavior that there was actually *less* need for parental control than had been surmised. He also concluded that the process of emancipation was substantially completed by the time the boys reached adolescence because their parents had encouraged the boys' independent behavior from early childhood on. (It should be noted here that Bandura's sample was limited geographically and could be overgeneralizing from too few statistics.) In response to the Freudian theory of endocrine stimulation and biological drive, Bandura points to cross-cultural studies that indicate that human sexuality is more profoundly influenced by social conditioning than by any physiological imperatives. Sexual tensions, he argues, are not an inevitable part of pubescence.

While Bandura is probably right in stating that an upsurge in hormonal secretions does not always entail a period of confusion and conflict, his emphasis upon social conditioning is a double-edged sword that can cut both ways. If we look at the total social setting into which today's adolescent is thrust, the sheer number of choices and life decisions he or she must make, and the alternatives from which to choose, we might well reach the opposite conclusion: that adolescence is a chaotic period and increasingly so for each subsequent wave of youth. The combination of newfound intellectual awareness and the incredibly broad scope of problems facing youth today can create within the adolescent the feelings of urgent crisis reflective of the global disorders of modern society.

SUMMARY

Modern adolescence is a complex process taking place in a complex world. Biological change alone poses a number of quandaries, even in simpler societies. Adolescents are acutely aware of growing toward the new status of adulthood, and they worry whether they are going about it properly, especially when they vary from physical norms. They strive for rigidly proscribed social norms, many of which are impossible to attain.

Although intense interest in sex and sexuality surfaces during this period, many of the factors which affect the adolescent's sexual development have been well established by his earlier socialization. The differences between the sexes already interposed by nature are exaggerated by the separate kinds of training given boys and girls during this period. Because girls of all class backgrounds are generally encouraged to lower their sights to a restricted range of adult roles, class differences are not as prominent in their sexual development as in that of boys. Boys' training is aimed at grooming them to take over a variety of positions in a male-dominated society.

Intellectually, adolescence is really a period of refinement rather than dramatic growth. Once formal operational thought has been mastered, further mental growth consists largely of new, and more difficult, areas of interest. Adolescent egocentrism is an interesting wrinkle in this development; it is caused by an imbalance between the adolescent's cognitive ability to comprehend other people's thoughts and his lack of experience in putting others' thoughts in proper perspective.

Sociologically, adolescents are in a contradictory situation. On the one hand, society regards them with adulation, glorifying youth, carefreeness, and leisure. On the other hand, most high schools are incredibly boring and alienating institutions, wasting their students' time in meaningless, depersonalized routines. The teenager has to cope with all this in an age of unprecedented complexity and precariousness, without the benefit of traditional wisdom or inspiring leadership at any level. And it is these young people who must grow up to solve the conflicts that threaten to destroy us all.

1. What functions does adolescence serve in American society? What functions might it serve in a utopian society?

2. Discuss the divergent development of male and female sexuality. How much of this development is biologically motivated and how much stems from other factors?

3. How would you characterize your own adolescence? Compare it to that of an older or younger sibling or acquaintance. Are any aspects of adolescence lingering in you and your peers as young adults?

4. Considering the quality and scope of adolescent cognition, what educational reforms would you suggest to help adolescents realize their intellectual potential more fully?

5. What kind of adolescence can you foresee for your own children, should you choose to have them? What will be your hardest tasks as a parent?

SUGGESTED READINGS

Douvan, E. & Adelson, J. *The adolescent experience.* New York: Wiley, 1966. The authors gather conclusions from considerable research in order to describe American adolescence. Much attention is given to social and emotional aspects of development during the period of adolescence.

Friedenberg, E. Z. *The vanishing adolescent.* Boston: Beacon Press, 1959. Edgar Friedenberg focuses much of his social critique on the institution of the American high school.

Goodman, P. *Growing up absurd.* New York: Random House, 1960.

_____. *Compulsory mis-education.* New York: Horizon Press, 1964. Both of these books are compelling social comments on the predicament of adolescence and youth.

"Twelve to sixteen: Early adolescence." *Daedalus.* Fall 1971, *100* (4). This particular issue of *Daedalus* features experts and commentators discussing various aspects of early adolescence. Nearly every article is outstanding. (This issue has been published separately as a book under the editorship of Jerome Kagan.)

In our complex American society, the period of adolescence is a paradox. On the one hand, the adolescent is approaching physical and intellectual maturity. He or she is a well-developed organism, capable of grappling with great physical and intellectual challenges. Were he or she in a simpler society than our own, he might carry home the buck for the hunting party or she might build the new home. Or together they might procreate the next generation. On the other hand, in our complex, industrialized society the adolescent is in a cultural box. He or she is isolated from the main processes of the community, rarely participating in the meaningful or productive or problem-solving work of the social group. Adolescence is a period of preparation, transition, delay, and sometimes even impotence in a world of enormous challenges, startling injustices, and highly visible social problems. From this cultural box the adolescent must emerge, and he must emerge with a personal identity, a set of values, and a culture. Each adolescent escapes from his own cultural box in his own way. But his identity, his values, and his culture are a solution, a production, and an act of creation derived from this paradox.

Adolescence and youth are not necessarily periods of instability. They comprise the time, often marked by experimentation, when the individual "tries on" many different roles and self-images to see how they fit. The changes and shifts—sometimes polar opposites—that occur make adolescence an exciting, though confusing, period. In recent years there has been considerable expansion of a youth culture. Over a prolonged period of time, adolescents together create their own culture from society's culture. A youth culture often expresses and dramatizes both the best and the worst of the larger culture. The youth culture holds up a mirror to society and dramatizes both the idealism and the reaction against some of society's dominant values. Sometimes the youth culture serves simultaneously as a fulfillment and an escape from aspects of the larger society. Observers have noted the sensitivity of the adolescent culture to larger problems within the society (Coleman, 1965, 1970; Otto & Otto, 1967). Adolescent fads and movements are sometimes bellwethers of the lulls and upheavals in the broader society—in small ways, with fads and fashions, or in larger issues of racism, wars, and political movements.

The adolescent and his culture act not only as a mirror and bellwether of the broader society but sometimes also as a catalyst for change in society. The impatience and energy of a youth phenomenon may highlight a problem such as the Vietnam War until the broader society cannot ignore it (Otto & Otto, 1967). The youth culture may voice what the older adult society is "too polite" or "too conservative" to say. Or conversely, the youth culture's vigorous adherence to one aspect of society may caricature that aspect so that it becomes grotesque, at least to some. There is no one youth culture. It involves many subcultures: high school athletic crowds, the motorcycle cult, the Jesus cult, the college campus culture, the rock music culture, the hippie culture, fraternities and sororities, the New Left, the drug culture, and so on. Each has its own patterns of values and behaviors. In fact, each is a solution to a certain kind of cultural box.

VALUES, IDEALS, AND MORAL DEVELOPMENT

One of the most important challenges of adolescence is the selection of a set of guiding values. This process is hardly new to the adolescent. The development of conscience and values begins very early in the socialization process, when the toddler is taught not to pull hair, lie, or steal. This early morality training, however, is quite different from the development of the value system of a mature adult. Many psychologists believe that processes such as modeling, identification, and rewards and punishment, which teach the young child to distinguish right from wrong, can go only so far. They are satisfactory only as a means of imposing an external morality on the child which he then internalizes. However, in order to become a mature adult, the individual must eventually reassess and analyze these principles to build a coherent set of values.

Also, the preadolescent child may be unable to construct his own value system, even if he should want to. Cognitive theorists point out that the individual must have the ability to make rational judgments about what is right in order to form a mature system of morality. The 5-year-old, or even the 11-year-old, they contend, simply does not have the mental capacity to form his own framework of these principles. It is necessary to be able to consider all of the possible alternatives, to have a cause-and-effect logic and a future orientation, and to be able to consider fully the hypothetical. The ability to consider fully all the consequences or implications of hypothetical alternatives is not reached until adolescence or a later stage (and sometimes not at all). These new intellectual abilities are an important reason why the adolescent years are so full of rapid changes in ideals, values, and attitudes.

The Development of Morality: Two Views of Adolescence

KOHLBERG'S MODEL. We saw in Chapter 5 that Kohlberg describes the development of morality as a six-stage process which depends heavily upon each person's cognitive abilities and experiences (see Chapter 5, Table 2). By the time they reach their teens, most children have outgrown the first stages of premoral development and are somewhere in the level of conventional role conformity. They may stay at this "Archie Bunker" level for the rest of their lives, especially if they receive no stimulation to think beyond this level. But Kohlberg found that if children participate in informal, stimulating discussions and experience moral conflict at the right time, they will be more likely to pass on to the next higher stage in the third level—that of self-accepted moral principles (Kohlberg, 1966).

Kohlberg and others have set up experimental "moral education" classes for children from all types of social backgrounds. The results, even with juvenile delinquents, strongly support the idea that moral judgment can be taught. The classes center around discussions of hypothetical moral dilemmas. The child is presented with a problem and is asked to give his own solution. If his answer is from level 4, the discussion leader suggests a level 5 solution to see if the child thinks it is a good alternate. The student almost always finds that this slightly more advanced reasoning is more attractive than his own, and through repeated discussions like this he sooner or later begins to form his own judgments at level 5. At this point, the discussion leader might start suggesting level 6 solutions as alternate ideas (Kohlberg, 1966).

Kohlberg's model and his experiments with "moral education" show several things. An adolescent's set of values depends partly upon his cognitive development. These values are, in part, a product of his experiences in making moral judgments; and if, during these years of high receptivity to new ideas, the individual receives a great deal of stimulation to solve moral problems at higher levels, then adolescence may be a time of considerable moral development.

One note of caution ought to be introduced here. Kohlberg's studies are based totally on moral judgments, not on moral behavior. The development of his scales has depended upon asking individuals to think about, and make rational judgments about, certain moral dilemmas. During adolescence, individuals develop considerable sophistication in this kind of moral judgment task. However, an individual's behavior may at times be inconsistent with his moral reasoning!

Kohlberg presents only one picture of the adolescent's values and the ways they change. Other psychologists look at adolescent values from other perspectives.

CARL ROGERS. Carl Rogers, whose ideas we considered briefly in Chapter 2, also sees adolescence as a potentially exciting time in the development of each individual's values (Rogers, 1964). For him, it is a time when, if the conditions are right, the child can learn to stand on his own feet, to trust his own values, and to believe in himself as the best judge of what is right and wrong for him.

According to Rogers, the modern world is a bewildering place for both the child and the adult. We once had strong rules, both moral and religious, to live by. But this old order of values has come under question as our thinking has become more scientific and relativistic. Besides this, media such as TV constantly assail us with many contradictory ideas and values. At one time or another all of us have wondered whom, or what, we should believe.

Rogers describes the development of a mature value system as a circular process of three stages. The first stage can be seen in the first months of life. The infant has his own "value system," which is both self-sufficient and flexible. He cries when his environment does not suit his tastes—when he is too hot, or lonely, or tired. He can change his values when he wants; he likes bananas one day, then decides that he is tired of them the next day. But the infant's values do not remain self-sufficient and flexible for long. As he grows older, he enters a second stage of values. He learns to love his parents; and in order to win their love (or avoid their disapproval), he forgets his own value system and adopts theirs. He stops chewing on magazines and shoes; he learns that it is "good" to use the potty seat. Later on, he studies hard instead of playing baseball so that he can "go to college and get a good job." He has learned to distrust his own values and to depend upon those of others instead. Because he cannot test these values with his own experience, he holds them rigidly, often without understanding why he does so.

What happens as the child grows older? Many persons remain at this second stage and depend upon others for a value system they may not even understand. But adolescence is a time of reevaluation and integration of attitudes and values for every individual; and some persons—but not all—are fortunate enough to emerge from this chaotic period with a higher set of values. If their experiences and abilities allow it, they are able to regain the "organismic," self-sufficient, and flexible value system they possessed at birth—with the important difference that this system is now also in touch with the needs of those around them. As Rogers sees it, only the self-sufficiency of a mature value system can keep modern man from being lost in the confusion and relativism of the world around him.

Rogers has not been the only one to note that we have lost touch with the traditional values of society. It is common knowledge, for instance, that church attendance has fallen and divorce rates have soared in the past few decades. Have any substitutes been found for the old institutions and the strict morality that once guided Americans in their daily lives? Some interesting studies have investigated the transformation of values in twentieth-century America, and an important sidelight of this research has been the study of the role that young people have played in trying to find new values.

In 1962, the Students for a Democratic Society adopted their famous Port Huron Statement (S.D.S., 1962). The old values of our society no longer reflect our needs, they said, and they called for a reevaluation of our morality to establish what is most important to us today.

The student organization had recognized a change which has been taking place in our society for many years (Getzels, 1972). The traditional values—the ethic of achievement; the future orientation of "doing without today so we can be better off tomorrow"; the emphasis on independence; and the old, respectable, puritan morality—are no longer relevant for many Americans. In fact, some of these traditional values were phased out years before the Port Huron Statement, for by the late 1940s the old Horatio Alger image was quite out of style. Instead, America seemed to look toward a more sociable, affable, but apathetic ideal, a standard which proved to be only temporary.

By the 1960s, people—and especially young people—were calling for a more meaningful value structure. The result has been that a new set of national values now seems to be evolving ("American Youth," 1969; Getzels, 1972). Since we are still in the middle of this transformation, it is difficult to say exactly what these new values are. But the directions in which we are moving seem unmistakable. Instead of the old work-success ethic, there is a growing concern with social responsibility. For example, even corporations are contributing to community goals such as a clean environment. Instead of building toward future achievements, people are looking more at what is relevant for them here and now. There is less emphasis on being independent and more stress on being authentic. And rather than adopt the puritan morality, many people consider it more important to have a personal moral commitment to their own ideals, whatever those ideals are. So, while the old order of traditional American values may have lost its meaning for many of us, a new ethic does seem to be taking its place.

Young people, particularly the older adolescents in college, have been among the first to reject the old values and adopt new ones. How much of these new ideals represents youthful flirtation with ivory-tower idealism? How deeply do the new values affect the rest of society?

A recent follow-up survey of young people found that many of the values and attitudes with which college students startled the world in the 1960s are now being adopted by the working class youth ("Changing Attitudes of Youth," 1974). Mainstream attitudes are starting to show widespread dissatisfaction with the political system and with big business, to reflect a relaxation of attitudes about sex, and to place less emphasis on formal religion. The attitudes of a few adolescents in the 1960s are becoming popular in the 1970s. There is little question that young people's receptivity to new ideas and values acts as a powerful force in changing the value structure of society.

Changing Values: The Individual Adolescent

We have been examining adolescent values principally from a sociological point of view, focusing on the ways these values both reflect and influence the social environment. But we have not looked closely at the individual and at the upheaval of values he often experiences during adolescence. Throughout the adolescent years the young person often exhibits sharp contrasts in mood, with rapid swings from one emotional extreme to another. The typical teenager is cynical one moment, idealistic the next; rebellious, then conforming; carefree, then staunchly serious. Is there any rhyme or reason underlying these abrupt shifts in attitude?

There are many reasons why adolescent value systems are so contradictory (Eisenman, 1973). The teenager is trying to understand himself, to come up with a self-definition he can be satisfied with over a period of time. He asks himself, "What should I be like?" From this question he generalizes to the rest of the world: "What should society (or the government, or the world) be like?" This process of generalization can lead the adolescent from self-definition to idealism. But self-definition can also turn the adolescent to cynicism and rebellion, because another way of carving out a self-image is to reject the values and attitudes of others. Teenagers want to establish themselves as individuals who are different from their parents, or from their teachers, or from the establishment. One of the strongest statements of independence an adolescent can make is to rebel against the persons exerting authority over him.

Another explanation of changing adolescent values is that teenage idealism is sometimes a reaction formation to growing up. The physical process of maturation is biologically irreversible, but the adolescent is not always sure he wants to grow up. Becoming an adult means becoming like his parents, entering society with all its burdens and faults. Teenage idealism provides an escape, if only a temporary one, from the responsibilities and imperfections of adulthood. Idealistic images of love and strict sexual asceticism are other common forms of escape which the teenager may use to cope with his emerging sexuality. Both such reaction formations involve a great deal of ambivalence, for growing up has its good points too. The result is that the teenager may be idealistic one moment and worldly-wise the next.

Society often makes it difficult for the individual to decide whether he is a child or an adult. Even if he feels grown-up, the teenager is usually looked upon as a child in an adult-oriented world. He is expected to be frivolous even when he does not want to be. For example, potential for making a genuine contribution to society often remains untapped until the youth has gone through the testing ground of college, military training, marriage, or work apprenticeship. It is hard enough for adolescents to learn to trust their own judgment and values. But when society compounds the difficulty by imposing stereotypes on them and blocking their problem solving, their actions, and their creativity, it is no wonder that adolescents find life confusing and contradictory in our culture.

RELATIONSHIPS AND IDENTITY

Just as he had to do as a child in the earlier periods of his life, the adolescent must work out his own personal identity within the context of relationships. However, new elements are introduced at this time. The newly emerging pattern of values must be reintegrated into the individual's personal identity and his interpersonal relationships. At the same time, the teenager must become accustomed to the process of biological maturation taking place within him as he changes physically from child to adult. There is a new awareness of himself as a sexual being. This sexual identity must be accepted, investigated, explored, and integrated into his relationships with his friends, his family, and finally with heterosexual partners.

Sexual Identity and Relationships

Early adolescents do not usually have to deal with problems of heterosexual intimacy on a very sophisticated level. Early adolescents need to be liked; they need to have a sense of self-esteem; and they feel

Early adolescence is a time for learning to relate to the opposite sex. (*Hella Hammid, Rapho/Photo Researchers.*)

strong pressures to conform with the peer group. An important element that is emerging in all of these areas is growing awareness of their own and friends' bodily changes. Sexual experimentation may be frequent or limited but full heterosexual intimacy usually is not achieved until later adolescence or even early adulthood.

THE FIRST YEARS OF ADOLESCENCE. In early adolescence, most relationships with the opposite sex are in groups or clubs. The pre-16-year-old usually prefers this group contact to the closer relationships of a dating system (Douvan & Adelson, 1966). "Hanging out" (sitting around doing very little but chatting, usually at a coffee shop or pizza parlor or other public place) is a popular pastime throughout adolescence, and it becomes increasingly coeducational as adolescence progresses. This type of interaction is a first step in learning to relate to the opposite sex. Early adolescence is often an awkward stage of testing, imagining, and discovering what it is like to function in coeducational groups and pairs. But it gives the adolescent a trial period when he can collect ideas and experiences with which to form basic attitudes about sex roles and sexual behavior without feeling pressure to become too deeply involved. During this period, he can start to examine his own and others' stereotyped images of the opposite sex.

RITUAL PATTERNS. Each historical period, each cultural group, each local community, and even each crowd may develop certain stereotyped patterns of behavior through which the adolescent may seek to try out heterosexual behavior. In some historical periods, "courtship behavior" was highly formalized, with extensive codes of appropriate conduct. Some recent courtship patterns, although seemingly informal, appear—to the observer at least—to have almost as many rules. Sometimes high conformity is required if an individual wishes to be "popular." But it is not necessarily true that "dating" or "going steady" or "cruising" follow the same patterns in one high school as in another. We shall now look at dating as one traditional way of getting to know members of the opposite sex.

Dating patterns change rather rapidly, and they tend to vary quite a bit from one community to the next and from one ethnic group to another. In the past few years, the formal "date" has been out of style, with close-knit coeducational groups or more informal pairing being more popular in most areas of this country. But the date is still a basic custom among some segments of American youth, and it serves a number of functions (and dysfunctions, too, as many argue) in helping the adolescent as he learns to relate to potential mates (Douvan & Adelson, 1966).

Some of us are accustomed to thinking of the date as a training ground for more mature relationships. It gives adolescents a chance to try out their identities, to learn which aspects of their personalities (the swinger, or the sincere idealist, or the bitter rebel) are most pleasing both to themselves and to members of the opposite sex. It also provides practice in the social customs, as adolescents learn to sustain conversations and to handle a variety of situations. Dates also give adolescents a chance for small doses of sexual experimentation which are limited (at least theoretically) by built-in safety catches, for there are strict mores dictating just how far partners can go without "going too far." And finally, the date is often a way of measuring popularity, the teenaged boy or girl who ranks as a "good date" usually is able to develop considerable self-esteem and self-confidence as a result of his or her adolescent successes.

Although all of these functions are important to the adolescent, the custom of dating as we know it in America is a mixed blessing (Douvan & Adelson, 1966). While we usually think of the dating system as helpful preparation for later, deeper relationships, the personal qualities that the system actually rewards (with popularity) are not always the ones that will make for a good marriage, or good parenting, or meaningful relationships in adulthood. The popular date is the one who can "keep the ball rolling" on a superficial level; but this is a skill which just does not apply to sustained adult relationships. In addition, the competition for dates and the desire to be popular can put considerable strain on the adolescent. Failure in dating is a powerful social censure. Yet "success" often means developing manipulative and eventually self-defeating interpersonal skills. In this sense, the cultural expectations of the dating system complicate the biological and psychological adjustments the individual must cope with and make the identity search of the adolescent years more painful and difficult than it might be.

Dating allows an adolescent a chance to try out her identity and to see what aspects of her personality are pleasing to the opposite sex. (*Dan Jury, Rapho/ Photo Researchers.*)

INTIMATE RELATIONSHIPS. Pressures to move on to a more serious dating level, such as "going steady," increase as the adolescent grows older. The closer relationships that develop in later adolescence are the result of many different forces. For one thing, adolescents are accustomed to dealing with each other on a superficial level. Through the ritualized dating system or "hanging out" they may acquire some degree of ease and comfort in associating with the opposite sex; yet they may feel bored or confined by so stereotyped a pattern of socializing. For another thing, there are sexual drives and curiosities. Intimate relationships seem a natural means of fulfillment in a society which places as much emphasis on sexuality as our does.

These are two important reasons why some individuals form more intimate attachments in later adolescence, but another factor is perhaps the most important of all. Teenagers have strong security needs, but neither the structure of our society nor the dating system provides outlets to fill these needs. During the adolescent years, the individual is expected to break away from his family, but he is not yet ready to form his own family unit. Sexual intimacy is one way of answering deep security needs, by establishing closeness with another person during a confusing and often lonely time of life. It is one solution to the particular adjustments which each adolescent must make. But it causes problems, too, for it brings the teenager face to face with his own sexuality, often before he knows how to deal with it. Normal interpersonal struggles of power and control, dominance and submission, love and exploitation, dependence and independence, anger and hostility—all may be acted out intensely in intimate adolescent sexual relationships. Adult society confuses things further; for adults expect the teenager to have self-control but do not take into account the needs of sexuality and loneliness that the adolescent is grappling with. Often the adolescent is expected to show unrealistic restraint, and if followed to the letter, this kind of restraint can lead to unhealthy levels of frustration, both in adolescence and later on in life (Josselyn, 1970).

Not all teenagers try to fulfill the particular needs of adolescence by forming intimate relationships, of course—although the past few decades have unquestionably brought much more tolerance toward sexual freedom both in attitudes and behavior (Sorenson, 1973). Rubin (1965) points out that despite widespread rumors about the "younger generation," adolescents differ in the way they view sex just as much as their parents do. Their outlooks range all the way from repressive asceticism (sex has no other purpose but procreation) to sexual anarchy (no holds barred, so long as nobody gets badly hurt). Since we seem to be in the middle of a great transformation of sexual values, there are no firm

Intimate relationships are often formed in late adolescence to fulfill sexual and security needs. *(Joel Gordon.)*

guidelines that adults can give teenagers to help them through the confusion of becoming sexually mature individuals. Therefore, adolescents are left to think out their own morality and develop their own views, and the different solutions they choose are products of their individual personalities, needs, and backgrounds (Sorenson, 1973).

Friendships While sexuality is an emerging dimension of teenage relationships, it is by no means the only one. Friendships are also tremendously important throughout the period of growing up. In late childhood, friendship patterns are often based on sharing particular activities, such as playing ball or fishing or bike riding. But during adolescence, friendships take on an even more crucial significance. As individuals become more and more independent of their families, they depend increasingly upon friendships (as well as coeducational partnerships) to provide emotional support and to serve as testing grounds for new values (Douvan & Adelson, 1966; Douvan & Gold, 1966). With his close friends, the adolescent is working out an identity. And to be able to accept this identity himself, the adolescent must feel that he is accepted and liked by others.

Between the ages of 12 and 16, children—especially girls—increasingly demand greater loyalty, conformity, and intimacy of their friends (Douvan & Adelson, 1966). Boys sometimes persist longer in the looser childhood pattern of activity-based or sport-based friendships. But girls' friendship patterns often become quite close, expressive of considerable feeling and intimacy.

At this age, children tend to select friends who are from a similar social class and who have similar mentality, interests, moral values, and social maturity. They are increasingly aware of peer groups too, and are concerned whether the group they belong to is "in" or "out" and whether it has the right reputation. Most high schools use different names to describe different kinds of groups, such as "greasers," "straights," "hippies," "freaks," or "jocks." Adolescents usually know which group they belong to, and they may be painfully aware of their resulting status and reputation. Once the adolescent has become established in one clique or group, he may find it difficult to join another, perhaps more desirable, group (Douvan & Gold, 1966). Socioeconomic and ethnic patterns may contribute to this group rigidity.

Adolescence is a time when the teenagers are learning who they are. Multifaceted identities start out as a collage of many self-images which are drawn from all the different relationships we have discussed above. A girl thinks of herself as either a leader or a follower within the context of her group; and in turn, she thinks of her group in terms of its status relative to other groups at school. A boy may have an idea of what he is like when he is with a friend; he may have another self-image that reflects the way he thinks members of the opposite sex view him. As time goes on, a boy or girl gradually fits all of these different pictures into a fairly consistent sense of identity. But in early adolescence especially, the sounding board provided by peers is of critical importance to the young person.

Adolescents react to their cultural dilemma in many different ways. Some become serious students; some immerse themselves in athletics; some drop out of school; some work; some get involved in crafts; some become "hippies"; and some choose to be activists. Each individual reacts in the way that best suits his needs for identity and independence. Collectively, adolescents come together in various subgroups and evolve their own particular youth culture. Like any other culture, a youth culture is a set of shared attitudes, values, and expectations. It may involve patterns of dress, ways of communicating, common language, and numerous patterns of acceptable or unacceptable behavior. Each subgroup—the high school athletes, the motorcycle cult, the sorority girls—has its own particular subculture. However, there seem to be certain commonalities within a youth culture. Coleman (1973) has identified five such characteristics—traits which he finds common to young people's attitudes and behaviors but not so common among adults.

YOUTH CULTURE

During adolescence, there is an increasing tendency to select friends with similar interests. *(Sepp Seitz, Magnum Photos.)*

First, the youth culture is *inward-looking*. Adolescents look to their inner selves and also to each other for many of their needs. Most of their heroes are from the youth culture, and even many of the products they use, such as records and clothes, are oriented toward youth. Second, the youth culture is characterized by a *psychic attachment* of its members. There is strong in-group solidarity among young people who have similar values and outlooks, and there are strong pressures to conform within the group. A third trait is a drive toward *autonomy*. In part this is caused by the youth culture's awareness of itself as a separate subculture; group members tend to glorify their peers who stand up against adult authority. A fourth characteristic is a *concern for the underdog,* perhaps a reaction to youth's own position in the social hierarchy. Fifth is *an interest in change,* perhaps because young people have little at stake in the status quo but considerable concern for the future.

These general characteristics, Coleman finds, are common to the youth culture, but not all young people express all of these traits, nor do they express them in the same way. Some subgroups of the youth culture have attracted considerable attention in the past few years, and we shall now look at a few of the more notable ones.

Politics, Activism, and Protest

One of the most conspicuous ways in which adolescents have established themselves as separate from the rest of society in the last decade has been by engaging in political dissent, most notably during the late 1960s. Most of the political activity—the student revolts, rallies, marches, and volunteer work—has been centered on college campuses, but the mood of dissent has been present even in high schools and junior high schools.

Some people tend to stereotype student dissenters, giving them labels such as "long-haired radicals" or "young hotheads." But adolescent protest has taken a variety of forms. Two important dimensions in each individual's basic outlook seem important in determining the degree to which, and the way in which, he will involve himself in trying to correct society's ills (Block, Haan, & Smith, 1973). The first is his interest in political and social issues around him; here the continuum stretches from total apathy at one extreme to strong commitment at the other. The second dimension is the degree to which the adolescent accepts or rejects the dominant societal values and the existing institutional authority.

Each individual's combination of these two dimensions represents his own personal solution to his need to fit into some cultural context. Block, Haan, and Smith (1973) suggest six basic types of reaction to describe the range of choices that adolescents may take with respect to social and political issues. The vast majority of young people are termed *politically apathetic*. They are in basic agreement with the values of the dominant society, and they are not involved in efforts to alter their environment. The *alienated* youth rejects society's values, but he refuses to become involved. Instead, he chooses to escape society by dropping out. The *individualist* accepts the social order and strives

Adolescent receptivity to new ideas can act as a powerful force in changing the value structure of society. *(Michael Lloyd Carlebach, Nancy Palmer Photo Agency.)*

to maintain the status quo. This type of conservative activist has been described as the "obedient rebel" (Schiff, 1964). The *constructivist* is also task-oriented, but he works actively to change social conditions for the better. While his commitment is very strong, he acts only within the legitimate social structure; he does not challenge the establishment as the activist often does. The *activist* rejects mainstream values to a greater degree than does the constructivist; but he thinks society can be saved and involves himself in "good works" in an effort to do this. A final type, the *dissenter*, resembles the activist in that he rejects his social and political environment. But unlike the activist, the dissenter is not involved in constructive change. His specialty is protest, and he is deeply committed to it.

Keniston (1967) has studied politically aware youths, and he makes a similar, but broader, distinction of two basic types of adolescent outlooks, based on degree of involvement. In the first group is the alienated dissenter, and in the second group is the activist. The *alienated dissenter* rejects modern society because of its dehumanizing effects, its lack of aesthetics, and its failure to provide fulfillment for the individual. He sees society as too sick to save, and so he settles on a solution that will save himself instead: he drops out. This particular solution has become more popular in the past few years. Taking a different point of view from the alienated dissenter, the *activist* thinks something can be done to improve conditions. He is involved and committed in a fight to save the world, society, a particular minority, or the environment.

What determines the way adolescents react to society or the social context in which they find themselves? Who will drop out, who will become an activist, and who will be comparatively satisfied with conditions as they are? Who will find personal issues more compelling than broader social issues? Several studies have investigated the personalities and family backgrounds of young people in an effort to answer these questions. Researchers have been especially successfull in learning about two groups: the activists and dissenters on college campuses.

The studies have shown that most politically active young people are superior students at school (Flacks, 1967; Heist, 1965) and they usually come from socially and educationally advantaged homes (Flacks, 1967; Smith, Haan, & Block, 1970). Their values and ideals tend to agree with those of their parents, who are often politically liberal themselves (Flacks, 1967; Keniston, 1968). Parents of activists are a bit more permissive than are parents of nonactivists; the activist parents stress rational approaches to childrearing and place a great deal of value on communicating with their children. In fact, the student movements of the 1960s have sometimes been blamed on Dr. Spock, because the kind of rational upbringing he popularized in the 1940s seems to have contributed directly to adolescent political expressiveness. According to this argument, children brought up "by Spock" learned to value dialogue and persuasion as instruments of change. As adolescents, they naturally attempted to use the same tactics as a means for changing social institutions. Studies show that dissenters have backgrounds similar to those of the activists, but their childhood home environments were usually less receptive to dialogue and less supportive of them as individuals. This important difference in the home situation seems to have been a crucial factor in the dissenters' decision to express political dissatisfaction by means of negative protest rather than by more constructive methods.

Studies of the value systems of activists and dissenters have made some interesting discoveries about the type of morality and the kinds of value judgments on which these students base their sense of commitment. Members of the Free Speech Movement (FSM) arrested at Berkeley were studied in an effort to determine where they fit into Kohlberg's levels of morality systems (Haan, Smith, & Block, 1968). The findings showed that a disproportionately high number of these activists had reached the highest levels of postconventional morality. Simultaneously, the findings show another disproportionate (but smaller) number of these arrestees base their actions on premoral levels of morality. Thus, this population of student activists contained extremes of both mature and immature individuals.

The vast majority of young people are neither activists nor dissenters, of course. Some research has looked at these groups, too, but the findings have not been nearly so complete or consistent. For example, the *individualists* tend to have conservative backgrounds; in one study they were predominately from Republican, Protestant families (Flacks, 1967). Some findings suggest that they are more accepting of, or submissive to, authority and more self-controlled than are the *activists* (Schiff, 1964). Less research has been devoted to the *constructivists;* but the few findings we have suggest that these young people are likely to come from less affluent families (Haan, Smith, & Block, 1968) and to have public school backgrounds (Gelineau & Kantor, 1964). Finally, alienated young people have been the hardest group of all to study, chiefly because they just do not wish to be researched. What findings there are show these individuals to be estranged from both family and society, often with a history of hostility toward their fathers (Keniston, 1965, 1970; Watts & Whittaker, 1968).

Certainly, many of the forms of protest and commitment come from the same psychological roots, and many of the differences between dissent and activism lie solely in the way they affect society—whether they eventually are accepted as legitimate, or whether they stimulate some positive change in society. There is no question that the commitment to change espoused by many young people can act as a vital force for needed change in society (McGovern, 1973). Adolescents have great potential as innovators because they have the advantage of perspective: they can look in on society from the outside, without being tied to the status quo.

In some historical periods, this special role of adolescents as innovators has acted as a safeguard against the dangers of unquestioning obedience to established authority. Research shows that when people allow authority figures to make moral judgments for them, then the people can easily commit deeds they would shrink from doing on their own (Milgram, 1974). But the "moral precocity" of some activist adolescents can have its dangers, too (Keniston, 1970). Young people— even those with postconventional value systems—do not always have the human experience necessary to apply their ideals realistically. The wrong application of the right ideals—what Pascal called "evil with a good conscience"—can have even more dangerous consequences than those of conformity. Involved young people have been a strong force in calling attention to changes that need to be made in society. And from the perspective of the 1970s, we are beginning to realize that many of their ideas are indeed having a positive effect on society's values.

The Counterculture   Although many of his ideas are being adopted by the mainstream of society, the student activist may be starting to become a thing of the past. In recent years the dropout—the alienated youth we mentioned briefly in the last section—has taken over center stage as society's problem child; and the counterculture has become the object of fear, scorn, ridicule, praise, and, most of all, considerable misinterpretation and stereotyping. What does the sociologist mean when he talks of the counterculture? What are the counterculture's social and psychological roots?

The roots of the counterculture are the same as those of political activism: dissatisfaction with the present system. But the counterculture reaction is on a much broader scale: it is an attempt to deny the "lethal culture" that exists and to remake it into an alternate life-style for an alternate culture (Roszak, 1969). How is this to be done? The counterculture aims to reorder the priorities and the values that exist in the established society. It puts personal rights above property rights, cooperation above competition, the individual over the machine, pleasure over discipline, and experiencing over conceptualizing (Slater, 1970; Yablonsky, 1968).

THE COUNTERCULTURE PHENOMENON. The counterculture embodies a general mood of alienation from the larger culture; but like the larger culture each subgroup expresses its own values in fairly consistent ways. Cross and Pruyn (1973) suggest several notable characteristics which they venture to call counterculture "institutions"! These include an appreciation of another person's individuality, honest business ethics, rock music, group marriage, free schools, and communes. They suggest that each such "institution" serves certain functions. For example, they see rock music as a unifying social lubricant which provides a vehicle both for social protest and for flaunting forbidden subjects such as sex and drugs. Another characteristic suggested by Cross and Pruyn is a pronounced dislike of the exploitation practiced by society's economic institutions such as banks and corporations. This they have termed an "anti-rip-off" attitude. *Transrationality,* or a reaction against the overly analytical, logical, scientific mode of thought, is suggested as another counterculture institution. Studying Eastern religions and seeking mystical experiences are just different aspects of the reaction against the impersonality of a scientific and techno-logical world. *Communes* have received a great deal of attention as counterculture institutions which offer an alternate life-style to that of the larger society. The commune may be centered around the counter-culture value of cooperation; members live together, sharing responsi-bilities, values, and usually property. Often the commune is situated on a small rural farm, and the members are concerned with economic self-sufficiency, ecology, crafts, and trying to "get back to the land," away from the impersonality and complexity of city life. Similarly, group marriage and free schools are intended to provide alternatives to the traditional marriage forms or to the impersonal atmosphere and pre-cepts of most mass-oriented schools and emphasize the emotional and social values of honest communication, personal growth, trust, and sharing.

The current literature has a number of alternative analyses of counter-culture phenomenon with widely divergent perspectives. One single analysis may be far too simplistic.

DRUG USE. If all the psychoactive compounds which are prescribed and unprescribed—the sleeping pills, diet pills, stimulants, alcohol, nic-otine, and caffeine—are counted, then one must conclude, as does Keniston (1968/69), that "the American who has never 'used' drugs is a statistical freak." In the last two decades, new types of drugs—partic-ularly the hallucinogens, which include marijuana, LSD, psilocybin, and mescaline—have been used for the sole purpose of altering mood or consciousness. And here the influence of the counterculture is important.

All of the counterculture institutions we have described above have a two-fold meaning: they are strong, positive reactions against the seem-ingly misplaced values of society, and they are personal ways of ex-pressing the alienation that many young people feel. In an important sense, the counterculture is not so much a mass movement as it is an accumulation of individual patterns of adjustment. These individual adjustment patterns may represent healthy growth and independence, with release from oppressive interpersonal or socioeconomic condi-tions, or they may signify pathological escape from life's demands.

Drugs are a part of some counterculture institutions because they can serve a number of functions when they are incorporated with counter-culture values. First, the dispensing of drugs is strictly controlled by law, so the very possession of drugs illegally becomes an expression of alienation. (Alcohol is forbidden to persons under 18.) Second, drugs provide an escape from the outside world to inner consciousness. They give the user a deeply personal, sometimes hedonistic, sometimes religious experience. Third, drugs act as a "social lubricant," establish-ing feelings of closeness between people who share the experience of using them. All drugs should not be considered together in one cate-gory. Their use and function, as well as their effects, differ markedly. We shall single out marijuana for particular comment.

Marijuana is in a class by itself as the least potent and most widely used narcotic substance. Keniston estimated that only about 5 percent of college students used marijuana in various forms—although the percentage has clearly increased since then. However, the use of "pot" or "grass" is not evenly distributed among college students or even among high school populations. It is more prevalent in the liberal arts colleges and the private universities than in state colleges, commu-nity colleges, vocational schools, or religious institutions. It is more prevalent at any given college in the arts and humanities than at the professional schools. Marijuana use is more widespread among the more intelligent students than among the less intelligent ones in both high schools and colleges. According to Keniston, the drug is often used as part of a generalized pattern of exploration of life experiences, a seek-

The use of drugs may be thought to be a reaction to society or an expression of alienation. *(Fred DeVan, Nancy Palmer Photo Agency.)*

ing of alternatives, and a searching for shared social and philosophical meaning, as well as to provide release from boredom, emptiness, or achievement pressures. Drug users, especially marijuana users, should be carefully defined. According to Keniston (1968/69) a "taster" is one who has tried marijuana but should not be counted as a "user." A "seeker" has smoked (or otherwise used) grass several times but does not use it as often as once a week and has not organized his life around it. A "head" (or "pothead," or "freak") smokes it at least weekly, and more likely several times a week or daily. He may or may not have dropped out of more regular activities with his peers. Even "heads" are not necessarily caught in a downward cycle. They may temporarily withdraw from the larger society to reexamine and reevaluate life only to reemerge 6 months to a year later with greater personality integration. Keniston (1968/69) describes one type of college drug user as follows:

> Unlike most seekers, heads are genuinely alienated from American society. Their defining characteristic is their generalized rejection of prevalent American values, which they criticize largely on cultural and humanistic grounds. American society is trashy, cheap, and commercial; it "dehumanizes" its members; its values of success, materialism, monetary accomplishment and achievement undercut more important spiritual values. . . . For heads, the goal is to find a way out of the "air-conditioned nightmare" of American society. What matters is the interior world, and, in the exploration of that world, drugs play a major role.

A second characteristic of many heads is a more or less intense feeling of estrangement from their own experience. Such students are highly aware of the masks, facades, and defenses people erect to protect themselves; they are critical of the social "games" and "role-playing" they see around them. They object to these games not only in others, but even more strongly in themselves. As a result, they feel compelled to root out any "defense" that might prevent awareness of inner life; self-deception, lack of self-awareness or "phoniness" are cardinal sins. (pp. 102 & 103)

There are, of course, many other reasons for drug use and many other drugs. Drugs may be used for "stimulus flooding," "psychological numbing," or for total withdrawal and avoidance. The use of alcohol among adolescents is clearly on the rise again, with many communities reporting serious problems of alcoholism. On the other hand, the use of "hard" drugs—heroin and other narcotics—seems to be declining, at least in some parts of the country. The use of each drug in each community has its own pattern of functions, of use or abuse, of expression of solidarity, of community, or of alienation.

In our discussion of activism and alienation, we have looked at the more extreme ways that some young people have chosen to voice their strong feelings of dissent. Both activism and the counterculture, despite their impact on the broader society, represent only a minority of adolescents, and it is misleading to imply that they represent the only ways in which adolescents set themselves apart from the dominant culture.

Mainstream Youth Culture

We have saved our discussion of mainstream youth culture for last, partly because it is more difficult to identify than the counterculture or the student political movement. One reason for this difficulty is that adolescent culture varies from one locale to another. What is mainstream in a midwestern suburb may not be mainstream at all in Atlanta, or San Francisco, or New York. Another reason is that many expressions of the youth culture are bits and pieces—such diverse manifestations as long hair and clothing fads (what one commentator called the "adolescent grooming phenomenon" of the 1960s [Havighurst, 1973a]), music and dances, styles of ornamentation, activities, in-groups and out-groups, language, and rules for behaving with each other and with adults. These different patterns may seem superficial to adults, but often they are central to the adolescent's self-expression.

Although it eludes description, the adolescent culture does differ from the dominant adult culture. In a sense, mainstream youth culture is a kind of mini-counterculture. It shares many roots with the counterculture: a concern with working out individual identities and rejecting the values of the broader society that do not fit; pressures for both conformity (especially in the early years) and autonomy; and a vital interest in the nature of interpersonal relationships. Adolescents in general place great importance on the way they can communicate with—and trust—their parents, their teachers, and their peers (Schmuck, 1965);

Expressions of youth culture. *(Bonnie Freer, Rapho/Photo Researchers.)*

and they are very concerned with the self-image which emerges from these relationships. In sum, mainstream adolescents, like activists and dropouts, are trying to find out who they are.

Many symbols of the youth culture, such as long hair, special jargon, rock music, and psychedelic posters, are popular badges of the adolescent's separateness from the adult world. But there is more to the youth culture than these pop symbols. Coleman (1970) suggests three ways of explaining the adolescent culture as it has evolved as a spin-off from the larger culture. In one way, some elements of the adolescent culture are a rational reaction against the "sickness" of society. We can see this by looking at popular youth heroes: many are young rebels or rock singers or writers who express alternatives to their parents' way of life. In another way, though, youth behavior is a cultural derivative of adult patterns—a teenager's interest in such material things as motorcycles or blue jeans, for example, is equivalent to an older person's interest in cars or fur coats. In a third sense, youth culture is a structural creation of the broader society. Adolescence itself is a creation of our society, as we saw earlier in this chapter. Whether the adolescent reacts to his special place in the world by dropping out, by crusading for change, or by less controversial means is a matter of individual circumstance, choice, and needs.

Throughout this chapter, we have talked about the particular needs of the adolescent and the different solutions that adolescents find to fill these needs. The major task of the period of adolescence is to "put it all together." This is nothing startlingly new, for we have seen again and again that we spend our whole lives, from the cradle to old age, trying to figure out who we are. But in adolescence, there is a new element in the way the individual forms a self-image. He now has new cognitive abilities that allow him to be self-reflective, analytical, and evaluative. He can now make choices about his future life. He can make increasingly important decisions about what he wants to be, how long he wants to go to school, what kinds of relationships he wants to have with friends and with dates. He is forming what Erikson (1962) calls an *ego identity*—an image of himself which for the first time has consistency both in the way he sees himself and the way that others see him.

This ego identity is not formed all at once at age 15, or 17, or 19. The adolescent's new cognitive powers give him the ability to reevaluate and reconsider his decisions about himself and others, and so he seems to be constantly changing his mind, making wide swings from one identity to another. Often his way of thinking about himself changes as adolescence progresses.

In early adolescence, the individual is self-centered, reflective, and self-absorbed. But his self-evaluations are highly dependent upon what others think of him—whether his high school friends see him as a joker, a "jock," or a square, and whether his parents see him as responsible or lazy. During these years, the teenager usually feels intense pressure to conform to group norms and expectations, and his self-image centers around how he fits in with a group or measures up to his peers. His value system, too, is highly dependent upon the values of those around him (Douvan & Adelson, 1966).

As the child grows older, the measuring stick with which he evaluates himself and those around him often changes. He is still self-absorbed, but his ideas about the way he fits into his world may now come more from his own discoveries about himself than from what he hears from others. His evaluations may reflect a sincere, idealistic, long-term commitment to ideals and values instead of short-term commitments to friends. The development of this new idealism is the reason why the first two years of college are often such a watershed or period of transformation for students in the way they see themselves and others and in the way they come to depend upon themselves. In part, this change is caused by the new, broader exposure to, and reaction to, the college atmosphere. But much of the change is also caused by the maturity of the rational processes—the new cognitive tools the adolescent can now bring to bear in evaluating himself.

Noncollege youths often go through the same dramatic transformation in the first few years after high school. In part, their change too is the result of adjusting to a new way of life: being socialized into a particular occupation; learning new rules and norms; watching the old circle of friends dissolve. Yet at the same time, the older adolescent who enters the work force often develops a more objective and independent outlook. His measuring stick, like the college student's, may become more individualistic.

In this chapter, we have been focusing much of our attention on high school and college students and on the youth movements that have centered on the campuses. But even though the noncollege, working youth does not face the awkward, artificial prolongation of childhood that confuses the college student, the adjustment process is every bit as complex. Particular problems center around teenage unemployment and the dull, repetitive jobs that adolescents are usually given. Cognitive maturity makes meaningful and significant work particularly important at this point in development (Dansereau, 1961; Goodman, 1960). Unemployment or meaningless work offers no challenge and denies the individual the opportunity to see the clear consequences of his efforts. This lack of significant work can be critically demeaning and demoralizing to the late adolescent, because the juxtaposition of an optimal state of biological, cognitive, and social maturity with seemingly trivial tasks makes an individual feel particularly disoriented. Often, the adolescent has no armor of numbness or carelessness to protect him against the frustration and lack of fulfillment. Needs for personality integration, for identity, and for self-fulfillment are particularly insistent during these years; and so the working adolescent, like the college student, is especially vulnerable and sensitive to an impersonal, mass, technological society.

The need for autonomy, the search for identity, and the need to develop a sense of integrity—are basic keys to adolescent behavior. If the teenager seems to act in eccentric or "adolescent" ways in our society, is it the adolescent who is peculiar? Or is the culture he lives in out of step?

SUMMARY   Adolescence is a time when the individual consolidates and integrates many elements of his personality and experience to become a more integrated person. We have looked at three key elements of this consolidation process.

One of these is building a value system. The adolescent's mature cognitive abilities allow him to look at himself, his beliefs, and his environment from a broad perspective. Some individuals use these abilities to build a mature and independent value system in the later years of adolescence—what Kohlberg calls postconventional morality and Rogers calls an "organismic" value system. But many others remain dependent upon external values and peer pressures throughout their lives.

A second element is the building of a personal identity. In the early teen years especially, relationships are very important in the development of a self-image. Adolescents use friendships and peer groups to test out aspects of their personality and interpersonal skills.

A third element of the period of adolescence is the collaborative creation of a youth culture. The modern world is a confusing place and more so for the adolescent, who is regarded neither as a child nor as an adult. Adolescents react to their lack of status in a complex world in different ways. A few become activists, committing themselves to positive values and trying to improve society. Activists exerted considerable influence on society in the 1960s; but political activism has become less popular in the 1970s, as more dissatisfied young people reject the dominant culture and adopt aspects of the counterculture. Most young people neither crusade nor fully drop out. They belong to a subgroup of youth culture which varies from place to place and from time to time. Activism, the counterculture, and numerous subcultures represent alternative solutions to the problem of finding an identity.

REVIEW QUESTIONS

1. What three explanations does Coleman offer for the development of youth culture?

2. How do peer friendships and ritual patterns help the adolescent develop a sense of identity?

3. Why is adolescence a particularly important time for the development of a set of values? Include Kohlberg's and Rogers's descriptions of a mature value system in your answer.

SUGGESTED READINGS

Adams, J. F. (Ed.). *Understanding adolescence* (2nd ed.). Boston: Allyn & Bacon, 1973. This second edition includes excellent articles combining both summary research and social critique of issues affecting adolescence.

Coleman, J. S., et al. *Youth: Transition to adulthood*. Report of the Panel on Youth of the President's Science Advisory Committee. Washington, D.C.: U.S. Government Printing Office, 1973. This report summarizes historical concerns about adolescence and central issues concerning adolescence and youth in today's world. Its recommendations include dramatic changes in the structure of school, work opportunities, and community involvement for youth.

Roszak, T. *The making of a counter-culture*. New York: Doubleday, 1968. This social analysis, already becoming a classic, describes the social groups comprising the cultural phenomenon called the counterculture.

Yablonsky, L. *The hippie trip*. New York: Pegasus, 1968. In the mid-1960s, Yablonsky was a participant-observer of the "hippies" in the Haight-Asbury district of San Francisco. His report is sensitive and sympathetic.

PART VII
ADULTHOOD AND AGING

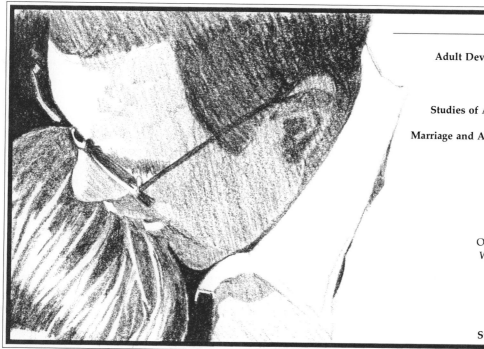

CHAPTER

19

EARLY ADULTHOOD: ROLES AND ISSUES

Development—or at least the potential for development—continues throughout the life span. Although some theorists have proposed that developmental stages occur in adulthood, the nature of the developmental process in maturity is somewhat different from that during childhood and adolescence (Havighurst, 1973b). Changes during the post-adolescent years are related more to social and cultural forces than to physical and cognitive development. In this section of the book, we shall focus upon the social milestones and cultural demands that provide the context for adult development.

Because the timing of social milestones (such as marriage, parenthood, the choosing of a career) varies from individual to individual, and because cultural demands differ according to nationality, socioeconomic status, and occupation, it is difficult, if not impossible, to pinpoint stages of adult development on the basis of age alone. Choice of occupation or the birth of a first child may occur at age 15 or 40. Marriage may take place during adolescence, early adulthood, old age—or not at all. Individuals' reactions to these events and the nature of the roles those individuals are required to assume will vary according to the demands and restrictions of their culture. One culture may require early marriage and childbearing, while another may frown upon such practices. As we have seen in earlier chapters, expectations for marital roles and parenting differ markedly from culture to culture.

In this chapter we shall examine the social and cultural milestones that generally, but not always, are reached in early adulthood; and we shall look at patterns of adaptation, integration, and reorganization associated with these milestones. In Chapter 20, we shall focus more on developmental theories, with particular emphasis on the interaction of developmental periods and life events.

ADULT DEVELOPMENT: MATURITY

When does adolescence end and adulthood begin? If we say that the attainment of maturity is the deciding factor, then we are still left with the problem of defining precisely what we mean by maturity. There are, of course, legal definitions within the social system. A person is mature enough to vote at age 18, according to the law; however, a United States senator must be at least 30 years old, and the presidency is open only to those age 35 and over. There are also informal social definitions of maturity; someone who is employed, is financially independent, or is a parent is generally considered a mature individual. Beyond these definitions, however, a vast array of psychological characteristics usually is associated with maturity: psychological independence and autonomy, independent decision making, and some degree of stability, wisdom, reliability, integrity, and compassion. Different investigators put different characteristics into the blend (Bischof, 1969), and different cultures demand different sets of responsibilities. Freud defined psychological maturity quite simply as the ability to work and to love.

Whatever combination of characteristics may be included in a definition of maturity, there is no clear age demarcation for its occurrence.

Studies of human behavior suggest that each of us has an internalized social clock by which we judge age-appropriate activities (Neugarten, 1968a). In other words, we have built-in expectations, constraints, and pressures for various stages in life. Although these boundaries may sometimes have a psychological base, they are more often social in nature. For example, if we should observe a couple dancing with total involvement at a rock music festival, we would probably have dramatically different reactions, depending upon whether the couple were age 25 or 55. We would interpret the motivations of the dancers quite differently, in accordance with their ages, and hence would act differently toward the couples.

Neugarten and Moore (1968) define three age periods or stages of adulthood: young adulthood (20s and early 30s), middle age (40s and 50s), and senescence (65 and over). But even these age guidelines are not always accurate indicators of a person's internalized judgment of behavior. Socioeconomic status, rural or urban setting, ethnic background, historical periods, wars, financial depression, or other life events—all may strongly influence the definitions, expectations, and pressures of adulthood. For example, middle age and old age usually occur earlier among the lower working classes than among the higher socioeconomic classes. If a man is dependent upon physical labor for his livelihood, he may feel that he has reached his prime at age 30 and old age by the time he is 50. A business or professional man, on the other hand, may judge himself—and is usually judged by others—according to his experience, mature judgment, and self-confidence; recognition and financial success may not come to him until he is in his 40s or early 50s, and his productivity may well continue into his late 60s. The age clock is set, in part, by social class; the higher the class, the more likely is the luxury of delay in the movement from one stage to another (Neugarten & Moore, 1968).

It is important to remember that the variation in definition and boundaries of maturity does not mean that the roles and issues of various periods of adulthood are unreal or unimportant. Many of these issues become part of the self-concept, and in adulthood the self-concept is central to the integration of the personality. Whether or not a person considers himself or herself to be in the prime of life, or to be fully autonomous, or to be among the decision makers in the immediate society is an important aspect of the self-concept. Individuals who feel that they should be autonomous or among the decision makers, but who perceive that they are not—that instead they are powerless, lost in a mass society, and caught in the cogs of an industrialized world—have a dramatically different set of realities to adapt to.

AGE CLOCKS

STUDIES OF ADULT DEVELOPMENT

The ideal way to study adult development is to combine both longitudinal and cross-sectional studies (see Chapter 1). It is important to look at individuals as they progress through their particular life spans; and it is also desirable to compare people at selective points in their lifes or at different ages yet at the same point in historical time (Block, 1971; Neugarten & Datan, 1973). For example, a person who is 30 years old is different from one who is 50; but being 50 in 1976 is different from being 50 in 1949.

If a country is at war, is undergoing a social upheaval, or is experiencing a financial depression, the effect of these events will differ for different age groups. During a depression, a 25-year-old may or may not be faced with the same demands as would a 45-year-old; neither would a 45-year-old necessarily face the same conditions, and consequently adapt in the same manner, as would a 65-year-old. How can we analyze such variations in effect across a population or within an individual? One way is to select several groups of individuals at different ages and study them at one point in time; these groups can then be followed and checked at regular intervals during several years. In this way, the cross-sectional approach can be combined with the longitudinal view.

MARRIAGE AND ALTERNATE LIFE-STYLES

One of the major tasks of young adulthood is to develop a relatively stable pattern of intimacy. This may be achieved through marriage or in a number of other life-styles. Each life-style has its own cultural demands, social roles, and stresses.

Marriage

Throughout many periods of history and in many cultural groups, a monogamous marriage has been the dominant life-style for a sizable percentage of the adult population. This form of marriage provides a certain stability for the rearing of children as well as a certain regularity and a shared set of expectations for the adult participants. Indeed, the institution of marriage is often one of the most clearly delineated social institutions in a society. Most cultures have specific premarital traditions such as dating, courting, and a period of engagement; rites of passage, such as a formal wedding, are imposed, and the roles of the participants within their new social state of marriage are rigorously defined.

In traditional Japan, the prescribed ritual leading up to marriage is an elaborate one that is often conducted through a go-between (in Japanese, the *nakohdo*). The use of a third party ensures that the match will be socially and economically "appropriate" and that neither party will lose face should one of the families reject the potential spouse (Vogel, 1961). In early twentieth-century Ireland, the "matchmaker" fulfilled a similar role (Arensberg, 1937). His function was that of a

The institution of marriage. (*Eli Reed, Nancy Palmer Photo Agency.*)

negotiator who sought concessions in the form of money, land, or live-
stock from both sets of parents until a mutually beneficial arrangement
was reached.

Although American marriages in general are relatively free of such
prenuptial investigation and negotiation, there still exist in this country strong constraints on relationships that violate social, economic,
religious, or racial boundaries. Community groups and social institutions, as well as parents, often frown upon mixed marriages or marriages outside of one's class, religion, ethnic background, or age group.
However, change not only is taking place but is beginning to be more
widely accepted. Recent studies indicate that one out of every five
Americans has dated someone of another race and that there are almost
half a million black-white marriages in the United States (Porterfield,

1973). As male-female roles continue to be redefined and as new marriage styles (noncontractual marriage, group marriage) are tried, many of the traditional prescriptions and taboos may begin to fade or give way to new taboos, constraints, or expectations.

The Family The family has often been studied from the point of view of the child, with emphasis upon the socialization patterns of the child and the cultural demands made upon him. However, the family continues to be a primary socializing agency or institution for the adult. Both the nuclear family structure (a father, a mother, and their children) and the extended family structure (usually at least three generations living together in one unit) place demands for new roles and relationships upon the adults involved.

An adult who marries into an extended family which has a close network of interrelationships must adapt and adjust to this new and rather intense group. However, adjustment is just as difficult for an individual accustomed to an extended kinship structure who marries into a nuclear family and moves far away from the extended family that has provided his major social context.

Families go through cycles, with certain functions demanded at various time periods. The first milestone, of course, is reached when the individual leaves his original family (the *family of orientation*). This separation may occur at the time of marriage, or it may occur earlier if the individual has opted for independence, either living alone or with a group of his peers. The second milestone is usually marriage, with all the attendant adjustments of establishing a relationship with a new individual or with a new family network. The most common third milestone is the birth of the first child and the beginning of parenthood. The occasion is sometimes referred to as the establishment of a *family of procreation*. There are still other milestones, such as the birth of the last child, the departure of the last child from the family, and the death of a spouse. In an extended family several of these cycles may interact, providing rehearsal and repetition and making each member's adjustment somewhat easier.

During the past 50 to 100 years, family cycles have changed in timing as well as in nature. Not only are people living longer now than was true in earlier years, but their ages at various points in the family cycle and the average length of time from one milestone to another have changed. (See Figure 15.) There has been some increase in the average period of time between marriage and the first child. There is also an increase in the period between the time the last child leaves home and the date of the parents' retirement or death; and this post-parental period seems to be continuing to grow longer.

COMMUNAL FAMILIES. Communal families fulfill many of the functions common to nuclear and extended families. They provide a context for interpersonal intimacy, establish rules or norms for interpersonal responsibility, and supply shared values and ideals for the development

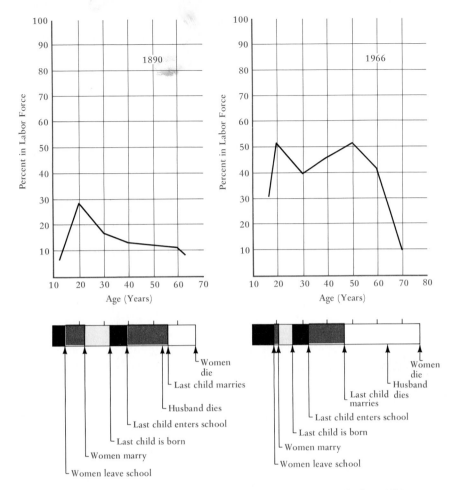

Figure 15 Work as related to the significant stages that occur in the lives of women. *(Sources: National Manpower Council.* **Womanpower.** *New York: Columbia University Press, 1957, p. 307. Right-hand portion of figure has been revised based on labor-force data taken from U.S. Department of Labor. 1967 manpower report. Washington, D.C.: U.S. Government Printing Office, 1967, Table A-2, p. 202; and on family cycle data taken from Glick, P.C., Heer, D.M., & Beresford, J.C. Family formation and family composition: Trends and prospects. In M. B. Sussman (Ed.),* **Sourcebook in marriage and the family** *(2nd ed.). New York: Houghton Mifflin, 1963, p. 12.*

of a life-style. For example, in the kibbutzim of Israel, kinship ties are psychological rather than biological; but the sense of responsibility and feelings of relationship among the members are just as strong as the ties of a biologically related family (Spiro, 1954). This is amply illustrated by the fact that individuals almost never marry someone with whom they have grown up in the kibbutz. Although there are no rules against their doing so, they seem to feel such kinship with one another that marriage within the group would carry some of the weight of incest.

One of the earliest experiments in communal living in the United States was begun in Putney, Vermont, in 1846 (Kephart, 1966). John

Communal families have become more popular in the last decade. (*Bonnie Freer, Rapho/ Photo Researchers.*)

Humphrey Noyes, a follower of the perfectionist doctrine (a belief that man could attain sinlessness, or perfection), established a community based on economic and sexual communism. Forced out of Vermont, Noyes took his followers to New York State where they settled near Oneida Creek and were thereafter known as the Oneida Community.

The world does not remember the Oneida Community for its economic communism nor for its practice of mutual criticism (a method of group problem solving), but for its system of complex marriage. Rightly or wrongly, just as the term "Mormon" signifies polygamy, so the term "Oneida" conjures up thoughts about the unique sex practices of the Colony. Noyes, himself, coined the term "free love," although he seems to have preferred the phrase "complex marriage" or, occasionally, "pantogamy." Realistically, the Oneida marital system can best be characterized as a combination of group marriage and community living. (Kephart, 1966, p. 486)

In 1877 Noyes turned the leadership of the community over to one of his sons; and two years later, Noyes himself left for Canada. Within a few months after his departure, the Oneida Community had ceased to exist. The strength of the group had evidently been built upon the man rather than upon the grand idea.

Present-day communal experiments have met with varying degrees of success. Where they are a result of a rather unfocused desire of a group of people to "do their own thing" away from the critical and constraining eye of the Establishment, they have often failed. They seem to be more successful when they are organized around a clear-cut purpose and include some system of rules and responsibilities, shared values, and ideals (Cross & Pruyn, 1973).

Wife and mother, husband and father, marriage and family, home and children—the list of coupled words with their implicit assumptions and expectations could go on forever. The strength of the coupling of such words indicates the strength of the stereotyped cultural demands. For many persons, the social pressure to assume the parenting role arises within themselves.

But parenthood requires new roles and responsibilities on the part of the mother and father. It creates demands for response on the part of the parents and provides a new social status for them (Hill & Aldous, 1969). And no matter how much social conditioning they have been exposed to, parenthood is the one milestone all individuals are probably quite unprepared to meet.

The initial adjustment to parenthood is likely to be dramatic. Learning nutrition and child care, going to the doctor for regular check-ups, buying baby clothes, choosing a name, deciding on breast-feeding or bottle-feeding—all of these are minor considerations for the new parents compared to their experience when the infant is born. The actual birth brings an onslaught of physical and emotional strains—disruption of sleep and routines, financial drain, and increased tension and conflict over responsibilities, possessiveness, and discipline. The mother is tired, the father feels neglected, and both experience a curtailment of their freedom. The closeness and companionship of husband and wife are diluted by the introduction of a new family member, and the focus of concern of either or both partners may shift to the baby (Komarovsky, 1964).

STAGES OF PARENTHOOD. Alice Rossi (1968) has analyzed adult development during parenthood in terms of four stages: the *anticipatory stage*, the *honeymoon stage*, the *plateau stage*, and the *disengagement* or *termination stage*. Where parenthood is concerned, the anticipatory stage refers to pregnancy and the new roles and perceptions that it requires. Husband and wife are now prospective parents and, as such, they face both domestic and external social adjustments. They must come to terms with the idea of being a family rather than a couple, and they must adjust to a new status within their community group.

Parenthood

The anticipatory stage of parenthood. (*Joel Gordon.*)

The honeymoon stage of parenthood is the period during which the parent-child attachment relationship is formed. Although difficult adjustments (catching up on lost sleep, coming to grips with the diminishment of husband-wife intimacy, and dealing with loss of freedom) have to be made during this time, the period is one of excitement over the formation of new relationships and a time of uncertainty over the meaning of parental love.

During the plateau stage, parents are involved in acting out their roles as father and mother. There are problems to be dealt with within the family and within the community. Socialization of the child, religious education, future family planning, involvement in the local schools, and participation in community organizations may all be a part of parenting.

The final stage—disengagement-termination—is usually thought to be reached when the last child is married or leaves home permanently. At this time, parenting involves letting go of major responsibilities to allow for child autonomy.

DEMANDS UPON PARENTS. The demands made upon parents vary with the age of the child. An infant's demands, for instance, are for almost total and constant nurturance. Satisfying this want is much easier for some parents than for others. For certain parents, the intense dependency requirements of the infant are overwhelming. At this stage of the child's development, as at any other, the particular needs that are paramount for the child tend to stimulate similar needs in the parents themselves. For example, some parents cannot bear to hear an infant cry. The baby's wails trigger the father's and mother's feelings of helplessness and dependency and some related feeling of anger associated with their own unacceptable dependency requirements. Other parents take their own dependency much more in stride as a normal, natural need of human beings.

The toddler has a quite different set of needs. He is struggling with his own individuality and autonomy; he is active in exploring and vigorous in his demands for both dependence and independence; he is intense and unreasonable in his refusals to obey commands. Again, these rather primitive needs of the toddler stimulate rather primitive needs in the parents, who may feel threatened by this willful, tyrannical, unreasonable creature. Every adult is frustrated at one time or another and is impatient enough to want to resort to a temper tantrum. Parents who have to work hard to subdue their own impulses in this direction may find a child's indulgence in bouts of temper totally unacceptable.

The important point to be made here is that each critical period for the child produces or reactivates a critical period in the parents (Benedek, 1970). The parents may be able to resolve their own conflicts at a new and more advanced level of integration, or they may simply be unable to cope with their aroused feelings. The conflicts may lead to the development of pathological problems by the parents, or to new family crises, or to overzealous disciplining of, or permissiveness toward, the child.

It must be remembered that parents who are unable to deal effectively with a child at one stage of his development may be quite good at dealing with him at another stage. For instance, parents who have extraordinary difficulty with an infant may manage to cope quite effectively with the preschool child or the adolescent. The reverse may also be true; the parent at ease with the helpless baby may have problems with an independent teenager. Parents should not feel incompetent or neurotic merely because they are having difficulty dealing with some aspects of their role as parents at any particular point in time. On the other hand, readily available, nonjudgmental help in parenting is often missing in our society at the crucial time it is needed.

Each critical period in a child's development produces a critical period in his parents' development. (*Hanna Schreiber, Rapho/Photo Researchers.*)

PARENTING IN EXTENDED FAMILIES AND COMMUNAL SETTINGS. Intensity of adjustment to parenthood and the intensity of psychic conflict and feelings of responsibility tend to be reduced in the extended family or communal family. In the kibbutzim in Israel, for example, responsibility for the physical care, religious training, education, and socialization of children is shared by the group (Spiro, 1954). The same type of sharing is usually found within the extended family, where grandparents, aunts, and uncles may assume some of the burden of child care.

MOTHERHOOD. Throughout most historical periods, there has been rather comfortable acceptance of the idea that motherhood is desirable for nearly all women. Starting with doll play in early childhood, females tend to move, or be moved, toward that ultimate event that will place them, in their own and society's eyes, in their "proper" role: motherhood. More recently, however, many women have realized that fulfillment does not have to include motherhood. The choice of motherhood is an absorbing and fulfilling role that tends to subordinate many other roles, at least for a while. But the concept of childbearing as the biological and psychological high point for all women has been oversold and arouses expectations for reward that are far beyond reality (McBride, 1973).

Most women cannot fulfill the idealized picture of motherhood put forth by the media and generally accepted by the culture. They then may feel a sense of failure and guilt when they compare themselves with such mythical standards. For example, mothers who work may feel that they are cheating their children, and society often reinforces that feeling. However, studies have shown that the working mother can be as effective in nurturing and caring for her children as the mother who stays home all day. The quality of the time a mother spends with her children is more important than the quantity (Hoffman, 1963; Stolz, 1960).

Singles

Thus far, we have assumed that all individuals have certain kinds of needs for belonging and sharing, for feeling secure in an interpersonal context, and for having meaningful and close relationships with significant others. However, there are various life-styles that lean toward greater autonomy and less permanent social structures for the solution of intimacy.

Singles will be defined here as those persons who have left the family of orientation and who are not involved in any long-term *formalized* alliance or collaboration with any other individual or group of individuals. Single status, however, does not imply a permanent or finite situation; it is a continuum and often merges into other alternatives.

There are a number of types of relationships other than heterosexual marriage that achieve many of the functions of intimacy and sharing usually associated with formal marriage. Increasingly, young adults are finding life-styles in which they live together in pairs or in small groups and work out patterns of interrelationships and responsibility, of closeness, warmth, and interpersonal intimacy. Some of these are homosexual living arrangements; others are heterosexual. Since they allow flexibility in working out individual roles and responsibilities, many of these relationships are much more satisfying and fulfilling than are the more traditional circumscribed and prescribed family relationships.

Although many singles are individuals who have never been married, many others are divorced or widowed persons who are currently single either by choice or by misfortune. As our culture has come more and more to view divorce as an acceptable, or even preferable, alternative to an unhappy marriage, our divorced population has grown. For example, in 1880, when divorce was looked upon as a rather shameful process, only 0.4 out of every 1,000 persons in the United States—or a total of 20,000—obtained a divorce. By 1974, however, the rate had climbed to 4.6 out of every 1,000 persons, for a total of 981,000 divorces (U.S. Department of Health, Education, and Welfare, 1975). Psychologists, religious counselors, and social service workers have endeavored to assist this swelling population of divorced persons in making the transition from marriage to single status. Singles bars, special resorts and cruises for single persons only, groups formed solely for the purpose of sharing life-style problems, books explaining how to divorce "creatively" and live happily ever after—all have been developed to be marketed to those who are recently widowed, divorced, or separated.

A divorced man and his child doing their household chores. (*Ray Ellis, Rapho/Photo Researchers.*)

The sudden change in status which follows the ending of a long-term, intimate relationship often causes more turmoil and requires more readjustment than an individual had anticipated. Obtaining a hotel room, securing a bank loan or a mortgage, adopting a child, and getting a department store charge account—all are more difficult for singles, and especially for single women, than for married couples. But for the person who becomes single after having been married, the problem is compounded by emotional trauma. Often, those who went from their family of orientation directly into marriage have quite literally never been on their own, and they are inexperienced in coping with the change in status which now confronts them. Their problems of adjustment are often underestimated both by the individuals themselves and by their family and friends. When loss of a partner and the accompanying grief are followed quickly by forced autonomy and the need for independent decision making, a newly single individual occasionally suffers a breakdown in physical or mental health.

WORK

An important characteristic of maturity and of adulthood has generally been considered the individual's ability to become involved in meaningful work, to take on the responsibilities that work or a career implies, and to provide a livelihood for himself and his dependents (Goodman, 1960). Although Freud defined the normal adult as someone able to love and to work, some apparently "normal" people regard work as merely a necessary evil. Individuals' attitudes toward work vary considerably according to social class, age, and sex. For some persons, work is merely something that must be done in order to survive; others view it as an opportunity to be productive, to gain self-esteem and respect, or to be creative. For still others, work may be an addiction—something they are driven to do or they must perform in order to feel adequate. A person may achieve a sense of pleasure, satisfaction, and fulfillment from work or may feel blocked, burdened, frustrated, and dehumanized by it (Keniston, 1963).

Most males are socialized to feel that their work is a central part of their identity (Goodman, 1960; Moore, 1969). Women, on the other hand, have a rather mixed socialization toward work. Some are clearly socialized to particular careers or to achievement; others see work as a rather unsatisfying alternative to marriage and motherhood. However, with changes in attitudes and with equal opportunities being made available to them, increasing numbers of women are joining the work force. By 1971, 50 percent of American women between the ages of 20 and 50 were employed outside the home (Neugarten & Moore, 1968).

There is a close relationship between an individual's occupational satisfaction and family satisfaction. A person who experiences frustration or a feeling of incompetence or depersonalization in one area will tend to seek satisfaction in the other. A man who is unhappy in his job

Some people view their work as an opportunity to gain self-esteem and to be creative. (*Sylvia Johnson, Woodfin Camp & Assoc.*)

will place great emphasis upon family harmony, while the man who is unhappy in his family situation will use his job as a substitute for interpersonal satisfaction.

The work cycle, like the family cycle, is defined by particular turning points or crises (Moore, 1969). The first major step consists of the entrance into the occupation. Later come changes in responsibility, dramatic promotions or reassignments, or changes in career. All of these may require a career plateau, which may come earlier and last longer than is desirable. Others encounter frequent or protracted periods of unemployment—often with intense financial, social, and psychological stress. Near the end of a career, a person may experience a decline in responsibility or authority as he approaches retirement, the final stage in the work cycle.

Work Cycles

There are several factors that have an impact on occupational choice. Social class, ethnic origin, intelligence, sex, race, or parental occupation can either provide opportunities or limit opportunities for a specific career. Although most people tend to focus upon an occupation during late adolescence or early adulthood, many of the social and psychological influences that direct their choice occurred in the early years of

Occupational Choice

A person's occupational choice may be influenced by various social and psychological factors which occurred in her childhood. (*Steve Eagle, Nancy Palmer Photo Agency.*)

childhood. A person's cognitive and emotional development, acquisition of attitudes and values, and achievement orientation are important to career choice and job success, and all of these take place long before the career choice is made. While we may like to think of occupational choice as primarily a rational decision, the evidence for this is rather slim (Moore, 1969).

Work and Life-Style

To a great extent, a person's work may determine his life-style. It may determine where he lives: East, West, city, country, suburb. It may determine his friendship patterns, level of sophistication, opinions, prejudices, and political affiliations. What appears to be a rather subtle socialization into a particular career may have an extraordinary impact on an individual's life.

Everyone who is either beginning a new job or continuing a career in a new company is faced with certain adjustments in routine and with new patterns for performance. Beyond this, however, is the need to discover the unwritten rules of the new work situation. What are the expectations for "appropriate clothing, speech, and topics of conversation"? Is conformity rewarded, or is individuality more admired? Are radical political and social ideas frowned upon? Is it necessary to live in a specific suburb and join a particular club in order to succeed? Sometimes the patterns are so clear and well known—for the shop foreman, for example, or for "the man in the gray flannel suit"—that we are aware of the norms and expectations and work roles almost without thinking.

Sometimes the process of transition into the career or new job is relatively smooth, if considerable preparation has been made prior to the actual work experience. In other situations, the transition to the occupation results in a kind of culture shock. The college student who spends a summer working in a factory or with a construction gang may experience this type of shock. Similarly, individuals who are given special opportunities to upgrade their careers dramatically may find the subtle demands for attitudinal adjustment much more overwhelming than the specific skills or knowledge necessary for job performance.

<hr>

SUMMARY

Although adult development is different in nature from childhood development, it is a process that is potentially as fraught with needs for adjustment and socialization as is the growth process during the earlier years. Adult development is more social and cultural than physical and cognitive, and it is usually measured in cycles or cultural milestones rather than in age periods.

Marriage and the establishment of alternate life-styles are some of the solutions to needs for security and intimacy. These family milestones mark the periods of adult development and require new adjustments and responsibilities. Single people face similar demands for growth and change and needs for close relationships with significant others. Some of these adjustments are made more difficult by social sanctions favoring marriage and the nuclear family.

One characteristic of the mature individual is his ability to become involved in meaningful work. As with other milestones in adult life, a career brings with it pressures and demands for adjustment. Although we think of occupational choice as occurring during the early adult years, factors that influence that choice are often set in the childhood years. The consequences of occupational choice are sometimes subtle, yet profound. Indeed, an individual's life-style is often determined by the career he has chosen to pursue.

<hr>

REVIEW QUESTIONS

1. Are your views on marriage and parenthood different from, or similar to, those of your parents? What factors have influenced your attitudes?

2. Various life-styles and family systems were discussed in this chapter. Which of them do you find most appealing? Give the reasons for your choices.

3. Interview (a) someone who is just starting a career, and (b) someone who has worked in the same occupational field for a number of years. Analyze their reactions to their work in terms of what you know about the work cycle and the factors that influence occupational choice.

What adjustment problems might the beginner have? How has the older worker's occupation influenced his life-style?

SUGGESTED READINGS

McBride, A. *The growth and development of mothers.* New York: Harper & Row, 1973. Motherhood is demanding and not for all women. In fact, it has been grossly oversold according to Angela McBride.

Packard, V. *The pyramid climbers.* New York: McGraw-Hill, 1962. In this vividly descriptive account, Packard looks at the roles and tactics of the young executive on the way up.

Toffler, A. *Future Shock.* New York: Bantam Books, 1971. Toffler's best seller highlights the dramatically increased pace of life and change which we currently face. Adjustment may result in the loss of a sense of time and reality.

20

THE MIDDLE YEARS OF ADULTHOOD: CONTINUITY AND CHANGE

In earlier chapters of this book, we have looked at childhood, adolescence, and young adulthood. We have seen the developmental steps by which a child becomes an individual who is reasonably set in his outlook and his personality. And we have seen the social milestones that mark the adolescent's entrance into the world of the adult—marriage, parenthood, a career.

After this, what happens? The period of adulthood may encompass as much as 75 percent of the life span. Does it pose any new challenges, or is it merely a time of living out the decisions made early in life, possibly making a few corrections here and there? How much continuity is there during these years—is John Smith the same person at age 55 that he was at 25? If not, what makes him change? Is it biological decline or a slowdown in intelligence, an accumulation of wisdom and experience or a narrowing of perspective? What aspects of change can he control, and what aspects are totally beyond his control?

These questions are important ones, but developmental psychologists have only recently started to look closely at what happens to people in middle and late life. In this chapter, we shall be looking at some of the discoveries that are being made about adults and discussing some of the common issues that need to be solved in adulthood. We shall look first at middle age: the challenges it poses and the elements of both continuity and change in the middle years. Then we shall review some developmental theories to see how adult growth fits into the overall perspective of lifelong development—how in some ways it is a continuation of the patterns established in the early years of life, and how in another sense it is a very different kind of personal growth.

MIDDLE AGE AS A DEVELOPMENTAL STAGE

"I saw some stunning girls on stage at a Las Vegas review. I was really having a good time until I realized, 'My God! My own daughter is old enough to be up there dancing with those girls!'"

When do people start thinking of themselves as middle-aged? What are the cues that tell a person that he is no longer young, and how does he react to this knowledge? There are many signals of middle age. Sometimes, as the quote above illustrates, middle age hits a person like a sudden slap in the face. At other times, the awareness of middle age is felt in quieter, more satisfying ways.

Chronologically, the span of middle age covers roughly the years from age 40 or 45 to age 60 or 65—but the period may be longer or shorter for different people. This variation occurs because there are so many different kinds of cues (Neugarten, 1968b). Some cues are social and positional. Middle age is a period of being in between, a kind of a bridge between two generations. It carries with it an awareness of being in a separate class not only from youngsters and young adults but also from retirees and aged people.

Other cues may be physical and biological. A man may suddenly

Individuals in the middle adult years become increasingly aware of their physical vulnerability. Often they will embark on exercise and sports programs. (*Bruce Anspach, EPA News Photo.*)

realize that his son is taller than he is, or a woman will find that her knitting is hampered by arthritis. There are psychological cues, too. There is the realization that certain basic decisions of career or family have already been made—that these patterns are set and must now be played out or fulfilled. There is no longer an unlimited horizon of endless possibilities in the future. Women tend to clock middle age according to the family cycle—when their children leave home or, if they have no children, when they would have left home if there had been a family. Men's cues often come from their careers—when they have reached positions of seniority or status, or when they realize they have lagged behind the goals they set for themselves as young adults.

Along with the social, biological, and psychological cues that tell a person she is no longer young, there often comes a feeling of satisfaction, a belief that she is now in the prime of life (Neugarten, 1968b). While physical activity may be more limited at this time, many people find that their combination of experience and self-knowledge gives them an ability to manage their own lives for the first time. They are able to make decisions about themselves and others with an ease and self-confidence that was beyond their grasp before. This is why the 40- to 60-year-old group has been called the "command generation," and why most of the decision makers in government, in corporations, and in society are within this age span.

Prime of Life or "Beginning of the End"?

Of course, not all middle-aged people make weighty decisions; many do not feel that they are in command of their own lives, let alone in command of others in their environment. And while presidents and eminent scholars are usually in this age group, there are quite a few people who seem to lose vitality after the age of 40. Frenkel-Brunswik (1963) does not see middle age as the period of the command generation. Instead, she sees it as a period of declining activity whose onset, around the age of 48, is usually marked by both biological crises (such as female and male menopause) and psychological crises.

Frenkel-Brunswik divides life into five stages. The first three are periods of the building up of life. They peak after age 30 when the individual is involved in more activities and interests than at any other time in life. The last two stages are periods of decline. At some point in the late 40s, the individual gradually reduces his activities. He takes on fewer new interests, and he starts to develop more physical ailments. Middle age, says Frenkel-Brunswik, ushers in this period of biological, social, and psychological decline—usually with a crisis of boredom, discouragement, or depression. Other theorists, laymen, and armchair analysts also see middle age as a time of particular strain.

Mid-Life Crisis   We have many half-humorous stereotypes that give a sort of layman's description of this period of crisis—the 53-year-old woman who suddenly redecorates her home in shocking pink, or the established career man who quits his job, leaves his wife, and joins a tribe of mystics. While the average 50-year-old is probably not about to do either of these things, developmental psychologists are starting to recognize that the period of middle age often is a time of reassessment and turmoil, if not dramatic change.

Different descriptions are used to identify this time of upheaval. According to one theory (Levinson et al., 1974), the personality changes quite profoundly during adulthood, and this change occurs in three stages. In his 20s, the individual faces the task of "getting into the adult world," exploring all the possible things he may want to do with his life. By the age of 30 or 32, he has become fairly committed to a few goals. He is now in the second stage of "settling down," working hard to reach his chosen goals. About the age of 40, though, the individual may begin to question, or at least put into perspective, the "driven" life he has been leading. If he has been successful in reaching his goals, he may suddenly ask, "Were they worth the struggle?" If he has not done what he wanted to do with his life, he may now become keenly aware that he does not have many more chances to change his lot.

This painful stage has been given a number of names. Levinson sees it as a time of growing pains which each person must pass through before he can go on to "become his own man." Other names for it are "mid-life transition" (Sheehy, 1974), "mid-career crisis" (Rogers, 1973), and "middle-age slump." Why does it happen? Many psychologists feel that just like the first stirrings of adolescence, the entrance into middle age is a period of profound change which requires people

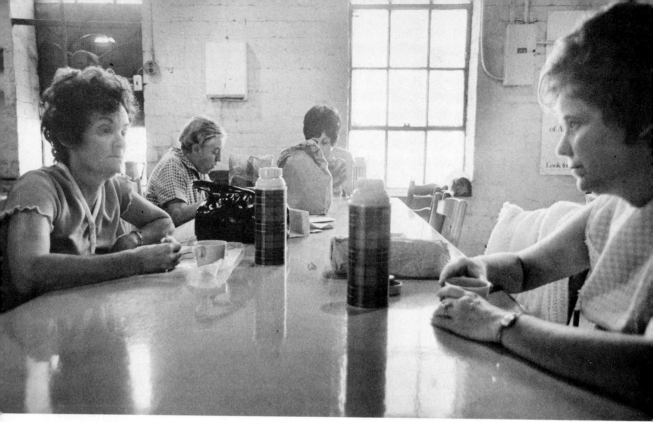

Middle age is a period of profound change which requires reassessment of one's abilities and limitations. (*Abigail Heyman, Magnum Photos.*)

to make some readjustments—and not always pleasant ones. There *has* to be a reassessment at this point, because suddenly there are a number of facts which force them to come face to face with their own limitations. They can no longer pretend that their physical stamina is boundless and stay up all night; they cannot use or abuse their bodies the way they used to do as youths. They have made choices about their life-styles that they are no longer free to change at will. The die is cast, whether they like it or not. Middle-aged people realize that they may have made mistakes in their lives. And they must increasingly put the blame on themselves, not on the upbringing they received from their parents, for whatever they have made of themselves (Gould, 1975).

At this time, too, extra demands are being made on them. If their parents are still alive, they are probably disabled enough to need their middle-aged children to act as parents to them. At the same time, the children of these middle-aged adults are probably going through a difficult stage of rebellion, testing new life-styles and criticizing their parents' judgment. There may be renewed awareness of world or community problems, perhaps accentuated by the younger generation's concern and then by painful realization of their own inability to solve them. Throughout this period, these individuals become aware of the approach of their own death and are frustrated that there is nothing they can do to stop the process of aging. How do they react? As Rogers (1973) describes it, they can choose between "flight and fight." Either way, this first serious contact with the notion of their own mortality adds to their troubles.

All of these different circumstances and realizations are the reasons why a crisis, change, or depression of some sort is almost inevitable at mid-life. But there are many specific areas—biological and intellectual functioning, and personality—where changes seem to take place at this time which contribute to the sense of being middle-aged. How much physical, mental, and personality change is there in adulthood, and how much stability is there?

CONTINUITY AND CHANGE IN MIDDLE AGE
Biological Continuity and Change

It used to be assumed that people reached the prime of life, at least in physical terms, at age 20 or shortly thereafter, and that from then on, the body declined. It was thought that while different functions and organs deteriorated at different rates, this deterioration began almost immediately after the body had fully matured. Many people still think that the body cells begin dying at a faster rate at some point in young adulthood, and that aging occurs because these cells are no longer replaced at as fast a rate as they deteriorate.

Do people begin aging almost as soon as they reach maturity? And is there an inevitable amount of deterioration that takes place by the age of 35, or 45, or 55? In some ways, there is bound to be some physical decline or slowing down during the years of middle age (Birren, 1959). The bone structure, for instance, stiffens and even shrinks a bit during the course of adulthood. This is the reason why some people may be shorter at their fortieth high school reunion than they were when they were students. Skin and muscles begin to lose some elasticity. There is a tendency to accumulate more subcutaneous fat, especially in certain areas like the midriff. There are more sensory defects during the adult years, too. Vision tends to be constant from adolescence to the 40s or early 50s, when visual acuity may begin to show signs of decline. However, nearsighted people often are able to see better in middle age than they could as young adults. There is an increased incidence of hearing problems during mid-adulthood, especially hearing loss in the upper frequencies. Long-term exposure to high levels of noise increases the likelihood of hearing loss. Therefore, some factory workers, and many city dwellers, may be particularly prone to hearing problems in later years. Similarly, taste, smell, pain, and other senses tend to become somewhat deadened with age.

Other biological functions, such as reaction time and sensorimotor skills, seem likely to slow down. Reaction time drops off slowly through-

The middle years of life are often not a time of physical decline. There is at least as much continuity as change. (*Ray Ellis, Rapho/Photo Researchers.*)

out adulthood, then more precipitously during old age. Motor skills do not necessarily decline. A man who chops firewood every week and the woman who plays tennis each afternoon will probably notice almost no slowdown in either efficiency or skill. But it becomes increasingly difficult to learn new skills. Sexual activity and interest usually remain high throughout middle age, especially in men (McCary, 1973; Pfeiffer, Verwoerdt, & Davis, 1972).

What causes the biological decline that often accompanies aging? There are numerous explanations. One is that aging is caused by the simple accumulation of wear and tear on the organism. Another is that it results from a reduced efficiency of the body chemistry or of the homeostatic balance. Another is that accumulated body wastes cause aging. And another is a theory of autoimmunity which says that organs begin to reject their own tissue. One final explanation is perhaps most important of all: the incidence of disease or accident. Each of these factors probably contributes to aging. By considering all of them together, we gain an overall picture of why body functions often begin to decline in the middle and late years of life.

But body functions do not always decline with age. Two 60-year-olds may look, act, and feel as if there is 30 year's difference in their ages. So, while statistics may show a decline in vision or hearing with age, it is important to remember that the figures reflect a statistical average, not a prediction for each individual. In fact, calculating how much aging of specific organs, systems, and functions can be expected in the average middle-aged person is very difficult. A great deal of the higher incidence of biological deterioration in middle age is caused by poor nutrition and health care in the individual's young life—a factor which many statistical averages do not consider. Other important causes of aging are environmental conditions such as air pollution; genetic factors such as early baldness or more serious inherited disabilities; and chronic illnesses which are found among certain races or classes of the population.

Each of these causes may affect only a limited segment of the population, but they combine to cause a decline in the *average* health statistics for the middle-aged group. However, this does not mean that physical decline is a part of the natural course during the years from 45 to 65. On the contrary, more sophisticated longitudinal studies show that most biological functions do not naturally decline at all in the healthy middle-aged adult. Their evidence points to the conclusion that this period is often not a time of physical decline, and that there is at least as much continuity as change in the middle years of life.

Continuity and Change in Intellectual Functioning

Just as people erroneously assume that physical decline is a necessary part of the natural course of middle age, many also mistakenly think that intelligence declines throughout adulthood. As in the case of some biological misconceptions, this wrong conclusion is caused to some degree by reliance upon research which uses cross-sectional averages without taking personal backgrounds into account (Schaie, 1970). For example, when IQ tests of bright, interested college students are compared with those of whatever 60-year-olds can be found in the neighborhood, the results show lower intelligence scores for the older group. Unfortunately, some studies are done in precisely this way! Clearly, for a comparison to be valid, the cross-sectional subjects must have comparable educational and socioeconomic backgrounds; and this comparable situation is difficult to achieve because college and even high school educations were not as common 20 or 30 years ago as they are today. For this reason, longitudinal studies which measure a person's intelligence at age 20 and then use the same instruments to measure that person's intelligence later in his life, give us much more dependable information about the individual's intellectual growth or decline.

What happens to intelligence as people get older? We may often find ourselves thinking that middle-aged people are less able to learn and perhaps are slower in general than young people. We also are aware that researchers, writers, and academicians often seem to reach their creative peak in middle age. Which of these pictures is accurate? Findings from some of the more recent studies relate some of the contradictory notions we have about intelligence in middle age.

Testable abilities such as word fluency, verbal understanding, reasoning, and space and number conception (Schaie, 1970) are used to measure intelligence. Some researchers have found it useful to divide such abilities into two kinds of intelligence, each of which behaves differently during middle age (Horn, 1970). The "learning" kind of intelligence—which is knowledge that accumulates through education and general acculturation—continues to increase throughout life. While its sharpest rate of growth is during childhood, it shows no decline at all in middle age or even old age. Elements such as verbal reasoning, vocabulary, and spatial perception remain stable or even broaden throughout adulthood. This fact helps to explain why scholars and scientists, whose work is based upon a great deal of accumulated knowledge and experience, are usually much more productive in their 40s, 50s, and even their 70s than they were in their 20s (Dennis, 1966).

But not all elements of intelligence continue to grow during life. "Fluid" intelligence is based upon the central nervous system's development, and it includes abilities such as motor speed, induction, memory, and figural relations. This kind of intelligence peaks early in adolescence, then begins to decline in many adults (Horn, 1970).

Thus, intelligence both increases and wanes with age. Some elements continue to develop throughout life, while others show signs of deterioration. Many psychologists are interested in the causes of decline— the reasons why some people think in radically different ways at the age of 60 from the way they thought at 20. Many factors are involved, and impairment of the nervous system is a primary cause. But at least one researcher (Schaie, 1958) thinks that continuity of intelligence over the life span may be linked strongly to another aspect of personality: the individual's overall flexibility. Evidence to support this hypothesis is still fairly scanty, but the suggestion that the stability of intelligence is associated with other areas of the personality is an interesting one which will be receiving more study. It also leads us to another question, and to another area of adult development. What happens to personality as people grow older?

Personality Continuity and Change

The "theory of disengagement" is a description of the changes that take place in personality through adulthood (Cumming & Henry, 1961; Neugarten, 1964). This theory pictures the process of aging as a gradual, mutual withdrawal of the individual from society and of society from the individual. As people grow older, their involvements and emotional attachments narrow first to a few friends or family; but eventually—often as a result of physical ailments—they become primarily preoccupied with themselves.

We cannot doubt that this theory describes what happens to many people as they grow older. And this stereotyped picture of the active, assertive young man who changes into a doddering, compliant, aged man has received some support from research (Neugarten, 1964;

Rosen & Bibring, 1968). But many psychologists think that the disengagement theory is not an accurate description of the aging process at all, because it treats aging too uniformly and sets "old age" apart as almost a separate segment of life unrelated to the rest of the developmental progression. (Perhaps it is also too easy a rationalization for isolating the aged!) If people are different during childhood, adolescence, and young adulthood, then why should they not age in very different ways, too (Maas & Kuypers, 1974)? Some longitudinal studies have looked at changes in personality occurring over a span of several years during adulthood. They give us some interesting pictures of the sharply different ways in which different people change as they grow older.

THE LONGITUDINAL STUDIES. One study (Maas & Kuypers, 1974) was an outgrowth of the Berkeley growth study. It began in 1928 as a study of children's development, collecting in-depth data on both children and their parents. When a follow-up of the children was made about 40 years later, the researchers decided to visit the parents, too, to see how they had changed. Among the total of 142 parents who were available for the second study, the researchers found a wide diversity both in the personalities of the older people and in their styles of growing old. They divided the personality types into several general categories: person-oriented mothers; autonomous mothers; fearful-ordering mothers; anxious-asserting mothers; person-oriented fathers; conservative-oriented fathers; and active-competent fathers. These types reflect general styles of outlook and of coping. They also show different degrees of social involvement and interests, of self-confidence and anxiety. For example, the person-oriented mother is outgoing, interested in others, dependable, self-confident, and relaxed. She had developed a successful method of coping with the changing world around her. The fearful-ordering mother has difficulty coping with aging. Instead, she is full of anxiety; she has few interests ("I don't have anything to live for anymore"); and, in effect, she has withdrawn into a very constricted life space.

A different longitudinal study was done in Kansas City, where subjects between the ages of 49 and 90 were interviewed over a span of 5½ years (Williams & Wirths, 1965). Like the Berkeley study, this research found that middle-aged and older adults, just as young people, have different outlooks and styles of interacting with their worlds.

A few general categories were drawn up to describe the various ways in which the subjects interacted with their environment. There are six self-explanatory types of life-styles: familism; couplehood; living fully; world of work (a more functional kind of interaction with the outside world than in living fully); living alone; and easing through life with minimal involvement. The first three styles represent a generally positive, highly satisfying relationship between the individual and his social context, a style the writers call *gemeinschaft*. For example, a widow of 72 describes herself as full of "wim, wam, and wigger." She had two husbands and both of them died, but she never seemed to lose her hold on life. She had always kept herself busy with children or employment or organizations, and she continued to fill her days with activities and social contacts.

The last three styles of interaction, called *gesellschaft*, reflect more withdrawal from the world; and individuals with these life-styles usually showed anomie, alienation, and isolation to some degree. The theory of disengagement would have predicted these as the dominant and more satisfying pattern. But the Kansas City study found that only 58 of its subjects fell into the *gesellschaft* set, while 110 subjects, the vast majority, had *gemeinschaft* life-styles.

PERSONALITY DEVELOPMENT AND SUCCESSFUL AGING. Both the Kansas City study and the Berkeley study in particular found continuity in personality between young adulthood and old age. Women who showed high anxiety as young mothers (the fearful-ordering and anxious-asserting types) were very consistent in showing the same characteristics in old age; and, in general, there was more continuity in women's personalities than in men's over the adult years. Perhaps this was because women had to develop styles of coping early, as they adjusted to important changes with the birth of their children and later with the children's leaving home. The findings also showed that the

A middle-aged woman instructs a younger employee. (*Mark Jury, Rapho/Photo Researchers.*)

individuals who began to withdraw from life in their later years had started to "disengage" even as young people, and that most of the highly energetic older people had always been very outward-oriented.

From these studies, a picture of successful aging emerges (Williams & Wirths, 1965). In large part, successful aging requires a series of good adjustments to the dramatic changes in life-style that take place during adulthood—forming intimate relationships, finding meaningful work, parenting, having children leave home, retiring, experiencing widowhood. What is a "good adjustment"? One of the most important elements seems to be an active exchange of energy between the individual and his environment. The well-adjusted individual is autonomous, rather than dependent, and can give as well as take. This balance of energy seems to be most vital and positive where the individual's life space—that is, the range and amplitude of his social contacts and interests—is realistically far-reaching and flexible. The person who has many interests is less concerned with withdrawing or disengaging. And if he is flexible enough to adjust to the changes that happen to him, then he is less likely to become lost or isolated when a loved one dies or when a broken hip forces him to take it easy. A final element in successful aging is, of course, satisfaction with life, and this usually accompanies the active energy exchange, the wide interests, and the flexibility of the most contented agers.

While the longitudinal studies give us a fairly good picture of adult personality development, they suggest a few qualifiers which the reader should keep in mind. First, the subjects of the studies are admittedly not quite run-of-the-mill. The kinds of people who are willing to volunteer for a series of in-depth interviews over a period of time are generally above average in both education and economic status. This second factor undoubtedly adds to the degree of life satisfaction in later years, for a comfortable economic situation allows people to divide their time as they like between work or responsibilities, and hobbies or recreation. The longitudinal subjects were also above average in health, a factor which may be related to their economic well-being.

Another qualifier is the element of bias in the researchers themselves. Social scientists are not always unbiased, and sometimes it is virtually impossible not to reflect some of the values of the cultural context. For example, some of the studies on authoritarian personality which followed World War II (Adorno et al., 1950) were done as objectively as possible, but they could not help but reflect some of the general horror with which people viewed German authoritarianism during the war.

The longitudinal studies, too, use thorough, scientific methods of collecting and analyzing data, but personal biases may still creep into the final interpretations and conclusions. The personality types delineated in the Berkeley study seem to rate some qualities as positive in men but negative in women. The active-competent father shares many traits with the anxious-assertive mother. But in the case of the woman, assertiveness means tension, restlessness, and dissatisfaction instead of confidence, directness, and capability. How much of this differentiation is caused by society itself—by the fact that assertive women may be made to feel anxious because they do not fit into the stereotype of the passive female? And how much represents a value judgment on the part of the researcher? Sometimes it is impossible to separate the study from its context.

Another area where value judgments seem to creep into studies of personality and aging is in the attempts to define successful aging. Who is to say what constitutes success for different personality types? Here, social research cannot be separated from the researchers' general overview of meaningful life.

Most of developmental theory has been concerned with the patterns which are set in the early years of life. There are some theories that relate to limited areas of adult development—for instance, mini-theories about leadership training and the like, or the Dale Carnegie type of self-improvement concept, or theory about specific changes that can be brought about by therapy. There are also theories advanced by biologists, sociologists, and anthropologists which describe how certain physical or cultural changes may affect adult life. But aside from a few longitudinal studies, there is relatively little theory or even hard data about how individual people change over their entire life spans.

LIFELONG DEVELOPMENT: THE ADULT YEARS
Theories of Adult Development

The main reason for this lack of data is that psychologists have only recently recognized that adults "grow," too. Jung (1933) was one of the first to emphasize the second half of life, when he talked about the need of older people to find meaning in their own lives. Frenkel-Brunswik's description of the five stages of life, which we mentioned earlier in this chapter, was another piece of pioneering work, as was Buhler's study of the role of goal setting in personality development (Bühler & Massarik, 1968). But none of these offers an all-encompassing theory of lifelong development.

PECK'S EXTENSION OF ERIKSON. Erikson did describe a lifelong process of development, as we saw in Chapter 2. When we looked at Erikson's eight ages of man earlier in this book, we dealt mainly with the first six developmental steps. But the later years of life also present important issues to each person, and Peck (1968) has been especially concerned with expanding Erikson's picture of the second half of life.

Peck's main criticism of Erikson has been that the eight ages of man stress the first 20 to 25 years of life too heavily. The six developmental issues of trust versus mistrust, autonomy versus doubt, initiative versus guilt, industry versus inferiority, identity versus role confusion, and intimacy versus isolation—all pose important conflicts that each individual must resolve in these early years. But what of the last 40 to 50 years of life?

During these later years, all of the earlier issues and their resolutions reappear from time to time. A sudden physical impairment such as a heart attack, may bring on struggles with autonomy, dependence, and crisis in the 45-year-old; the death of a husband may renew strong intimacy needs in a woman. In fact, each major life adjustment necessitates some revisions and reevaluations of old solutions to problems. In addition, Erikson describes two new developmental issues or conflicts that arise in adulthood: a seventh issue of generativity versus self-absorption, and an eighth issue of integrity versus despair. In the seventh stage, the individual either finds satisfying, productive outlets for his energies or sinks into boredom and stagnation; and in the eighth stage, he looks upon his life either with satisfaction or with despair.

Peck agrees that these seventh and eighth stages are important developmental issues in adult life. But he thinks that there are too many altogether new issues arising in these years to be summed up in only two developmental tasks. (In practice there is actually only one task, for the issue of generativity is often resolved by persons when they are in their 30s.) During this time, some critical changes take place in every individual's life. Events such as children leaving home, career stagnation, and retirement force each person to redirect his energies toward new interests. Physical disabilities may put a crimp in activities which were once important sources of satisfaction. The death of a loved one may leave a great emotional void. Unemployment, social upheaval, and changes in financial status may place constraints on a once stable lifestyle. In an attempt to account for these special challenges of adult life, Peck proposes seven issues or conflicts of adult development.

The first four issues are particularly important in middle age. As his physical stamina and health begin to wane, the individual must make an adjustment, shifting a good part of his energies into mental instead of physical activities. Peck calls this adjustment *valuing wisdom versus valuing physical powers*. A second developmental task is to find a new balance between *socializing versus sexualizing* in human relationships. This, too, is an adjustment which is imposed on the individual by social constraints as well as by biological changes; his changing physical state makes him redefine his relationships with both men and women to stress companionship rather than sexual intimacy or competitiveness. A third dimension is *cathectic (or emotional) flexibility versus cathectic impoverishment*. Emotional flexibility, as we saw earlier in some of the longitudinal studies, underlies all of the adjustments people must make in middle age, as families and friends split up and as old interests and jobs stop being the central focus of life. In the same way, *mental flexibility versus mental rigidity* is another basic conflict where the ability to make adjustments underlies all of the changes of the adult years. Mental flexibility means avoiding the inclination to become too set in one's ways or too cautious to be open to new ideas. Mental rigidity is the tendency to become dominated by one's experiences and old judgments—to decide, for example, that "I've disapproved of democrats (or communists, or Catholics) all my life, so I don't see why I should change my mind now."

A sense of competency at his work and the respect of fellow workers contribute to a person's feeling of self-esteem. (*Franz Kraus, DPI.*)

Three additional dimensions are particularly important in the years of old age, but the individual is already beginning to deal with these issues during middle age. The first of these is *ego differentiation versus work-role preoccupation*. If an individual bases his definition of his own worth upon his job (or family), then retirement, or a change in occupation, or the children's leaving home will produce an enormous gulf in which the individual is likely to flounder. The second conflict, *body transcendence versus body preoccupation*, centers around the individual's ability to keep from becoming too preoccupied with the increasing aches, pains, and physical annoyances that accompany age. A third dimension particularly important in old age is *ego transcendence versus ego preoccupation*. This requires the ability to avoid becoming mired in thoughts of death (the "night of the ego," as Peck calls it). The successful ager, as in Erikson's theory, transcends the prospect of his own extinction by becoming involved in the younger generation—the legacy that will outlive him after he is gone.

Like the earlier ages of man which Erikson described, none of Peck's dimensions is confined just to middle age or old age. The decisions made early in life act as building blocks for all the solutions of the adult years, and the middle-aged man is already starting to resolve the issues of old age. In fact, research suggests that the period from age 50 to 60 is often a critical time for making many of the adjustments which will determine the way the individual lives out the rest of his years (Peck & Berkowitz, 1964). Cross-sectional data show that subjects in their 50s measured lower on satisfaction with life and on feelings of effectiveness in dealing with their environment than people in either their 40s or their 60s—a finding that seems at least tentatively to support the picture of the middle-age slump or mid-career crisis we saw earlier in this chapter.

LOEVINGER'S STAGES OF EGO DEVELOPMENT. Another picture of personality development has received a good deal of attention in the past few years, and it provides a way of looking at lifelong growth that is an alternate to the theory of Peck and Erikson.

Loevinger's stages of ego development are not so much a theory as a set of descriptive stages that have roots in many theories and also have strong theoretical implications. The development of the ego, or self-concept, is described in six stages which begin after the infant has recognized himself as a being separate from his mother. Each of the six stages is prerequisite for the next, but Loevinger assumes that few people actually reach the last stage of full ego integration.

The first stage is the *impulse-ridden* stage. The young child controls himself only when he anticipates external punishments or controls. His main concern is to gratify his wants and needs. The second stage is the *opportunistic* stage. Now the individual sees more order in the social world, but he attempts to bend it to fit his own desires. He is still exploitative; but since he recognizes the value of expediency too, he may often appear to be self-controlled. An example is the 5-year-old who controls his desire to steal his older brother's cookie because he knows he will be hit if he is caught.

Stage three is the *conformist* stage. Here the structure and order of society begins to take on a meaning of its own for the individual. Rules are followed because they are there; and disobedience causes feelings of shame because the individual knows that others disapprove. It becomes part of the self-concept to be able to conform and to obey the rules of society. In the *conscientious* stage, the individual has gone a step farther. He has developed a set of principles for himself which he uses to guide his own ideals, actions, and achievements. Instead of shame, he now feels genuine guilt for his transgressions.

In the *autonomous* stage, the individual's evolving principles for himself are somewhat apart from the social world in which he lives. This situation may present a sort of conflict of interests, where the individual must deal with the difference between his own needs, principles, and duties and those demanded by society. The final, *integrated* stage represents the individual's resolution of the conflicting demands which posed problems in the fifth stage. This reconciliation allows him to be at ease with himself and to have an integrated sense of identity or ego. Few people reach this stage. When they do, it is usually late in life, after many years of accumulated experience, wisdom, and self-knowledge.

Through his experience as a father, a man may gain new perspectives about his own feelings. (*Bill Mahan, Rapho/Photo Researchers.*)

Loevinger's stages have much in common with Kohlberg's stages of moral development. Both see personality growth as being heavily influenced by cognitive or intellectual functions: the adult develops by thinking about himself, setting up ideals and rules for himself, and then attempting to meet these expectations. Both Kohlberg and Loevinger see that the degree of integrity in the individual's self-demands increases along a continuum of greater and greater maturity. They see behavior not simply in terms of adaptability or conformity to the social order, but in terms of individual growth. Loevinger's picture of ego development has elements of other theories besides Kohlberg's. It draws heavily from psychoanalytic theory and particularly from more recent ego psychology. The early stages reflect the ego's incorporation of the social code; the later stages represent a rational balance of forces. Finally, the theory shares many ideas with the humanistic views of development that we saw in Chapter 2, especially Maslow's idea of man's lifelong striving toward autonomy, integrity, and self-actualization.

Loevinger's stages of ego development share some common elements with Peck's theory, too. Both are pictures of lifelong development. In this they differ from childhood developmental theory, which stresses external forces—the reinforcement, punishment, and modeling with which parents, teachers, and even TV programs socialize the youngster—as the major factors in individual growth. Instead, Peck and Loevinger emphasize the role of thought and the rational processes in personal growth. As students of adult development, they give more of the initiative to the adult, putting heavy emphasis on the integrative function of the self-concept and identifying specific elements of the self-concept (such as flexibility or autonomy) which seem to be the most crucial in personality development.

Personality Repair or Continued Growth?

There has been a good deal of controversy among personality theorists, clinical psychologists, and psychiatrists as to the nature of personality development during adulthood. Throughout this chapter, we have been looking at the ways in which people change and the ways they stay the same during the years of middle age. Is the primary task of adult personality development the reintegration and repair of personality, or is adulthood also a time of new growth and change?

Many people assume that adult personality development is mostly a process of repair, working out problems caused by faulty development in the earlier stages. The assumption is that most of us were somewhat "bent out of shape" by our early socialization or development. Some people were overly inhibited, overly restrained, or burdened with unreasonable expectations, excessive guilt, or anxiety. Others were undersocialized, allowed to live in relative chaos with inadequate controls and conflicting social demands. According to this view, the task of adult development is to iron out the old conflicts of dependency and autonomy, to correct old coping problems, and to overcome conditioned anxieties. This is a pretty pessimistic view of human beings, for it sees adults—like old dogs who cannot learn new tricks—as being able to do little more than repair old mistakes.

In contrast to this view, some theorists, and probably many more in recent years, see adult development as potentially a process of continued growth. This view of lifelong development owes much to the humanistic psychology branch. In Maslow's terms, the individual is constantly "becoming." He never arrives at a point where he can say, "This is me," with finality—not at age 30, not at 40, not even at 70. O'Connell & O'Connell (1974) suggest four key dimensions to this process of becoming. First, we never stop learning who we are and what our world is all about. Second, we never stop growing in awareness of our emotional needs and the emotional needs of others. Third, we never stop trying to be ourselves and to direct our own destinies. And fourth, we never stop trying to find a meaningful and comfortable fit between ourselves and our world.

Personality integration can be a lifelong process which begins with birth and ends with death. The thoroughly integrated, fully functioning

Adult development can be a process of continued growth. (*Betty Moriarty.*)

18-year-old is not the same organism, nor has he reached the same stage of maturity or integration or autonomy, as the 50- or 60-year-old who has continued growing for another 30 or 40 years. The woman from the Kansas City study who was still full of "wim, wam, and wigger" at 72 had never stopped changing and growing to meet the challenges presented by the changes in herself and in her environment. Theorists like Peck, Loevinger, Maslow, and Kohlberg see adult development as more than a process of repair. They view it as a process of genuine growth in the later, as well as the early, years of life; and the evidence we have seen in this chapter seems to support this picture of lifelong growth.

Middle age covers roughly the years from age 40 to 65, although there are so many kinds of social, biological, and psychological cues that different people may think of themselves as middle-aged at different ages. It is a time for the individual to adjust to the realization that he is no longer young and his future no longer holds unlimited possibilities. The result is that middle age often includes a time of crisis.

SUMMARY

There are elements of both continuity and change in the years of adulthood. Biologically, body abilities may begin to slow down in certain ways, but there is often no need for physical decline to accompany middle age unless accidents, disease, poor nutrition, or poor health care interfere. Many aspects of intelligence continue to develop throughout middle age, although presumably the fluid intelligence begins to decline in many adults. Longitudinal studies show that some threads of personality change little throughout life, especially tendencies toward high anxiety. In other ways, people may change a great deal with age. Their satisfaction with their lives is an important element in their aging successfully.

Unlike child development psychology, most lifelong development theory assigns the individual much of the initiative for his own growth during the adult years. Theorists like Peck and Loevinger stress the challenges of adulthood and the kinds of qualities, such as the ability to adjust to change, that help the individual to continue to grow long after the age of 30.

REVIEW QUESTIONS

1. How does adult development differ from personality development in childhood?

2. What are the elements of continuity and change in intelligence during the adult years?

3. Drawing upon the work of Peck and Loevinger and upon the longitudinal studies, describe the personality elements which enable an individual to age successfully.

4. What is the mid-career crisis and why does it happen?

SUGGESTED READINGS

Huyck, M. H. *Growing older.* Englewood Cliffs, N.J.: Prentice-Hall, 1974. Many of the issues and controversies of middle age and aging are discussed.

Maslow, A. H. *Toward a psychology of being.* New York: Van Nostrand, 1968. This classic work by the well-known humanist discusses many of the issues adults must cope with in order to develop fully as human beings.

May, R. *Man's search for himself.* New York: New American Library, 1953. As a writer of the "third force," May suggests that one advantage of this age of insecurity and confusion is that man must search within himself for strength and direction.

21

AGING, RETIREMENT, AND REFLECTION

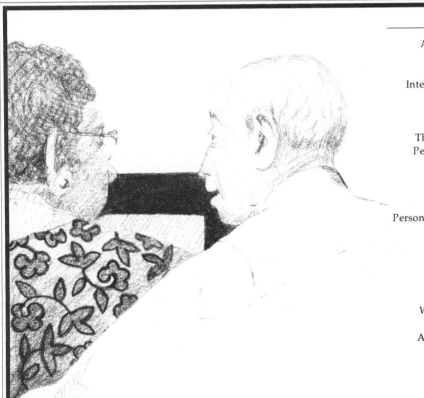

What is it like to grow old? To many people, the prospects are so grim that they do not ever want to find out. Some recent research showed that nearly 25 percent of persons interviewed wanted to die before their time (Kastenbaum, 1971). In fact, most people today seem to view old age almost as a state of marginal existence. They fear the loss of energy, creativity, flexibility, sexuality, physical mobility, memory, and even intelligence, which they think goes hand-in-hand with great age.

In our society, the elderly have a higher poverty rate and a lower education level than most of the population. Nursing homes have recently gained notoriety as places where old people have been taken advantage of and have been given enough care to subsist but little reason to want to live. And until recent minority movements began to voice the needs of the aged, most people assumed that the elderly were not even able to speak for themselves. No wonder old age seems such a horrible fate to many people!

But people have not always dreaded growing old. In the Bible, elders were usually considered to possess great wisdom and stature. In many societies, such as the American Indian tribes, the old have traditionally been venerated as the wise elders, the transmitters of the culture, the storehouse of the historical past. In Thailand, age is the greatest determinant of status and old people are given seats of honor everywhere, from public meetings to the family dinner table (Cowgill, 1972b). Even a century ago in our own culture, the elderly received more respect than they do today. Why is it that there seems to be no place for old people in the modern world?

One reason is that there are so many more older people today than there ever were before (Neugarten, 1970). Modern medicine helps many to survive serious illnesses. A side effect of this is that many people live on with serious impairments which necessitate constant medical care. Another reason is that the Social Security Act of 1935 set an arbitrary cutoff point at age 65 to determine who is old. Ever since then, many healthy 65-year-olds who would otherwise have 5, 10, or even 20 more good years of productivity have found themselves out of the work force instead, with little to keep themselves occupied (Cowgill, 1972a; de Beauvoir, 1972; Neugarten, 1970, 1971). There has been such a lack of interest in the aged, too, that until the past few years there was almost no research at all on old people. Neugarten (1970) uses the word *age-ism* to describe this attitude of indifference and neglect with which the American society and many other modern societies view the elderly.

In this chapter, we shall try to answer some questions about the last years of life. Is the old person really just a "shadow of his former self"? How do people react to being old—do 65-year-olds still want to die before their time? And what kind of advice can the developmental psychologist (and the old person himself) give society regarding ways to meet the needs of the elderly? We carry with us many attitudes and stereotypes about the aged that color our thoughts, our actions, and our social policies but are not necessarily true. We shall devote most of this chapter to finding out what is, in fact, the truth about growing old.

What happens in 45 years to change a 25-year-old quarterback into a sedentary, fragile old man of 70? What elements of the aging process are predictable, and which are caused by totally unpredictable factors? To answer these questions, we shall look at several different causes of physical aging.

As we saw in Chapter 3, some of the reasons people age are genetic. We inherit many of the more obvious changes in physical appearance that take place with aging. The aging of identical twins, for instance, points out how clear and predictable are such characteristics as balding, the accumulation of wrinkles, or the tendency to shrink a few inches. Longevity also seems to be related to genetic factors, because long-lived parents are more likely to have children who will live to a ripe old age.

A number of biological factors are important, too. Some biological changes seem to be fairly predictable. Decreased energy level, the body's reduced ability to recover from stress, and a lessening of sensory efficiency are very likely to accompany the aging process. Deafness is an example of a sensory defect to which older people are prone,

AGING: CHANGES IN THE BODY AND THE MIND
Physical Aging and Illness

A person's evaluation of his own health is very subjective, often differing considerably from his doctor's evaluation. (*Bruce Roberts, Rapho/Photo Researchers.*)

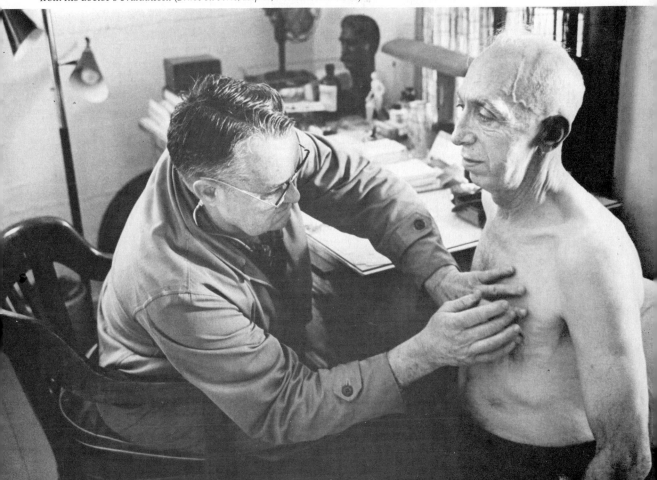

especially with regard to higher frequency tones. Less than 1 percent of individuals aged 10 to 19 have a hearing loss of 45 decibels for tones above 3,520 cycles per second (the higher sounds we make in speech, including the sounds such as s, sh, ch, and f), but 45 percent of men over 60 have a high frequency hearing loss of at least this magnitude (Shock, 1952b). The rate of blindness and loss of visual acuity increases sharply after the age of 60. Both visual and hearing impairment may have important effects on the individual, because his perception, and therefore his ability to communicate, is hindered. Poor hearing may have an especially isolating effect, for it is not always as correctable as is visual impairment. Another sense to decline with age is the sense of smell. In addition, both fine motor coordination and the speed of reaction time tend to decrease with age (Botwinik, 1970; Shock, 1952a).

These sensory and motor slowdowns commonly accompany age. But not all old people show these signs of aging, so we cannot say that the predictable biological course of nature is the only explanation for physical aging. In fact, many of the defects and problems of old age are the result of interference with the course of nature (see Chapter 20). Many people who become deaf in old age have had some kind of accident or illness——for example, a firecracker which went off too close to the ear in childhood—which started at least the initial phases of deafness earlier in life. Similarly, for most sensory deficiencies and defects of the internal organs, there have been individual precipitating events which began the process of decline. Lifelong smokers may develop cancer in later years; an old woman with back problems may have begun to suffer strain as a young mother picking up her children; a 65-year-old man with heart trouble may have had early warning signs with a brief illness at the age of 40. Therefore, we cannot conclude that the biological changes that come about with age are all predictable. The kind of life the individual has lead, the types of illnesses or accidents that he has experienced, and the number of years he had to live in order to undergo many such experiences—all add together to cause him to age and to age in ways that are different from anyone else.

Just as important as the physical changes that affect the individual is the psychological impact of these changes: the way the individual's image of himself changes. If the older person is aware of his creaking joints, the brittleness of his bones, his shortness of breath, and his longer reaction time, he will probably need to change certain attitudes about himself. Some activities, such as driving a car, he may eventually have to stop completely. In other activities, he may become more cautious; he may feel more awkward doing them or derive less pleasure from them than he used to. He may cut down on his after-dinner constitutionals, for example, because he feels weak and fears catching cold out-of-doors.

Sometimes the individual's physical changes force him to make major psychological adjustments. This is especially true in cases where aging seems to occur suddenly. After a prolonged illness or a serious fall, the individual may find that he has turned into an old man overnight, before he is ready. He is not able to regain his usual energy level, muscle tone, and quickness of thought or action. The suddenness of such a drastic change may cause considerable confusion, stress, and frustration.

Much of aging is the result of a combination of physical and psychological factors and cognitive decline. One phenomenon, called "imminence of death," shows how these elements can be so simultaneous that it is impossible to categorize which causes which. Imminence of death is a marked decline which sometimes occurs in the last year or so before death. It does not always follow the same pattern. In fact, one of the first ways it was noted was when a nurse at a home for the aged said she could predict which patients would die soon because they "just seemed to act differently" (Lieberman, 1965). Studies have tried to pinpoint the individual changes which cause them to act differently. These persons show a marked decline in several areas of cognitive functioning, such as memory span and ability to organize and integrate stimuli, as well as more generalized deterioration in reaction time, general energy level, and the ability to cope with the demands of the environment (Lieberman, 1965; Reimanis & Green, 1971; Sanderson & Inglis, 1961).

It is clear that psychological factors are significant in the sharp physical and mental declines before death. Within 2 years after the death of a spouse, for example, there is a high death rate for the surviving widow or widower. The psychological sense of loss seems to be a direct cause of biological decline. In other senses, psychological shrinkage is caused by physical and cognitive deterioration. Certain biological and physical aging processes, once they get started, may snowball rapidly, causing the individual to withdraw into himself in the last months of life. It was thought that this withdrawal was caused by a sudden preoccupation with physical problems, but at least one researcher thinks it has a different origin (Lieberman, 1965). The individual has to make such an overwhelming effort to cope with the disruption and disequilibrium of his whole body system that he has no energy to interact with other people. Thus, psychological factors are both causes and effects of many of the steep declines in the last months of life.

Many cultural and intellectual functions do not decline at all with old age. (*Irene Bayer/ Monkmeyer.*)

Most of us have a preconception of aging as a time of intellectual demise. The epitome of this stereotype is the senile old woman who cannot remember how to finish the sentence she has just started, or who has erased 70 years of her life by thinking she is a child of 10 again. As we saw in Chapter 20, many cross-sectional studies which ignored differences in education or economic level reinforced the picture of cognitive decline, if not senility, as part of the aging process.

How accurate is the preconception of mental decline in old age? Recent research shows that many intellectual functions do not decline at all in old age, but one key function does degenerate. And the weakening of this function, short-term memory, makes the older person seem to slow down in many other mental processes.

Intellectual and Cognitive Changes with Age

SHORT-TERM MEMORY AND DECLINES IN LEARNING. There are two types of memory. Long-term memory involves information and experiences which have been accumulated over years. This kind of memory usually holds up quite well with age. Short-term memory (STM) is the type we use to remember a phone number from the time we look it up to the time we dial it. It is similar to a limited storage area that holds information for a relatively brief period of time until we can code and store it. Older people often report considerable difficulty with STM. They cannot remember a phone number; they forget the name of someone to whom they were just introduced. They have difficulty following long, involved directions, filling out forms, and taking tests which are geared to a faster, younger pace of thinking. This difficulty with STM hampers older people in some intelligence tests.

Short-term memory is central to several learning processes that would otherwise not decline with age (Welford, 1958). Processes of synthesis, analysis, comparison, and other kinds of organization often do not break down at all with age. The problem in learning occurs, instead, because the individual loses the pieces of information before he is able to process, code, or store them. This is especially true when there is some complication in remembering or organizing information. Some experiments (Kirchner, 1958) tested both old and young people by having them face a row of 12 lights which went on and off randomly, 1 at a time. When subjects were asked to press a key below the light that had just flicked off, older people did about as well as the younger subjects. But when subjects were asked to press the button "one back"— the button below the next-to-the-last light to go off—or "two back," or "three back," older people did significantly worse. This indicates that problems with STM in old age are not so much in simple recall as in the process of retaining information through interference or shifts in attention (Kirchner, 1958; Welford, 1958, 1964).

COGNITIVE STABILITY AND INDIVIDUAL DIFFERENCES. While the decline of STM affects many areas of the older person's functioning, there are also many areas where mental performance does not naturally decline at all with age. Verbal facility continues very well. And certain factors of judgment, most areas of learning retention, and many well-practiced verbal abilities, such as those used in a lifelong profession, seem to be sustained quite well even in advanced age (Arenburg, 1973).

In the areas of intelligence performance that do seem to decline with age, a few important facts should also be considered. There is very wide individual variation in the rates of deterioration, so that despite the averages, many 70-year-olds are perfectly able to do better on intelligence tests than many 30-year-olds. Individuals who have received a great deal of education tend to show greater resistance to decline; so do people with high intelligence. Recent programs like the Third Age College in Toulouse, France, and Fordham University's College at Sixty in New York are designed to give older people a chance to continue learning. Perhaps the use of continuing education will be the answer to the problem of keeping older people in good mental condition and prolonging their vital interests and cognitive abilities.

Another factor besides educational level is the individual's history of disease or accidents. The person who has had a serious stroke has probably suffered serious damage because of insufficient oxygen in certain centers of the brain. As a result, he may lose some skills such as speaking or walking, or some areas of the memory may simply be blacked out. These functions have to be completely relearned. This kind of disability is not part of the normal aging process at all; but it is far more common in older people than younger people, and it is a very important contributor to the decline in cognitive and psychomotor functions found in testing older populations.

PERSONALITY AND AGING

Problems of ill health, poverty, deterioration of vision, and loss of memory are common burdens of the elderly. We tend to think that people just have to learn to cope with these handicaps. But for the older person who cannot expect ever to work his way out of these problems, they mean severe restrictions on his autonomy. They require the individual to make adjustment from thinking of himself as his own person to realizing that he must depend upon others. The person who formerly took care of his own needs but now must ask others to help, even in simple tasks like getting dressed, feels demeaned and even dehumanized. Whether he must learn to live with massive or minor inconveniences, the individual usually finds that being old is not easy.

Some people adjust well, others do not. Peck's term "body preoccupation" (see Chapter 20) and Shanas's term "health pessimism" (Shanas et al., 1968) describe the tendency of some old people to become overwhelmed by the limitations of their bodies. "Body transcendence" describes the ability to find life satisfying despite changes in health; "health optimism" describes a similar state, although the term refers more specifically to the individual who often resorts to pretending his health problems do not exist.

Findings indicate that the older person's physical evaluation is often a good measure of his psychological well-being (Shanas et al., 1968). Many elderly people have real ailments but consider them as "little aches and pains." Others are in relatively good health but magnify the minor problems that they have. The sicker people think they are, the more lonely and alienated they are likely to be. What determines the way people adjust to the physical and emotional problems of old age?

The level of interest in the world and receptivity to new ideas reflect individual personality patterns more than chronological age. (*Betsy Wyckoff.*)

Theories of Adjustment to Aging

There are only a few major theories of adjustment to aging—most of them little more than hypothesized explanations—and we shall look briefly at three of them. The *theory of disengagement*, as we saw in Chapter 20, sees the process of aging as a mutual withdrawal of the

Activity level varies widely among the elderly just as it does among people of other ages. It is generally continuous with the pattern of the earlier years. *(Joel Gordon.)*

individual from society and of society from the individual (Cumming & Henry, 1961). According to the theory, this withdrawal is natural and even beneficial, because the aging individual's shrinking of life space is suited to his decreased physical and psychic energy. Thus, while social and emotional involvements and outside interests and activities become less important, the individual still maintains a feeling of life satisfaction because his investments still fill his decreased needs.

The *activity theory* presents a different picture of old age. According to this theory, the pattern of withdrawal that characterizes many persons' last years is the result of society's withdrawing from those individuals, usually against their wishes. Older people stay most satisfied with life if they remain active and involved, resisting the isolating effects of social attitudes toward the aged. According to the activity theory, the older person is gratified by his ability to adjust to his changing life. People who retire must find substitutes for their work; individuals who lose a spouse must try to find new friends to fill the emotional gap.

The *role exit theory* (Blau, 1973) says essentially the same thing as the activity theory, but from a more sociological perspective. It describes old age as a time when a number of roles are terminated (and when others must be found as substitutes). A role exit is the cessation of a stable pattern of social interaction, and old age is characterized by many such exits. Friends die; children and grandchildren move far away; physical ailments curtail activities; monetary restrictions force the individual to move to a small apartment in a strange neighborhood. Most of these role exits truly signal the end of lifetime attachments. When one exit follows another in rapid succession, as they often do in old age, the cumulative effect can be devastating. Role exit describes only part of the process though, for the individual must try to adjust to his losses by finding new, substitute interests. Where he succeeds in finding replacements, the process is one of both role exit and renewal.

FITTING THE THEORIES TO REALITY. All of these theories describe changes and adjustments that are central to the later years of life. Each points toward its own notion of how the successful ager adapts to old age. The disengagement theory supports a natural and satisfying slowdown, while both the activity theory and the role exit theory see a high level of involvement as the key to successful aging. Most research, such as the longitudinal studies we saw in Chapter 20, considers high activity to be the best way for the older person to transcend the physical and cognitive declines and the role exits of old age.

But high activity may not be the answer for all older people (Maddox, 1968a; Neugarten, 1965). The person who has been happily involved in personal interests all his life, without much social interaction, will feel awkward and unhappy if he suddenly feels he must start joining organizations and making social calls at age 70. There are as many different personality types in old age as there are in youth.

Some individuals may be happier if they remain disengaged from the outside world, rather than participate actively in it.

Bernice Neugarten (1965) studied several people who were between the ages of 70 and 79. She found that there were a number of different personality types in the group, and that each type had different needs for interacting with the social environment. Some individuals, whom she termed the "reorganizers," were highly active and happy in their social involvements. They fit the picture described by the activity and role exit theories. So did another group, the "holders-on." These people kept frenetically, but happily, active, thinking that this was the only way to ward off old age. But not everyone needed to be active to stay happy. The "focused" persons had sharply narrowed their fields of activity as they grew older, devoting their energies to just one or two roles such as being a grandfather or tending the backyard garden. Despite their reduced activity, these people were highly satisfied with their life-styles. Another group, the "disengaged," were content with almost no social interaction at all. This rocking-chair approach to old age involves a voluntary withdrawal from previous role commitments. While this role may be antithetical to the theories of high involvement, some older people are content with it.

Personality Changes in Later Life

While there are few universal personality changes that occur in later life, some researchers have studied whether any distinct pattern of personality change can be observed as people grow old. One study used Thematic Apperception Test (TAT) cards to determine the way middle-aged and older men from the Kansas City longitudinal sample (see Chapter 20) viewed their world (Gutman, 1964). It found that the 40-year-old man tended to view his environment as being within his control, rewarding boldness and risk taking; he saw himself as possessing energy equal to the challenges presented by the outside world. In contrast, the 60-year-old saw the world as more complex and dangerous, no longer within his power and to be changed according to his will. Instead, he saw himself conforming and accommodating to his environment. Gutman called this the shift from *active* to *passive mastery*.

Other studies which used TAT scores to evaluate the Kansas City sample found other patterns of universal change with age. They noticed trends toward increased eccentricity and lessened sensitivity to others over the middle and late years of life (Shukin & Neugarten, 1964). They observed a tendency toward inner preoccupation (Neugarten & Gutman, 1964) and a decreased ability to deal with challenging situations or wide ranges of stimuli (Neugarten & Gutman, 1964; Rosen & Neugarten, 1964). In general, these studies all showed a gradual shrinking of life space as the individual approaches and enters old age.

Does this mean that there are universal patterns of change? From the evidence we have, the kinds of patterns which show up seem to depend upon the type of methodology used. Other studies of the same Kansas City sample (see Chapters 1, 2, and 8) employed the interview

Emotional ties and the responsibility for another person may have a greater effect on adjustment than chronogical age. *(Grete Mannheim/DPI.)*

technique, a methodology aimed at measuring the individual's ability to get along with his environment as well as the "inner space" evaluated in TAT scores. These studies showed far greater disparity among various personality types within each group than between different age groups. They showed no consistent change in life orientation and values from middle to old age. Instead, personal factors such as work status, health, financial soundness, and marital status had the greatest impact upon the individual's outlook and activities.

RETIREMENT   Of all the events which influence a person's later years, retirement has perhaps the greatest impact. It is a way of life in old age. It is so important that in our society at least, we tend to define old age as synonymous with retirement from the work force (Cowgill, 1972a). We usually think of old age as beginning at age 65, when people generally become eligible for full social security and other benefits. Clearly, retirement is a kind of rite of passage in our society. It marks the step from a productive maturity to a nonproductive old age (Maddox, 1968b).

But although we think of retirement as a sort of universal marker, by no means does it have the same effect on everyone. Women, especially, are not always affected by retirement. For some who have worked all their lives, it truly does mean a major change. But other women have never worked; and still others have moved in and out of the work force all their lives. They have had a chance to adjust to a less structured life at home. For some of these women, the major adjustment to retirement may be in getting used to having the husband around the house all day. Because retirement is not something that all women go through, there has been relatively little research on how the experience affects women. More is known about the effect of retirement on men.

A number of conditions seem to be important in determining how different men react to retirement (Maddox, 1968b). One important consideration is health. A great number of retirees leave the work force because of ill health. The 60-year-old man who leaves his job after having a heart attack may be unable to find new work after he recuperates. This kind of forced retirement can be frustrating and stressful. Poor health also limits the ways an individual can spend his leisure hours; hence, it makes retirement an unpleasant time of life for those who retire voluntarily, too.

Physical, Social, and Economic Conditions

Most men leave the work force more or less willingly, and a few variables seem to be important in their adjustment to their new way of life. Economic status is one crucial factor. A few individuals have no accumulated savings and no pensions. To them, retirement means permanent impoverishment. For most people, retirement does not mean real economic deprivation, but it often does require learning to live on half their former income. If this retrenchment cuts deeply into the individual's favorite pastimes or lifelong retirement dreams, he may feel sharply restricted in his last years of life.

Another condition affecting retirement is the individual's lifelong attitude about work. Our society is characterized by an almost religious devotion to work (Tilgher, 1962). Many men have spent so much time at their jobs that their whole sense of worth and self-esteem is tied to their work. Their leisure-time activities have been superficial, lacking much meaning. Retirement for these men means *disengagement* from the important, valuable, productive stream of life. Disengagement seems to be especially hard for people who have never developed ways of finding satisfaction outside of their jobs—in hobbies, reading, continued education, or involvement in organizations. In general, the persons who fail to develop hobbies or leisure-time interests have lower levels of education, lower economic status, and little political or organizational prestige; but the professional individual or the business executive may also have difficulty organizing his retirement years.

It is clear that social and economic circumstances have an important impact on an individual's adjustment to retirement. But even in the same social conditions, different people react differently to being retired.

Personality Adjustment to Retirement

Older people often maintain a relatively high level of social involvement which contributes to a sense of well-being. *(Joel Gordon.)*

One piece of research has suggested that personality types determine a person's reaction to retirement (Reichard, Livson, & Petersen, 1968). It tentatively identifies five different personality types.

Among the well-adjusted, the largest group are the "mature"—those who have no regrets about their past lives and who accept their present circumstances realistically. They make the best of old age by finding genuine satisfaction in their activities and friendships. A second group of "rocking-chair men" welcomed old age as a time when they were free to sit back, relax, and do nothing. They, too, seemed to find genuine satisfaction—but in passivity, instead of activity. The third group, the "armored," used activity as a way of fending off old age. They developed a highly satisfying life-style in the years after retirement, but this system served as a defense against anxieties about feeling old.

Other individuals found little satisfaction in retirement. Some poor adjusters, the "angry men," bitterly blamed others for their own failures in life. Others, the "self-haters," blamed themselves.

Whether an individual reacts well or poorly to retirement is the result of a combination of different factors: his outlook on life and work; his health; his economic status; his needs for a sense of fulfillment; his flexibility; and his personal history. If the individual has led an involved, highly active life, he is likely to carve out a busy retirement for himself. If he has led a disordered life, with little central meaning, then retirement is apt to be unsatisfying and even dehumanizing. In an important sense, retirement is the culmination of a lifetime (de Beauvoir, 1972).

If retirement has an overriding impact on the individual's later years of life, the approach of death is even more significant. Death happens to everyone. But few of us are able to fully face the thought of our own extinction, especially by natural causes (Kübler-Ross, 1969). In our unconscious minds, we can think of our own death only as something that is done to us by an outside force—as an accident, or someone's deliberate act. But it is almost impossible to imagine growing old and dying quietly in bed, "not with a bang, but a whimper."

But as people do grow old, the realization comes that death is not far off. And hard as it is to imagine, the fact of death's imminence is increasingly in the older person's mind. As young people, we have the luxury of being able to push such thoughts aside as irrelevant. But in old age, thoughts of death are very relevant. How do old people react?

There has been relatively little attention given to this tremendous adjustment until recent years, perhaps because many psychologists and doctors themselves ignore death and dying. But a few researchers have given the process a good deal of thought and study. As we saw in Chapter 5, Kübler-Ross (1969) describes five stages in the process of adjusting to the idea of death. The first reaction to the knowledge of approaching death is denial: the person simply refuses to believe it can happen to him. After this come stages of anger, bargaining, depression, and finally, acceptance.

THE LIFE REVIEW. Butler (1968, 1971) has another perspective on death. He sees a process of life review as the most important part of the individual's adjustment to his own death. The life review is a universal process. Both old and young people who know they will die soon look back upon their lives, rehashing old conflicts and reliving old pleasures and pains. They review the meaning and importance of their existence.

Most of us are familiar with the tendency of old people to talk about the way things were, or about what they used to think, hope, or dream. Elderly people also dream about death and judgment. We often dismiss such occurrences as garrulousness or flights of fancy. But according to Butler, this kind of life review is a very important step in the lifelong growth of the individual. There is probably no other time of life when there is as strong a force toward self-awareness as there is in old age. The older person is constantly reviewing, assessing, and evaluating his life, and often this process leads to real personality growth. (However, growth does not always follow, for sometimes the individual dies before the review is completed, and sometimes the review leads to deep terrors and pathologies.) So, while the older person may seem to be living in the past, he is also actively involved in growing, by resolving old conflicts, reestablishing meaning in his life, and even discovering new truths about himself. Like Erikson's

Reminiscence serves an important function in the elderly and is integral to the level of one's life. Reassessment of the past may lead to greater acceptance of one's life as having been worthwhile and meaningful, or to despair that one's life has been unfulfilled. (*Sigrid Owen/DPI*)

eighth stage of integrity versus despair, the life review is just one more step in the lifelong process of active growth of the individual's ego.

While Butler sees the life review as usually happening over a period of time, others report that even the actual experience of dying also includes for some a sort of split-second life review. People who have thought they were dying—who fell from a height, or were hit by a car, or almost drowned—report that in what they expected to be the last seconds of their existence, their mental processes accelerated. They went through three stages of experience: resistance; then life review, where the ego seemed to split from the body as the individual watched his life pass before him; and finally transcendence, where the individual passed beyond his personal history and felt a sense of serenity and oneness with the universe (Noyes, cited in Goodall, 1972).

The Right to a "Good Death" While we still know little about the experience of dying, the suggestion that there may be a final feeling of transcendence raises some important questions about death in our society. If death is a natural, positive experience, do we have a right to tamper with it? Do we rob the individual of a dignified death if we artificially maintain his life systems beyond the point where he can ever regain consciousness? Is there a point at which a person is meant to die, and would it be better to let nature take its course at this point? Do we prolong life because *we* fear death, even though the patient himself may be at peace and ready to die? These questions have been given a great deal of attention in recent years, and many thoughtful people are starting to demand a "right to die." The "Living Will" prepared by the Euthanasia Educational Council (see Figure 16) is one example of an effort to assure some individual autonomy even in the last stages of life.

There are other complaints about the attitude toward death in our society. We seem to be remarkably good at providing medical care to the dying patient—the medication, the instruments, the life support systems. But what kind of personal care do we give him? We are extremely poor at dealing head-on with the worries and thoughts of the dying patient. Terminally ill individuals are often treated as less than human by those around them. They are isolated from their loved ones in a sterile environment; decisions are made for them, without regard for their wishes; they are rarely told what their treatments

Figure 16 "A Living Will." It is a formal request prepared by the Euthanasia Educational Council. It informs the signer's family, or others who may be concerned, of the signer's wish to avoid the use of "heroic measures" to maintain life in the event of irreversible illness. (Reprinted with permission of the Euthanasia Educational Council, 250 West 57th Street, New York, NY 10019.)

TO MY FAMILY, MY PHYSICIAN, MY LAWYER, MY CLERGYMAN
TO ANY MEDICAL FACILITY IN WHOSE CARE I HAPPEN TO BE
TO ANY INDIVIDUAL WHO MAY BECOME RESPONSIBLE FOR MY HEALTH, WELFARE OR AFFAIRS

Death is as much a reality as birth, growth, maturity and old age—it is the one certainty of life. If the time comes when I, _____ can no longer take part in decisions for my own future, let this statement stand as an expression of my wishes, while I am still of sound mind.

If the situation should arise in which there is no reasonable expectation of my recovery from physical or mental disability, I request that I be allowed to die and not be kept alive by artificial means or "heroic measures". I do not fear death itself as much as the indignities of deterioration, dependence and hopeless pain. I, therefore, ask that medication be mercifully administered to me to alleviate suffering even though this may hasten the moment of death.

This request is made after careful consideration. I hope you who care for me will feel morally bound to follow its mandate. I recognize that this appears to place a heavy responsibility upon you, but it is with the intention of relieving you of such responsibility and of placing it upon myself in accordance with my strong convictions, that this statement is made.

Signed _____

Date _____

Witness _____

Witness _____

Copies of this request have been given to _____

_____

_____

_____

are for; and if they become upset or rebellious, they are simply sedated (Kübler-Ross, 1969). Compared to the terrifying cold atmosphere of the hospital, it seems a luxury to die the old-fashioned way at home, surrounded by familiar faces and objects.

According to Weisman (1972), dying people are surrounded by a "conspiracy of silence" in our society. Terminally ill patients usually suspect that they are dying, and they often want to talk about it. But their loved ones, their nurses, and their doctors are so uncomfortable with death themselves that they do all they can to avoid the subject. As a result, the patient has nowhere to turn for honest answers and real support. He is not allowed to deal honestly with himself, and others will not discuss what is happening with him. He is left confused and isolated, unable to make peace with himself.

Weisman thinks that besides being allowed to come to terms with the truth, the dying patient can be given some measures of autonomy. Being permitted to state how much medication he wants, for instance, can give the individual a sense that he still controls some aspects of his own life. This is very important for the patient who may otherwise feel he is being swept along by forces totally out of his control. In fact, some research indicates that almost any animal—whether a rat, a dog, or a cockroach—often simply relinquishes life if it feels it has lost control of its destiny (Seligman, 1974). In an experiment where rats were put in water to see how long they could swim, some lasted for as long as 60 hours while a few sank below the surface and drowned almost instantly. What caused the different reactions? The rats that died quickly had been restrained before being put in the water; those that kept on struggling did not sense that there was no use in trying to survive. Something similar happens when people are put into nursing homes or hospitals prematurely and feel they can no longer control their own lives in any meaningful way. They respond, just like any other animal, by giving up the struggle.

One of the best accounts of what the experience of death can mean came from a person who was actually dying. When Ernest Becker was interviewed in 1974 (Keen, 1974), he was hospitalized in the last stage of terminal cancer. During his life, he had written a great deal about facing up to death, so he was aware of what he was experiencing on many psychological, philosophical, and theological levels. Becker had passed through several stages of adjusting to his own death, and by the time of the interview he might be characterized as having reached the stage of transcendence which Weisman, Kübler-Ross, and Butler talk about. His own resolution was a religious one: "What makes death easier is . . . to know that . . . beyond what is happening to us there is the fact of the tremendous creative energies of the cosmos that are using us for some purposes we don't know" (Keen, 1974, p. 78). Other individuals may use a slightly different philosophy to come to terms with their own death. But in any case, Becker's testimony is a compelling argument for allowing people to work out their own personal resolution to face death in dignity and peace.

In 1900, about 4 percent of the population was over the age of 65. Today, this figure has risen to almost 10 percent, and it is still growing. Despite the bright picture presented by increasing life expectancy of the average American though, other statistics are not so hopeful (U.S. Department of Housing and Urban Development, 1973).

Of the 95 percent of older people who are not institutionalized, more than one-quarter (mostly women) live alone and about two-thirds live in family households where they are the same generation as the household heads. In other words, there is considerable age segregation in the living arrangements of even the older people who are not institutionalized. Living conditions are also relatively worse for the aged than for the rest of society.

Statistics show that a high proportion of older people are below the poverty level. In 1970, 19.2 percent of elderly heads of families lived in families with incomes below the poverty level, as compared to only 9.4 percent of heads of families under age 65. One side effect of this situation is that older people often have trouble getting adequate nutrition because of the high cost of food. Transportation, too, may be a severe problem for the elderly, especially in rural areas where distances are great and public transportation is often minimal.

In many ways, our society is simply not geared for the kinds of lives that the elderly must lead. We have made medical advances that allow people to live longer than ever before, but we do not seem to know what to do with them after we have saved their lives. Too little allowance is made for the person who is no longer earning a living, who cannot walk long distances or drive a car, or who may have physical or mental disabilities that keep him from communicating with others.

The institutional care we give our older people is a good reflection of the overall attitude of our society toward the aged. In the past few years, nursing homes have received wide attention as boring, meaningless places where people often have little else to do but wait for the end of their lives. Senile wards in mental hospitals are even worse. One of the most shocking things about nursing homes has been the unwillingness of people on the outside to show real concern for what happens in these institutions. Even people who are entrusting a parent to the care of a home rarely ask about the nurse-patient ratio, about the kinds of creative facilities or physical therapy equipment available, or even about the frequency of doctors' visits (Jacoby, 1974). And the government has provided federal money without enforcing high standards of care. In fact, federal standards were lowered in 1974; therefore, in some sense our concern for the aged seems to be moving backward, not forward. This picture is in striking contrast to the treatment of venerable patriarchs and matriarchs in many societies.

Alternatives for the Aged in our Society

What alternatives are available to make life easier for older people? Some nursing homes do have high standards which they adhere to voluntarily. They provide services to rehabilitate patients, not just to sustain them. But they also pay their staffs more, so they cost more and need more federal money. There are other options, too, for the elderly in good health. Retirement communities allow older people to live together, under the assumption that they will enjoy sharing interests and activities in a physically safe environment. But for most older people, these communities are not the answer because they isolate the elderly from the rest of the world. Other ideas are being tried by organizations such as the Gray Panthers and the Quakers. An experiment which seems to be quite successful is the Quaker concept of "life centers" in Philadelphia, where older people live with students and people of other ages in an old mansion having many rooms. They share costs, housework, meals, and, more importantly, conversation on a communal basis.

Besides better living arrangements, the lot of older people can be improved in other ways. Many suggestions have been made for lifelong education. In the current period of a knowledge explosion, most people find that their formal education has become obsolete by the time they reach 40. The aged as a group have a very low education level. The idea of taking special training at any age to learn a job skill, or to acquire knowledge, or to learn satisfying ways of spending leisure time may be an excellent method of making life more meaningful for the aged—and for everyone else as well.

In other areas, answers must be found to ease some of the simple needs of the aged (Eisdorfer, 1975). Insufficient money is the older person's most frequent complaint. Social security and other supplementary income programs should be reevaluated. Health is also a major problem. Three-quarters of all individuals over 65 have some chronic disease (not all of them serious); and about 37 percent have some health disability which interferes either with work or with leisure activities. Much more research is needed on how to make life more comfortable after the age of 65. Other problems are how to allay fears many older people have about safety, especially in urban areas, and fears about prolonged deteriorating illness—both sources of high anxiety in older people. A more educated, protective, and supportive attitude among the rest of society could ease some of these fears.

All of these are areas where society should give more attention to the needs of the aged; but they are also areas where older people can be an important resource for themselves and for others. Often, older people are unaware of the services and benefits available to them as senior citizens; better use of media such as television can help to inform them of their rights. Even more effective as a means of self-help are organizations like the Gray Panthers (actually, a coalition of the aged with young people who are also victims of indifference and neglect) which bring older people together as a political and social force. This group rightly sees the aged as an almost untapped resource

Living in the same communities, the old and the young may benefit from each other's experience. *(Joel Gordon.)*

in our society. Its members are working to give older people more autonomy in deciding whether they want to keep on working instead of retiring. They are also trying to give older people a chance to work for social improvements, not only for the aged but for everyone. In this, the Gray Panthers have shown that the very weaknesses of some older people can be a great source of strength for social change. One badly crippled elderly woman made a great impact in Philadelphia by publicly demonstrating that the urban transportation system could not accommodate the weak or the old. For example, the steps for boarding buses were too high. Finally, organizations like the Gray Panthers are giving older people a better self-image—something long neglected in a world which equates youth with beauty, maturity with power, and age with obsolescence (Gray Panther power, 1975).

Improving the lot of older people requires many changes. It means making government more aware of the financial needs of older people and of the inadequacy of some public services. It means making the aged aware that even though they have lost their youth, they can still be creative, productive, sensitive, and sensual individuals. And it means educating everyone to a realization that old age is still a part of life, be it a culmination, fulfillment, or travesty.

1. Referring to the work of Weisman, Butler, Kübler-Ross, and others, show how old age and even death can be an experience of personal growth and integration.

2. How does intelligence seem to be affected by age? In what ways does it decline, and in what areas does it remain fairly stable?

3. What factors are involved in a person's adjustment to retirement and old age? Contrast Neugarten's and Reichard's views of retirement with the theories of disengagement and activity.

SUGGESTED
READINGS

de Beauvoir, S. *The coming of age* (Patrick O'Brian, trans.). New York: Putnam, 1972. Simone de Beauvoir, who has written compelling descriptions of women's issues, now attacks society's age prejudices.

Kübler-Ross, E. (Ed.). *Death: The final stage of growth.* Englewood Cliffs, N.J.: Prentice-Hall, 1975. This collection expresses the issues and processes of coping fully with death.

Saul, S. *Aging: An album of people growing old.* New York: Wiley, 1974. A kaleidoscope of items, feelings, issues, and individual styles of living and coping in the last decades of life.

Accommodation The need to adjust or modify one's schema because new information fails to fit the existing schema.

Acquired Adaptation A change in behavior stimulated by repeatedly presenting an organism with the same situation or circumstance.

Activity Theory A theory that views the withdrawal characterizing many people's last years as primarily the result of society withdrawing from the individual.

Aging Biological evolution beyond the point of optimal maturity.

Aggression Hostile or angry feelings where there is intent to hurt or destroy.

Alleles A pair of genes, found on corresponding chromosomes, that affect the same trait.

Amniotic Sac A protective covering, filled with fluid, that forms around the developing prenatal organism.

Anal Stage The second stage of development in psychoanalytic theory during which primary erogenous interest centers around the child's anus.

Anxiety A generalized feeling of uneasiness without cause.

Assimilation The process of making new information part of one's existing schema or framework of experience.

Associative Flow Undirected forms of thinking characteristic of daydreaming, dreaming, or creative thought.

Attachment The process of developing the first relationship between infant and primary caretaker.

Authoritarian A style of parenting that is warm, controlling, and somewhat detached.

Authoritative A style of parenting that combines high controls with warmth, receptivity, and encouragement.

Autism A schizophrenic condition characterized by extreme fantasies and loss of contact with reality.

Autosomes The chromosomes of a cell, excluding the sex-determining chromosomes.

Behavior Contagion The tendency to exhibit similar behavior to those around you.

Behavioral Objectives The kinds of knowledge and skills that one can expect to achieve after a specific amount of instruction.

Blastula The hollow sphere of cells, with an accumulation of fluid in the center, that forms several days after conception.

Cephlo-Caudal Trend The observable trend of an embryo to develop in a head-to-tail direction.

Chorion A protective outer sac that develops from tissue surrounding the embryo.

Chromosome A chainlike structure, found in the nucleus of a cell, that contains the genes.

Classical Conditioning See respondent conditioning.

Cleavage The division of cells.

Cloning The regeneration of a plant or organism from one of its somatic cells.

Competence Motivation A need to achieve in order to feel effective as an individual.

Concrete Operational Period The third stage in Piaget's cognitive theory during which the 7- to 11-year-old child begins to think logically although his thinking is still limited to what he sees.

Conditioned Stimulus A previously neutral stimulus that acquires the ability to elicit a response after repeated pairings with an unconditioned stimulus.

Conservation A cognitive ability described by Piaget as occurring with concrete operations; the time when a child begins to understand the physical properties of matter.

Construct Validity How well the data generated by a test or study enables us to draw conclusions about the nature of the particular construct being tested.

Convergent Thinking A type of thought aimed at finding a single, logical solution to a problem.

Counterconditioning A procedure in which an incompatible response is conditioned and will compete with or eliminate an undesired response.

Criterion-Referenced Test A test that evaluates an individual's performance in relation to his previous performance on the same test.

Critical Period The only point in time when a particular environmental factor can have an effect.

Crossing Over A process occurring prior to meiosis in which a segment of a chromosome breaks off and exchanges places with a corresponding segment on another chromosome of the pair, greatly increasing the possible combinations in each sperm or ovum.

Cross-Sectional Study A study in which different individuals of different age groups are selected and studied at the same time.

Cumulative Theory of Learning A theory that sees learning as a cumulative process where complex principles are formed from the interaction of simpler skills.

Defense Mechanisms Any of the techniques used to shield oneself against anxiety-producing situations.

Defensive Identification Freud's term for adopting characteristics of the same-sex parent in order to win the affection and attention of the opposite-sex parent.

Denial The refusal to admit that an anxiety-producing situation exists or that an anxiety-producing event happened.

Dependent Variable The variable in an experiment that changes as a result of manipulating the independent variable.

Desensitization A technique of behavior therapy in which anxiety about a specific object or situation is gradually reduced.

Deterministic The view that man's values, attitudes, behaviors, and emotional responses are determined by past or present environmental factors.

Deviation IQ A measure of intelligence quotient derived from a statistical table comparing an individual's score with scores of other subjects the same age.

Differentiation A process of perceptual learning in which the distinctive features of an object or its variance from other similar objects are observed. Also, the process of undifferentiated cells taking on specialized functions.

Displacement A defense mechanism in which a person or object is substituted for the actual source of anxiety.

Divergent Thinking A type of thought aimed at finding several correct solutions to the same problem.

Dizygotic Twins See fraternal twins.

DNA Deoxyribonucleic acid, a complex molecule found in the genes that contains the "blueprint" to regulate the functioning and development of an organism.

Ectoderm The upper layer of embryonic cells after differentiation; the cells which develop into the skin, sense organs, and nervous system.

Ectomorph A body type that is characterized by tallness, thinness, and fragility.

Egocentrism The failure to distinguish between one's own perceptions and the perceptions of others.

Ego Identity Erikson's term for an image of self that a person develops which has consistency over a period of time.

Elaborated Language Basil Bernstein's term for language characteristic of the middle and upper classes that is syntactically more complex and more sophisticated than restricted language.

Elicited Response In respondent conditioning, a particular response that is encouraged by a stimulus or set of conditions.

Embryonic Period A period generally considered to take place from the end of the germinal period to the end of the second month after conception when major structural changes are occurring in the developing embryo.

Emitted Response In operant conditioning, a response generated by an organism acting on the environment; for example, pressing a bar in a Skinner box to obtain reinforcement.

Enactive Stage The first stage of Bruner's cognitive theory during which the child represents objects and events through physical action.

Endoderm The lower layer of embryonic cells after differentiation; the cells which develop into the circulatory, muscular, and skeletal systems.

Endomorph A body type characterized by a round, soft, and fat body.

Equilibration The process of finding a balance between accommodation and assimilation.

Ethnocentrism The tendency to assume that one's own beliefs, perceptions, and values are normal and that the beliefs, perceptions, and values of others are substandard or inferior.

Ethology The study of complex instinctual behavior in animals in an evolutionary framework.

Extrinsic Motivation Motivation that comes from an outside source—parental encouragement, peer competition, etc.

Fetal Period The final period of prenatal development from the beginning of the third month after gestation to birth when the embryo, now a fetus, begins to function.

Formal Operational Period The fourth and final stage of Piaget's cognitive theory, beginning at 12 to 15 years of age, and characterized by logical thinking and a grasp of abstract concepts.

Fraternal Twins Also called dizygotic twins; twins which result from two or more sperm each fertilizing a separate ovum.

Functional Fixedness The tendency to see only limited uses for a particular object, making it difficult to consider the object for different kinds of functions.

Functional Subordination The integration of a number of separate simple actions or schema into a more complex pattern of behavior.

Gemeinschaft A style of highly satisfying living characterized by a generally positive outlook and active involvement.

Gene Complex DNA molecules appearing on the chromosome and responsible for the hereditary transmission of traits.

Genital Period According to psychoanalytic theory, the period of normal adult sexual behavior beginning with the onset of puberty.

Genotype The genetic makeup responsible for a given trait.

Germinal Period The period of very rapid cell division, lasting approximately one week from the time of conception.

Gesellschaft A life-style in which the individual is somewhat withdrawn, alienated, or isolated.

Gestation Period The total period of time from conception to birth; 266 days on the average.

Grasp Reflex The closing of a neonate's fingers in reaction to an object, such as a pencil, placed in the palm of the neonate's hand.

Habituation The process of becoming accustomed to certain kinds of stimuli so that they are no longer responded to.

Holophrastic Speech Single words used in the early stages of language acquisition to convey full sentences.

Iconic Stage The second stage of Bruner's cognitive theory during which a child develops the use of imagery in picturing things to himself.

Identical Twins Also called monozygotic twins; two or more offspring who develop from a single fertilized ovum.

Identification Taking on the behaviors and qualities of a respected person that one would like to emulate.

Implantation The time when the developing prenatal organism becomes embedded in the uterine wall after its descent through the Fallopian tubes.

Imprinting A form of early instinctual learning that has been of primary concern to ethologists.

Independent Variable The variable that is manipulated or changed in an experiment to observe the effects on the dependent variable.

Intelligence Quotient The ratio between an individual's mental age and chronological age; derived by dividing mental age by chronological age and multiplying by 100.

Internalization The incorporation of mores, values, attitudes, ideas, or beliefs of others or society as one's own.

Intrinsic Motivation Motivation that is internal, such as self-satisfaction.

Intuitive The second part of the preoperational period, roughly from ages 5 to 7, when a child is able to separate mental from physical reality and understand multiple points of view.

Karyotype A photograph of a cell's chromosomes arranged in pairs by graduated length.

Language Acquisition Device (LAD) A term used by linguist Noam Chomsky to describe an innate mental ability to learn language.

Law of Effect Proposed by Edward Thorndike; the law states that the consequences of an act will alter the frequency of the act itself.

Learning Disability Extreme difficulty in learning, relative to one's peers, in the absence of detectable physiological abnormality.

Longitudinal Study A study in which there is a continued observation of the same subjects at various ages.

Mapping The process of determining the gene or genes responsible for genetic traits or defects and the position of these genes along their chromosomes.

Maturation The physical development of an organism as it grows toward fulfilling its genetic potential.

Mechanistic A model that views man as a function of his learning—similar to a machine with input (stimuli) and output (response).

Meiosis The process of cellular division which, through two divisions, results in four cells, each containing half the number of chromosomes of the parent cell.

Menarche The time of first menstruation.

Mesoderm A middle layer of embryonic cells after differentiation; the cells eventually develop into the digestive system.

Mesomorph A body type characterized by more than average musculature.

Minimal Brain Dysfunction A difficult to detect physiological cause for some learning disabilities.

Mitosis The process of cellular division that results in two cells identical to the parent cell.

Modeling Imitation of a respected person or persons.

Molding A temporary misshaping or elongation of a neonate's head caused by pressure on the soft bones during the birth process.

Monozygotic Twins See identical twins.

Moro Reflex The newborn's startle reaction, characterized by the extension of both arms to the sides with fingers outstretched, followed by retraction to the midline of the body.

Morphemes The minimal units of meaning in a language consisting of phonemes which are combined to form basic words, prefixes, and suffixes.

Mutation A genetic mistake occurring during the duplication of a cell.

Neonate The term used to describe a newborn baby; usually defined as the period from birth to the end of the first month of life.

Nonreversal Shift In discrimination learning experiments, a change to a different dimension than was previously correct (as from square to circle).

Non-Sex-Linked Traits Traits caused by genes on the non-sex-determining chromosomes (autosomes).

Norm-Referenced Test A test that compares an individual's performance with the performance of others in the same age group.

Object Permanence The assumption that objects continue to exist when they are out of sight, touch, or some other perceptual contact.

Observational Learning Learning that takes place by observing another person's behavior and its consequences.

Operant Conditioning A type of conditioning that occurs when an organism is reinforced for emitting a response.

Optimal Period A period during which a particular environmental factor will have a heightened effect on development.

Oral Stage The first stage of development in psychoanalytic theory during which the primary erogenous interest centers around the mouth and sucking.

Ovulation The release of the ovum into one of the two Fallopian tubes occurring approximately fourteen days after conception.

Ovum The female sex cell (or gamete).

Perception The process of extracting meaningful information from stimulation of the senses.

Phallic Stage The third stage of development in psychoanalytic theory during which the genitals are the source of erogenous pleasure.

Phenotype The observable physical trait of an individual (such as eye color) that results from a particular combination of genes.

Phonemes The basic vowel and consonant sounds that exist in a language.

Pivot Grammar Two-word speech of young children combining a pivot word with an open word (also called X-word).

Polygenic A trait caused by an interaction of several genes or gene pairs.

Positive Reinforcement Providing a reward of something pleasurable following an action or response.

Preconceptual The first part of the preoperational period, lasting roughly from age 2 to age 4, in which there is a new use of symbols and symbolic play.

Pregenital Period The first part of infantile psychosexual development encompassing the oral, anal, and phallic stages.

Preoperational Period The second stage of Piaget's cognitive theory during which the child from 2 to 7 develops symbolic images for representing the world around him.

Primary Circular Reactions Biological and reflexive actions such as thumb-sucking that occur initially by accident in stage two of the sensorimotor period but then come under the infant's control.

Projection A defense mechanism in which one attributes one's own undesirable thoughts or actions to someone else.

Psychosexual Stages Freudian theory of developmental stages characterized by the area where erotic feelings are organized.

Psychosocial Stages The eight stages of developmental conflict in Erikson's theory of personality development.

Proximal-Distal Trend The term applied to the observable trend of an embryo to develop outward from the centerline.

Qualitative Growth A change in function during development such as in the digestive system of an infant, which gradually becomes able to digest solid food.

Quantitative Growth An increase in size (such as height) or number (such as increased number of cells) but not in function.

Rationalization Making unacceptable thoughts or behaviors more acceptable by attributing to them a socially acceptable explanation.

Reaction Formation The adoption of attitudes and behaviors that reflect an exaggerated opposite of unacceptable feelings an individual may have.

Regression A way of coping with an anxiety-producing situation by reverting to earlier, more childish or babyish behaviors.

Reliability The repeatability of an observation or test instrument on different occasions with comparable results.

Repression An extreme form of denial in which an anxiety-producing event or situation is completely erased from consciousness.

Respondent Conditioning A type of learning in which a previously neutral stimulus becomes a conditioned stimulus through repeated pairings with an unconditioned stimulus such as food.

Restricted Language Basil Bernstein's term for language characteristic of lower-class persons that is shorter, syntactically simpler, and less sophisticated than elaborated language.

Reversal Shift In discrimination learning experiments, a change to the opposite end of the same dimension (as from small to large).

RNA Ribonucleic acid, a chemical manufactured by DNA that aids in protein synthesis.

Role Exit Theory A theory that describes old age as a time when a number of roles are terminated and when other substitute roles must be found.

Rooting Reflex The neonate's reaction of moving his mouth toward the stimulus when touched on the cheek.

Schemata A term of Piaget that refers to the structure or framework into which one's experiences are integrated.

Secondary Circular Reactions Reactions that occur in the third stage of the sensorimotor period when an infant uses behaviors learned through primary circular reactions to act indirectly on the environment.

Semantics The study of meaning conveyed in language.

Senescence Old age.

Sensation The stimulation of the sense organs by physical or chemical energies.

Sensorimotor Period The first stage of Piaget's cognitive theory in which the child from birth to 2 years seeks to integrate perceptions and bodily motions.

Sex-Linked Traits Traits caused by genes on either of the sex-determining chromosomes.

Shaping Systematically reinforcing successive approximations to a desired act.

Social Learning Theory A theory that investigates the acquisition of traits, values, attitudes, and behaviors through the observation of models.

Socialization The lifelong process by which an individual acquires the beliefs, attitudes, customs, values, roles, and expectations of a culture or social group.

Sociogram A chart of the network of relationships occurring in a group.

Sociometric Techniques Techniques that are used to measure attitudes of social acceptance or rejection among members of a group.

Sperm The male sex cell (or gamete).

Stepping Reflex A reflexive reaction in which a neonate appears to be walking when held vertically with feet against a hard surface and moved from side to side.

Structuralism A branch of psychology characterized by a concern for the structure of thought with an emphasis on basic units of experience and their interactions and combinations.

Sucking Reflex The natural tendency of an infant to suck when an object such as a finger or nipple is placed in its mouth.

Surprise Paradigm The startle reaction resulting from the presentation of a novel or unexpected stimulus.

Symbolic Stage The third and final stage of Bruner's cognitive theory during which a child uses symbolic language to relate the real and the abstract.

Syntax The rules for combining words and morphemes to form basic words and sentences.

Teratology Literally "the study of monsters"; applies to the study of any agent that disturbs development and produces abnormalities.

Tertiary Circular Reactions Reactions that occur in stage five of the sensorimotor period and are characterized by a child busily exploring and manipulating different means to the same end, or investigating one activity for a variety of results.

Theory of Disengagement A theory that views aging as a mutual withdrawal of an individual from society and society from the individual.

Token Economy A technique used to modify maladaptive behavior by reinforcing desired behaviors with tokens that can later be exchanged for food or privileges.

Tonic Neck Reflex An infant's reaction to having his head turned sharply to one side—he reacts by extending the arm and leg on the same side and flexing the arm and leg on the opposite side.

Transductive Reasoning A term of Piaget that refers to a preoperational child's tendency to use associative reasoning rather than induction or deduction

Validity The degree to which a test measures the variable it was designed to measure.

Visual Cliff An experimental apparatus used to test depth perception of infants or animals in simulating an abrupt drop-off.

Withdrawal Avoiding an anxiety-producing situation; a common defense mechanism in children.

Zygote A fertilized ovum.

Adams, J. F. Adolescents in an age of crisis. In J. F. Adams (Ed.), *Understanding adolescence* (2nd ed.). Boston: Allyn & Bacon, 1973.

Adorno, T. W., et al. *The authoritarian personality*. New York: Harper & Brothers, 1950.

Ainsworth, M. D. S. *Infancy in Uganda: Infant care and the growth of love*. Baltimore: Johns Hopkins University Press, 1967.

Ainsworth, M. D. S. The development of infant-mother attachment. In B. M. Caldwell & H. N. Ricciuti (Eds.), *Review of child development research* (Vol. 3). Chicago: University of Chicago Press, 1973.

Alexander, T. Psychologists are rediscovering the mind. *Fortune*, November 1970, pp. 108–111ff.

Ames, L. B. Don't push your preschooler. *Family Circle*, December 1971.

Anastasi, A. Heredity, environment, and the question of "How?" *Psychological Review*, 1958, *65*, 197–208.

Angrist, S. S. The study of sex roles. *Journal of Social Issues*, 1969, *25* (1), 215–232.

Apgar, V. Proposal for a new method of evaluating the newborn infant. *Anesthesia and Analgesia*, 1953, *32*, 260–267.

Arenberg, D. Cognition and aging: Verbal learning, memory, and problem solving. In C. Eisdorfer & M. P. Lawton (Eds.), *The psychology of adult development and aging*. Washington, D. C.: American Psychological Association, 1973.

Arensberg, C. M. *The Irish countryman*. New York: Macmillan, 1937.

Aries, P. [*Centuries of childhood*] (R. Baldick, trans.). New York: Knopf, 1960.

Ashton-Warner, S. *Teacher*. New York: Bantam Books, 1971.

Atkinson, J. W., & Feather, N. T. *A theory of achievement motivation*. New York: Wiley, 1966.

Ausubel, F., Beckwith, J., & Janssen, K. The politics of genetic engineering: Who decides who's defective? *Psychology Today*, June 1974, p. 30ff.

Babson, S. G., & Benson, R. C. *Primer on prematurity and high-risk pregnancy*. St. Louis: Mosby, 1966.

Baird, D. The epidemiology of prematurity. *Journal of Pediatrics*, 1964, *65*, 909–924.

Bakan, D. Adolescence in America: From idea to social fact. *Daedalus*, 1971, *100*, 979–995.

Baldwin, A. L. The effect of home environment on nursery school behavior. *Child Development*, 1949, *20*, 49–61.

Ball, W., & Tronick, E. Infant responses to impending collision: Optical and real. *Science*, 1971, *171*, 818–820.

Bandura, A. The stormy decade: Fact or fiction? *Psychology in the Schools*, 1964, *1*, 224–231.

Bandura, A. The role of modeling processes in personality development. In W. W. Hartup & N. L. Smothergill (Eds.), *The young child: Reviews of research* (Vol. 1). Washington, D. C.: National Association for the Education of Young Children, 1967.

Bandura, A. *Principles of behavior modification*. New York: Holt, Rinehart & Winston, 1969.

Bandura, A., Ross, D., & Ross, S. A. Transmission of aggression through imitation of aggressive models. *Journal of Abnormal and Social Psychology*, 1961, *63*, 575–582.

Bandura, A., Ross, D., & Ross, S. A comparative test of the status envy, social power, and secondary reinforcement theories of identificatory learning. *Journal of Abnormal and Social Psychology*, 1963, 67, 527–534. (a)

Bandura, A., Ross, D., & Ross, S. A. Imitation of film-mediated aggressive models. *Journal of Abnormal and Social Psychology*, 1963, *66*, 3–11. (b)

Bandura, A., Ross, D., & Ross, S. A. Vicarious reinforcement and imitative learning. *Journal of Abnormal and Social Psychology*, 1963, *67*, 601–607. (c)

Bandura, A., & Walters, R. H. *Adolescent aggression*. New York: Ronald Press, 1959.

Bandura, A., & Walters, R. H. *Social learning and personality development*. New York: Holt, Rinehart & Winston, 1963.

Baratz, J. C. Teaching reading in an urban Negro school system. In F. Williams (Ed.), *Language and poverty*. Chicago: Markham, 1970.

Barker, R. G., Dembo, T., & Lewin, K. Frustration and regression. In R. G. Barker, J. S. Kounin & H. F. Wright (Eds.), *Child behavior and development*. New York: McGraw-Hill, 1943.

Baumrind, D. Socialization and instrumental competence in young children. In W. W. Hartup (Ed.), *The young child: Reviews of research* (Vol. 2). Washington, D. C.: National Association for the Education of Young Children, 1972.

Bayer, L. M., & Bayley, N. *Growth Diagnosis*. Chicago: University of Chicago Press, 1959.

Bayley, N. Consistency and variability in the growth of intelligence from birth to eighteen years. *Journal of Genetic Psychology*, 1949, *75*, 165–196.

Bayley, N. Research in child development: A longitudinal perspective. *Merrill-Palmer Quarterly*, 1965, *11*, 183–208.

Bayley, N. Learning in adulthood: The role of intelligence. In H. J. Klausmeier & C. W. Harris (Eds.), *Analysis of concept learning*. New York: Academic Press, 1966.

Bayley, N. *Bayley scales of infant development*. New York: Psychological Corporation, 1969.

Becker, S. W., Lerner, M. J., & Carroll, J. Conformity as

a function of birth order and type of group pressure: A verification. *Journal of Personality and Social Psychology*, 1966, *3*, 242–244.

Becker, W. C. Consequences of different kinds of parental discipline. In M. L. Hoffman & L. W. Hoffman (Eds.), *Review of child developmental research* (Vol. 1). New York: Russell Sage Foundation, 1964.

Beller, E. K. Dependency and independence in young children. *Journal of Genetic Psychology*, 1955, *87*, 25–35.

Bellugi, U. Learning the language. *Psychology Today*, December 1970, pp. 32–38.

Bellugi, U., & Brown, R. (Eds.), The acquisition of language. *Monographs of the Society for Research in Child Development*, 1964, 29(1).

Benedek, T. Parenthood during the life cycle. In E. J. Anthony & T. Benedek (Eds.), *Parenthood: Its psychology and psychopathology*. Boston: Little, Brown, 1970.

Bereiter, C., & Engelmann, S. *Teaching disadvantaged children in the preschool*. Englewood Cliffs, N. J.: Prentice-Hall, 1966.

Berger, B. M., Hackett, B. M., & Millar, R. M. Child-rearing practices of the communal family. In R. M. Kanter (Comp.), *Communes: Creating and managing the collective life*. New York: Harper & Row, 1973.

Berko, J. The child's learning of English morphology. *Word*, 1958, *14*, 150–177.

Bermant, G. Sisterhood is beautiful: a conversation with Alice S. Rossi. *Psychology Today*, August 1972, pp. 40–46ff.

Bernstein, B. Elaborated and restricted codes: Their social origins and some consequences. In A. G. Smith (Ed.), *Communication and culture*. New York: Holt, Rinehart & Winston, 1966.

Bernstein, B. A sociolinguistic approach to socialization: With some reference to educability. In F. Williams (Ed.), *Language and poverty*. Chicago: Markham, 1970.

Berscheid, E., Walster, E., & Bohrnstedt, G. Body image. *Psychology Today*, November 1973, 119–123ff.

Binet, A., & Simon, T. Méthodes nouvelles pour le diagnostic du niveau intellectual des anormaux. *L'Année Psychologique*, 1905, *11*, 191–244.

Binet, A., & Simon, T. [*The development of intelligence in children*] (E. S. Kite, trans.). Baltimore: Williams & Wilkins, 1916.

Birch, H. G. Health and the education of socially disadvantaged children. *Developmental Medicine and Child Neurology*, 1968, *10*, 580–599.

Birch, H. G., & Gussow, J. D. *Disadvantaged children: Health, nutrition and school failure*. New York: Harcourt Brace Jovanovich, 1970.

Birch, H. G., & Rabinowitz, H. S. The negative effect of previous experience on productive thinking. *Journal of Experimental Psychology*, 1951, *41*, 121–125.

Birren, J. E. (Ed.). *Handbook of aging and the individual*. Chicago: University of Chicago Press, 1959.

Bischof, L. J. *Adult psychology*. New York: Harper & Row, 1969.

Blank, M. Cognitive functions of language in the pre-

school years. *Developmental Psychology*, 1974, *10*, 229–245.

Blau, Z. S. *Old age in a changing society*. New York: New Viewpoints, 1973.

Block, J. *Lives through time*. Berkeley, Calif.: Bancroft Books, 1971.

Block, J. H., Haan, N., & Smith, M. B. Activism and apathy in contemporary adolescents. In J. F. Adams (Ed.), *Understanding adolescence* (2nd ed.). Boston: Allyn & Bacon, 1973.

Bloom, B. S., & Krathwohl, D. R. *Taxonomy of educational objectives. Handbook I: The cognitive domain.* New York: David McKay, 1956.

Bloom, L. *Language development: Form and function in emerging grammars*. Cambridge: M.I.T. Press, 1970.

Bloom, L. Why not pivot grammar? *Journal of Speech and Hearing Disorders*, 1971, *36*, 40–50.

Blos, P. The child analyst looks at the young adolescent. *Daedalus*, 1971, *100*, 961–978.

Bossard, J. H. S., & Boll, E. S. Personality roles in the large family. *Child Development*, 1955, *26*, 71–78.

Bossard, J. H. S., & Boll, E. S. *The sociology of child development*. New York: Harper & Brothers, 1960.

Botwinick, J. *Cognitive processes in maturity and old age*. New York: Springer, 1967.

Botwinick, J. Geropsychology. *Annual Review of Psychology*, 1970, 239–272.

Bower, T. G. R. The object in the world of the infant. *Scientific American*, October 1971, pp. 30–38.

Bower, T. G. R. *Development in infancy*. San Francisco: Freeman, 1974.

Bowes, W. A., Jr. Obstetrical medication and infant outcome: A review of the literature. *Monographs of the Society for Research in Child Development*, 1970, *35* (4, Serial No. 137).

Bowlby, J. Separation anxiety. *International Journal of Psychoanalysis*, 1960, *41*, 89–113.

Bowlby, J. *Attachment*. New York: Basic Books, 1969.

Boyd, G. F. The levels of aspiration of White and Negro children in a non-segregated elementary school. *Journal of Social Psychology*, 1952, *36*, 191–196.

Brackbill, Y., & Koltsova, M. M. Conditioning and learning. In Y. Brackbill (Ed.), *Infancy and early childhood: A handbook and guide to human development.* New York: Free Press, 1967.

Braine, M. D. S. The ontogeny of English phrase structure: The first phase. *Language*, 1963, *39*, 1–13.

Braine, M. D. S., Heimer, C. B., Wortis, H., & Freedman, A. M. Factors associated with impairment of the early development of prematures. *Monographs of the Society for Research in Child Development*, 1966, *31* (4, Serial No. 106).

Brazelton, T. B. *Infants and mothers: Differences in development*. New York: Dell, 1969.

Brazelton, T. B., Freedman, D., Horowitz, F. D., Koslowoski, B., Robey, M., Ricciuti, M., & Sameroff, A. *Neonatal behavioral assessment scale*. In press.

Breckenridge, M. E., & Vincent, E. L. *Child development*. Philadelphia: Saunders, 1955.

Broderick, C. B. Social heterosexual development among urban Negroes and Whites. *Journal of Marriage and* the Family, 1965, 27, 200–203.

Bronfenbrenner, U. The changing Soviet family. In D. R. Brown (Ed.), The role and status of women in the Soviet Union. New York: Teachers College, Columbia University Press, 1968.

Bronfenbrenner, U. Two worlds of childhood: U.S. and U.S.S.R. New York: Russell Sage Foundation, 1970.

Brown, P., & Elliott, R. Control of aggression in a nursery school class. Journal of Experimental Child Psychology, 1965, 2, 103–107.

Brown, R. Social psychology. New York: Free Press, 1965.

Brown, R. A first language: The early stages. Cambridge: Harvard University Press, 1973.

Brown, R., & Lenneberg, E. H. A study in language and cognition. Journal of Abnormal and Social Psychology, 1954, 49, 454–462.

Bruner, J. S. The process of education. Cambridge: Harvard University Press, 1960.

Bruner, J. S. The growth of mind. American Psychologist, 1965, 20, 1007–1017. (a)

Bruner, J. S. On Knowing: Essays for the left hand. New York: Atheneum, 1965. (b)

Bruner, J. S. Toward a theory of instruction. Cambridge: Belknap Press of Harvard University Press, 1966.

Bruner, J. S. Eye, hand and mind. In D. Elkind & J. H. Flavell (Eds.), Studies in cognitive development: Essays in honor of Jean Piaget. New York: Oxford University Press, 1969.

Bruner, J. S. The relevance of education. New York: Norton, 1971.

Bruner, J. S. Beyond the information given: Studies in the psychology of knowing. New York: Norton, 1973.

Bruner, J. S., Olver, R. R., & Greenfield, P. M. Studies in cognitive growth. New York: Wiley, 1966.

Bühler, C., & Massarik, F. (Eds.). The course of human life: A study of goals in the humanistic perspective. New York: Springer, 1968.

Burnham, A. S. The heroin babies are going cold turkey. New York Times Magazine, January 9, 1971, p. 18ff.

Butler, R. N. The life review: An interpretation of reminiscence in the aged. In B. L. Neugarten (Ed.), Middle age and aging. Chicago: University of Chicago Press, 1968.

Butler, R. N. Age: The life review. Psychology Today, December 1971, pp. 49–51f.

Calder, R. Food supplementation for prevention of malnutrition in the pre-school child. In National Research Council, Pre-school child malnutrition: Primary deterrent to Human progress. Washington, D. C.: National Academy of Sciences, 1966.

Caldwell, B. M. China notes. Society for Research in Child Development Newsletter, Fall 1974, pp. 4f.

Campos, J. J., Langer, A., & Krowitz, A. Cardiac responses on the visual cliff in prelocomotor human infants. Science, 1970, 170, 196–197.

Carmichael, L. The onset and early development of behavior. In P. H. Mussen (Ed.), Carmichael's manual of child psychology (3rd ed.) (Vol. 1). New York: Wiley, 1970.

Castaneda, A. Reaction time and response amplitude as a function of anxiety and stimulus intensity. Journal of Abnormal and Social Psychology, 1956, 53, 225–228.

Caudill, W., & Weinstein, H. Maternal care and infant behavior in Japan and America. Psychiatry, 1969, 32, 12–43.

Changing attitudes of youth on sex, patriotism, work. U.S. News and World Report, June 3, 1974, pp. 66–67.

Chen, E., & Cobb, S. Family structure in relation to health and disease: A review of the literature. Journal of Chronic Diseases, 1960, 12, 544–567.

Chess, S. Temperament in the normal infant. In J. Hellmuth (Ed.), The exceptional infant (Vol. 1). Seattle: Special Child Publications, 1967.

Chomsky, C. The acquisition of syntax from 5 to 10. Cambridge: M.I.T. Press, 1969.

Chomsky, N. (Review of Verbal behavior by B. F. Skinner). Language, 1959, 35, 26–58.

Chukovsky, K. From two to five. (M. Morton, Ed. & trans.). Berkeley: University of California Press, 1963.

Church, J. (Ed.). Three babies: Biographies of cognitive development. New York: Random House, 1966.

Clark, K. B., & Clark, M. P. Racial identification and preference in Negro children. In T. M. Newcomb & E. L. Hartley (Eds.), Readings in social psychology. New York: Holt, Rinehart & Winston, 1947.

Cloward, R. A., & Ohlin, L. E. Delinquency and opportunity: A theory of delinquent gangs. Glencoe, Ill.: Free Press, 1960.

Cohen, A. K. Delinquent boys. Glencoe, Ill.: Free Press, 1955.

Cole, M., & Bruner, J. S. Cultural differences and inferences about psychological processes. American Psychologist, 1971, 26, 867–876.

Coleman, J. S. Social change: Impact on the adolescent. Bulletin of the National Association of Secondary School Principals, 1965, 49(300), 11–14.

Coleman, J. S. Interpretations of adolescent culture. In J. Zubin & A. Freedman (Eds.), The Psychopathology of adolescence. New York: Grune & Stratton, 1970.

Coleman, J. S. Bremner, R. H., Clark, B. R., Davis, J. B., Eichorn, D. H., Griliches, Z., Kett, J. F., Ryder, N. B., Doering, Z. B., & Mays, J. M. Youth: Transition to adulthood (Report of the Panel on Youth of the President's Science Advisory Committee). Chicago: University of Chicago Press, 1974.

Coles, R. Children of crisis. Boston: Little, Brown, 1967.

Coles, R. Like it is in the alley. Daedalus, 1968, 97, 1315–1330.

Collard, R. R. Personal communication and private tapes, 1974.

Collard, R. R., & Rydberg, J. E. Generalization of habituation to properties of objects in human infants. Proceedings of the 80th Annual Convention of the American Psychological Association, 1972.

Conger, J. J. A world they never knew: The family and social change. Daedalus, 1971, 100, 1105–1138.

Coster, G. Scientific American, November 1962, p. 44.

Coursin, D. B. Nutrition and brain development in infants. Merrill-Palmer Quarterly, 1972, 18, 177–202.

Cowan, P. A., & Walters, R. H. Studies of reinforcement of aggression: I. Effects of scheduling. Child Develop-

ment, 1963, *34*, 543–551.

Cowgill, D. O. Aging in American society. In D. O. Cowgill & L. D. Holmes (Eds.), *Aging and modernization*. New York: Appleton-Century-Crofts, 1972. (a)

Cowgill, D. O. The role and status of the aged in Thailand. In D. O. Cowgill & L. D. Holmes (Eds.), *Aging and modernization*. New York: Appleton-Century-Crofts, 1972. (b)

Craig, G. J., & Garney, P. *Attachment and separation behavior in the second and third years*. Unpublished manuscript, University of Massachusetts, 1972.

Cratty, B. J. *Perceptual and motor development in infants and children*. New York: Macmillan, 1970.

Cravioto, J., & Robles, B. Evolution of adaptive and motor behavior during rehabilitation from kwashiorkor. *American Journal of Orthopsychiatry*, 1965, *35*, 449–464.

Cross, H. J., & Pruyn, E. L. Youth and the counterculture. In J. F. Adams (Ed.), *Understanding adolescence* (2nd ed.). Boston: Allyn & Bacon, 1973.

Cumming, E., & Henry, W. E. *Growing old: The process of disengagement*. New York: Basic Books, 1961.

Cutter, I. S., & Viets, H. *A short history of midwifery*. Philadelphia: Saunders, 1964.

Dansereau, H. K. Work and the teen-ager. *Annals of the American Academy of Political and Social Sciences*, 1961, *338*, 44–52.

Davis, C. D., & Morrone, F. A. An objective evaluation of a prepared childbirth program. *American Journal of Obstetrics and Gynecology*, 1962, *84*, 1196.

Davis, C. M. Results of the self-selection of diets by young children. *Canadian Medical Association Journal*, 1939, *41*, 257–261.

Davis, H. V., Sears, R. R., Miller, H. C., & Brodbeck, A. J. Effects of cup, bottle, and breast feeding on oral activities of newborn infants. *Pediatrics*, 1948, *2*, 549–558.

Dean, R. F. A. Nutrition and growth. *Modern Problems in Pediatrics*, 1962, *7*, 191–198.

De Beauvoir, S. Old age: End product of a faulty system. *Saturday Review*, April 8, 1972, pp. 38–45.

DeCharms, R., & Moeller, G. H. Values expressed in American children's readers: 1800–1950. *Journal of Abnormal and Social Psychology*, 1962, *64*, 136–142.

DeMause, L. (Ed.). *The history of childhood*. New York: Psychohistory Press, 1974.

Dennis, W. A description and classification of the responses of the newborn infant. *Psychological Bulletin*, 1934, *31*, 5–22.

Dennis, W. Causes of retardation among institutional children: Iran. *Journal of Genetic Psychology*, 1960, *96*, 47–59.

Dennis, W. Creative productivity between the ages of 20 and 80 years. *Journal of Gerontology*, 1966, *21* (1), 1–8.

Dennis, W. *Children of the crèche*. New York: Appleton-Century-Crofts, 1973.

Dennis, W., & Najarian, P. Infant development under environmental handicap. *Psychological Monographs*, 1957, *71* 7, Whole No. 436).

Deutsch, M. Minority group and class status as related to social and personality factors in scholastic achievement. *Monograph of the Society of Applied Anthropology*, 1960, No. 2.

Deutsch, M., Fishman, J. A., Kogan, L., North, R., & Whiteman, M. Guidelines for testing minority group children. *Journal of Social Issues*, 1964, *20*(2), 129–145.

Dewey, J. *Art as experience*. New York: Putnam, 1958.

Dewey, J. *Democracy and education*. New York: Macmillan, 1961.

Dick-Read, G. *Childbirth without fear*. New York: Harper & Brothers, 1953.

Dimondstein, G. *Exploring the arts with children*. New York: Macmillan, 1974.

Dollard, J., Doob, L. W., Miller, N. E., Mowrer, O. H., & Sears, R. R. *Frustration and aggression*. New Haven: Yale University Press, 1939.

Dollard, J., & Miller, N. E. *Personality and psychotherapy: An analysis in terms of learning, thinking, and culture*. New York: McGraw-Hill, 1950.

Doman, G. *How to teach your baby to read*. New York: Random House, 1964.

Doris, J., & Cooper, L. Brightness discrimination in infancy. *Journal of Experimental Child Psychology*, 1966, *3*, 31–39.

Douvan, E., & Adelson, J. B. *The adolescent experience*. New York: Wiley, 1966.

Douvan, E., & Gold, M. Modal patterns in American adolescence. In L. W. Hoffman & M. L. Hoffman (Eds.), *Review of child development research* (Vol. 2). New York: Russell Sage Foundation, 1966.

Duncker, K. [On problem-solving] (L. S. Lees, trans.). *Psychological Monographs*, 1945, *58*(5, Whole No. 270).

Dwyer, J., & Mayer, J. Psychological effects of variations in physical appearance during adolescence. *Adolescence*, 1968–69, *3*, 353–380.

Eisdorfer, C. Resources for the aged reflect strongly held social myths. *The Center Magazine*, March-April 1975, pp. 12–18.

Eisenberg, L. A developmental approach to adolescence. *Children*, 1965, *12*, 131–135.

Eisenman, R. Values and attitudes in adolescence. In J. F. Adams (Ed.), *Understanding adolescence* (2nd ed.). Boston: Allyn & Bacon, 1973.

Elkind, D. Egocentrism in adolescence. *Child Development*, 1967, *38*, 1025–1034.

Elkind, D. Giant in the nursery: Jean Piaget. *New York Times Magazine*, May 26, 1968.

Elkind, D. Erik Erikson's eight ages of man. *New York Times Magazine*, April 5, 1970, pp. 1ff.

Elkind, D. *A sympathetic understanding of the child six to sixteen*. Boston: Allyn & Bacon, 1971.

Elkind, D. Misunderstandings about how children learn. *Today's Education*, March 1972, pp. 18–20.

Epstein, S. The self-concept revisited: Or a theory of a theory. *American Psychologist*, 1973, *28*, 404–416.

Erikson, E. H. The problem of ego identity. In E. H. Erikson (Ed.), Identity and the life cycle: Selected papers. *Psychological Issues Monograph*, 1959, No. 1.

Erikson, E. H. Youth: Fidelity and diversity. *Daedalus*, 1962, *91*, 5–27.

Erikson, E. H. *Childhood and society*. New York: Norton, 1963.

Evans, E. D. *Contemporary influences in early childhood education* (2nd ed.). New York: Holt, Rinehart & Winston, 1975.

Fantz, R. L. Pattern vision in young infants. *Psychological Record*, 1958, *8*, 43–47.

Fantz, R. L. The origin of form perception. *Scientific American*, May 1961, pp. 66–72.

Fantz, R. L., Ordy, J. M., & Udelf, M. S. Maturation of pattern vision in infants during the first six months. *Journal of Comparative and Physiological Psychology*, 1962, *55*, 907–917.

Fantz, R. L. Visual perception and experience in early infancy: A look at the hidden side of behavior development. In H. W. Stevenson, E. H. Hess, & H. L. Rheingold (Eds.), *Early behavior: Comparative and developmental approaches*. New York: Wiley, 1967.

Farber, J. *The student as nigger*. New York: Pocket Books, 1970.

Feldman, C., & Shen, M. *Some language-related cognitive advantages of bilingual five-year-olds*. Paper presented at the meeting of the Society for Research in Child Development, Santa Monica, Calif., March 1969.

Feshbach, S., & Singer, R. D. *Television and aggression: An experimental field study*. San Francisco: Jossey-Bass, 1971.

Flacks, R. The liberated generation: An exploration of the roots of student protest. *Journal of Social Issues*, 1967, *23*(3), 52–75.

Flavell, J. H. *The developmental psychology of Jean Piaget*. Princeton: Van Nostrand Reinhold, 1963.

Flavell, J. H. Cognitive changes in adulthood. In L. R. Goulet & P. B. Baltes (Eds.), *Life-span developmental psychology: Research and theory*. New York: Academic Press, 1970.

Fleming, E. S., & Anttonen, R. G. Teacher expectancy as related to the academic and personal growth of primary-age children. *Monographs of the Society for Research in Child Development*, 1971, *36*(5, Serial No. 145).

Forman, G. E. *The early growth of logic in children: Influences from the bilateral symmetry of human anatomy*. Paper presented at the conference of the Society for Research in Child Development, Philadelphia, April 1972.

Fortune, January 1969. (A special issue on American youth)

Fraiberg, S. H. *The magic years*. New York: Scribners, 1959.

Frank, L. K. *On the importance of infancy*. New York: Random House, 1966.

Frankenburg, W. K., & Dodds, J. B. The Denver developmental screening test. *Journal of Pediatrics*, 1967, *71*, 181–191.

Frazier, A., & Lisonbee, L. K. Adolescent concerns with physique. *School Review*, 1950, *58*, 397–405.

Freda, V. J., Gorman, J. G., & Pollack, W. Rh factor: Prevention of isoimmunization and clinical trial on mothers. *Science*, 1966, *151*, 828–830.

Frenkel-Brunswik, E. A study of prejudice in children. *Human Relations*, 1948, *1*(3), 295–306.

Frenkel-Brunswik, E. Adjustments and reorientation in the course of the life span. In R. G. Kuhlen & G. G. Thompson (Eds.), *Psychological studies of human development* (2nd ed.). New York: Appleton-Century-Crofts, 1963.

Freud, A. *The ego and the mechanisms of defense*. London: Hogarth, 1949.

Freud, S. [*The ego and the id*] (J. Riviere, trans.). London: Hogarth Press, 1947. (Originally published, 1923.)

Friedenberg, E. Z. *The vanishing adolescent*. Boston: Beacon Press, 1959.

Friedlander, B. Z. Receptive language development in infancy: Issues and problems. *Merrill-Palmer Quarterly*, 1970, *16*, 7–51.

Friedrich, L. K., & Stein, A. H. Aggressive and prosocial television programs and the natural behavior of preschool children. *Monographs of the Society for Research in Child Development*, 1973, *38*(4, Serial No. 151).

Furth, H. G. Linguistic deficiency and thinking: Research with deaf subjects 1964–1969. *Psychological Bulletin*, 1971, *76*, 58–72.

Gage, N. L. Paradigms for research on teaching. In N. L. Gage (Ed.), *Handbook of research on teaching*. Chicago: Rand McNally, 1963.

Gagné, R. M. *The condition of learning*. New York: Holt, Rinehart & Winston, 1965.

Gallagher, J. McC. Cognitive development and learning in the adolescent. In J. F. Adams (Ed.), *Understanding adolescence* (2nd ed.). Boston: Allyn & Bacon, 1973.

Gardner, E. F., & Thompson, G. G. *Syracuse Scale of Social Relations: Elementary, junior high, and senior high school levels*. Yonkers, N. Y.: World, 1958.

Gardner, H. *The arts and human development: A psychological study of the artistic process*. New York: Wiley-Interscience, 1973. (a)

Gardner, H. *The quest for mind: Piaget, Lévi-Strauss, and the structuralist movement*. New York: Random House, 1973. (b)

Garrison, K. C. Psychological development. In J. F. Adams (Ed.), *Understanding adolescence* (2nd ed.). Boston: Allyn & Bacon, 1973.

Geertz, H. The vocabulary of emotion: A study of Javanese socialization processes. *Psychiatry*, 1959, *22*, 225–237.

Gelineau, V. A., & Kantor, D. Pro-social commitment among college students. *Journal of Social Issues*, 1964, *20*(4), 112–130.

Gerbner, G. Violence in television drama: Trends and symbolic functions. In G. A. Comstock & E. A. Rubinstein (Eds.), *Television and social behavior*. (Vol. 1). Washington, D. C.: U.S. Government Printing Office, 1972.

Gesell, A. *The first five years of life: The preschool years*. New York: Harper & Brothers, 1940.

Gesell, A., & Ilg, F. L. *The child from five to ten*. New York: Harper & Brothers, 1946.

Gesell, A., Ilg, F. L., & Ames, L. B. *Youth: The years*

from ten to sixteen. New York: Harper & Row, 1956.

Getzels, J. W. On the transformation of values: A decade after Port Huron. *School Review,* 1972, *80,* 505–518.

Getzels, J. W., & Jackson, P. W. The highly intelligent and the highly creative adolescent: A summary of some research findings. In C. W. Taylor (Ed.), *The Third (1959) University of Utah Research Conference on the Identification of Creative Scientific Talent.* Salt Lake City: University of Utah Press, 1959.

Getzels, J. W., & Jackson, P. W. *Creativity and intelligence: Explorations with gifted students.* New York: Wiley, 1962.

Gewirtz, J. L. Three determinants of attention-seeking in young children. *Monographs of the Society for Research in Child Development,* 1954, *19*(2, Serial No. 59).

Gibson, E. J. *Principles of perceptual learning and development.* New York: Appleton-Century-Crofts, 1969.

Gibson, E. J., & Walk, R. D. The "visual cliff". *Scientific American,* April 1960, pp. 64–71.

Glaser, R. Instructional technology and the measurement of learning outcomes: Some questions. *American Psychologist,* 1963, *18,* 519–521.

Glick, P. C., Heer, D. M., & Beresford, J. C. Family formation and family composition: Trends and prospects. In M. B. Sussman (Ed.), *Sourcebook in marriage and the family* (2nd ed.). New York: Houghton Mifflin, 1963.

Glidewell, J. C., Kantor, M. B., Smith, L. M., & Stringer, L. A. Socialization and social structure in the classroom. In L. W. Hoffman & M. L. Hoffman (Eds.), *Review of child development research* (Vol. 2). New York: Russell Sage Foundation, 1966.

Glueck, S., & Glueck, E. T. *Unraveling juvenile delinquency.* New York: Commonwealth Fund, 1950.

Glueck, S., & Glueck, E. T. *Physique and delinquency.* New York: Harper & Brothers, 1956.

Golann, S. E. Psychological study of creativity. *Psychological Bulletin,* 1963, *60,* 548–565.

Goldberg, S. Infant care and growth in urban Zambia. *Human Development,* 1972, *15,* 77–89.

Goldberg, S., & Lewis, M. Play behavior in the year-old infant: Early sex differences. *Child Development,* 1969, *40,* 21–31.

Goodman, M. E. *Race awareness in young children.* Cambridge, Mass.: Addison-Wesley, 1952.

Goodman, N., Richardson, S. A., Dornbusch, S. M., & Hastorf, A. H. Variant reactions to physical disabilities. *American Sociological Review,* 1963, *28,* 429–435.

Goodman, P. *Growing up absurd.* New York: Random House, 1960.

Goslin, D. A. (Ed.). *Handbook of socialization theory and research.* Chicago: Rand McNally, 1969.

Gould, R. L. Adult life stages: Growth toward self-tolerance. *Psychology Today,* February 1975, pp. 74–78.

Gratch, G. A study of the relative dominance of vision and touch in six-month-old infants. *Child Development,* 1972, *43,* 615–623.

Gratch, G., & Landers, W. F. Stage IV of Piaget's theory of infant object concepts: A longitudinal study. *Child Development,* 1971, *42,* 359–372.

Gray Panther power. An interview with Maggie Kuhn. *The Center Magazine,* March-April 1975, pp. 21–25.

Gray, S. W., & Klaus, R. A. The early training project: A seventh year report. *Child Development,* 1970, *41,* 909–924.

Greenberg, M., Pelliteri, O., & Barton, J. Frequency of defects in infants whose mothers had rubella during pregnancy. *Journal of the American Medical Association,* 1957, *165,* 675–678.

Grimes, J. W., & Allinsmith, W. Compulsivity, anxiety, and school achievement. *Merrill-Palmer Quarterly,* 1961, *7,* 247–271.

Grimm, E. R. Psychological and social factors in pregnancy, delivery, and outcome. In S. A. Richardson & A. F. Guttmacher (Eds.), *Childbearing: Its social and psychological aspects.* Baltimore: Williams & Wilkins, 1967.

Gross, B., & Gross, R. A little bit of chaos. *Saturday Review,* May 16, 1970, pp. 71–73ff.

Guilford, J. P. Three faces of intellect. *American Psychologist,* 1959, *14,* 469–479.

Guilford, J. P. Creativity: Yesterday, today, and tomorrow. *Journal of Creative Behavior,* 1967, *1,* 3–14. (a)

Guilford, J. P. *The nature of human intelligence.* New York: McGraw-Hill, 1967. (b)

Gutierrez de Pineda, V. Organizacion social en la Guajira. Bogota: *Rev. Institute Etnolog. Nac.,* 1948, *3.*

Gutmann, D. L. An exploration of ego configurations in middle and later life. In B. L. Neugarten *Personality in middle and late life: Empirical studies.* New York: Atherton Press, 1964.

Haan, N., Smith, M. B., & Block, J. Moral reasoning of young adults: Political-social behavior, family background, and personality correlates. *Journal of Personality and Social Psychology,* 1968, *10,* 183–201.

Haggard, E. A. Socialization, personality, and achievement in gifted children. *School Review,* 1957, *65,* 388–414.

Haimowitz, N. R. Development patterns: Birth to five years. In M. L. Haimowitz & N. R. Haimowitz (Eds.), *Human development: Selected readings* (3rd ed.). New York: Thomas Y. Crowell, 1973.

Hamachek, D. E. Development and dynamics of the adolescent self. In J. F. Adams (Ed.), *Understanding adolescence* (2nd ed.). Boston: Allyn & Bacon, 1973.

Harlow, H. F. Love in infant monkeys. *Scientific American,* June 1959, pp. 68–74.

Harlow, H. F., & Harlow, M. K. Social deprivation in monkeys. *Scientific American,* November 1962, pp. 137–146.

Harper, P. A., Fischer, L. K., & Rider, R. V. Neurological and intellectual status of prematures at three to five years of age. *Journal of Pediatrics,* 1959, *55,* 679–690.

Harris, D. B. *Goodenough-Harris drawing test* (manual). New York: Harcourt, Brace & World, 1963.

Hartup, W. W. Nurturance and nurturance-withdrawal in relation to the dependency behavior of preschool children. *Child Development*, 1958, *29*, 191–201.

Hartup, W. W. Dependence and independence. In H. W. Stevenson, J. Kagan & C. Spiker (Eds.), *Child psychology*. Chicago: National Society for the Study of Education, 1963.

Hartup, W. W. Friendship status and the effectiveness of peers as reinforcing agents. *Journal of Experimental Child Psychology*, 1964, *1*, 154–162.

Hartup, W. W. Peer interaction and social organization. In P. H. Mussen (Ed.), *Carmichael's manual of child psychology* (3rd ed.) (Vol. 2). New York: Wiley, 1970. (a)

Hartup, W. W. Peer relations. In T. D. Spencer & N. Kass (Eds.), *Perspectives in child psychology: Research and review*. New York: McGraw-Hill, 1970. (b)

Havighurst, R. J. A cross-cultural view of adolescence. In J. F. Adams (Ed.), *Understanding adolescence* (2nd ed.). Boston: Allyn & Bacon, 1973. (a)

Havighurst, R. J. History of developmental psychology: Socialization and personality development through the life span. In P. B. Baltes & K. W. Schaie (Eds.), *Life-span developmental psychology: Personality and socialization*. New York: Academic Press, 1973. (b)

Haynes, H., White, B. L., & Held, R. Visual accommodation in human infants. *Science*, 1965, *148*, 528–530.

Healy, W., & Bronner, A. F. *Delinquents and criminals, their making and unmaking: Studies in two American cities*. New York: Macmillan, 1926.

Heathers, G. Emotional dependence and independence in nursery school play. *Journal of Genetic Psychology*, 1955, *87*, 37–57.

Hebb, D. O. *A textbook of psychology*. Philadelphia: Saunders, 1966.

Heist, P. Intellect and commitment: The faces of discontent. In O. W. Knorr & W. J. Minter (Eds.), *Order and freedom on campus*. Boulder, Colo.: Western Interstate Commission for Higher Education, 1965.

Herron, R. E., & Sutton-Smith, B. *Child's play*. New York: Wiley, 1971.

Hertzig, M. E., Birch, H. G., Thomas, A., & Mendez, O. A. Class and ethnic differences in the responsiveness of preschool children to cognitive demands. *Monographs of the Society for Research in Child Development*, 1968, *33*(1, Serial No. 117).

Hess, E. H. Ethology and developmental psychology. In P. H. Mussen (Ed.), *Carmichael's manual of child psychology* (3rd ed.) (Vol. 1). New York: Wiley, 1970.

Hess, E. H. "Imprinting" in a natural laboratory. *Scientific American*, August 1972, pp. 24–31.

Hetherington, E. M. Effects of paternal absence on sex-typed behaviors in Negro and White preadolescent males. *Journal of Personality and Social Psychology*, 1966, *4*, 87–91.

Hetherington, E. M., & Deur, J. L. The effects of father absence on child development. In W. W. Hartup (Ed.), *The young child: Reviews of research* (Vol. 2). Washington, D. C.: National Association for the Education of Young Children, 1972.

Hilgard, E. R., & Bower, G. H. *Theories of learning* (3rd ed.). New York: Appleton-Century-Crofts, 1966.

Hill, R., & Aldous, J. Socialization for marriage and parenthood. In D. A. Goslin (Ed.), *Handbook of socialization theory and research*. Chicago: Rand McNally, 1969.

Hilton, B., Callahan, D., Harris, M., Condliffe, P., Berkley, B. (Eds.). *Ethical issues in human genetics: Genetic counseling and the use of genetic knowledge*. New York: Plenum, 1973.

Hindley, C. B., Filliozat, A. M., Klackenberg, G., Nicolet-Meister, D., & Sand, E. A. Differences in age of walking in five European longitudinal samples. *Human Biology*, 1966, *38*(4), 364–379.

Hoffman, L. W. Research findings on the effects of maternal employment on the child. In I. Nye & L. W. Hoffman (Eds.), *The employed mothers in America*. Chicago: Rand McNally, 1963.

Hoffman, M. L. Moral development. In P. H. Mussen (Ed.), *Carmichael's manual of child psychology* (3rd ed.) (Vol. 2). New York: Wiley, 1970.

Holt, J. *How children fail*. New York: Dell, 1964.

Hooker, D. *The prenatal origin of behavior*. Lawrence: University of Kansas Press, 1952.

Horn, J. L. Organization of data on life-span development of human abilities. In L. R. Goulet & P. B. Baltes (Eds.), *Life-span developmental psychology: Research and theory*. New York: Academic Press, 1970.

Horowitz, F. D., & Paden, L. Y. The effectiveness of environmental intervention programs. In B. M. Caldwell & H. N. Ricciuti (Eds.), *Review of child development research* (Vol. 3). Chicago: University of Chicago Press, 1973.

Hunt, J. McV. *Intelligence and experience*. New York: Ronald Press, 1961.

Hunt, J. McV. The psychological basis for using preschool enrichment as an antidote for cultural deprivation. *Merrill-Palmer Quarterly*, 1964, *10*, 209–248.

Hutcheson, R. H., Jr. Iron deficiency anemia in Tennessee among rural poor children. *Public Health Reports*, 1968, *83*, 939–943.

Hutt, C. Sex differences in human development. *Human Development*, 1972, *15*, 153–170.

Huxley, A. *Brave new world*. New York: Harper & Brothers, 1932.

Illich, I. *Deschooling society*. New York: Harper & Row, 1972.

Inhelder, B, & Piaget, J. [*The growth of logical thinking: From childhood to adolescence*] (A. Parsons & S. Milgram, trans.). New York: Basic Books, 1958.

Isaacs, S. *Intellectual growth in young children*. London: Routledge & Kegan Paul, 1930.

Jacoby, S. Waiting for the end: On nursing homes. *New York Times Magazine*, March 31, 1974, p. 13ff.

Jelliffe, D. B., Jelliffe, E. F. P., García, L., & De Barrios, G. The children of the San Blas Indians of Panama. *Journal of Pediatrics*, 1961, *59*, 271–285.

Jensen, A. R. How much can we boost IQ and scholastic achievement? *Harvard Educational Review*, 1969, *39*, 1–123.

Jersild, A. T., & Holmes, F. B. *Children's fears* (Child Development Monographs No. 20). New York: Teachers College, Columbia University Press, 1935.

Jones, H. E. Intelligence and problem-solving. In J. E. Birren (Ed.), *Handbook of aging and the individual*. Chicago: University of Chicago Press, 1959.

Jones, K., Shainbergh, L., & Byer, C. *Dimensions: A changing concept of health* (2nd ed.). San Francisco: Canfield Press, 1974.

Jones, M. C., & Bayley, N. Physical maturing among boys as related to behavior. *Journal of Educational Psychology*, 1950, *41*, 129–148.

Joos, M. Language and the school child. *Harvard Educational Review*, 1964, *34*, 203–210.

Jessner, L., Weigert, E., & Foy, J. L. The development of parental attitudes during pregnancy. In E. J. Anthony & T. Benedek (Eds.), *Parenthood: Its psychology and psychopathology*. Boston: Little, Brown, 1970.

Josselyn, I. M. Sexual identity crises in the life cycle. In G. H. Seward & R. C. Williamson (Eds.), *Sex roles in changing society*. New York: Random House, 1970.

Jung, C. G. [*Modern man in search of a soul*.] (W. S. Dell & C. F. Baynes, trans.). New York: Harcourt, Brace & World, 1933.

Kagan, J. The concept of identification. *Psychological Review*, 1958, *65*, 296–305.

Kagan, J. Inadequate evidence and illogical conclusions. *Harvard Educational Review*, 1969, *39*, 274–277.

Kagan, J. *Change and continuity in infancy*. New York: Wiley, 1971.

Kagan, J., & Moss, H. A. The stability of passive and dependent behavior from childhood through adulthood. *Child Development*, 1960, *31*, 577–591.

Kagan, J., & Moss, H. A. *Birth to maturity: A study in psychological development*. New York: Wiley, 1962.

Kallmann, F. J., & Sander, G. Twin studies on senescence. *American Journal of Psychiatry*, 1949, *106*, 29–36.

Kalnins, I. V., & Bruner, J. S. Infant sucking used to change the clarity of a visual display. In L. J. Stone, H. T. Smith & L. B. Murphy (Eds.), *The competent infant: Research and commentary*. New York: Basic Books, 1973.

Karlson, A. L. *A naturalistic method for assessing cognitive acquisition of young children participating in preschool programs*. Unpublished doctoral dissertation, University of Chicago, 1972.

Karnes, M. B., Studley, W. M., Wright, W. R., & Hodgins, A. S. An approach for working with mothers of disadvantaged preschool children. *Merrill-Palmer Quarterly*, 1968, *14*, 174–184.

Kastenbaum, R. Age: Getting there ahead of time. *Psychology Today*, December 1971, pp. 52–54ff.

Keen S. The heroics of everyday life: A theorist of death confronts his own end. *Psychology Today*, April 1974, pp. 71–75ff.

Keller, F. S. *Learning: Reinforcement theory* (2nd ed.). New York: Random House, 1969.

Kellogg, R. *Analyzing children's art*. Palo Alto, Calif.: National Press, 1970.

Kendler, H. H., & Kendler, T. S. Vertical and horizontal processes in problem solving. *Psychological Review*, 1962, *69*, 1–16.

Kendler, T. S. Development of mediating responses in children. In J. C. Wright & J. Kagan (Eds.), Basic cognitive processes in children. *Monographs of the Society for Research in Child Development*, 1963, *28*(2, Serial No. 86).

Kendler, T. S., & Kendler, H. H. Reversal and nonreversal shifts in kindergarten children. *Journal of Experimental Psychology*, 1959, *58*, 56–60.

Keniston, K. Social change and youth in America. In E. H. Erikson (Ed.), *Youth: Change and challenge*. New York: Basic Books, 1963.

Keniston, K. *The uncommitted: Alienated youth in American Society*. New York: Harcourt, Brace & World, 1965.

Keniston, K. The sources of student dissent. *Journal of Social Issues*, 1967, *23*(3), 108–137.

Keniston, K. *Young radicals: Notes on committed youth*. New York: Harcourt, Brace & World, 1968.

Keniston, K. Student activism, moral development, and morality. *American Journal of Orthopsychiatry*, 1970, *40*, 577–592.

Kephart, W. M. The Oneida community. In W. M. Kephart (Ed.), *The family, society, and the individual* (2nd ed.). Boston: Houghton Mifflin, 1966.

Kessen, W. *The child*. New York: Wiley, 1965.

Kessler, J. W. *Psychopathology of childhood*. Englewood Cliffs, N. J.: Prentice-Hall, 1966.

Kimmel, D. C. *Adulthood and aging: An interdisciplinary developmental view*. New York: Wiley, 1974.

Kirchner, W. K. Age differences in short-term retention of rapidly changing information. *Journal of Experimental Psychology*, 1958, *55*, 352–358.

Klima, E. S., & Bellugi, U. Syntactic regularities. In J. Lyons & R. J. Wales (Eds.), *Psycholinguistics papers*. Edinburgh: University of Edinburgh Press, 1966.

Knobloch, H., & Pasamanick, B. (Eds.). *Gesell and Amatruda's developmental diagnosis* (3rd ed.). New York: Harper & Row, 1974.

Knobloch, H., Pasamanick, B., Harper, P. A., & Rider, R. V. The effect of prematurity on health and growth. *American Journal of Public Health*, 1959, *49*, 1164–1173.

Koch, H. L. Sibling influence on children's speech. *Journal of Speech Disabilities*, 1956, *21*, 322–328. (a)

Koch, H. L. Sissiness and tomboyishness in relation to sibling characteristics. *Journal of Genetic Psychology*, 1956, *88*, 231–244. (b)

Koegh, J. F. *Motor performance of elementary school children*. Physical Education Department, University of California, Los Angeles, 1965. (Monograph)

Kogan, B. A. *Health*. New York: Harcourt Brace Jovanovich, 1970.

Kohl, H. *36 children*. New York: Norton, 1968.

Kohlberg, L. The development of children's orientations toward a moral order. I. Sequence in the development of moral thought. *Vita Humana*, 1963, *6*, 11–33 (S. Karger, Basel 1963).

Kohlberg, L. Development of moral character and moral ideology. In M. L. Hoffman & L. W. Hoffman (Eds.), *Review of child development research* (Vol. 1). New York: Russell Sage Foundation, 1964.

Kohlberg, L. Moral education in the schools: A developmental view. *School Review*, 1966, *74*, 1–30.

Kohlberg, L., & Mayer, R. Development as the aim of education. *Harvard Educational Review*, 1972, *42*, 449–496.

Kollmann, F. J., & Jarvik, L. F. Individual differences in constitution and genetic background. In J. Birren (Ed.), *Handbook of aging and the individual*. Chicago: University of Chicago Press, 1959.

Komarovsky, M. *Blue-collar marriage*. New York: Random House, 1964.

Kozol, J. *Death at an early age*. New York: Bantam Books, 1970.

Kraus, P. E. *Yesterday's children: A longitudinal study of children from kindergarten into the adult years*. New York: Wiley-Interscience, 1973.

Kübler-Ross, E. *On death and dying*. New York: Macmillan, 1969.

Kuhlen, R. G., & Houlihan, N. B. Adolescent heterosexual interest in 1942 and 1963. *Child Development*, 1965, *36*, 1049–1052.

Labov, W. The logic of nonstandard English. In F. Williams (Ed.), *Language and poverty*. Chicago: Markham, 1970.

Lamaze, F. *Painless childbirth: The Lamaze method*. Chicago: Regnery, 1970.

Leifer, A. D., & Roberts, D. F. Children's responses to television violence. In J. P. Murray, E. A. Rubinstein & G. A. Comstock (Eds.), *Television and social behavior* (Vol. 2). Washington, D. C.: U.S. Government Printing Office, 1972.

Levinson, D. J., Darrow, C. M., Klein, E. B., Levinson, M. H., & McKee, B. The psychosocial development of men in early adulthood and the mid-life transition. In D. F. Ricks, A. Thomas, & M. Roff (Eds.), *Life history research in psychopathology* (Vol. 3). Minneapolis: University of Minnesota Press, 1974.

Levy, D. M. Experiments on the sucking reflex and social behavior in dogs. *American Journal of Orthopsychiatry*, 1934, *4*, 203–224.

Levy, D. M. On instinct-satiation: An experiment on the pecking behavior of chickens. *Journal of Genetic Psychology*, 1938, *18*, 327–348.

Levy, D. M. *Maternal overprotection*. New York: Columbia University Press, 1943.

Lieberman, M. A. Psychological correlates of impending death: Some preliminary observations. *Journal of Gerontology*, 1965, *20*(2), 181–190.

Liebert, R. M., Neale, J. M., & Davidson, E. S. *The early window: Effects of television on children and youth*. New York: Pergamon Press, 1973.

Liebert, R. M., Poulos, R. W., & Strauss, G. D. *Developmental psychology*. Englewood Cliffs, N. J.: Prentice-Hall, 1974.

Linton, D. *Scientific American*, May 1961, p. 66.

Lorenz, K. Z. *King Solomon's ring*. New York: Thomas Y. Crowell, 1952.

Lövaas, O. I. Effect of exposure to symbolic aggression on aggressive behavior. *Child Development*, 1962, *32*, 37–44.

Luria, A. R. *The role of speech in the regulation of normal and abnormal behavior*. New York: Liveright, 1961.

Maas, H. S., & Kuypers, J. A. *From thirty to seventy: A forty-year longitudinal study of adult life styles & personality*. San Francisco: Jossey-Bass, 1974.

Maccoby, E. E., & Feldman, S. S. Mother-attachment and stranger-reactions in the third year of life. *Monographs of the Society for Research in Child Development*, 1972, *37*(1, Serial No. 146).

Maccoby, E. E. & Jacklin, C. N. What we know and don't know about sex differences. *Psychology Today*, December 1974, pp. 109–112.

Maddox, G. L. Persistence of life style among the elderly: A longitudinal study of patterns of social activity in relation to life satisfaction. In B. L. Neugarten (Ed.), *Middle age and aging*. Chicago: University of Chicago Press, 1968. (a)

Maddox, G. L. Retirement as a social event in the United States. In B. L. Neugarten (Ed.), *Middle age and aging*. Chicago: University of Chicago Press, 1968. (b)

Maehr, M. L. Culture and achievement motivation. *American Psychologist*, 1974, *29*, 887–896.

Mann, I. *Development of the human eye* (3rd ed.). New York: Grune & Stratton, 1964.

Marshall, W. A. The body. In R. R. Sears & S. S. Feldman (Eds.), *The seven ages of man*. Los Altos, Calif.: William Kaufman, 1973.

Maslow, A. H. *Motivation and personality*. New York: Harper & Brothers, 1954.

Maslow, A. H. *Toward a psychology of being* (2nd ed.). Princeton: Van Nostrand Reinhold, 1968.

McArthur, C. Personalities of first and second children. *Psychiatry*, 1956, *19*, 47–54.

McBride, A. B. *The growth and development of mothers*. New York: Harper & Row, 1973.

McCall, R. B. Smiling and vocalization in infants as indices of perceptual-cognitive processes. *Merrill-Palmer Quarterly*, 1972, *18*, 341–347.

McCarthy, J. J., & McCarthy, J. F. *Learning disabilities*. Boston: Allyn & Bacon, 1969.

McCary, J. L. *Human sexuality*. New York: Van Nostrand Rheinhold, 1973.

McClelland, D. C. Some social consequences of achievement motivation. In M. R. Jones (Ed.), *Nebraska Symposium on Motivation* (Vol. 3). Lincoln: University of Nebraska Press, 1955.

McCord, W., McCord, J., & Zola, I. K. *Origins of crime*. New York: Columbia University Press, 1959.

McCreary-Juhasz, A. How accurate are student evaluations of the extent of their knowledge of human sexuality? *Journal of School Health*, 1967, *37*, 409–412.

McDonald, R. L., Gynther, M. D., & Christakos, A. C. Relations between maternal anxiety and obstetric complications. *Psychosomatic Medicine*, 1963, *25*, 357–363.

McGlothlin, W. H. Drug use and abuse. *Annual Review of Psychology*, 1975, *26*, 45–64.

McGovern, G. S. The need for involved youth. In J. F. Adams (Ed.), *Understanding adolescence* (2nd ed.). Boston: Allyn & Bacon, 1973.

McNeill, D. *The acquisition of language: The study of developmental psycholinguistics*. New York: Harper

& Row, 1972.

Mead, G. H. *Mind, self, and society: From the stand-point of a social behaviorist.* Chicago: University of Chicago Press, 1934.

Mead, M. *Coming of age in Samoa.* New York: William Morrow, 1928.

Mead, M. Children and ritual in Bali. In M. Mead & M. Wolfenstein (Eds.), *Childhood in contemporary cultures.* Chicago: University of Chicago Press, 1955.

Mead, M. A new understanding of childhood. *Redbook,* January 1972, pp. 49f.

Mead, M., & Calas, E. Child-training ideals in a post-revolutionary context: Soviet Russia. In M. Mead & M. Wolfenstein (Eds.), *Childhood in contemporary cultures.* Chicago: University of Chicago Press, 1955.

Mead, M., & Newton, N. Cultural patterning of peri-natal behavior. In S. A. Richardson & A. F. Gutt-macher (Eds.), *Childbearing: Its social and psychological aspects.* Baltimore: Williams & Wilkins, 1967.

Merton, R. K. *Social theory and social structure* (Rev. ed.). Glencoe, Ill.: Free Press, 1957.

Milgram, S. *Obedience to authority: An experimental view.* New York: Harper & Row, 1974.

Miller, W. B. Lower class culture as a generating milieu of gang delinquency. *Journal of Social Issues,* 1958, *14*(3), 5–19.

Mischel, W. Sex-typing and socialization. In P. H. Mussen (Ed.), *Carmichael's manual of child psychology* (3rd ed.) (Vol. 2). New York: Wiley, 1970.

Money, J., & Ehrhardt, A. A. *Man and woman, boy and girl.* Baltimore: Johns Hopkins University Press, 1972.

Montagu, M. F. A. Constitutional and prenatal factors in infant and child health. In M. J. Senn (Ed.), *Symposium on the healthy personality.* Josiah Macy Jr. Foundation, 1950.

Montessori, M. [*The Montessori method: Scientific pedagogy as applied to child education in children's houses*] (Anne E. George, trans.). New York: Stokes, 1912.

Moore, O. K., & Anderson, A. R. The Responsive Environments Project. In R. D. Hess & R. M. Bear (Eds.), *Early education: Current theory, research, and action.* Chicago: Aldine, 1968.

Moore, R. S., & Moore, D. R. The dangers of early schooling. *Harper's Magazine,* July 1972, pp. 58–62.

Moore, W. E. Occupational socialization. In D. A. Goslin (Ed.), *Handbook of socialization theory and research.* Chicago: Rand McNally, 1969.

Moreno, J. L. *Who shall survive?* Washington, D. C.: Nervous and Mental Diseases Publishing Co., 1934.

Morison, R. S. Dying. *Scientific American,* March 1973, pp. 54–60.

Mowbray, C. T., & Luria, Z. Effects of labeling on children's visual imagery. *Developmental Psychology,* 1973, *9,* 1–8.

Murphy, L. B. *The widening world of childhood: Paths toward mastery.* New York: Basic Books, 1962.

Mussen, P. H., & Jones, M. C. Self-conceptions, motivations, and interpersonal attitudes of late- and early-maturing boys. *Child Development,* 1957, *28,* 243–256.

National Manpower Council. *Womanpower.* New York: Columbia University Press, 1957.

Neill, A. S. *Summerhill: A radical approach to child rearing.* New York: Hart, 1960.

Neugarten, B. L. *Personality in middle and late life: Empirical studies.* New York: Atherton Press, 1964.

Neugarten, B. L. Personality and patterns of aging. *Gawein,* 1965, *13,* 249–256.

Neugarten, B. L. Adult personality: Toward a psychology of the life cycle. In B. L. Neugarten (Ed.), *Middle age and aging.* Chicago: University of Chicago Press, 1968. (a)

Neugarten, B. L. The awareness of middle age. In B. L. Neugarten (Ed.), *Middle age and aging.* Chicago: University of Chicago Press, 1968. (b)

Neugarten, B. L. Continuities and discontinuities of psychological issues into adult life. *Human Development,* 1969, *12,* 121–130.

Neugarten, B. L. The old and the young in modern societies, *American Behavioral Scientist,* 1970, *14,* 13–24.

Neugarten, B. L. Grow old along with me! The best is yet to be. *Psychology Today,* December 1971, pp. 45–48ff.

Neugarten, B. L., & Datan, N. Sociological perspectives on the life cycle. In P. B. Baltes & K. W. Schaie (Eds.), *Life-span developmental psychology: Personality and socialization.* New York: Academic Press, 1973.

Neugarten, B. L., & Gutmann, D. L. Age-sex roles and personality in middle age: A thematic apperception study. In B. L. Neugarten *Personality in middle and late life: Empirical studies.* New York: Atherton Press, 1964.

Neugarten, B. L., & Moore, J. W. The changing age-status system. In B. L. Neugarten (Ed.), *Middle age and aging.* Chicago: University of Chicago Press, 1968.

O'Connell, V., & O'Connell, A. *Choice and change: An introduction to the psychology of growth.* Englewood Cliffs, N. J.: Prentice-Hall, 1974.

O'Leary, K. D., & Drabman, R. Token reinforcement programs in the classroom: A review. *Psychological Bulletin,* 1971, *75,* 379–398.

Olim, E. G. The self-actualizing person in the fully functioning family: A humanistic viewpoint. *Family Coordinator,* July 1968, pp. 141–148.

Olim, E. G. Maternal language styles and cognitive development of children. In F. Williams (Ed.), *Language and poverty.* Chicago: Markham, 1970.

Olim, E. G., Hess, R. D., & Shipman, V. C. Maternal language styles and their implications for children's cognitive development. In *The effect of maternal behavior on cognitive development and impulsivity.* Symposium presented at the meeting of the American Psychological Association, Chicago, September 1965. (a)

Olim, E. G., Hess, R. D., & Shipman, V. C. Relationships between mothers' abstract language style and abstraction styles of urban preschool children. Paper presented at the meeting of the Midwestern Psychological Association, Chicago, March 1965. (b)

Olim, E. G., Hess, R. D., & Shipman, V. C. Role of

mothers' language styles in mediating their preschool children's cognitive development. *School Review*, 1967, *75*, 414–424.

Olton, R. M., & Crutchfield, R. S. Developing the skills of productive thinking. In P. H. Mussen, J. Langer & M. Covington (Eds.), *Trends and issues in developmental psychology.* New York: Holt, Rinehart & Winston, 1969.

Omark, D. R., & Edelman, M. S. *The development of early Social interaction: An ethological approach.* A paper presented at a meeting of the National Laboratory of Early Childhood Education, Committee on Human Development, University of Chicago, January, 1969.

Opie, I., & Opie, P. *The love and language of school children.* London: Oxford University Press, 1959.

Ostrovsky, E. S. *Children without men* (2nd ed.). New York: Collier Books, 1962.

Otto, H. A., & Otto, S. T. A new perspective of the adolescent. *Psychology in the Schools*, 1967, *4*, 76–81.

Palermo, D. S. Racial comparisons and additional normative data on the Children's Manifest Anxiety Scale. *Child Development*, 1959, *30*, 53–57.

Papousek, H. Conditioned head rotation reflexes in infants in the first months of life. *Acta Paediatrica Scandinavica*, 1961, *50*, 565–576.

Parke, R. D. Some effects of punishment on children's behavior. In W. W. Hartup (Ed.), *The young child: Reviews of research* (Vol. 2). Washington, D. C.: National Association for the Education of Young Children, 1972.

Parten, M. B. Social participation among pre-school children. *Journal of Abnormal and Social Psychology*, 1932–33, *27*, 243–269.

Pavlov, I. P. [*Lectures on conditioned reflexes.*] (W. H. Gantt, trans.). New York: International Publishers, 1928.

Peck, R. C. Psychological developments in the second half of life. In B. L. Neugarten (Ed.), *Middle age and aging.* Chicago: University of Chicago Press, 1968.

Peck, R. F., & Berkowitz, H. Personality and adjustment in middle age. In B. L. Neugarten *Personality in middle and late life: Empirical studies.* New York: Atherton Press, 1964.

Peel, E. A. Intellectual growth during adolescence. *Educational Review*, 1965, *17*, 169–180.

Pfeiffer, E., Verwoerdt, A., & Davis, G. C. Sexual behavior in middle life. *American Journal of Psychiatry*, 1972, *128*, 1262–1267.

Pfeiffer, J. (Ed.). *The cell.* New York: Time-Life Books, 1964.

Phillips, J. L., Jr. *The origins of intellect: Piaget's theory.* San Francisco: Freeman, 1969.

Piaget, J. [*The moral judgment of the child*] (M. Gabain, trans.). New York: Free Press, 1965. (Originally published, 1932.)

Piaget, J. [*The origins of intelligence in children*] (M. Cook, trans.). New York: International Universities Press, 1952. (Originally published, 1936.)

Piaget, J. [*The psychology of intelligence*]. (M. Percy & D. E. Berlyne, trans.). New York: Harcourt Brace, 1950.

Piaget, J. *Play, dreams and imitation in childhood.* New York: Norton, 1951.

Piaget, J. *The child's conception of number.* London: Routledge & Kegan Paul, 1952.

Piaget, J. [*The construction of reality in the child.*] (M. Cook, trans.). New York: Basic Books, 1954.

Piaget, J. The stages of intellectual development of the child. *Bulletin of Menninger Clinic*, 1962, *26*(3), 120–145.

Pines, M. Infants are smarter than anybody thinks. *New York Times Magazine*, November 29, 1970, pp. 1ff.

Pines, M. A child's mind is shaped before age 2. *Life*, December 17, 1971, pp. 63ff.

Plowden, B. *Children and their primary schools: A report of the Central Advisory Council for Education in England* (Vol. 1). London: Her Majesty's Stationery Office, 1967.

Plumb, J. H. The great change in children. *Horizon*, Winter 1971, pp. 4–12.

Porterfield, E. Mixed marriage. *Psychology Today*, January 1973, pp. 71–78.

Pratt, K. C. The neonate. In L. Carmichael (Ed.), *Manual of child psychology* (2nd ed.). New York: Wiley, 1954.

Prechtl, H., & Beintema, D. *The neurological examination of the full term newborn infant* (Clinics in Developmental Medicine Series No. 12). Philadelphia: Lippincott, 1965.

Proshansky, H. M. The development of intergroup attitudes. In L. W. Hoffman & M. L. Hoffman (Eds.), *Review of child development research* (Vol. 2). New York: Russell Sage Foundation, 1966.

Rabkin, L. Y., & Rabkin, K. Children of the kibbutz. *Psychology Today*, September 1969, pp. 40–46.

Radke, M. J., & Trager, H. G. Children's perceptions of the social roles of Negroes and Whites. *Journal of Psychology*, 1950, *29*, 3–33.

Radke, M. J., Trager, H. G., & Davis, H. Social perceptions and attitudes of children. *Genetic Psychology Monographs*, 1949, *40*, 327–447.

Rainwater, L. Crucible of identity: The Negro lower-class family. *Daedalus*, 1966, *95*, 172–216.

Rank, O. *The trauma of birth.* New York: London: Routledge & Kegan Paul, 1929.

Raven, J. C. *Standard progressive matrices* (manual). New York: Psychological Corporation, 1958.

Read, K. H. *The nursery school: A human relationships laboratory* (5th ed.). Philadelphia: Saunders, 1971.

Rebelsky, F. G. Infancy in two cultures. *Nederlands Tijdschrift voor de Psychologie*, 1967, 379–385.

Reichard, S., Livson, F., & Petersen, P. G. Adjustment to retirement. In B. L. Neugarten (Ed.), *Middle age and aging.* Chicago: University of Chicago Press, 1968.

Reimanis, G., & Green, R. F. Imminence of death and intellectual decrement in the aging. *Developmental Psychology*, 1971, *5*, 270–272.

Reinach, L. de. *Lelaos.* Paris: A. Charles, 1901.

Rheingold, H. L. Gewirtz, J. L., & Ross, H. W. Social conditioning of vocalizations in the infant. *Journal of Comparative and Physiological Psychology*, 1959,

52, 68–73.

Robertson, J., & Bowlby, J. Responses of young children to separation from their mothers. *Courrier du Centre Internationale de l'Enfance*, 1952, 2, 131–142.

Robinson, W. P., & Rackstraw, S. J. *A question of answers* (Vols. 1 & 2). London: Routledge & Kegan Paul, 1972.

Roff, M., & Sells, S. B. Relations between intelligence and sociometric status in groups differing in sex and socio-economic background. *Psychological Reports*, 1965, 16, 511–516.

Rogers, C. R. *On becoming a person*. New York: Houghton Mifflin, 1961.

Rogers, C. R. Toward a modern approach to values: The valuing process in the mature person. *Journal of Abnormal and Social Psychology*, 1964, 68, 160–167.

Rogers, K. The mid-career crisis. *Saturday Review*, January 20, 1973, pp. 37–38.

Rosen, J. L., & Bibring, G. L. Psychological reactions of hospitalized male patients to a heart attack: Age and social-class differences. In B. L. Neugarten (Ed.), *Middle age and aging*. Chicago: University of Chicago Press, 1968.

Rosen, J. L., & Neugarten, B. L. Ego functions in middle and later years: A thematic aperception study. In B. L. Neugarten *Personality in middle and late life: Empirical studies*. New York: Atherton Press, 1964.

Rosenbaum, A., Churchill, J. A., Shakhashiri, Z. A., & Moody, R. L. Neuropsychologic outcome of children whose mothers had proteinuria during pregnancy: A report from the collaborative study of Cerebral Palsy. *Obstetrics and Gynecology*, 1969, 33, 118–123.

Rosenfeld, A. If Oedipus' parents had only known. *Saturday Review*, September 7, 1974, pp. 49f. (a)

Rosenfeld, A. Starve the child, famish the future. *Saturday Review*, March 23, 1974, p. 59. (b)

Rosenthal, R., & Jacobson, L. *Pygmalion in the classroom: Teacher expectation & pupil's intellectual development*. New York: Harper & Row, 1968.

Rossi, A. S. Transition to parenthood. *Journal of Marriage and the family*, 1968, 30, 26–39.

Roszak, T. *The making of a counter-culture*. New York: Doubleday, 1969.

Rubin, I. Transition in sex values—Implications for the education of adolescents. *Journal of Marriage and the Family*, 1965, 27, 185–189.

Ruebush, B. K. Interfering and facilitating effects of test anxiety. *Journal of Abnormal and Social Psychology*, 1960, 60, 205–212.

Ruebush, B. K. Anxiety. In H. W. Stevenson, J. Kagan & C. Spiker (Eds.), *Sixty-second Yearbook of the National Society for the Study of Education. Part I: Child psychology*. Chicago: University of Chicago Press, 1963.

Rugh, R., & Shettles, L. B. *From conception to birth: The drama of life's beginnings*. New York: Harper & Row, 1971.

Sanderson, R. E., & Inglis, J. Learning and mortality in elderly psychiatric patients. *Journal of Gerontology*, 1961, 16, 375–376.

Santrock, J. W. Relation of type and onset of father absence to cognitive development. *Child Development*, 1972, 43, 455–469.

Sarason, S. B., Davidson, K. S., Lighthall, F. F., Waite, R. R., & Ruebush, B. K. *Anxiety in elementary school children: A report of research*. New York: Wiley, 1960.

Sarason, S. B., Hill, K. T., & Zimbardo, P. G. Longitudinal study of the relationship of test anxiety to performance on intelligence and achievement tests. *Monographs of the Society for Research in Child Development*, 1964, 29 (7, Serial No. 98).

Scammon, R. E. The measurement of the body in childhood. In J. A. Harris, C. M. Jackson, D. G. Paterson, & R. E. Scammon (Eds.), *The measurement of man*. Minneapolis: University of Minnesota Press, 1930.

Schaie, K. W. Rigidity-flexibility and intelligence: A cross-sectional study of the adult life span from 20 to 70 years. *Psychological Monographs*, 1958, 72 (9, Whole No. 462).

Schaie, K. W. A reinterpretation of age related changes in cognitive structure and functioning. In L. R. Goulet & P. B. Baltes (Eds.), *Life-span developmental psychology: Research and theory*. New York: Academic Press, 1970.

Schiff, L. F. The obedient rebels: A study of college conversions to conservatism. *Journal of Social Issues*, 1964, 20(4), 74–95.

Schmuck, R. Concerns of contemporary adolescents. *National Association of Secondary School Principals Bulletin*, 1965, 49(300), 19–28.

Schopler, E. *Visual and tactual receptor preferences in normal and schizophrenic children*. Unpublished doctoral dissertation, University of Chicago, 1964.

Sears, P. S. Doll play aggression in normal young children: Influence of sex, age, sibling status, father's absence. *Psychological Monographs*, 1951, 65 (6, Whole No. 323).

Sears, R. R. Ordinal position in the family as a psychological variable. *American Sociological Review*, 1950, 15, 397–401.

Sears, R. R. Dependency motivation. In M. R. Jones (Ed.), *The Nebraska Symposium on Motivation* (Vol. 11). Lincoln: University of Nebraska Press, 1963.

Sears, R. R., Maccoby, E. E., & Levin, H. *Patterns of childrearing*. Evanston, Ill.: Row Peterson, 1957.

Sears, R. R., Rau, I., & Alpert, R. *Identification and child rearing*. Stanford: Stanford University Press, 1965.

Seligman, M. E. P. Submissive death: Giving up on life. *Psychology Today*, May 1974, pp. 80–85.

Seligman, M. E. P., Maier, S. F., & Solomon, R. L. Unpredictable and uncontrollable aversive events. In F. R. Brush (Ed.), *Aversive conditioning and learning*. New York: Academic Press, 1971.

Sever, J. L. Rubella as a teratogen. In D. H. M. Woollan (Ed.), *Advances in teratology* (Vol. 2) London: Logos, 1967.

Severin, F. T. What humanistic psychology is about. *Newsletter Feature Supplement*. San Francisco: Association for Humanistic Psychology, July 1974.

Seymour, D. Z. Black children, black speech. *Common-*

weal, November 19, 1971, pp. 175–178.

Shanas, E., Townsend, P., Wedderburn, D., Friis, H., Milhoj, P., & Stehouwer, J. The psychology of health. In B. L. Neugarten (Ed.), *Middle age and aging*. Chicago: University of Chicago Press, 1968.

Sheehy, G. Catch-30 and other predictable crises of growing up adult. *New York Magazine*, February 18, 1974, pp. 30–46f.

Sheldon, W. H. *The varieties of temperament: A psychology of constitutional differences*. New York: Harper & Brothers, 1942.

Sherif, M., Harvey, O. J., White, B. J., Hood, W. B., & Sherif, C. W. *Intergroup conflict and cooperation: The robber's cave experiment*. Norman: University of Oklahoma Press, 1961.

Sherif, M., & Sherif, C. W. *Groups in harmony and tension*. New York: Harper & Brothers, 1953.

Shirley, M. M. *The first two years: A study of twenty-five babies* (Institute of Child Welfare Monograph No. 7) (Vol. 1). Minneapolis: University of Minnesota Press, 1931.

Shirley, M. M. *The first two years: A study of twenty-five babies* (Institute of Child Welfare Monograph No. 7) (Vol. 2). Minneapolis: University of Minnesota Press, 1933.

Shock, N. W. Aging and psychological adjustment. *Review of Educational Research*. 1952, 22, 439–458. (a)

Shock, N. W. Aging of homostatic mechanisms. In A. I. Lansing (Ed.), *Cowdry's problems of aging* (3rd ed.). Baltimore: Williams & Wilkins, 1952. (b)

Shukin, A., & Neugarten, B. L. Personality and social interaction. In B. L. Neugarten *Personality in middle and late life: Empirical studies*. New York: Atherton Press, 1964.

Sidel, R. *Women and child care in China: A firsthand report*. New York: Hill & Wang, 1972.

Siegler, R. S., & Liebert, R. M. Effects of presenting relevant rules and complete feedback on the conservation of liquid quantity task. *Developmental Psychology*, 1972, 7, 133–138. (a)

Siegler, R. S., & Liebert, R. M. Learning of liquid quantity relationships as a function of rules and feedback, number of training problems, and age of subject. *Proceedings of the 80th Annual Convention of the American Psychological Association*, 1972, 7, 117–118. (b)

Simon, W., & Gagnon, J. H. On psychosexual development. In D. A. Goslin (Ed.), *Handbook of socialization theory and research*. Chicago: Rand McNally, 1969.

Simpson, W. J. A Preliminary report on cigarette smoking and the incidence of prematurity. *American Journal of Obstetrics and Gynecology*, 1957, 73, 808–815.

Siqueland, E. R., & DeLucia, C. A. Visual reinforcement of nonnutritive sucking in human infants. *Science*, 1969, 165, 1144–1146.

Siqueland, E. R., & Lipsitt, L. P. Conditioned head-turning in human newborns. *Journal of Experimental Child Psychology*, 1966, 3, 356–376.

Skinner, B. F. *The technology of teaching*. New York: Appleton-Century-Crofts, 1968.

Skinner, B. F. *Beyond freedom and dignity*. New York: Knopf, 1971.

Slater, P. E. *The pursuit of loneliness: American culture at the breaking point*. Boston: Beacon Press, 1970.

Slobin, D. I. They learn the same way all around the world. *Psychology Today*, July 1972, pp. 71–74f.

Smedslund, J. The acquisition of conservation of substance and weight in children. *Scandinavian Journal of Psychology*, 1961, 2, 11–20.

Smith, F. *Understanding reading: A psycholinguistic analysis of reading & learning*. New York: Holt, Rinehart & Winston, 1971.

Smith, M. B., Haan, N., & Block, J. Social-psychological aspects of student activism. *Youth and Society*, 1970, 1, 261–288.

Smith, M. E. An investigation of the development of the sentence and the extent of vocabulary in young children. *University of Iowa Studies in Child Welfare*, 1926, 3(5), 268–269.

Sontag, L. W., Baker, C. T., & Nelson, V. L. Mental growth and personality development: A longitudinal study. *Monographs of the Society for Research in Child Development*, 1958, 23(2, Serial No. 68).

Sorenson, R. C. *Adolescent sexuality in contemporary America: Personal values and sexual behavior, ages 13–19*. New York: World, 1973.

Spearman, C. "General intelligence" objectively determined and measured. *American Journal of Psychology*, 1904, 15, 201–293.

Spiro, M. E. Is the family universal?—The Israeli case. *American Anthropologist*, 1954, 56, 839–846.

Spiro, M. E. *Children of the kibbutz: A study in child training and personality*. New York: Schocken Books, 1965.

Spitz, R. A., & Cobliner, W. G. *The first year of life*. New York: International Universities Press, 1966.

Spivak, G., & Shure, M. B *Social adjustment of young children: A cognitive approach to solving real-life problems*. San Francisco: Jossey-Bass, 1973.

Stephens, W. N. *The family in cross-cultural perspective*. New York: Holt, Rinehart & Winston, 1963.

Sternglass, E. J. Cancer: Relation of prenatal radiation to development of the disease in childhood. *Science*, 1963, 140, 1102–1104.

Stolz, L. M. *Father relations of war-born children*. Stanford: Stanford University Press, 1954.

Stolz, L. M. Effects of maternal employment on children: Evidence from research. *Child Development*, 1960, 31, 749–782.

Stone, J. G. *Play and playgrounds*. Washington, D. C.: National Association for the Education of Young Children, 1970.

Stone, L. J., Smith, H. T., & Murphy, L. B. (Eds.). *The competent infant: Research and commentary*. New York: Basic Books, 1973.

Stott, L. H., & Ball, R. S. Infant and preschool mental tests: Review and evaluation. *Monographs of the Society for Research in Child Development*, 1965, 30(3, Serial No. 101).

Students for a Democratic Society. *Port Huron Statement*, 1962.

Summer scholars at work: Bridging the intelligence test gap. *Newsweek*, July 15, 1968, pp. 51–52.

Sunley, R. Early nineteenth-century American literature on child rearing. In M. Mead & M. Wolfstein (Eds.), *Childhood in contemporary cultures*. Chicago: University of Chicago Press, 1955.

Sutton-Smith, B. A formal analysis of game meaning. *Western Folklore*, 1958, *18*, 13–24.

Sutton-Smith, B., & Rosenberg, B. G. *The sibling*. New York: Holt, Rinehart & Winston, 1970.

Taft, L. T., & Cohen, H. J. Neonatal and infant reflexology. In J. Hellmuth (Ed.), *The exceptional infant* (Vol. 1). Seattle: Special Child Publications, 1967.

Tanner, J. M. *Growth at adolescence* (2nd ed.). Oxford: Blackwell Scientific Publications, 1962.

Tanner, J. M. The regulation of human growth. *Child Development*, 1963, *34*, 817–847.

Tanner, J. M. Physical growth. In P. H. Mussen (Ed.), *Carmichael's manual of child psychology* (3rd ed.) (Vol. 1). New York: Wiley, 1970.

Tanner, J. M. Sequence, tempo, and individual variation in the growth and development of boys and girls aged twelve to sixteen. *Daedalus*, 1971, *100*, 907–930.

Tanner, J. M. Growing up. *Scientific American*, September 1973, p. 40.

Taussig, H. B. The thalidomide syndrome. *Scientific American*, August 1962, pp. 29–35.

Taylor, R. G. Personality traits and discrepant achievement: A review. *Journal of Counseling Psychology*, 1964, *11*, 76–82.

Terman, L., & Merrill, M. *Stanford-Binet intelligence scale*. Houghton Mifflin, 1960.

Thorndike, E. L. *Animal intelligence*. New York: Macmillan, 1911.

Thurstone, L. L. Primary mental abilities. *Psychometric Monographs*, 1938, No. 1.

Tilgher, A. Work through the ages. In S. Nosow & W. H. Form (Eds.), *Man, work, and society*. New York: Basic Books, 1962.

Toffler, A. *Future shock*. New York: Random House, 1970.

Torrance, E. P. *Guiding creative talent*. Englewood Cliffs, N. J.: Prentice-Hall, 1962.

Torrance, E. P. The creative personality and the ideal pupil. *Teachers College Record*, 1963, *65*, 220–226.

Translating genetic code. *New York Times*, September 15, 1974, Section 4, p. 11.

Turnbull, C. M. *The mountain people*. New York: Simon & Schuster, 1972.

U.S. Department of Health, Education, and Welfare. *Births, marriages, divorces, and deaths for February 1975* (DHEW Publication No. [HRA] 75–1120) (Monthly Vital Statistics Report, Vol. 24, No. 2). Rockville, Md.: Health Resources Administration, 1975.

U.S. Department of Housing and Urban Development. *Older Americans: Facts about incomes and housing*. Washington, D. C.: U.S. Government Printing Office, 1973.

U.S. Department of Labor. *1967 manpower report*. Washington, D.C.: U.S. Government Printing Office, 1967.

Uzgiris, I. C. Patterns of cognitive development in infancy. *Merrill-Palmer Quarterly*, 1973, *19*, 181–204.

Valadian, I., Stuart, H. C., & Reed, R. B. Studies of illnesses of children followed from birth to eighteen years. *Monographs of the Society for Research in Child Development*, 1961, *26*(3, Serial No. 81).

Van Baal, J. *Déma. Description and analysis of Marind Anim culture, South New Guinea*. The Hague: Martinus Nijhoff, 1966.

Vogel, E. The go-between in a developing society: The case of the Japanese marriage arranger. *Human Organization*, 1961, *20*, 112–120.

Vore, D. A. Prenatal nutrition and postnatal intellectual development. *Merrill-Palmer Quarterly*, 1973, *19*, 253–260.

Vulliamy, D. G. *The newborn child* (3rd ed.). Edinburgh: Churchill Livingstone, 1973.

Vygotsky, L. S. [*Thought and language*] (E. Hanfmann & G. Vaker, Eds. and trans.). Cambridge: M.I.T. Press, 1962.

Walker, R. N. Body build and behavior in young children: II. Body build and parents' ratings. *Child Development*, 1963, *34*, 1–23.

Wallach, M. A., & Kogan, N. A new look at the creativity-intelligence distinction. *Journal of Personality*, 1965, *33*, 348–369.

Ward, M. C. *Them children: A study in language learning*. New York: Holt, Rinehart & Winston, 1971.

Watson, E. H., & Lowrey, G. H. *Growth and development of children* (5th ed.). Chicago: Year Book Medical Publishers, 1967.

Watson, G. Some personality differences in children related to strict or permissive parental discipline. *Journal of Psychology*, 1957, *44*, 227–249.

Watson, J. B., & Rayner, R. Conditioned emotional reactions. *Journal of Experimental Psychology*, 1920, *3*, 1–14.

Watson, J. D., & Crick, F. H. C. Molecular structure of nucleic acids. *Nature*, 1953, *171*, 737–738.

Watson, J. S. Smiling, cooing, and "the game". *Merrill-Palmer Quarterly*, 1972, *18*, 323–339.

Watson, J. S., & Ramey, C. T. Reactions to response-contingent stimulation in early infancy. *Merrill-Palmer Quarterly*, 1972, *18*, 219–227.

Watts, W. A., & Whittaker, D. Profile of a nonconformist youth culture: A study of Berkeley nonstudents. *Sociology of Education*, 1968, *41*, 178–200.

Wechsler, D. *Wechsler intelligence scale for children*. New York: Psychological Corporation, 1949.

Wechsler, D. *Wechsler adult intelligence scale* (manual). New York: Psychological Corporation, 1955.

Wechsler, D. *Wechsler preschool and primary scale of intelligence*. New York: Psychological Corporation, 1967.

Wechsler, D. *Wechsler intelligence scale for children—revised*. New York: Psychological Corporation, 1974.

Weikart, D. P., Rogers, L., Adcock, C. *The cognitively oriented curriculum* (An ERIC-NAEYC publication in early childhood education). Urbana: University of Illinois, 1971.

Weisman, A. D. *On dying and denying: A psychiatric*

study of terminality. New York: Behavioral Publications, 1972.

Welford, A. T. *Ageing and human skill.* New York: Oxford University Press, 1958.

Welford, A. T. Experimental psychology in the study of ageing. *British Medical Bulletin*, 1964, *20*, 65–69.

Wender, P. H. *Minimal brain dysfunction in children.* New York: Wiley, 1971.

Westinghouse Learning Corporation. *The impact of Head Start: An evaluation of the effects of Head Start experience on children's cognitive and affective development* (Preliminary draft). Columbus: Westinghouse Learning Corporation, Ohio University, 1969.

White, B. L. An analysis of excellent early educational practices: Preliminary report. *Interchange: A Journal of Educational Studies*, 1971, *2*(2), 86–87. (a)

White, B. L. *Human infants: Experience and psychological development.* Englewood Cliffs, N. J.: Prentice-Hall, 1971. (b)

White, B. L., Castle, P., & Held, R. Observations on the development of visually-directed reaching. *Child Development*, 1964, *35*, 349–364.

White, B. L., & Held, R. Plasticity of sensorimotor development in the human infant. In J. F. Rosenblith & W. Allinsmith (Eds.), *Causes of behavior: Readings in child development and educational psychology.* Boston: Allyn & Bacon, 1966.

White, B. L., & Watts, J. C. *Experience and environment: Major influences on the development of the young child.* (Vol. 1). Englewood Cliffs, N. J.: Prentice-Hall, 1973.

White, R. W. Motivation reconsidered: The concept of competence. *Psychological Review*, 1959, *66*, 297–333.

White, S. H. Evidence for a hierarchical arrangement of learning processes. In L. P. Lipsitt & C. C. Spiker (Eds.), *Advances in child development and behavior* (Vol. 2). New York: Academic Press, 1965.

Whiting, B. B. (Ed.). *Six cultures: Studies of child rearing.* New York: Wiley, 1963.

Whiting, J. W. M., & Child, I. L. *Child training and personality: A cross cultural study,* New Haven: Yale University Press, 1953.

Williams, F. (Ed.). *Language and poverty.* Chicago: Markham, 1970. (a)

Williams, F. Some preliminaries and prospects. In F. Williams (Ed.), *Language and poverty.* Chicago: Markham, 1970. (b)

Williams, R. H., & Wirths, C. G. *Lives through the years: Styles of life and successful aging.* New York: Atherton Press, 1965.

Williams, R. L. The silent mugging of the black community. *Psychology Today*, May 1974, pp. 32–34ff.

Winchester, A. M. *Human Genetics.* Columbus, Ohio: Charles E. Merrill, 1971.

Winder, A. E., & Angus, D. L. *Adolescence: Contemporary studies.* New York: American Book, 1968.

Wolfe, T. *The web and the rock.* New York: Harper & Brothers, 1939.

Wolfenstein, M. The emergence of fun morality. *Journal of Social Issues*, 1951, *7*(4), 15–25.

Wolff, P. H. Observations on newborn infants. *Psychosomatic Medicine*, 1959, *21*, 110–118.

Wolpe, J., Salter, A., & Reyna, L. J. (Eds.). *The conditioning therapies: The challenge in psychotherapy.* New York: Holt, Rinehart & Winston, 1964.

Wodcock, L. P. *The life and ways of the two-year-old.* New York: Basic Books, 1941.

Wyden, B. Growth: 45 crucial months. *Life*, December 17, 1971, pp. 93f.

Yablonsky, L. *The hippie trip.* New York: Pegasus, 1968.

Yarrow, L. J., & Pedersen, F. A. Attachment: Its origins and course. In W. W. Hartup (Ed.), *The young child: Reviews of research* (Vol. 2). Washington, D. C.: National Associatoin for the Education of Young Children, 1972.

Yarrow, L. J., Rubenstein, J. L., Pedersen, F. A., & Jankowski, J. J. Dimensions of early stimulation and their differential effects on infant development. *Merrill-Palmer Quarterly*, 1972, *18*, 205–218.

Yarrow, M. R., Scott, P. M., & Waxler, C. Z. Learning concern for others. *Developmental Psychology*, 1973, *8*, 240–260.

Zamenhof, S., Van Marthens, E., & Grauel, L. DNA (cell number) in neonatal brain. *Science*, 1971, *172*, 850–851.

SUBJECT INDEX

role exit theory of aging, 458
rooting reflex, 146

schema(ta), 33
school: environment, 324–325; free versus mass-oriented, 402; Montessori, 314
segregation by age, 379
self, development of, 95–100
self-absorption versus generativity, 41, 444
self-actualization, 43
self-awareness, development of, 96–98, 217
self-concept, 98–100
self-esteem, and personality, 360
self-evaluation, 277–278
self-fulfilling prophecy, 326
self-fulfillment, 95; adolescent, 408
self-reports, 20
self theories, 43
semantics, 225
senescence, 52
sensation, 66
sensorimotor intelligence: and object permanence, 193–195; and perceptual competence, 190–195; and symbolic representation, 195; and visually guided reach, 192–193
sensorimotor period, 34
sensory capacities, 148–149
sensory pleasure, 262
sensuality, and sexual curiosity, 273–274
sex-linked inheritance, 163–164
sex-linked traits, 163–164
sex-role identity, 169–172
sex-role socialization, 170–172
sexual curiosity, and sensuality, 273–274
sexual identity, 373–375
sexual identity and relationships, adolescent, 391–396
sexualizing versus socializing, 444
sexual maturity, 368–375; biological changes, 368–371
shape stage, 258
shaping, 29
shift, reversal versus nonreversal, 301
short-term memory, and age, 456
siblings, 346–347
sibling status, 346
singles, 424–426
social isolates, 352
socialization: and aggression, 94–95; and culture, 166–169; defined, 12–13; direct reward, punishment, and, 90–91; and identification, 93–94; and modeling, 91, 93; sex-role, 170–172
socializers, peers as, 309–311
socializing versus sexualizing, 444
social learning theory, 30
social planning for aged, 467–469
social responsiveness, 205
Social Security Act (1935), 452
social studies, 335–336
sociogram, 352
sociometric techniques, 352
solitary play, 309
somatic cells, 156
speech, holophrastic, 230
sperm, 118
Stanford-Binet test, 74–76, 77
stars, 352
status: minority group, 356–357; in peer group, 352–354; sibling, 346
stepping reflex, 146
stimulation, variety and complexity of, 197

structuralists, 32
Students for a Democratic Society, Port Huron Statement, 389
successive approximations, 29
sucking reflex, 146
surprise paradigm, 190
symbolic representation, 195
symbolic stage, 36
symbolic thought, 253
syntax, 225
Syracuse Scale of Social Relations, 353

Tay-Sachs disease, 164
Teacher (Ashton-Warner), 334
teaching: art, 261; diagnostic-prescriptive, 325; machines, 29–30
television, and aggression, 287–289
teratology, 126
terminal illness, 465–466
terms, definition of, 17
tests: aim of, 327–328; criterion-referenced, 325; norm-referenced, 325; use of, 326; see also intelligence; intelligence tests
Thematic Apperception Test (TAT), 459
36 Children (Kohl), 336
thought: changing, 300–305; changes in style of, 376–378; convergent, 329; creativity and, 328–330; divergent, 329; egocentric, 253; enactive, 252; formal operational, 376; growth of, 252–257; iconic, 253; intuitive, 302–303; irreversible, 253; operational, 376; preoperational, 253–256; productive, and creativity, 328–330; symbolic, 253
timing, 196–197; learning, maturation, and, 14
toilet training, 215–216
token economy, 30
tonic neck reflex, 145
toxemia, 140
traits: non-sex-linked, 164–165; sex-linked, 163–164
transductive reasoning, 254
transformation, 256
transrationality, and counterculture, 402
triangle, 352
triggering, 202
trust versus mistrust, 39
Turner's syndrome, 162
twins, fraternal versus identical, 119

understanding, as science goal, 21
unemployment, teenage, 408

validity, 77
values, and moral development, 387–391
The Vanishing Adolescent (Friedenberg), 380
vas deferens, 123
verbal mediation, 298
vernix caseosa, 124

The Web and the Rock (Wolfe), 156
Wechsler Adult Intelligence Scale, 76
Wechsler Intelligence Scale for Children, 74, 76
Wechsler Preschool and Primary Scale of Intelligence, 76
Westinghouse Learning Corporation, 313
wisdom versus physical powers, valuing, 444
withdrawal, 271
work, 426; cycles of, 427; and life-style, 428–429; and occupational choice, 427–428
work-role preoccupation versus ego differentiation, 445

youth culture, 397–398; and counterculture, 402–405; mainstream, 405–406; and protest, 398–401